9.50

new deal mosaic

ROOSEVELT CONFERS with his NATIONAL EMERGENCY COUNCIL

·1933-1936·

EDITED BY

Lester G. Seligman

Elmer E. Cornwell, Jr.

UNIVERSITY OF OREGON BOOKS

Eugene, Oregon . 1965

dedication

This book is affectionately dedicated
to our children, Susan and David
Seligman and Alison and Joan
Cornwell. May they learn, through
this volume, something of a critical and
challenging period in American
history. It is the period which shaped
the world in which they grew up.

preface

Students of the American presidency will welcome the
publication of the Proceedings of the National Emergency
Council for the years of the New Deal. They fill an important
gap in our knowledge of how a president functions when
privately conferring with a group of his top administrators.
Few other such records have ever been made available.
There are diaries and inside accounts, but despite the degree
of truth these accounts contain, there is always the gnawing
doubt in the mind of the scholar that they might also
contain self-justifying distortions.

Here in the crisp, vivid words of the Proceedings one finds
President Roosevelt speaking, often in full candor, concerning some of the political and administrative problems
he confronted in the exciting early years of the New Deal.
It is the confidential nature of the Proceedings that gives them
their value, since the President could speak so much more
freely at the Council meetings than at his press conferences.
There is the added value that in the Council Proceedings,
as well as in the Press Conference Proceedings, one does not
need to fathom what might have been the spontaneous
remarks of the President as between what might have been
prepared for him by advisers, as one must do in connection
with his formal speeches.

I can see many uses to which historians, political scientists,
and other behavioral scientists may wish to put this material.
It is useful to biographers, to students of public administration,
and to persons interested in studying group relationships.
For the casual reader, the Proceedings bring to life some of
the exciting moments of the New Deal.

FRANK FREIDEL

vii

acknowledgment

From the day in the National Archives in Washington, D.C., when we first read these Proceedings of the National Emergency Council, until the date of this publication, several years have elapsed. During this time, we jointly, and persistently, traced the path of this agency, now dead twenty-eight years. The tracks of a governmental body that flashed cometlike into great prominence for a very short period of time, and then descended into obscurity, were not altogether easy to follow. Some of the participants could be interviewed; official documents and newspaper files were consulted for the background of the agency and its influence on national administration.

Professor Seligman wrote the Introduction and Professor Cornwell prepared the editors' notes and footnotes that appear throughout the volume.

We are particularly grateful to Dr. Herman Kahn, former director of the Franklin D. Roosevelt Library, for his assistance, and to Professor John M. Gaus of Harvard University for his early interest and encouragement. We thank George N. Belknap, University editor, and members of his editorial staff, Kenneth Metzler and Catherine Lauris, for their assistance.

LESTER G. SELIGMAN
ELMER E. CORNWELL, JR.

contents

Preface _____ vii

Introduction _____ xiii

MEETING NO. 1 December 19, 1933_____ 1

NO. 2 January 9, 1934_____ 26

NO. 3 January 23, 1934_____ 48

NO. 4 February 6, 1934_____ 79

NO. 5 February 20, 1934_____ 100

NO. 6 March 6, 1934_____ 136

NO. 7 March 20, 1934_____ 161

NO. 8 April 17, 1934_____ 180

NO. 9 May 1, 1934_____ 191

NO. 10 June 26, 1934_____ 220

NO. 11 July 10, 1934_____ 232

NO. 12 July 24, 1934_____ 247

NO. 13 August 7, 1934_____ 263

NO. 14 August 21, 1934_____ 271

NO. 15 October 2, 1934_____ 286

NO. 16 October 16, 1934_____ 299

NO. 17 October 30, 1934_____ 316

NO. 18 November 13, 1934_____ 340

NO. 19 December 11, 1934_____ 350

NO. 20 December 20, 1934_____ 381

NO. 21 January 8, 1935_____ 400

NO. 22 January 22, 1935_____ 415

NO. 23 February 5, 1935_____ 425

NO. 24 February 19, 1935_____ 441

NO. 25 March 12, 1935_____ 452

NO. 26 April 23, 1935_____ 461

NO. 27 August 6, 1935_____ 475

NO. 28 December 17, 1935_____ 481

NO. 29 January 28, 1936_____ 502

NO. 30 March 3, 1936_____ 523

NO. 31 April 28, 1936_____ 534

APPENDIX A Biographical Notes_____ 553

B Rules and Regulations_____ 570

C Brief Chronology_____ 572

Index of Subjects_____ 577

introduction

A U.S. Senate subcommitte of the Committee on Government
Operations not long ago conducted hearings on the
adequacy for national security of our national governmental
machinery. Being subject to review and critical appraisal
is the way in which the various foreign policy agencies and
the military are coordinated by the chief executive. The
National Security Council received particular attention
because it is charged principally with integrating and defining
national defense policy. All this calls to mind an
administrative experiment of thirty years ago, designed to
achieve, amidst domestic crisis, policy coordination of our
bureaucracy. It was 1933 to be exact, a watershed date in
American history. The administrative experiment was
called the National Emergency Council.[1]
We remember 1933 as a time of deep economic crisis when
the national administration vigorously attempted to recover
national economic stability. A new president had just been
inaugurated after four years of an economic depression more
profound than any in our history. "No previous depression
in the history of the country had ever been so protracted;
none before had been devoid of capacity to liquidate itself."[2]
The first term of the New Deal faced the task of devising
policies that would restore production, investment,
employment, consumer spending, and, above all, public
morale.

---

[1] The Proceedings of the National Emergency Council are found in the
National Archives and Records Service in Washington, D.C. There is
no record of who transcribed the proceedings. Efforts were made by
the editors to trace the identity of the secretary who took verbatim
notes—but no one remembers.
Appended to the originals of the typed transcripts of the meetings of
the National Emergency Council were the texts of the often lengthy
reports, charts, and other materials, which had been prepared for each
meeting, and which were referred to in the course of the discussion.
It would neither have been practical nor particularly useful to attempt
to reprint all of these in full. Since most of them dealt with weekly or
monthly summaries of agency progress or with problems of no more
than passing contemporary interest, their omission detracts little from
the value of the transcripts themselves. As a result, however, a few
allusions in the transcripts may remain partially obscure. Where these
ambiguities relate to important matters of more than transient interest,
footnotes have been inserted to explain the reference. To avoid unduly
encumbering the transcripts, these notes were deliberately held to
a minimum.
[2] Walton Hamilton, *America in Crisis*, ed. Daniel Aaron (New York,
1952), p. 275.

new deal mosaic

Devising and initiating policies for economic recovery was only half the battle. Their proper management and implementation were no less important and no less difficult. Except for the example of President Wilson's National Industrial Advisory Council during World War I, there was little administrative precedent for what the Roosevelt Administration was trying to do. There was neither a corpus of wisdom nor a reserve of experienced personnel ready to direct this effort. Neither was there administrative machinery for a massive and far-reaching program.

The keystones of New Deal recovery policy in 1933 were a few agencies: NRA, AAA, CWA, and FERA. NRA, through its voluntary codes, hoped to mobilize employers to increase employment, production, and prices, and thereby spur renewed industrial activity. The AAA was designed to raise farm prices and prevent farm surpluses that would depress prices through a program of crop allotment. FERA was charged with giving direct relief to the indigent and unemployed. CWA inaugurated a public works program to stimulate the construction and durable goods industries to increase employment. TVA, HOLC, and banking legislation rounded out this initial recovery program. The whole strategy was as much a fillip to public psychology as it was to economic behavior. It was recognized that regenerated morale and confidence was indispensable to any economic recovery.

This New Deal program was thus a synthesis of many components. When these are considered individually, they appear neither new nor radical. The roots of NRA can certainly be found, in part, in Herbert Hoover's policy of fostering the growth of trade associations. So it was with other New Deal policies that are by hindsight and historical perspective far less "radical" than they seemed or were regarded.

NRA and AAA, the two principal efforts, were congenial to the desires of organized business and organized farm interests. The "marketing agreements" of AAA and the "codes" of NRA were endorsed by the U.S. Chamber of Commerce and the Farm Bureau Federation. The Public Works policies were perhaps not "self-liquidating," but they did not threaten fundamentals of the economic system. TVA was a new venture because it permitted government to market power in addition to producing it. However, its reclamation and agricultural assistance features were in keeping with long-

introduction

established objectives. Roosevelt's political conception seemed
to be to use government to restore the stakes in the economy
(and in society) of every economic group. He articulated a
concept of the concert of interests, a consensus built by coalition
of interest. Roosevelt was trying to heal breeches rather
than to unleash social indignation.

The New Deal was not, properly speaking, an "ideology." Its
rationale was the need for more governmental responsibility
and control to sustain the established goals of American
society. At the time, it appeared that there *was* a new national
program which supported this endeavor.

The severest test was administrative, as new programs
overlapped, criss-crossed, and blocked one another. There was,
therefore, a great need for an over-all coordinating body. It
was in hopes of accomplishing this that Roosevelt organized an
Executive Council in July 1933. At the outset the Council
was an enlarged cabinet, with Frank Walker, Roosevelt's
able and trusted friend, its executive secretary. The purpose
of the council was to "provide for the orderly presentation
of business and coordinate interagency problems of organization and work of the new governmental agencies." The
Executive Council proved too cumbersome for effective
discussion and so on November 17, 1933, Roosevelt created
the *National Emergency Council*. (It is the proceedings of
this Council that are printed herein.)

NEC was greeted on all sides with enthusiasm as a much-
needed planning agency that would bring cohesion and
clarity to the New Deal administration. The breadth of the
purposes of the new agency were made clear in the Executive
Order which launched it:

Whereas the Congress of the United States has declared the existence
of an acute national economic emergency which affects the national
public interest and welfare, and

Whereas, in order to meet the said emergency and to provide the relief
necessary to protect the general welfare of the people, the Congress of the
United States has enacted legislation including, among other statutes, the
National Industrial Recovery Act of June 16, 1933 (Public No. 67,
73d Congress), the Agricultural Adjustment Act of May 12, 1933
(Public No. 10, 73d Congress) and the Federal Emergency Act of
May 12, 1933 (Public No. 15, 73d Congress); and

Whereas it is deemed expedient and necessary that an organization be
created for the purpose of coordinating and making more efficient and
productive the work of the numerous field agencies of the Government
established under, and for the purpose of carrying into effect, the provisions of the said legislation;

Now, therefore, by virtue of the authority invested in me by the aforesaid legislation, there is hereby created an organization which shall be known as the National Emergency Council, at the head of which shall be an Executive Director who shall be appointed by the President and shall receive a salary to be fixed by him at not to exceed $10,000.00 per annum. The Council shall be composed of the following and such other members as the President may designate:

The Secretary of the Interior
  (Administrator of Public Works)
The Secretary of Agriculture
The Secretary of Commerce
The Secretary of Labor
The Administrator of Agricultural Adjustment
The Administrator of Federal Emergency Relief
The Chairman of the Home Owners Loan Corporation
The Governor of the Farm Credit Administration
A representative of the Consumers' Council

The members of the Council shall act in a capacity advisory to the President and the Executive Director and shall serve without compensation.

The functions and duties of the Council shall be prescribed by the President, and such rules and regulations as may be necessary to effectuate the purposes for which the Council is created shall be prescribed by the Executive Director and approved by the President.

The Executive Director is authorized to execute the functions and to perform the duties vested in the Council by the President through such persons as the Executive Director shall designate, and he is further authorized to prescribe such rules and regulations as he may deem necessary to supplement, amplify or carry out the purposes and intent of such rules and regulations as may be prescribed by him and approved by the President under the provisions of this Order.

The Executive Director may appoint, subject to the approval of the President, without regard to the Civil Service laws or the Classification Act of 1923, as amended, fix the compensation and prescribe the duties and authority of such officials and employees, and make such expenditures (including expenditures for personal services, and rent at the seat of the Government and elsewhere, for law books and books of reference, and for paper, binding, and printing) as may be necessary to carry into effect the provisions of this Order. The Executive Director may also with the consent of any board, commission, independent establishment, or executive department of the Government, including any field service thereof, avail himself of the services of the officials, employees, and the facilities thereof and, with the consent of the State or municipality concerned, may utilize such State and local officials and employees as he may deem necessary.

For the purposes of this Order, the sum of $10,000 is hereby allocated to the National Emergency Council from the appropriation authorized by Section 200 of the National Recovery Act and made by the Fourth Deficiency Act, fiscal year 1933, approved June 16, 1933 (Public No. 77, 73d Congress).

introduction

All volunteer field agencies established under, and for the purpose of effectuating, the provisions of the aforesaid legislation, are hereby abolished, this provision to become effective thirty days from the date of this Order; and thereafter all functions theretofore performed by said agencies and considered necessary by the Executive Director for carrying out the purposes of this Order shall be assumed and performed by the Council.

In an early step, a central statistical board headed by Dr. Winfield Riefler was established as part of NEC in July 1934. The board was to assure standardized statistical reporting by all administrative agencies.

The course of the National Emergency Council was inevitably bound up closely with NRA. The National Recovery Act became law on June 16, 1933. When Roosevelt affixed his signature to the legislation, he said "history probably will record the National Industrial Recovery Act as the most important and far-reaching legislation ever enacted by the American Congress,"[3] to achieve its objectives of increasing payrolls, public spending, raise prices and provide for greater economic stability.

The scope of NRA was far-reaching. Its jurisdiction embraced the range of industrial and trade activity from the animal soft hair industry to retail trade. In time, some 546 codes of fair competition were formulated and approved; some 11,000 administrative orders were issued interpreting the codes; some 139 administrative orders were issued on administrative procedure and some 70 presidential executive orders were promulgated dealing with rights, procedures, and privileges under NRA.[4] The administration of NRA became a huge network suffused by the drive and energy of its first director, the colorful General Hugh Johnson, a protegé of Bernard Baruch. Bureaucratic conflicts and overlapping abounded among the several new recovery agencies. For example, NRA's regulations pertaining to the timber industry affected FHA in its drive for home remodeling and the public works slum clearance projects of PWA.

To harness NRA and its associates in recovery (AAA, FERA, CCC, CWA) as a team appeared imperative. Several efforts were made. Roosevelt's first try was to subordinate Hugh Johnson to a Special Industrial Recovery Board, as a kind of

[3] Leverett Lyon, *et al.*, *The National Recovery Administration* (Brookings: 1935), p. 3.
[4] Lyon, *et al.*, *op. cit.* p. 30.

Board of Directors of NRA. The members of that board were from established departments for the most part—the Secretary of Commerce (Daniel Roper) as chairman; the Attorney General (Homer Cummings); Secretary of Interior (Harold Ickes); Secretary of Labor (Frances Perkins); the Director of the Budget (Lewis Douglas); the Administrator of Industrial Recovery (Hugh Johnson); and the Chairman of the Federal Trade Commission (Garland Ferguson).

This special Industrial Recovery Board was to be a general policy board, designed to put NRA under the canopy of interrelated programs in the various departments and agencies. The Cabinet members and other government officials who comprised the board proved too busy, and so the board failed to fulfill its function. As one observer noted: "No policies were arrived at or promulgated, and the Board was soon lost in the fast-shifting NRA scene."[5]

As a result, in the month following the creation of NEC, Roosevelt transferred the functions of the Special Industrial Recovery Board to NEC in hopes that the latter might serve as policy coordinator over NRA. But the change met with no greater success. Leverett Lyon and his associates who studied NRA administration concluded "that the exact relationship between the National Emergency Council and NRA was never clearly defined . . . there is no evidence that it functioned any more effectively as a general control agency for the NRA than did the Special Industrial Recovery Board."[6]

NRA was reorganized in September 1934, and a five-member board was named by the President to replace the single administrator. This board was placed under an Industrial Emergency Committee, charged with general supervision of NRA activities. In a major reorganization in October 1934,[7] this Industrial Emergency Committee was in turn made a sub-committee of the National Emergency Council by executive order. The same Order then merged the Executive Council, the Industrial Emergency Committee, and the National Emergency Council into a single agency under the title of National Emergency Council, with Donald Richberg, former general counsel of NRA, as its director.

The same executive order reorganized the National Emer-

---

[5] Lyon, *et, al., op. cit.,* pp. 43, 44.
[6] *Ibid.,* p. 61.
[7] Executive Order 6889-A dated Oct. 29, 1934.

gency Council and gave sweeping powers to its director.
These powers, it was pointed out at the time, "are too great
for any one man, or any one governmental machine, no matter
how large or smooth running."[8] As broad as these powers
were, they could be reduced to impotence unless the President
gave his directors full support. Mr. Richberg served only
until April 1935, having left NEC to head up the reorganized
NRA organization. Frank C. Walker returned as executive
director of the National Emergency Council, taking on
the additional duties of director of the Division of Applications and Information to "coordinate" matters of dispute
between FERA and PWA. Walker's comings and goings
as head of NEC came to an end with his resignation in
December 1935.

Walker's departure marked the virtual end of NEC, though
Walker's assistant, Mr. Alverson, continued to serve in this
nominal capacity. The agency continued a perfunctory
existence. "The President no longer presided, and agency
heads left attendance at meetings to their subordinates."[9] By
the time the Roosevelt second term began, the "emergency"
had abated and many of the early New Deal agencies had
been abolished or were so well established as to make NEC
methods futile or needless.[10] NEC continued its legal exist-
ance, to be formally abolished in July 1939, when executive
reorganization plan No. 1 became effective.

THE STRUCTURE OF THE NEC

The staff and functions of the National Emergency Council
changed at various times throughout its existence. For the most
part, its organization consisted of the following: The Office
of the Executive Director; Office of the Administrative Assistant and General Counsel; Office of the Executive Assistant;
Office of the Chief Clerk; the Field Operations Division and
Forty-eight State Directors, the United States Information
Service, and an Editorial and Distribution Section.

The National Emergency Council met every two weeks on
Tuesday. Its meetings were based upon an agenda prepared
by the executive director of the Council in consultation
with the President. It was decided that each agency would

---

[8] *New York Times*, Nov. 2, 1934.
[9] R. Neustadt, *Presidential Clearance of Legislation*, Ph.D. Thesis
(Harvard, 1950), p. 50.
[10] Neustadt, *ibid.*

submit progress reports to each of the other agencies so that all might be informed and bring misunderstandings and conflicts for discussion at meetings. Since the President presided, problems could thus be brought for his decision. Such was the basic design of the Council, but as the reader will notice, practice deviated from these plans.

THE FUNCTIONS OF NEC

The meetings were filled with discussions of a variety of topics. Those at which Roosevelt spoke "off-the-cuff" on New Deal policy are perhaps the most revealing available. Excerpts of Roosevelt's press conferences and several volumes of memoirs and recollection have been published, but these NEC Proceedings are the only verbatim accounts of his discussions with colleagues.[11] In these Proceedings, Roosevelt is found discussing TVA in a manner that makes startlingly clear the broad perspective in which he envisioned that massive program. In almost didactic monologues, the goals of housing policy, power policy, etc., are expressed with great clarity. When Roosevelt speaks about his concern for the underprivileged in society, he gives eloquent expression to his humane sentiments. When the President instructs his colleagues on how to handle Congress and the Washington press, we are given a revealing portrait of the adroit and experienced politician with a sure touch for manipulation. When Roosevelt sets forth the importance of the Council's role in clearing all legislative proposals by all departments and agencies so that the Administration may speak with one voice to Congress, he indicates his firm grasp of the methods and values of forceful administrative coordination. The toughness of the President as chief executive is seen clearly in these passages. If Roosevelt's term of office came to be characterized as administratively somewhat chaotic, these proceedings indicate that such untidiness was perhaps more deliberate than the result of negligence. F.D.R. regarded administrative tidiness as subject always to political or programmatic considerations. He frequently reminds his colleagues that public acceptance, not conformity to administrative canon, is the best indicator of policy success.

A leitmotif of these proceedings is Roosevelt's overriding

---

[11] These proceedings are the closest approximation in U.S. history of the type of discussions that characterize cabinet meetings.

concern with his lines of communication with the public.
Under the National Emergency Council, a network of field
organizations in all states and counties had been created.
Roosevelt saw these not only as administrative instruments,
but as a channel for regular reports on "how things were
going." He expected these reports to contain judgments
as to whether the public was pleased, and secondly, whether
the administration of the programs was coherent. Characteristically, Roosevelt did not place sole reliance on these. He
solicited reports from state and local political leaders and many
other sensitive observers. Perhaps no other president was so
attuned to public opinion, or so conscientiously invited the
public to communicate with him.

Apart from significant discussions by Roosevelt himself, the
considerations of major issues by all the participants are
often trenchant and revealing. Housing policy and banking
policy, relief, farm policy, labor organization, railroads, the
relationship between federal, state, and local government—the
gamut of public affairs were discussed at various times at
Council meetings. As broad as was his perspective, these
conferences give us a revealing portrait of both the variety
of parochial positions and complexity of motives and considerations that enter into responsible decision-making.

Yet, as a means of top level policy determination and administrative coordination, the National Emergency Council
proved disappointing.[12] In reading these Proceedings, one
observes a progressive degeneration of meetings. Toward
the end, Cabinet members and agency heads absented themselves more frequently and sent principal subordinates to
record their "interest." Why did this happen? The reasons
are various and significant.

First, as was indicated, the New Deal program was itself not
internally consistent. For example, the reclamation purposes
of TVA contradicted the crop control features of AAA.
The monopoly-facilitating policies of NRA were at odds
with economic expansion. At any given time, the New Deal
administration contained many conflicting policies and outlooks
about the relations between government and the economy.
It is sometimes said that there was a left and right wing in
the New Deal higher circles. This is an oversimplification.
The lines of policy difference were more varied and complex

---

[12] With few exceptions all such efforts at top level coordination have
proven failures. OWMR is perhaps the single exception.

than can be exhausted by these two classifications. At odds
with each other were blocs and personalities ranging over
a wide political spectrum. Cordell Hull represented one policy
line, Frankfurter, another; Tugwell, still another. In paired
disagreements were Moley vs. Perkins, Henry Wallace vs.
George Peek, Ickes vs. Hopkins, etc. The New Deal in its
highest circles almost mirrored the wide range of views held
by *both* its public supporters and detractors. It could hardly
be expected that an agency like the NEC could resolve these.
NEC could serve initially to ventilate differences, but after a
while, as the patterns of opposition crystallized, NEC would
come to rest on a plateau of the noncontroversial. Administrative
opponents sought private meetings with F.D.R., or worked
through intramural negotiation and bargaining. In time,
avoidance of the forum afforded by Council meetings
was regarded as necessary to the fulfillment of the particular
objectives of its members.

Second, Cabinet and agency heads were inclined to resist the
idea of coordination, because coordination threatened special
departmental prerogatives and interests.[13] Each agency and
department and their subunits developed close ties with the
interest groups they served, and worked together with blocs
in Congress. Although the NEC arose at a time when
emergency agencies were just crystallizing such patterns,
older departments had these relationships ingrained. Who
wanted coordination? In a sense, no one but the President—
cabinet departments and bureaus found they could pursue
their own policies most effectively by (1) by-passing the
President if necessary, or (2) enlisting the President's personal
support, plus alliances with Congress and interest groups. To
illustrate the point, one of the significant decisions of NEC was

---

[13] To illustrate this point, the following entry in Ickes' diary is significant:
"The National Emergency Council held a meeting at two o'clock and
it was evident that Richberg has been getting in some fine work. He is
steadily building up his own power, and he acted today like the fair-haired
boy of the Administration. He looked like the cat that had swallowed the
canary. He is gathering under his control all of the various interdepartmental committees, although why the Director of an Emergency Council
should have anything to do with committees that attach to the permanent
branches of the Government is more than I can understand. He also
suggested the possibility of eliminating all, or a large number, of the various
legal staffs of the Departments, and a committee was appointed, under the
chairmanship of the Department of Justice, to canvass this situation.
If an attempt is made to abolish the Solicitor's office in this department, I
shall certainly put up a stiff fight." *The Secret Diary of Harold L. Ickes*
(New York, 1953), Vol I, pp. 242-243.

introduction

the requirement that each executive agency clear its legislative proposals through the NEC to prevent overlapping and conflict in administration policy before Congress. The agencies failed to comply. E. E. Witte, who reviewed the function of NEC in this matter of legislative clearance, reported, "The total number of proposed bills which passed through the office of the Executive Director of the NEC was much smaller in the 1936 session than in the 1935 session ... There is much reason to believe that a major factor in the decrease in the number of measures cleared through the National Emergency Council was the failure of departments to comply with the requirements of the Budget Circular. Very few of the principal acts of this congressional session were cleared with the Executive Director of the National Emergency Council. Nearly all of the clearance work of this officer on this session affected only minor departmental bills, and many bills even of this description were not cleared at all."[14] From the beginning, the Interstate Commerce Commission, headed by Joseph Eastman, refused to submit legislative proposals to the NEC on the grounds that the ICC was an independent regulatory commission not directly or primarily responsible to the President. The lively exchange on this point between the President and Mr. Eastman is reported in these proceedings.

Third, NEC was not the exclusive agency for policy advice or the achievement of coordination. It is true that Cabinet meetings were held less frequently during the early stages of NEC. But the President had his inner circle of advisers— Ray Molcy, Rexford Tugwell, Donald Richberg, Bernard Baruch, Louis Howe, and others whom he relied upon for advice and the work of negotiation. The NEC was an impressive formal device, but it was only one framework— there were always other more informal methods for the attainment of some objective. The diaries of Harold Ickes, Robert Sherwood's *Roosevelt and Hopkins,* Henry Morgenthau's diaries, Rexford Tugwell's writings, and those of Frances Perkins make clear that NEC was never, for them or *for the President,* the sole or prime channel for coordination and communication.

Roosevelt was no rigid adherent of the staff concept like

---

[14] E. E. Witte, *The Preparation of Proposed Legislative Measures,* President's Committee on Administrative Management (U.S. Government Printing Office, 1937), pp. 366-367.

Mr. Eisenhower. He wanted coordination, but not to the degree that it would tie his hands. He kept his doors open to wrangling bureaucrats so that *he* would have the choices to make, as to whether to mollify them, discipline them, or give them enough rope to hang themselves. All our information on the inner bureaucratic life of the New Deal indicates that Roosevelt was a master juggler, who always made sure that he personally retained control. We can surmise from Roosevelt's administrative behavior that he employed coordinative devices to satisfy some clamor for administrative tidiness, but also because he wanted to shake up administrative arrangements when they became troublesome. In the case of NEC, it served a useful purpose of putting Hugh Johnson under some cover.

Fourth, the NEC never had enough staff to carry out its decisions. It was a nerve center without adequate nerve endings. The director had to work largely with the apparatus of departments and agencies and numerous overlapping interdepartmental committees. The departments were left free to fulfill pledges of support or not. Without adequate staff, the NEC was restricted to stating policy but was never equipped to follow through.

Fifth, the executive directors of the NEC, Frank Walker and then Donald Richberg, never enjoyed the status of "chief of staff," that their position appeared to be. All experience indicates that the effectiveness of cabinet-like bodies like the NEC depends greatly upon the role of their principal administrative chief. The prime source of the authority of such an official is his relationship with the President. His voice is respected solely because when he speaks, it is the President who is heard. When he no longer enjoys close and full support of the President, then his voice is reduced to a whisper. Both Walker and Richberg, the two directors of NEC, began their work with great fanfare. The President publicly announced his fullest support and confidence. This honeymoon was shortlived; slowly, Roosevelt gave cues that they were not presidential surrogates. Department and agency heads, only too eager to whittle down this barrier to the President, lent their full support to the deterioration of their authority. After a time, they became progressively ignored. "Frank Walker was, by his own confession, mainly a trouble shooter."[15]

---

[15] W. Y. Elliott, *The Need for Constitutional Reform* (New York, 1935), p. 100.

introduction

Donald Richberg has stated in retrospect (not without some of the bitterness that seemed characteristic of those who fell —or slid— from power in Roosevelt's administration), "My function was to develop an agenda in preparation for the meetings of the various subjects that ought to be discussed in such a gathering, and that the President wanted discussed. And I sometimes had as much as five or ten minutes [*sic!*] with the President before a meeting to go over the agenda with him. You can see what profound consideration was given to the preparation of the agenda."[16] Richberg's directives were not listened to by agency and department heads.

In part because, "His offices were not in the White House. Many officials of the administration were found to have more ready access to the President's ear than Richberg. Policies were made and approved by the President without Richberg's knowledge. Department heads found they could ignore him with impunity."[17]

The pattern of rapid ascent and descent from influence that Richberg exemplified was almost a New Deal administrative syndrome. Ray Moley, Corcoran, Donald Nelson, Knudson, and many others, experienced it. Roosevelt and his policies attracted many able, and ambitious, individuals. They were already susceptible to Potomac fever, and Roosevelt made use of them and they became politically vulnerable. As a result, the administrative apparatus constantly demanded "new blood" and "new faces." This circulation among the administrative elite arose from conditions endemic to the Rooseveltian political milieu.

A new personality might be given a high-powered position in a new administrative agency, whose course would turn out to be fraught with political dangers. After a period, when the person was "shot full of holes" by indignant Congressmen, or interest group leaders or the press, he became a political liability and had to be dropped. Another pattern involved the eager beaver who began to have dreams of glory and entertained the notion of challenging the President. The demise of such individuals was quick.

NEC failures in coordinating the highest levels were translated into confusion and conflict among its state and local offices. It was one of NEC's prime objectives from its inception to establish an effective field organization for the recovery

---

[16] Proceedings of the *Institute of Public Affairs*, 1952 (University of Virginia, 1952), p. 15.

[17] H. Somers, *Presidential Agency* (Harvard, 1950), pp. 207-208.

agencies. It recognized that efficient administration on the Washington level needs organization at the state and local levels. James Fesler, who surveyed these state offices of NEC in 1937, found that their problems of cooperation were directly traceable to the difficulties in Washington. He concluded that "coordination in the field is far less important than coordination at Washington. It is true that administration comes into contact with the public in the field, but the point of contact is not necessarily the point of treatment of the disease of lack of coordination."[18]

Sixth, and this cannot be overemphasized, the NEC was born in emergency and operated amidst emergency. As recovery agencies burgeoned in 1933 and 1934, there was an urgent need for some instrumentality to tie them together. The sheer tempo of events, their dramatic impact on the country, the experimental character of many programs manned by ardent but inexperienced administrators, made some overriding Presidential control imperative. The President needed to "school" his inexperienced administrators.

By 1935, there was a cooling off—agencies were more settled, procedures more established and the crisis atmosphere had abated somewhat. It was obvious to all that NEC was no precedent for a permanent solution. The "super-cabinet" method had shown that coordination and clearance could be better accomplished perhaps by the strengthening of the President's personal staff rather than by collegial bodies.[19]

What the President needed, his Committee on Administrative Management declared (and Roosevelt fully endorsed), was personal "help"—permanent and competent staff. Directly responsible and loyal to him, such a staff could furnish the liaison, reporting, advising, coordination, and managerial assistance he needed. Such recommendations took effect in White House and Executive office reorganization in 1939. The celebrated six Presidential assistants, with a "passion for anonymity" were ushered in.

By 1935 and 1936, there was also a shift in New Deal policy. The immediate program that gave NEC birth had changed.

---

[18] *Report with Special Studies*, President's Committee on Administrative Management (Washington, D.C., 1937), p. 292.

[19] Louis Brownlow, the chairman of the President's Committee on Administrative Management in a letter to the editors stated: "President Roosevelt's experience with the National Emergency Council was the prime reason for the creation of the President's Committee on Administrative Management."

introduction

Some time during that period, the policies that underlay
NRA were abandoned. In the Schechter case in 1935, the
Supreme Court declared NRA unconstitutional. The judicial
opinion was not altogether unwelcome in New Deal circles.
By that time, NRA had proved at best a mixed blessing,
and certainly no magic path to economic recovery. In its
attempt to mobilize the nation's industry through voluntary
codes, NRA had brought many problems in its wake—
monopoly and a raft of enforcement difficulties that belied
the "voluntary" character of NRA. The concert-of-interests
policy, in which NRA was a keystone, gave way to a "shift
to the left." Anti-monopoly policy, "soak-the-rich" taxes,
pro-labor legislation, social security were the prime objectives of new policy. The idea of a grand national coalition was
abandoned for the more restricted coalition of labor, lower
middle-class, urban, ethnic groups, and the unorganized.
The White House circle was changing, and perhaps there
was less need for an over-all council. President Roosevelt
was to emphasize executive leadership and power, not
government by councils.

THE ACHIEVEMENTS OF NEC

We have attempted to put NEC in some perspective; perhaps
with the indulgence of hindsight, its failings and weaknesses
have been exaggerated.[20] On balance, NEC was guilty of
failure to fulfill only unwarranted expectations. Its inadequacies
must be judged as an instrument in a total administrative
and political system. Its achievements were notable and
significant. First, it succeeded in accomplishing a
measure of policy and administrative coordination at a
critical time. It served as a much-needed forum for clearance
of many problems during an experimental period. It was
an ongoing conference for planning and clarification of
objectives. Second, significant policies like our banking and
housing, and Federal Reserve policies originated in NEC
decisions. New Deal housing policy, HOLC, FHA, and PWA
were policies declared by NEC. Third, NEC created consumer advisory councils which were an important attempt to
enlist consumer interest in government policy and to give the
public a voice in government administration. Fourth, it set up

---

[20] Those disrespectful of NEC spoke of it as the New Deal "Town
Meeting," of "The blue and the gay," or "Of Thee I Sing" after the then
current musical comedy which satirized the presidency.

a network of state and local emergency councils which provided a useful lesson in government decentralization. When during World War II, the Government once again embarked on economic regulation through price control and rationing, the lessons of these field offices were not lost. These NEC councils proved valuable laboratories to study the problems involved in any decentralized administration. The NEC experience with State Emergency Councils glaringly revealed the impact of conflicts and overlapping of Washington policy on the "firing line." This network of field offices was a line of communication that kept Washington soberly aware of its errors. Fifth, NEC inaugurated the policy of requiring executive agencies to clear their legislative proposals with the President—an important procedure in achieving executive policy coordination. That procedure, now administered by the Bureau of the Budget, has become a keystone in the structure of presidential policy formation. Sixth, the decision to publish a governmental manual was an important step in keeping the public informed as government grew more complex. Today, the *U. S. Government Organization Manual* is issued annually and is an indispensable means to an informed citizenry. Seventh, the NEC performed a useful role in connection with the proper handling of personnel hired to staff the new emergency agencies at a time of rapid expansion of personnel. The action of its classification unit "resulted in much more uniformity of salary policies throughout the emergency agencies than would have obtained in the absence of any central review."[21]

The full worth of NEC eludes the sum of particular achievements. The question we must put is a functional one. How great was its contribution to the clarification of purposes and means? What difficulties might have arisen had it not existed? Such assessments can not be made with either precision or accuracy. In those crisis years, NEC was a "school" for policy-makers, giving some structure to the range of programs that resisted formalization. The educative experience by any pragmatic test paid off. For all its administrative untidiness, the New Deal hammered through new structural changes in the United States.

A PORTRAIT OF F.D.R.

In the NEC proceedings, a portrait of Roosevelt is revealed in discussion with his Cabinet and leading associates. There

---

[21] President's Committee on Administrative Management, *op. cit.,* p. 86.

introduction

have been descriptions of this man in various contexts and in many roles—as legislative leader, as public tribune, as leader of his party. The unique contribution of these proceedings is their presentation of a completely candid picture of Roosevelt reacting spontaneously to his associates. These verbatim proceedings therefore communicate in a special way the flavor of his personality. Roosevelt's elan—his infectious optimism and enthusiasm comes forth clearly. That he was a skillful compromiser is indicated here, as well as his ability to be firm in resolution. In these meetings, he is a man of more basic conviction than has so far been appreciated. Yet, his "political" side—deviating, hedging, mollifying, cajoling, and persuading—is also apparent. One is forced to conclude that with Roosevelt ends and means were never separable, as they should not be with the responsible democratic politician.

Here then is a primary document on presidential leadership in time of crisis. A public leader has as many images as he has an audience and as there are perspectives from which he may be observed. Here we see the man confronted with decision and consensus in the unique setting of his "cabinet." In this context, there are no walled-off distinctions between politics, and administration, domestic and foreign policy, etc. All the lines of the political network converge. Leadership expresses itself as negotiation and (at best) synthesis rather than the mythical and dramatic conceptions of our political folk-lore. Leadership is also at once the multi-roled work and contribution of one man, and yet inextricably an organizational product.

This brief introduction attempts to indicate the many perspectives to which these Proceedings contribute. The significance of this agency and its meetings lie beyond its successes or failures. There is more continuity in our national political life than is conveyed by the surface of our day-to-day politics. The halting experience of NEC was an important antecedent to abiding developments. As an account of an administrative experiment and historic events, it recreates a period whose mood, policies, and personalities are still fresh in memory and impact.

LESTER G. SELIGMAN

Held in the Cabinet Room of the Executive Offices,
The White House, Tuesday, December 19, 1933, at 2:00 p.m.

_____

Present: the President of the United States; the Attorney General;
the Secretary of Agriculture; the Secretary of Commerce; the Secretary
of Labor; the Hon. Harold M. Stephens, Assistant Attorney General;
the Hon. E. Willard Jensen, Assistant Secretary of the Special Industrial
Recovery Board; the Administrator of Agricultural Adjustment
Administration; the Administrator of Federal Emergency Relief; the
Hon. Charles H. March, Chairman, Federal Trade Commission; the Hon.
G. C. Haas, Deputy Governor of the Farm Credit Administration; the
Administrator for Industrial Recovery; the Chairman of the Home
Owners' Loan Corporation; the Executive Director.

_____

[This initial meeting of the National Emergency Council is
of special interest to the general reader, and of even greater
interest to students of top level government policy coordination.
The formal rules and regulations drawn up for the functioning
of NEC are printed as Appendix B and contain an attempt to
crystallize on paper the expectations regarding the agency.
F.D.R.'s discussion in the early part of this meeting provides
a supplement to these formalized aspirations. He seems to have
had three primary functions in mind for NEC, which he here
expresses. First and foremost, he wanted a place where discussion
of policies and problems could be carried on that he might
absorb and use in resolving the issues involved. That he expected
NEC as such to _make_ policy decisions on major questions
seems unlikely from the tenor of his remarks here. Secondly,
he saw NEC, and particularly its director, as an agency for
relieving him of the burden of settling inter-agency
conflicts and problems. Finally, he saw NEC as the apex of
a pyramid of state committees made up of representatives
of emergency activities and agencies, and headed by state
directors of NEC who could coordinate the emergency
work in each state.
The major problem discussed in this first meeting was the
up-flow of information to the President and to the departments and agencies in Washington, which could serve as
checks on progress and guides to action. This concern with
administrative intelligence was unique in the history of
national administrations, as was the urgent need for

statistical information as a guide for government policy. We shall refer again to the special importance of statistical data.—Editors' Note.]

THE PRESIDENT: This is a very exclusive little organization. The general thought, as you know, in organizing this Emergency Council is to centralize the work of putting the country back on its feet, especially in the relationship of that work to the general public, and Frank Walker has prepared a statement. I think he might as well go ahead and read it so as to orient us before we discuss it. The Emergency Council is not so big that we cannot have some discussion, which I think is a good thing. The other organization, the Executive Council,[1] which will meet on alternate Tuesdays, is excellent for information but it is too big for us to have much discussion. I think this is a much more practical unit than the larger one on this emergency work. Go ahead, Frank.

MR. WALKER:[2] [Mr. Walker read the Executive Order, which is in the Introduction.]

In addition to that, the question that has not been determined is with reference to a consumer representative.

THE PRESIDENT: That is on the list to be talked over. Now have you that proposed statement by me?

MR. WALKER: I didn't write that out.

THE PRESIDENT: There is another matter in connection with the need of this National Emergency Council that occurred to me and which may not have occurred to you, and that is that Congress is coming in about two weeks. I have been comparatively free since the sixteenth day of June to act as sort of father to all the new agencies that have come, and I have been only too glad to do it. I think things have run along in an exceedingly happy way; but there are limits to the number of hours in my day, and there have been, of course, a great many matters of what might be called quite frankly, not minor details, but lesser problems that I have handled in the past but which I cannot continue to handle while Congress is here. When Congress is

---

[1] The Executive Council was created July 11, 1933, and merged with the National Emergency Council on Oct. 29, 1934. Its membership did not differ greatly from that of the NEC itself.

[2] Appendix A is an alphabetical list of persons who appear or are prominently mentioned in the meetings. Brief biographical notes give background, position in the administration, and subsequent career. The names are not individually footnoted; the reader may refer to the Appendix when necessary.

here, I have probably on the average of between three and four hours a day of conferences with congressional leaders, with committees, with individual senators and congressmen who want something for their districts, and so forth, and during that time I cannot devote to the administration end of the government quite the same time I can devote when Congress is away.

Now, all of this recovery program I think is going along very well, and it is quite remarkable to me that we have not had more overlapping and clashes and problems where one or more agencies get mixed up with some other agency. It is extraordinary the way we have kept the various channels free from interference from other channels; but the time has come when I have got to have somebody to act as sort of alter ego for me during the congressional session, going around and acting as my legs and ears and eyes and making certain—what might be called suggestions. I would not call them decisions, because we don't do things that way, but working out these things in such a way that they will not come up to me during the session of Congress.

The first suggestion I have is that Frank has made one mistake in this preliminary report and the suggestions, and that is that he has described the Council as being headed by an *acting* executive director. I think it is much better to leave out the word "acting." He is the executive director. That is the first practical suggestion to be made today. Frank has been doing this work for me and doing an extraordinarily good piece of work. I think we would all feel very happy if he would leave off that word "acting" and run this show for us until such time as your wife insists that you come back to New York, and then I want to speak to her first! (*Laughter*)

MR. WALKER: We tried to follow that idea of "suggestion."

THE PRESIDENT: If we go ahead with this, it will give a meeting every two weeks, and I will try to come into these meetings. If I am not here, Frank will preside over them. If I can come, I certainly will.

As I said before, with such a small number we can have general discussion around the table, which is of very great value; and at the same time, in between, the executive director can work out this problem out in the three thousand counties of the United States, and the forty-eight states, each with their organization. The thing has been that we have organized an awful lot of local committees. Almost everybody in the government has a local representative in almost every county. Their name is legion. I think we can tie the whole thing in together.

This first came up with the idea of creating a bureau of information. That was the suggestion, I think, of Mrs. Rumsey, that there should be a bureau of information in every county. The more we thought it over the more we thought we could extend it and consolidate certain functions in a comparatively small number of hands. Then General Johnson suggested that we tie the whole thing in with his enforcement work of NRA. That seemed to be a perfectly pious idea, so now we have this conception of a well-centralized organization in every state, with a state director and with a county organization, that will be directly responsible to this National Emergency Council. Of course that does not mean that when that particular organization is functioning on NRA it will not communicate directly with General Johnson; it should. And when functioning on farm mortgages it would confer with Chester Davis, and so on with everybody else.

The duties as set forth here are very simple. I suppose we may have to have more rules and regulations as we go on.

MR. WALKER: Our experience will teach us how many agencies are needed, and then we can establish them.

THE PRESIDENT: Yes, as you go along. I don't think we want in the Council itself much paper work. What do you think?

MR. WALKER: I think the experience of the Special NRA Board[3] would be very helpful. They have had a lot of problems before them, handled by the Secretary of Commerce.

THE PRESIDENT: You know the meetings that we usually have on Tuesdays of the Executive Council are so big and there is so much paper work that it takes an hour and a half to two hours to get through it. It is more informative than anything else. It gives me an excellent picture of every branch of the government. But my idea is that this particular group should keep the paper work down to a minimum and have as much discussion as possible. Do you think that is good?

MR. WALKER: I think so.

THE PRESIDENT: What do you all think of it? Somebody start in and talk.

---

[3] The Special Industrial Recovery Board was created June 16, 1933, as a supervisory policy board for the NRA administrator, Gen. Hugh Johnson. The board consisted of various members of the Cabinet whose departments related to NRA work. It was absorbed by NEC by Executive Order, Dec. 18, 1933, the day before this meeting.

4

SECRETARY ROPER: The Executive Secretary has referred to our Board. I assume that it is in order now to suggest that our Board be absorbed by this Council.

THE PRESIDENT: We can do that perfectly well.

MR. WALKER: I think that was done by Executive Order.

SECRETARY ROPER: I take it that it will be necessary to preserve the records of this old Board, and to that end I suggest this resolution:

Resolved, That the National Emergency Council adopt in toto and continue in full force and effect the resolutions and rules and regulations heretofore adopted, made, or established by the National Recovery Board.

That could be modified, but the idea there is to avoid any misunderstanding as to what is to be done about the policies that have been agreed upon by our Board. This just brings them over into this Council; of course they can be changed, but this simply brings the records over.

THE PRESIDENT: I do not know what your resolutions were, so I cannot very well pass on that.

SECRETARY ROPER: It is just a matter of bringing over the records.

JUDGE STEPHENS: I have been in all the meetings, and I should like to speak in favor of that resolution. We have had a great many questions relating to statistical data and compliance organization on which subcommittees worked, and finally worked out policies, and the record of those policies would save a lot of investigation. Is that your idea?

SECRETARY ROPER: Exactly!

THE PRESIDENT: How would you word it?

SECRETARY ROPER: Resolved, That the National Emergency Council adopt in toto and continue in full force and effect the rules and regulations and forms heretofore adopted by the Special Industrial Recovery Board.

GENERAL JOHNSON: I think that is all right. I think I would be the principal person concerned if there were any objection to that, and I think it is all right.

MR. WALKER: There would not be any rules in conflict with this here, would there?

COMMISSIONER MARCH: If there were, we could repeal them.

ATTORNEY GENERAL CUMMINGS: I think it would be very well to adopt that and then have a survey made as to exactly what has been done with a view to making any changes necessary to harmonize the program.

THE PRESIDENT: We could put in there "continue in full force and effect *subject to change.*" Any objections? I hear none. Passed.

MR. WALKER: According to the Executive Order, the rules are to be approved by the President.

THE PRESIDENT: Those rules that you read. Are there any suggestions? Do you want me to read them again? They are not very long . . . .
Now there you have left off the consumers' representative.

MR. WALKER: Yes, sir.

THE PRESIDENT: What do you think of putting the consumers' representative on?

GENERAL JOHNSON: I think there is a great deal of misunderstanding about that. The real consumers' representative in this suggestion is the President of the United States, and when you attempt to select somebody and say that they represent the consumers it is a very difficult thing. I think we should select somebody and have them here so that it can always be said that they have an office.

THE PRESIDENT: What do you think, Frances?

SECRETARY PERKINS: I talked to Mrs. Rumsey about this, and I think that the real consumer problem is to make the actual consumers—the human beings—vocative in some kind of organization small enough and near enough to them in their locals so that gradually, over a period of years, they can find a channel through which they can express what their real local problem is. The economists can analyze some of these problems, but they are never the problems that the people in the lumber camps in Maine feel is their problem. It is, therefore, pretty important in setting up this organization to plan for the gradual development of simple, human organizations through which the people of that locality can give voice to their peculiar economic problem as consumers. They get their political voice when they vote on election day, but they get no channel through which to express themselves on these problems.

THE PRESIDENT: Ought not that to be a permanent person?

GENERAL JOHNSON: The organization is to receive complaints and see that they get action, and therefore the consumer does have a voice right there.

MR. WALKER: What we have in mind is having these various county committees and breaking them up into subcommittees, one of which would be a consumers' subcommittee before whom all the consumers could register their thoughts and ideas.
I think it is going to be necessary to have some machinery down here in Washington to provide the information for them.

THE PRESIDENT: Wouldn't that be somebody at your right hand—an assistant to the executive director, in other words?

MR. WALKER: You have a Consumers' Advisory Board[4] in existence, headed by Mrs. Rumsey. In Agricultural Adjustment, you have somebody. I think, looking after that, all the way down. As the Secretary of Labor suggested, I think there should be some place down in the field—in the counties and various localities—where the consumer will have an opportunity to make protest, or to be vocative, as she suggests.

THE PRESIDENT: Don't you want somebody in Washington, at your right hand, to tie all that in together?

MR. WALKER: I do. And I think we should have somebody representing the consumer on this Council, and the same person should head up the consumers' work.

THE PRESIDENT: In other words, you would not take anybody from an existing government position.

MR. WALKER: Somebody like Mrs. Rumsey.[5]

THE PRESIDENT: And we would turn him or her over to you to act as your representative on all these county and local problems.

MR. WALKER: Yes, sir.

THE PRESIDENT: And that one person would come here to this table with you.

GENERAL JOHNSON: I think that would be fine. I think that is exactly the way to do it.

MR. FAHEY: Don't you think it is desirable, from the standpoint of these consumer groups, to have them feel that they are appropriately represented at the top?

THE PRESIDENT: What do you think about it?

GENERAL JOHNSON: I would be all in favor of it. I raised the question originally. Henry [Wallace] has a consumers' [counsel],[6] and we have a consumers' advisory board.

THE PRESIDENT: What do you think, Frances?

SECRETARY PERKINS: It is well-known that Mary Rumsey is a very close personal friend of mine, and I think my views would be colored by personal affection.

SECRETARY WALLACE: I would suggest that you give her [Mrs. Rumsey] the opportunity to designate an alternate who might perhaps be someone in her council or in our organization.

GENERAL JOHNSON: It might be a good thing to have somebody in your organization because that is a separate body. They have consumers' problems from another angle.

MR. WALKER: My thought was to try to coordinate that council between

---

[4] Consumers' Advisory Board of NRA, Mary H. Rumsey, chairman.
[5] Mrs. Rumsey later joined the NEC as Adviser on Consumer Problems.
[6] Frederic C. Howe was the Consumers' Counsel in the Agricultural Adjustment Administration, 1933-1935.

7

NRA and Agricultural Adjustment, and in the absence of the representative as chosen, let them select a delegate in her place who comes from the Agricultural Administration. They surely should be coordinated, I should think.

ATTORNEY GENERAL CUMMINGS: Is Mrs. Sabin[7] in public work at all?

THE PRESIDENT: I don't think so.

MR. WALKER: The suggestion came from various members of the Board that some had sent delegates to sit in their place who had no authority to act for the department.

THE PRESIDENT: I am inclined to think that, as I have given up the Tuesday Cabinet Meeting and substituted the Executive Council meeting on Tuesday, so that this does not make any more meetings, but brings the Executive Council one Tuesday and the Emergency Council the next, the actual people should come themselves rather than have assistants come.

MR. FAHEY: I think that is very important.

THE PRESIDENT: It is very important to have the actual heads come themselves.

SECRETARY PERKINS: There are, Mr. President, a lot of occasions when one has to be away, and other occasions when someone in one's department knows more on a matter to be considered than the head of the department. There are occasions when that is the appropriate thing. For instance, if statistical matters are under discussion, it would be better that I send Dr. Lubin.

THE PRESIDENT: I think assistants might come for the purpose of giving information and advice, but not for the purpose of voting or participating in the actions of the Council. I think that should be the office of the original members.

MR. FAHEY: That could be controlled by the preparation of an agenda for the fixed meetings and placing it in the hands of everybody in advance, so that members would be put on notice in time to decide whether to send an alternate or bring someone for a particular purpose.

There is one other suggestion: you spoke about paper work; so far as a lot of these reports are concerned—in the distribution of reports that have to be considered in advance—I think it would be of great value in each case if they could be accompanied by a very brief summary attached to the front page, because the things all of us are required to do under present conditions are so numerous that it is simply overwhelming.

THE PRESIDENT: In the Tuesday meeting of the Executive Council, the summary in the end generally runs to five pages, but that

---

[7] Perhaps Mrs. Charles H. Sabin (see Appendix A).

	is the summary of 30 to 40 pages.
MR. WALKER:	Sometimes 50 pages.
SECRETARY PERKINS:	I myself have found that general survey very informative. I think it is vital to us to see the whole rather than exclusively the part under our control.
GENERAL JOHNSON:	We get that at the other meeting.
THE PRESIDENT:	In No. 1, you would add "the representative of the Consumers' Council."[8]
GENERAL JOHNSON:	The difficulty with that is that the Secretary of Agriculture calls his consumers' organization "The Consumers' Council."
MR. WALKER:	We were to have Consumers' Councils in the various localities where we think they are going to be necessary.
SECRETARY PERKINS:	As a matter of fact, I don't think the word *representative* can possibly be used. Why not say "an individual to present consumers' problems," or something like that?
THE PRESIDENT:	But they would have to have some kind of title on paper.
MR. WALKER:	According to the Act, the Executive Director has authority to appoint a representative of the county consumers' council.
SECRETARY ROPER:	Why not put in the word *county?*
MR. FAHEY:	Why not make that plural—*consumers' councils?*
THE PRESIDENT:	The Representative of the Consumers' Councils.
SECRETARY PERKINS:	In the present state of news which has been recently stimulated to an interest in this matter, I think you might get the counties at once getting together and organizing themselves for a purpose which you do not now anticipate, and that you might get some extraordinary suggestions pouring in here that would have no relation. This person will be developing consumers' councils. They do not exist at the present time. Isn't that right?
MR. WALKER:	Yes.
SECRETARY PERKINS:	Could you use a word that would make it clear that this is a representative of the problems of consumers?
GENERAL JOHNSON:	Why not say "Counsel for Consumers"?
SECRETARY WALLACE:	Why not say "Consumers' Representative of NRA and AAA"?
THE PRESIDENT:	I think Hugh's idea is pretty good—"Counsel for Consumers," and stop right there.

---

[8] Whenever the Proceedings record that lengthy reports were read at these meetings, interspersed with questions and comments, the report itself will not be reproduced; and only occasionally, where issues were or remain of particular interest, will there be any explanatory or background material in the notes. The editors think that the value for the present-day reader of these portions of the meetings lies not in the details but in the breadth and complexity of the matters discussed, and the interest taken by the President and the members of the Council in them. Any omission from the original transcripts is indicated by an ellipsis.

GENERAL JOHNSON: That doesn't tie you up.

ATTORNEY GENERAL CUMMINGS: "Adviser" would be a better term.

MR. WALKER: That gives an official title that could be used, "Chairman of the Consumers' Advisory Board."

THE PRESIDENT: That is under NRA.

ATTORNEY GENERAL CUMMINGS: I suggest the word "adviser."

GENERAL JOHNSON: That is better.

SECRETARY PERKINS: "Adviser on Consumer Problems." . . .

THE PRESIDENT: That is the best yet. Stick in at the bottom, under No. 1, "Adviser on Consumers' Problems." . . . .
You want, in addition to that, not only the word "conflict" But also "where they run parallel" or words to that effect . . . .
I made a suggestion there to Frank—this goes back to the old Wilson administration—that the Council should every other Tuesday lunch together at the Cosmos Club or some place like that at one o'clock and stay there until 2:30 or 3:00 —whatever length of time is necessary—and then come over here. All have to have lunch somewhere. If you do not go out to lunch, you ought to—not that we all do—and then come over and meet with me. What do you think of that idea?

MR. WALKER: I think there might be clearer discussion in the presence of the President.

SECRETARY PERKINS: Long experience has taught me to distrust lunch conferences; I think they are awfully unsatisfactory. I should rather tell everybody to go and have his lunch at 12 o'clock and meet at one. Most people can get lunch before one-thirty. Our meetings would function better.

THE PRESIDENT: The tendency is to go to sleep after lunch.

ATTORNEY GENERAL CUMMINGS: I think two o'clock is a safer hour. I do not usually find it possible to get away from my office before one, get a ten-minute bite, and get here at two o'clock.

THE PRESIDENT: That would be all right to meet here in this room at two o'clock and I would come in at three. (*The President then read down to the point about members absenting themselves.*) That is the question I raised. I think it is a question as to how far we should delegate full authority to our assistants. What do you think?

MR. WALKER: If they do not delegate them, then they have to come.

COMMISSIONER MARCH: There are times when it is impossible to be here.

THE PRESIDENT: Then send a representative.

SECRETARY ROPER: Your idea is to eliminate that, then?

THE PRESIDENT: "Any member absent from Washington at the time of a meeting shall delegate a representative with full authority to act."

SECRETARY PERKINS: I think that is exactly right.

SECRETARY ROPER: All right.

SECRETARY PERKINS: Absent or ill.

SECRETARY ROPER: You are not supposed to be ill in Washington.

SECRETARY PERKINS: Not in this salubrious climate!

(The President then read down to the point about fixing compensation of employees.)

THE PRESIDENT: That means of the Council; it doesn't mean that you are going to fix the compensation of Hugh Johnson's employees.

MR. WALKER: Oh, no. Those are all subject to your approval.

THE PRESIDENT: That is all right.

GENERAL JOHNSON: Why wouldn't it be better to have that "subject to the disapproval of the President," because otherwise everything that is done still has to be brought to you. That would take up as much of your time as if you had not invented this device.

THE PRESIDENT: Instead of saying "subject to the approval or disapproval," leave all this out in this *A-B-C-D* and then put at the end, "Actions of the Executive Director shall be subject to such approval as the President may from time to time require."

GENERAL JOHNSON: I think that is very much better.

THE PRESIDENT: That covers the whole thing.

MR. HOPKINS: Will these rules get to the press? If so, it seems to me the use of the word "conflict" is unfortunate. It would be better to speak of affirmative things and not assume there may be conflicts.

ATTORNEY GENERAL CUMMINGS: They are pretty sure to get it sooner or later.

THE PRESIDENT: What is another word for that word "'conflict?'"

SECRETARY WALLACE: Promote harmony.

ATTORNEY GENERAL CUMMINGS: Require further coordination.

THE PRESIDENT: Require coordination or consolidation. That is in Sec. 2(d) at the end. It occurs somewhere else, too; 5(a), "subject to the approval of the President in all matters wherein any conflict of policies or activities between the various agencies exists." I would say there, "on all matters relating to the coordination or consolidation of policies or activities between the various agencies."

Are there any more suggestions on the rules and regulations?[9] If not, we will assume that they are adopted as read and corrected.

(At this point, a few words of inaudible conversation passed between Mr. Walker and the President.)

THE PRESIDENT: I am going to put it up to the members of the Cabinet. Frank

---

[9] These rules and regulations are printed as Appendix B to this volume.

suggests that in my absence, the senior member of the Cabinet should preside. I don't think any of you people will object to having Frank preside. He is in touch with it all.

ATTORNEY GENERAL CUMMINGS: I haven't the slightest objection not only to his presiding but doing all the work! (*Laughter*)

THE PRESIDENT: The first suggestion of the executive director is vetoed! (*More laughter*) Have you any other happy thought?

MR. WALKER: Not now.

THE PRESIDENT: Before we go on, I think you ought to show the chart.

MR. WALKER: I didn't bring the chart because it was merely tentative with references to our local organization. I made this suggestion, that it might be well to have these state directors come on here the middle of January and have somebody from each department advise them in a short talk about the activities of each department, and give them all the information we had at that time, and perhaps get suggestions as to the need in communities for making a survey now. I do not think it is going to be necessary to go into every county, and as I said before, I think experience should teach us in how many communities we want to go. Our chart will be prepared in accordance with that at a later date. I thought that if it was agreeable after the various heads of departments advise the state directors, the President would later address them at some place convenient to the President.[10]

THE PRESIDENT: You would have them come on about the middle of January?

MR. WALKER: That is my suggestion.

THE PRESIDENT: The next meeting we would have here would be Tuesday the second. The next meeting would be the sixteenth of January. Why don't we have that right after the sixteenth of January? That gives us two meetings in which to get things pretty well organized before that.

COMMISSIONER MARCH: About the twentieth, Mr. President?

THE PRESIDENT: Yes.

MR. WALKER ...: These suggestions will go in writing later to the departmental heads.

...It has come to our attention by the survey that many letters go to various heads of departments where they do not belong, and there is considerable delay with reference to this mail and instead of being handled within two or three or four days, it is often held up for two or three weeks. If we establish this liaison activity, where there is doubt, reference to the chart will show where a letter should be directed,

---

[10] The state NEC directors met on Jan. 31, 1934.

and if a letter comes to the wrong department it will be immediately sent on. A lot of correspondence comes to departmental heads, and they, to use the language of the Army, sort of "pass the buck" and do not try to send it through the correct channel quickly. With a liaison officer established in each department this would be avoided.... We have no uniform index to rules and regulations, and it seems to me that one can be developed so that in seeking information it will be uniform and standardized. We have the services of the Congressional Library index men who can do this kind of work and bring about a uniformity that can be very helpful....

In other words, I think we have a lot of committees in existence that should either be eliminated, abolished, or consolidated, and if any of the departmental heads desire to retain them, I think it might be well to set forth the reasons for their retention.[11] A memorandum on that, if it is agreeable, will go out.

THE PRESIDENT: Anything else?

MR. WALKER: Nothing more that I can think of.

THE PRESIDENT: There is one thing I would like to have a little discussion on, and that is, it is tremendously important for every one of us to get a cross section from, let us say, every one of the forty-eight states, as to how the whole recovery program is working out. We haven't got it today. I don't know how to get it. Various of you have agents in the field appointed on some one particular phase. Harry Hopkins may have a relief agent that is doing checking-up work in some given area. That relief agent gives not only a picture of how Harry's relief work is getting on, but he also reports, let us say, that the Farm Credit work is going terribly slowly, or that the Home Credit work is going extraordinarily well, or that the NRA is unpopular, and so forth and so on. There is no doubt that man can give me, or any of us, a fairly comprehensive picture of the state. But now I have a mental picture based on insufficient information,—a dab here, a dab there, and a dab somewhere else, but it gives a mental picture. As to how ten-cent cotton is working in Georgia; I would not have

---

[11] NEC undertook a survey of the numerous interdepartmental committees that had either sprung up to achieve coordination in the early days of the New Deal, or were left over from previous administrations. See the transcript for the meeting of Dec. 11, 1934, for further discussion of this matter. See also, E. H. Hobbs, *Behind the President* (Washington, D.C., 1954), p. 126.

known how it was working unless I had gone down there.
I spent two weeks there, and I know.

COMMISSIONER MARCH: That is a good illustration.

THE PRESIDENT: How can we all get the picture of what I saw in Georgia?

SECRETARY ROPER: We can get it through this organization we are setting up now.

SECRETARY PERKINS: When you made the original call for the Governors Conference on the sixth of March,[12] didn't you have in mind utilizing that council to get cooperation with the various branches of the federal government and to give you just that kind of report by a trusted agent in every state—not the governor, but someone on which you and the governor mutually agreed? And you will remember that we discussed the need in the state of New York of what we called a super-statistician or a super-economist to be looking over the whole state for you when you were governor. The agencies in some states are good and in others they are not good.

THE PRESIDENT: Take four states that are contiguous: North and South Dakota, Minnesota, and Wisconsin. In North Dakota, Langer, the governor, is loud-mouthed, unpopular in his own state, rotten state organization for relief work, no public works planning, nothing else, plays to the gallery most unsuccessfully. We could not do anything there through the Langer organization. South Dakota, Tom Berry, cowboy, darned good fellow all through the state; they need relief terribly; the situation is pitiful in South Dakota in many parts, but their machinery is clicking and everything is going fine. In Minnesota, Olson, playing for Olson all the way through—everything is for Olson. Not so bad in some things, but it is Olson machinery. In Wisconsin, the governor is Schmedeman, just a plain weak sister run by a fellow named Crowley; Schmedeman, scared to get off the train for fear somebody will blow up a milk factory in his face. Tom Berry said, "Don't get off here, go on through; I will take care of you in South Dakota!" Schmedeman afraid to walk down the streets in his own state! Herring is a distinctly weak governor in Iowa, but his relief work, and some other machinery in the state, is doing pretty well. I don't know how far we can go unless we modify that original plan, put it up to the effective governors, and in other states, not have anything to do with them.

SECRETARY PERKINS: Have them do it on your plan. There is a great educative force in getting them to make a survey and having them fall down

---

[12] Governors' Conference at the White House, March 6, 1933. *Public Papers and Addresses of Franklin D. Roosevelt: 1933. The Year of Crisis.* (New York, 1938), pp. 18-24.

14

on it. It calls to their attention locally the things they ought to know about, but don't know, and then you can, through Mr. Walker, you can send in some effective agent of the federal government to assist them where they do not know how to do it and so teach them how; and where they are not able to do it at all, he could bring back the picture himself. I think you have an effective instrument which has long been needed.

THE PRESIDENT: The governor of Oklahoma—let him know why it is he is out in the cold. You haven't got a complete picture of how the NRA is working?

GENERAL JOHNSON: No, but we get a tremendous number of pieces of mail every day, and every piece is opened and digested twice a week, and an analysis of the telegrams comes in every day. That is not broken down as to states, but you get a pretty good idea. Some are highly critical, some constructive and some destructive, but it gives you a good idea, right up to the minute too, for the telegraphic analysis comes in the day after it is received.

THE PRESIDENT: How could we tie in on that plan? What machinery would we need?

GENERAL JOHNSON: I think you are going to have the most perfect machinery covering every state and every county in the country.

SECRETARY PERKINS: In the Department of Labor, I am already doing that with state departments of labor, utilizing an information service on our matters through state departments where they are able to get it, and we are trying to build that up. I think they have relief departments, agricultural departments, and other entities of government that you could utilize; and supplement them, using this Emergency Council—using Mr. Walker's well-known diplomatic techniques for approach to these governors who are not entirely harmonious. I think somebody ought to think out with Mr. Walker a very careful analysis of what it is you wish to know—what are the facts you ought to know in order to judge of the situation in every particular state and ask them to give you the information and to get it regularly at stated intervals. And then provide them with a method of getting it, if they do not have it.

SECRETARY ROPER: We have 26 representatives of the Department of Commerce through the country.

THE PRESIDENT: Suppose we make some bad selections of state directors?

ATTORNEY GENERAL CUMMINGS: Why don't you consider appointing liaison officers who would report from each state independent from the group?

15

THE PRESIDENT: That is one of the functions of the state director. I am groping for something that will give me the information I need.

MR. FAHEY: I wonder if your best method to consider on that is not the possibility of using some well-selected field men operating from here directly under Mr. Walker and reporting back. The difficulty of depending on state directors is not alone that you will have a certain proportion of weak ones, but all the rest will be reporting that they are doing a first-class job.

ATTORNEY GENERAL CUMMINGS: That is the same idea I had.

MR. FAHEY: You have great variations in the conditions in the states. Suppose you had twelve men, one for each Federal Reserve district, and each one keeping an eye on the states in his group, getting specific information and checking up from independent sources.

THE PRESIDENT: The difficulty is this: the operations are so tremendously extensive that I do not know how one man can cover them all. In the Kansas City Federal Reserve District there are six or seven states. A man going out there would be checking, we will say, in the first place, on Harry Hopkins' relief work. That would be a terrific job. He would be checking on NRA in all those states, and that would be terrific; and he would be checking on AAA in those states, and checking on Farm Credit and Home Credit. What I was wondering is this: it would take, not a statistician, but a fellow who would go through things and give us a simple report. Suppose Frank [Walker] had under him some good man who would get each week a report from each one of the forty-eight state directors. That is No. 1.

Let us say the state director in Iowa sends a report of all the activities in Iowa as he saw them. At the same time you would send a report to this man under Frank as to how the Home Loan was working in each of the forty-eight states; then the same thing with AAA, same thing with NRA. In other words, General Johnson would send to him each week or each two weeks an estimate of the situation in the NRA in every state. All that this fellow would have to do would be to consolidate those estimates of the situation. If he could get this on a big sheet of paper every two weeks, it would be a pretty good idea. To be sure, you would not have the outside idea. How to get the outside point of view, I do not know.

GENERAL JOHNSON: I neglected to say that it so happens that the president of

Dun & Bradstreet[13] is the head of one of our divisions. He has had his organization render reports at stated intervals. Those reports can be used, but there is some question of the propriety of using private reports.

THE PRESIDENT: I think that would be fine to use it. Every Sunday morning I get the *New York Times*; on the editorial page, there is a large editorial that says "just too bad," and that is all it says, but it takes two columns to say it. Then turn to the financial page, and you find a large financial article which says, "We don't know where we are going, we don't know what the administration's policy is." On the next page, you begin to get reports, the wire stories, from all over the country; and out of 50 wire stories, 49 localities say things are going fine, and the fiftieth says, "While there has not been much change this week, things are not any worse."

This is the sort of thing that gets my goat. I would like to have a better picture.

MR. HAAS: May I make a suggestion, Mr. President? I believe a statistician could give you a picture of bank deposits by states by months; automobile registrations by states by months; electric power and light figures; and could make up an index of agricultural income in the state of Georgia, say, where the income increased so much; Secretary Wallace's cotton payments, so much; farm mortgages, so much; relief, so much; so you would have a picture of actual recovery correlated with the activity of the Relief Administration.

THE PRESIDENT: We want three things. First, we want to check up and see how the government operations are getting along; that is a checkup on ourselves—how is Harry getting along with relief; we all want to know that.

The second is what you talked about, the actual financial conditions, using financial in the very, very broad meaning of the term.

And the third is public opinion.

Well, now, the three may not check at all. You may have a rotten public opinion with good financial conditions and good administrative conditions. We want to check on all those things.

SECRETARY WALLACE: Harry Hopkins has a smart girl that circulates around the country and gets closer to the people than anybody else.

THE PRESIDENT: I think Lorena Hickox's [Hickok] reports have been perfectly grand. She is trained to follow a trail; she is after quail and she

---

13 Arthur D. Whiteside (see Appendix A).

won't flush a rabbit. Do you see the point? Lorena Hickox [Hickok] goes right after it, but I have got to have somebody with a broader knowledge and a broader point of view. She would not know anything about Home Loan.

MR. FAHEY: My suggestion, Mr. President, was based on our experience.

THE PRESIDENT: Do you think you can get twelve people in this country able to handle the work around over a big district in such a way that we could take their judgment?

MR. FAHEY: It all depends on the character of the person. If people are really trained to investigate and observe, that is one thing. In connection with this recent experience of ours, the fact of the matter is that since the middle of November we have only begun to find out where we stand as a result of getting competent men out in the field. We found every one of these state directors trying to send in figures and reports that indicate he is doing a great job, and you don't know what the truth is until you dig down underneath and really find out what people think. The fact is, it is important to get this reflection of nationwide public opinion. A lot of states have sources of information that can be tapped—there is no question about it. In any event, I think that phase of it is worthy of study and perhaps experiment, but it depends altogether on the kind of people that can be put on the job.

THE PRESIDENT: It takes almost a superhuman person to do that.

MR. FAHEY: I would not say so. The men are doing it without any great difficulty.

THE PRESIDENT: They are doing it from the statistical point of view.

MR. FAHEY: They report on the outstanding developments in the state, and they manage to present a pretty fair picture of the state conditions.

MR. HOPKINS: I wonder if Mr. Walker has considered getting all the reports sent in by the field people of all departments referring to any state or city and having those analyzed, and see what kind of written reports are coming in from the field. I have an idea that there are a great many written reports which Mr. Walker should have that might bring to light a great deal of information which doesn't get around at all. I wonder what reports are coming in from state people now.

GENERAL JOHNSON: [Winfield] Riefler is supposed to do that, and I think he does a pretty good job.

MR. HOPKINS: There must be federal agents that are meeting these state officers all the time and writing letters and memoranda and reports as to what someone said to them. You have got to have judgment as to whether they know what they are talking about, but I imagine there is a great deal more information.

SECRETARY ROPER: Mr. President, there is a great deal more in our files than we ourselves know. Mr. Jensen has been the secretary of our Board, and I can send him through the Department of Commerce and he can bring you very reliable information.

THE PRESIDENT: Frank has to have someone who will tie that information all together.

SECRETARY WALLACE: It seems to me that the writings of newspaper reporters located at hot spots would be worth more than all the material dug out of reports which would be very much behind.

I think we ought to be posted on these things very promptly.

THE PRESIDENT: Information that is a month old, or even two weeks old, is not very valuable. That is not a bad idea of Henry's to try to get some good newspaperman in every state to give us a bird's-eye view.

GENERAL JOHNSON: You analyzed this into three divisions, and I don't think the same man can do all three of them. On the purely statistical matter, if it is proper to use a private institution, I think Dun & Bradstreet could give us better information than anybody else in the country.

THE PRESIDENT: What do you think of the idea of having some newspaperman do it?

MR. FAHEY: It would be difficult to find the right kind.

THE PRESIDENT: Do you know such a newspaperman in the state of Massachusetts?

MR. FAHEY: I am afraid not.

MR. WALKER: H——right (?) [sic] could give a good idea.

THE PRESIDENT: Yes, on the City of New York; but as soon as you get north of the Bronx County line he doesn't know the difference between Chautauqua County and Cataragus County; he doesn't know where they are.

MR. WALKER: In setting up these various agencies in these committees and councils in the localities, I think we might be able to find personnel that would be helpful.

TTORNEY GENERAL CUMMINGS: You might be able to break it up, and instead of going by state lines go by regions. For instance, in New York you might have somebody take Greater New York and someone also Upper New York, or even have Upper New York divided into two or three segments. States that are homogeneous could be covered by one person. But a Chicago reporter isn't very familiar with southern Illinois. You would have to have two or three men in Illinois, and

19

you would have to have two or three men in Ohio; but in a state like Delaware or Connecticut or Rhode Island, one man could do it.

SECRETARY WALLACE: A man wouldn't need to give his full time to it.

ATTORNEY GENERAL CUMMINGS: I think the newspaper idea of finding out bad spots would be very helpful.

THE PRESIDENT: Yes, on public opinion.

MR. HOPKINS: If we could get together with Mr. Walker, we might be able to agree on the right person to send these reports in. It may not be the state director; he may not be a good reporter; he may be inarticulate. But I think throughout the country, we have people who are identified with this administration among whom we could find one or two or three who could regularly write Mr. Walker a confidential memorandum. I believe we could pick those people out now without much difficulty. We have some of our people in ten or twelve states —people identified with our administration—who have a very broad point of view, and who could make a very useful statement once a month or once in two weeks. I think that must be true in all departments of the government; and they would be happy to do it.

THE PRESIDENT: Hugh, would Dun & Bradstreet let us have that for nothing?

GENERAL JOHNSON: Yes, sir; they have been furnishing me all that free.

THE PRESIDENT: Their staff is very good.

GENERAL JOHNSON: I think it is the best there is.

THE PRESIDENT: Just about the statistical end—nothing else—the way money is moving, bank credits, department stores, chain stores, and so on.

SECRETARY WALLACE: Dr. Riefler's Federal Reserve folks get that right along.

SECRETARY ROPER: A letter from Will Rogers says conditions have improved wonderfully in the last two weeks.

THE PRESIDENT: Christmas sales are up eighteen per cent.

SECRETARY PERKINS: Agricultural implement sales are up seven and one-half per cent since September.

THE PRESIDENT: We really haven't got anywhere on this. I think we ought to set up some kind of machinery, bearing in mind those three things. First, how well the administrative work is going; and here would be my thought. Ask every one of the government agencies affected to send in to some person selected by the executive director a report, by states, relating to their own work. In other words, for instance, Harry would say, "Iowa, good; South Dakota, excellent; North Dakota, bad," and so on, purely from the administrative point of view.

Harry's point of view would be, "Am I doing my job for my department in that state?" And then grade himself or mark himself on it. That gives the point of view of each of these agents. That is the first thing. Then, your executive directors in each state would serve as at least a partial check on how it is going. That is the administrative end, No. 1.

And let us leave the statistical end to Riefler and Dun & Bradstreet, Riefler to report on alternate Tuesdays; and as the head of Dun & Bradstreet is working for Hugh, have Hugh get that confidential information and give it to Frank every two weeks, so as to get the Dun & Bradstreet checkup.

Then, No. 3, on the point of view of the public, I suggest that we try an experiment, and that is that Frank should try in half a dozen localities, perhaps, to find some individual, either a newspaperman or otherwise, for a test period of perhaps a month to give us the point of view of the public as to how we are doing.

And then see if you can work out a combination of all these things on about two pages, 24 states to a page, about two lines to a state. You can boil it down.

SECRETARY ROPER: Do I understand that the regular departments would be expected to make reports from any agencies they have?

THE PRESIDENT: No, I don't think so.

SECRETARY ROPER: Just the emergency administrations?

THE PRESIDENT: Yes, just the emergency agencies.

SECRETARY PERKINS: We break down every month the employees and payrolls. We could always provide that.

THE PRESIDENT: That would come in through Riefler.

SECRETARY PERKINS: He doesn't get that. We break it down and we only give it out to the states themselves.

GENERAL JOHNSON: Should not Riefler get from all departments of the government a breakdown by states of their figures?

THE PRESIDENT: Riefler should do that, too. That would cover it pretty well through an experimental period of perhaps a month, just so we have something every two weeks that is pretty well up to date.

MR. WALKER: A breakdown such as the Secretary of Labor mentions would be very helpful.

THE PRESIDENT: Yes, it would.

MR. HOPKINS: Would you like very interesting personal letters from people out in the field that are articulate, well written—well-known people—would you be interested in having those in his office?

THE PRESIDENT: I should say it depended on the letter and the length thereof.

21

For instance, some that you have been sending over to me. Of course, there are pages and pages and pages, and in reading pages about a couple of counties in Nebraska, I get the idea that the relief is going pretty well, but she has run into somebody who says that the revolt against NRA is about to result in bloodshed, and it takes two pages to tell the story about that. If that could be summarized and sent to Frank, that would be an excellent thing, because Frank would then pass it over to General Johnson that somebody had been out in a couple of counties in Nebraska and said they are about to take up arms against NRA. He would be glad to know that, but he doesn't want to read through all four pages. Can that be done?

MR. HOPKINS: All right.

THE PRESIDENT: Don't you think there is a lot in that?

MR. HOPKINS: Yes, sir.

THE PRESIDENT: I am tremendously interested in such things as this: The *Saturday Evening Post* finds a mother and nine children in bed while the tenth child wears the family clothing to go to the shop.

GENERAL JOHNSON: I can send the digest of correspondence covering four or five thousand letters a day, and also many complaints on that very thing.

THE PRESIDENT: If one of your letters from out around the country says these relief agents are eating all the food themselves, or something like that, it ought to get to Harry.

SECRETARY ROPER: The newspaper digest that is gotten out by the Democratic headquarters is very interesting. Of course, Mr. Walker will have access to that.

May I mention another matter, Mr. President? In order that there may be no misunderstanding when our Special Recovery Board is absorbed by this Council, I think General Johnson should be treated as all the other heads of these units. This Board has been approving his personnel journals from week to week, but I assume now that General Johnson is put on a level with all the others, and that there is no need to have those personnel sheets approved by anybody but General Johnson.

THE PRESIDENT: No, very soon the whole thing is going in like every other department, because we are becoming permanent.

GENERAL JOHNSON: I would prefer to have the Secretary of Commerce go on approving our suggested salaries as he has in the past.

THE PRESIDENT: Do it that way, then, until we put the thing under the Director of the Budget and the Comptroller General.

GENERAL JOHNSON: All right, sir.

THE PRESIDENT: I want to do that before Congress meets so that in case Congress raises a question I can say we have regularized everything.

One other question on your state directors. Can we pay them? What are you going to do about that?

MR. WALKER: We gave a lot of consideration to that. We thought we might succeed in getting volunteers. However, we queried some of the prospective directors, and it seems to me we cannot make fish of one and flesh of another. I think it is necessary to them; and, if it is agreeable, we have fixed the salaries at no less than $4,000 and not in excess of $6,000. In the larger states, we have fixed the salary at $6,000—Pennsylvania, New York, and Illinois—and in the smaller states, $4,000.

THE PRESIDENT: And you will make some savings on existing committees.

MR. WALKER: Yes, sir.

GENERAL JOHNSON: Isn't it all right to accept volunteer service?

MR. WALKER: If they want to waive their salary, I think they can do that. I think we have to establish a rule with reference to it. The question came up with reference to some men who are about on the border line. If one man would volunteer to serve without compensation, others might do it too, but it might pinch one man while to another it wouldn't mean a thing.

THE PRESIDENT: I don't think there will be any complaint from the country if we pay them. This is really going to save at least a portion of the money now being spent on these various committees by abolishing them and consolidating them; and the second point is that this also carries with it the permanent enforcement program of NRA and AAA, and to a certain extent might be called enforcement problems of relief, because relief has to be enforced or checked up to see that the right people are getting it.

SECRETARY ROPER: The difficulty is not so much in salaries as in expenses.

THE PRESIDENT: That's it; we have to keep the expenses down to a minimum.

MR. HOPKINS: Some governors do not get $4,000, and you have a few states where you are making that the minimum. We have run into that where no state official gets as much as $4,000.

SECRETARY ROPER: But that is to cover all expenses.

MR. WALKER: No, that is salary.

THE PRESIDENT: Are there any states where the governor gets less than $4,000?

SECRETARY PERKINS: The governor of Maine gets $2,000.

THE PRESIDENT: But he has a darn nice house and servants.

MR. WALKER: The sum necessary to bring about compliance machinery was estimated at $10,000,000.

GENERAL JOHNSON: That estimate was made on the theory that the worst might happen—that there would be very little voluntary service.

MR. WALKER: We are not going to reach anything like that; and besides, the machinery we are setting up in the states will have to be set up for compliance by NRA and AAA. All the functions are going to be added to the state directors and the state machinery. As we are starting out now, it will not approach near to the $10,000,000 estimate.

GENERAL JOHNSON: That was for the entire period of the Act, not for just one year.

THE PRESIDENT: I don't think $4,000 is too much. Do you, Harry?

MR. HOPKINS: You may run into a local situation that will cause a lot of trouble.

SECRETARY PERKINS: I don't think I would set a minimum. If you are going to accept volunteer service at all, I think you are very unlikely to get a man to volunteer for a $4,000 job. He would not consider that a very important job, and there is a curious vanity that relates to the amount of money a job gets.

MR. WALKER: The original plan did not include salary. It was put on the basis of personal service to the government. But we had quite a few inquiries with reference to what the salaries were going to be. Those who were interested made it evident there was a need for salary in their case.

SECRETARY ROPER: Have you looked into the National Council of Defense program to see how that was conducted?[14]

MR. WALKER: Yes, we have.

ATTORNEY GENERAL CUMMINGS: Offering a salary of $6,000 gives you a grip on the situation and enables you to select your man. It enables you to keep the organization under control; it requires him to work and has many advantages. I am strongly in favor of paying a salary not to exceed $6,000.

MR. HOPKINS: Are you asking state directors to give full time?

MR. WALKER: Our letter of query indicated that we wanted full-time service. And the compliance work is of a type that will require intelligence, integrity, and a lot of service in that work alone. In addition to that, there will be the setting up of machinery throughout the state and the general supervision. We have been trying to get a high type of individual, and I think we will get into the position where the NRA will

[14] The National Council of Defense was established by President Wilson to oversee the war mobilization program during World War I.

require a considerable amount of time. It cannot be somebody who is not going to sit in at the hearings any time NRA controversies come up. It cannot be an honorary man. He must be a director, present and supervising the hearings and investigations. I don't think your machinery is going to function without that type.

THE PRESIDENT: If you can get somebody for less than $4,000, all right. Do you have anything else?

TORNEY GENERAL CUMMINGS: What will be the order of these meetings—the Executive Council and the Emergency Council?

THE PRESIDENT: The Executive Council will meet next week.

TORNEY GENERAL CUMMINGS: Then they alternate.

THE PRESIDENT: Yes; I thought we would hold the Cabinet meeting this week on Thursday instead of Friday, because some people want to get away. Would you like to have the Executive Council on Wednesday or Thursday—say Wednesday?

TORNEY GENERAL CUMMINGS: It makes no difference to me.

THE PRESIDENT: I think we better do that.

MR. WALKER: Wednesday?

THE PRESIDENT: Yes.

MR. WALKER: How about those committees that we contemplate eliminating eventually. We thought we would break the ground for it, and the suggestion is that the President send out these messages to NRA committees.

GENERAL JOHNSON: I think we ought to thank them.

THE PRESIDENT: I do, too. I don't have to sign these, do I?

GENERAL JOHNSON: No, most of them are just to be printed and addressed to the committee. I think we ought to send out word to the compliance boards that they are supposed to stay on until they are released; but I can do that by telegram.

THE PRESIDENT: We will now adjourn for two weeks.

Meeting adjourned at 4:05 p.m.

Proceedings of the National Emergency Council

meeting no. 2
January 9, 1934

Held in the Cabinet Room of the Executive Offices, The White House, Tuesday, January 9, 1934, at 2:00 p.m.

Present: the Attorney General; the Secretary of the Interior; the Secretary of Agriculture; the Secretary of Commerce; the Secretary of Labor; the Director of the Budget; the Administrator of Agricultural Adjustment; the Administrator of Federal Emergency Relief; the Hon. Charles H. March, Chairman, Federal Trade Commission; the Administrator for Industrial Recovery; the Chairman of the Home Owners' Loan Corporation; the Adviser on Consumer Problems, Mrs. Mary H. Rumsey; Dr. Paul Douglas, Chief of the Bureau of Economics of the Consumers' Council; Lieut. K. Johnston, National Recovery Administration; the Executive Director.

[The spirit of experimentation with new ideas and organizational forms that was characteristic of the early days of the New Deal is vividly conveyed in this meeting. The philosophies and outlooks of some of the central New Deal figures emerge in their own words here, as they will in later meetings. Note especially Hopkins' pleas for caution and conservatism, and Miss Perkins' eloquent plea for grass roots democracy. The NEC functioned here primarily as a forum for the discussion of procedural problems. No decisions came forth (and in the absence of the President, it was probably not possible to arrive at decisions). The suggestion to set up a committee of those concerned was the standard resolution for many questions raised. NEC also began to function here as a channel of information to the members about agency activities; for example, the discussion of consumers councils by Professor Paul Douglas.—Editors' Note.]

MR. WALKER: If it is agreeable, I think we will proceed. The first thing we have on the agenda is the regulations of the Council as amended by the President and adopted at the last meeting; but the change is so slight that if it is agreeable I do not think there is any need of going over them again, unless someone was absent or wants to have them read. I think it is unnecessary at this time.

26

The first order of business we have is "Consideration of Proposed Consumers' Councils" presented by the Adviser on Consumer Problems. Did you want Professor Douglas with you?

MRS. RUMSEY: Yes. I have copies of the memorandum, if you would like to read them. (*Mrs. Rumsey then passed out several copies of her memorandum.*) The Consumers' Board has been advocating three things, and it is on the basis of those three problems that we have our report ready. This is Dr. [Paul] Douglas, who is the director of what we call the Bureau of Economic Education, and he will give the details of the plan we have.

MR. WALKER: Your report seems quite extensive, and I wondered if it might be agreeable to the Council to have Mr. Douglas outline his views with reference to the organization of the Consumers' Council. It might obviate the necessity of going through the entire report.

DR. DOUGLAS: We have mapped out several sets of functions for the Consumers' County Councils: to attempt to adjust price complaints, to act as a channel through which information to consumers may be distributed, to help express the consumer's point of view on public policy, and to cooperate with the CWA [Civil Works Administration]. We had planned to have at least seven members, and in larger counties, where there is a population of over 100,000, the membership should be somewhat larger. We have obtained about 15,000 suggestions for membership on these county councils which we have gathered from a large variety of sources, and the standards which we have tried to impose on membership have been that persons should be in sympathy with the liberal purposes of the administration, should be competent, able, and honest, and should generally represent consumers' interests, not mercantile, banking, or industrial interests. We are ready to make recommendations on 16 states with a total of 900 counties of the 3,100, and we will be ready within a week or ten days to make recommendations of at least 2,800. We ask that the various state directors should choose their chairmen from the lists which we submit and also choose at least one other member from the lists which we submit from the counties over 100,000 in population. If for any good reason, the state directors believe that none of the names which we submit are satisfactory, then they should have the privilege of suggesting their names, but we ask, in order that the appointments may be unified, that our approval

27

be obtained before the appointment is finally effective.

So much for the chairmen. We ask that the other members of the Consumers' Council appointed by the chairmen be chosen from certain occupational groups; that one member should be from an organization of women actively interested in consumers' problems; another member would be county agent; another, a home demonstration agent; another, a dirt farmer, with emphasis on the *dirt*; fifth, a manual worker; sixth, a housewife of moderate or less than moderate means; and seventh, a member from some organization of consumers. We believe that in addition to those already suggested, there should be field agents to stimulate the work of the county councils. In the smaller states, the field agents may well take care also of the other county councils—other local groups— and in the larger states, it would seem to be desirable to have someone under the state director who would specialize in the consumers' problems, and we ask that the Bureau of Economic Education and Consumers' Advisory Board should bear the primary responsibility of selecting these field agents; and finally, we ask that the Bureau of Economic Education and Consumers' Advisory Board be given authority with the Director of the National Emergency Council to prepare information which is necessary to go to the councils.

MR. WALKER: Do you want to be heard now?

MRS. RUMSEY: In connection with the formation of the county councils, we discussed with Mr. Hopkins several months ago the possibility of securing from him secretaries for the county councils in the Civil Works Administration. Whether the secretary would be for the whole county or not is not in our province to decide.

The small budget of $25,000 is for Dr. Douglas' central organization in Washington and should, we feel, come from one of two sources—the AAA or the NRA, though I am not at all qualified to judge whether that is possible.

The other point is with reference to this Price Increase Committee[1] which has been operating with General Johnson and handling complaints and making analyses of facts as they come in, various facts gathered from the different statistical bureaus of the government. The Price Increase Committee

---

[1] The Price Increase Committee may have been the "complaint committee" (on prices) of the NRA Consumers' Advisory Board, whose chairman was Mrs. Hugh S. Johnson, wife of the NRA administrator. See *New York Times*, Aug. 9, 1933, p. 2, col. 5.

will cooperate with Federal Trade [Commission], Bureau of Standards, and others. Other sources of consumers' statistics are available, but there has been too little effort to cooperate. That is the other budget of $25,000 we are asking for over and above the very small amount being spent on that now. There is nothing in Washington to which the consumers' complaints can come and be analyzed to decide whether it is the fault of the retailer, the wholesaler, or the manufacturer. We have reports on seven or eight major commodities, and we want this Price Increase Committee established to act as a sieve through which the complaints can be handed down to the Federal Trade Commission or the Department of Justice. That is a budget of $25,000. I do not know where it should come from, myself. It is a consumer problem—essentially a consumer problem based on the AAA and the NRA.

MR. WALKER: I might suggest to the council for the purpose of enlightening them as to the reasons for setting up the agenda as I have that it has become necessary now for the National Recovery Administration to set up its compliance machinery, and there are requests coming from various emergency departments of the government—from the Consumers' Council, the Home Owners' Loan, Federal Emergency Relief and unemployment relief—for a large number of committees, and some of these people want budgets to carry on their work. I think the thing that we should advise upon is the question, first, as to the character of the machinery necessary to adopt, and second, look to it with a view to ascertaining whether or not we cannot eliminate a large number of these committees; and also give serious consideration to the economy of it. I know the Consumers' Council is desirous of setting up machinery that may come in conflict with the National Recovery Administration, insofar as its operation is concerned, and it seems to me the orderly thing first to do would be to ascertain what sort of machinery the National Recovery Administration contemplates setting up. We would like to hear from General Johnson on that, and then try to get the rest of our program to comply with that.

GENERAL JOHNSON: We are starting out with a state director in each state who will be paid and two assistants who will be paid. State and district recovery boards merge into one. Then there is a local organization and compliance board that we can make out of our existing organization of volunteer workers. They will not be paid. Briefly, that's it. Does that cover it sufficiently?

29

new deal mosaic

MR. WALKER: I thought it might be well to advise the Council of as much detail as possible. If it is worthwhile, I think it might be well to give some rather definite ideas of the plans. If there is no objection, we will have Lieutenant Johnson [Kilbourne Johnston, son of Hugh Johnson][2] outline his view of it. In this connection, I think we should get as many suggestions from the various agencies that are involved as possible with reference to the whole problem.

LIEUTENANT JOHNS[T]ON: The organization within the National Recovery Administration consists of four—no, five—industry divisions now that take care of what could be called normal code administration—that is, planning and progress in the industry—and, also, they will attempt to adjust all complaints which come up to them from industry agencies.

On the other hand, we have the Compliance Division under the direction of William H. Davis, the National Compliance Director, who is charged with the responsibility of attempting to adjust all complaints where industry has no machinery for the adjustment of complaints. That is, often industry is not even organized in trade associations sufficiently to be able to handle complaints of trade practice violations, and in practically no instance has industry any organization appropriate for the adjustment of labor complaints. In order to provide for machinery to adjust complaints as they arise out in the field, it is proposed to have field offices of the Compliance Division. In fact, right now we have 53 such offices. At present, these are under those who were district managers of the Department of Commerce, the Bureau of Foreign and Domestic Commerce, and they have at these offices local officers and a skeleton clerical staff.

The temporary regulations provide that all complaints of code violations should go to these local officers and there they will either be adjusted by the NRA compliance field machinery or they will be referred over to the code authority in the industry if the code authority has any adjustment machinery in the field. If the code authority has in the field any organization for handling complaints, they will always attempt to adjust the complaint through that machinery. In order to provide that an industry shall not adjust complaints unless they have a proper organization, there is also in Washington

---

[2] The stenographer taking notes at the meeting was apparently unaware that father and son spelled the surname differently. See Hugh S. Johnson, *The Blue Eagle from Egg to Earth* (New York, 1935), p. 4.

an NRA adjustment organization consisting of representatives of the Department of Labor and labor advisory boards of the industry divisions. That is, briefly, the Trade Association Division; and industries are required, as soon as their code is passed, to coordinate with a plan whereby they will provide machinery for the adjustment of complaints.

If this plan is approved, it may be approved in one of two ways. Complaints may be referred to them; that means that the complaint shall go to them after a copy has been made by our field setup, and they will be allowed ten days or two weeks, depending on the nature of the complaint and the distance involved. Then, if they fail to adjust it, it will come back to the state director. That is one method. The other method is where an industry has already been operating and has been satisfactorily adjusting complaints for some time. For instance, under the bituminous coal code authority, complaints go first to the local agency of the code authority, and up until it hits the industry relations board of the code authority. Then if the complaint is still unadjusted, so that there is still an outstanding controverted issue, either because of the complainant not being satisfied or because the respondent claims the adjustment reached is not fair to him, they always have appeal to the National Recovery Administration.

In the first instance, where the code authority handles it, it will come up to the divisional administrator. If he cannot adjust it, it goes to the National Compliance Board; and if that Board is unable to settle it, it is provided that it be turned over to the Federal Trade Commission or the Attorney General. We have provided for liaison men with the Federal Trade Commission and the Attorney General, who will decide which is the proper one to handle the case. Most trade practice violations would go to the Federal Trade and most violations of labor provisions would go to the Attorney General.

This fits in with the field agencies. It is proposed that the state director in this setup will have a chief assistant who will be known as the labor compliance adviser. Plans have been worked out with the Secretary of Labor whereby, to the fullest extent possible, the state labor departments will be utilized. It may even be provided that the head of the state labor department will be the labor compliance adviser in that state. That is, roughly, the setup.

MR. WALKER: For the enlightenment of the council, will you give us your views of the National Recovery Administration with reference to the consumer problem? What views, if any, do you have with reference to that? I think you have had several discussions with Mrs. Rumsey and also with the Agricultural Adjustment Administration.

LIEUTENANT JOHNS[T]ON: On page 27 of the regulations, there should be a change in the last two lines, with reference to price increases. That would only be practical where the code specifically provides for inhibiting unwarranted price increases. The retail code has it and several others do. If there is no provision in the code, it is proposed that under the county councils will be set up a subcommittee known as the Consumers' Council; and Mrs. Rumsey can tell you more about that than I can. Colonel Howe[3] asked that a plan be prepared for the speedy adjustment of consumer complaints where the consumer claimed there was unwarranted price increase in retail stores. There are two different ways in which it could be handled. It was thought those complaints could be referred to the consumers' sub-committee. An alternative method would be provided under the retail code.

SECRETARY PERKINS: The consumers' subcommittee would be under what?

DR. DOUGLAS: The National Emergency Council.

SECRETARY PERKINS: In the field of operations, where does it belong?

GENERAL JOHNSON: It does not appear on this chart.

SECRETARY PERKINS: My idea is that it would not appear on this chart unless there was a provision in the code to that effect. If there is, it would be handled just as trade practices on this chart. Otherwise, it would be registered with the state director.

MR. WALKER: Madam Secretary, do you have any suggestions with reference to where your department fits into this, both from the consumer end and from the NRA compliance or adjustment end?

SECRETARY PERKINS: The statistical division has made a study of retail and whole-sale prices, and of course that function could be carried on with great value to any consumer committee this council might set up, and could be expanded or modified in any way that they needed. That could be a joint enterprise, and I think there has been preliminary conference to such an extent that we are all aware what is to be done.

On the compliance proposal, I think the Department of Labor's function and place in it is clear, and I think we have an understanding of it as in the nature of an advisory

---

[3] Apparently Frederic C. Howe, not Louis McHenry Howe.

cooperative agency in carrying on independent functions and acting as critic of the machinery as developed locally and talking with the NRA upon the adequacy of the machinery. That is, we will get a different kind of complaints as to the adequacy of the machinery, and I think that can be easily worked out.

In studying over these regulations, which I had opportunity only late last night to examine, I am somewhat puzzled, I think, by the setup within the state offices of a very large legal staff and an enormous responsibility placed upon persons called legal advisers who seem to take the authority out of the hands of the state director, who would be the one to whom we would naturally look, I should suppose, for the final word with regard to complaints, and I am wondering if that has been studied sufficiently. We may find ourselves just with a large committee of young attorneys in every state who were doing a lot of analytical work that perhaps does not need to be done if we regard these adjustments as being made between people who are in their right minds and know what the general purpose is.

MR. WALKER: You are referring to the legal adviser selected for each state?

SECRETARY PERKINS: Yes; and the complaints, under the regulations, all go to the legal adviser. He sorts them and says to whom they will go, and rejects some of them. In other words, I put myself always in the position of the state labor commissioner who might find himself the legal adviser for adjustment, and I find he will learn from outside sources that a complaint has been made about a violation of a code, and that it has been rejected and he never heard of it. He is going to be not only extremely embarrassed, but sooner or later he will be extremely angry. If he is the director, he is to be charged with the responsibility for it. While he will want legal advice, I don't think the manual should say just what the legal adviser will do for him.

SECRETARY ICKES: Why shouldn't it go to the director and have him refer it where he desires?

GENERAL JOHNSON: The state director is the boss. But that function is needed there, as a matter of fact, according to our experience. Of course, it would not need to be the same in every state. I have no very strong view about it.

SECRETARY PERKINS: If you happen to have in a given state a very strong director, he will use his legal adviser as he chooses; but on the other hand, if we draw a very weak man, he will rely more and more on his legal adviser. I think it would be awfully unfortunate

	to define in the manual just what these people are going to do. You might find a slowing up of the process; moreover, you could easily provide for a very large legal staff.
GENERAL JOHNSON:	There isn't supposed to be more than one.
SECRETARY PERKINS:	He has to sort the complaints and write digests. I should prefer to see the thing grow; if in a given state, they need a strong legal staff, give it to them. That will develop as the work goes on in that state.
GENERAL JOHNSON:	This is not fished out of the air; it is what we are doing now. This is not a new invention; it is writing down the experience we have had.
SECRETARY PERKINS:	Now this is going to grow into a much more orderly routine procedure. It is going to be more like enforcing the hours of labor and the child labor laws in any state. It would be a very peculiar and almost comic situation to have a legal adviser standing between the commissioner and the people who had violated the law.
LIEUTENANT JOHNS[T]ON:	The examining of legal complaints is a legal function. In working up the office routine (page nine of the regulations), the matter of complaints came in. Many of them do not belong in the office, such as crank complaints; many of them can be picked out just by looking at a list. That is a clerical job. What we thought was that a young lawyer of two or three years of legal experience would be the sorter of complaints and throw them into the proper category rather than a clerk. When the mail reaches the desk of the mail clerk, it will be first looked at to see whether it is a trade practice or a labor complaint, and then it will be referred to the labor compliance director. Undoubtedly he will be too busy to go through all that mail and read through letters that are merely crank complaints.
SECRETARY ICKES:	Why does that have to be set up in your rules and regulations?
GENERAL JOHNSON:	I don't think it does.
SECRETARY ICKES:	I am inclined to agree with the Secretary of Labor. You give your lawyer an undue importance of authority which he derives from the code.
GENERAL JOHNSON:	It was not intended to do that.
SECRETARY ICKES:	They ought to go to the director and let him work out the details.
SECRETARY PERKINS:	Why do we describe the duties in a manual which is issued in advance of there being any organization?
LIEUTENANT JOHNS[T]ON:	There is an organization.
MR. WALKER:	There are some 26 organizations, are there not?

LIEUTENANT JOHNS[T]ON: There are 53 organizations, but only 26 have legal advisers functioning.

SECRETARY PERKINS: This is too much "cut-and-dried" in advance. I see this thing as it would appear in the community where the complaint arises, and I think it will create a very unfavorable opinion in the country when a long manual goes out specifiying the duties of every person and specifying the route that complaints must take. Any compliance director worth his salt is going to resent this routine matter of the legal adviser looking over the complaints before he gets them. He ought to be the one to say how that should be done.

LIEUTENANT JOHNS[T]ON: This is merely a suggestion of office routine to take the burden off.

SECRETARY PERKINS: In one place the manual provides that the compliance officer shall be given a digest of complaints. I know the way some people make up a digest the compliance officer will never know the scandal inherent in the situation. He should take it raw, rather than go on blindly.

LIEUTENANT JOHNS[T]ON: It was a labor-saving plan. Many of these men have not had the benefit of experience in this. We have been handling these complaints ever since last July, and we have found that having lawyers sift out a lot of material that never should go to a person in a responsible position is a very good plan. Of course, it is up to the person in the responsible position to see that it is carried out.

SECRETARY ROPER: Is it not likely that these offices will be classified into different groups in accordance with the volume of business naturally coming before them? Wouldn't the points being brought up here be met if you were to issue two lines of instructions, one dealing with the general principles involved and another devoted to points that are discovered to be necessary? Human nature is human nature, and especially in rural districts; and when the average man in a small community, if you please, gets hold of an outline so complete as this he thinks he better act accordingly. It is a suggestion to him to make his office just as important as possible. We find that all along the line. I believe you can meet that situation by dividing your instructions into two pamphlets instead of one, one with initial instructions governing until you see how this business is classified, and then you will prepare your instructions in accordance with that lineup.

LIEUTENANT JOHNS[T]ON: We could well leave this part out. The only thing we want to do is to insure the speedy handling of complaints by the field officers.

35

SECRETARY ROPER: If you do not go into too much detail, you will get splendid suggestions from the people themselves. They will hesitate to give you the suggestions after you have covered every detail.

GENERAL JOHNSON: There seems to be some misapprehension as to what this is. It is merely crystallizing the practice of months that we are shaping up in a new way.

MR. WALKER: My thought was to have this discussion in view of the fact that the consumers' representative contemplates setting up certain machinery; and in addition to that, Mr. Secretary of Agriculture, your department has already set up, as I understand it, some fifty consumers' committees, and I understand your department also contemplates continuing this practice, and it seem to me that we might work out some plan whereby we could have the whole scheme fit in together. Do you have any ideas how that is going to function so far as your department is concerned, Mr. Wallace?

SECRETARY WALLACE: Our concern has been much more with the consumers' committees than with the compliance committees. They are largely, I would say, at the present time rather of a propaganda nature; [they] do not have any very definite functions except of an educational nature to let the folks in their communities know the objectives of our Act and to report certain complaints. There is nothing we do except clear up the misunderstanding. It is not a very clear-cut functioning thing yet, these local committees that have been set up.

MR. WALKER: I thought if we could get a picture of this, we might avoid duplication to a large extent. We know the NRA consumers' committees are distinct from the AAA.

MRS. RUMSEY: Mr. Howell has worked with us on this.

MR. WALKER: Some of his machinery is set up now. Does your plan contemplate absorbing his?

MRS. RUMSEY: Yes, Mr. Howell wishes it that way.

MR. WALKER: I do not understand that from his report.

MRS. RUMSEY: The two could be combined.

DIRECTOR DOUGLAS: What is a consumer?[4]

MRS. RUMSEY: We have taken the position that the consumer is one who purchases the product of industry. I would like Dr. Douglas to explain that.

---

[4] Budget Director Lewis Douglas' opposition to the Economic Recovery Program of the administration—specifically NRA—manifests itself in the proceedings of the NEC for the first time at this meeting. Subsequent meetings record some of the clashes of view and policy differences which led ultimately to Douglas' resignation.

DIRECTOR DOUGLAS: Do I understand that the purpose of this is to teach those who buy in the industry—educate them with respect to prices?

MRS. RUMSEY: Yes.

DIRECTOR DOUGLAS: And do you propose to include in that the consumption by individuals, or groups of individuals, or corporations or municipalities or states? Suppose you educate all of them with respect to the purchase of structural steel, bolts, nuts, and so on. According to your definition they would be consumers.

DR. DOUGLAS: In our activities on codes, we take the position that we represent the purchaser, and, therefore, in the case of leather we would say we represent the shoe manufacturer; but these committees are to deal with the ultimate purchasers of consumers' goods.

DIRECTOR DOUGLAS: The definition of consumer is not definite. How do you protect the purchaser in the codes—by fixing prices?

DR. DOUGLAS: Oh, no. Where a code is submitted which may have adverse effects on the purchaser of that product, even though he be himself a manufacturer, we scrutinize the code with respect to the interests of the purchaser of that product; but that is in the legislative process in the NRA. The point we are discussing this afternoon is the organization out in the field, the purchasers of consumers' goods and services.

DIRECTOR DOUGLAS: I must confess that, like one of the stockholders in one of the Insull companies, I do not understand the distinction you draw between the various types of consumers, and I do not understand the distinction between the various types of consumption. It is my own stupidity that keeps me from understanding.

DR. DOUGLAS: No, it is my error in exposition.

ATTORNEY GENERAL CUMMINGS: It is also a different type of enterprise.

DIRECTOR DOUGLAS: Possibly.

MR. HOPKINS: Mr. Walker, it seems to me you said in the beginning of this meeting you thought there were too many committees.

MR. WALKER: No, not too many committees; but it seems to me some of this work is liable to overlap if we do not get this ironed out. In addition to that, the Home Owners' Loan has some committees they are setting up, and we should get their discussion, too.

MR. HOPKINS: It seems to me we are getting the cart before the horse in discussing this. I think the local committees fall into two groups, one for permanent activities of the government—

and by permanent activities I mean those to last three or four years—and the other for temporary activities which we would like to see discontinued as soon as possible. If we are talking about temporary activities, then it seems to me the fewer local committees appointed from Washington the better; and we should not be trying to integrate these temporary committees into a permanent scheme of local committees. If it is a permanent organization of government, is it a job that requires a local administration or is it one that can be administered from Washington without local units? I think there is some loose thinking on the part of all of us as to whether or not we need a local committee. I am convinced that there have been a lot of local committees that probably never should have been appointed at all. The more I think about this, the more I become afraid of throwing into these local committees from Washington a whole flock of activities and things to do. I think we ought to think very clearly as to whether these things are not state functions. I think the General has a plan here of something that is clearly a national function that has to be done by Washington; but when you think of a lot of these other things, you raise some questions as to whether it should be run by the national government by appointing local people. I think these states have some pretty fine organizations, and a lot of the things we are talking about the states want to do. I think we could have a very interesting debate as to whether or not it is the function of the national government to organize consumers' groups. Is it possible for the federal government to organize a militant consumers' group that has power? Let us not fool ourselves about this volunteer business. You are going to build up a very expensive organization.[5]

SECRETARY ICKES: Each one is going to want a secretary.

MR. HOPKINS: We are talking about this broad scheme of the national government getting its work coordinated through all these things down into the local counties. I think we are going to run into a whale of a bill if it is done right. And I think there is danger of some of us wanting to load responsibilities on that local committee so that this thing gets integrated

---

[5] It is interesting to note that Hopkins' views were strongly favorable to control by the states; his observations on the problems of federally controlled consumer committees derive special significance in the light of the difficulties experienced during other government programs. On this point, see E. Pendleton Herring, *Public Administration and the Public Interest* (New York, 1935), ch. XV.

permanently, when, as a matter of fact, we may be thinking of a temporary matter. No relief committees in the United States have been appointed from Washington; they have all been appointed by local people. We join money with them. I would hate to see that become centralized. If it is, there would be great danger of our holding the bag. I think this is of very great importance. On everything else besides the General's plans there have been questions in my mind—I have seen all this list of these committees—as to whether the national government should be directly appointing committees in every county in the United States. I think we need a full and frank discussion as to whether consumers' committees should be appointed from Washington.

MRS. RUMSEY: The ideal was that the state directors would appoint those.

MR. HOPKINS: Are they state officers? Are they government committees? They get their power from Washington. I am not opposed to it, but I think these things ought to be talked through when it comes to appointing 3,300 committees. The Civil Works Administration is to be mobilized by the fifteenth of April or the first of May. I do not believe an emergency organization should pay administrative salaries. I also have some feelings about throwing all our eggs in this one basket. Then, I think, too, you need to have a unified command here; you cannot have these state directors taking orders from fifteen different people, unless we in turn are not reporting to Mr. Walker. I am not sure that would not be a bad thing for us to do. I think politically this has a good deal of dynamite in it and they are going to say we built up an enormous machine all over the United States. Whether true or not, that is what they are going to say.

As to that information service—after sitting in on a good many discussions of that, it still doesn't carry conviction with me that I know that is something the government ought to do. I do not quite get convinced about it.

SECRETARY ICKES: We have had some experience with Public Works that might have a bearing here. We started out originally to set up a Public Works Board with three in each state, and I am frank to say if I could get rid of every one of them I would do it. They have not been necessary. They have not done anything the state engineer could not have done. They have cluttered up the works. They started in modestly with a secretary for the board and they keep expanding—more and more personnel. They are all seized with a desire—practically all of them—to travel from one end of the state to the other; and they travel interstate although their functions are limited to state lines. Some of them can't travel without their private secretary—even to Washington where we can supply them amply. I am inclined to agree with Mr. Hopkins. You are going to build up a great organization here with the idea that you are decentralizing, just as we did in Public Works. You are going to add to your expense. You are going to complicate the thing—going to be so busy running the machinery and seeing the machinery work that you will get mighty little out of it in the way of results. I believe in a strong central organization. That is the reason I question this matter of rules and regulations prescribing in detail what your setup in the state is to be. If anybody should offer me a state directorship, with a book of rules like that, I would decline with thanks.

SECRETARY PERKINS: Do I gather that Mr. Ickes' remarks run to the whole conception of this Emergency Council and the centralizing of all the functions of the various emergency functions in one organization?

SECRETARY ICKES: I am not familiar enough with it. This is the first meeting of this group I have attended.[6] I am impressed with what Mr. Hopkins says about merging all these functions and having half a dozen bosses here in Washington.

SECRETARY PERKINS: They must head up in that individual group that has responsibility for the particular function. The theory was that this council, with Mr. Walker as its head, would make a clearing house of these various functions. Those in the states, although taking orders, would nevertheless take orders from Mr. Walker with regard to the relationship of one function to another so that they would be harmonized. If it was a matter of just what account to render, they take orders from you; but if the Public Works rule in one instance was entirely out of harmony with the Agricultural Adjustment rule with regard to the day of rendering accounts, they would consult Mr. Walker about that, and he would straighten out what was probably a purely technical difference here.

SECRETARY ICKES: But suppose your state director is representing in his state several of our Washington departments and independent offices, and he gets, more or less simultaneously, instructions from three or four of them as to particular matters; how is

[6] Ickes' qualified remark at this point ripened into only grudging acceptance of the NEC. See the Ickes' diaries, *The First Thousand Days*, (New York, 1954), pp. 197f., 242.

40

he going to decide which is more imoprtant, which is to have precedence, which to have the greater amount of his time, and all the rest of it? And yet you are holding a man here who issues the instructions with respect to his department responsible for proper administration.[7]

MR. WALKER: May I suggest, Mr. Secretary, the thing that inspired it largely was the very objection that was just suggested by Mr. Hopkins. It seemed that we had so many committees being appointed by so many various departments, and it seemed there had become quite a bit of overlapping. What we were trying to do at the outset was to avoid duplication and overlapping, and it was not the function at any time to have the state director guide the destinies of the various emergency agencies out in the field, but rather to eliminate a lot of the committees being appointed, and use him to ascertain what was really necessary and require a report back.

SECRETARY ICKES: You get rid of overlapping in that event, but won't you substitute for it confusion and want of responsibility?

MR. WALKER: You have to set up your NRA machinery for compliance.

SECRETARY ICKES: I don't see how you can do it in the states any more than you can combine it all here.

SECRETARY PERKINS: They all combine here in the President. I think the President saw the need of this from the great confusion which the average citizen has. The small man in the relatively small community takes a daily paper which is local, and it is full of information and misinformation about local affairs and a little bit of information from Washington. He has become confused. He has a problem about his mortgage, and he keeps the hardware store, and he is responsible for operating under certain codes, and he is a buyer of milk and butter and eggs and cheesecloth, and he has consumers' problems. He finds prices rising. He has people connected with him who need relief, and he doesn't know how to help them. In other words, he has to follow a very long and tedious route to connect with all the various agencies.

SECRETARY ICKES: I think they can be grouped; but I do not think they can all be put effectively under one organization. I do not know whether it is contemplated to tie up the Public Works organization.

---

[7] Ickes' point accurately foretells one of the weaknesses of the field organization of NEC, clearly disclosed by the President's Committee on Administrative Management (see *Report with Special Studies*, Washington, 1937, pp. 282-287), and a more general problem in government field coordination.

MR. WALKER: The state director was to take charge in the field of the information bureaus that would be set up in each state. The number of information bureaus that are to be set up in the states is not to be determined at this time, but determined by experience, and after consultation with the men in the field and after a survey and report from them as to what is necessary. There is a lot of duplication of material, information, and data. There is an absence mostly of information with reference to all the emergency measures in the field. Practically all the agencies are sending out a lot of information and there is a lot of duplication going on, and it seems that in the field there is no very well defined information nor are people well informed as to what relief they may obtain from various agencies throughout the country. The only duties thus far outlined for the state director are to head up the compliance machinery of the National Recovery Administration, make a survey in the field as to the needs, and also have charge of information, and set it up when he makes his report and it is determined here that it is necessary to set it up in that field. He is also to report back here with reference to his views as to what is going on. He cannot interfere with any departments of the government at all. It was never contemplated that he should. It was thought advisable to find out the extent of overlapping or interference and whether or not things are functioning properly. At no time was it supposed to be supervisory. I have never heard of any such thing, except with the NRA.

SECRETARY ICKES: Won't it be inevitably supervisory before we get through with it?

MR. WALKER: I think that would be a mistake.

SECRETARY ICKES: I agree with you.

MR. WALKER: We have now the Home Owners' Loan in the field contemplating setting up various committees. Agricultural Adjustment has been setting up committees. NRA have had a number of committees, and it was contemplating setting up consumers' councils throughout the country. It seems to me that before all these things are done we should survey the danger and see what is the best plan to adopt in setting up this machinery, and see how much can be avoided, and eliminating a lot that is now in existence. So far as this information bureau is concerned, it seems to me we have machinery in the field now without setting up any new machinery.

SECRETARY WALLACE: The people we are setting up are directing themselves to a very particular problem. We have committees dealing with wheat and corn and hog campaigns. I do not see how this would be of the slightest use or obviate in any way the necessity of our committees.

MR. WALKER: How about the consumers' thing?

SECRETARY WALLACE: The consumers' thing is not much of a thing, really. Recognizing the type of meeting they would hold, I just came to the conclusion that while they might furnish a good mailing list to folks that are especially interested and probably worthwhile as long as it didn't cost anything, that nevertheless the thing had no great, astonishing possibilities so far as our work was concerned. It seemed to me that most of our consumers' work would be done just about as well without them.

SECRETARY PERKINS: I think we ought to think of this in addressing ourselves to the subject, however; that we must keep in mind that this country is an experiment in democratic government. It is quite as true as in Abraham Lincoln's day that we are testing "whether any nation so conceived can long endure." One of the very complicated problems in democratic government is to have all moderately efficient and at the same time really have participation in popular thinking; and this kind of organization, somewhat awkward as it may be, is a part of the technique of keeping our government in the hands of the people. It is the modern substitute for the old town meeting and the old talk around the stove. None of these programs will be very successful, except for a short time while people are frightened, unless there is a real participation by people who have been thinking about the subject and have been slowly absorbing the information which those of us at Washington have had predigested for us and have talked over time and again. As they know somebody who is on these committees they slowly come to gather the information which makes them intelligent on the subject, and they are therefore able to think in terms of the particular town in which they live about as intelligently on how to handle the problem as anybody here in Washington. I think eventually they think of it much more clearly than does the person who stays only at the central point of government. To me that is the principal reason for the development of these consumers' committees. The idea of the function of consumption in the economic scheme as an essential balance to the problem of production and distribution is a new idea. The very fact that we are all vague when Mr. Douglas challenges us is an illustration of how new that idea is. We now recognize that it ought to be understood by government and provided for by government so that no injustice shall be done to the citizens in their capacity as consumers, even though perfect justice is being done to them in their capacity as manufacturers.

I should be very much alarmed to allow groups of militant consumers to rise and take their part. It seems to me that that just goes directly in the opposite direction from the thing we are aiming at now, which is to make a government which has a weigh-up of all human problems and some place where human problems can be registered. The citizens in their capacity as consumers face certain problems—problems chiefly of being able to get enough of the things they want. I think it is rather important to develop that function carefully and cautiously but with the full participation of the people even though it is awkward in its organization.

SECRETARY ROPER: May I ask how long this meeting is likely to continue, as I have an important engagement, and will have to go.

MR. WALKER: There are two or three more matters I think we ought to discuss. (*Secretary Roper then excused himself from the Council.*)

GENERAL JOHNSON: This manual of regulations has nothing to do with anything except NRA.

MR. WALKER: My thought in having that submitted here was so that there would be no interference by the Consumers' Council.

MRS. RUMSEY: General Johnson and I are in complete accord about this. I agree with the Secretary of Labor, and I would like to add, with reference to Mr. Wallace's suggestion with reference to the high-pressure groups throughout the country, that I thought he meant that they should be helped, too.

SECRETARY WALLACE: I agree with you quite fully. It is just a question as to the part they take in it. I do not see how it could be of very great service to the AAA. It is up to us to gather certain information as to pyramiding of costs and other information of that sort. I don't think that we in the Agricultural Adjustment Administration require the elaborate machinery which is here contemplated. From the standpoint of the entire government, I can see a very real need for some expression of the consumers' interests.

MRS. RUMSEY: There are two points I would like to make: We have had complaints, of course, against processing taxes,[8] and you must have received complaints against retail prices. The second point is that the councils formed by Colonel [Frederic C.] Howe of the Better Business Bureaus he has said himself were rather abortive.[9]

MR. WALKER: May we hear from the Home Owners' Loan? Didn't you contemplate setting up local committees?

MR. FAHEY: The Home Owners' Loan Act originally, while it was in Congress, contemplated including in the law provisions for county committees and state committees. There was considerable support for that idea, but it was dropped at the last moment and left to the Board to determine how far it should go. That was wise, for the Home Owners' Loan does not need committees in every county, and they should not be set up, in our judgment. About a dozen states have been organized with state committees, and suggestions for a good many others have been presented to the Board, and we held them up until it was settled what was going to be done in this council so far as committees are concerned. The state committees which have been appointed have in most instances been rather helpful in bringing about a better understanding on the part of mortgagees of what was intended by this Act. California and Massachusetts are notable examples where the work of these committees was most influential in overcoming the resistance of savings banks and other mortgage institutions. They have been quite successful in those two states and some others. In some of the smaller communities, local committees have been helpful along similar lines where a mortgagor was meeting with resistance from the mortgagee and our manager could not make any headway and the intervention of influential citizens helped to compose their differences.

Another very important work of some of the committees has been prevailing on mortgagees to refinance mortgages and not turn them over to us at all. It has been very helpful because of course we do not want to take any more of these mortgages than necessary. In one state, as many as 40 per cent of the applications have been adjusted through local managers and with the help of committees of this sort.

---

[8] The processing taxes, levied by the government on processing of agricultural commodities under the first Agricultural Adjustment Act, were to finance the subsidies paid farmers for curtailing production.
[9] See article headed "Publicity Planned to Curb Profiteers," *New York Times*, Aug. 4, 1933, p. 8, col. 5.

We suspended the organization of any more committees, as I explained. I think it is rather a separate function. I do not know just how it could be fitted into a state committee. If it could be done, we certainly would welcome it. There are some states where we are not particularly anxious to appoint state committees and do not feel that we need them. There are many such counties. But where the need exists, it would be well to establish them as soon as possible. How far it would be necessary to place them under the state director I think it is impossible to say. As it is now, they are working with our organization. I may add that there is no question that many have been very helpful in bringing about a better understanding between the mortgagee and the home owners and to understand where our ability to help them stops.

MR. WALKER: If it is agreeable, I thought we might, in order to bring this thing better before us, have a committee of the people involved in this and let them sit down and deliberate and set up some plan, if we are going to set up a consumers' council of large proportions, and if we are going to find out how it is going to function; and then the question arises with reference to all these various committees now in existence. What would the council think of selecting a committee to report back to the next meeting, including the NRA, the Labor Department, a consumer representative, Agriculture, Home Loan, and the Budget. Is your budget contemplating what it did some little time ago, General?

GENERAL JOHNSON: We have never been able to make out a very definite budget.

MR. WALKER: On the basis of two and one-half millions of dollars?

GENERAL JOHNSON: Yes, but with the remark, nobody could tell.

MR. WALKER: A million and a half for the consumers' budget?

MRS. RUMSEY: Yes.

MR. WALKER: Would it be agreeable to the Council to select only the ones really involved in this particular matter?

SECRETARY ICKES: I think that is a good way to handle it.

GENERAL JOHNSON: Is there any good reason why we could not go ahead with our organization? We are suffering terribly from delaying so long.

MR. WALKER: My understanding is that it is a matter to be submitted to the President. I think you are waiting for his approval now.

COMMISSIONER MARCH: Did I understand that this state director is largely to give information, without directing?

MR. WALKER: He is to head up the compliance machinery of the National Recovery Administration and also head up the information service in the state.

The President suggested that he would rather be excused this afternoon if we did not need him. I sent back word I didn't think it would be necessary for him to appear today.

By the way, I think the Attorney General should be represented on that committee.

ATTORNEY GENERAL CUMMINGS: All right.

Meeting adjourned at 3:35 p.m.

Held in the Cabinet Room of the Executive Offices,
The White House, Tuesday, January 23, 1934, at 2:00 p.m.

Present: the President of the United States; the Vice-President of the
United States; the Attorney General; the Secretary of the Interior;
the Secretary of Agriculture; the Secretary of Commerce; the Secretary
of Labor; the Director of the Budget; the Administrator of Agricultural
Adjustment; the Administrator of Federal Emergency Relief; the
Administrator for Industrial Recovery; the Chairman of the Board of
the Home Owners' Loan Corporation; the Governor of the Farm
Credit Administration; the Hon. Garland S. Ferguson, Chairman,
Federal Trade Commission; the Hon. Charles H. March, former
Chairman, Federal Trade Commission; the Adviser on Consumer
Problems, Mrs. Mary H. Rumsey; the Economic Adviser; the
Executive Director.

[In this long meeting, the spectrum of possible functions for
NEC as a coordinating agency is covered. The first few
subjects taken up are housekeeping problems—a census
of pamphlets being issued by the government and the
matter of the Government Manual. The Manual remains today
as a minor monument to the work of the NEC. The Council,
even on these minor matters, did not appear to be a formal
decision-making body, but seemed to move vaguely toward
informal consensus. On page 60, Secretary Perkins starts
an interesting though inconclusive discussion of the role
of the NEC and the place of the President in its functioning.
After F.D.R.'s entrance, there is a brief discussion
of future credit policy. With this, the Council reaches
the opposite pole from that of detailed housekeeping
matters—still with issues raised but hardly resolved.
Throughout this meeting, the dual problem of philosophical
coordination within the administration and the transmission of
the administration objectives to the field staff and public is
considered. The kaleidoscope of views and outlooks that
was the New Deal comes alive as some members of the group,
like the Attorney General, are caught up in the spirit of the
administration effort, and others manifest the growing
skepticism of Budget Director Douglas.—Editors' Note.]

MR. WALKER: The first matter on the agenda is a report by the executive
director on the use of pamphlets by the various departments

of the government. A preliminary survey has been made with reference to that, and I thought it might be well to call it to the attention of the various departments and see what, if any, ideas you have in reference to it.

Production of Government printed material could be aided by the development of a more readily recognizable Government publication style which would be to the public a guarantee of authenticity. Distribution would be materially helped through the central mailing list, properly classified and revised daily by a competent staff. The cost of such maintenance of a central mailing list would be much less than that now expended separately by the various Government departments and agencies.

Figures based on 20 out of 42 Government agencies reporting, show that approximately 95 per cent of all publications are factual.

Of these 20, only 2, the Post Office Department and the Civil Service Commission, issued historical treatises.

Only 3, the Post Office Department, the Federal Home Loan Bank Board, and the Inland Waterways Corporation, issued printed matter of a propaganda nature.

STYLES.

Government printed matter is prepared as follows:

1. Mimeograph.
2. Light paper binding.
3. Heavy paper binding.
4. Cloth.
5. Buckram.

SUBJECT MATTER.

The subject matter of Government printed material is as follows:

1. Factual.
2. Historical.
3. Propaganda.
4. Press releases.

ISSUANCE.

Government printed matter is issued as follows:

1. Daily—The intermittent issuance of press releases by emergency organizations.
2. Weekly—The press releases of the State Department.
3. Monthly,—by the State Department, the United States Board of Tax Appeals, and the Federal Emergency Relief Administration.
4. Quarterly,—by the State Department, Foreign Service and Diplomatic.
5. Semi-annual.
6. Annual,—Annual Reports.

Only 10 of the departments furnishing information published rules and regulations for their Department. Only 4 have complete indexes of their publications.

All emergency organizations issue masses of mimeograph material at irregular intervals, as many as six different orders being published in one day by one organization. These are mostly instructions and press releases. Only eight of the agencies covered furnished a complete list of publications.

A complete analysis of Government publications will be presented to the Council as soon as its collection can be completed.

I wonder if any members of the Council have any ideas with reference to what can be done or any suggestions as to what may be advisable with reference to this problem. It doesn't seem to have any head or tail to it, and it is becoming more and more cumbersome and heavy every day, and also quite expensive.

SECRETARY PERKINS: Shouldn't there be some critical analysis of these publications? I know that in the Department of Labor my own thought was that there were too many publications, and I set up a little interdepartmental committee to analyze and classify the desirability of any future publications. Of course, there was nothing to be done about those already printed. It has proved helpful and much of the material that has been prepared, instead of being printed, has been circulated in its original mimeographed form, and a digest has been circulated, largely to the press. We have not printed pamphlets at all. It is purely material of interest to a few, and it may be interesting only in a very diluted form.

SECRETARY WALLACE: We have found it necessary to increase our publications enormously since the AAA was put into effect and we have had the problem of reaching millions of farmers. I do not know of any possible way of avoiding it. It is specific and definite in nature, and I do not know of any way to get around it.

MR. WALKER: The observation is that some of the publications go out without proper supervision from the heads of departments.

ATTORNEY GENERAL CUMMINGS: Does your report indicate how these publications are allocated amongst the various departments of the government?

MR. WALKER: I am starting the survey now, and I want to get the ideas of the Council. It is really a great task. It seems to me it is best to get some order out of the thing, but I do not want to proceed unless the heads of departments think it is a good plan.

SECRETARY ROPER: In the Department of Commerce, this is one of the first tasks we set for ourselves, and we have two groups studying it. One is the Business Advisory Council, and I believe Mr. [John H.] Fahey has that in hand for our Council. We have also a departmental committee. We have made some considerable progress with it. We have found it necessary to enlarge our study so as to include the study of forms. We find that many of our forms—I mean the forms which we turn out of a questionnaire nature—are out of date; so we are making a study of forms with a view to trying to get the information in simpler form and so give the public as little trouble as possible in that connection. It is quite a study.

And, as I say, we have our departmental group charged with it—three men; and over above that we have the major line of study being pursued, I think, by Mr. Fahey. Am I correct, Mr. Fahey?

MR. FAHEY: Yes; a subcommittee has been working on that, Mr. Secretary. They took that up back last August; and without going into the details of their studies and recommendations, my recollection is that they effected some 15 or 20 per cent of eliminations of things that had been standard for many years. I was going to ask, Mr. Chairman, if any analysis is available of that 89 million pamphlets, etc., on hand which would give an indication as to what might be avoided in over-production in the future.

MR. WALKER: I did not want to go too far into an analysis of this unless I felt that the members of the Council felt it would be advisable. I felt that there might be some sort of central agency that could coordinate some of it and standardize and make it uniform. There is now no standard of uniformity.

MR. FAHEY: I think there is a lot of wisdom in that suggestion. The effectiveness of any printed matter depends considerably on its appearance and a lot of the material put out by the government is so dead and uninviting that I think it fails of its purpose. It may contain facts and be of value to those who are intensely interested and therefore dig into these publications; but I think there are a lot of them that fail of their purpose for two reasons: (1) because they are not interesting in appearance, and (2) because there is a tendency to select lists out of hand and send things out regardless, assuming that a whole lot of people on the list will be interested. Again, I think mailing lists, just as in private business, are apt to be very inaccurate, and it would be well if you could provide some central control for mailing lists so far as groups of people you want to reach is concerned, and plan for some central distribution that way. I believe investigation would disclose that there is a good deal of duplication in that respect. I found we had lists of all the clergymen in the United States and all the lawyers and real estate dealers and all that sort of thing. As it was started, they just assumed that tens of thousands of things should be sent out to all of them, regardless of what was sent, and we stopped that.

MR. WALKER: Our survey showed that in one week 60 per cent of some

35,000 pieces of mail had been misdirected and returned to the Post Office.

MR. FAHEY: I believe you would find that is due to the fact that you have lists that have been revised and changed—that have not been in use for years, and a lot of the people are dead.

MR. WALKER: Does anybody else have any suggestion or thought in regard to this, as to whether or not we should pursue this further and make a more complete survey and classification? It is going to be quite a task to classify all this material. I would not want to go into it unless it seemed to be the opinion of the council that it would be worthwhile. If a majority of the heads of departments think that they ought to regulate this themselves, that is perfectly agreeable to me.

ATTORNEY GENERAL CUMMINGS: As far as my department is concerned, I suspect it doesn't figure very largely in this total.

MR. WALKER: I would not imagine so.

ATTORNEY GENERAL CUMMINGS: It is a matter of indifference to me.

SECRETARY ROPER: The Department of Commerce has no objection.

MR. WALKER: Unless there is objection, then we will carry on the survey and make a more complete report.

For the examination of the Members of The National Emergency Council there is presented herewith preliminary copies of the projected daily revised manual of "Emergency Recovery Facilities and Agencies." It is intended to make this book available in the field as the basis of factual information to be provided every citizen who cares to inquire.

The Manual[1] as presented is incomplete in that it does not include any material affecting the National Recovery Administration. That material is in the course of final checking and at the present moment is awaiting final approval by the Administrator for Industrial Recovery.

As you will see the book is of a loose-leaf type which will permit its revision as often as changes in the various Emergency Agencies occur, daily if necessary. The attention of the Members is called in particular to the index which is designed to provide a ready answer to almost any inquiry presented to a field representative of the Federal Government.

In addition it is proposed to add an index of Rules and Regulations in force in the various departments and agencies of the government. This will provide a simple system by which a citizen can determine which rules and regulations of the government affect him and obtain

---

[1] The Council here considers the publication of a manual of government activities. Subsequent meetings show its development into the *U.S. Government Organization Manual* as we know it. A looseleaf volume covering just the emergency agencies was issued for 1934; an expanded but still looseleaf, manual, designed for constant revision and covering all departments, was issued in 1935 and 1936. The 1937 issue served until 1939, when the first permanently bound edition came out.

them without wading through a mass of material and writing to half a dozen agencies.

I would like to pass them around and get any suggestions you may have with reference to them.

SECRETARY WALLACE: Have you considered using the reverse of the Great Seal which has on it the pyramid and under that the words, *Novis Ordo Secularum* [*Novus Ordo Seclorum*, A New Order of the Ages], which means a good deal.

SECRETARY PERKINS: Really?

SECRETARY ROPER: I think we ought to use the reverse. This is the era we have been looking forward to.

SECRETARY PERKINS: Have you thought of the possible laughter that might follow the issuance of a textbook or guide? These are already made up, aren't they?—they are not dummies?

MR. WALKER: No, these are dummies.

SECRETARY PERKINS: To call it a guide is bad psychology.

MR. WALKER: We have only this number made up.

SECRETARY PERKINS: You are not adding the regular departments of the government at all?

MR. WALKER: These are only the emergency activities. If we added the regular departments of the government, we would have quite a task on our hands.

SECRETARY PERKINS: This is on a loose-leaf basis and you can add to it if that seems advisable.

MR. WALKER: Five thousand copies will cost about $6,000, and to keep them up daily, the service would cost about $13,000 a year.

SECRETARY PERKINS: Perhaps this is the time for me to make a suggestion—

MR. WALKER: We have to have some sort of National Industrial Recovery service covering compliance boards and copies of the rules and regulations kept up to date, and any changes made in the other departments. This matter is approved by the head of each department and a member of the legal staff.

SECRETARY ROPER: I think the general idea is all right, Mr. Chairman. As I look at this, it seems to me if you could have the general lines of information which is permanent here in these various agencies put into solid form rather than loose-leaf and then follow up the loose-leaf with the daily additions, it would look a little more permanent and would be a little more useful to me, it seems. I find that in dealing with such things the spikes wear through the loose leaves. I presume this would not likely change—it seems very definite—and I think this could be put into a form that would be what we call solid and then have the daily additions go in the loose-leaf form. The general idea, I think is all right.

53

SECRETARY PERKINS: I have been thinking for some time of recommending that the government publish a regular weekly or monthly bulletin in order to keep the world and those who deal with the government up-to-date. You know the type of thing in the European countries called the Official Gazette, where they have been operating many years under councils and boards. We are doing almost that same thing. I mean, the rules and regulations in certain administrative departments have the force and effect of law so far as the prosperity of the citizens is concerned. Any one of us who has dealt with the general public knows it is almost impossible for an average citizen to come here and really know what he ought to do. He shops around and bothers a great number of people in order to find out what the rulings are to fit his case. Even competent counsel cannot tell him, because they are hidden away, and there ought to be some place where all the orders and regulations authorized by any divisions of the government, and the Executive Orders of the President, are included, and perhaps some other interesting and important material such as dates of meetings of committeees of Congress, day of meetings of the courts, and all that sort of thing, as a guide to the citizen who wants to find his way through the intricacies of the government. It is sometimes very difficult for a well-intentioned citizen to know what he ought to do. He doesn't know about the original order or the addition. It is very confusing to many people who honestly wish to conduct their business and private affairs in conformity with the latest rules and regulations.

MR. WALKER: All rules and regulations are to be filed at the office of the National Emergency Council[2] and then they will be forwarded to your state directors, and they will be in touch with the various organizations. There is a great deal of confusion. People do not know what the definite, specific rulings are with reference to so many matters, and if we are to be helpful at all we will have to give them something very definite and specific.

SECRETARY ICKES: Do you want all our regulations filed with you?

MR. WALKER: I think that will have to be determined.

---

[2] Suggestions of this sort, here and subsequently, foreshadowed the establishment of the Federal Register by the Federal Register Act of July 26, 1935. Clearly, the Administration was aware of the problem before it had become an issue in Congress and the courts.

SECRETARY ICKES: There are various orders appointing regional committees of one sort and another and general orders.

MR. WALKER: This manual has not been adopted as yet, and that is why I want to pass it around to the heads of departments and see what suggestions you have with reference to it. The state directors will have to be informed with reference to these matters; and so far as these information bureaus are concerned the same thing is going to apply. I was talking with a man in New York this morning and he said most of the work done by the Compliance Boards and members of NRA in New York, for instance, is handing out information with reference to all departments of the government, and that a major portion of the correspondence is of that nature. They have very considerable difficulty in knowing how to answer a lot of it. They have no definite guide. He said many questions arise with reference to Home Owners' Loan, Public Works, Civil Works, Federal Emergency Relief, and so on. Do you have any suggestions with reference to this, General, in view of the fact a good portion of the rules and regulations coming out will be NRA?

GENERAL JOHNSON: We think it will cut out a lot of correspondence, which is the bulk of the work. Of course, I cannot speak with reference to the other departments.

MR. WALKER: As far as the NRA is concerned, you are quite favorable, then. It seems to me the expense is not going to be great, in view of what can be accomplished by it.

SECRETARY WALLACE: Do you need a motion from this group to go ahead with it?

MR. WALKER: No, I thought if there are no objections we will proceed with them. We have gone into it quite extensively, and it was taken up with the President before we began. If any of you people have any ideas or suggestions, we will be very glad to entertain them.

The next thing on the agenda is the tentative program for the conference of state directors.[3] I think we have some copies of it here, and we would like to have you people glance it over and give us any suggestions you may have with reference to it. It is contemplated that we will have the head of every department appear before the state directors as a body and give them some definite ideas with reference to each activity that is involved. The major portion of the time I think will be spent with the National Recovery Administration in going

---

[3] State NEC directors first met on Jan. 31, 1934.

over its instructions and rules and regulations.

SECRETARY ROPER: In order that we may be as effective as possible and not duplicate, will you assign the exact subject or territory which we are to cover? I see you have the Secretary of Commerce down for 30 minutes on Wednesday, January 31. Just what phase of it would you like for me to discuss? That question may be also in the minds of others.

MR. WALKER: So far as each department is concerned, we thought it would be well to have the state directors advised with reference to the important matters; for instance, the working of the Home Owners' Loan, the Reconstruction Finance Corporation, and Public Works, any ideas the Secretary of Labor had with reference to her department, and the National Recovery rules and regulations. We thought it would be helpful to them to have some discussion from every one of the heads of departments. The main thing would be, especially with reference to the Home Owners' Loan and National Recovery Administration, to advise them with reference to the rules and regulations; and so far as the other departments are concerned, it would be for them to decide what message they wanted to convey, or whether or not they wanted to go on the program.

SECRETARY PERKINS: Mr. Chairman, do you want us to discuss the actual work which these directors are to do for our departments, or do you want to make just glittering speeches?

MR. WALKER: I think there are only a few departments that they can be helpful with. In other words, they will have charge of the information bureaus in their own states, and anything that is of an informative character with reference to any of the departments, I think they should be appraised of.

SECRETARY PERKINS: You mean on the actual basis of programs. I notice in this you put the Secretary of Commerce down to speak on business conditions and future economic forecasts, which would be a simple thing to do in 30 minutes! He might not like to take the responsibility for too broken an outline.

MR. WALKER: These are merely suggestions. We thought there should be some variety on the program so that they will not be wearied with instructive matter.

SECRETARY ROPER: Let me make this suggestion: I will be glad to make some outline. There should be some coordination so that we may the more effectively cover the field as you would like to have it covered. I would like to suggest that the thing that is uppermost in my mind is to make sure that there is a line of demarcation drawn between what I regard as permanent or ordinary and extraordinary facilities of government. I am thinking now strictly in terms of the Department of Commerce and the way in which it must continue to run in serving the public regardless of what we now call our emergency.

MR. WALKER: What we would like to have is instructive discussion from each of the emergency activities and I suppose from the Home Owners' Loan, for the benefit of the state directors, who are going to set up these information bureaus. In view of the fact that there are other members of the Emergency Council who are not directly involved, we have reserved a place for them tentatively, having in mind that they might have something to present to the state directors when they are here. This is merely tentative, and I would like to have from each department some suggestion as to what, if anything, they want to present to the Council, so there will not be confusion.

SECRETARY ROPER: I will be glad to submit—say, by Monday, if you please—a memorandum of what I think I ought to say.

SECRETARY PERKINS: I think it is highly desirable, just thinking of that first day, that rather than give them a purely speculative prediction as to future business and economic conditions, what they really need is a description of the recovery program so that at the very outset they see all of its parts fitted together and recognize that there is underlying all these various activities a purpose and plan, and it is out of the more or less coordinated operation of all of them that we expect to get some measure of recovery. They will be treated, as the days go on, to very detailed instructions as to how they are supposed to operate under each one. They probably lack a rounded conception of the whole recovery program,—in fact, we all lack it. Someone like Mr. Roper, for instance, might explain the relationship of heavy expenditures on one side and reduced budgets on the other.

SECRETARY ROPER: It seems to me if a little attention is given to coordinating this and making it fit into a pattern, as the Secretary of Labor says, what we shall say might be a very valuable document.

SECRETARY PERKINS: To us.

SECRETARY ROPER: And to some people outside. I think it could be made a very useful document; that is, if you are given time to put it into the pattern and make sure that we are not duplicating.

MR. WALKER: I thought at the outset of dropping a word as to the scope of the conference, and I was going to have the President give them a general talk, which he has agreed to do, on the program.

57

SECRETARY PERKINS: At four o'clock on Friday?

MR. WALKER: Yes.

SECRETARY PERKINS: My idea is that the President will come in toward the end. He will not take much time. He will furnish the patriotic inspiration and other points of view with which they will go ahead with the work; but somewhere they ought to get a rather carefully-worked-out mosaic of the whole program, and I think it is too much to ask the President to prepare such a rounded statement. I think it would be quite a burden to do that.

MR. WALKER: It is quite a task for anybody.

SECRETARY PERKINS: I think it ought to be done.

SECRETARY ROPER: Inasmuch as this is an initial meeting, they would take such a pattern back with them. They would read that and digest it. I think it is an opportunity, Mr. Chairman.

SECRETARY PERKINS: The relationship of the Public Works program to the whole Recovery Program, the relationship of CWA and Public Works and the relationship of CWA and other things, ought to be made clear; and also the relationship of industrial and agricultural recovery. Mr. Roper would be admirably suited to do that.

SECRETARY ROPER: I made a talk recently before the Real Estate Boards at Philadelphia. I went over there with a talk undertaking to show them how we wanted to cooperate with them in the study of real estate, which I thought would be of interest to them. But really the thing they were interested in—which rather surprised me and Mr. Vanderlip who followed me and spoke with me—was not really that, but the policy of the Administration. For instance, they said, "Are we trying to get business back on its own initiative, or, is the government going to continue to concentrate the operation of business in Washington?" I was amazed at the number of inquiries that came to me about that; and what I had to say I thought seemed the most interesting feature of the talk. And my correspondence indicates that from all over the country. I believe the people are getting nervous about that. I did not know it before. It has been impressed on me very much indeed. I think you are now creating an agency that is to sell the purposes and plans of this administration to the people, not for any other purpose than to keep the people informed as to how they should react and how they should cooperate. We cannot put any of this over without the cooperation of the public, and we ought to take the public in that way into a desire to get the facts, and having gotten the facts, to inspire them too with a willingness to assist in educating the public.

MR. WALKER: I think that is true so far as the dissemination of factual information is concerned, and we will have to be awfully careful how this should be presented.

SECRETARY ROPER: True; and that is why I am suggesting now that you work this out according to a pattern.

MR. FAHEY: It seems to me this suggestion made by the Secretary of Labor is a very consistent one—bringing these people together to give them a general outline of this whole problem and an understanding of the separate parts of it. It seems to me very consistent, therefore, that at the outset provision should be made for a general statement which will make clear the fact that the Recovery Program is a program and that there are reasons for the separate things that are being done here; that you are not dependent upon any one thing, but it is the combination of all that will have its effect. Also, it would seem to me consistent, in view of what Secretary Roper has said, that if it could be made clear in this connection that this is essentially an emergency to carry us over a certain period and bridge a gap and lay the foundation for greater activity and initiative on the part of the people themselves, that too would be useful. If there were a proper statement of that sort, and then, consistent with this program, an explanation of the several parts of the program, it would give an understanding to these assembled directors that they would not get in any other way; and if the President then came in at the end of that program it would send them along with a certain spirit of enthusiasm which would certainly contribute in a very large way to the success of the whole thing.

There is one other suggestion I want to raise, and that is whether it is your intention to provide for questions from the floor on these several subjects, because I imagine that in a number of cases there will be those among the directors who will have some thoughts that have not been made entirely clear as to the purposes in a particular case; and if you get them to ask questions you can give them a very much clearer understanding of what you are driving at. It makes a considerable difference in the time assigned here on some of these administrations.

MR. WALKER: Just a minute, please. The President wishes to know whether or not you would like to have him and the Vice-President come to the meeting. It seems to me there are consumer problems to be discussed, and I doubt if there is anything to be accomplished by the President being here; so unless there is suggestion otherwise it seems to me we will not have any need of him at this time.

SECRETARY PERKINS: Aren't we likely to turn ourselves into a kind of large executive committee if we do not look out, and discuss here with all these people just purely executive functions? When the President comes in we talk about policies. He doesn't care who makes the speech. He keeps on what I think is the purpose of this Council, mainly the determination of policy and the measure of success of the various policies. And should we not, perhaps, divest ourselves in our larger group of so much of this executive detail? I think it is important for us to be in touch with him from time to time, and for him to be in touch with the agencies of government.

MR. WALKER: It is perfectly agreeable to me.

DIRECTOR DOUGLAS: I don't know what there is to discuss.

MR. WALKER: The matter of this conference is quite important.

SECRETARY ROPER: The meeting is one week off. It seems to me that is a very vital thing to the success of the program.

MR. WALKER: The tentative general outline of the program was discussed with the President before it was submitted to the Council.

SECRETARY ROPER: All right, then.

MR. WALKER: Do you think we should ask the President to come in?

SECRETARY PERKINS: That is for you to say. I think it might be bad for us and might be bad for the President if we separate him from this Council.

MR. WALKER: It seems to me the important thing for us after this is the consumer problem, and I do not think there is any necessity of his being here for that.

SECRETARY PERKINS: When we established these meetings we had been meeting for some months regularly with the President, Tuesdays, at which time the President kept himself in touch with the emergency activities of the government by reading a very much digested report, which was his method of gaining this information for himself. He then established the practice of having a kind of report made upon weekly conditions as reflected by various economic indices, the digest of a number of statistical tables which are available if anybody bothered to study them. As a basis of that we came, not to a conclusion, but simply to a kind of policy with the President with regard to certain activities of government. I felt that was valuable, and I feel there is danger of losing that contact which was really very important for us, and I think, in the long run, for the President.

SECRETARY ROPER: Would this line up with the thought? Suppose we give fifteen minutes to the discussion of the consumer situation and then, say at three-fifteen or three-twenty have the President come in?

MR. WALKER: The only reason I suggested it was that he made it known that during the time Congress is here he wanted to avoid as much as possible making some of these decisions that he wanted the Council to make for him. The last time he did not come, and it was his own wish that he might not have to come unless we absolutely needed him. He didn't want to make some of these decisions and would like to pass them on to us and have them made by us and relieve him during the session of Congress.

SECRETARY PERKINS: Decisions about what? We do not make any decisions.

MR. WALKER: He calls them suggestions; and he wants us to abide by them if the Council can agree upon them. He wanted suggestions which amounted to decisions.

SECRETARY ROPER: I suggest that you proceed to the discussion of the consumer problem.

MR. WALKER: Have you a report on the Consumers' Councils? And then the Administrator for National Recovery will have a statement

GENERAL JOHNSON: No, the matter was presented to me about 11 o'clock this morning, and I suggested that it lay over for a week, because we haven't had a chance to do anything.

MR. WALKER: We had a meeting last week attended by Lieutenant Johnston. and at that time we agreed on allowing $25,000 to the Consumers' Council for expenditure by them; and since then I have understood that your department had changed its views with reference to the policy the Consumers' Council should follow.

GENERAL JOHNSON: That was left for discussion with me, but it was too little time for me to offer an opinion.

MRS. RUMSEY: Who brought up the question for discussion?

MR. WALKER: We had a report.

SECRETARY PERKINS: Is the report ready?

MR. WALKER: The report is ready, but I understood the National Recovery Administration had some new ideas. Is that right, General?

GENERAL JOHNSON: The ideas are pretty vague, because I didn't get the report until a short time ago. I do not know that I have any disagreement.

MRS. RUMSEY: We had a subcommittee meeting last week. Since that I have heard nothing more; and this report is based on that resolution.

MR. WALKER: The question is, what authority shall be given to the Consumers' Advisory Council, and how far shall we go with reference to these Consumer Councils?

SECRETARY PERKINS: Wasn't there a report made by that subcommittee?

MR. WALKER: Mrs. Rumsey is making the report now. The subcommittee authorized the expenditure of $25,000. I would like to have Mrs. Rumsey report at this time.

SECRETARY PERKINS: It was a regular subcommittee; what did it report?

MR. WALKER: That we authorized $25,000 to be expended by the Consumers' Council. As to the matter of procedure, there can be no definite report by the committee because General Johnson has a plan he is outlining, and Mrs. Rumsey has some ideas as to how she wants to spend the $25,000.

GENERAL JOHNSON: I would suggest that Mrs. Rumsey's plan be presented.

MR. WALKER: That is what I thought.

SECRETARY PERKINS: I thought that we took a very clear position. We spent a lot of time on it. My remembrance of it—I didn't write it down— was that the subcommittee agreed to report to this Council its belief that $25,000 should be set aside and earmarked for the development of Consumers' Councils, and that function should be carried on by Mrs. Rumsey and any assistants whom she saw fit to employ—I think she stated she was employing Dr. Douglas; and we agreed not to segregate it because of our belief that one could not foresee exactly what would be the best plans to utilize this money, and if we tried to support a nationwide organization, we might find we had spread the money very thin and had something very cumbersome to operate.

MR. WALKER: That is correct. But all we did was to authorize the $25,000, the procedure was to be submitted by Mrs. Rumsey, and she has the plan she is submittting now. May we have your report?

MRS. RUMSEY [reading]:

LOCAL CONSUMERS' COUNCILS

In accordance with our last conference on the subject, we present herewith our revised suggestions for the creation of a Consumers' Division of the National Emergency Council.

I. PURPOSE

The Consumers' Division of the National Emergency Council is to serve as the coordinating agency for the work of the Consumers' Advisory Board of the NRA and the Consumers' Council of the AAA, insofar as it does not relate directly to the drafting and revision of codes and marketing agreements under the respective jurisdictions of the NRA and the AAA.

The Division's functions shall be primarily to help coordinate and unify the policies and administration of matters affecting consumers. These are to be specifically along the lines of:

(A) Developing local Consumers' Councils, which shall have the following general functions:

(1) To aid in the adjustment of consumers complaints of undue price increases.

(2) To act as a channel through which information to the consumers may be distributed.

(B) Of setting up a Fair Price Committee to deal effectively with consumers' complaints of undue price increases.

II. PROGRAM OF ACTION

(A-1) Wherever possible, and provided there is need for them in the particular communities concerned, the Consumers' Division should utilize as Local Councils coming under its jurisdiction, such Councils as have already been initiated by the Consumers' Council of the AAA, together with other Consumers' groups already in existence, which give promise of vitality. As and when experience shows the need and desirability of setting up additional local Councils throughout the country, these will be set up under rules and regulations approved by the Executive Director.

(A-2) The preparation of the factual economic information should be taken over and incorporated in the Consumer Division of the National Emergency Council, which will thereafter supervise its activities.

(B) The Fair Price Committee shall cooperate with and coordinate the consumers' statistics, not only of the NRA and the AAA, but of Bureaus of permanent Government Departments and Commissions, such as the Bureau of Labor Statistics of the Department of Labor; the Bureaus of Foreign and Domestic Commerce and of Standards of the Department of Commerce; the Bureaus of Home Economics and of Agricultural Economics of the Department of Agriculture; the Tariff Commission and the Federal Trade Commission. A large volume of consumer statistics is at present available in these Departments and Commissions and this Fair Price Committee would serve primarily to apply this valuable material to consumers' complaints and problems. Thus a centralized study of price increases as an economic guide to check consumers' complaints will be established, and will educate the consumer to understand a fair price.

III. COST

The cost of the Consumers' Division is to be at the rate of $50,000 a year, exclusive only of printing expense and of office space, this sum to be divided equally between the work of developing local Consumers' Councils and the work of the Fair Price Committee. Though the Division will be under the supervision and jurisdiction of the National Emergency Council, through its Executive Director, it will be housed, as a separate entity, in the Commerce Building, or in such other quarters as the Executive Director may hereafter direct.

The members of the local councils are to serve without pay, but are to be given the franking privilege, and wherever possible room is to be found for them in Government buildings.

IV. SUPERVISION

As previously stated, the Division will be under the supervision of the National Emergency Council, through its Executive Director; and all matters affecting its personnel and functions will, therefore, naturally come under the jurisdiction of the Executive Director.

Mr. Paul H. Douglas, or his successor, is to be the Administrative head of the work in organizing local Consumers' Councils, and Mr. Dexter Keezer, Executive Director of the Consumers' Advisory Board, is to be the Chairman of the Fair Price Committee. They are to be assisted in the formulation of recommendations to be made from time to time to the Executive Committee composed of Mrs. Mary H. Rumsey, as Chairman, Mr. Fred Howe, Consumers' Counsel of the AAA, Mr. Winfield Riefler, Chairman of the Central Statistical Board, Mr. Douglas, and Mr. Keezer. These will form the Executive Committee of the Consumers' Division of the National Emergency Council.

V. SELECTION OF MEMBERS OF LOCAL COUNCILS

It is contemplated that the personnel of such presently existing local Councils as may be utilized under the plan herein set forth, will be retained. Replacements and substitutions, as well as the appointment of the personnel of Councils newly to be created, will be under rules and regulations approved by the Executive Director.

IV. ECONOMIC AND STATISTICAL INFORMATION

The material to be circulated to consumers shall, to as large a degree as possible, be prepared by the Consumers' Division with the assistance of existing governmental agencies. All such material, as well as all press releases and other publicity matter, shall be cleared through the Office of the Executive Director of the National Emergency Council.

DIRECTOR DOUGLAS: They are to be given the franking privilege?

MRS. RUMSEY: Yes.

MR. WALKER: General Johnson, do you have anything to suggest at this time?

GENERAL JOHNSON: No. It was only presented to me this forenoon.

MRS. RUMSEY: This was not prepared until one o'clock; and when was it sent to you?

MR. WALKER: The question arises now as to how much jurisdiction will be given to the Consumers' Councils, so that there will be no conflict with the National Recovery Administration. As I understand it, you would rather postpone this.

GENERAL JOHNSON: I don't know that I have any objections at all; but I have not given it much study, and I am not prepared to speak on it.

DIRECTOR DOUGLAS: I think it might be well to let General Johnson examine that.

MR. WALKER: That is the reason that we cannot have any action today.

SECRETARY PERKINS: Several of us gave a lot of time to this at that afternoon meeting, and I wonder if we could not now obviate the necessity of still further meetings on that same subject by agreeing to give General Johnson two days to examine the material and then give you or somebody else the power to authorize it.

MR. DAVIS: May we see copies of this also?

MR. WALKER: Yes. You were invited to that meeting.

MR. DAVIS: The invitation came at four o'clock of the day it was to convene.

MR. WALKER: I notified you the day before, at the Executive Council.

MR. DAVIS: I don't recall that.

DIRECTOR DOUGLAS: I will not be on any group that will be considering the subject, and I would like to voice a reservation that I have with reference to the use of the franking privilege by the Consumers' Council.

MR. WALKER: I would like to hear it.

DIRECTOR DOUGLAS: I think a good deal of criticism may develop if the frank is used by it.

MR. WALKER: Do you mind giving us your reasons for that, Mr. Douglas?

DIRECTOR DOUGLAS: I am not clear in my own mind as to exactly what this is to do, this Consumers' Council. I am not quite clear as to how it is to accomplish its purpose. If there is to be a good deal of writing and mailing of material, I can conceive not only this Council, but the branch of it, being charged with developing into a political body for the purpose of engendering faith in the Democratic principles, and the use of the frank for that purpose I think would be quite a serious thing.

MR. WALKER: Do you think that charge could be made if it was confined to the activity of the consumers' work, trying to adjust consumers' complaints of extraordinary prices? Don't you think there is some need, Mr. Douglas, of some sort of forum where consumers can register their views with reference to exorbitant prices? That is what these Consumers' Councils contemplate—providing such a forum and presenting to the code authority and the state directors and the compliance boards their complaints with reference to exorbitant prices and increases that are unwarranted.

DIRECTOR DOUGLAS: That raises a question of prices in general. I can see very easily how a great deal of criticism might arise over the use of the frank for that purpose. The Compliance Board is an official body which, under the NRA, has certain powers. What powers has this? It is an educational organization, isn't it? Isn't that its purpose?

MR. WALKER: To function under the NRA. They have a representative on the code authority—a consumer representative; isn't that right, General?

GENERAL JOHNSON: Yes, advisory. That has nothing to do with this, however.

65

SECRETARY WALLACE: We have mailed out an immense amount of educational material to producers in various phases of our program.

DIRECTOR DOUGLAS: Here you are setting up an organization all over the country. It could very easily develop—and probably will, at certain times—into political instruments.

SECRETARY ROPER: Would it be effective and satisfy the situation if the use of the frank were confined to correspondence with Washington?

MRS. RUMSEY: That is the way it was intended to be. Everything is under the direction of General Johnson and Mr. Walker.

SECRETARY ROPER: It might give the notion that the local group might conduct their correspondence with consumers in other parts of their districts and for that purpose use the frank. That is the impression I got from hearing this. I presume you did too, Mr. Director.

DIRECTOR DOUGLAS: Yes.

SECRETARY PERKINS: They will have their headquarters at some central city and they will have a complaint in writing and they will answer it by mail and make the inquiries which they find necessary to make in order to follow up that complaint.

ATTORNEY GENERAL CUMMINGS: I have not participated very much in this discussion but I want to go on record as being very strongly persuaded that the movement which is contemplated by these arrangements that Mrs. Rumsey is making is of the highest consequence. I think we would be derelict in our duties and make a terrible strategic error if we failed in the first place to give what is regarded as a voiceless group opportunity to be heard and to voice their complaints; but I think it goes deeper than that; I think we are trying to set up in this country a certain approach, as it were, to industrial and economic problems, and no matter how well-conceived they may be or how earnestly promulgated, half the efficiency of what we are doing will be destroyed unless the public is in a receptive mood. This is educational, not just a machine we are setting up and that we hope these people will believe in; but part of our duty is to make it apparent that this is an organization that should be believed in and should be supported. If you neglect the educational aspects of this problem—neglect to take advantage of every possible opportunity to inculcate the idea that here is a sound project that we are all committed to as a nation, you will be wasting a powerful motive to support this program.

I do not want to see this whole thing broken down by secret criticism, by people here and there gathering in groups and talking against what the government is trying to do, with nobody answering them, with no little centers where information can be disseminated. I am in favor of going the limit on it, and I am in favor of using the government frank as far as we can do so lawfully, because I think that this is a legitimate function. It is not political, unless you conceive that every governmental activity is political. It certainly is not partisan.

I just simply want to say that I think we have devoted too much of our thought to the idea of making what we are doing agreeable to the people we are trying to service. Therefore, I want to go on record as very strongly in favor of this little bite into the problem. I don't think it goes half far enough. I think we could go miles and miles and miles beyond what Mrs. Rumsey is contemplating, which is a very mild program. And if in some technical way it overlaps some function that General Johnson has, that can easily be ironed out. I am not talking about those defects. I am talking about a program. I think we must proceed along this line or we will all live to regret it.

DIRECTOR DOUGLAS: What program?

ATTORNEY GENERAL CUMMINGS: I am so sorry I was unable to make myself clear! There cannot be any mortal doubt as to what I mean, and that is this program—if you don't know what the program is, I don't know who does—the whole program of the administration of NRA, Public Works, and all the things that have to do with the reconstruction of our country and the establishment of a new approach to the economic problems through different types of machinery; but everybody knows what I am talking about.

DIRECTOR DOUGLAS: With respect to the use of the frank for a purpose which I was not clear about—

ATTORNEY GENERAL CUMMINGS: My notion about it is that this part of the program is just as essential as any other part, and if we have the right to use the frank in the Agricultural Department and the NRA department we have a right to use it in this other department.

SECRETARY ROPER: I do not believe there is any doubt about that. The thing is, how can we keep the use of this frank in the hands of persons who rightfully are entitled to the frank? For instance, just how far down the line are these people under oath and thereby woven into the entire program to which you refer.

MR. WALKER: My suggestion, Mr. Secretary, is that these rules and regulations are subject to the approval of the Emergency

67

Council, and will be submitted, naturally, to the correct legal officer of the government. Don't you think that would iron it out?

SECRETARY ROPER: I should think so.

MR. WALKER: We will have to face now or in the immediate future the question of how far we can give jurisdiction to this consumer board; and in view of the fact that the General is not prepared at this time to give us his version of that, I think we will have to postpone that matter.

GENERAL JOHNSON: I would like to make it quite clear that I agree with every word that the Attorney General said. I have been accused of setting up 8,000 committees, and I don't think my part of the program could have been put through without that. We have now to set up something in place of that. It was the President's idea that there should be some sort of information service in every part of the country. I am not in opposition to that.

ATTORNEY GENERAL CUMMINGS: I want the details worked out. But as to the big program, I am very strongly for it.

MR. WALKER: The main point we will have to clarify is a question of how far you can let these Consumers' Councils go. It is a very vital problem.

SECRETARY PERKINS: Isn't that one of the items where we will have to learn a good deal by experience?

MR. WALKER: Yes, and not establish our councils too broadcast and go at it rather gradually.

MR. MARCH: Doesn't the Consumers' Councils tie in with the NRA?

MR. WALKER: There is going to be a place where they disagree.

GENERAL JOHNSON: There are two groups.

MR. WALKER: The time may come very shortly when they will be as far apart as the north and south poles.

PRESIDENT ROOSEVELT: Well, Mr. Chairman, how are you coming?

MR. WALKER: We have several matters on the agenda.

PRESIDENT ROOSEVELT: What do you want to talk about, especially?

MR. WALKER: There is one thing we might get your ideas on. The state directors' meeting is coming on the 31st of January, and we have prepared a tentative program.

PRESIDENT ROOSEVELT: How has the appointment of the state directors been taken?

MR. WALKER: Generally, I should say, very well. There was some criticism before that it looked as though we were setting up a political machine. I have not seen much of that since.

PRESIDENT ROOSEVELT: Yes, that was eliminated.

VICE-PRESIDENT GARNER: There would be two angles to that.

PRESIDENT ROOSEVELT: We appointed six or seven Republicans.

SECRETARY PERKINS: That is what makes all the trouble!

VICE-PRESIDENT GARNER: The Democrats say we appointed too many Republicans and the Republicans say we appointed too many Democrats.

MR. WALKER: Our first discussion was with reference to the number of pamphlets. I think we found out that on a certain day of June, 1933, we had 87,581,111 copies of various pamphlets and publications, and that the Government Printing Office advises there were 58,000,000 copies printed during the year.

VICE-PRESIDENT GARNER: [President Herbert] Hoover used to send out enough to fill every wastebasket in the country!

MR. WALKER: We discussed a survey to standardize material and form, and make uniform mailing lists so that they can be used by each department.

PRESIDENT ROOSEVELT: Have you done anything about planning to use local newspapers for dissemination? They would be tickled to death to help.

MR. WALKER: I talked with three or four men without telling what I wanted, and I didn't get very good results.

PRESIDENT ROOSEVELT: I am inclined to think that every county paper in the country would be glad to tell about the setting up of the state and county organizations.

MR. WALKER: The President suggested here before that we select some newspaperman in each locality to give us some idea of what is going on. I thought that was what you meant. I think we can get cooperation.

SECRETARY WALLACE: We will use them to the limit in the Triple A.

PRESIDENT ROOSEVELT: As long as it doesn't look like canned stuff.

MR. WALKER: The President suggested at our first meeting, I think, that we might try to select some newspaperman in each state to inform us what is going on.

It was suggested by the Secretary of Labor with reference to the meeting of the state directors that we might have somebody outline the general program. I think she suggested that the Secretary of Commerce do that, so as to give them at the opening meeting a general idea of the entire program—how each part fitted into the other. I think she might better explain it.

SECRETARY PERKINS: I am afraid I am moved to that by the large number of young ladies and young gentlemen who have sought an interview with me in the last month because they are writing an essay in school or college or a master's thesis or something else on the subject of the total national recovery program. It struck me that it might be well for us if we each one attempted to set down what it is. There would be some authoritative source which would obtain it for each one of us, individually, and for these state directors who are now going to be the source of all wisdom.

PRESIDENT ROOSEVELT: Suppose I offer a prize for the best essay from this group— a trip to Bermuda!

SECRETARY PERKINS: I have several submitted by the high school students. They are very good, too.

PRESIDENT ROOSEVELT: That is not very far off.

MR. WALKER: A week from tomorrow.

PRESIDENT ROOSEVELT: Do you want me to see them?

MR. WALKER: We agreed upon that. We set you down for—

PRESIDENT ROOSEVELT: When?

MR. WALKER: Friday at four o'clock.

PRESIDENT ROOSEVELT: Will you prepare something for me to say?

MR. WALKER: I don't know whether you will accept it or not!

PRESIDENT ROOSEVELT: I would like to have an outline.

MR. WALKER: I suggested that you might give an inspiring speech, but the Secretary of Labor thought that would be asking too much for you.

PRESIDENT ROOSEVELT: I think you have a great many evangelists down here on the list already! (*Laughter*)

MR. WALKER: The last matter taken up before you came in is the consumer question, which, to my mind, is very important. We had a subcommittee meeting the other day at which we recommended the setting aside of $25,000 for the Consumers' Council, and an additional $25,000 for research work on price fixing; and the question arises, what jurisdiction can be given to the Consumers' Council so that there will be no conflict with the NRA? It seems we will be running into something like that very soon. I think we will have another meeting on that in the near future. We did not get very far on it today.

PRESIDENT ROOSEVELT: What are the plans suggested on it?

MRS. RUMSEY: I think it was your suggestion that there should be local groups, and adequate organization for the consumer to voice his grievances. The idea would be to have a volunteer organization set up, with Dr. Douglas as the administrative head to organize it; and then to have a fair price committee.

PRESIDENT ROOSEVELT: Do you see any objection to that general plan, Hugh?

GENERAL JOHNSON: No. There is a technical question, and I didn't see this report until today; I don't think I am prepared to discuss it. We have just finished setting up an organization for a somewhat similar purpose and I have not had a chance to compare the two things. I asked for a day or two in which to look it over.

PRESIDENT ROOSEVELT: Most problems of unfair prices would probably be settled without any appeal to anybody. Isn't that so?

MRS. RUMSEY: That is exactly the feeling we have about it; but there should be somebody for them to look to.

PRESIDENT ROOSEVELT: Would they go to the state director or jump to Washington?

MRS. RUMSEY: They would jump to the fair price committee.

PRESIDENT ROOSEVELT: I think it is a good thing to make the localities responsible; let the localities fix up their own trouble.

MR. WALKER: The Attorney General spoke about educating the American people not only on the consumer problem but also on the general program. We discussed the question of how far we can permit the Consumers' Councils to use the franking privilege.

ATTORNEY GENERAL CUMMINGS: I think we should go as far as we can in making it easy for these organizations to function, and therefore we should use the franking privilege as far as we can without violating either the law or good taste. There are, of course, limits to which we can go. I think that can be worked out very easily through some committee or through our board after a little thought.

As I indicated, I feel very strongly that we should make a vital feature of this program concerning the consumers, not only to permit a voiceless group to have a voice, but also so that they may feel themselves part of a great program; and if we neglect the educational features of it we will be storing up trouble for ourselves. That, in substance, is my viewpoint.

DIRECTOR DOUGLAS: I raised the question about the use of the frank, Mr. President. This recommendation reads, "The members of the local councils are to serve without pay, but are to be given the franking privilege." I have never seen the report before, and I still raise the question after having seen it. I can still imagine that there might be, and probably would be, very serious charges brought that these people serving without pay on these local Consumers' Councils all over the United States would be using the frank for political purposes. You can well see how that might happen, particularly during a campaign year; and I would hate to see you subject yourself to that charge. These are not paid employees of the government. They are local Consumers' Councils, the members of which are not on the federal payroll at all. There has been a good deal of agitation about the misuse of the frank.

PRESIDENT ROOSEVELT: Will they have any paid employees that the government pays?

MRS. RUMSEY: Only the central office at Washington under Dr. Douglas. We had no idea that the local citizens would use the frank.

DIRECTOR DOUGLAS: That is what it says.

MR. WALKER: It would be essential that they use that or there would not be the saving. We are not providing stamps for them.

SECRETARY PERKINS: Surely there can be rules and regulations that will limit it.

GENERAL JOHNSON: It will depend on the law.

DIRECTOR DOUGLAS: And the material that is to be sent out under the frank.

MR. WALKER: The President was not at the last meeting. The question came up on volunteer committees being created by various organizations, whether it would be well to clear those committees first through the National Emergency Council or whether each department should make its decision itself. The survey showed we had a very large number of volunteer committees throughout the country, and some of the departments contemplated setting up new and additional ones, some volunteer and some otherwise. We didn't reach a decision on it.

PRESIDENT ROOSEVELT: What sort of committees are being set up by the departments?

MR. WALKER: There are a lot in existence now.

PRESIDENT ROOSEVELT: I thought the whole original idea was to tie them all into a central group and subdivide them into subcommittees so that they would all meet together occasionally. Wasn't that the first idea?

SECRETARY PERKINS: The problem I think was to whom these people are to be responsible. Each of these departments has established some local people to give them advice and to carry on. Now the state director of the Emergency Council is being appointed. Is the committee of the Home Owners' Loan Association, for instance, going to continue to report directly to the Home Owners' Loan or are they going to take their orders from the new state director? And there is the reluctance on the part of most of us to break down this relationship between the departments that have an administrative duty and their local representatives in the field, even if those representatives are volunteer. I think that they should continue to report to the agencies of the central government somewhat as in the past, but that locally for the purposes of clearance and cooperation they would gradually build into the organization under the state director. It would have to be a gradual transfer, and each function of the government will have to determine how far he can operate through the state director.

PRESIDENT ROOSEVELT: The important thing is to have the people in the Home Loan and Labor and Agriculture meet every once in so often and tell each other what each group has been doing. Gradually you will get a smaller number of people concerned and better cooperation. I think it is all right to report as they are doing now to Home Loan and Agriculture, so long as they meet. It is the getting together that counts more than anything else. Take the average man, where there are several different government organizations, and he doesn't know what the other fellow is doing.

SECRETARY ROPER: You want to do in the country what you are doing here.

PRESIDENT ROOSEVELT: Yes.

SECRETARY PERKINS: Where the state director is a vigorous person he will almost immediately make that thing begin to function; and undoubtedly he will be an admirable check on the information and advice now being given us. I do not believe, Mr. Walker, there will be any long difficulties there.

PRESIDENT ROOSEVELT: Are you going to tell the state directors just how to go about that sort of thing?

MR. WALKER: That is a question of policy. The only powers and duties given under the rules and regulations we have adopted are the authority that comes from the National Recovery Administration. The state director is chairman in charge of compliance, and in addition to that he is going to supervise the work of the Consumers' Councils in the state and also set up certain information bureaus in the state. That is the only jurisdiction we have extended to him to date. The thought seemed to be that after we got to know them better perhaps we could extend their supervisory powers in different directions; but these are the only powers given to them at the outset. It seems to me that is the best way to start out.

PRESIDENT ROOSEVELT: There is one question that has occurred to me. What do you propose to do with the thousands of complaints that are coming in from various parts of the United States that various functions of the government are being used for political purposes? When the report comes in that selfish people of either party are trying to use, we will say, CWA to build up a political machine, are you going to give the state director the job of finding out whether that is true or false?

MR. WALKER: I think, being in charge of the information bureau, complaints are likely to come to him, and I suppose he will forward them on.

PRESIDENT ROOSEVELT: What do you think about it?

73

MR. HOPKINS: He is going to need a very large staff if he is going to do that. If you put that job on him right off the bat, it seems to me he is going to get away from his main business to start with. He will be swamped. We get thousands of those charges every day. Republicans make charges against Democrats, and Democrats charge the Republicans. It costs three or four hundred dollars to run one of those charges down and really find out the facts. You cannot take anybody's word for that. I think it would be unwise to put that job on him at first.

MR. WALKER: Suppose we confine their jurisdiction to the three things mentioned at the outset.

PRESIDENT ROOSEVELT: Has the Secretary of the Interior given us enough money to keep on going?

SECRETARY ICKES: They appropriated it.

MR. WALKER: They earmarked it.

PRESIDENT ROOSEVELT: Is there anything else you want to take up? I think it is going to be an interesting meeting. Is it to be open to the press?

MR. WALKER: I don't see how you are going to avoid that; do you? I surely think we would subject ourselves to criticism if we did not open it to the press.

SECRETARY PERKINS: How can you take up the details of procedure with the newspapers hanging around? You have to have some meeting open to the press, but certainly some of the meetings should not be.

PRESIDENT ROOSEVELT: How many children are coming to school—forty-eight?[4]

MR. WALKER: Forty-nine—an extra one from New York.

PRESIDENT ROOSEVELT: I think Frances is right. I don't think we ought to have all these sessions open. For instance, here you have the first day, Wednesday; you have your outline, and Dan's outline and Frances' outline and Johnson's outline. Those can all be open to the press perfectly well because they are four speeches. If you are going to have discussion, no.

SECRETARY PERKINS: The function Mr. Walker has assigned me, with regard to employment, comes down to being a highly technical set of instructions. If the press is present, I shall, of course, not tell them to keep their hands off anything. At the same time, in the conference, they will have to be told not to interfere with the employment service.

ATTORNEY GENERAL CUMMINGS: You could have an executive session.

PRESIDENT ROOSEVELT: On that first day, why don't you have in your outline the

---

[4] The "school" and "children" images here are characteristic of F.D.R., who on more than one occasion equated his role as a political leader with that of a teacher.

purpose and scope, which will be more or less formal documents, and then go right into executive session and stay in executive session until Friday at four o'clock.

MR. WALKER: The time that you appear.

PRESIDENT ROOSEVELT: Yes.

MR. WALKER: I think that is a good suggestion.

PRESIDENT ROOSEVELT: Just have those two sessions open to the press. The Secretary of Labor is right. There are a lot of things to be taken up with the directors without the press being present.

MR. WALKER: I thought we would have General Johnson give one of the opening talks and let his instructions come later.

PRESIDENT ROOSEVELT: Are you ready to use some picturesque language?

GENERAL JOHNSON: I think I better cut some of it out.

PRESIDENT ROOSEVELT: Appeal to their imagination in picturesque language, and then you can talk to them naturally.

MR. WALKER: I would like to start them out with a little sip. What are the President's thoughts with reference to the suggestion of the Secretary of Labor that somebody should open the general picture of the program to them? Should that be given privately or publicly? I thought whoever does that would have to be very careful not to make it appear as a political effort.

SECRETARY ROPER: He is looking at me! (*Laughter*)

SECRETARY PERKINS: He is a good enough politician to be trusted.

MR. WALKER: If anyone is going to be trusted, I don't know of a better one.

SECRETARY ROPER: We think of submitting these talks in advance so as not to step on each other's toes, so that at the end of this conference it might be well to have these talks assembled. It might be they would form a complete survey which the directors could take back with them.

PRESIDENT ROOSEVELT: There is one thing that should be worked in, and that is that they should be told all the different things the government cannot do. That doesn't appear here at all. You know, we are getting requests practically to finance the entire United States. There are individuals who want $500 to start raising chickens, and from there up to the corporation that wants to borrow money to meet its payroll; from there up to the railroad that has to refund its bonds coming due; from there up to the municipality that says the wicked banks won't let us have any money; and from there down to the individual who says he is entitled to work, the white collar man, from the individual all the way up the scale. There is a general feeling that it is up to the government to take care of everybody, financially and otherwise—the artists, musicians, painters, and brass bands. One brass band asked to be financed on a trip around the country. These directors are going to be asked to lend their support to tapping the Treasury of the United States in some new way. I think somebody in one of these sessions should present a manual of don'ts to the various directors to tell them what the government can't and won't do.

One very simple illustration is CWA,[5] which is so popular and successful that the letters and telegrams are coming in from the Governor of New York down to the humblest citizen demanding that CWA continue on at least an equal scale, and possibly a greater scale, all the way through the summer. If we continue CWA through the summer, it is going to cost seven or eight million dollars, and secondly, it will become a habit with the country. We want to get away from CWA as soon as we can. The CWA ends the end of April, and next winter, if there is still a great deal of relief needed, the matter can be taken up again. But they must know that it is going to end this year at the end of April. We cannot carry CWA through the summer. We all agree there has got to be a limit to CWA and the people must look toward the time when it will have ended. We have to assume more or less that things are going to straighten themselves out. We must not take the position that we are going to have permanent depression in this country, and it is very important that we have somebody to say that quite forcefully to these people.

SECRETARY ROPER: I covered that point quite fully the other night in the talk at Philadelphia.

PRESIDENT ROOSEVELT: Nobody is going to starve during the warm weather.

MR. WALKER: The best man I know of for that is Lew Douglas!

VICE-PRESIDENT GARNER: What about Harry Hopkins? (*Laughter*)

PRESIDENT ROOSEVELT: I think there are somewhere around 110 or 111 banks that did not come in under the federal insurance plan, for the simple reason that they were "busted" to the tune of 25, 50, or 75 per cent, and they are all squawking. It is just too bad! The government is not handing out money to depositors just because the bank happens to have gone wrong a couple of

---

[5] Civil Works Administration was established Nov. 9, 1933, to provide regular jobs on public works for four million unemployed men and women. Its functions more or less merged with those of WPA, after July 1, 1934.

years ago. Closed banks—two thousand of them—we are helping to pay off the depositors so that they can get their money quickly; but that is a different thing. We cannot get them a hundred cents on the dollar, however. The bank in Atlantic City is making an awful squawk at ten cents on the dollar. They had a defaulting president, a defaulting cashier, and several defaulting directors who looted the bank. I think somebody ought to give an awfully mean talk—a thoroughly mean, hard-boiled talk—about the things they cannot expect. Otherwise, it will cause us more trouble down here. Will you try to arrange to have somebody do that?

MR. WALKER: At the National Emergency Council office, we have lots of requests. One was from a motion picture concern for the Reconstruction Finance Corporation to finance their picture productions for the year, and Reconstruction Finance gets plenty of them. Public Works get plenty of requests, matters that Public Works cannot take care of. If we could get a list from Public Works and Civil Works of these requests they had to deny, that would make a very good series of don'ts.

SECRETARY PERKINS: We have come to the point where we all want to say no; but do you remember last spring when private industry wanted the government to take it over, instead of saying, "No, no," a program was substituted in which they had a definite part, and now they are ready to run it. Haven't you almost the same thing now, with your private credit, your banks, your municipalities? Somebody has got to formulate a plan in which they can begin to function. Once they have begun, they will function properly. I have thought for a long time it was somebody's duty to think creatively in that field, just as many people thought creatively in the field of industry and the field of agriculture.[6] Nobody has been thinking creatively in the field of finance.

PRESIDENT ROOSEVELT: When they start to study a plan for that, there should be an effort made to provide for private finance to a greater extent than is possible at the present time and have a system of appeals. It is a rather interesting thing that the twelve Federal Reserve Banks have a right to make direct loans to an individual industry, but they have never done it in any one of the twelve districts. When an industry, say in Poughkeepsie, New York, tries to get a loan and gets turned down by the local bankers, if they go down to the Federal

---

[6] Reference to the NRA program for industry, and the AAA program for agriculture.

Reserve Bank, they are told that their local bank has turned them down, and that is the end. They can't go any further. The thought is to create some kind of appellate division by which an appeal can be taken from the Federal Reserve Bank to Washington, and then on investigation, if Washington finds that they have been turned down in an unjustified way, Washington will say to the local bank, "Here, it is up to you to take care of this thing; and if you don't take care of it, the government will, and we will show you up."

VICE-PRESIDENT GARNER: And if the local bank fails to take care of it, you would send them to the Federal Reserve Bank and say, "The local bank is unable to take care of it; you take care of it."

PRESIDENT ROOSEVELT: I have Harry Hopkins and Jesse Jones and Harold Ickes—Harold doesn't know it yet—working out a plan of that kind. I think it is possible to work something out.

MR. MARCH: That is a wonderful plan, Mr. President.

Meeting closed at 4:20 p.m.

Proceedings of the National Emergency Council

meeting no. 4
February 6, 1934

Held in the Cabinet Room of the Executive Offices, the White House, Tuesday, February 6, 1934, at 2:15 p.m.

Present: the Attorney General; the Secretary of Agriculture; the Secretary of Commerce; the Secretary of Labor; the Honorable Edward F. McGrady, Assistant Secretary of Labor; the Director of the Budget; the Administrator of Agricultural Adjustment; the Administrator of Federal Emergency Relief; the Chairman of the Board of the Home Owners' Loan Corporation; the Deputy Governor, Farm Credit Administration; the Honorable Garland S. Ferguson, Chairman, Federal Trade Commission; the Adviser on Consumer Problems, Mrs. Mary H. Rumsey; the Economic Adviser; the Executive Director.

[This meeting shows NEC effectively integrating government activity. We find evidence of valuable subcommittee spade-work for future substantive policy determinations, as in the discussion of housing led by Mr. Fahey. Had this kind of activity become firmly established in the NEC, its usefulness as a policy coordinator would have been immense. One of the most significant long-range contributions to emerge from the Council's deliberations—the centralization of review of proposed legislation which ultimately centered in the Bureau of the Budget—is clearly germinated in this meeting. Though no final decision could be taken in the absence of the President, the issues involved were clearly set forth.

Statistical data collection as a concern of government arose with the first large scale effort in American history to deal governmentally with an economic depression. The advent of the counter-cyclical theories of J. M. Keynes, Mr. Riefler's activities, and other developments inevitably paved the way for the establishment of the Council of Economic Advisers of today.[1]—Editors' Note.]

MR. WALKER: We may as well proceed, although there are two or three absent.

The first thing I will present for your information is the report on the meeting of the state directors, which was held last week [Mr. Walker then read the report]. . . .

[1] See L. Seligman, "Presidential Leadership: the Inner Circle and Institutionalization," *Journal of Politics* XVIII, No. 3 (Aug. 1956), 410-426.

I may state that it was the personal observation of the Director that we have a very fine type of [state] director. I venture the opinion they were about 80 per cent efficient, which I think is a pretty good record. They all seemed very intelligent, high-class fellows, all very enthusiastic about work, and they all seemed quite amazed at the breadth of the program. A good many of them were surprised at the confidence and understanding that each of the various heads of the departments seemed to have with reference to their work; and many of them were very much surprised that the program was in detail, as broad as it is.

A good many things were discussed during the conference concerning which the directors seemed to know little or nothing. They did not know the government was going into a lot of things discussed and concerning which a great deal is being done, not only here, but throughout the country. Now we have a report from Mr. Riefler.

MR. RIEFLER: This is a report on the feasibility of setting up some coordinating work.[2]

A composite summary of the various emergency activities of the government for use of the Executive Council and the Emergency Council could be built up along the following three lines:

A. *Persons affected by emergency activities.* Last week a chart was presented to the Executive Council showing monthly changes in total public employment since January 1, 1933. This series could be supplemented in two directions, first, by a comparable series showing the number of persons receiving relief, the number of farmers receiving disbursements through the AAA, the number of persons obtaining loans through the Farm Credit Administration, the Federal Home Owners Loan Corporation, etc., and, secondly, by a series showing total private employment in manufacturing, mining, public utilities, etc.

It would also be possible to build up comparable figures for the most important of these items by states. These state figures, since some of the reports are not available by states and others, when they are available, are sometimes subject to a considerable margin of error.

In using these figures, it should be remembered that a grand total of all of the persons enumerated under each of these heads could not be compared directly with the total population of the country, since some individuals would have been counted twice.

B. *Emergency Disbursements.* It would be possible to build up fairly

---

[2] Mr. Riefler's report is the first of numerous references in these meetings to the continuing and important problem of government: the collection of adequate statistics and data on which to evaluate programs. Discussion of this problem in the meetings to follow provides an interesting study in the evolution of government statistical work and of the realization of the need for such data.

comparable national and state totals of expenditures along the same general lines. Such expenditures would have to be classified according to their character, i.e., refunding disbursements, such as RFC loans to financial institutions on collateral, differ widely from PWA loans for new construction, and both of these items differ further from direct expenditures for relief. It probably would be difficult to build up complete totals along these lines by states showing the total of all disbursements in significant categories, but the major disbursement items could be handled.

C. Overhead Expenses. The Emergency Council might obtain from each of the emergency agencies a summary of its overhead expenses, showing separately (1) salaries, (2) wages, and (3) expenses for equipment, rental, supplies, etc. This would serve to guide the council on the administrative phases of its work.

If the Council desires to organize current co-ordinating information of this kind, I would suggest that an Executive Committee be formed to decide in more detail on the general character of the reports to be prepared, and also to arrange specifically for their compilation.

This is simply a summary of what could be done. I think all the reports that come in could be, if we got at it, put on a much more comparable basis so that a person could see the progress of the Recovery movement agencies with each other and by putting it on state lines could see what the conditions are.

It would be very difficult to develop it rapidly because there are a great many problems to be met; but I think some rather interesting comparable totals can be gotten together.

MR. WALKER: Any discussion with reference to this?

SECRETARY PERKINS: I don't think I altogether understand just what the purpose is. Is it to give us a measuring stick for the progress of recovery?

MR. RIEFLER: Yes.

SECRETARY PERKINS: If that can be done, I think it is very important to do it. I am always impressed with our inability to measure the results attained. Your office this morning sent over to me for some information for appearance before a committee this afternoon, I think, and they wanted to know the total number of unemployed, the total of employed, the production in various industries and sales and all that sort of thing. This information is not on a comparable basis and it is very misleading to a person who doesn't know this. Many people would like to know those things and I think it would be very valuable in measuring our recovery. In the matter of employment and unemployment alone, we are likely to fall into grave error at some point in considering one situation and not recognize the causes of distress in another direction. For instance, I have just learned during the past week that in some areas about a third less agricultural laborers are going to be employed this year than last year; but they will not show up in anybody's records of employment and unemployment and all those things are very confusing. I think we must get this on a comparable basis. Do you think it can be done in a short time?

MR. RIEFLER: Not in a short time. What we have to do is to work out a form which will be accurate in outlining the activities of the agencies and also getting one that will be on a comparable basis with the others so we can build up totals. I think that a lot can be done and make it very interesting.

SECRETARY PERKINS: I think it is very important to tackle it. I was challenged this morning when a newspaperman asked me how many people would be out of work by June first. I said that I didn't know and that nobody knew, but he said that Mr. Hopkins told him that there would be four million people out of work by June first. I don't know what he is talking about and we haven't any basis upon which we can either rest for comparable material for the present, or base a prediction for the future. I think if you can manage it, Mr. Walker, to establish such an enterprise on a sound basis is very important.

MR. WALKER: For the information of the Secretary of Commerce, who was a little late coming in, I would say we are discussing the report Mr. Riefler has submitted with reference to getting such reports from the various emergency organizations as to make a picture showing the persons affected by the emergency activities, the departments themselves and also concerning the overhead of the various emergency agencies.

SECRETARY ROPER: I must apologize for being a little late, Mr. Chairman, but I had conferences I could not escape from.

DIRECTOR DOUGLAS: Is the purpose of this to coordinate the whole picture?

MR. RIEFLER: It is to present a coordinated picture so that the different parts can be judged against the whole. As I read the reports from the different agencies, I have no perspective with which to compare them. I think that we can gradually work that material into perspective so that we can weigh it by states and dovetail them into each other.

DIRECTOR DOUGLAS: There are three items—first, the number of people affected; secondly, disbursements—

MR. RIEFLER: I think we ought to have a pretty clear, rounded picture of the different types of disbursements; for instance, loans on existing collateral that soar up in the existing credit structure rather than give anybody a job, are very different from PWA loans. I think we ought to be able to classify all these

	different activities and get some idea of how they are run.
DIRECTOR DOUGLAS:	And the third item is overhead. Is it one of the objects of the second and third items in that memorandum to exercise some control over expenses?
MR. RIEFLER:	That is entirely up to the Council.
MR. WALKER:	That is one of the things up for discussion—one of the reasons I had this report presented to the Council.
MR. FAHEY:	I would like to ask Mr. Reifler how soon it might be possible to get a picture—even if not accurate and only an estimate—as to how many people there are unemployed at present or likely to be in a month or so, and in what directions. That is, how many are employed in the building trade, for instance. What I am thinking about is this: after all, our fundamental problem is getting people back to work, and we are trying in many directions to bring this about. It seems to me it would be very useful if we could examine these several efforts and their direct relation to the possibilities of re-employing people now unemployed. I do not know whether this is a proper place to bring it up but there is a question which arises in connection with our problem on this matter of housing.
MR. WALKER:	I put that on the agenda for discussion to follow this.
MR. FAHEY:	All right then, let it lie over until we reach it.
SECRETARY ROPER:	There is another phase of this situation, as I understand from your discussion, that I would like to call attention to. It is all right for us to be careful in our canvass and get accurate statistics of unemployed, for instance, but I would like to have that paralleled by the results under the old system at the same time, because I would not want the public, you see, to misunderstand the situation. In other words, the public has in its mind a certain result from certain sources. That result we will assume, just for the sake of argument, may not have been built up through the canvass of the same source that you will now more accurately canvass, if you please. The result would be that probably we would show a great many more unemployed, you understand, as a basis of comparison with the old figures which are in the public mind. Therefore, if I may try to make myself a little clearer, you would want, in presenting this, to safeguard against the possibility of our injuring our own cause by showing a figure that would not be comparable with the figures already in the public mind. Do you understand what I mean? For instance, there are some people who have reached the conclusion—I have discussed it with my associate, the Secretary of Labor, and

I don't know that I have in my mind who put it there, whether Mr. Hoover or somebody else—but I have crystalized a certain notion that there are a certain number of people who are always out of employment. I was told on one occasion that it was about four million. That may have been entirely wrong, and yet it is going to affect the approach to our problem here, so that I believe, sir, we ought to try to effect the comparison in two ways.

MR. WALKER: My thought in bringing this up for discussion was more to draw out information for the benefit of the Council than for public information.

SECRETARY ROPER: This is different.

MR. WALKER: The picture we want is not a picture for the public, but precisely for our own selves.

ATTORNEY GENERAL CUMMINGS: I suppose it is a sort of a progress chart, as it were, for our own purposes and to guide us along the most feasible lines. The thing about it that rather appeals to me is your reference to the analysis of overhead expenses. I don't know what that situation is, but I suspect that the overhead expenses are running pretty strong, and if the information that you would collate would give something upon which to base some possible control in that respect, it might be very well worth-while; but that is only one aspect of the situation.

DIRECTOR DOUGLAS: Mr. Chairman, I think that these reports should be confidential in nature and should not be given to the public, either directly or indirectly.

SECRETARY ROPER: That is fine.

DIRECTOR DOUGLAS: Secondly, if this is designed for the purpose of maintaining some control as to overhead, to which the Attorney General has referred, and over the general emergency expenditures, I think it is an absolute essential. Certainly it is if there is going to be any effective financing program conducted by the Treasury. It is easy enough to spend money, but it is very difficult to raise the money to spend. If there is going to be a coordinated program, there has to be some control over the expenditures. You can't spend unless you are able to finance your spending (some governments have, but it has been disastrous).

I think it would be a very illuminating picture, Mr. Chairman, to find out how many American citizens are being subsidized by American money—maybe fifteen millions, maybe more.

MR. WALKER: Anybody else wish to be heard further on this subject?

SECRETARY WALLACE: I would like to see the thing broadened out, which might well be within Mr. Riefler's province, to make some kind of study of the balance that could be maintained between the various productive forces, and have it as near as possible up-to-date—an index of profits, an index of labor, and amount received by agriculture; and also set up a kind of balance between productive forces and consumptive forces, between labor and agriculture and between profits—a situation which could be kept going, which would be self-perpetuating without undue call on the government for money. I would sort of like to have some concept, to know what we are shooting at, representing all the productive forces.

SECRETARY PERKINS: I think that is very important, and we don't actually know what constitutes balance today—a balance that can be maintained—do we?

SECRETARY ROPER: Is it within the purview of this committee to look into the future and find out just what we propose to do, for instance, a year from now? In other words, what efforts are going to be made toward spurring industry to take on people; to what extent are we going to permit capital to assist in financing experts; to what extent I may be permitted to bring forward a very serious problem touching subsidization of the merchant marine—as to what is to be the policy in that connection; and as to what is to be the policy in the other phase which I am studying today, namely, air mail? There is just a multitude of things here that enter into a fundamental study. We are faced today by two conditions; one is an emergency condition which we are trying to meet, but there is also a long term planning program which is just as important. In fact, if we don't care for that, the emergency will continue. It seems to me that it might be within the purview of this committee to have a subcommittee, if you please, that would be studying that phase of it, because we are trying to get on what you would call a normal basis.

MR. HOPKINS: It seems very wise and extremely important; I wonder if it would not be wise if we had a group which we might name which would present in the most specific outline a plan of approach to this whole matter. I should like to move that a committee be appointed by the chairman to bring in a report at the earliest possible moment.

MR. FAHEY: I second it.

SECRETARY PERKINS: Doesn't Mr. Riefler's report cover it? I have a feeling that the next thing to do is to begin to do it. It is very hard to make a plan in this case in advance. You have to see what your material is, how you can utilize it, and what needs to be supplemented.

DIRECTOR DOUGLAS: I should think there would be a good many details to be worked out—for instance, who is going to do it?

SECRETARY ROPER: Mr. Riefler could head this and could be authorized to call in anybody that he wants to cooperate with him.

DIRECTOR DOUGLAS: I think there are a great many details.

MR. WALKER: This is the thought that came to me: it seems to me the important thing we need to try now is to have our information coming in to us and have it as full and complete from the various departments as we can so that Mr. Riefler can correlate and coordinate it for us. It seems to me that we have no information with reference to overhead of any particular emergency activity, and I don't know how far either the President or the Council would want to go in setting up any sort of control for the various emergency agencies.

DIRECTOR DOUGLAS: There is a certain amount of information referred to in Mr. Riefler's memorandum which is now submitted weekly to the Treasury Department. In order to avoid duplication, I think the thing really should be surveyed in some detail; otherwise, there will be duplication of effort.

MR. RIEFLER: Yes, we ought to clear up those things.

DIRECTOR DOUGLAS: There are also some administrative details in that rather broad statement of the objectives.

MR. WALKER: If there is no objection, the chair will appoint such a committee and I would like to give a little thought to it, so if it's agreeable to everybody, I will do it in the immediate future so that it can start to function.

The next question is the matter that was suggested by Mr. Fahey, with reference to the housing problem.

MR. FAHEY: Mr. Chairman, it is logically a part of the discussion. You will recall that some weeks ago, out of the discussion here in the Council, the President asked me to act as chairman of a committee to organize a meeting of representatives of the Federal Reserve Board, the Treasury, insurance companies, savings banks, building and loan associations, and national banks to get from them and consider with them what might be done to stimulate the activity of private interests in dealing with the construction problem as a whole, and particularly with its relation to private housing. Consistent with that resolution we first had a meeting at the Federal Reserve Board and brought together the representatives of those several interests; out of that a subcommittee was formed. At the first meeting the consensus of opinion of the representatives of those financial interests was that they did not see how anything much could be done with the problem of employment in construction industries as it related to modernization of homes and new construction, except by government aid or government backing. Mr. [Jesse] Jones and Governor [Eugene R.] Black and some of us suggested to them that that attitude was quite consistent with that of many interests that were coming down here and wanting the government to aid this, that, and the other, and the question was if the time had not arrived when private interests ought to be ready to take hold and do something.

They agreed that they would get together some figures as to their resources and also examine further the possibilities of help so far as they were concerned, and meet with us again. That second meeting was held at the office of the Reconstruction Finance Corporation a week ago Friday. We had about 25 representatives of savings banks especially and a large number of insurance executives. On that occasion they agreed that a survey of their resources indicated that they had considerable money available which they could use this year and which they were ready to use, but that they were very definitely restricted as to how they could use it because of the laws of the several states. In many instances they could advance only 50 per cent, and that on first mortgages. In some of the other states they could go as high as 66⅔ per cent, either on new construction or modernization. They were agreed that the greatest demand was for modernization and repairs, which had fallen to a very low percentage of anything like normal.

I ought to explain that, in advance of these meetings, we also put in a night with the representatives of the Recovery Administration, Labor, Public Works, and various others interested in this subject of housing and there we found considerable conflict of opinion as to how much demand there was for new construction. But again there was pretty general agreement that there was very considerable opportunity for modernization, and for the board to employ a very considerable number of people also in that direction.

Out of this last conference a week ago Friday, as I started to say, the insurance and other interests agreed that so far as first mortgage money was concerned they could contribute a good deal, and they were prepared to; and they could meet that demand, at least in part, although they felt they would have to be rather cautious about it. For the rest, however, they were of the unanimous opinion that they could do nothing and that if anything really was to be accomplished it would have to be under government auspices. It is out of that that a suggestion arose that the Home Owners' Loan Corporation, out of its own resources, should first of all undertake to do what it could to meet the demand for modernization in connection with homes which it is taking over; and secondly, it should try to find a way to make some money available to the private institutions—that is, the savings banks, building and loan associations, and the insurance companies—for use on both modernization and new construction, the idea being that with their facilities all over the country, and their experiences, they could utilize that money to advantage and supplement it with their own but that anything placed at their disposal should be with the stipulation that it was for specific purposes, not for withdrawal or their own liability or anything of that sort; and the other suggestion in connection with the program was that, through the Home Loan Bank System, we might also supplement the resources of the banks in agreement with the Reconstruction Finance Corporation through the medium of preferred stock, and keep them from issuing bonds and putting them on the market under present circumstances. That program is still under consideration, having been checked with the Director of the Budget and with the Treasury Department, and in a preliminary way, with the representatives of the House and Senate committees, but it is not yet worked out.

Out of all these, we were somewhat confused and puzzled by the fact that we find a dozen or fifteen different government agencies all interested and involved, in one way or another, in this particular problem as affecting construction industries and especially in the field of housing. You will recall that as this was put up to us in the first place, it was limited to the question of contacting the private financial institutions and finding out what they were prepared to do; but the question arises as to whether some steps ought not to be taken for a consideration of this problem by all the government agencies which have an interest in it, and have a survey made for the purpose of determining whether the stimulation of employment in this particular direction, because of its relation to the construction industry and effect on the market, is something that ought to be considered in a special way and entirely apart from such incidental contributions as the Home Owners' Loan Corporation is able to make, and in those directions entirely outside our areas. The Department of Agriculture is affected; the Farm Credit Administration—so far as farm homes are concerned; then you have the slum-clearance project, and you have the subsistence homesteads problem. A number of groups have been interested in the possibility of correlating all of these several agencies into one comprehensive program.

Meanwhile, we face the necessity of dealing with some projects up in Congress represented by bills which call for the appropriation of from two to three billion dollars to deal with this problem; and those demands are backed by several organized industries which claim they have already received commitments of a substantial portion of both the House and Senate in support of large appropriations of that sort. I think that there is no question that some very vigorous demands are going to be presented in that direction. I wanted to repeat here the question as to whether it might not be well if the chairman, or somebody, assumed the task of bringing together the representatives of these several departments and bureaus of the government which have a common interest in this whole problem, to see if a survey of it on their part might result in some recommendation to this Council that the Council will need to consider.[3]

SECRETARY ROPER: Which would be the departments?

MR. FAHEY: Well, your own department, for example, is involved. I have here a rather incomplete list of those that we have found. Financially interested in the housing are the Farm Credit Administration, Home Owners' Loan Corporation, Savings and Loan Associations, Housing Division of the Public Works Administration, Reconstruction Finance Corporation, and Subsistence Homesteads in the Department of the Interior. In addition to that, there is the Rehabilitation Division of the Reconstruction Finance Corporation, Farm Homes in the Department of Agriculture, and the Construction Division

---

[3] This and the ensuing discussion of problems of coordination in the area of housing foreshadows the establishment, following the passage of the National Housing Act (Public Law 479, 73rd Congress) in June 1934, of a Better Housing Division within the NEC. The functions of this division were taken over in Nov. 1934 by the Federal Housing Administration, which was also created by the National Housing Act.

of the Bureau of Foreign and Domestic Commerce. Aside from all that, the Tennessee Valley Authority is interested in a part of this problem, and the Army Housing Unit in the War Department is another one. On the statistical side, you have the Bureau of Labor Statistics, the Housing Division of the Bureau of Standards in the Department of Commerce, and the Employment Stabilization Board. The Bureau of the Census is also doing some work on the statistical side, and the Bureau of Mortgages in the Interior Department on materials; the Bureau of Industrial Research is doing some work with reference to construction corporation income; the Comptroller of the Currency is dealing with it from the angle of banking and building and loan associations, and the Interstate Commerce Commission is dealing with it from the standpoint of freight on construction materials. And then you have the Civil Works Administration, as well. It also comes into the picture in the Recovery Administration in connection with a number of codes; and also the Department of Labor, from the standpoint of labor, is interested in a very large way.

There have been five general conventions and conferences of the organizations interested in home building and construction here and in New York, and Cleveland within the last six weeks. I don't know to what extent they are shooting at the other departments, but we get them frequently. Hardly a day passes that we do not have a delegation backed up by four or five congressmen.

The lumber people have held five different conventions, and the material people have held four or five more. The Home and Community Builders National Association met here last week on Tuesday. They had a convention here on this subject, and presented a raft of statistics; and only a couple of weeks before, we had the other one at the Willard Hotel, and several of them have permanent agencies housed here with their own staffs, and they are just at work day after day on that problem.

MR. WALKER: The housing division of Public Works has a little fund of $25,000,000.

MR. FAHEY: The United States Housing Corporation has an inheritance of half a million dollars that it doesn't know what to do with, but I understand numerous departments are clutching at that as a last straw. I don't know what will be done with it.

DIRECTOR DOUGLAS: On this general subject, an agreement was reached last week between the Home Owners' Loan Corporation, the Treasury, the Budget, and the White House under which the Home Owners' Loan Corporation asked a broadening of its powers from Congress so as to permit a hundred million to two hundred million dollars to be raised through the sale of Home Owners' Loan Corporation bonds, the sum so raised to be used for the purpose of extending loans for modernization of homes. That is a direct approach to that particular phase of the general construction problem.

With respect to the interest which the ICC has, and the Department of Commerce, the Department of Agriculture, and various other departments, their interest is not really directly toward the construction problem. The ICC's interest is one of freight rates, and that of the Labor Stabilization Board is one of determining what the employment situation is. The Farm Credit Administration's program is a somewhat different one. That was the agreement reached with respect to a direct approach to this problem. It was decided, as I recollect, that for the time being, that was ample for the purpose of experimenting in this field, and that nothing further would now be done. It appears to me that if all these various agencies which have a remote interest in the general problem, but an interest which is not directly associated with the stimulation of trade, were congregated together, we might have to construct another Commerce Building, Mr. Secretary.

SECRETARY ROPER: You could add to this building, I suppose. Since we are discussing the question here—throwing our thoughts into a basket—in line with what Mr. Fahey and the Director of the Budget said, let me call attention to one phase of the situation which confronts me, and which, I believe, this Council might give consideration to. I am flooded with bills of many kinds asking my opinion as to whether this venture or the other would, in my opinion, be wise or unwise or practicable. Now, I like to look at ourselves as all one family just occupying different rooms in the same house. I believe, sir, it would be very wise indeed, at this time, if these bills could be channeled, before opinions are given, through a common source.[4] Now I have at least a couple of dozen, and my opinion should not

---

[4] The beginning of proposals to have clearance of legislation through the President's office. For a detailed discussion of the evolution of legislative clearance, see Richard Neustadt, "Presidency and Legislation: The Growth of Central Clearance," *American Political Science Review* XLVIII (Sept., 1954), 641.

govern about these things, even when they affect the Department of Commerce primarily. They have a continuing expense which enters into the problem. If the Director of the Budget, for instance—I am just thinking out loud—could be charged by this Council with the responsibility of looking these over—if it isn't asking too much—I think it ought to be done. I don't believe I have any right to pass an opinion as to whether the government should do this, that, or the other without it should channel through a common mouth here, like the Director of the Budget.

DIRECTOR DOUGLAS: There are generally two questions involved with respect to legislation. The first question has to do with the desirability of the particular purpose of the act. That, it seems to me, is something that the department should pass on.

SECRETARY ROPER: Oh yes, we can pass on that by a memorandum to you.

DIRECTOR DOUGLAS: The second question, as generally involved, is the question of expense and whether or not the expenditure necessitated by the act is consistent with the financial program of the President. With respect to that phase of it, some time ago, by the direction of the President, all legislation submitted to the executive departments for report was to be finally passed through the Bureau of the Budget, its sole function being to simply answer the question, "Is this in conflict with the financial program of the President, or isn't it?"

SECRETARY ROPER: Many of these enterprises are all right, but the point is, are they worth while at this time?

DIRECTOR DOUGLAS: And can we afford them?

SECRETARY ROPER: Yes, and can we afford them. I can say, "Yes, this is a good thing, it is all right, we would like to have it," but a person cannot have all he wants in the world at this particular time. I think you ought to pass on that—in cooperation with the head of the department or bureau, of course.

DIRECTOR DOUGLAS: I had thought that in so far as the expense is concerned, they were now being submitted to the Bureau.

SECRETARY ROPER: But they do not always state the expenses; you have to make a careful research to get at that.

DIRECTOR DOUGLAS: Oh yes, there will be a great many acts that have the expense hidden.

MR. WALKER: How do you suggest controlling that?

SECRETARY ROPER: I would suggest that before the head of a department passes upon a measure of the type we have referred to, we call the letter which we are issuing in reply to the congressman or committee to the attention of the Bureau of the Budget.

ATTORNEY GENERAL CUMMINGS: I believe, Mr. Roper, that there is an Executive Order extant on that now.

SECRETARY ROPER: Only when the expense is exposed, as I might say. Many of these are simply establishing a new venture or new unit or new investigation or something of that kind.

SECRETARY WALLACE: Everything involves expense; that would mean that the Director of the Budget should pass on every particle of legislation.

MR. WALKER: That could be changed to apply to all legislation instead of as the Order now stands.

ATTORNEY GENERAL CUMMINGS: What is your understanding of the present Order, Mr. Douglas?

DIRECTOR DOUGLAS: My understanding is that wherever legislation authorizes an appropriation, it has to be submitted to the Bureau of the Budget to determine whether or not that is in conflict with the financial program of the President.

ATTORNEY GENERAL CUMMINGS: That is exactly my understanding; you don't think that quite enough, Mr. Roper?

SECRETARY ROPER: I am only bringing this up; it seems to me we are liable to give the congressman or the committee an argument to do something that carries a hidden necessity, you understand, for an appropriation.

DIRECTOR DOUGLAS: May I ask a question? There is one act that occurs to me in connection with the Deposit Insurance Corporation. Would that direct the performance of any duties on the part of the federal government which would increase the expenditures to the government aside from the $150,000,000 for the Deposit Insurance Corporation? Or another one: Did the Securities Act specify anything more than the appropriations?

COMMISSIONER FERGUSON: Two hundred fifty thousand dollars.

DIRECTOR DOUGLAS: I mean in the way of authorization. It simply imposed upon you the responsibility of doing certain things—charged you with them.

ATTORNEY GENERAL CUMMINGS: How are the appropriations handled?

DIRECTOR DOUGLAS: They have been charged with that responsibility.

COMMISSIONER FERGUSON: There was an appropriation of $250,000.

ATTORNEY GENERAL CUMMINGS: That was made in the regular routine.

DIRECTOR DOUGLAS: Next year they get $500,000 more, although the Act itself did not authorize the appropriation necessary to make the provisions of the Act effective; so really what the Secretary of Commerce is saying is that frequently legislation, while not containing an expressed authorization is, nevertheless an implicit authorization for an appropriation.

93

COMMISSIONER FERGUSON: It very often comes up in a resolution. Very often the Senate or the House will pass a resolution directing the Federal Trade Commission to make a certain investigation and no appropriation is made for it. That, of course, involves the expenditure of money and sometimes has caused us to bring a deficit. For instance, the public utilities investigation—in order to carry out that work, we had to create a deficit and then later on Congress appropriated the fund in a deficiency bill.

ATTORNEY GENERAL CUMMINGS: Isn't the line of demarcation rather simply whether the particular act is going to require a hitherto unconsidered appropriation? Now for instance, there is a whole realm of legislative enactments—I know there are in my department and I presume there are in others—which are technical, changing a statute, putting in words or taking some words out; but I don't consider those as involving appropriations because even if you could conceive that they might cost a little more somewhere along the line, it would all fall within the general appropriation anyhow. I suppose you would not need to bother with those.

SECRETARY ROPER: Certainly not. Let me mention this, within the four walls of the room; strange to say, California has admitted that they do have earthquakes out there, and now we are importuned in our Coast and Geodetic Survey to examine the buildings to determine whether the structures are of such a nature as to withstand earthquakes. That is something new and I just mention that as one of the things, like Commissioner Ferguson says, that come up every day. Shall we undertake that work or not? We will have to say the work is proper and necessary.

ATTORNEY GENERAL CUMMINGS: Doesn't it all come down to this—whether you can do it out of your regular appropriation, whether you have enough money to do it?

SECRETARY ROPER: It really comes down to that.

COMMISSIONER FERGUSON: The policy we are pursuing now is when a resolution passed by Congress involves the expenditure of funds not contemplated in our annual appropriation, to submit an estimate to the Director of the Budget for the funds necessary to carry out this work. And if the funds are eventually not appropriated, we cannot do it.

SECRETARY ROPER: Whenever the thing takes the form that [it] has taken in the Coast and Geodetic survey, we can handle it in that way but when it is a matter of approving something that is of a new type, if we have the money we can do it and if we haven't we can't do it. I didn't mean to take up your time unduly;

I just mentioned this thing as one point to be kept in mind.

DIRECTOR DOUGLAS: There is the Geological Survey.

SECRETARY ROPER: Yes, and this is the Coast and Geodetic Survey.

DIRECTOR DOUGLAS: The Geological Survey can do that very work.

SECRETARY ROPER: We have the testing machinery.

DIRECTOR DOUGLAS: Well, so do they.

MR. WALKER: I don't know as we want to swamp the Director of the Budget with considering all the contemplated legislation before Congress.

SECRETARY PERKINS: I think any department knows, when it sees a bill that requires performance of certain duties, whether or not those duties can be performed without a substantial increase in the appropriation; and when it is obvious that the bill requires a duty or performance that will go way beyond the present appropriation, I should think the thing to do would be to make a memorandum to that effect, that the purpose is good but that it would require an appropriation of not less than so much more for the first year, and so much for the second and third years, and in that way submit it to the Director of the Budget.

SECRETARY ROPER: I think that would be perfect. Here is another interesting thing coming to us; you know the scientists think that internal cancer may be cured provided they can get sufficient ray power developed. We are asked to laboratory these tests which will cost, according to the best estimates, probably as much as $250,000. Now they are asking me to go before the Public Works and get that. That is all right and I will endeavor to present that, but I am keeping in mind also the thought that the continuing overhead expense becomes an important question in many of these things. If we can get the money for the tests I am speaking of—the earthquake tests —that is all right, as they may not, probably, be continuous, but the scientific laboratory which carries this extra voltage, which will cost about $250,000—in the interest of humanity it makes a very great appeal to me, and I have a wonderful report that will give probably a new conception of this— it does involve continuing expense.

MR. WALKER: It would not be improper for us to suggest that measures which do require new appropriations be submitted to the Director of the Budget. There could not be any objection to that, could there? And that might revive a lot of people around to follow that practice, isn't that true?

DIRECTOR DOUGLAS: I don't know the extent to which the old Executive Order has been followed by the departments. Supposing I look up that old Executive Order and see what it expressly says and what its implications are.

SECRETARY ROPER: That would refer to cases where we are getting money to establish a particular facility which will carry continuing expense into the future, I take it.

ATTORNEY GENERAL CUMMINGS: I think the thing to do is to get a copy of the Executive Order and find out what scope it covers now; we would not want to be in the position of rendering an Executive Order by some resolution of our own, so suppose we start right by finding out where are now. I am perfectly willing to hunt up the Executive Order, and advise Mr. Walker as to what it means, if there is any ambiguity about it.

MR. WALKER: I imagine the Director of the Budget has it.

DIRECTOR DOUGLAS: Yes, I have the old Executive Order.

ATTORNEY GENERAL CUMMINGS: If you have any doubt as to whether that covers the things we are talking about, I shall be glad to confer with you on it.

DIRECTOR DOUGLAS: Suppose we leave it that way and I will get in touch with you. I am reasonably certain that the Bureau of the Budget does not want every piece of legislation passed through it.

ATTORNEY GENERAL CUMMINGS: I will wait until I hear from you.

DIRECTOR DOUGLAS: I do think there is one suggestion that might relieve a great deal of work in the departments. Congressmen as individuals very frequently write to departments and ask what the attitude of the department would be toward a bill which that congressman or his friends may have introduced. I think that it is desirable to be courteous to the members of Congress, but I don't think that an executive department ought to be called on for a report until the committee having jurisdiction over that has requested it.

ATTORNEY GENERAL CUMMINGS: It is an invariable rule in my department that we never give opinions to Congress on any matters until requested by the President or through some executive head of department; and sometimes, for the sake of avoiding circumlocution or being too technical and too tied up with red tape, where they are really looking for constructive help, I have sometimes had memoranda of law prepared and sent along for what they may be worth. I am very careful to avoid giving opinions to Congress as to what legislation they can enact and what they should enact and all that sort of thing because I might find myself in a very embarrassing position later, being called upon to advise upon that very thing after it had taken some modified form.

DIRECTOR DOUGLAS: There is a great difference too, so far as the executive depart- ments are concerned, between submitting a report on a bill to a committee which has requested it and submitting a report to an individual congressman who has requested it.

SECRETARY WALLACE: An individual senator called up this morning. He was interested in a Senate resolution providing for an inquiry into the so-called milk or dairy combine. He said he under- stood certain of my statements indicated I might be in sympathy, and if I was, would I please write a letter indicating my attitude in regard to this resolution.

MR. WALKER: I suppose you don't desire any particular action on this suggestion?

Going back to this housing matter, is it your thought that the matter of housing has been definitely solved by the conference held at the White House?

DIRECTOR DOUGLAS: At least temporarily.

MR. FAHEY: My question about it was this. I agree with Mr. Douglas about that, of course; I am not thinking in terms of additional appropriations, so far as this year is concerned; but as we have been dealing with this problem we have come in contact with a number of departments and bureaus here, all of which have some interest in some phase of the housing problem. The question I am raising is whether it would not be desirable to go a little further in just canvassing private interests as to their relation to this problem and whether it might not be well to bring together these several groups to consider the problems presented by housing as a whole, as against future developments.

MR. WALKER: Didn't the President appoint you as chairman of the committee?

MR. FAHEY: Yes, but it was just in relation to the private financial interests. I might say in that connection—I have not had opportunity to take it up with RFC or the Comptroller—that one of the points raised by the private financial interests is that they are not as free as they might like to be in making money available for housing or for loans to small industries or loans to industry generally, because they claim that the requirements of the Comptroller relative to loans are at present so stringent that they do not feel like being at all liberal in the character of the loans they make those institutions which have taken Reconstruction Finance Corporation preferred stock. They say that they are called upon to make such elaborate reports every two weeks with reference to their use of the money

97

at their disposal and such restrictions are put upon their use that they are not getting very much help out of that situation. That is only one phase of it and that perhaps can be cleared up by direct contact with the Comptroller and RFC; but there is a broader question here as to whether any means may be devised which will stimulate greater liberality on the part of private lending agencies. But the immediate question I was raising was whether it was worth while to broaden our undertaking here and get together for further consideration of the problem of those directly interested in government departments as to whether anything further ought to be looked forward to, so far as the housing problem is concerned.

MR. WALKER: Do you recommend there is a necessity for that?

MR. FAHEY: I think it would be very useful to be forehanded about it and provide an exchange of views of these several departments and divisions.

MR. WALKER: Couldn't you start that, yourself, as the chairman?

MR. FAHEY: I would rather somebody else would do it. I have plenty on my hands, but if that is your wish, all right.

MR. WALKER: If there is no objection now that you have gone into it, I could have a talk with you and maybe we could set up a committee, if that is agreeable to the Council. Do you think there is need of immediate action on that?

MR. FAHEY: I think the sooner such a group could be brought together the better, within the next week or two.

MR. WALKER: Then we will consider the selection of a committee, if there is no objection.
Is there anything further? The President will not be here today. I do not think he will be in the Executive Offices until tomorrow. He has a slight cold, but is much improved.

SECRETARY PERKINS: Is there a report ready on that matter we have been laboring on the past two weeks?

MR. WALKER: The consumer question?

SECRETARY PERKINS: Yes.

MR. WALKER: I thought there was no necessity of reporting and so advised the consumer representative. We have authorized an expenditure of the monies and I think we have full authority to go ahead with that, so I know of no objection to going ahead. Do you?

SECRETARY PERKINS: No. I think it is all right.

MR. WALKER: I think it is within our authority to proceed with it and I so advised before the meeting.

If there is nothing further, I would like to suggest that the Secretary of Labor, Director of the Budget, the Director of the Relief, and the Interpreting Economist remain for a few minutes after this meeting and get organized as a committee so we can get the thing started. It will take only a few minutes.

Meeting adjourned at 3:30 p.m.

Proceedings of the National Emergency Council

meeting no. 5
February 20, 1934

Held in the Cabinet Room of the Executive Offices,
The White House, Tuesday, February 20, 1934, at 2:05 p.m.

Present: the Attorney General; the Secretary of Commerce; the Secretary of Labor; the Director of the Budget; the Administrator of Agricultural Adjustment; the Administrator of Federal Emergency Relief; the Administrator for Industrial Recovery; the Chairman of the Board of the Home Owners' Loan Corporation; the Governor of Farm Credit Administration; the Honorable Garland S. Ferguson, Chairman, Federal Trade Commission; the Adviser on Consumer Problems, Mrs. Mary H. Rumsey; the Honorable Oscar L. Chapman, Assistant Secretary of the Interior; the Assistant Secretary of Agriculture; the Honorable Thomas C. Blaisdell, Assistant Director of the Consumers Council; the Economic Adviser; the Executive Director.

[The discussions in this meeting point up clearly the pressing need for top level coordination of policy in a total administrative program. The report made on the agricultural program and the discussion that ensued were doubtless of value as a means of informing the participants of what was being done in fields other than their own. The report also raised problems of inter-program conflict in objectives, such as the adverse impact on employment of agricultural labor produced by the acreage restrictions, and the consequent additional drain on the relief programs of other agencies. Quite clearly, NEC did not provide a mechanism for resolving this program incompatibility. In the absence of the President, the possibility that it might have done so was further diminished. Unless NEC were to provide such a mechanism, its coordinating function could hardly amount to more than a forum for raising problems and exchanging information.—Editor's Note.]

MR. WALKER: Here is a memorandum from the Federal Emergency Relief Administrator [Harry Hopkins]:

In planning a program for the coming year, it seems to be important that there be made available information on the following points:

(1) How many men may be employed directly and indirectly in public works by months and by states and cities.

(2) How many men and women not now employed will be employed

by private industries. For example, how many additional men will be employed in the automobile industry, in the steel trade, by railroads, by factories, and what is the basis of these estimates.

(3) How many men will be displaced from gainful employment as a result of reducing the crop acreage.

I think we have started to get some of those figures, and in view of the fact that there will be a report by Mr. Riefler, I would suggest that we hear from him now.

MR. RIEFLER: We are already getting the aggregate figures together as to the number of persons employed and payrolls under the CWA, TVA, CCC, and other emergency activities and we are trying to bring in regular governmental activities also where we can get the material. The forecast of future employment under PWA, as far as direct employment is concerned, is being worked out and we are getting fairly good results on it now.

The question of number of workers displaced by the agricultural program we have not touched at all. I don't know whether agriculture has done anything on it or not, but we can try to get in contact with them. I am not familiar with that. I will get in touch with them and see.

Dun & Bradstreet's have prepared a report every two weeks for the use of the Council on business failures. It is the only source of these figures and they are very good. I have had copies of the report given to each one of you, and I have a short summary here . . . .

MR. WALKER: It was the suggestion of some of the members that we take up consideration of some of the problems concerning agriculture.

DR. TUGWELL: I suppose everybody is familiar with what I might say in general. We all realize that our approach to the agricultural problem is indicated in the wording of the Agricultural Adjustment Act. We felt that adjustment was necessary, and all our activities have been directed toward adjustment. We believed improvement depended on our ability to adjust production to consuming ability within the country. Of course, we are just as much interested in the increase of the consumer's ability to pay as anything else, but we also have felt that maladjustment of prices—particularly agricultural prices as a group—as against industrial prices as a group—had to be corrected, and the only way to do that was to reduce the surpluses of agricultural commodities and really balance what it is necessary to produce in order to meet the visible

101

market—not an imaginary one—as farmers have been trying to do in the past. In order to do this we have been proceeding in ways which I think are pretty much familiar to all of you, through taking land out of production, by payment, and in general trying to adjust production to consumption. This is the general plan on which we have worked; but in talking with Mr. Davis, being directly concerned with the adjustment administration work, I know he would be in a better position than myself to give you a general picture of the operations of the Act.[1]

MR. DAVIS: Mr. Chairman, when Congress passed the Adjustment Act it made known our objectives to establish and maintain such a balance between the production and the consumption of agricultural products as would restore farm prices to the prewar relationship with the prices of articles, goods, and services that farmers buy. That is, it is not directly a mandate to raise prices, but it is to raise prices by securing an adjustment between the production and consumption of these commodities as will support those prices, and to approach that price relationship as rapidly as feasible in view of the current consumptive power through the economic conditions that we contend with.

In the Act itself, which is simply a broad grant of powers to the agricultural department, there was no specific method laid out for any commodity. It indicated two lines on which we might work; first, the line that applied to the so-called basic commodities—and basic commodities under the Act simply means a convenient legal definition applied to seven commodities—wheat, cotton, corn, and hogs, tobacco, rice, and milk and its products. With those basic commodities the department is authorized to proceed with powers much broader than powers that may be applied to the other commodities. Those powers include the right to enter into contracts with individual producers to bring about adjustment in acreage of wheat, corn, rice, and tobacco, and breeding activities in the case of hogs and dairy cattle, that will tend to make the adjustment which is good for the industry as a whole.

I think it ought to be clear that under the pressure of economic

---

[1] For a general discussion of the agricultural policies of the early New Deal, see Arthur M. Schlesinger, Jr., *The Age of Roosevelt: The Coming of the New Deal* (Boston, 1957), pp. 27-84; see also Rexford G. Tugwell, *The Democratic Roosevelt* (Garden City, 1957), *passim*.

forces, the individual farmer will respond in a way which means his survival, but is bad for the industry as a whole. Take cotton, for example. When the price went low under the pressure of excessive supply, the tendency was for the grower who has his fixed charges and other costs, to increase his production by the number of units which when sold at that price would give the money he needed. That is destructive to the industry as a whole. The object of that first line of approach—the making of contracts with individual farmers—is to put them in a position that will make it worth while for them to make the adjustments which are good for the industry as a whole. To do that, we have to be in a position to add to their income—that is, the income of the farmers who enter into the contract with us—through payments in addition to the price of their produce, so that their position as cooperators will be more favorable than the position of the man who stays outside the program and does not make adjustments.

No single method can be applied to that first plan relating to the basic commodities, so called. No single method applies equally well to each of the seven commodities. I want to say that out of the seven, we have in effect now far-reaching and effective programs for six of the seven, the six being wheat, cotton, corn and hogs, tobacco, and rice. With milk and its products, we have groups within the administration working with groups outside in the development of a far-reaching national program of adjustment of dairy production to the current market needs which we believe will tend to stabilize and improve the income of all the dairy producers. That program will not be out in the country for a little while yet.

Mr. Chairman, in developing these programs, since there is no specific rule for action, our policy has been to meet first with the interested group and the representatives who know something about it, develop a tentative plan that would be applicable to a particular commodity, and when we have the plan in tentative shape then go out in regional conferences and group meetings, submit the plan to the producers and other interests affected, let them criticize it, and bring back their criticisms and develop a program which can be put into effect.

When the Act was passed on May 12, cotton planting had practically been completed; in fact, it was beginning to mature in certain sections of the South. We faced the situation where the world had more than a year's supply of American cotton on hand with a crop in prospect that promised to be greater than a normal crop. In other words, there was enough American cotton to pass into the markets of the world, without growing any crop at all in 1933, to keep the mills of the world busy. That was the situation we faced. The price of cotton was down around five or six cents a pound. There was no doubt in the minds of the cotton South, nor in our minds, that if the 1933 crop of cotton had been permitted to mature, had been harvested and put on the market, the price of cotton would have sunk to levels far below what this country had ever dreamed of; so, working in cooperation with the southern cotton producers, we developed and adopted the drastic move for 1933 to prevent the maturity of such a crop as was then in prospect. We set out to take out of production approximately ten million acres or fourteen million bales of cotton. The report of the division of crop and livestock of the department indicates that we cut the crop, which otherwise would have amounted to about seventeen million bales, down to approximately thirteen million bales. We secured one million, forty-two thousand individual contracts and something in excess of the ten million acres we set out to get. That land was actually taken out of production, and partially as a result of that 1933 campaign, partially as a result of the plans made for the 1934 campaign, partially as a result of monetary policies and partly due to the loan policy adopted on cotton, the price of cotton has approximately doubled to the farmer and the total income to the South from cotton for the 1933 crop approximately doubled. That is, it went to about eight hundred fifty million where it had been four hundred twenty-five million the year before for a crop of substantially the same size.

With wheat, the weather conditions prevailing in the wheat belt made it unnecessary to carry out an equally drastic treatment of wheat, although the carryover condition was fully as serious. Approximately three hundred eighty million bushels of American wheat were carried over to the time the first of the 1933 crop was ready for harvest. That is about three times the normal carryover of American wheat on the market. The price had reached a point so low that the statistician reported it to be the lowest price since Queen Elizabeth's day. However, the weather conditions seemed to promise to cut the total yield in this country to the point that emergency treatment was not necessary; but after discussing the problem with the wheat growers and wheat cooperatives, we adopted a plan which is based on the voluntary domestic allotment plan as applied to wheat. It was a three-year program, that is, to cover reductions for 1934 and 1935 to an extent determined by the Secretary of Agriculture with payments extending over 1933, 1934, and 1935.

We have just completed the review of 1,740 counties growing wheat in the United States which entered into the program, and have passed for payment all of those 1,740 counties except one. Under that wheat plan, approximately 80 per cent of the wheat acreage in the United States entered into this contract, and taking the areas that are largely wheat growing districts, I would say the percentage ran about 90 per cent. The sign-up was not so heavy in states east of the Mississippi, in regions where wheat is not so important as a commercial crop, but is mainly used for feed or local grinding.

We asked for the 1934 plan a 15 per cent reduction. Owing to the fact that only 80 per cent of the wheat farmers are in this plan and owing to the fact that there was some increase in the regions outside the main wheat areas, it looks as though we will have in the neighborhood of 10 per cent reduction on the three-year plan which we adopted as a result of the 15 per cent agreement. The spring wheat is not yet planted. It will be impossible to say just what the reduction or adjustment will be in wheat until the spring plantings are in. About that time, as you know, the international conference of the wheat exporting and importing nations are attempting to arrive at an agreement on world-wide curtailment for exporting nations and, among the importing nations, a falling away from the program they have been developing of building up quotas and import restrictions to the point that export was equal. The United States is the only nation which has definitely moved to put a check-rein on wheat.

The total benefit payments distributed directly to cotton producers in land rental amounted to $112,000,000 with an additional amount estimated at about $48,000,000 dollars, making a total of $160,000,000 in what we call benefits. I will not go into the detail of that unless somebody wants me to.

QUESTION: How many acres?

MR. DAVIS: The total number of bales is 2,400,000. About a third of a bale to the acre; but those options were on the bale basis rather than the acre basis.

On wheat, the total amount of benefits payments distributed on the first year's program amount to about $102,000,000. That is our present estimate.

I should have said that to finance these payments, which are really addition to income, the law provides for processing taxes which may be applied to these basic commodities. The processing tax is stated in the law to be an amount which represents the difference between the current average farm price as determined by the latest statistics available in the department, and the so-called parity price. The parity price is the prewar price for a farm unit, multiplied by the current index of articles the farmers buy. The law permits the secretary to assess a lower rate or determine a lower rate of tax if certain results would follow from imposing the full measure of difference between parity and current price; but in the case of cotton and in the case of wheat, the tax imposed amounted to what was then the full difference between the current farm price and parity. The consumers' protection on these basic commodities lies in the fact that the current market price plus the tax cannot exceed the prewar exchange relationship in price. That is, the consumer is paying no more when he pays the market price plus the tax. The law fixes the limit to which the tax can go.

I will sketch over these basic commodities. In the case of tobacco, we have to adopt six separate programs. There were six distinct types, each one requiring different treatment. The first one was the cigar leaf tobacco. There we employed a method somewhat similar to that with cotton. We contracted with the tobacco growers to take out of production a certain portion of the cigar leaf tobacco crop in prospect for 1933. When we came to the bright tobacco, which is the most important of the tobacco crops grown in this country, the crop was approaching maturity and we did not attempt to interfere with the production in 1933, but did put on a sign-up campaign among the growers to be effective in 1934. We have approximately 98 per cent of the total acreage under contract for 1934.

At the same time, we entered into marketing agreements with the domestic buyers under a section of the law which I will discuss later, under which they agreed to take a certain quantity of bright tobacco, the quantity being what they had consumed in domestic manufacture during the twelve previous months plus about 75,000,000 pounds in addition. They agreed to pay that parity price. As a result of that program, the income of the bright tobacco growers increased from about $40,000,000 in 1932, to around $117,000,000 in 1933.

As I said, there are six different tobacco programs all based on rental or benefit payments or both financed by the processing tax. Unless the group is interested, I will not go into the details of those programs—six different ones on tobacco.

On rice, we [chose] a different method, which was possible because we were unable to get 100 per cent of the rice mills into a marketing agreement. The approach to the rice problem is different. The mills agreed to pay the parity price for rice, which was about double the price in 1932. For 1934, owing to the loss of export outlets, some reduction of the program on rice has to take place. We have, under this agreement, an arrangement whereby the rice mills agreed to pay the parity price, but to pay it in two parts. We have two agreements. One for the south and one for California. Under one of the agreements they will pay, say, 70 per cent, the so-called parity price, when the rice is delivered. They turn the other 30 or 40 per cent, as the case may be, in to a trust fund in the Department of Agriculture. When the grower markets his crop he gets the 70 or the 60 per cent and the trust fund then is held for distribution to those farmers who have cooperated in making the 20 per cent reduction in their acreage this year. By that plan we avoid the use of the processing tax mechanism entirely.

The problem with reference to corn and hogs is a difficult one. They have to be treated together. The situation in connection with the hog supply was much like that in connection with cotton. The spring farrowings reported for 1933 showed a great increase. The price of hogs was at a disastrously low level, yet with livestock it takes a long time to bring about the adjustment which would affect the price. The producers themselves brought in a plan for emergency treatment which it was felt would lower receipts of hogs this winter to the point that we could begin to move the prices forward.

As a result of that campaign we purchased some 600,000,000 head of small pigs, and some 200,000,000 sows due to farrow and all animals large enough to process for meat were

processed, and the meat turned over to emergency relief—
about 100,000,000 pounds; and that program, of course,
is financed by advances from the Treasury to be repaid by
the processing tax. That was purely an emergency program.
By fall, we had worked out the broad outlines of the corn
and hog program to a reduction of the corn acreage by
approximately 20 per cent, a reduction in the number of litters
to be farrowed in 1934 spring and fall by 25 per cent; and a
reduction in volume of hogs marketed 25 per cent. Under
that program, both corn and hogs combined, let us assume
100 per cent cooperation—which will not be the case—the total
amount of benefit payments will approximate $350,000,000.
The sign-up on that campaign is still under way. We had
a report today that Iowa, having approximately 160,000 hog
producers, has reported a sign-up of 130,000. We expect to
have better than a 90 per cent sign-up in the main hog producing states. To finance that, we started in with a processing
tax of fifty cents, moved it up to a dollar, then a dollar and
fifty cents, and on March first to $2.25.

There was complaint that the processing tax was being taken
out of the farmer. The figures show, however, that from
September to the present moment in this present current year
as compared with last year, we have received larger receipts
of hogs this year than last and the price, with the exception
of the first week in September, has been uniformly higher in
the face of heavier receipts. In addition to that, this tax has
been collected and stored up for distribution to the growers
who cooperate. An important factor in the success of the
plan has been the splendid cooperation we have had from the
Federal Emergency Relief Administration in buying hogs for
relief distribution. I think your estimates, Harry, are that
there will be a total of 400,000,000 pounds of pork distributed
by April 30, going to all sections of the United States to
increase the meat rations of the unemployed. We purchased
the live hogs out of the processing tax income and the
Federal Emergency attends to the processing cost. In general,
that is the division. We were buying, up to the first of
February, approximately 23,000 head of hogs a day—that is,
Mr. Hopkins was buying them—and they were being processed.
Anticipating there would be some shock on February first
when the extra fifty-cent tax went into effect, we arranged,
in our cooperation with the Emergency Relief, to increase
our purchases by 10,000 head a day. The price started sky-

rocketing pretty rapidly at that time. We are trying to hold
the market steady until we iron out the present situation.
I think that illustrates, in general, the type of approach we
make to production adjustments.

On crops, the crop value in 1933 was approximately 55 per
cent higher than the crop value in 1932. That doesn't include
livestock, which is slower to adjust and slower to respond
to treatment. It will take some time before the increase can
be brought about in livestock. That is one line of approach
under the Adjustment Act. The other is through marketing
agreements which the Secretary of Agriculture is authorized
to enter into with processers, associations of producers, and
others who are engaged in the handling of agricultural
commodities. That treatment is not limited to the so-called
basic commodities. Under that we have entered into some 35
or 40 marketing agreements. Each one is a problem in itself.
It is a little difficult to apply any uniform principle; but some
of them have been particularly successful and I think on the
whole they represent a worthwhile approach to the problems
of these special groups that we cannot reach through a nationwide adjustment program. For instance, the first agreement
was the cling peach agreement with the peach canners of
California. The peach growers in 1933 received $5,000,000,
approximately, as compared with less than $1,000,000 in 1932.
The growers themselves attribute that largely to the operation
of the marketing agreement.

Up in the Pacific Northwest, we entered into what we called
the Northwest Fruit Agreement which got into operation
late in the season. It did not work perfectly, yet the growers
estimated that their increase in income amounts to approximately $10,000,000 this year as compared with what it would
otherwise have been.

We have agreements in effect for the three areas producing
citrus fruits. There are a number of them in prospect.
When the Act was passed, the maturity of these crops was
almost upon us and there was not time to develop marketing
agreements with the crops we would have liked to develop.
The toughest problem has been milk and dairy products.
When we first came down here, the representatives of the
distributors were camped right at the door of the office asking
that these marketing agreements be entered into immediately,
and after seven months' experience with the agreements we
entered into, it is our conclusion that we were on the wrong

track. Fundamentally, we don't think those milk marketing agreements can change the general price level. We think the price level of dairy products has to be moved up through adjustment of supply and demand, and that you cannot correct the situation with little islands of territory which are brought up to the price level. The problem of enforcement is so difficult that it would almost be impossible. We find, too, that those first agreements included fixed consumer prices. Our experience is that we have to take into consideration the fact that these agreements arrive at a consumer's price as a result of bargaining between distributors and producers, and when they agree it means that the price has been established to the satisfaction of the distributors. The distributors won't sign unless the margin is satisfactory to them. The government has not the power over the new industry that it might have over a public utility. We do not have the power to examine or correct uneconomic capital structure margins, but we were asked to enforce those prices nevertheless. We finally concluded, with respect to them, that we would attempt to fix no consumer prices at all, that we would depend on licenses; that we were to establish a uniform and fair producers price, ask our distributors to pay that price; ask them to carry their proportionate share of the surplus, and let competition take care of the consumers' price unless there is an unreasonable advance, in which case we would establish a maximum price for the protection of the consumer.

I think, Mr. Chairman, in general that takes a kind of hop, skip, and jump at the whole program. I believe we will come nearer getting at what the men and women present have in mind if they will ask questions.

I might say that it is estimated that the total program for the current year will distribute in rental and benefit payments about seven hundred sixty [million] dollars, not allowing for the general program on dairy cattle and not allowing for beef cattle. If beef cattle are included, I would say the total will probably run in excess of a billion dollars. Those benefit payments are not the end in themselves. They are a welcome addition to the current income of the farmers, but they are paid in order to make it worthwhile for the farmer to adjust his production so as that the group of producers who are growing the same products will be in line with the market plans. The market plans are flexible.

Of course, we recognize that we cannot step these prices up

any faster than consumers' purchasing power can take them, and that is particularly true of the perishable commodities where the demand is elastic.

I would like to submit to any questions that the group would like to ask.

SECRETARY PERKINS: I would like to ask whether or not, in making this very interesting survey, you have along with it any estimates of the number of persons formerly employed as agricultural laborers or finding their chief employment as tenant farmers who would be dislocated from their usual means of making a living.

MR. DAVIS: Dividing the program into two parts—that which has taken place in the past and what may happen in the future—I would say I do not believe there has been any displacement up to date as the result of the past program. I imagine your question is particularly directed to the cotton South.

SECRETARY PERKINS: Cotton and rice, both; I have had inquiries about both.

MR. DAVIS: I do not anticipate that there will be any considerable change in rice. The program calls for a twenty per cent adjustment in production. The total income will be greater than would be possible without the rice adjustment. In cotton, we accepted the measurements which the South itself placed on the extent of reduction desirable for 1934. It is not a continuing program but an emergency move to bring down excessive carryover to the point that the price for cotton can be ironed out. They set the reduction at 40 per cent. That is pretty drastic. I cannot give you any estimate as to the amount of labor that will be displaced. I know that the men from the South who represent cotton in the administration in the department, as well as our extension directors of the state in charge of the program in their state, do not believe that sharecroppers or tenant farmers will be displaced as a result of the program. Many of them believe that there will be just as much demand for field laborers down there this year as there will be people. They point to the CWA, and they say that if Mr. Hopkins continues to pay anything like the wages he has been paying they could not keep the field men on the cotton farms with an army, but I am not in a position to give an estimate as to the number; however, as Mr. Riefler has inquired, we will attempt to get the best estimate.

DR. TUGWELL: I don't think it probably would be possible for us before the year; we could count up after the year. I think you are quite right when you speak of it as "dislocation." If we

111

succeed in doing what we are trying to do we are not only raising the total income of the South but the total income of the country; and if we succeed in doing that, there is more employment for somebody.

SECRETARY PERKINS: But you have to take care of it eventually. There is a period of dislocation that is very serious in the suffering and distress it brings to particular areas and particular groups of people.

DR. TUGWELL: I would not try to minimize that at all.

MR. HOPKINS: As a result of plowing under cotton, thousands of people were displaced in the cotton districts of the South, and went on relief rolls. Our relief people, on evidence that the planters gave them, are telling us that we are going to have to take care of tens of thousands of people who are going to be displaced one way or another as a result of the cotton program. We also have to bear this in mind about the rice business; when you speak of the same amount of money coming back to the rice people, to whom does it go? Not to the laborers.

SECRETARY PERKINS: Nor to tenant farmers. They tell me they are not getting any share. Formerly three tenants took care of a piece of land. Now, one of them is cut off.

MR. DAVIS: It is a 20 per cent reduction. It would scarcely amount to one out of three; and of course the tenant farmer gets the same increase of price on his share of the crop as the land owner.

SECRETARY PERKINS: He says he does not have any crop because the owner decides not to plant his particular patch.

MR. DAVIS: That might be true in some instances. I question whether it would be widespread. Twenty per cent is the maximum reduction we are asking for. That is one out of five, and since there is a twenty per cent reduction, the practice will be to take twenty per cent out of each farm.

DR. TUGWELL: I don't think there is any disposition on our part to resent criticism. On the other hand, I think you have to keep in mind what would be the alternative. I am sure, if this succeeds, that somehow or other people are going to be better off. We have had some difficulty about contracts. Nobody has worked harder on tenant-farmer contracts than Mr. Davis and myself have, and we have not succeeded in settling the matter. It is very hard to know what to do.

MR. DAVIS: I might say on that, that we held up the cotton plan for two months during which time I was in a daily battle against what I might call the solid representation of the South; because you notice a sharp difference in their view of this problem when you get south of the line. As a result of holding out on that we did get many modifications of the contracts in the interest of the tenant farmer and laborer. We had a modification made so that the managing share tenant gets half of the land rental and three-fourths of the parity payment. We had the provision written in that no cropper shall lose his right to live on the farm and have a certain acreage to use for family maintenance. They cannot move people off the farms as a result of this campaign. They agreed to keep them on there and furnish them mule power and land for their family living. They agreed that insofar as possible, they will keep the same number of tenant farmers employed as they had in former years; and yet we face this alternative, Miss Perkins. Supposing we had made an ironclad contract and said "You must pay half your land rent to your tenant share cropper." There would have been no tenant share cropper; they would have all been turned off and hired as day laborers. If we had had any provision in the contract that they must employ the same number of tenant farmers and made that ironclad we would not have had the contract signed. We would not have had the reduction. We have written everything into that contract we could for protection. Just what the displacement will amount to I do not know.

SECRETARY PERKINS: There is no way of estimating, is there?

MR. DAVIS: Reports from the people who are handling it would give us some idea, but I don't know how good it will be. They tell me that their good field hands are going to be kept because they won't permit a one-year radical reduction to lose the services of their good tenants. I just asked Mr. Trent—who is in charge of the production division, who comes from Oklahoma and who stood with me in this work over the contracts, a very fair man—for his estimate. I could have brought it with me. He believes that on the whole the land-lords are going to operate this very equitably and fairly, which of course differs from the reports Harry has on the situation. They claim, also, that when they can get free food or cash employment there is a powerful inducement to these colored men and women to move off their regular employment and move to town. They do not see anything in it except that Uncle Sam is furnishing free living, and it looks pretty good to them.

These tenant farmers work on an average of about 125 days out of a year. That is the amount of labor that it requires to make a cotton crop, harvest and market it. Most of them, under the worst conditions of the plantation system, have their home furnished, medical care, and some degree of schooling furnished as a result of 125 days of labor. If you attempt to put that on the day's pay basis—if you give them a day wage for those 125 days—that would give them the same return in annual income and annual keep; but your day labor would undoubtedly be unreasonably high. I throw those things out as a part of the picture.

SECRETARY ROPER: Mr. Davis, may I ask what is your method of supervising and determining whether this program is going to be carried out in bona fide fashion, and whether you are really succeeding by reduction of acreage in reducing production? I think you will find that in many localities there will be a disposition to increase the fertilizer as well as the cultivation. At least in my portion of the South we have very greatly increased production through cultivation methods so that we produce more when we plant less. That is, we care for it better. We plow it more times, if you please, and keep it in better condition. We have advanced the maturity of cotton by two weeks in my time through improved methods and through more intelligent application and use of fertilizer. We must not fool ourselves by thinking we can reduce cotton production by getting acreage reduction. We can easily cut out ten per cent of the cotton acreage and produce just as much cotton in fact, more. If our associates here do not object, I would like very much to know whether those features are being cared for and whether we are really going to secure the results we are seeking.

MR. DAVIS: The machinery for enforcement is through the county production associations. The democratic method is for each county to police its own reduction.
On the second part, Mr. Secretary, Senator [John H.] Bankhead is arranging to take care of that for us in his bill.

SECRETARY ROPER: That is a very good bill—the ginning bill.

MR. DAVIS: It is a bill for a tax on any quantity marketed in excess of a base allotment.

SECRETARY ROPER: In other words, the man may produce as much as he wants but he can only gin a certain amount?

MR. DAVIS: He can produce as much as he wants to, but if he markets above a certain portion, which is his share of the nine-and-one-half-million-bale crop, he is going to have to pay a tax.

SECRETARY ROPER: Take the man who produces and gins ten bales of cotton extra and that cotton is carried home to his own warehouse, subject, as I understand, for sale the next year. How are you going to keep track of that?

MR. DAVIS: The draft of the Bankhead law I saw provides for identification of the bales at the gin on which the tax is not being paid with what they call an undetachable marker. The tax must be paid before the rest is moved.

SECRETARY PERKINS: To what extent is agricultural labor a factor in these other programs—tobacco, corn and hogs, wheat, etc.?

MR. DAVIS: Not much in corn and hogs. It might be a factor in some types of tobacco. I would say that it is not changed materially by wheat. A fifteen per cent reduction in a field does not change the situation much. I think the chief one is cotton.

SECRETARY PERKINS: Do you anticipate that it will be on that basis, that there will be fifteen per cent reduction in a field, or will there rather be a general reduction by leaving out of cultivation entirely a considerable acreage which will reduce the labor costs?

MR. DAVIS: You mean in wheat?

SECRETARY PERKINS: Yes.

MR. DAVIS: It will be the fifteen per cent reduction in the individual farmer's planting.

SECRETARY PERKINS: The same amount of labor?

MR. DAVIS: Yes, approximately so.

DR. TUGWELL: Of course, in the long run the situation is probably very different.

SECRETARY PERKINS: Oh yes, I can see that.

DR. TUGWELL: We certainly don't think we are entering upon a period of general limitations. This is merely temporary.

MR. MYERS: It seems to me the problem of labor displacement in connection with tobacco is quite simple. It is raised very largely by families that get a wage and a share of the crop. They are called sometimes tenants, but actually they are wage earners.

SECRETARY PERKINS: Isn't that true of the corn and hog areas?

MR. DAVIS: The status of the tenant farmer in connection with the production of corn and hogs is very different from that of those in the raising of tobacco and cotton. Secretary Roper mentioned that a more intensive system of farming might be adopted where the acreage is reduced. That means more intensive use of labor. If they move to more intensive cultivation, there will not be the displacement of labor to the extent that you fear. On the other hand, there are idle acres which cannot be left without attention. They will be planted in erosion-preventing or soil-building crops, or home-

115

feed crops, and that will take labor. Of course Harry [Hopkins] has had reports from his people. I think some of the general interest in this is stimulated by the article which I saw in *Harper's* magazine.[2] I think they exaggerate the condition considerably, from what our people report to us.

MR. WALKER: They do seem to make quite a plausible argument. I have heard a number of people speak of it. I would not want to exaggerate, but I think at least 25 people have asked me if I read the article in *Harper's* about agricultural adjustment, and asked what I thought of its efficacy. The article referred to 800,000 being displaced. Is that correct?

MR. DAVIS: That is correct.

MR. WALKER: I also heard some criticism of the fact the administration is putting money in at the top and forgetting the fellow down below. They do make quite a plausible argument. I was wondering if you thought it worth while to give it consideration?

MR. DAVIS: We have given it a lot of consideration since this whole cotton program came up, before there was any criticism. Dr. Tugwell will agree, I think, that that was the livest topic we had during September and October.

It is not true that the money is going in at the top, because the object of readjustment is to bring about a relationship between supply and demand that will restore the prewar purchasing power of the commodity. The tenant farmer and the cropper get their income from the price of the product. As this program operates to improve the price of their product they get a benefit, the same as the land owner. The average cropper gets half the crop for his labor. Let us say as a result of this program—I don't think this program is to be credited with the complete price improvement, but as a result of combining the programs the price of cotton has doubled. The tenant farmer who gets half the crop has had the value of each bale doubled. In addition to that, we allow a parity payment guaranteed to be not less than $5.00 a bale and we hope the collections will permit it to be more. That goes to the cropper—half of the so-called parity payment—and in addition he gets the price improvement also. The benefits go either directly to the land in the case of land rental or in the case of improvement in price of commodity, it goes directly to everybody who has a hand in raising it.

---

[2] Webster Powell and Addison T. Cutler, "Tightening the Cotton Belt," *Harper's* (Feb. 1934).

MR. MYERS: Your reduction in cotton and tobacco may be negatived by fertilizer. Are these local associations attempting to induce local sources to reduce loans made to insure normal use of fertilizer?

MR. DAVIS: You know the arrangement worked out in California in cooperation with you and other private agencies.

MR. MYERS: It might be mentioned that in financing crops through the Farm Credit Administration, we are restricting the financing to farmers who are cooperating in this program or who are "okayed" by the local association as not attempting to defeat it. I wondered if any effort is being made with local banks or mercantile establishments?

MR. DAVIS: Yes indeed there is. In the Memphis territory, they tell me that practically 100 per cent of the lending agencies have agreed to cooperate along these lines.

MR. MYERS: We had an inquiry about this. The intermediate credit banks wanted to cooperate, but felt there was a very widespread desire to use more fertilizer, and they wanted to know how far they could go. It falls back to your local control associations to see that producers live up to the spirit of the agreement.

MR. DAVIS: In the tobacco contracts we have a clause limiting the use of fertilizer. That was another thing we attempted with the cotton people and they were a unit in claiming that it was impracticable of enforcement. They claim you can use a stronger fertilizer and not apply more pounds to the acre. They thought it was impracticable to control it.

SECRETARY ROPER: Dollars per acre would cover that.

MR. DAVIS: That might result in a sharp restriction in the quantity sold. They tell me that the price of fertilizer this year is considerably higher than last year. They consider it, rightly or wrongly, an effort to stabilize the industry. Changing the plan to dollars per acre might result in a sharp curtailment.

I had two or three questions handed to me by Mrs. Rumsey, who followed literally your suggestion that questions be prepared to guide the discussion. The first one is as follows: "How is this temporary emergency program being related to a long-term program for general increase in the consumption of farm products rather than a net long-term decrease in the domestic use of farm products?"

Now I suppose there is not a day passes but what some group comes to see us to ask if we will not cooperate in an "eat-more-cheese," or "wheat," or "meat" or some other

117

campaign. We have had to take the position that the human stomach is more or less inelastic, and that the only way we can attack that is as the general recovery program advances and gives the consumer more purchasing power. As there is an increase in payrolls, there will be a tendency to increase the consumption of milk, fresh vegetables and fruit, and all that sort of thing, which would be very helpful; of course, if we had a fairly uniform distribution of wealth in this country so that no family had less than $2500 a year, our problem would be infinitely simpler than it is; but we are dealing with the realities of the situation and will have to permit consumption to expand as it can.

SECRETARY PERKINS: Is there any record of the decrease in consumption in any one of these products?

MR. DAVIS: Oh yes, as a result of decreased purchasing power, that is very definitely related to pork, beef, and milk and other dairy products.

SECRETARY PERKINS: One realizes that is true, but do you have the actual records?

MR. FAHEY: Swift printed a chart on that some days ago. There was a page in *Time*[3] not more than a week or so ago which showed the relationship very definitely.

MR. DAVIS: Another question was this: "Is it not probable that there are increased returns for farmers in certain farm products by the expansion of production rather than a decrease in production?"[4] There may be some, but I think the economic pressure of the last few years has forced the farmers to shift over into the lines of production that are relatively profitable to as great an extent as they possibly can. Lower returns for livestock and grain caused more farmers to shift into dairy production and intensified the problem there.

MR. CHAPMAN: Would you say a word about [Howard] Tolley's studies?

MR. DAVIS: I should have brought that into the main discussion. We recognize ours is an emergency adjustment act and emergency program. We want to point our activities far in the direction of a permanent national policy for agriculture and plan an organization that gets away from the emergency phase which none of us like.

---

[3] Mr. Fahey may have had in mind the following item: *Time*, Vol. XXIII, No. 5, Jan. 29, 1934, p. 43.
[4] Underlying this discussion is, of course the issue of whether an agricultural program should be framed on the basis of restricting production and hence adequate price levels, or by leaving production unregulated and finding some other means of providing adequate income for the farmer.

After Dr. Tolley had organized our special crop section, we asked him to head up the program planning division. He is planning to build up a nucleus there that is to examine long-time phases of this program and get things established on a sounder basis of land utilization in the country. I think one thing we may get to will be one contract covering a farm and attempting to hold that farm in the best kind of balanced production possible instead of having one farmer signing three or four different contracts, overlapping for special commodities. Do you have any particular commodity in mind?

MR. CHAPMAN: I was thinking of Tolley's studies of the possible consumption of milk. He made a very considerable study on the basis of balanced diet and reported that there was a tremendous market there which could be made available as soon as purchasing power rises.

MR. DAVIS: That is an economic question. I think we have to have the payrolls up before we can move into much heavier consumption of dairy products. As fast as that comes about you will have a safety valve that will reach all through agriculture.

DR. TUGWELL: Do you remember the chart for the liberal diet? With the population as it is at present we would need about 13 per cent less acres than we have now under production.

MR. MYERS: With no exports.

MR. DAVIS: I think with exports as they are.

SECRETARY PERKINS: Thirteen per cent less acreage. That anticipates the efficient use of land in production.

MR. DAVIS: I wonder if you realize what is taking place in agriculture.

SECRETARY PERKINS: None of us do. It is fascinating.

MR. DAVIS: Prior to the war, we were employing great areas in production of agricultural products which moved abroad in the payment of the foreign debt, but the war wiped that out. We woke up after the war—and the awakening took place some time after—to the realization that foreign markets did not exist. We continued to lend money abroad to finance those foreign nations in their purchase of our agricultural products until 1928, when it was cut off. The shift from debtor to creditor nation just wiped out a large part of the foreign demand, not mentioning the nationalistic tendencies which led nations to try to bring themselves into a self-sufficient position. Our problem now is, "What are we willing to take in exchange in this country?" It is a very serious question. You can leave export out of the picture except with cotton and tobacco.

About the same time, we developed gasoline and oil power to take the place of horse and mule power used on the farms and in the cities; and it is estimated that from twenty-five to thirty-five million acres that had in the past been used to produce feed for horses and mules was not needed; and that was transferred to the oil fields. The only outlet for those acres was to turn them into meat, beef, and pork.

I realize the shock on tenants and labor, but these adjustments are absolutely necessary. The whole social and economic structure has got to absorb that shock.

SECRETARY PERKINS: Mr. Davis, do you know anything about this Smith bill that provides $150,000,000?[5]

MR. DAVIS: I just heard about it.

SECRETARY PERKINS: Is it true that it has been reported out of the Senate?

MR. DAVIS: I have no doubt of it. There is one point here on revenues. I asked that they get from the Treasury the report on the collections up to date of processing taxes. The total up to the first of February collected was $184,062,000. That is largely from cotton and wheat. The total for cotton was $96,234,000 and for wheat $63,000,000. I would say that is running a little in excess of our estimate.

MR. WALKER: When do you expect to wind up on this?

MR. DAVIS: There were $760,000,000 for the program. We are just getting into the corn and hog program, and that will be balanced by collections on the processing tax.

MR. WALKER: At one time the department contemplated making considerable profit.

MR. DAVIS: I think our cotton options do show a profit which will pay the expenses, probably a little more; but the Farm Credit Administration says we bought the cotton too cheap.

DR. TUGWELL: To what extent have price-fixing agreements by manufacturers and distributors and unrelated industries been responsible for the increased prices? The farmers believe that the NRA code has been responsible for that. I don't know.

MRS. RUMSEY: Is it wages or price fixing?

MR. DAVIS: They do not differentiate much. They say the result of codes is to increase the price of overalls. We hear more of that than anything else.

DR. TUGWELL: We don't know whether it is added costs or price fixing.

MR. DAVIS: I think this is true, that taking as a whole 1933 over 1932, the

---

[5] A bill introduced by Senator Ellison D. ("Cotton Ed") Smith (Dem., S.C.) to help alleviate the depression by distributing cotton products to the needy. The bill (S.2500, 73rd Congress, 2nd Session) was reported out on Feb. 19, 1934, but was never debated nor acted upon.

farm income has shown a relatively higher increase than payrolls have.

DR. TUGWELL: As a whole.

MR. DAVIS: Yes, as a whole. Here is another question from Mrs. Rumsey: "To what extent will the proposed dairy program result in an actual net decrease in the consumption of dairy products?"

GENERAL JOHNSON: That is an unanswerable question. In the first place, the question is as to what extent they have raised prices. We had a price hearing on that and those studies are just coming through now. We broke it down into those cases of evidence of undue price increases. I have not seen the study. There are some cases, no doubt; but people seem to forget that NRA did not get into active operation until after the first of September. So far as the living increase is concerned, there wasn't any. The cost of living was lower at the end of December than at the end of August.

MR. DAVIS: I pointed that out to the delegation in here Saturday from the northwestern farm groups. As I stated while you were out, General, they centered their case on the price of overalls, and then they wanted to know why we could not do for agriculture what was being done for industry. I made the statement that I thought the increase of agriculture income for 1933 was relatively greater than the increase in labor payrolls in 1933 over 1932. I believe that is correct.

GENERAL JOHNSON: I think it is. Of course, the case of the overalls is a bad one.

SECRETARY PERKINS: Of course, there is a tendency on the part of the people to believe that the lowest price in history is the right price.

GENERAL JOHNSON: It is the sort of price that was creating the depression.

MR. DAVIS: I pointed this out, and it is true, that in the case of the raise in the price of overalls it was not the rise in raw materials that did it. The cotton price, both per unit and total income, was more than doubled.

GENERAL JOHNSON: Payrolls in cotton were pyramided.

MR. DAVIS: There are one or two other quetsions.

MR. WALKER: Go ahead.

MR. DAVIS: On the question of increase in dairy products, personally I don't think it is necessary to relate the price increase to payrolls. The farmer would not be benefited by doubling the price if the consumption falls down proportionately. That would not increase his income at all. The dairy program has got to move along with the whole national recovery program. It cannot outstrip it a great deal. I think we can stop the trend toward surplus increases of butter which, in turn, have

121

a price influence on the whole dairy structure. It is not possible to raise dairy prices out of line with the consumers' purchasing power.

The next question is this: "Has the Department of Agriculture explored fully the possibilities of removing this temporary emergency surplus by stimulating actual consumption through the distribution of fluid milk by welfare agencies, hospitals, and schools at surplus prices, plus minimum handling charges?"

As to butter, with Mr. Hopkins' cooperation we did take off the market for distribution to the needy enough stored butter to bring the commercial storage stocks down in line with the five-year average. There was a very serious butter situation.

As to whole milk, we have given some consideration to that. We would like to see local communities and dairy associations cooperate with relief organizations so that they could furnish milk for relief purposes. We can encourage local farmers to turn their surplus milk over for such distribution; but I find quite a militant spirit among some of the farmers in a way opposing the idea that it is up to the farmer to finance the federal relief work. For instance, Harry, a delegation of five from the wheat area in the Pacific Northwest presented us with a demand that we support an amendment to do away with the exemption from processing tax for food for relief purposes. They claim what you were doing is taking away from the farmer the income and turning it over to relief. I mention this as an extreme view with which we are not in sympathy. We took the position that is actually increasing the consumption, because Mr. Hopkins' dollars go further if he doesn't have to pay the tax.

SECRETARY PERKINS: Is there anything at all in the idea that increased volume of milk production reduces the cost and so makes it possible to sell the milk at a lower price and make a profit to the farmer on the greater volume?

MR. DAVIS: I don't believe you can generalize that. Suppose you increase your production by adding more low-grade cows; then you have reached the point where your returns diminish.

SECRETARY PERKINS: Can the farmer, with the same overhead, increase his output and make a profit on larger volume? If milk would come down in price, consumption would increase. Milk is a very expensive item.

MR. MYERS: The real answer is in the question as to how much consumption would be increased. You must have figures on that, Rex [Tugwell]. If you drop the price of milk two or three cents, the increase in consumption would be very responsive.

MR. WALKER: That would affect the small producer.

SECRETARY PERKINS: If the farmer has a small barn, but frequently he has a larger barn. He is constantly decreasing his production. The barn and the labor and general overhead go right on without regard to the number of quarts. I have always been under the impression that the milk distributing companies are responsible for the price.

MR. MYERS: Comparing production costs and distribution costs, distribution would be reduced more rapidly. Distribution costs are a very important part of the picture.

MR. DAVIS: More quarts could be put on drivers' wagons.

SECRETARY PERKINS: Isn't it extremely important to the farmer that distribution costs be cut so that the consumer can consume more?

MR. DAVIS: I think it is the most important element.

SECRETARY PERKINS: Is anybody in the world working on it?

MR. DAVIS: We would like to find some city that would undertake the municipal distribution of milk as a demonstration.

SECRETARY PERKINS: It would take some city that hasn't a distributing company.

MR. DAVIS: Washington, D.C. is under federal jurisdiction. Perhaps we could try it here.

SECRETARY ROPER: There are three milk men on my block.

SECRETARY PERKINS: In New York three or four sometimes go over the same stairs.

MR. WALKER: Any further questions?

MR. HOPKINS: Is any agency of government able to loan money to farmers for stock feed? If not, cattle and horses are going to starve to death.

MR. MYERS: Insofar as they have a basis for credit, we can do it.

MR. WALKER: It is one of the cases of "passing the buck."

MR. DAVIS: We have had it up before us there and there just isn't any fund available for us to do it. Harry has spent all that is available to him. I think money has to be made available for that.

MR. HOPKINS: We have power under the Act to give seed wheat to farmers that can't get a loan. But if there are very many of those, we will be in trouble.

MR. MYERS: We have a crop loan that will shortly be signed so that we can make loans to farmers to buy seed.

MR. WALKER: Yours is a grant, isn't it?

MR. HOPKINS: No.

MR. MYERS: The terms of this Act provide not more than a million dollars

123

for stock feed, but the difficulty is that it requires a first mortgage on live stock, and the people who have the greatest need already have their live stock mortgaged.

MR. WALKER: Isn't that a matter to be adjusted by the Farm Credit and the Federal Relief Administration? It is a problem that will have to be solved.

MR. HOPKINS: It is on us right now.
Is it proper to ask whether the Executive Department of the government is in favor of or opposed to the Smith bill appropriating $150,000,000 to buy cotton to be made into cloth to be given to the poor?[6]

MR. WALKER: What have you to say about that, Mr. Secretary of Agriculture?

DR. TUGWELL: We would be glad to get rid of the cotton; but is there any reason why $150,000,000 for cotton should be segregated from the rest?

SECRETARY PERKINS: Is there any special need?

DR. TUGWELL: I think it is a mistake.

MR. HOPKINS: We could not use any such sum as that.

MR. DAVIS: Following that same proportion of $150,000,000 for cotton, Congress is going to be faced with the demand that the same thing be carried through the whole list.

SECRETARY PERKINS: They will be wanting to distribute cigarettes to the poor next, Harry! (*Laughter*).

MR. WALKER: It might be appropriate here to make the suggestion, since Mr. Hopkins asked what the position of the Administration is, that the President asked me to advise you that he is tied up on another matter and would not come in. He asked if I would give this message; he thought it might be well for the departmental heads to advise any representatives of theirs who go before Congress or the Senate to be in accord with the ideas of the departmental heads.

SECRETARY PERKINS: Did I say the wrong thing the other day?

MR. WALKER: Someone went before Congress the other day and said the Agricultural Department was opposed to the cotton policy.

MR. DAVIS: I knew what was coming, all right. This gentleman is one of the rugged individualists. He went before them to explain the cotton option plan. After that he would say, "Now, speaking as an individual and not as a representative of the Department of Agriculture," and then he would proceed to tear into the Bankhead bill.

SECRETARY PERKINS: I would like to know what to do. I went up there on a labor matter and they took me out into the tariff and the

---

[6] See note, p. 120.

       devaluation of the dollar. I was talking about unemployment in Washington. It is a very embarrassing situation. They have you there. They ask you questions, and if you appear to evade the questions they can accuse you of contempt.

MR. WALKER: This man pretended to represent the Agricultural Department and spoke for the Department.

DR. TUGWELL: But he said, "Now speaking as an individual" every time.

MR. DAVIS: He watched that.

MR. WALKER: There is another one about Mr. Weaver on the sugar question. He said, "This is the first step in eliminating the sugar beet industry." The President has the sugar beet men with him now; he had to waste an hour to convince them.

SECRETARY PERKINS: To what extent are we bound to allow subordinates of the department to go up there? They get somebody who knows all about his subject and isn't aware of the political difficulties, and they get him up there in all innocence. He gives his personal views, not realizing the significance. Must we send Mr. Weaver, or anybody else in my department, if they ask for him?[7]

DR. TUGWELL: The Senators establish relationships with these people themselves. Mr. Davis knew about this only a short time before.

SECRETARY PERKINS: Nobody in my department can go before a committee in Congress without seeing me first.

MR. WALKER: That might not be a good rule to have in writing, but it is a good rule all the same.

DR. TUGWELL: In the instance of Mr. Weaver, the case was very peculiar. He did not actually say anything which was not our governmental policy.

MR. DAVIS: He did see me before he went up. The notice did not come to me. They called him direct from the committee. He came over to see me but he didn't tell me he was going to say anything like this. One of the smart Republicans led him out on a limb!

MR. WALKER: It might be well to suggest that some of them submerge their individualism.

MR. HOPKINS: There are 6,600,000 families—over twenty million people—getting public benefits through CWA and relief. It is my opinion that we have substantially more employment now than we had at this time a year ago. In spite of that, we have a very heavy load of people in need. The reason is that the

---

[7] A frank, and fairly rare, recorded discussion of a problem in executive-legislative relations that has been a continuing one in American government.

longer people remain unemployed, the larger the percentage of those needing help. We have a plan for the year based on certain premises. Upon these premises, however, various members of the government are in no sense agreed. For instance, it is our judgment there is going to be a substantial number of people going to work through Public Works; but there is a wide difference of opinion as to how many there will be. It is extremely important, it seems to me, that we have these estimates on Public Works that can be substantially correct, but as to direct and indirect employment.

We are also counting on the usual seasonal increase of employment; and we are also counting very heavily on the fact that we have been giving benefits to a great many farmers and tenant farmers who will not require it during the summer; and finally, we are counting on a real increase of employment through the Recovery Program. Our program of $950,000,000 is based on the assumption that we are going to have to take care of between two and one-half and three million families, on the average, per month.

MR. FAHEY: Through what period?

MR. HOPKINS: Through next winter. It will vary, of course.

MR. FAHEY: How long will it run?

MR. HOPKINS: Probably through March of next year.

MR. FAHEY: You can take care of them that long?

MR. HOPKINS: Yes; though there are economists in the government that tell me these estimates of mine are ridiculous—that no such number of men are going to work—and this becomes a matter of realism. We drop 570,000 men next Friday that don't go back to work, and 400,000 more will be off a week from Thursday.

We are dealing now with the problem of unemployment, a problem which has always been a great political problem. Up to the present moment, our plans have been such that we believe it has been substantially met through this winter. I may be all wrong in this projection of mine.

DR. TUGWELL: Two and one-half to three million families?

MR. HOPKINS: Yes, that number unemployed.

SECRETARY ROPER: How many people?

MR. HOPKINS: About twelve million people.

DR. TUGWELL: What is the relationship of unemployment to 1928?

MR. HOPKINS: In terms of need, this is fifteen times as many as were in need in 1929. That provides for a drop of a million and a half

families at this moment in need down to two and one-half
or three million families in June. It seems to me it is very
important that the government have its data on this point and on
all these points submitted so that there is a substantial meeing of
minds. This represents a personal opinion of my own. I have
a conviction that a great many people are working now that
were not a year ago. I believe there is going to be a pick-up.
I may be wrong about it. It seems to me that the government
needs to have a meeting of minds. There is a good deal of
disturbance as to my dropping 570,000 men. I have been
asked, "Where in the world did you pick up these estimates?"
I said, "Public Works, seasonal factory, farming, and the
Recovery Program." They say, "Where is your statistical
basis? Where are they going to get jobs? Are the automobile
industry and steel and railroads going to employ them? In
what parts of the country are these people going to be
employed? What about Cleveland and Detroit? We still
have 45,000 unemployment in Detroit today."
I think it is a political matter and the danger of letting the
President down on this employment business is a very serious
matter. If some of us should do some wrong guessing, we
will find on our hands a much larger number of people. I
cannot prove this up to the hilt, especially in some spots.
I am weakening a little on this Public Works business, as to
the numbers to get jobs there. I have been one of those
who have always discounted a lot of this unemployment.
It seems to me this question of how fast these people are
going to work, where they are going to work, and the
projection is tremendously vital to the President and his
immediate program, irrespective of the whole Recovery
Program. This business is a relief factor. This job I am doing
has nothing to do with the fundamental Recovery Program.
I think it is very vital in the terms of human interest and
political implications for this administration; I don't want to
find that I have left the President out on a limb in this.
I would like to see the statistical data on the Public Works
and seasonal thing; I think the farm thing is going to be
almost impossible to get. I think we are going to get a big
drop on farm laborers and tenant farmers. We hear that
everywhere people are being hired, but statistics are hard
to get. We get it from all over the country that about four
million have been taken on through an enormous number
of employment bureaus.

SECRETARY PERKINS: Four million taken on out of ten million registrations.

MR. HOPKINS: It is a real responsibility. The whole hope of this large number of people is in this Administration. We must not let them down.

SECRETARY PERKINS: You know these figures show there was another decline in January.

MR. HOPKINS: You would expect that, wouldn't you?

SECRETARY PERKINS: Yes.

MR. HOPKINS: January usually declines.

SECRETARY PERKINS: But nevertheless if we had two and three-fourths million re-employment at the peak of this recovery, it is now about two million.

GENERAL JOHNSON: What industries?

SECRETARY PERKINS: It was in almost everything. Out of 95 that report regularly, I think only 10 or 12 showed an increase. As a matter of fact, the figures do not show any response that there may have been to the January increase in production, because that practically all takes place in the last two weeks and our figures are collected for the week including the fifteenth. Steel went up very much in January, and we don't reflect that at all in our employment figures. Agriculture is still way up. The increase in the number of persons employed in the manufacture of agricultural implements is very significant. We got an increase, also, in the manufacture of hardware.

GENERAL JOHNSON: We are going to have all the code authorities here on the fifth of March.[8] We are going to make an awful effort to cut hours and increase the weekly wage by ten per cent. If we are successful, that will mean a million more employment.

SECRETARY PERKINS: A very large number of industries are now showing a movement into the black. I have been thinking a great deal of this same matter of the necessity of knowing what are the probabilities of reemployment and where these probabilities lie; and it is probably quite true that we do not show the actual employment there has been. We ought to correlate almost immediately all our active forces, including this institution we know as the Reemployment Service,[9] with its 3,500 branches, within the next few weeks—the only agency of government that is really in a position to make an intensive

---

[8] A national conference, Mar. 4-7, 1934, at which the President spoke.
[9] The Reemployment Service was an agency of the United States Employment Service, established June 6, 1933. The purpose was, particularly, to supply lists of workers eligible for employment on public works projects.

128

inquiry in their own districts as to what are the likelihoods of employment opportunities in private employment. What would you think of that?

SECRETARY ROPER: That is a very good suggestion.

MR. WALKER: I have a report here; but before going into that, I will ask Mr. Riefler what he would say would be the quickest and most accurate way to get a real picture of this. Take Public Works, for instance; some may not know that this committee appointed can do nothing but report progress to date. We attempted to start moving in that general direction, but we haven't gotten nearly as far in it as we would have liked, in view of what Mr. Hopkins has just suggested, which does paint a rather critical picture from a good many angles. What would you think would be the best and most effective way?

MR. RIEFLER: I appointed a committee this morning to get together on that— one member from Miss Perkins' department, one from the Treasury, one from Mr. Hopkins' department, and one from my own. But most of the things Mr. Hopkins brings up do not lend themselves to a definite, scientific technique by which you can say so many people will be at work at a certain time in Toledo and so many in Detroit.

SECRETARY PERKINS: Do you think if an inquiry were made by each of the 3,500 offices of the Reemployment Service, they could give a good estimate of the number of people they will probably employ within the next three months? I mean putting into the hands of those 3,500 people who are located in the counties a questionnaire to which they must obtain the answers from the employers in their community on a specific basis, asking how many will the Jones and Smith Company take on. I see it as a device which we would be glad to carry out, because it will train our people in the technique of exercising judgment and putting them into very good relationship with the employer groups. We would be glad to do it on the grounds of the training it will give our people, if it has any validity at all. It is guesswork at the best. The important thing is really to integrate the program of relief of all types with a program that at least is intelligently anticipated for reemployment.

MR. RIEFLER: It seems to me so.

MR. WALKER: Mr. Douglas, you have certain reports coming in weekly.

DIRECTOR DOUGLAS: But they are not coming in in the form which was requested.

MR. WALKER: Have you provided a cushion for yourself on this if you are off a million or a million and a half?

129

MR. HOPKINS: No, but this is our projection of this thing. The government has projected a policy of unemployment relief beginning with spring for two and one-half million people in need.
It is a very important decision to make. Some of my friends think it will be many more than that, so I am asking for whatever statistical data on this point we can get. I think we have to assume a great deal in regard to this matter.

SECRETARY PERKINS: How are you estimating it—that a million families will go back on some kind of agricultural way of earning a living?

MR. HOPKINS: At the peak of the winter we had six million, six hundred thousand.

MR. FAHEY: When?

MR. HOPKINS: In January.

MR. FAHEY: How does that compare with last March?

MR. HOPKINS: We had six million, six hundred thousand families getting benefits from the government—CWA and relief. It is my judgment that four million, five hundred thousand families are at this moment in need.

MR. FAHEY: What is the figure of last March?

MR. HOPKINS: About the same.

MR. FAHEY: You mean you have about the same number as last March?

MR. HOPKINS: Yes, in spite of the numbers that have been employed. The longer unemployment lasts, the higher the percentage of unemployed that get on relief rolls. With four and one-half million families in need in the month of January, that is going to drop down to between two and one-half and three million families, from May first on through next winter.

MR. WALKER: What is the operation figure for last year?

MR. HOPKINS: We moved down every month from March to September. We got below three million in September.

MR. FAHEY: How good a figure have you as to number of persons unemployed as of the first of the year?

MR. HOPKINS: We have closer to a figure than ever before through the registration of Civil Works. It is my opinion that you should count the four million people on Civil Works as bona fide unemployment people. We have another half million on relief that are able-bodied unemployed. There were about six million more who applied for jobs than got them. About four million represent bona fide unemployment people; the rest represent the farmers, farm laborers, duplicate registrations, and perhaps another half million. So I believe we can talk in terms of nine million unemployed people. People will estimate that up and down about a million. Then if you want to, you can lop at once two or three million people who are always unemployed. I personally throw out at once another million or million and a half of farmers and farm laborers.

SECRETARY ROPER: Reducing it then to about six million.

MR. HOPKINS: With the increase in employment, we find a higher percentage in need. Relief now compared with a year ago does not mean anything. If we have four and one-half million in need now, I believe it can be dropped to two and one-half or three million.

MR. WALKER: Increased efficiency has been a very considerable factor that came through the depression. During the depression, people got out a much higher production than they did in 1928.

GENERAL JOHNSON: It is the other way in the steel industry.

DIRECTOR DOUGLAS: There has been very little replacement during the depression. Don't you think that it is very difficult, generally speaking, almost impossible to project into the future what employment will be by private enterprise? I think it would be very reasonable to say that if the capital market were opened you would get that reemployment and possibly more. If, however, the present barriers to the operating capital market remain, I think it a question as to whether or not you will get it.

MR. HOPKINS: We have to meet a need head-on.

MR. WALKER: Aren't there some pretty well agreed-upon factors between direct and indirect employment?[10] General Motors has a very good figure; they say that for every man directly employed there are four indirectly employed. Isn't that true in a number of industries?

MR. RIEFLER: I think the problem of direct and indirect employment is always the flow of goods.

MR. WALKER: General Motors say they will take on a hundred thousand people at the factory. For June, July, and August, you can figure four hundred thousand men indirectly employed.

GENERAL JOHNSON: There is not another industry like it.

MR. FAHEY: I wanted to ask Mr. Hopkins or anybody else, assuming that there are six million unemployed at present, whether we have any reliable breakdown of the classes.

MR. HOPKINS: There are three million families on relief and we are getting the occupational history of all those people.

MR. FAHEY: How soon will you have that?

---

[10] An interesting foreshadowing of the Keynes multiplier theory (which did not appear until later), which sought to establish a reasonably accurate method of estimating the indirect effects on unemployment of a given amount spent directly on public or private investment.

MR. HOPKINS: In probably another week.

SECRETARY PERKINS: The ten million who registered for the CWA work also gave their occupational and industrial background on the cards which they filled out; so we can know on a much larger and unchecked group to what trade they consider themselves attached.

MR. FAHEY: I think that will be very helpful.

SECRETARY PERKINS: Has any consideration ever been given to the utilization of extension of credit of RFC to enterprises the value of which will be measured somewhat, at least, by their ability to give immediate or large employment?

MR. WALKER [reading]:[11] State Directors have begun to report on actual conditions affecting the Recovery program in their respective states. These reports are of unusual value because the Directors are forming their opinions from an independent and impartial viewpoint.

In addition they have transmitted complaints and criticisms, made to them in connection with local conditions. These have been forwarded by this office to the departments and agencies concerned, with the request that they be investigated and that the action taken in each case be reported back to the Executive Director of the National Emergency Council.

The majority of the complaints and criticisms concern the administration of the Emergency Agencies by local officials, particularly in the Civil Works program. There has been very little adverse comment on the administration of the Emergency Agencies in Washington.

The State Directors report as follows:

NRA

COLORADO	General misunderstanding reported. Public to date lacks authentic information.
KANSAS	Director reports general improvement in code compliance.
MARYLAND	Violence attends picketing of Munson Line at Baltimore; code should be expedited.
MICHIGAN	Director reports general complaints that small business suffers, that employers hamper collective bargaining; labor trouble predicted.
NEBRASKA	Manufacturers Association head says small industries in that area suffering by enforced increased cost of production which is at level with urban industrial centers; decentralized code authorities suggested with power to except small units in areas of low living cost; economic planning to protect small unit suggested. Uniform regulations suggested to stop spending of Federal funds with non-complying concerns.
SOUTH CAROLINA	Delay in dealing with flagrant violators has caused

---

[11] This rather lengthy report has been left in the final editing of the transcript less for its intrinsic interest than as an example of the type of information flowing in from the field to the NEC staff.

public to feel code enforcement is lacking. Local code authorities hampered by failure of National authorities to inform and advise them; local code authorities include men interested in other codes; re-check of personnel suggested.

TENNESSEE — Director reports cooling interest, but no compliance troubles.

WISCONSIN — Four strikes, 1,150 shoe and 1,800 furniture employees, picketing with no violence; Sheboygan, Milwaukee, Beaver Dam, and Kenosha affected.

CWA

COLORADO — Single State Administrator instead of committee is eliminating criticism.

FLORIDA — State official reported as refusing to investigate graft charges in Union County; much favoritism prevalent; many needing relief barred by registration rules.

IOWA — Compensation director reported operating insurance business, using CWA quarters and staff. Many complaints of political preference.

KANSAS — Program inadequate; greater rotation of labor needed.

KENTUCKY — State Administrator using politics. Louisville Republican organization claimed beneficiary.

LOUISIANA — Work hampered by politics; many complaints received.

MINNESOTA — Mayor of St. Paul claims political credit for CWA. Suggested CWA be continued in drought area.

MISSISSIPPI — Greater rotation urged as substitute for cutting off CWA. Suggested wage scales be gradually lowered.

MISSOURI — Workers forced to buy from CWA board member; favoritism permits men with other jobs on CWA; entire families on payroll; much politics in Green County where Republican county committee chairman passes on all CWA jobs. Department of Justice action urged.

NEVADA — State Administrator reported using jobs for political machine. Caliente employment head using CWA to improve own property and political organization.

RHODE ISLAND — Cranston man says he is barred by CWA because he is Mason and Baptist.

TENNESSEE — Merchants cannot collect $1,500,000 for goods because incorrect forms were used under emergency instructions from Washington. Suggested CWA take no farm labor after season opens April 1.

VIRGINIA — General concern that industry will not be able to absorb CWA men.

FERA

MARYLAND — Petty graft in coal for unemployed in Baltimore; District Attorney acting.

TENNESSEE — Director says relief effective despite complaints.

PWA

COLORADO — Discouragement because bond requirements regarded

	too severe.
KANSAS	Operating efficiently. One hundred ten projects approved.
MINNESOTA	Suggested that program be speeded up for men laid off by CWA.
TENNESSEE	In Shelby County, two contracts let to high bidders who were county CWA officials; much criticism of this. Few projects approved; result that transferring labor from CWA will be delayed.

RFC

KENTUCKY	Reported loan to Frankfort shoe company refused despite good security; 400 employees affected.
NEBRASKA	Industrial concerns with good collateral cannot get loans from Omaha banks.
TENNESSEE	Small business cannot get loans because of rigid credit rules of Federal Reserve System.

HOLC

COLORADO	Criticism allayed since loans have gone up to 50 a day.
OKLAHOMA	Government home repair funds going to non-NRA concerns.
TENNESSEE	Doing good work. No complaints.

AAA

| KANSAS | Wheat allotment money is great relief. |
| TENNESSEE | Recovery program stimulated by AAA help to cotton farmers. |

FARM CREDIT ADMINISTRATION

| KANSAS | Confidence in farm regions returning as agencies function very effectively. |

NATIONAL REEMPLOYMENT SERVICE

| NEBRASKA | Investigation of Douglas County Reemployment Service needed to clear up inefficiency and favoritism. |

GENERAL

MARYLAND	State is backward in using Recovery Agencies.
SOUTH DAKOTA	Cooperation pledged by state constitutional officials.
TENNESSEE	Governor, state commissioners, and heads of emergency agencies cooperate with State Director.

That is a digest of the early suggestions coming in.

GENERAL JOHNSON: Is that the report from the 48 state directors?

MR. WALKER: This is just for your general information.

SECRETARY ROPER: It seems to me that these men, in the light of what Mr. Hopkins has told us, are thinking exclusively of the emergency. They might very well render great service in getting various concerns to say whether they are alive to this situation and endeavoring to get people back to work. You know there is a great deal of information that could be gotten through

134

this source if they could see that their proposition in working out the emergency had also to dovetail into the long-term program.

The meeting adjourned at 4:35 p.m.

Proceedings of the National Emergency Council

meeting no. 6
March 6, 1934

Held in the Cabinet Room of the Executive Offices, The White House, Tuesday, March 6, 1934, at 2:35 p.m.

Present: the Attorney General; the Secretary of Agriculture; the Secretary of Commerce; the Secretary of Labor; the Director of the Budget; the Honorable Oscar L. Chapman, Assistant Secretary of the Interior; the Chairman of the Board of the Home Owners' Loan Corporation; the Governor of the Farm Credit Administration; the Honorable Frank Healy, Assistant Compliance Director of National Recovery Administration; the Honorable H. R. Tolley, Assistant Administrator of Agricultural Adjustment Administration; the Honorable Charles H. March, Federal Trade Commission; the Adviser on Consumer Problems, Mrs. Mary Rumsey; the Economic Adviser; the Honorable Fred A. Ironside, Jr., Special Assistant; the Executive Director.
The President of the United States came in at 3:10 p.m.

[This meeting provides a test for NEC. Lewis Douglas (together with Comptroller General McCarl) held views sharply at variance with some administration policies. On the issue of the Executive Order discussed here, they oppose the carrying out of an important part of one of those policies. The NEC, again functioning without F.D.R.'s presence, could do no more than bring the disagreement into the open. Even after the President entered the meeting and was made fully aware of the problem, the issue was bypassed rather than resolved. At this high policy level, only Presidential action could have been effective (in all probability the removal of Douglas would have been necessary), and if a President in such circumstances declines to act, the rift must remain. Eventually (September 1, 1934), Douglas resigned, and though he declined to state the reasons, his basic disagreement with administration policies was common knowledge. It appears that F.D.R. did not take the initiative but was willing to tolerate Douglas' disagreement as long as the latter was willing to remain in the Administration.
With the less important yet significant issue of gearing government procurement to economic fluctuations, the matter was raised, discussed, and, in effect, resolved by the President when he referred the matter to Walker to follow up. The essential question about an experiment in coordination like NEC is: what can one reasonably expect from it and what is unreasonable to expect?—Editors' Note.]

MR. WALKER: Shall we proceed with the meeting? The first matter we have on the agenda is the state directors' report which I think might, if it is not too lengthy, be of some interest. It will give a general idea of what is going through the minds of the state directors and what problems they are running into.

Transmitted herewith is a cross-section of the conditions, progress, and defections of the Recovery Program as reported by the State Directors of the National Emergency Council.

Most of the reports are critical, with the view of correcting the weaknesses in various places.

Although many instances of ineffective administration of the Recovery Program still exist, in general there is an improvement in conditions since the last reports to the Council two weeks ago. This is in part due to the new impetus given the program by the State Directors themselves and the stimulus resulting from the NRA Code Authority Conference and the critical forum which preceded it.

The Directors report as follows:

NRA

CALIFORNIA	Washington dilatory in handling code violations.
LOUISIANA	Personal contact with employers needed.
MARYLAND	Imperative need for decisive action to obtain compliance. Consumers losing interest. Business men fear compliance will not be enforced. Hagerstown coal dealer who lost Blue Eagle supplying postoffice with coal.
MASSACHUSETTS	State Director calls conferences to arbitrate difficulties. He protests Labor Compliance Officer's final authority over investigators.
MINNESOTA	Complaints that eastern manufacturers get code advantage.
MONTANA	General improvement although chiselers active and employees restive. Jefferson County mine to close if new union is not dissolved. Campaign to combat apathy towards NRA planned.
NEBRASKA	Low bidder, not complying with NRA accepted by Quartermaster Corps. Suggested uniform instructions on this be given Government purchasing agents. Wholesalers collecting alleged "NRA tax" from retailer, discrediting whole program. Lancaster County Compliance Code reorganized to eliminate inefficiency and bitterness. Unfair trade practice adjusted by State Director. Small business man aided by NRA. Dakota County farmers optimistic. Omaha bank clearings gain leads country.
NORTH CAROLINA	State Director ignored in Labor Compliance appointment.
PENNSYLVANIA	State Politics ensnarls Labor Compliance appointment.
SOUTH CAROLINA	Proposed state NRA enforcement ensnarls recovery in local politics. Members of Code Authority destroying confidence by not complying themselves.

137

TENNESSEE	Memphis public opinion very good. Nashville manufacturers state NRA helps small business. Disapprove price fixing codes.
TEXAS	Legislature in special session considers ineffective state recovery measure.
WISCONSIN	Labor troubles increasing; one strike of 1800 settled; additional ones involving 3500 at Racine and Milwaukee.

CWA

ARIZONA	Many general complaints.
ARKANSAS	State purchasing agent states he must accept low bid even if non-NRA.
FLORIDA	Five members of CWA advisory committee resign, charge extravagance and high salaries. Many projects of little permanent good. Favorites on higher payrolls.
GEORGIA	Collusion alleged in contract awarded without notice to low bidder on Atlanta U. S. Naval Armory.
IOWA	Nine Cedar Rapids City foremen transferred to CWA with 166 per cent pay increase.
KENTUCKY	Slowness in redeeming vouchers for groceries results in wholesaler refusing to accept vouchers at par from retailers. Lack of cooperation with State Board of Health handicaps both organizations. General criticism of high wages.
LOUISIANA	Personal and political motives in CWA work.
MINNESOTA	CWA generally effective. Freeborn County protests CWA reduction. Causing great hardships in unemployment since local industries are reducing their forces.
MISSOURI	Administration has good record. Independent check-up of complaints might alleviate criticism.
NEW MEXICO	Stated CWA is major unemployment relief and business aid. Continuance needed until improved business or PWA absorbs men.
NORTH DAKOTA	Well-to-do farmers getting Federal land loans and allotment checks are on CWA rolls.
OREGON	Delay in naming State Director for CWA causes unrest.
RHODE ISLAND	Administration good. Political complaints unsupported by concrete cases.
TENNESSEE	Press praises benefits of CWA. Urges payment for goods supplied to CWA. Miners who quit jobs for CWA now back at work. Four hundred men laid off at Chattanooga storm CWA headquarters. One-hundred-seventy-five discharged men march on CWA headquarters in Memphis demanding relief. Disbanded only after being promised direct relief.
WISCONSIN	Complaints of delay in paying for materials.

PWA

MARYLAND	Survey needed to determine number of CWA men to be absorbed by PWA since balance not employed by industry will be on relief.
MISSOURI	Effect on employment should be apparent shortly.

TENNESSEE	Work on sixteen projects will begin soon. Suggested that State Director be furnished details of works projects submitted and anticipated employment. Considerable delay reported in getting projects approved.

FERA

KENTUCKY	Administration and general results effected good.
NEBRASKA	Dawes County Republicans dominate relief instead of equal party representation.
TENNESSEE	Local branches will care for families of discharged CWA workers.

AAA

KENTUCKY	State pleased with work.
LOUISIANA	Many complaints on delay in completing codes. Failure of milk agreement causing prices 20 per cent lower than March 1933.
MONTANA	Program confused. Dairy Products Association wishes to form temporary organization under marketing agreements until Code is approved.
NEVADA	Uncertainty on dairy marketing agreements causing anxiety.
TENNESSEE	Sign up on cotton reduction contracts exceeding expectations. Farmers using more fertilizer to make up for reduced acreage. State Director suggests no loans be made for buying fertilizer.

ECW

NEVADA	Only 50 per cent of applicants placed. More camps needed.

HOLC

KENTUCKY	Appears to be functioning well.
MISSOURI	Excellent. Approximately 2750 loans closed.

RFC

MONTANA	Charged that Deposit Liquidation Board Committee in ninth Federal Reserve District discriminates against small banks.
MISSOURI	Many requests about loans to small businesses who cannot borrow directly from RFC.

FEDERAL RESERVE SYSTEM

TENNESSEE	Poor credit to small business retards recovery program.

NATIONAL REEMPLOYMENT SERVICE

FLORIDA	State Director states that because of inferior labor drawn from CWA or PWA lists, one project is costing over four times as much as it should.
NEBRASKA	Two men discharged in Omaha because not members of union.

TVA

TENNESSEE	Fourteen thousand men employed at Norris. Farmers

protest prices they are offered for their land.

GENERAL

KANSAS	Suggested that all Agencies file with State Director detailed reports. Would give him information on which to handle complaints.
OKLAHOMA	Strong feeling state has not received its share of Federal aid.

Through the medium of the State Directors and the Washington office of the National Emergency Council many of the acute cases of misunderstanding or maladministration have been adjusted.

In the nineteen-day period from February 15 to March 6, fifty-three complaints or serious problems affecting twelve of the major Emergency Agencies were transmitted by the Washington office to the agencies affected. Of these, twenty-eight have been adjusted and their files closed. An additional seven have been partially adjusted but are retained in the current files pending further action.

Only seven problems are still pending after the ten-day period suggested for adjustment by the Council.

We are getting very full and complete reports from our state administrators and most of them seem quite anxious to be a little more effective and broaden their jurisdiction, but I think we will have to go a little slowly on that matter.

The report of the committee on NRA compliance in government contracts will be read by Mr. Ironside.

MR. IRONSIDE [reading]: *Subject: NRA Compliance with Respect to the Spending of Federal Funds.* For the purpose of bringing about compliance to codes and agreements by Government contractors, Executive Order No. 6246 of August 10, 1933, was promulgated. By the terms of this Order every contract "for supplies" entered into by the United States, or any of its agencies or instrumentalities, was required to contain a provision under which the contractor engaged to comply with all the provisions of the applicable codes, or if there were no approved codes, then with the President's Re-employment Agreement. Furthermore, if the contractor failed to comply with these provisions the Government retained the right to terminate the contract.

Correspondence received by the Executive Director indicates:

(a) That Government funds are being spent with firms which are not complying with NRA codes and agreements, and

(b) That confusion exists with respect to regulations designed to bring about compliance by contractors with NRA codes and agreements.

The following illustrations are submitted:

1. Letter from the Associated General Contractors of America, Inc., Washington, D.C.: PWA contract form superseding the standard form of contract developed by the Interdepartmental Board of Contract and Adjustments has resulted in uncertainties, particularly re wage and hour clauses. The Associated General Contractors of America, Inc., anxious to work with NRA in standardizing interpretations and requirements.

2. Letter from O. H. Sunwinkel, Commissioner of the Nebraska Manufacturers' Association, Lincoln, Nebraska: Nebraska manufacturer making stove, furnace, and range repairs has submitted bids on such repairs to the Quartermaster Corps. A statement was sent to all bidders that they must agree to comply with all provisions of codes of fair competition, or to the PRA.[1] In spite of this, bids varied so much that PRA complying firms say their competitors could have been paying "little or nothing to labor."

3. Letter from the Yonkers Truckmen's Association, 78 No. Broadway, N.Y.: Conflict between CWA and NRA. CWA asked the Truckmen's Association to submit bids for truck hire on Make Work Projects. Underbid by Plaza Sand and Stone Co. The Truckmen's Association code was in Washington ready for signature before date of proposals but signature was held up due to one clause re price of labor. Code has now been signed by the President, effective February 27. CWA bids for trucks terminated February 15. The Association wants CWA to readvertise its bids so as to make only Code complying concerns eligible, because Plaza Sand and Stone Co., is paying 50¢ an hour while code requires 74¢.

4. Letter from Iowa State Director for NEC: Readvertisement of bids on Des Moines bridge project asked because bidders receiving contract not complying with NRA. This project is largest in the State and its consequences will be far reaching with respect to compliance. The greatest breakdown in NRA compliance is stated to be the conflict of authority between Washington officials.

5. Letter from Maine NRA Office Manager: Only instructions received by CWA State Director are to accept the lowest bid, Maine Compliance Office uncertain whether bidders must conform to NRA.

6. Letters from Nebraska State Director for the NEC: Considerable misconception on part of Government purchasing agencies; some are under the impression they can purchase supplies and give contracts to firms that are not working under the NRA. Wants instructions sent out to all Government purchasing agencies, calling attention to Section 53, Part 2 of Bulletin No. 51 PWA, providing "No bids shall be received from any director who has not signed and complied with the applicable approved Code of Fair Competition adopted under Title One of the National Recovery Act, or the Trade or Subdivision thereof concerned, or if there be no such approved code of competition, who has not signed and complied with the provisions of the President's Reemployment Agreement."

7. Letter from Messrs. Macfarlane & Monroe, 90 Broad Street, New York City: Clients confused by varying forms of Government orders. Firm wants copies of orders to government purchasing agencies relative to conformity with code provisions, or PRA.

8. Letter from Painters Local, No. 342. The Union painters in Lubbock, Texas state that they are unable to obtain a fair proportion of the work done with money loaned by the Home Owners' Loan Corporation for repairs because the work is given to men who are not regular painters and who pay wages even lower than Union painters operating under

---

[1] President's Reemployment Service. See note 9, p. 128, and note 2, p. 274.

NRA codes or agreements, whose scale is 25¢ per hour less than Government scale for skilled labor.

9. Letter from F. B. Stever, Oklahoma City, Oklahoma: States that loans by Home Owners' Loan Corporation for home repairs are spent with firms whose prices, forced down by unfair competition, result in inferior materials, workmanship, and wages below NRA levels, which has resulted in letting of contracts to non-NRA firms.

10. Letter from Arizona State Director for the NEC: Reports that the Purchasing agent for CWA states that he must accept the low bidder even though it is known that the low bidder is not complying with NRA.

11. Letter from Vermont Commissioner of Forestry: U.S. Army gives bids for shoe repairs and lumber to non-NRA firms or those whose prices are below minimum code price.

12. Memorandum from Maryland State Director for NEC: Blue Eagle removed from H. L. Mills for non-compliance with codes other than Coal Code. He supplies Hagerstown Post Office with coal.

It is recommended:

1. That an Executive Order be promulgated requiring in substance that all Federal funds granted, loaned, or otherwise disbursed, should be conditioned on the recipients' compliance with NRA codes or agreements.

2. That regulations for the carrying into effect of this Order be promulgated by the National Emergency Council, and that such regulations be substantially similar in principle to the regulations of the PWA Bulletin 51, Part II, Section 53.

3. That violations of such Executive Order or such regulations be promptly reported to the National Recovery Administration.

MR. FAHEY: Will a copy of that report be sent around to members of the council? There are a good many things in there that, it seems to me, if taken up by the separate administrations, could be acted upon at once.

MR. WALKER: Perhaps we might be able to get a little more concrete action. We have had a number of complaints from National Recovery Administration. Mr. Healy, perhaps, could give you the general attitude of National Recovery Administration with reference to it. It seems there has been very little attempt at compliance with the Executive Order. A general Executive Order was prepared by the Attorney General, I think, which has not been signed. I think Mr. Healy might like to make some suggestions with reference to it. It seemed to me when I was going over the Executive Order that the language was so clear there was no need for rules and regulations, but in view of the fact that so many complaints have been received, I think we should give this matter our careful attention and try to work it out very definitely. Have you something to say along that line, Mr. Healy?

MR. HEALY: I think you have covered it very well. The great difficulty is with the people in the field. They are not close enough to Washington to have an exact idea as to what the policy is, and policies are determined according to each man's individual view. The contractors coming into Washington, however, do complain that when they go to the Public Works Administration for the contract they find one set of regulations, and in the War Department, another, and in the Treasury Department, another. Different wage scales have something to do with that, but there are other conditions referring to National Recovery Administration compliance which are sources of their complaints. One department will require an affidavit, another a certificate, another will have the compliance certificate written into the invitation to bid, another into the contract. In the case of the War Department and the Forestry Department, we have the peculiar situation of their contracts requiring compliance with the approved applicable code and the Adjutant General of the Army sending an order to all special bases advising them that the Comptroller General has ruled that price posting and purchasing requirements of codes do not apply to the United States.[2] The Forest Department includes the restriction as to codes in its invitation to bid, I believe, but encloses in the envelope a slip quoting from the Comptroller General to the effect that bidders are not required to comply with National Recovery Administration conditions. We daily have two or three inquiries from the field from dealers asking if they must comply with the code in bidding for the United States and referring to the Comptroller General's decision. We have to give them a rather split answer and state that we are familiar with the Comptroller General's opinion and that he did rule that government sellers were not bound by all of the terms of the code, but that the law-enforcing body, as headed by the Attorney General, takes a different view, and that the Comptroller General does not try the criminal prosecution. In that way we let the man take his choice between the Comptroller and the Attorney General.

MR. WALKER: The question of departmental heads asking for exceptions

---

[2] For a discussion of one of these prior decisions by the Comptroller General, see the account in the *New York Times*, Dec. 2, 1933, p. 5. This conflict between the views of the Comptroller General and the Attorney General is an excellent example of an institutional condition that would defy many efforts at coordination.

has been called to my attention. Have you any written requests of that?

MR. HEALY: Exceptions to the codes?

MR. WALKER: Yes. Have you had any difficulty along that line?

MR. HEALY: No, that is a misunderstanding. Under the proposed Executive Order there will be need for exceptions. For instance, the Canal Zone is covered by the law, but there are very few American concerns in the Canal Zone—in fact, none, if I am informed correctly. All those concerns are in the Panama Republic.

MR. WALKER: You don't think there will be any need of consulting the heads of emergency organizations with reference to their requests for exceptions?

MR. HEALY: I should not think so. That will develop according to the general departmental business. Each department will undoubtedly develop a great many exceptions needed for their respective divisions.

MR. WALKER: As I remember, there have been a good many violations in the field concerning which governmental agencies have never reported to the National Recovery Administration, but which have come to you in indirect fashion.

MR. HEALY: Yes, that very frequently happens. Mr. Chapman has just advised me of one that he had taken care of, of which we had not been informed.

SECRETARY PERKINS: Mr. Chairman, I think it might be well for you to discuss with the Secretary of War the whole matter of the policy with the Army in regard to doing work with its Public Works money and paying less than the regular wages that are agreed upon for other public work. A great many of the strikes we are called upon to adjudicate turn out to be that the Army has followed its usual practice of the lowest price possible without regard to what the wage for that particular phase of work was fixed at on Public Works, and there is a lack of coordination that is embarrassing. I think if you would look into that it might be a useful work of coordination.

MR. HEALY: We have run into that same feature in a number of cases where the Army and also Public Roads are complying strictly with the minimum by Public Works regulations and are in some cases using it as a chisel to cut down the prevailing wage scale in the country. The Army is spending its own appropriation from Public Works allotments, and is buying for the Civilian Conservation Corps camps. They have three different sets of conditions, and there are just that many

144

sets of conditions which the contractors have to meet. There is bitter complaint from the contractors that they cannot deal with the government of the United States without meeting just as many conditions as there are departments, and sometimes two or three in the same department.[3] Civilian Conservation Corps funds are spent by the Army. Any violation of the codes, without regard to the character of the violation, is promptly stepped on through the Civilian Conservation Corps. On the other hand, there are funds spent by the Army in cases where the Adjutant General has advised them that the seller has to pay no attention to that feature of the codes.

ATTORNEY GENERAL CUMMINGS: Let me inquire, if I may, whether you think that the difficulty can be cured by each department forming regulations, or whether we have to have a new Executive Order to start with.

MR. HEALY: We have to have a new Executive Order to start with.

ATTORNEY GENERAL CUMMINGS: What is the present status of that Executive Order? Do you know where it is?

MR. HEALY: The last I heard it had been returned by your office with a statement from Comptroller General McCarl. He had criticized it and the criticism had been sent to your office and you had replied to it.

ATTORNEY GENERAL CUMMINGS: As I recall the situation, there were two Executive Orders of similar import. One originated in the National Recovery Administration, and the other originated in some other department—I have forgotten which one—but apparently they took a different course. One of them went to McCarl first, apparently, and one went to Mr. [Lewis] Douglas. When they came to me I had both of them: one with the criticisms of Mr. McCarl, the other with the criticisms of Mr. Douglas; and I then had a meeting with some of the interested parties, and somewhat changed the order that had been previously prepared by your department in collaboration with ours, and sent the whole thing over to the President because it involved a question of policy—a rather fundamental one. Personally, it is very clear to me what ought to be done—just as clear as a bell what ought to be done—but somehow it doesn't get done. I don't know where it sticks or what causes it to stick.

---

[3] The President had issued an Executive Order on Aug. 10, 1933, requiring that all contractors supplying the government must conform to the NRA codes. A new Executive Order was issued ten days after this meeting, on Mar. 15, 1934, and provided for exceptions in cases approved by NRA when necessary to protect the government from excessive bids.

MR. HEALY:	The lack of it is the weakest spot in compliance.
MR. WALKER:	I cannot find out where it is.
ATTORNEY GENERAL CUMMINGS:	Perhaps it has been lost in transit. Suppose, out of abundance of caution, I check up from my records, and if I have not sent it over, I will. If I have sent it over, I will supply you with a copy of it.
MR. WALKER:	What would be your idea, generally, with reference to the best way to proceed? Wouldn't it be well for us to appoint a small committee and draft an order and let the National Recovery Administration make such suggestions to your department as you and they think best, and then pass on them?
ATTORNEY GENERAL CUMMINGS:	Well, we have really done all that. Our understanding is that the objections of the Comptroller General are rather fundamental. He seems to cling to the notion that the lowest bidder is in a preferred position, no matter who he is or whether he complies or not. My notion is entirely different. I don't think we ought to do business with anybody that is not complying with the National Recovery Administration, because it seems to me inconceivable that you can make a program succeed unless the government supports it. It doesn't seem to be open to debate in my mind. However, there are others who do not take that view of it. One of them is the Comptroller General, and so to submit it again to him means to reinvite the same criticisms. I think it has got to the stage where it is for this board or the President to say what should be done. Maybe the President would like to have this board suggest to him how the board feels about it; or perhaps you'd better take it up informally with the President after you have acquainted yourself with the situation.
SECRETARY PERKINS:	What control have we over who bids?
ATTORNEY GENERAL CUMMINGS:	The proposed Executive Order, as it was finally drafted, promulgated a rule under which no bid was to be received unless it was submitted by a person who had complied. There was a little debate on that question as to whether everybody could bid, and then the man who got the bid could comply. It seemed to me that that was an indefensible position, because a man should not be permitted to gamble with the chance of getting a contract and complying for that contract and still continuing to violate all the plans of the Administration if he did not get it. I think we ought to lay down a fundamental doctrine that we do not do business with people who do not do business with the government. It all comes down to that, just as clear as two and two make four.

146

SECRETARY PERKINS: What would happen in these circumstances? Suppose they have complied, and establish by records that they have complied with the rules as to working conditions, etc., and they get a large government contract. Thereupon they take on a large number of extra employees, beyond those whom they originally held, in order to handle this contract, and they then chisel by not complying on that particular contract. Could you cancel that contract?

ATTORNEY GENERAL CUMMINGS: Oh, yes.

SECRETARY PERKINS: Even though they had previously complied and had gotten the award?

ATTORNEY GENERAL CUMMINGS: My impression is that they lay themselves open to all the penalties, but the contract itself can be cancelled.

MR. HEALY: The order requires that only those who have complied shall receive the invitation to bid, and that there be a provision for forfeiture in case of noncompliance.

ATTORNEY GENERAL CUMMINGS: It was intended to be drastic. (*The Attorney General then read a large part of the proposed Executive Order.*)

MR. WALKER: We are discussing, Mr. Douglas (*Mr. Douglas had just arrived*), a complaint by National Recovery Administration directed to the various department heads of the government and governmental agencies, especially in the field, to the effect that they are failing to comply with the Executive Orders issued by the President, and are contracting with people who are not complying with National Recovery Administration regulations. We have a number of complaints as to the Quartermaster, Civil Works Administration, Home Owners' Loan Corporation, Post Office Department, and others that they have failed to comply with that Executive Order. I understand you have some ideas on this subject.

DIRECTOR DOUGLAS: I think two Executive Orders have been drafted. The first was not acted upon and we reported adversely on it. The second we reported adversely on and it was referred back to us with the request that we get together with the Attorney General and the Comptroller General and General Johnson. The Comptroller General has been away and won't be back for three or four days. The Attorney General was away until last Saturday.

ATTORNEY GENERAL CUMMINGS: That probably explains what became of the order. My recollection, Lewis, was that these two orders came over, and one seemed to have with it a memorandum from you.

DIRECTOR DOUGLAS: That's right.

147

ATTORNEY GENERAL CUMMINGS: And the other had a memorandum by the Comptroller General.

DIRECTOR DOUGLAS: That was the first order.

ATTORNEY GENERAL CUMMINGS: There were two orders.

DIRECTOR DOUGLAS: That's right.

ATTORNEY GENERAL CUMMINGS: And the last I knew of this I had before me those two orders and those two memorandums; and it lay in my mind that I had somewhat modified the first order and sent it back to the President with my comments, and that is the last I heard of it, and that was before I went South.

DIRECTOR DOUGLAS: Then it came back to me the day on which you went South, the same day on which the Comptroller General left for a ten-day vacation. The President had a note on it—and I spoke to him about it afterwards—to get in touch with you, General Johnson, and the Comptroller General and see if we could not iron out the difficulties.

MR. WALKER: It seems to be the consensus of opinion of most of those present that they are in favor of the order. Did you register any objection to it, Mr. Douglas?

DIRECTOR DOUGLAS: The order, as it seemed to us, as I recollect, imposed on any administrator of a federal agency a right to waive provisions of the order; that was one thing to which I took objection. The other thing to which we took objection was that there was a provision which required all sub-contractors to have signed the code and to have given evidence of their compliance with the code.

MR. WALKER: Have you any objection to the principles of the order?

DIRECTOR DOUGLAS: There was a third objection—

MR. WALKER: I think we are quite generally agreed that an order of this character should be executed. It is just a question of form; I think we might properly leave that with the Attorney General and some of the objectors.

DIRECTOR DOUGLAS: We had a third objection to the fundamental principle of the whole thing, and that is that it would increase costs, that in a large measure it gave protection to the large and relatively inefficient producers as against the smaller and more efficient producers.[4]

---

[4] The root of the divergence of views between Budget Director Douglas and the Administration on recovery policies here emerges. This kind of basic difference in approach and philosophy among members of a coordinating body such as NEC raises a problem of "coordination" that is quite clearly beyond the capacity of the group itself to deal with. Some concept of "collective responsibility" for broad policy would seem to be a prerequisite.

MR. WALKER: How are we going to justify our attitude if the government does not comply with NRA?

DIRECTOR DOUGLAS: I don't know, sir; but anyway these things go through us and we give our honest opinion. I frankly don't see how there is going to be much revival of the heavy goods if prices are increased.

SECRETARY PERKINS: Would you give us your objections in detail?

DIRECTOR DOUGLAS: I will see that you get them.

SECRETARY PERKINS: We are not in the business of deciding whether the National Recovery Administration is right in its principle. I think it is a question, as the Attorney General says, whether the government shall abide by its own rules.

DIRECTOR DOUGLAS: That is right, but these Executive Orders come through us and we are asked to register our opinion.

MR. WALKER: Don't you think the only question we should discuss is the matter of fundamental principle? I don't think we should burden the Council with the question of form.

SECRETARY PERKINS: Mr. Douglas objects to the fundamental principle.

DIRECTOR DOUGLAS: I do; but I am just one member of the Council. This goes deeper than whether or not the government shall comply with the National Recovery Administration or whether the governmental contractor shall comply. It goes to the very principle of the National Recovery Administration itself, and I frankly do not see how there is going to be very much revival if you increase prices of manufactured articles.

SECRETARY PERKINS: Isn't the question whether or not the government should obey its own rules quite distinct from what we think about how recovery should be effected?

DIRECTOR DOUGLAS: That is true.

SECRETARY PERKINS: What objections, then, would you have to an Executive Order that imposed upon the government compliance with its own rules?

DIRECTOR DOUGLAS: They have only a corner of the show. I do not approve of the increased cost to the government incident to the carrying out of this program.

ATTORNEY GENERAL CUMMINGS: That is practically McCarl's argument.

DIRECTOR DOUGLAS: I don't make the decision. My opinion may be wrong. It may cut across certain fundamental policies of the Administration.

ATTORNEY GENERAL CUMMINGS: Do you see any advantage to be gained, Mr. Douglas, by any conference between you and me and McCarl and Johnson where apparently our differences are so fundamental? Johnson and I would undoubtedly maintain that the thing was entirely proper and could not be objected to on any logical ground, in fact, that it would be illogical and almost stultifying not to do it. You and McCarl would probably take the contrary view.

DIRECTOR DOUGLAS: Waiving for the moment the discussion of the principle, I think there are some details of the order that we could agree upon. I think both orders, as they came to us, contained provisions which grant extraordinarily large powers to the administrator or agency which let the contract.

ATTORNEY GENERAL CUMMINGS: I shall be perfectly willing to sit in conference if there is any hope of agreement.

DIRECTOR DOUGLAS: I think there might be.

ATTORNEY GENERAL CUMMINGS: If there is no objection, Mr. Walker, I should be glad to see this Council go on record as in favor of the issuance of an Executive Order substantially along those lines.

MR. WALKER: Are there any other objectors to the fundamental principles to be heard from?

(President Roosevelt came in at this point.)

PRESIDENT ROOSEVELT: Well, go right ahead.

MR. WALKER: Mr. President, we are just discussing a complaint registered by NRA with reference to failure of certain departments and agencies of the government to comply with Executive Orders issued sometime ago by the President, requiring all departments of the government to purchase supplies from and contract only with people complying with NRA. It was thought necessary to extend or modify that order or broaden its powers. Apparently the order has become lost some place. There seems to be a difference of opinion with the Attorney General and General Johnson on one side, and the Director of the Budget and General McCarl on the other.

SECRETARY PERKINS: And it cannot be reconciled.

MR. WALKER: That leaves it right in the President's lap!

PRESIDENT ROOSEVELT: You mean the Comptroller General and the Attorney General do not agree on that?

DIRECTOR DOUGLAS: Mr. President, there is apparently a fundamental difference as to principle. I, for example, do not see how there is going to be very much recovery if by increasing costs we force up prices of manufactured articles. I stated that in a memorandum to you, I think. The question arose as to whether or not, in compliance with your note to me, any benefit might flow from a conference between the Attorney General, the Comptroller General, and myself with respect to the order. I said that, waiving the question of principle, there are some details in the order that I think might be ironed out.

150

PRESIDENT ROOSEVELT: In a nutshell, what was the order as drafted by the Director of Procurement?

DIRECTOR DOUGLAS: The order came from Public Works through General Johnson to me and to the Attorney General and back to you and then back to me on the day on which the Attorney General left, and the Comptroller General likewise.

(The President then looked over the order.)

PRESIDENT ROOSEVELT: Why did the Comptroller General object?

ATTORNEY GENERAL CUMMINGS: Because he said it does not give the lowest bidder the right to have the job, and he interprets the lowest bidder as anybody who bids, whether he is a complier or not. That restricts the government to doing business only with those who comply with NRA.

PRESIDENT ROOSEVELT: Why shouldn't they comply with NRA?

ATTORNEY GENERAL CUMMINGS: I don't see any objection.

PRESIDENT ROOSEVELT: Why should not people comply with National Recovery Administration?

DIRECTOR DOUGLAS: As I told you before, I think it retards recovery to increase cost.

PRESIDENT ROOSEVELT: Then NRA is wrong!

DIRECTOR DOUGLAS: I think, as it is being administered, it is.

PRESIDENT ROOSEVELT: But, unfortunately, it is government policy.

DIRECTOR DOUGLAS: I recognize that.

PRESIDENT ROOSEVELT: I think if we accept that as government policy, we have to go along with it.

DIRECTOR DOUGLAS: I think there might be some advantage in a conference between the Attorney General, the Comptroller General, General Johnson, and myself with respect to the details of the order.

ATTORNEY GENERAL CUMMINGS: I would not want to talk about whether the NRA is any good or not.

PRESIDENT ROOSEVELT: Let us waive the question whether the NRA is right or not, and talk over the details.

ATTORNEY GENERAL CUMMINGS: Those details which I suspect Mr. Douglas and Comptroller General McCarl would object to are the real teeth in the order. The order was purposely drafted in drastic terms so there could not be any doubt what contractors were expected to do, and what government officials were expected to do. There has been so much confusion and so many different forms of compliance and so many unfortunate rulings from the Comptroller General on this question of low bids that we tried to clear it up in an Executive Order. The challenge of Mr. Douglas is a fundamental one and has to do with

151

some powers that he thinks are a little excessive. Am I stating that correctly?

DIRECTOR DOUGLAS: That is right.

ATTORNEY GENERAL CUMMINGS: I don't know that I would be willing to yield very much on it.

DIRECTOR DOUGLAS: The administrator is given power to waive the provisions according to his discretion.

ATTORNEY GENERAL CUMMINGS: The Executive Order provides the power of the administrator to waive upon recommendation of the department affected. There are conceivable cases where you might have to make some exceptions. One illustration was where farmers along a railroad cut ties on their property, and they want to sell them to the railroad. They have been doing it for years.

PRESIDENT ROOSEVELT: I am one of them. I cut ties in the winter with my farm hands.

ATTORNEY GENERAL CUMMINGS: That illustration came up, and it justified the slight flexibility. I should not think you would want to object to flexibility.

DIRECTOR DOUGLAS: I think it gives terrific power to any executive. There is no limitation upon his power to waive.

SECRETARY PERKINS: You can waive it for anything?

DIRECTOR DOUGLAS: Exactly.

MR. HEALY: On any recommendation that affects the department.

DIRECTOR DOUGLAS: Not as the Executive Order came to me. I think it referred to the administrator in any executive department.

PRESIDENT ROOSEVELT: The Administrator for Industrial Recovery may make exceptions in specific cases, or otherwise, under this order, whenever such action shall be recommended by an agency of the United States—regular department or any other agency.

DIRECTOR DOUGLAS: I don't think that is the form in which it came to me.

ATTORNEY GENERAL CUMMINGS: I changed some things to clear them up.

PRESIDENT ROOSEVELT: Why don't you show that to the Comptroller General, but don't take up any questions that involve the general principle.

ATTORNEY GENERAL CUMMINGS: All right, sir.

MR. WALKER: In that connection, too, Mr. President, it seems to me we will have to provide further rules and regulations with respect to Executive Orders—draft uniform rules and regulations.

PRESIDENT ROOSEVELT: Why doesn't that whole thing fall under the Director of Procurement?[5] Doesn't almost everything pass through him?

ATTORNEY GENERAL CUMMINGS: My theory about it, sir, is that this should be done first. This will probably straighten out 75 per cent of our troubles. It is not conceivable it will straighten them all out. We may

---

[5] Probably refers to the head of the Treasury Department's Procurement Division, established by Executive Order 6166, June 10, 1933, renamed the Bureau of Federal Supply in 1947, and transferred to the General Services Administration in 1949.

152

have to have some coordination. Mr. Peoples may want to make some regulations and Mr. Walker may have to confer with different heads on details. I don't think you better begin to draft subsidary orders until you see what happens to this.

SECRETARY PERKINS: Certain supplies have been purchased from firms that do not obey the state labor laws, and they frequently violate on government orders.

TORNEY GENERAL CUMMINGS: That was another reason.

SECRETARY PERKINS: Is that covered?

PRESIDENT ROOSEVELT: The flexibility permits it.

MR. CHAPMAN: I think that is a good thing to take care of the majority of the problems involved.

TORNEY GENERAL CUMMINGS: I will sit in with you any time you want.

DIRECTOR DOUGLAS: All right, sir; tomorrow sometime?

TORNEY GENERAL CUMMINGS: Yes.

MR. FAHEY: What machinery is provided here to bring promptly to the attention of the several administrations affected any complaints as to failure to act? For example, some affecting the Home Owners' Loan Corporation we never heard about before. That is the first complaint I have heard from any part of the United States.

PRESIDENT ROOSEVELT: Copies of Executive Orders are supposed to go to every organization.

MR. FAHEY: The Executive Orders come to us but the complaint had not reached me.

MR. WALKER: For instance, the Hagerstown Post Office is buying coal from a man who lost his Blue Eagle.

PRESIDENT ROOSEVELT: Is that coal bought through the procurement officers?

MR. WALKER: I don't think so.

PRESIDENT ROOSEVELT: Who buys that coal?

MR. WALKER: I think the department itself does that. It seems to me those moneys could be followed right through for stricter compliance with National Recovery Administration.

MR. FAHEY: When complaints of this sort come in, there ought to be an arrangement by which they are sent along to us or anybody else involved.

PRESIDENT ROOSEVELT: Will you check on that and see that it gets routed to the right department?

MR. WALKER: The Emergency Council could help.

MR. FAHEY: I don't think it matters so long as it is looked after.

MR. HEALY: We send them to Mr. Walker whenever there is any doubt as to where complaints should go.

153

MR. FAHEY: This particular discussion brings up one other thought. It hasn't anything in particular to do with this, but does have to do with the question of government purchasing and employment. There has been a good deal of complaint from time to time that government needs, both national and in the states, have never been properly anticipated with the result that orders from the government on many occasions and orders from states come into the market at a time when they cause confusion, force overtime, night employment, and all that sort of thing; and in a great many cases if that situation were studied and purchasing were planned better, a lot of that confusion could be avoided and it would help very materially as far as stabilizing of employment is concerned. I do not know whether we have ever had anything done about it, but it is something that ought to be explored.

SECRETARY PERKINS: Government orders should come in so they could be made up in the slack season.

PRESIDENT ROOSEVELT: One of the difficulties is that funds become available on the first of July almost everywhere. The result is that bids are requested at the end of May or beginning of June, and you get an enormous number of government contracts of all kinds in the early part of July; it piles everything in at the same time of the year. I think it is a very pious idea that we should try to spread it through the year so that it will not conflict.

MR. FAHEY: No real attempt has ever been made to work it out, and in certain industries it causes great confusion and excessive cost. Take the manufacturers of school books, for instance; they know from year to year what they are going to be. But orders are not brought in until the eleventh hour, and as a result they have to bring in a lot of extra people, a large number of them inexperienced, which results in excessive costs and interference with the general employment market in a great many communities. There are similar experiences so far as a great many government supplies are concerned, such as stationery, furniture, and so on. A very large part of it could be anticipated with proper planning. I don't know what can be done about it but I think it would be worthwhile to study the question.

PRESIDENT ROOSEVELT: Most of our annual supplies are bought through the Procurement Office. I should think Admiral Peoples could divide up his supplies into classifications and, let us say, classify all stationery together, and then send for the manufacturers of

154

stationery and get them down here and ask them what their problems are as to times of delivery, and see if he can work out a method of asking for deliveries which will fit in with the average of their idle-time schedules. Isn't that a job for the Procurement Director?

DIRECTOR DOUGLAS: I should think so, sir.

MR. FAHEY: Do you think, Mr. President, it might be possible to devise any system by which the several states might also be asked to look into the situation and see what could be done? I think it is pretty appropriate right now because inventories are down so low in every direction the country over that it is easy to upset the market and cause it to rise with resulting confusion all over the lot.

PRESIDENT ROOSEVELT: I think Admiral Peoples could make a preliminary survey on it and then possibly he could ask the procurement officers of the different states to come down to a conference in Washington. Will you speak to Peoples about that?

MR. WALKER: Yes, sir.

SECRETARY PERKINS: The regular habit of the American people is always to indulge in our most extravagant public building at the height of the rush in the building industry, and so pay more than necessary.

MR. WALKER: Next on the agenda is a report by Mr. Riefler on the question of employment.

MR. RIEFLER: First is the report of Dun & Bradstreet on insolvency. I will summarize it:

Business failures have continued to decline in recent weeks, according to a special report prepared for the Council by Dun & Bradstreet. In February as a whole there were less than half as many failures as were reported a year ago. This improvement in stability of business concerns was general throughout the country, but was especially noticeable in the Southern States. In rural areas insolvencies were at a relatively lower rate, as compared with 1933, than in the cities.

The record of failures under NRA codes shows in every case a mortality rate of considerably less than one per cent. Our experience with information classified by codes is yet too limited to know whether current rates are exceptional or average. As in January, heavy insolvency rates, compared with other code industries, continued among men's clothing manufacturers and retail jewelers, both rather small industrial groups.

(*Mr. Riefler then passed around to the members of the Council the "Current Analysis of Primary Trends" dated March 3, 1934, and also the chart on "Employment and Unemployment in the United States."*)

The general structure of this chart is to show the whole population available for employment in the United States. It starts with 1930 to 1933. The top line, gradually rising, represents the number of people assumed to be available for work. The top section is the amount of unemployed. The gray section represents employment of the various groups such as industry and transportation, agriculture trade, management and miscellaneous. The black area is the direct employment of the three recovery agencies—the PWA, CCC and CWA. The chart goes up to January 15.

In January 1934, the American Federation of Labor estimated that there were approximately 50,000,000 people in this country available for work; an increase of about 2,000,000 since 1930. Of these 38,330,000 had regular jobs, leaving about 11,700,000 without regular occupations in private industry, in agriculture or in permanent government service. Against this may be counted the 4,640,000 men and women at work in the Civilian Conservation Corps, Public Works Administration and Civil Works Administration organizations in mid-January when Civil Works Administration activity was at its height. The net difference is about 7,000,000. However, it cannot be assumed that all of the people on the payrolls of the three recovery agencies were previously counted among the unemployed, particularly in agricultural sections.

Since the middle of January the course of employment is not known with any precision. CWA reduced its rolls by nearly 300,000 up to February 15, and another 270,000 by February 22, and PWA activities, especially on road work, have been retarded by bad weather. It appears from preliminary reports that all of this reduction has been absorbed by a corresponding increase in employment in private industry, particularly in those industrial areas in which factory operations are increasing rapidly.

The estimates of employment and unemployment shown on the chart have been made by good statistical procedure and are based upon all available information on employment, principally reports collected by governmental agencies. How much the total figures are in error no one can say until another census of occupations and employment is taken. So far as really accurate statistics go, we have reliable monthly figures covering only about 40 per cent of the gainfully employed.

PRESIDENT ROOSEVELT: That is an awfully interesting chart. Are you going to keep that up from month to month?

MR. RIEFLER: Oh, yes.

PRESIDENT ROOSEVELT: What do your preliminary figures show on February 15?

SECRETARY PERKINS: We have preliminary figures that are very good. They may be somewhat out of the way, but they show a very large increase in employment in February over January. The preliminary figures show 6.1 in employment and 11.02 in payrolls. That should not be murmured because it may be a point higher or two points lower but even so, if it is four points off it is very large. The average for ten years' increase for the month of February is about one. If it remains six we will have made up in one month almost the whole sag of the seasonal decline at the end of the year.

MR. RIEFLER: Payrolls entirely.

SECRETARY PERKINS: Yes, payrolls, entirely. Of course it is uncertain, but the big step-up in the month of February almost leads us to the conclusion that March will also be up. March is naturally a higher month than February.

PRESIDENT ROOSEVELT: And is April up over March?

SECRETARY PERKINS: No, not usually.

PRESIDENT ROOSEVELT: About the same?

SECRETARY PERKINS: About the same or slightly below. March is a peak month; but if April maintains its relative position with regard to March, it is entirely good. There are certain seasonal factors in March. It catches the last of one season, and the beginning of another season.

MR. FAHEY: I want to ask, in connection with that block entitled "Industry and Transportation" if there is any breakdown available by classes there. That is, what the employment is in transportation, for example, in 1930, and also in construction.

MR. RIEFLER: That block is the one where the figures are most complete.

SECRETARY PERKINS: That table gives it in detail.

MR. FAHEY: I would like very much to get it. What have you, roughly, with reference to the construction industry?

MR. RIEFLER: Just guessing, down about 60 per cent and possibly as much as 80 per cent, depending on whether you are thinking of residential work or maintenance work. Maintenance is construction labor. According to the different definitions, the decline is between 60 and 80 per cent.

MR. FAHEY: I am curious about that. So far as separate residential construction is concerned, it has been reported to be down about 9½ per cent.

MR. RIEFLER: The contracts are down about 90 per cent; between 90 and 80 per cent on residential construction alone.

MR. WALKER: Are you going to report on the stimulation of housing?

MR. RIEFLER: I have a short report here on the housing plan:

The Committee on Stimulation of Housing has continued to work along the lines discussed at last week's meeting of the Executive Council. During the past week, particular emphasis has been placed upon checking the plan for opening the mortgage market through a Federal Mutual Mortgage Insurance Corporation. A preliminary draft of a bill incorporating the main features of this plan has been submitted to various leaders in the mortgage field. In addition Mr. Walker and Mr. Riefler went to New York last Friday to discuss the plan with Mr. Henry Bruere, Mr. Charles Miller, Mr. James Perkins, and a representative group of the heads of leading mutual savings banks in New York State. This group promised to study the proposal and give a definite opinion on

157

its merits at a second meeting to be held this weekend.

The Committee has also met with representatives of various other groups interested in real estate financing.

Plans for setting up an organization to conduct a national modernization drive are being developed. At the present time the greatest difficulty in connection with this part of the program is to find a method of financing small home loans on an installment basis without expense to the government.

MR. WALKER: It looks as though we are not going to get any aid from the government on the modernization plan except the cost of personnel. We are trying to have it worked out to see if we can start a plan without any financial aid, and a good many of those we have consulted encourage us very much. I think we have a very good opportunity.

PRESIDENT ROOSEVELT: What would we pay for our share of that running campaign? Could that be done out of Hopkins' funds?

MR. WALKER: I don't know of any place else we could get the money. I think it would cost close around a million dollars.

PRESIDENT ROOSEVELT: Did you talk with Hopkins?

MR. WALKER: Yes, also with Mr. Ickes. We have consulted every department. The Secretary of Agriculture sees the great need for a modernization campaign.

PRESIDENT ROOSEVELT: Would that logically come out of Hopkins' funds or out of Harold's funds?

SECRETARY WALLACE: I think it would come out of Harry's funds.

PRESIDENT ROOSEVELT: Is it Public Works or Relief?

SECRETARY WALLACE: Both.

MR. WALKER: Both have agreed that they will help.

PRESIDENT ROOSEVELT: What do you think, Lew?

DIRECTOR DOUGLAS: I should think most of it would probably come out of Public Works, Mr. President. I can see how some of it might come out of Civil Works as a natural result of the employment that Harry is giving just as an incident to it.

PRESIDENT ROOSEVELT: I don't think Public Works has a million dollars.

DIRECTOR DOUGLAS: They have a reserve, Mr. President. I think Mr. Ickes has a reserve. He is guarding that with great care.

MR. CHAPMAN: Most of it is already earmarked.

MR. WALKER: He indicated he would work it out with Mr. Hopkins and with me.

SECRETARY PERKINS: Just one thing more. It was very unfortunate publicity with regard to this conference. In that publicity it was announced that labor would take a 20 per cent reduction. Of course labor was never consulted, and we were very much surprised to learn that. It will be infinitely more difficult now to even make the proposal. I have had a great many letters from all over the country from various unions that indicated that of course they would not take 20 per cent reductions, and that it might have been negotiated before on the basis of guaranteeing a certain number of weeks' work; and on the basis also that there was to be a corresponding increase in the profits on supplies, transportation, and contracting.

MR. WALKER: At the opening we suggested that it was a confidential meeting; but Arthur Krock had a story the next three or four days.[6]

SECRETARY PERKINS: Who was there?

MR. WALKER: About twenty people; twenty people are acting on this housing thing, from the government—Agricultural Adjustment, RFC, Public Works, Federal Emergency Relief, etc.

SECRETARY PERKINS: Were twenty people at the meeting?

MR. WALKER: About twenty, I think. That 20 per cent was merely for the purpose of illustration.

SECRETARY PERKINS: I know what took place, and it was a perfectly appropriate thing to discuss.

MR. WALKER: Everybody thinks Riefler and I are going to try to cut wages.

SECRETARY PERKINS: It is very unfortunate that anything got out about it.

DIRECTOR DOUGLAS: I know that Arthur Krock, shortly after the meeting, called me on the phone and told me he had the entire story of a meeting that was held in the Department of Commerce, and he understood that I was opposed to a million dollars which the Home Owners' Loan Corporation wanted. I told him that was an old story about the million dollars and that it was no longer a matter of controversy. That was the first time I knew anybody had said anything about the meeting. I said, "Arthur, if you are writing that story, leave the million dollars out of it."

MR. FAHEY: As the Chairman has said, at that meeting special emphasis was placed upon the necessity of regarding the whole thing as being confidential. The Chairman not only emphasized that, but I did, and it was agreed upon. Nothing about Home Owners' or this million dollars ever came up in that meeting— not a word. It is very apparent that somebody who is familiar with the details of that plan gave it to Krock or somebody else, because the details showed that.

SECRETARY PERKINS: I think you ought to ask everybody. Some of these younger

---

[6] The news story mentioned here seems to be one headlined: "Ask Cut Rate Plan to Improve Homes," which appeared on page three of the *New York Times* for Mar. 2, 1934.

	people have a great propensity to talk about things.
PRESIDENT ROOSEVELT:	How many were there?
MR. WALKER:	About eighteen, I imagine, all government people. I don't think it was done designedly. A reporter will get a little from one and then something from another and then say he has the whole story.
	Of course we have had to discuss this with various other people, getting advice and suggestions. We have had a number of commissions down here. The National Real Estate Association and the savings bank men have been down here; and insurance companies have been down here discussing the mortgage feature of this, and it is rather difficult to keep it quiet.
SECRETARY ROPER:	Colonel Howe sent his regards to the members of the Council and said he had very definitely in mind to make the report you are expecting from him, and would be able to report at the next meeting.
MR. WALKER:	The President does not expect there will be any opportunity to get any money from Congress to aid in the overhead financing of this modernization drive, even if we do get the banks to go along on it in a considerable amount.
PRESIDENT ROOSEVELT:	The banks have plenty of money.
MR. WALKER:	The overhead costs of those short loans of a year or a year and a half would take all of their earnings from the cash they advance.
PRESIDENT ROOSEVELT:	I wonder if it is necessary that the overhead be so great.
MR. WALKER:	That is the experience of those who have handled that short term financing. The experience teaches that it cannot be handled for less than six, and some think it goes as high as 12 per cent. Some of the men think we will not be able to do it without some assistance of that kind, and others disagree. If we get the mortgage thing going I think that is going to be a great thing—one of the best things that has been done.
PRESIDENT ROOSEVELT:	That overhead is largely unnecessary or fictitious. You see the fellow on the street, you don't have to go after him.
MR. WALKER:	I think we would have to concentrate on these bankers and tell them your ideas.
PRESIDENT ROOSEVELT:	I would suggest that in the larger communities they begin by reducing the bank presidents' salaries!

Meeting adjourned about 3:45 p.m.

160

Held in the Cabinet Room of the Executive Offices,
The White House, Tuesday, March 20, 1934, at 2:20 p.m.

Present: the President of the United States; the Attorney General;
the Secretary of Agriculture; the Secretary of Commerce; the Secretary
of Labor; the Director of Bureau of the Budget; the Honorable Marriner
S. Eccles, the Undersecretary of the Treasury; the Honorable Oscar
L. Chapman, Assistant Secretary of the Interior; the Administrator of
Agricultural Adjustment; the Administrator of Federal Emergency Relief;
the Chairman of the Board of the Home Owners' Loan Corporation;
the Governor of the Farm Credit Administration; the Honorable
Garland S. Ferguson, Jr., Chairman, Federal Trade Commission; the
Adviser on Consumer Problems; the Economic Adviser; the Honorable
Fred A. Ironside, Jr., Special Assistant; the Executive Director.

[Two additional facets of NEC as a policy-making/policy-
coordinating body are illustrated in this meeting. The first,
its function as a sympathetic audience to F.D.R. His discussion
of the impact of NRA on small businessmen did not really
reach the level of a formal policy decision. It was F.D.R.
thinking out loud about some NRA problems that had been
developing. Other members of the group contributed off-the-
cuff data and opinions and no decision was reached save
that the matter required further investigation. Informal and
inconclusive as this discussion was, this should not be
underestimated in assessing NEC's contribution to policy-
making.

We also see NEC operating as a kind of informal holding
company for subgroups and *ad hoc* committees (like that
planning the housing campaign), which dealt with specific
problems of coordination or policy recommendation.—
Editors' Note.]

MR. WALKER: Shall we begin, gentlemen? I have three or four short reports
which I thought we would go over before the President
comes in. He said he would like to come in after about fifteen
minutes. The reports of the state directors and the housing
report I will hold up until the President's arrival.
The first report is on the Information Service we have
just launched.... [1]

---

[1] The United States Information Service was established in Mar., 1934,
as a division of the NEC, to function as a central clearing house for
information on phases of governmental activity. It turned up later as the
Division of Public Inquiries of OWI during the war. It survived as part of
the Office of Government Reports until 1947 when that was liquidated.

We will send you a written memorandum in connection with the request that you notify all your department assistants and employees in reference to the existence of this Information Service.

MR. FAHEY: Mr. Chairman, on that question I wonder if you have thought of the possible advantage of especially notifying all of the daily newspapers and weekly newspapers of the country of the opening of that bureau, and that any inquiries they have they may address there. I do not know whether that would conflict with your state bureaus. It seems to me it probably would not.

MR. WALKER: In that connection we have notified all of the Washington correspondents, and all of the Washington papers, and we have prepared a press release for the use of the state directors. That did not bring it right down into each and every city, so we depended upon the state directors to publicize it. We are going to have an Information Service in each state as well.

MR. FAHEY: It might bring about some conflict with your information bureaus in each state—I do not know—but in the ordinary course of business a good many inquiries come in to the newspapers, through their letter-box columns and otherwise, asking for information about governmental affairs, and their method has been in the past usually to write direct to the bureaus and make inquiry or to inquire through their correspondent here if they have one; and it seems to me that the existence of a centralized bureau is something that might well be brought to the attention of the managing editors of these newspapers.

MR. WALKER: There are not enough of them to make it a serious matter. I think we can do that. I think it is a good suggestion.

MR. FAHEY: It is easy enough to get a list of managing editors of all the newspapers in the country, and a letter sent to the responsible man on the paper is something that ought to go to him and have his attention.

SECRETARY ROPER: Supplementing what Mr. Fahey says, I am wondering whether it might not be well to acquaint ourselves with the number of services like the Haskins Service here. That type of service is constantly receiving inquiries and we ought to endeavor to put them into the right channel to get the information to answer those inquiries. Haskins, I think, when he doesn't get enough inquiries, makes up some. He has a field service that covers a considerable area. I think there are a number of such special-column services throughout the country and I believe that the clipping bureau under Colonel Howe in our building[2]—I forget the name of the lady in charge, but I am sure she could acquaint your personnel with the number of such services and the managers of such services. I believe that is a very important point.

There are so many of these young fellows running these local inquiries for the press that haven't had the experience they should have. As an illustration, I was called up some nights ago and asked to tell a certain young man what the primary system is. That just shows how much needed this thing is. I think that is all.

MR. WALKER: We shall be very glad to follow the suggestions.... We would like to get a little advice from some of you present with reference to whether or not we should provide the senators and members of Congress with this manual.[3] We have had a number of requests from them. They cost us about eighty cents apiece, but the upkeep is going to be considerably more. I would like to get an expression from the Attorney General, and the Secretaries of Commerce, Labor, and Agriculture at least, as to whether we should provide all the members of Congress and the senators with these manuals.

ATTORNEY GENERAL CUMMINGS: How many will be published? I mean how frequently.

MR. WALKER: We keep them up to date. It is a loose-leaf document. We are keeping up to date with the new rules and regulations going out from each of the departments—keeping it a current affair.

ATTORNEY GENERAL CUMMINGS: You might supply it to those congressmen and senators who would like to have it.

MR. WALKER: If we send it to some and others did not get it, there might be a fuss about it.

ATTORNEY GENERAL CUMMINGS: You might consider asking them whether they would like to have it and if so supply it to them.

MR. WALKER: How many requests have we had from that direction?

MR. IRONSIDE: About 25, sir.

ATTORNEY GENERAL CUMMINGS: They are clearly entitled to it, I should think, but a good

---

[2] This became known as Louis Howe's "Daily Bugle"—a little newspaper composed of clippings from the daily press and circulated by Howe to the President and government officials. The clippings came from about 750 newspapers published in every city with a population of 25,000 or more. F.D.R. was kept informed of public reactions as none of his predecessors had been. See W. F. Binkley, *The President and Congress* (New York, 1947), p. 249.

[3] The loose-leaf predecessor to the *U.S. Government Organization Manual*, containing concise descriptions of the functions of all government agencies with particular emphasis upon the emergency agencies. See earlier note, p. 52.

many might not use it.

MR. WALKER: It has been provided for the Congressional Library.

DIRECTOR DOUGLAS: I should think that ought to be supplied to congressmen and senators.

ATTORNEY GENERAL CUMMINGS: You might circularize them and say that the manuals will be supplied to those who ask for them so that they will know they are getting something worth while, and treat it as something more than just a routine matter.

SECRETARY ROPER: I think that is about right. Are we furnishing them to libraries, for instance?

MR. WALKER: Not to public libraries. We are asking for a ruling of the Comptroller General on account of the loose-leaf feature of the manuals. We have no ruling yet as to what we can sell it to the public for. He will give us a decision on that. When we get that decision we will fix a price on it.

Here is a report of the work of the Consumers' Council. Next is the adjustment of complaints by the National Emergency Council . . . .

The President asked to be called in when we are ready to proceed with the report of the state directors. Following that we have the Housing Report, so I will tell the President we are ready for him.

DIRECTOR DOUGLAS: While we are waiting would you like me to read a report on the question of personnel in Emergency agencies?

MR. WALKER: I think you might go ahead with that.

DIRECTOR DOUGLAS: You remember you authorized a special committee some time ago to look into the question of classification of employees of Emergency organizations. The Comptroller General has made several rulings in connection with it. (*Director Douglas then read part of his report before the President arrived.*)

PRESIDENT ROOSEVELT: Well, how far have you gone?

MR. WALKER: The Director of the Budget is just reporting on the classification of personnel. I don't know whether the President wants to go into that.

PRESIDENT ROOSEVELT: Have you something definite on that?

DIRECTOR DOUGLAS: Yes, a final recommendation subject to your approval.

PRESIDENT ROOSEVELT: If everybody will agree on it I probably will too. Go ahead.

DIRECTOR DOUGLAS (*After going over the main points of his report again*): Now, if the Emergency Council agrees with these recommendations, we will be very glad to submit them then to the President for an Executive Order. There is one further recommendation and that is that the old Order, No. 6440, which you signed last fall classifying these positions, be modified in one further

respect, and that is that the salaries be "not in excess of."
The reason for that is that there are certain emergency
employees, as coast and geodetic survey, where it is not
desirable to pay the salaries fixed by that schedule. If the
order reads "not in excess of" there can still be paid to those
employees less than the amount provided in that schedule.
I think that is advisable.

To summarize the recommendations they are, first that there
be set up some control; second, that there be certain groups
exempted; and third, that the order read, "not in excess of."[4]

ORNEY GENERAL CUMMINGS: Does that skirt around the rule of the Comptroller General?

DIRECTOR DOUGLAS: It has been worked out in connection with the Comptroller
General.

PRESIDENT ROOSEVELT: Has anybody any thoughts on that? Is there anybody whose
organization will be so affected that it will have to be
completely reorganized?

ORNEY GENERAL CUMMINGS: It sounds all right, but it hits in so many unexpected directions
that I would like to study it.

SECRETARY ROPER: I would like to have a copy of it.

PRESIDENT ROOSEVELT: Can you get a copy to everybody, and get action so that I
can take action before I go away a week from today?

DIRECTOR DOUGLAS: I think so.

PRESIDENT ROOSEVELT: There is one thing I want to inject here—something that
affects NRA and the consumers and the general policies of
the codes, very materially in a great many respects, and the
Labor Department and others. We are going ahead on these
codes with a general rule of thumb in regard to wages, and
of course I have been seeing a great many people—not as
many as you have been seeing in NRA, for instance—but a
great many who are representing the small manufacturers
of the country, people who have their plants in small
communities—and I am talking about small communities.
There seems to be a general feeling among them that they are
being driven to the wall because in that small community
they have to pay under the code and under the general
standard scale of the industry a rate of pay which is a much
larger finance than that carried in the large communities.
They make this point, and it is worthwhile considering (I do
not know whether the figures are anywhere near correct or

---

[4] For a discussion of the control functions, regarding emergency
personnel, of the Executive Council and its successor, the National
Emergency Council, see President's Committee on Administrative
Management, *Report with Special Studies* (Washington, 1937), p. 86 ff.

not), that one reason why in the small communities of the country that have small plants with 10, 20, 30, 40, or 50 employees the burden is heavier than in the large communities is the obvious economic reason that rents and food in those communities cost that much less. There is a good deal of fundamental economy in connection with this. The girl, for instance, who is getting $12.00 in a Georgia cotton mill in a town of 3,500 population is getting infinitely more than the girl in Fall River who is getting $13.00. There is no question about that. In that particular community, the small cotton mill is driven out of business because they haven't got the organization and size of the larger cotton mill about 30 miles away in La Grange, Georgia, where they have 30,000 people and a large consolidated plant. The little fellow is being driven out because of the scale in the small community. Of course that is one thing we want to avoid.

The other general idea is that we want to lift the level of Georgia because it has been too low; but is it worthwhile doing it if we are going to drive out the small employers of labor? It is a question of the big community against the little community, big business against little business. Very careful study ought to be given to it. I do not know that you have given very much study to that, Mary [Rumsey], in NRA. I do know Miss Perkins has given a good deal of study to it.

MRS. RUMSEY: That question has to be handled separately.

SECRETARY PERKINS: I don't think we ought to keep our minds riveted upon the desirability of the small enterprise. If you are going to impose a standard, it ought to be imposed for other reasons than simply the size of the industry. It ought to be based on the needs of the community and the productive capacity and purchasing power of the workers in it. I think it ought to be studied with great care but not necessarily with the thought in mind of preserving the small industries. Frequently it is not desirable, except as an emergency measure. I would recognize it as an emergency measure not to wipe out a small, inefficient mill because it would upset a whole community, and you should postpone the time of upsetting that community until a later time when there is more opportunity for employment.

PRESIDENT ROOSEVELT: I would not use the term "small, inefficient mill" because the small mill may be an efficient mill, but it has not the volume of goods to sell. Its overhead is especially high for its volume of production.

SECRETARY PERKINS: They vary a great deal between themselves. Some are efficient and some inefficient. Some of them, if they are permitted to pay the lower labor costs, have an unfair advantage over the others. I think those things require extraordinarily careful study.

SECRETARY WALLACE: Isn't it a question of real wages as compared with monetary wages?

SECRETARY PERKINS: That is quite true, but there is this other factor. When you come to the production of cotton cloth, if the labor cost is not equalized, you get the advantage in the production and in the sale of the yardage from those mills that happen to be located in the small communities where a low monetary wage is paid.

PRESIDENT ROOSEVELT: Perhaps cotton is not a fair criterion to take, because the smallest cotton mill is a large employer of labor. No cotton mill employs as low as 80 people.

MR. FERGUSON: The Federal Trade Commission is making an investigation in regard to sawmills, particularly in the South, right along that line. A number of complaints came in to NRA that sawmills were being forced out of business on account of the codes, and the NRA requested us to make an investigation. We have now about six men going through the Southern states where the small mills are located. We should have that invesigation in a short time.

SECRETARY ROPER: I think you put your finger on the right spot when you say it must be studied from the standpoint of the difference in the expense of living.

PRESIDENT ROOSEVELT: Of course, there is one school of thought that says in spite of the very complicated factors in working up an index the whole thing can be sifted down to about two factors; one is rent and the other is food.

SECRETARY WALLACE: And there are some intangibles that you cannot measure.

PRESIDENT ROOSEVELT: But you can reduce the number of factors—intangible and all the other things—to a small number.

SECRETARY WALLACE: There are certain compensations which these workers have in smaller places which are not enjoyed in larger places.

MR. RIEFLER: I have some figures indicating that large plants are increasing and small plants decreasing. I have asked for more figures and we can try to find out from other places.

SECRETARY ROPER: I have had a number of complaints from the knitting industries, especially in the mountain regions of Tennessee and Kentucky, and the information I get is that there is a tendency brought about by this condition to drive the small industry to the large center, which is directly opposed to the thing we wish to do.

SECRETARY PERKINS: How does it do that?

SECRETARY ROPER: Because they cannot adjust themselves because of this differential in the small centers, and they are closing their plants, and the business is going into the large centers. It is a matter that requires very careful consideration.

PRESIDENT ROOSEVELT: I think it is something that should be given immediate study, and also we have to take into consideration from the Subsistence Homesteads point of view, moving people out of stranded centers. They are trying to encourage the small industries in the small towns. I had the National Manufacturers Association in this afternoon, and I asked them five questions. They were talking about Section 7a, and objections to the Wagner Bill.[5] I said, "I have been in touch with you people now for about 23 years. So far as I know, the National Manufacturers Association has never made a study or taken a stand on minimum wage during that entire period; has never made a study or taken a stand on lowering hours which were excessive during that entire period; you have never made a study or taken a stand on child labor; you have never made a study or taken a stand on workman's compensation, except adversely; you have never made a study or taken a stand on unemployment insurance, except adversely. That is a very simple record of your Association for the past 23 years. Correct me if I am wrong." They said, "No, you are right." I said, "What do you think of the concentation of more people in the big centers?" They said, "We have never studied that." I said, "Why the hell haven't you?" They said, "We are, in the main, in favor of decentralization of industry." I said, "Why don't you study it?" They said, "All right, we will go out and study that."

That has been the attitude of the National Manufacturers Association and the United States Chamber of Commerce during all the time they have been in existence. I believe we can get them to come along with us on this. It is a great bunch, but you have to "talk turkey" to them.

What is the effect of the codes at the present time on forcing the little fellows in the little community, not the little fellow

[5] The reference is to Section 7a of the National Industrial Recovery Act which, among other things, guaranteed labor the right to organize. The Wagner Bill was an early version of the proposal which was finally enacted in 1935 as the National Labor Relations Act.

in the big community? That is a different thing, but the man who employs 50 people or less—don't you think that is a pretty good figure to take?

SECRETARY PERKINS: We must remember that the great bulk of employment in this country comes from employers who employ large numbers.

MR. FAHEY: Is it more than half?

SECRETARY PERKINS: I think it is considerably more than half. At this moment my memory doesn't quite serve me for the country as a whole, but in the industrial states it is much over half.

MR. FAHEY: I am quite confident that is not so in all of them.

PRESIDENT ROOSEVELT: How many people do you have to employ to get under the codes?

SECRETARY PERKINS: Five or more, I think.

PRESIDENT ROOSEVELT: You have to have some measure for those from six to fifty.

MR. RIEFLER: In towns of 2,500 and less.

PRESIDENT ROOSEVELT: I would say 5,000 or less.

SECRETARY PERKINS: But that is where you get a large number of small employers.

PRESIDENT ROOSEVELT: I am not talking about five people or less. Take the case of a knitting mill in Troy, New York, where they make sweaters and they employ thirty people. They claim that they have been put out of business. It is just one little tiny knitting mill that makes sweaters.

MR. FAHEY: Mr. President, there certainly can be no debate on the proposal that the issue raised ought to have careful study and as quickly as possible because it is having an effect. How widespread it is, it is perhaps difficult to say, but it is having an effect and it is a great question whether it is in the common interest that a substantial number of such establishments should be forced out of business. There can be no doubt that under present circumstances they are being snuffed out in the smaller communities, and they have a tremendous effect on the economic conditions in those communities. Take the state of Massachusetts. You may recall, I said a few weeks ago we have approximately 9,900 industries classified, on which Massachusetts has been gathering figures for many, many years, and of that 9,900-odd (it is almost 10,000), less than 200 of them employ in excess of 500 people in normal times, but more than half of the employees are in smaller groups. As I recall it, about 30 per cent employ less than a hundred. Of course, in our state, industry developed quite actively in the smaller towns and the whole town was built about the industry, and then one or two more added; and when you undermine those, the effect upon the valuation and everything social in the place is widespread. Your schools are curtailed and a number of teachers thrown out of employment and that sort of thing. There was one very sharp illustration of that in Fitchburg, which is a small city, about 30,000. When a couple of yarn mills shut down, and a manufacturing company also, school teachers were thrown out of work and all that sort of thing. It had a disastrous effect. The same thing happened in Clinton and a dozen other towns of fifteen or sixteen thousand inhabitants. The distress of the people has been tremendous.

My point is just this. As you were saying a while ago, it may be that under more normal circumstances there would be reasons for not bothering our heads about these industries if they would go out in the natural course of events; but in present circumstances, if they are snuffed out rapidly they aggravate the problem in every way.

SECRETARY PERKINS: That, of course, was the main reason for such clauses in the codes that limit production. The limitation of production was meant to preserve just exactly these small industries which were being rapidly put out of the picture under the situation a year ago. I think you are right that it should be studied carefully at this time. I assumed that was being done.

PRESIDENT ROOSEVELT: We have this committee on small industries that is at work at the present time. Mr. Darrow is, I think, the chairman of it.[6]

SECRETARY PERKINS: We have accumulated in the Department of Labor certain very important information which we have been collecting and putting together for the purpose of guiding our own work, some of which relates to this problem, and I have been thinking of saying to Mr. Riefler that I wished he would go over it with us and decide what use, if any, ought to be made of the study up to this time. It is not to be given out to the public at this time.

SECRETARY WALLACE: Mr. Darrow is not well-equipped for doing this work.

PRESIDENT ROOSEVELT: No, he is not.

---

[6] The real issue here is whether or not NRA codes were operating to foster monopoly. The National Recovery Review Board, headed by the celebrated trial lawyer, Clarence Darrow, was set up Mar. 7, 1934, to learn if any of the NRA codes were "designed to promote monopolies or to eliminate or oppress small enterprises or operate to discriminate against them." See Basil Rauch, *The History of the New Deal* (New York, 1944), pp. 123-126 for a discussion of this committee and the reorganization of the NRA that followed its report. See also Arthur M. Schlesinger, Jr., *The Age of Roosevelt: The Coming of the New Deal* (Boston, 1959), pp. 132-135.

MR. ECCLES: The small industries haven't the capital to keep going. The large industries are possibly operating at a loss just as the small ones are, but the large industries are well-financed, and they are able to continue in spite of the loss and take advantage of the situation as to eliminate the small industries; whereas if there was sufficient employment and volume of business, the little industry would survive as well as the large industry.

SECRETARY PERKINS: The little industry springs up in times of great production.

PRESIDENT ROOSEVELT: There are a lot of little industries which have been going a long time which are being squeezed out by unfair practices. Right next to my home town, where Mr. Ogden Mills comes from, they have had a great many years a family in the third generation of running an ice tool factory, making tools for harvesting natural ice. For many years, they had a very nice business and employed an average of 16 people to whom they paid about $100 a month. They could rent houses there for $10.00 a month, nice little houses. While in Poughkeepsie, about 12 miles away, houses were $20.00 a month. In the smaller town, milk was 5¢ a quart while in Poughkeepsie it was 12¢ a quart. So their $100 a month was at least equivalent of $125 or $130 a month in a big city only 12 miles away. In about 1929, some big steel tool company started in and dumped their big company tools into the market of this small company and put them out of business. The big company was selling below cost in order to do that.

SECRETARY PERKINS: Electric refrigeration has something to do with it, too.

PRESIDENT ROOSEVELT: There is just as much use for natural ice as there was years ago. That was not a factor entering into this case.

DIRECTOR DOUGLAS: In the credit banks making loans to small industries, the working capital of the larger corporations had been diminished by about 25 per cent, whereas the working capital of the smaller corporations had been diminished 48 per cent during the depression. That may be a contributing cause. There may be a whole lot of things that enter into the situation. In the same study, as I recall the figures—I don't want to say that these are the figures, but as I recall—70 per cent of the industries in the country employ 250 men or less. I was wondering whether instead of limiting to 50 employees it might not be better to set the number of employees a little higher than 50.

MR. FAHEY: I think that is very desirable, because the small industries are apparently not necessarily those which have only a handful of employees. From a competitive standpoint in many lines, the industry that is doing a business of a couple of million dollars a year is a small industry in comparison with its competitor which is doing beyond two or three hundred million dollars a year.

DIRECTOR DOUGLAS: I don't know whether that has any bearing on the limitation of 50 employees or whether it might be desirable to increase the number.

PRESIDENT ROOSEVELT: Would you make it a hundred or less?

SECRETARY PERKINS: I think you better leave it pretty free for a committee to handle. They will break it down into two or three groups.

PRESIDENT ROOSEVELT: I would not go over a hundred.

SECRETARY PERKINS: Three hundred is a small industry.

PRESIDENT ROOSEVELT: If you have 300 employees in one plant, you are in a fair-sized community right away.

SECRETARY PERKINS: It makes a very nice industrial unit, though.

PRESIDENT ROOSEVELT: I am thinking of the little fellow. Frank will get in touch with General Johnson on this thing.

ATTORNEY GENERAL CUMMINGS: The Connecticut Valley is full of little factories of 20, 25, or 30 employees. They have been there for generations in some instances, and they are having a pretty tough time.

PRESIDENT ROOSEVELT: What is the next question?

MR. WALKER: I have a question here of great importance.

PRESIDENT ROOSEVELT: The report from the state directors?

MR. WALKER: Yes, about the emergency activities.

(President Roosevelt then read the memorandum.) ...

PRESIDENT ROOSEVELT: Do we have a check on the complaints they make here?

MR. WALKER: We keep a list of all the complaints received and all complaints adjusted. As soon as the complaint comes in, it goes directly to the agency involved, with a request for action. We get a report back from the state director about the action.

PRESIDENT ROOSEVELT: What is the next thing?

MR. WALKER: The next thing is the Housing Report.... [which was read by the President]. We would like to get some action on that today.

We have taken this up with the committee, Mr. President, and have gone into it quite thoroughly. I think it is the unanimous opinion of the committee at this time that we should go ahead with this. The recommendation is made that the Emergency Council start organizing this. We think if it is going to be started, it should be started immediately.

PRESIDENT ROOSEVELT: This would cost the federal government nothing except the million dollars for the campaign?

MR. WALKER: Yes, sir, it would have to be handled by the credit agencies out in the field. We have discussed it with the Treasury, the CWA, and others, and the only money we are asking for is $1,000,000 for the overhead cost.

PRESIDENT ROOSEVELT: Did the committee consider the matter of improving homes in the various states?

MR. WALKER: We have had discussions with the savings bank institutions, with the insurance people, with a number of banks, and also with practically every member of the Emergency Council— at least every member who is active in the housing campaign. It was discussed with a number of credit agencies, building and loan associations, and also with people who had been in contact with the campaign in Philadelphia. We also have reports on the Rochester and Cleveland campaigns. We had men from the Philadelphia campaign at the Council meeting a week ago, and they are very anxious to take part in this. They went through it a year ago, starting in February, and the campaign ran until the end of July, and they got pledges of about $21,000,000 with about 90 per cent fulfillment.

THE PRESIDENT: What do you think, John? You are in the home end of it.

MR. FAHEY: Mr. President, from the standpoint of employment and the whole Recovery program, I don't think there is anything quite so important as stimulating the revival of the construction industry; and the largest part is in the field of housing, without any question. I think it is true that a campaign throughout the country in connection with such an effort can be very helpful if it is well-organized and we don't go too far. Frankly, I don't believe that such a campaign will be safe or wise unless we clear the financial channels and see that the money is coming in. If we started such a thing and the financing was not forthcoming, it would have a very disastrous effect, in my opinion. It would be unsafe and unwise unless enough force is put behind it to make it go over, because if it fails, by next fall you would have to face very serious results from it. I do believe—and I think the discussion so far has given us some confidence in it—that plans can be worked out to stimulate the private lending agencies into action here. But frankly, Mr. President, I don't believe that that will come about without some type of government backing. How little backing we can give without risk is something that we have got to explore; but I do think we might just as well realize at the beginning that some risk has got to be taken in some way, either through the working out of a new

173

mortgage instrument such as suggested here and on which very interesting progress is being made, or some type of backing of commercial banks to stampede them into use of unused funds. The quicker we can get at that the better, in my judgment, because time is running against us. Spring will be here before we know it.

PRESIDENT ROOSEVELT: We talked two weeks ago about the timing of this. Someone made the suggestion that more work should be planned during the winter time.

MR. FAHEY: That is true, but no matter what we do now, any effort undertaken will go along so far into the end of the year, if it is cumulative as it should be, that I would like to see a large part of the results on this come after August, but I do think you can get a good deal of action this spring and summer and take up some of the slack caused by the dropping off of CWA.

PRESIDENT ROOSEVELT: You suggest, then, first a unified housing agency.

MR. WALKER: That is for the long term.

PRESIDENT ROOSEVELT: Then we can leave that out for the present. Then you come to mortgage legislation. That committee on legislation would develop the plans for financing.

MR. FAHEY: There is a question of policies. It is going to take a little time, and I think the planning should go hand in hand, because I assume that in less than two weeks after you have a financial plan which is acceptable, you want to be ready to go just as fast as you can. Consequently, the time saved in making the plans to go along with it is very useful.

PRESIDENT ROOSEVELT: What about your finance committee?

MR. WALKER: In discussing it, we suggested that the Director of the Budget act on that, and let him pick up his own committee. Then there would be the committee on reduction of costs of modernization and repair.

MR. FAHEY: In the discussion of this committee setup which was finished last night, it was suggested that the chairman, Mr. Walker, might find it desirable to consolidate some of them.

PRESIDENT ROOSEVELT: If No. 6 and No. 2 could be put together it might save trouble, and the same with No. 8. Why can't that be in with No. 5?[7]

MR. WALKER: That is good.

---

[7] Two types of committees seem to have functioned under NEC—interdepartmental coordinating committees (both *ad hoc*, and standing committees later brought in under NEC), and committees set up to do policy-planning spade work.

SECRETARY PERKINS: It is really community planning; it is not reduction of costs.

PRESIDENT ROOSEVELT: Does anybody wish to be heard in the negative?

SECRETARY PERKINS: I think this is likely to be just another thing in which none of us are responsible and which we will work on when we have time and inclination. It needs continual attention. It needs to be somebody's main concern. Otherwise, we will be helpful and do what we can and then forget about it.

DIRECTOR DOUGLAS: Aren't these committees just for the purpose of organizing the campaign? I would suspect that after the organization had been completed, the initial movement would probably come, and I think should come, from forces or agencies outside of the government rather than from agencies within the government so that it does not have the color of a ballyhoo campaign originating within the administration. I think that is a protection for you, Mr. President.

PRESIDENT ROOSEVELT: There is good psychology in that. We are doing this at the request of a lot of people and it happens to work in with the government plan.

DIRECTOR DOUGLAS: After that is done, the administration can baptize it and support it, and the driving force and responsibility would then be imposed on outside agencies.

MR. FAHEY: You have to tie them together. If you give them a start, you have the lumber and material and other people here who are ready to use funds of their own in their own particular direction. But you have to unite them in a common effort and see that they do not conflict.

PRESIDENT ROOSEVELT: Henry, what do you think?

SECRETARY WALLACE: I think there is a long-time planning effect, and I am inclined to agree with Lew that we should get as much initiative from outside as possible. I think it is going to be rather essential to have that million dollars in order to coordinate the thing. Time is very much the essence of it, if this is going to come in and fill up the gap after the first of August.

PRESIDENT ROOSEVELT: Your thought is that we should go ahead and appoint these committees and have them work four or five days and have them bring in a definite report two weeks from today with a definite plan.

MR. WALKER: We might do it a week from today, before you leave. We could get these committees started and functioning, elect some outstanding person to head the whole thing up and effect the organization after we get our plans ready, and then go on into the outside field for most of our committees. I think that would be a very effective way of doing it. I think

175

	we can elect somebody from outside, somebody from heavy industries.
SECRETARY PERKINS:	I think it may offer the way to start something that will be very important to us later. It is the beginning of a plan on which we can build. I think it is essential to begin now.
PRESIDENT ROOSEVELT:	What do you know about Charles Edison?
SECRETARY PERKINS:	Nothing very important.
PRESIDENT ROOSEVELT:	Not very heavy?
SECRETARY PERKINS:	He has loomed large in the NRA councils because he has sold himself as the leader of New Jersey, but, of course, New Jersey doesn't know that he is its leader. At least, that is the report that comes to me. He is not being heard of in New Jersey.
PRESIDENT ROOSEVELT:	After these committees are ready to bring in what might be called a consolidated report, if we can get some awfully good man to tie the whole thing together, that is what we want to do.
SECRETARY PERKINS:	I told you the other day who I thought it should be.
PRESIDENT ROOSEVELT:	And thereby hang several tales.
MR. WALKER:	Mr. [Edward A.] Filene is coming in to talk to us. He has made a very interesting tour of the country, and we promised him he would have a chance to say a few words to the Emergency Council in regard to what he had seen, and make any suggestions he would like to make. He might be helpful in making certain surveys. If you want to avail yourselves of the service of his organization, just call on him. He wants to do something for us. He is a great friend of Mr. Fahey's.[8]
SECRETARY ROPER:	It is very important that this be properly interpreted to the people.
PRESIDENT ROOSEVELT:	I would say no publicity yet.
MR. WALKER:	The article two or three weeks ago was the only thing.
PRESIDENT ROOSEVELT:	I think we should be terribly careful.
MR. FAHEY:	I think it is important that it should be understood that no publicity will be released on this until you approve it. There is one other warning I should like to offer, and that is, I doubt if we are going to have financial plans next week.
PRESIDENT ROOSEVELT:	But let's try for it. (*The President then left the room.*)

[8] Edward A. Filene was a wealthy Boston merchant and business man of liberal views who was an ardent supporter of President Roosevelt and his policies. He was director of NRA for Massachusetts. He made many radio and other addresses in support of the President and his program, going so far at one point as to rent at his own expense 55 bill boards in and around Boston which urged public support for F.D.R. He is a good example of the kind of enthusiasm the New Deal and Roosevelt himself aroused in otherwise disinterested individuals.

176

MR. FAHEY: Do we understand that we have the President's approval of these preliminary steps?

MR. WALKER: That is what the President says.

Mr. Filene is going to make a report.... We told Mr. Filene we would give him 15 minutes to give us a report on his trip.

MR. FILENE: What happened, I made a trip west, making a study of business in the big cities, and when I came back and reported to the President on it, he asked me to serve with the Emergency Council; but there seems to have been some mistake about it and Mr. Walker, with his efficient and kindly heart, let me down easily. I ought not to take up your time; I don't see any reason why I should. I will just get out, as there is evidently some mistake or misunderstanding. The President spoke to Mr. McIntyre. I don't think the mistake was wholly on my part, but I am serving the NRA with all my time and energy. I do think the best service I could do now is to let you do your own business without forcing on you my observation, which is what most of it is in these reports which I have prepared. Don't you think that is the best way to handle the situation?

MR. WALKER: I think the members would like to get your observations, Mr. Filene.

ORNEY GENERAL CUMMINGS: Have you copies enough so that they can be distributed to the members? I would like to see the report, and I would be very glad to hear a few words from Mr. Filene as to the high spots.

MR. FAHEY: I think that would be very helpful.

MR. FILENE: There is nothing in the world that will make me diminish my efforts for the Recovery Act and the new program. If there is no mistake—

MR. WALKER: I don't think there is any mistake, Mr. Filene. You came here at my request. I don't think there is any mistake about it at all.

MR. FILENE: This trip of mine was made through Chicago, St. Louis, Kansas City, Denver, Salt Lake City, San Francisco, Los Angeles, Dallas, Houston, New Orleans, Atlanta, Louisville, Cincinatti, and Cleveland. I made a statement of it for General Johnson's labor meeting that he had called, and presented it to the President. The study was a thorough one in every city. The Chambers of Commerce arranged for groups of business men to attend prearranged meetings running up from 150 to 200. In Chicago, for instance, the vice-president of one of the big banks of the country got together a group of picked leaders; there were 14 of them.

In every city, the heads of the labor movement were by pre-arrangement in attendance at meetings lasting one or two hours. These meetings represented the best cross-section in the country of white-collar and other workers, so that it was a fairly good study. I think probably I got a good cross-section of what the opinion of the country is. The opinion that will be most valuable to you is that the country is definitely behind the President's Recovery plan; anything the President makes the people understand he wants, they will not oppose. Even in elections, no man can win if he tries to make a fight on the basis of his opposition to the President. That was the first thing. Then the next thing is that the old Blue Eagle is largely disappearing, and there is a definite and immediate need of a new eagle—the Code Eagle[9]—and if it is pushed vigorously with a radio statement of the President and General Johnson, the people are ready to get behind it again; and in this case, you could get them to get the Eagle habit and buy only at the Eagle stores, which would be not only good in itself, but would be a source of strength in the future for carrying out the plans of the President.

There was a general backing of the President's monetary policy. A lot of people said—bankers as well as business men—that they do not understand it, but it is working well, and they are for it. There was practically no opposition.

There was opposition to the Security Act,[10] but that was largely confined to the bankers and secretaries of Chambers of Commerce and some of the leading officers of Chambers of Commerce, and it is my conclusion that what is needed is a further program of public enlightenment.

The great danger that was developed everywhere was the labor question. There was very bitter feeling about the lack of enforcement of codes and there was a definite feeling on the part of a great many that labor should not be allowed to organize,[11] the traditional thinking being that labor unions had no right of existence, while business men insisted that they had a right to organize and be represented by lawyers; but labor has not convinced business men that they are doing their duty in allowing labor to get much control, because they claim that labor cannot control its own members

[9] Filene refers to the need for securing better compliance with NRA codes.
[10] The Securities Act, passed May 27, 1933, was designed to protect the public from misrepresentation and manipulation in the issuance of stock.
[11] Section 7a of the National Industrial Recovery Act permitted collective bargaining by unions.

adequately, and that especially some of the new unions have very radical red elements; and labor leaders themselves admit that things are being done by uninformed new leaders that are inimical to the best interests of labor.

The greater enforcement of codes has got to come; and that means that there is an over-centralization of power in the Recovery Act; and my recognition of the evidence on this trip shows that the power should be in every state put under one man with ample power and ample backing, and that he should be promptly fired if he could not do the job adequately, because there is no time to let a man experiment. Such men can be found.

Meeting adjourned at 4:30 p.m.

Held in the Cabinet Room of the Executive Offices,
The White House, Tuesday, April 17, 1934, at 2:07 p.m.

Present: the Secretary of Commerce; the Secretary of Labor; the
Director of the Bureau of the Budget; the Honorable Harold M. Stephens,
Assistant Attorney General; the Honorable John Dickinson, Assistant
Secretary of Commerce; the Administrator of Agricultural Adjustment;
the Administrator of Federal Emergency Relief; the Chairman of the
Board of the Home Owners' Loan Corporation; the Governor of the Farm
Credit Administration; the Honorable Garland S. Ferguson Jr., Chairman
of the Federal Trade Commission; the Honorable Ewin Lamar Davis,
Vice-Chairman of the Federal Trade Commission; the Adviser on
Consumer Problems; the Honorable Dexter Keezer, Chief of the
Consumers Division, National Emergency Council; the Economic
Adviser; the Executive Director.

[The President did not attend this meeting and as a result—
(note Executive Director Walker's final comment)—rather
minor "housekeeping" questions were considered rather than
matters of major importance. Not all of the subjects raised
were trivial, however. For example, the idea for a "Gazette" to
bring together all Executive Orders in one accessible publication foreshadowed the establishment of the *Federal Register*
by an act of Congress in July 1935. Yet in general, this
meeting illustrates that the presence or absence of the President
at NEC sessions had much to do with the importance of the
business transacted. His absence meant that important matters
were saved for a later occasion, and also diminished the
interest of the participants in the discussions.—Editors' Note.]

MR. WALKER: I think we might as well proceed, in view of the fact that
some members of the Cabinet are attending the luncheon
being given to the President of Haiti.
First on the agenda is the report on the Information
Service . . . .
The schedule indicates distribution of mail from all except
five states. We are receiving very fine cooperation from a
great many of the departments with reference to this, and
the service is broadening out very considerably in the past
two or three weeks as it goes on.
We have a suggestion from the Department of Commerce
with reference to an official gazette . . . .

Mr. Dickinson is here. The suggestion came from the Department of Commerce, from him and the Secretary, and we might hear from him on it at this point.

MR. DICKINSON: I don't think really, Mr. Director, there is very much more to say beyond what is contained in your report. I don't know that the Department of Commerce is really the proper agency to take the lead in this matter, but what it has done was purely informal and after consultation with Judge Stephens, from the Department of Justice, who is familiar with this general problem.

So many proclamations and Executive Orders and departmental regulations that have the force of law are coming out every day that many of the public officials who are expected to administer them cannot keep up with them because they come from scattered and separate places and oftentimes it is difficult to find out which ones have been superseded by others or have been repealed. That is true especially of the field offices of the government, the District Attorneys, the Federal Courts, and collectors of customs. But it is also true, to a very considerable extent, of the offices right here in Washington. The new rules are not supplied to public officials in other departments with any permanence or regularity, and, in consequence, a great many inquiries come in here to Washington from the field that ought not to have to come in. And the people here in Washington themselves are kept in confusion on the matter. An official gazette,[1] if supplemented by appropriate cumulative indices, would indicate which are in effect and which had been superceded. Also, the gazette would serve as a medium for the publication of official notices which now are oftentimes published in very irregular ways in the newspapers or other ways.

Of course, with the Director of the Budget sitting down here at the end of the table, the matter of expense becomes of special importance; but I think it would be possible to publish a gazette of this kind certainly for less than $100,000 a year, which might very well be entirely recovered because a lot of this stuff is published already. The only thing is that

---

[1] Forerunner of the *Federal Register* provided for by act of Congress following criticism of the haphazard handling of Executive Orders and the like. The Federal Register Act was signed by the President on July 26, 1935. Responsibility for the task was lodged with the National Archives which had, in turn, been set up in June 1934. The Department of Commerce, which originated this gazette idea, was therefore not involved when the idea was finally implemented.

181

it is published in irregular, sporadic places where you don't know where to look for it—one department prints its stuff in one way and another department prints its material in another way—and if it were all brought together you would not be spending any more money than you are spending now. There would be a saving in the public notices, and you could get a very considerable number of subscriptions from lawyers and people of that kind who would be interested in having the gazette; I suggest that in all probability it might very well come out even, without any expense to the government; and when you reflect that the *Congressional Record* costs nearly a million dollars a year, it is a question whether this expenditure of $25,000 or $50,000 might not more than make up for what it costs by the convenience.

MR. WALKER: This suggestion came from your Department, Mr. Secretary of Commerce. Do you have any suggestions with reference to it?

SECRETARY ROPER: I think my very efficient Assistant Secretary has presented the case. It is only a suggestion for the good of the cause and at this time for the purpose of getting our minds to meet on the proper disposition of it.

JUDGE STEPHENS: Speaking for the Department of Justice, I think it is highly desirable to publish the rules and regulations and Executive Orders.

MR. WALKER: It is suggested, by the way, that the Director of the Budget be made one of a committee of several to give the matter consideration; do you have any suggestions with reference to it, Mr. Douglas?

DIRECTOR DOUGLAS: No. The subject is new to me as it has been brought up this afternoon. I think, offhand, it is a very desirable thing to do. There should be a corresponding reduction in the cost of printing for the various departments, however.

MR. DICKINSON: Absolutely.

MR. WALKER: The suggestion is made that the committee be appointed, composed of representatives of members of the Executive Council, and that this committee should include Mr. Haykin, Chief, Division of Documents of the Library of Congress, and Cyril Wynne, Chief, Division of Research and Publications, Department of State; this committee to include the Director of the Budget, and to consider the financing of the gazette as well as other features such as the contents, the department or organization to edit and publish the gazette, and the method of compilation of material. So, if there is no objection—

SECRETARY PERKINS: I would suggest that the word gazette be avoided. We can call it a bulletin or something of that kind which has the same meaning; but an official gazette is associated in most minds with orders which have the binding effect of law issued by a government which has police power over its people. And I think that if we can avoid the use of that word we will avoid the uneasiness that might be associated with it and a good deal of flippant criticism.

MR. WALKER: My idea of it is associated with barber shops: the *Police Gazette.* (*Laughter*) I think the committee might take that thought of the Secretary under advisement. If it is agreeable, then, the Director will appoint the committee and ask them to report on it at the next meeting of the National Emergency Council. We will include on the committee the ones suggested by the report from the Department of Commerce.

SECRETARY ROPER: In handling a matter of this character, are we supposed to be confined to the estimate of the Government Printing Office as to costs, or in this case would we be permitted to go outside and get estimates? I ask that question because of the fact that I think something must be done about the Government Printing Office. Their costs are excessive, as we have found in the Patent Office. Our estimate for the Patent Office printing was $1,235,000. We are now getting that done next year for $900,000, a saving of between $400,000 and $500,000. We have been thinking of trying to establish a differential as it were— that is, the suggestion has been made—up to 20 per cent in favor of the Government Printing Office. But it runs very much higher than that now. That is a matter that will require at some time, if the Director of the Budget hasn't already begun it, very careful investigation.

JUDGE STEPHENS: The cost of printing our briefs by the Government Printing Office is substantially larger than if we had them privately printed.

SECRETARY ROPER: I don't understand it myself.

MR. FERGUSON: Our expenses are very great in the printing of briefs in our cases.

SECRETARY ROPER: The Bureau of Patents has very heavy printing expenses, but when in one bureau of the Department you save about $450,000, it becomes worthy of very careful investigation.

DIRECTOR DOUGLAS: Wasn't that due to the particular kind of work the Patent Office was having done?

SECRETARY ROPER: Yes, but we found outside people who were willing to do it much cheaper.

183

DIRECTOR DOUGLAS: As I recollect, that was looked into a year ago when I was on a committee of the House and we ran into a provision of the law—that is my recollection—which, with a few exceptions, required printing to be done in the Government Printing Office. We did find in the Patent Office and in several other different agencies that apparently the printing could be done by private enterprises cheaper than in the Government Printing Office.

SECRETARY ROPER: I can understand that in the early years of the Government Printing Office, when naturally they wanted to build up that very important service, how that law could have gotten on the statute books; but we have outlived it, in my opinion.

SECRETARY PERKINS: Isn't there any way to make the Government Printing Office do cheaper work?

SECRETARY ROPER: I believe there is, Madam Secretary.

DIRECTOR DOUGLAS: The Government Printing Office has just sent a notice, I think, to all the government agencies to the effect that the cost of printing will be increased ten per cent as a result of a section in the independent offices bill which made mandatory the payment of wages for 48 hours although the hours themselves were only 40. That is one of the reasons why the Government Printing Office is more expensive, by reason of the various statutes passed by Congress with respect to the employees.

SECRETARY PERKINS: Is it an independent establishment?

DIRECTOR DOUGLAS: No, it is a legislative establishment.

SECRETARY ROPER: Created jointly by the two houses.

MR. WALKER: Doesn't some of the jurisdiction come under the Treasury and the Bureau of Engraving and Printing?

DIRECTOR DOUGLAS: That is quite different from the Government Printing Office.

MR. WALKER: You had some experience, Mr. Ferguson.

MR. FERGUSON: Yes, our records and briefs printed for the Circuit Courts of Appeals are most expensive. We sometimes feel embarrassed about carrying the case on because of the expense involved. It seems almost an impossible thing to do. We have had cases where the cost of printing briefs runs to several thousand dollars.

DIRECTOR DOUGLAS: Time and a half for overtime, 48 hours' pay for 40 hours' work, night differentials, and a great many other things that apply to the Government Printing Office do not apply to private publishing houses.

SECRETARY PERKINS: Those all apply except the 48 hours' pay for 40 hours' work.

DIRECTOR DOUGLAS: I understood that was true in only a few of them.

SECRETARY PERKINS: It ought to be in all of them. It is a differential that is customary.

MR. WALKER: In this connection, while we are discussing printing, you remember some time ago the Council authorized the survey of all periodicals published by the government. In that connection we have not succeeded in getting any information from the four following departments: Department of the Interior, Department of Labor, Federal Emergency Relief Administration, and Public Works Administration....

SECRETARY PERKINS: Did anybody send a written notice, or were we supposed to remember it?

MR. WALKER: Written notices were sent and several departments were prodded several times, but the information has not been forthcoming.

SECRETARY PERKINS: Regular publications?

MR. WALKER: Yes.

DIRECTOR DOUGLAS: I think the Bureau of the Budget submitted a report on that last July or August, and the appropriations for printing so substantially reduced the number of publications in the various departments that many of the publications which heretofore existed are now not being published at all. I think there was a report, as I recollect it, that we submitted last July or August as to limitations on expense of regular department appropriations for this year and appropriations for 1935. Maybe that information is already available.

MR. WALKER: I think they had that report before them in making the survey.

The state directors' report is quite extensive, but here is a short resumé of it which I will read....

The report is very extensive and we are sending a copy of the report that has applications to each agency to the particular agency.

Here is a report on the Manual. I would like to get some observations from some of the Council with reference to certain features of it....[2]

The United States Conference of Mayors have asked for copies of the Manual for the purpose of setting up information services in the city halls of 188 cities involved, which cities have a population of 80,000 or more, and we hesitate in sending them out until we get an expression from some members of the Council as to whether or not it would be a

---

[2] The publication which later became the *U. S. Government Organization Manual.* It was first published in a looseleaf binder, but after a few years assumed its present general format.

politic thing to do to scatter them among agencies of that character, and whether or not there would be any criticism on it. Have you any ideas with reference to that, Mr. Secretary of Commerce? Do you think there would be any objection to using city halls as information bureaus?

SECRETARY ROPER: Is that a suggestion from your state directors?

MR. WALKER: No, this is a request from the Conference of Mayors.

SECRETARY ROPER: Would it be in accordance with the wishes of the state directors, or would they feel that the authority was being taken away from them?

MR. WALKER: I would not think so.

SECRETARY ROPER: If the state directors are in accord with it, I think it would be the thing to do.

MR. DICKINSON: Distribution might be made through them.

SECRETARY ROPER: I think that they ought to be kept informed. I must think they would approve of it. If you could distribute through them, they would feel that they were kept in touch with it.

MR. WALKER: We have no control over these at all, and they are kept up currently, with any amendments and modifications.

SECRETARY ROPER: If you do that through your state directors, I should think you would have control to a certain extent. Are you going to charge them?

MR. WALKER: Personally, I would see no objection.

SECRETARY ROPER: Whom do you charge?

MR. WALKER: We have had many requests from private individuals, corporations, and law firms. We felt that the public should pay for them, and we have an opinion from the Comptroller General as to the price. The price is fixed by law, the limit being that they shall not be sold at a profit.

SECRETARY ROPER: I think it is all right for you to operate through the state directors.

MR. FAHEY: Would that involve having offices in the city halls?

MR. WALKER: Each city would conduct them itself.

MR. FAHEY: The office of the state director would not be located in the city hall?

MR. WALKER: Oh no, the mayors say they have many requests for information with reference to federal activities, and they want to set up information services of their own in their city halls.

Some little time since, we started the Consumers' Council on its way and Mr. Keezer was appointed under Mrs. Rumsey to take charge. We have a report from him at this time with reference to what has been done and the policy that is being pursued.[3]

MR. KEEZER: The only thing I can offer in the way of a report is with reference to Bulletin No. 1. Under this bulletin we have been operating only a little more than a week. This sets forth the rules and regulations governing the Consumers Division of the National Emergency Council. Under this division a week ago Saturday, letters went out over Mr. Walker's signature, appointing 112 chairmen of Consumers' county councils. These chairmen were approved by the state directors after a process of selection which involved recommendations from, I think, all representative organizations. The plan initially is to start approximately 200 of these councils and to do two things—furnish them factual information about the work of the consumer agencies in Washington, and ask them to send to the Consumers' Division information—again, factual and strictly factual—about the development in their communities of interest particularly to consumers. The rules and regulations have been very rigorously drawn, principally with a view to keeping the 200 councils initially to be undertaken as closely to the purpose as possible.

The Consumers' Division will also have another activity, that of coordinating the handling of price complaints by the AAA and NRA. We find it is possible, particularly in the NRA where I have been working, to have far more effective handling if there were a central agency. In the Fair Price Section we are undertaking the setting up of these 112 councils. I should have explained that that number was fixed at 200 because that number of nominees had been approved by the State Directors of the National Emergency Council. Thus far, there have been 18 acceptances and 30 rejections. Just why there have been so many rejections we are not sure, but it may be that the work involved is too difficult, and because the facilities offered (which do not include pay of any kind) are not sufficient to permit them to undertake the work with the assurance that they can succeed.

We felt that in starting the councils they must be rigorously controlled in the matter of making a factual reporting service.

---

[3] As the context below shows, Walker was apparently referring to the Consumers' Division of the National Emergency Council, which, with other agencies concerned with the problems of the consumer, was transferred to the Consumers' Division in the NRA as of July 30, 1935, and thence to the Department of Labor in Dec. 1935.

We are now at work on a number of bulletins which will explain to them what the consumers' agencies are doing here and a number of bulletins for more restricted use, asking them to report to us the developments. We are asking them to find out about certain developments in relation to coal prices. I think, Mr. Walker, that perhaps covers the work to date. I have copies of this preliminary bulletin, which I believe rather fully outlines the undertaking, for those who might want to have them.

SECRETARY ROPER: I would like to have a copy of it. (*Mr. Keezer then passed out copies to various members of the Council.*) . . .

MR. WALKER: Are there any questions or observations in reference to the Consumer Council problems?

MRS. RUMSEY: Mr. Director, I think it might be wise to state the relation of these county councils to the compliance machinery of the NRA and the State Directors. Shall I do that?

MR. WALKER: Yes, that is perfectly agreeable.

MRS. RUMSEY: The state directors and also the code authorities have jurisdiction over consumer complaints if they have within their code provisions which provide for too high increase in prices. Under those codes, complaints would have to be routed to the code authorities as well as the state directors and consumers' agency of the National Emergency Council.
I think only about six codes have actual provisions which prohibit too high price rises.

MR. WALKER: Next is the report of the Economic Adviser.

MR. RIEFLER: About three weeks ago, the President raised the question of the small industries in small towns and we have a report here on that . . . .
If the Council wants us to go forward with this and wants to spend the money, I think that by far the best material can be gotten by taking those returns from the Census Bureau. It is simply a question whether they are punched in such a way that you can get any classification you want. The cost would be about $10,000 to get this additional information.

SECRETARY PERKINS: How important do you think it is to know it?

MR. RIEFLER: I think that it would be rather important in this case. It seems to me when you get to the work of compiling a national census of manufacturers you ought not to tabulate it by hand and simply bring out the total. It seems to me the added cost of punching by machines so that any inquiry that comes up in the future can be qickly sorted through it at almost no additional cost would be a tremendous economy. I should think that material ought to be tabulated by machine in the first place so that it will be available later as the questions arise.

MR. WALKER: That expense would have to be borne by the Council?

MR. RIEFLER: I should think the NRA would be the proper source of expense in this case because it would be largely for their use.

MR. WALKER: I know the President is very anxious to get the information.

MR. RIEFLER: This will give it for 1932. The cost of getting the information of small firms is very great. All your current statistics are based on the largest firms in the industry where you can get the largest statistical representation at the least cost.

SECRETARY PERKINS: What differences, in general, do you think there are between the small firm and the large firm?

MR. RIEFLER: This material is so meager that it simply shows no conclusive results.

SECRETARY PERKINS: Do you think there are any conclusive results?

MR. RIEFLER: I think there might be in particular industries, but not generalized for all industries.

MR. WALKER: There has been quite a wave over the country about small industries being seriously affected by the NRA.

SECRETARY PERKINS: You can always get sympathy by using the word small. With little industries you feel as you do about a little puppy. Frequently it has no more reason for receiving sympathy because it is small. There is a lot of misunderstanding of that problem. In many situations there are too many small industries, too many small firms for any sensible plan of production and distribution. They just carry out the ambition of individuals to be in business for themselves rather than for somebody else. In many industries it makes for uneconomic production, distribution, and higher costs, and results in a great many bankruptcies and a good deal of over-turn and unsteadiness in production.

MR. WALKER: Can you furnish any authoritative figures on industry?

MR. RIEFLER: The decrease in failures is in favor of the large firms though the difference is only slight, one being 53 per cent and the other 50 per cent.

Dun & Bradstreet have prepared their usual fortnightly report for the Council. This report is prepared especially for us . . . .

They have asked us whether we want them to continue preparing these reports every two weeks. I would suggest that once a month would be perfectly satisfactory, if we want it as frequently as that.

MR. WALKER: That would come under your department, I should say. Do you think this would show any real trend by getting the 1933 figures?

MR. RIEFLER: You cannot tell what we would get from the census of manufactures for 1933 which covers practically all plants. Questionnaires to the small plants go out by mail, whereas they follow up the returns from the large plants. The returns from the small plants are not quite as representative. By an analysis of the figures by months from January through December 1933, it ought to be possible to squeeze everything that could be gotten out of the material to see whether the codes did affect small industries more seriously than the large industries in the matter of raising their wages and shortening their hours, and whether that was reflected in the differences in the increase in the amount of work they did. I cannot see any other way in which as much material can be gotten on the problem as cheaply. I think it would be the cheapest and best way to get the information. Whether it would be anything conclusive, I do not know.

MR. WALKER: There were one or two other matters, but the President is entertaining the President of Haiti today, and he asked that two or three other matters go over until next week. Is there anything further to be brought up? If there is nothing further, we will adjourn.

Meeting adjourned at 2:55 p.m.

Held in the Cabinet Room of the Executive Offices,
The White House, Tuesday, May 1, 1934, at 2:25 p.m.

Present: the President of the United States; the Secretary of the
Treasury; the Attorney General; the Secretary of the Interior; the
Secretary of Agriculture; the Secretary of Commerce; the Secretary of
Labor; the Honorable Ebert K. Burlew, Administrative Assistant of
the Interior; the Director of the Bureau of the Budget; the Administrator
of Agricultural Adjustment; the Administrator of Federal Emergency
Relief; the Administrator for Industrial Recovery; the Chairman of the
Board of the Home Owners' Loan Corporation; the Governor of the
Farm Credit Administration; the Chairman of the Federal Trade
Commission; the Adviser on Consumer Problems; the Economic
Adviser; the Executive Director.

[This is a particularly interesting meeting—and a lengthy one.
During the first half, the President was absent. The first items
of business were: the acute shortage of office space for some
of the new emergency agencies, and an Executive Order
requiring agencies of this same sort to bring their personnel
classification and compensation systems into line with civil
service practices even though such personnel were not covered
by civil service. These two issues highlight the growing
pains of the federal government under the New Deal.
The bulk of the meeting related to germinating plans for
broadening the intervention of the national government in the
area of home mortgage insurance. At issue were mortgages
for new construction, for repairs and renovations, and the
refinancing of mortgages on older existing buildings.
Opportunity is given the reader to watch the NEC filling,
in large part, the coordinating role for which it had been
created. Recorded here are some phases of a discussion which
had been going on among the agencies for some time,
and which had turned up fundamental disagreements. The
President, who enters during the discussion, tries through
his questioning to pinpoint the difference of view, and
eventually supplies an interim compromise regarding the
unresolved issues; he characteristically enjoins: "Frank
[Walker], get them in a room and tell them no lunch unless
they agree."—Editors' Note.]

MR. WALKER: I am awfully sorry for being late, but it was the President who held me up. I am not responsible.

SECRETARY PERKINS: We almost left.

MR. WALKER: There is a very extensive report here from the state directors. We have a digest consisting of two pages which covers the high lights of it ....

I think there is no need of reading the general report.

The Executive Council and the Emergency Council are confronted with the problem of what they are going to do about space. That of course depends a great deal on how far the National Emergency Council is going to go.

We have a report here. I do not know that it is necessary to read it at this time ....

We have an opportunity to go into the building of the Department of Justice. We are branching out to a very considerable extent and if the housing coordination remains with the Emergency Council—and it seems as though it will— we are going to need further space. I wanted to bring this to the attention of the Council, that we can get 20,000 square feet at the Department of Justice Building and it looks to me as though, if we are going to carry on further, we will need that amount of space. We are using approximately 12 or 13,000 feet now. The Attorney General has very generously consented to set aside some space for us.

ATTORNEY GENERAL CUMMINGS: I think we could spare at least 22,000 square feet. Would that help you?

MR. WALKER: I think with the work of the Executive Council and the Emergency Council branching out with the long term housing plan and an intermediate plan to be taken care of, it seems to me we will need all that space.

MR. FAHEY: Is that in the old building?

ATTORNEY GENERAL CUMMINGS: No.

MR. WALKER: It is in the new building. We have a Consumers' Council Organization also.

ATTORNEY GENERAL CUMMINGS: We are expecting to get into the new building shortly after the first of June. That is the latest report.

MR. FAHEY: I don't know what you are going to do meanwhile. We have been terribly overcrowded for room, and we have had it up with the Public Buildings and Parks Division as to allotment of space and we are at the point where we have got to go to Baltimore and get out of town, if we get any room in which to operate.

MR. WALKER: I took up with the President the problem today. We didn't reach a decision. I advised him that I have been in touch with Secretary Ickes on two or three occasions and your Mr. Jones, I think, has made a complete survey. I am satisfied that with all the records you have down there—notes and mortgages and some of your files being kept out in the halls—that you are overcrowded, and with summer coming on that is a very bad situation.

MR. FAHEY: It is disgraceful.

ORNEY GENERAL CUMMINGS: Did you plan to go into some of the buildings the Department of Justice vacates?

MR. FAHEY: We have no right to do so except with the approval of the Public Parks and Grounds Division. We have been trying to get more space ever since last October. We finally got into the Post Office Building so far as the Executive Staff is concerned. We have no room for several hundred people to work on loan examinations and legal papers. We have 30,000 sets of loan papers on hand and no place to put people to work on them. We cannot keep up with our work, and we have no place to install additional machinery, and no relief whatever has been afforded.[1] We have been all over the city surveying this situation, and it seems to me that so far as the government workers as a whole are concerned, you will have to look far ahead or in another twelve months you will be worse off than you are now. Certainly there is no room for expansion of our work. I don't know where it will be possible to get space in which to undertake the modernization work—you or anybody else. It was supposed that the Department of Labor buildings would be free some time around the first of July. We might be able to get along temporarily until then, but I understand the latest word is that it is not clear when they will be ready.

SECRETARY PERKINS: I think it will be about the first of July.

MR. FAHEY: I will bet it will be two months more.

SECRETARY PERKINS: They told us the new building would be ready the first of January, and it has been postponed two months. It is now nearing completion, but there is no furniture for it.

MR. FAHEY: You will have to wait about six weeks for furniture.

ORNEY GENERAL CUMMINGS: I don't think we will get our furniture until next fall, maybe December. We will have to take the old stuff. We will have to close our building two or three days to fumigate it and get rid of the bedbugs and things. It is terrible over there, but we will have to use it. We hate to take a lot of undesirable

---

[1] The agency under discussion was the Home Owners' Loan Corporation.

MR. WALKER:	inhabitants from the old building to the new one!
	There was some discussion about making a purchase.
MR. FAHEY:	Yes, we can; and as it stands right now, that seems to be the only way out for us unless we can get relief pretty quick.
MR. WALKER:	I understand you can get the Acacia building, but that would not house your entire organization.
MR. FAHEY:	No, but it would take care of the people we cannot put to work now. It would save our going to Baltimore or somewhere which would be very expensive and also very inefficient.
MR. WALKER:	Are you familiar with the situation, Mr. Burlew?[2]
MR. BURLEW:	No, I am not.
MR. WALKER:	I asked the Secretary to be here, and he said that he would be here later.
MR. BURLEW:	Our building is as overcrowded as any. After these new buildings are occupied, we will still have about $800,000 in rentals. We had planned to use all the other buildings for which we had money to pay rentals—Labor buildings and Justice—but that will not give us the relief we still need.
MR. WALKER:	I believe there is an absolute necessity to do something for the Home Owners' Loan Corporation. They are keeping their records, notes, and things of that kind out in the halls. Some of the employees are working in halls.
MR. FAHEY:	Yes, conditions are wholly unsatisfactory.
MR. BURLEW:	The appropriation committee does not see the need of other buildings. They think this is all temporary, and we can get along with what we have.
MR. WALKER:	You could purchase a building.
MR. FAHEY:	Yes, we can under the law.
MR. WALKER:	We have had this matter up for six months, and do not seem to get any place on it. It needs immediate solution. Perhaps after the Secretary comes, we might have a meeting after the Council meeting, if that will be agreeable to you.
MR. FAHEY:	All right. I do think, Mr. Chairman, in view of the attitude of the appropriations committee, that it would be very helpful if the facts could be assembled and then brought to their attention. I think you are going to encounter some difficulty as in the past; the need develops and when it is upon you, then it is too late to do anything about it.
MR. BURLEW:	We have already compiled that.
MR. WALKER:	If there is no objection, I think the Council may take the

[2] Ebert K. Burlew was temporarily representing his superior, Secretary of the Interior Ickes.

space offered by the Department of Justice.

The next matter before us is the proposed Executive Order on personnel classification .... A copy of this has been sent to all members of the Council with a request that if they have any questions they will bring them up at this time.[3]

DIRECTOR DOUGLAS: That request was made in March.

MR. WALKER: They have been notified that this is the last opportunity.

MR. FAHEY: This is with reference to the proposed draft?

DIRECTOR DOUGLAS: This draft has not been submitted to the Attorney General; but if it meets with the approval of the Council, it will be.

A part of the Executive Order was drafted in the Attorney General's office—that part on page five. In substance, it carries into effect the recommendations of March 26; it provides that the salaries paid shall be in amounts "not in excess of those in the salary standardization schedule." The words "not in excess" were inserted to take care of situations which exist in a good many of the emergency agencies, such as the National Recovery Administration, the Home Owners' Loan Corporation, and some others, in which salaries are being paid for the classified positions referred to in the order, but not as high as the rates prescribed in the Executive Order.

If each emergency organization is compelled to pay a salary for classified positions at the rate prescribed in the salary standardization schedule, the cost to the government will be substantially greater than it is now. The language "not in excess of" was put in the first part of the order. There are certain organizations exempted, such as the Tennessee Valley Authority and its affiliates, employees of the Federal Coordinator of Transportation, all common laborers, unskilled, and skilled or semi-skilled laborers, and others, in order to conform to an opinion of the Comptroller General, including also enrollees of Emergency Conservation Works and employees of the Federal Civil Works Administration, and the Federal Emergency Relief Administration, as well as all other persons engaged in similar employment or employed under similar circumstances as the groups of employees described, three, four, and five.

---

[3] Apparently this draft became Executive Order 6746, issued June 21, 1934. Since this dated well before the first volume of the *Federal Register* was issued, it cannot readily be checked. The best description of the Order is probably the citation in the *Catalog of Public Documents*, 1933-34, p. 1146 f: "Executive order, rates of compensation of government employees in emergency agencies, etc., not subject to classification act as amended."

SECRETARY ROPER: On page four, where the figures are in parentheses ($600.00) as against $840.00—what does that mean?

DIRECTOR DOUGLAS: Those are the salaries paid under the amended classification act.

SECRETARY ROPER: You mean $600.00?

DIRECTOR DOUGLAS: That's right. That position of CAF 10 is for a salary of $3,500 and CAF 11 is $3,800.

SECRETARY ROPER: Pursuing the amended classification act?

DIRECTOR DOUGLAS: No, on a salary standardization under the second column. All employees of regular departments being paid out of Emergency funds will be subject to this classification.

MR. FAHEY: What number is that?

SECRETARY ROPER: We are discussing page four.

ATTORNEY GENERAL CUMMINGS: What was that last observation?

DIRECTOR DOUGLAS: All employees of the regular establishments which are paid from Emergency funds—that was the part of the order you sent over—

ATTORNEY GENERAL CUMMINGS: Yes.

DIRECTOR DOUGLAS: —are to be subject to the same classification.

MR. BURLEW: We have finished with the classification for Public Works, and have been ready to put it into effect for two months. We think we now have the way, but if that has to be reviewed, it means we will carry on until next fall. If a new agency is set up, they would hardly accept the classification of the previous agency.

DIRECTOR DOUGLAS: That was set up by the old committee, wasn't it?

MR. BURLEW: Yes; if those were to stand, I think the classification would be all right, but if we have to have another, the employees will not get their five per cent.

DIRECTOR DOUGLAS: On page two, these words are used: "Subject to review and revision by the Executive Council utilizing the services of such Federal Agencies as it may designate." I suppose that classification already having been reviewed and approved, the Executive Council would not take any further steps.

MR. BURLEW: We were planning to put it into effect May 1.

DIRECTOR DOUGLAS: If you want a further review and decision, you could order it. It is up to the Executive Council as to whether or not it be done. As far as I know the situation, I would not recommend it. There must be some check somewhere on the classification. You see, the Comptroller General ruled that each agency had the power to classify under the Executive Order. There should be some check on that. Since these agencies are emergency agencies, we felt the authority to review and check should be vested in the Executive Council.

MR. BURLEW: That would be all right—

DIRECTOR DOUGLAS: It is our thoughts that the authoritative review would be used only as discrepancies appeared in the light of experience.

MR. BURLEW: In the case of Public Works, the total is an increase of only $250,000 for the entire staff to receive the five per cent. There is not much extravagance there. I think the office of the Comptroller General and the Civil Service Commission could well be used as a check.

DIRECTOR DOUGLAS: The Comptroller General has refused to allow the committee of the Executive Council to pass on his employees.

MR. DAVIS: In our situation, Mr. Douglas, we are rapidly completing the classification under the Classification Act of 1923.

DIRECTOR DOUGLAS: Those are permanent employees.

MR. DAVIS: We have, I would say, about 85 per cent of our temporary group classified and 90 per cent of the permanent ones. We expect shortly to have all but 33 positions classified, and those will be excepted as experts under the language of our Act. Is the permanent classification subject to review here?

DIRECTOR DOUGLAS: Yes, unless Congress revises that. I think that takes care of your difficulty, doesn't it?

GENERAL JOHNSON: I am not sure.

DIRECTOR DOUGLAS: You don't have to pay them $8,000. You can pay $6,900.

ﾗRNEY GENERAL CUMMINGS: Why is that, Mr. Douglas?

DIRECTOR DOUGLAS: On page two it says "amounts not in excess of those prescribed in the following salary standardization schedule." According to that, a man need not receive $8,000. He may receive only $7,000, but he cannot receive more than $8,000. A good many employees were brought down here under agreements which created a sort of moral obligation to pay so much. They are stepped up into the grade requiring that salary. Then they would have to be paid $8,000 because they agreed to come for $7,000. If the Executive Council approves of this Executive Order, it will go to the Attorney General in the regular way.

MR. BURLEW: Could you have intermediate steps?

DIRECTOR DOUGLAS: Yes, so far as salaries are concerned, but not so far as grades are concerned.

MR. BURLEW: We cannot increase salaries by reclassification. The Comptroller General's decision to the Administrator on Saturday says you cannot increase salaries by reclassification.

DIRECTOR DOUGLAS: I had not seen that.

MR. BURLEW: I have the original here. That followed the Attorney General's recent opinion and the Executive Order of March 27. That Executive Order authorized the increases of salary.

197

ATTORNEY GENERAL CUMMINGS:	Is there a direct conflict there?
MR. BURLEW:	Yes, sir, very direct; and he had the Attorney General's opinion before him at the time. He overruled the Attorney General. They continue to suspend our salary accounts. I don't think this has been published yet. It is quite long.
SECRETARY ROPER:	There is an interesting point, Mr. Attorney General; I am taking the position in our department that any matter requiring legal interpretation shall pass from our solicitor to you. There has been a tendency, as you know, to take it up with other officials, including the Comptroller General. Is that proper procedure?
ATTORNEY GENERAL CUMMINGS:	There is no doubt that it is.
MR. BURLEW:	When I presented this last opinion, they maintained it was not a matter upon which he should rule—the spending of funds. They paid no attention to it.
DIRECTOR DOUGLAS:	That was under the then existing Executive Order of March 27.
MR. BURLEW:	The Order of March 27 was gotten up primarily to authorize the purchase of automobiles. We included the personal services.
MR. WALKER:	Would it be agreeable to the Director of the Budget to delay action until next Tuesday? I would like to get into this housing matter.
DIRECTOR DOUGLAS:	Unless there is some objection to the points of the Executive Order by some member of the Executive Council, I see no reason why the Executive Council cannot approve it and let the thing go on through.
SECRETARY ROPER:	And refer it to the Attorney General.
DIRECTOR DOUGLAS:	Yes, and then to the State Department.
SECRETARY ICKES:	I think we have already lost in efficiency much more than the Comptroller General will make up in any saving he will effect. We are just running around. It is not fair.
DIRECTOR DOUGLAS:	This thing has been batting around from bush to bush and limb to limb since March 26. I would like to see it cleared up, and get it on its way. If there is an objection to the contents of the Executive Order, I think it ought to be stated, and if there is no objection, I think it ought to be put on its way.
MR. WALKER:	The Executive Council did approve this before.
DIRECTOR DOUGLAS:	No, this was submitted to the Executive Council on March 26 with a request that objections be stated. I have heard no objections.
SECRETARY ROPER:	I move the approval of the Executive Order and

	its reference to the Attorney General.
MR. BURLEW:	I think the whole picture is changed. We have gotten out two previous Executive Orders that did not get us anywhere.
DIRECTOR DOUGLAS:	If the Council will approve of this Executive Order, the legal end of it can be taken care of subsequently.
ORNEY GENERAL CUMMINGS:	If we are unable to iron out the legal situation we will have to come back. I see no objection to Mr. Roper's motion.
GENERAL JOHNSON:	We started out with very low salaries. We are now getting into a situation where we are going to have to pay more. Do you see any objection to this?
DIRECTOR DOUGLAS:	No, I do not.
MR. BURLEW:	That does not relieve the situation as to suspension.
GENERAL JOHNSON:	Isn't there another way besides classification?
MR. BURLEW:	Yes, you can hire a new man, but your whole payroll has been suspended.
MR. FAHEY:	What can we do, Mr. Douglas? So far as we are concerned, there are some types of work that do not seem to come within the classification. We are troubled about that somewhat.
ORNEY GENERAL CUMMINGS:	The Chairman raises the question that this is the Emergency Council meeting, and some members of the Executive Council are not present. I think that motion should be recast to the effect that this Council has no objection to it.
MR. BURLEW:	Mr. Douglas thinks that the authority to review will not be exercised unless a review is necessary in particular instances; that in cases such as Public Works, it will be allowed to stand unless some point is raised which will require review.
DIRECTOR DOUGLAS:	May I elaborate on that? The Comptroller General has ruled that each independent establishment has the power to classify. The Comptroller General has not raised the question of revision, and this expressly vests in the Executive Council the right to revise and use any agency which it may see fit to use for that purpose. I personally think that the Civil Service Commission and the Comptroller's office ought to be able to do that work.
MR. BURLEW:	The Civil Service Commission cannot do it in a reasonable time.
DIRECTOR DOUGLAS:	The check is on the payroll. That is where you get your check, and the Comptroller General is the one who passes on that.
ORNEY GENERAL CUMMINGS:	The mere fact that he passes on the payroll does not authorize him to pass on the legal questions as to whether or not certain things should be done.
DIRECTOR DOUGLAS:	Certainly not, Mr. Attorney General.
ORNEY GENERAL CUMMINGS:	That is where he overstepped his authority. I will say this

199

for the Comptroller General, although I hold no brief for him, and that is that he is not entirely to blame because many of these agencies around here have asked him legal questions. If they keep up that practice you can hardly blame him for answering.

SECRETARY ICKES: We don't do it in our department.

DIRECTOR DOUGLAS: As I understand it, this will start on its way.

MR. FAHEY: I wanted to make this reservation, if I might; we have run into so many difficulties on this that I would like to check with my people on this proposed draft and telephone you in the morning.

MR. WALKER: Is that agreeable to you, Mr. Director?

DIRECTOR DOUGLAS: I don't know what it was, so I will say no. (*Laughter*)

MR. FAHEY: I said I just wanted to check up on it with my people and phone you in the morning.

DIRECTOR DOUGLAS: Certainly!

ATTORNEY GENERAL CUMMINGS: What was the date of the Comptroller's opinion?

MR. BURLEW: April 28.

MR. WALKER: In view of the fact that the National Emergency Council is bringing the modernization plan and the new mortgage insurance plan within its jurisdiction, I thought we might bring you up to date as to the status of our proposed plans at this moment. As you will remember, a committee of 15 consisting of all the heads of departments directly connected with either plan met with the President, at which time we thought we were all in accord with general principles. Since that time some things have arisen that need some adjustment and some decision. It seems now that we are all in accord upon going ahead with the modernization plan, and the President today signed an Order that was suggested by the Director of the Budget and by the Attorney General authorizing the Administrator of Public Works to give a million dollars to the National Emergency Council for the purpose of modernization plans.

SECRETARY ICKES: Did he tell us where we were going to get it?

MR. WALKER: He signed the order to be delivered to you before the day is over. That will be your work, Mr. Administrator.
Insofar as the insurance plan is concerned, the Chairman of the Home Owners' Loan Board is not entirely in accord with some of the views of the rest of the members of the Council, and of the committee. I think we are all in accord except the Home Owners' Loan.
The President had hoped that we would not need legislation.

However, we are all in accord that legislation is necessary. The proposed legislation will take up both the Emergency plan or modernization plan and also such revisions and amendments as are necessary to have the No. 2 plan go through. In addition to that there are some modifications made since our last meeting. One which was suggested by the Secretary of the Treasury, and that is the second plan—the No. 2 plan—will be modified so that insofar as existing mortgages are concerned, the limit will be one billion dollars of insured mortgages on the basis of 50 per cent appraisal.

MR. FAHEY: You mean existing mortgages?

MR. WALKER: Yes, taking in the insurance plan. This is the recommendation of the Secretary of the Treasury, and so far as future construction is concerned, a time limit was placed upon it of three years. There are two other features involved. One is the question of the Home Owners' Loan, which plan, I understand, is to be worked out between the Home Owners' Loan and the Reconstruction Finance Corporation for $500,000,000 for the Home Owners' Loan. Then we are confronted with the situation of whether or not any legislation will be proposed insofar as the insurance of building and loan associations is concerned. It seems to me that we need an early decision as to whether or not we are going to go ahead with the modernization plan, and with the mortgage insurance plan. The President, I think, has in mind having Mr. Hopkins act as director of the modernization and insurance plan if both go through, and I would like to see some discussion as to whether or not we are going to go ahead with it. My suggestion would be that we go ahead with both plans and try to have the Treasury work out with the Home Owners' Loan the question of insuring building and loan associations. In the meantime, I don't think that should hold up the other two plans. If the Treasury cannot agree with the Home Owners' Loan let them submit their plans at a later date. It seems to me we should make a decision at once because we are going to require legislation, and we should have our legislation submitted in final form to the Attorney General and the legal advisers of the agencies involved. We feel that can be done within 24 hours. The earlier plans have been approved by the Attorney General and by the other legal advisers. If there is any discussion I think we should hear it now, and at the end of the discussion I

201

think we should submit it to the President for final action.[4]

MR. FAHEY: Mr. Chairman, so far as we are concerned, we are in real agreement so far as the organization plan is concerned, but we are not in agreement so far as the insurance plan is concerned. The suggestion thus made about insuring the different mortgages is a new one. We have been discussing this plan and discussing it, up to Friday evening; there were various suggestions made as to changes which we thought might overcome some of the objections made to it. In that discussion, as we understood it, the idea of insuring the different mortgages had been eliminated and the proposal was to experiment with this insurance on new construction, which we felt would not be objectionable and which might work out all right. Frankly, our board regards the insurance of individual mortgages as very much of an experiment, and pretty near every direction in which we have moved and made inquiry with reference to it, we find a great deal of doubt as to its feasibility. We know, and we have distinctly told the Treasury and those who have discussed it, that the Federal Home Loan Bank Board was the board named in the Act which would carry on the work. It has seemed out of the question for us, with our machinery, to undertake in any reasonable time to appraise existing properties to be insured under that act. Under that proposal the appraisal system of the country simply is not authorized to do it. Certainly our organization is not capable of doing it, and I would say, out of our experience, it is a physical impossibility to put together an organization that could do it within a year. It would take all that time. I have no doubt that the Farm Credit Administration has had much the same experience that we have in the matter of appraisals—probably more difficulty in some respects; but we know that so far as we are concerned, we haven't any organization which would justify us for one minute in saying that the United States Government or any authority representing the government should take responsibility for guaranteeing mortgages on the basis of any appraisals which can be made by our organization at the present time.

The other side of it is just this; that so far as we are concerned,

---

[4] Another discussion of the housing problem and the coordination of government efforts in this area. Legislative action contemplated here was directly related to the National Housing Act (Public Law 479, 73rd Congress), approved June 27, 1934. Subsequently, the Better Housing Division of the National Emergency Council came into existence.

this last year we brought forward the proposal of the members of our banking system and of the savings banks who have not gone into the deposit insurance proposition, who wanted some form of insurance which would protect them from competition of the savings departments of national banks and of such savings banks as have gone into the deposit insurance, and prevent further undermining of their resources and put them in a position to serve their communities and provide mortgage funds. They are still suffering from that competition and it represents a very real difficulty. In the judgment of our board, as a result of long consideration of this thing and conferences with representative groups of bank commissioners whom we have had down here and a great many different delegations, we are running a very serious risk, so far as next year is concerned, if some device cannot be developed under which the flow of savings into the treasury of these associations may be resumed. We think it is a pretty important matter, since these associations take care of about 65 per cent of the workers' homes of the country, so far as financing them is concerned, and we certainly would not feel like approving a type of insurance concerning which we are very doubtful, unless we saw some way at the same time to afford some protection to these 2,400 bank members of ours. It is sure to produce a serious crisis if we do that. That is where we stand on it. We would like to see the experiment made.

MR. WALKER: This did not contemplate abandonment of working out some plan.

MR. FAHEY: No, but you have to tie the two together, and in my own judgment you cannot submit any legislation without precipitating a controversy over it right off. This particular matter has been under discussion up there in the committee. We held them off when we first went up there on the amendment that has already been made to our Act, and I very greatly doubt if you could get the one insurance plan by without providing for the other.

MR. WALKER: What do you propose?

MR. FAHEY: I think we ought to have kept on to see if we could not reach a meeting of minds on it.

MR. WALKER: We have been trying for three months but haven't gotten very far.

MR. FAHEY: As bearing on our whole economic and financial situation I think a real solution of this mortgage problem is of the

203

greatest importance. There is something like $35,000,000,000 of mortgage indebtedness outstanding in this country.

It is the greatest single block of indebtedness we have— $21,000,000,000 on homes alone of less than $20,000 in value. We have done a very considerable piece of work so far as the farm homes are concerned, but we haven't done anything corresponding with it so far as the other homes are concerned. We are still getting this amounting [*sic*] demand for loans and no gain in the situation so far as your building and loan associations are concerned, or your savings banks. Now, unless steps are taken to remedy the situation, as we see it now, we are going to have a greatly increased demand for more relief through Home Owners' Loan Corporation by next spring. We think the two go together. We do not see how you can separate them.

MR. WALKER: What are your thoughts, Mr. Hopkins?

MR. HOPKINS: I have been on most of these conferences from the beginning and it seems to me that this represents the judgment of the group that has been considering it with the exception of the Home Owners' Loan. It seems to me there is a fundamental difference of opinion.

MR. FAHEY: There certainly is!

MR. HOPKINS: But this does represent the opinion of the committee and the group that has been working on it, and it seems to me that the fact that the Home Owners' Loan objects to it should be presented to the President, as I presume Mr. Walker has already done, and let him decide it.

MR. FAHEY: That is perfectly agreeable to me. The point about it is that unfortunately the Federal Home Loan Bank Board is the institution that happens to be up against it as far as the mortgage situation is concerned, and is dealing with these folks every week in the year. Consequently, we cannot fail to be impressed with the seriousness of the problem. Your difficulty on the other side is that if anybody will tell me who the institutions are who are going to use your new insurance plan, I would be interested to know it. There just simply is no conclusive evidence on that point right now—not a bit in all these discussions. Your insurance companies are not going to do it. Savings banks are not. Are the national banks going to use it?

MR. WALKER: We have debated that for a considerable time.

MR. FAHEY: Yes, and they have not produced any evidence, Mr. Chairman. I am just willing to be shown on this and I would like to be shown.

MR. WALKER: There is a difference of opinion. Mr. Secretary, what are your thoughts?

SECRETARY MORGENTHAU: I took a short course in this this morning. We have two problems here. One is to get new housing, and the other is to divert the flood of mortgages coming to the Home Owners' Loan into private hands. Mr. Eccles has been on this for three months. The thing I would like to satisfy myself on, if it is agreeable to Mr. Fahey and the President, is the question of what you are doing to put on the brakes. I think I would like to send some people over there to review about a thousand of the last mortgages that have gone out.

MR. FAHEY: Surely!

SECRETARY MORGENTHAU: If that is agreeable, possibly there is some way of putting the brakes on.

MR. FAHEY: There is no difficulty about putting the brakes on. The original policy was the anxiety to afford relief and get the money. We have done that. If the policy is to reverse the process we can do that; but what the effect is going to be, so far as the public and the mortgage situation is concerned, is something else. All we can do is report the facts as we see them. We may be completely wrong as to the fact, but plainly our duty is to report what we see.

SECRETARY MORGENTHAU: I would like to see some of your two billion dollars held for cases where people are about to lose their homes.

MR. FAHEY· The steps which may be taken are those which are authorized under the law, and that is to put more definite restrictions on the question of relief, and crack down harder on that. That can be done; but we have some 400,000 applications that have gone through the period of appraisals and are approaching examination. That will represent the absorption of a large part of the remaining funds which we have. Of the greatly increased applications which have been coming in, we are satisfied that quite a substantial portion of these are prompted by the banks themselves. For example, we got this information—some of it came to us only yesterday, and I have not had an opportunity to take it up with the Comptroller of the Currency—that the bank examiners have been after the national banks to cut down their mortgage loans. We have cases of their going to the mortgagors and demanding that they file applications with us. We have headed that off. In one state—Massachusetts—the bank commissioner sent out orders to all state banks through his examiners that they were up to the limit of seven per cent loans and demanding that they cut those limits down, and they immediately turned around on us and filed a lot of applications. These we threw out. We persuaded the bank commissioners to issue some letters to the banks stopping that. Those impositions on the corporation are easy enough to stop, we believe. Improved organizations will help us a good deal on that, we think. But on the basis of our best estimate, just moving along as we are now without going any higher, as it would normally so far as closing loans are concerned, because we are now close to about fifty millions a week, it would be up to sixty or seventy millions very shortly if we did not do anything but just let it take its normal course. That would run us out of money about September fifteenth. Meanwhile the applications are continuing to come in at the rate of four hundred million or five hundred million a month. There is no sign of let-up on that. A considerable part of that is due to the fact that as these savings institutions or savings banks and building and loan associations and the savings department of state banks have mortgages mature, they are not renewing them, and they cannot renew them.

MR. WALKER: Shall we ask the President to come in now?

MR. FAHEY: I think we had better attempt to thrash this out in a small group.

MR. WALKER: This does not prevent you and the Treasury working out your insurance plan.

MR. FAHEY: No, if we can agree on joint plans we are perfectly agreeable. We cannot do it.

MR. WALKER: You would oppose the mortgage insurance plan?

MR. FAHEY: Yes, I don't want to take the responsibility of appraising the billion dollars worth of existing mortgages. We cannot do that. We won't do it. It cannot be done.

MR. JONES: I would like it understood that we are making no plans about the $6,500,000,000. We could not do it without legislation. Nothing is being done about that.

MR. WALKER: It is being discussed. It will have to be worked out by somebody.

MR. JONES: We are making no move in it at all.

MR. WALKER: Something will have to be done about it.

MR. JONES: We cannot lend under the present law, and you cannot borrow under the present law. All he can do is to have his limits raised. When he gets that it is a question whether we buy bonds or the market buys them. That will have to be worked out. He would have to get his law approved or amended, and then we would have to be able to get the money.

MR. WALKER: We want to keep in mind that this meeting is strictly confidential. We cannot be too careful about that.

MR. JONES: Was that one million from the Secretary of the Interior, or one billion?

MR. WALKER: It was a million.

SECRETARY ROPER: Do you have to announce the fact that you are starting out with one million?

MR. WALKER: No, it is not an Executive Order.

SECRETARY PERKINS: That looks so small!

MR. WALKER: That is just the cost of conducting the campaign. We don't contemplate making reference to that.

MR. JONES: Is that capital stock?

MR. WALKER: No, cost of overhead of the modernization campaign.

SECRETARY PERKINS: Where is the other money coming from? There is no sense in spending a million dollars for overhead unless the rest of the money can be secured.

MR. WALKER: We hope to get private capital. The government is going to guarantee up to 20 per cent. That is the plan outlined for the modernization.

PRESIDENT ROOSEVELT *(who had just come in at this point)*: Well, people, how many insurance companies have you organized so far?

MR. WALKER: We are just where we started. Mr. President, there are two matters on which we are not in accord. We thought we were in accord the last time we met with you. The first one is with reference to mortgage insurance. Everybody seems in accord with that plan except the Home Owners' Loan, and the Home Owners' Loan has a contemplated plan that we do not seem to be able to agree upon. They contemplate insurance of building and loan associations which the Treasury has been trying to work out with them for the last week or ten days. It seems to be at an impasse on that. We felt we should go ahead with our housing plan, insofar as the modernization plan is concerned, and also insofar as the mortgage insurance is concerned, and permit the Treasury and the Home Owners' Loan to try to work out their plan with reference to building and loan associations.

PRESIDENT ROOSEVELT: In other words, take the first and the second, and go ahead with them.

MR. WALKER: Yes, the third can be done by Executive Order, getting the housing agencies under one authority.

207

new deal mosaic

PRESIDENT ROOSEVELT: The first is repairs and additions. Do we need any law to go ahead with that?

MR. WALKER: I think we are all agreed that we need law for both plans.

ATTORNEY GENERAL CUMMINGS: That is the trouble.

MR. WALKER: We submitted that to the Attorney General.

ATTORNEY GENERAL CUMMINGS: We have been working on that.

MR. WALKER: There are more amendments which I would like to bring to your attention.

PRESIDENT ROOSEVELT: What, in a nut shell, is the difference on the home building loans between the two schools of thought?

MR. FAHEY: The difference is this, Mr. President. One is a proposal of a Federal Mortgage Insurance Corporation which would insure individual mortgages both up to a billion dollars of old mortgages, and the individual mortgages on new construction. In our view, there are a great many difficulties in the application of that theory. It might be worked out. The idea of the application to the insurance principle we think has some attractive possibilities, but since it represents a complete change in the whole mortgage situation of the country, our theory is that nothing very important is to be expected of it presently. It is going to take time to work out any such thing, and too, we say without any hesitation that so far as our undertaking the responsibility of having approved and examined a billion dollars' worth of mortgages already made, and appraising them for insurance, we know that we have no organization capable of doing that; that an appraisal organization to operate on a nationwide basis to do that sort of thing does not exist; that the whole appraisal situation is very weak at its best; and that when it comes to insuring rents of that kind, they are to be approached, in our judgment, with a great deal of caution.

We do think that it might be possible to make the beginning on new construction and that you could then work it out. That phase of it, of applying to old construction, we did not understand was left in the picture when our discussion ended last Friday.

On the other insurance plans, the situation is this. You will remember that last fall when deposit insurance was just coming into effect, the Bank Commissioner of New York was greatly alarmed. They have between 350 and 400 millions in building and loan associations, and they have been steadily losing ground. They and the other commissioners of Pennsylvania, Illinois, Ohio, and Indiana have been appealing to us, and also the Bank Commissioner of Massachusetts, to try to consider some sort of insurance that could apply to these home thrift associations which would eliminate the possibility of their funds being drained away. They became very much excited before Christmas and I finally issued one of those fool statements that did not say anything, but it mollified them. Some of the commissioners came down here and had a three-day conference with us on the subject, and representatives of building and loan people of more than 40 members spent a very considerable time on this thing, and their only solution of it was a plan to insure or guarantee the solvency of these institutions; that is, that the insurance provided for should not be drawn upon unless and until an association went into liquidation. These institutions are very strongly in favor of that plan. The Treasury did not like our original bill, and the billion dollars we were looking for then, and it was dropped out. These are the two plans.

We have in this banking system now over 2,400 members. That increase has all come practically since last May. They represent about three and one half billion dollars of assets. These building and loan associations supply the mortgages for about 65 per cent of the small homes of the country.

Our view is that if you allow them to go on and be drained of their resources, and unable to get any new funds, we are going to face another avalanche of mortgages and demands.

PRESIDENT ROOSEVELT: How are they being drained of funds?

MR. FAHEY: In this way—as their shares mature their people come around and demand payment, and they either pay in part or in full. A great many of them are unable to pay in full, and because of that they are getting no new savings at all. Nothing new is coming in.

PRESIDENT ROOSEVELT: What rate have they for paying?

MR. FAHEY: Their share holders get three and a half, four, and, in some cases, four and one-half per cent.

PRESIDENT ROOSEVELT: Why all that spread?

MR. FAHEY: It takes a spread of about one and a half per cent to do business, but, of course, in the areas where they are getting seven and one-half per cent, they are paying more for their money.

PRESIDENT ROOSEVELT: Is it your impression that the overhead is altogether too high on these building and loan associations?

MR. FAHEY: Most of them are pretty modest.

RNEY GENERAL CUMMINGS: They have to take care of losses.

MR. FAHEY: Yes.

PRESIDENT ROOSEVELT: What does the Treasurer think?

SECRETARY MORGENTHAU: Mr. President, Mr. Walker asked me to come over this afternoon. Mr. Eccles has been on this thing for about three months. Almost worked himself out. This is an emergency program and we have about come to the end of the—what shall I say?—the end of the road on this thing, and the important thing is, can we go on indefinitely refinancing at a lower interest rate all the small home mortgages in the United States, and don't we have to take steps to divert this into private channels?

Before you came in, I asked Mr. Fahey whether he had taken any steps to put the brakes on so that we could save some of the two billion dollars for the sole purpose of keeping people from losing their homes. I asked if I could go over there and see whether I could not put the brakes on to save at least $500,000,000 for the sole purpose of saving their homes from being taken away from them. I took a short course of an hour and a half on this subject this morning with Mr. Hopkins and Mr. Walker, and we have been all over it. I think Mr. Fahey will have to say that he has had plenty of time to argue on this thing back and forth, and I think we have come to the place where we have to make a decision.

MR. FAHEY: On that point I beg to differ with you. A draft of this bill was never available until last week. The draft of the plan was submitted a week or ten days ago, and it has been discussed and under examination as something that should be submitted for criticism and discussion. That is the process it has been going through.

PRESIDENT ROOSEVELT: Shouldn't we differentiate between two very different subjects —one, financing of new homes, and two, refinancing of homes already in existence? Or have we already done that?

SECRETARY MORGENTHAU: Yes, that has been put up to Mr. Fahey.

MR. FAHEY: We were not invited in on this discussion today at all.

SECRETARY MORGENTHAU: I can say that everybody that was there this morning agreed to this—Harry and everybody else there—that if they set up a billion dollars for homes already in existence, and offered to insure those mortgages under this plan which has been worked out, that that was a channel which would divert the flood which is on Mr. Fahey, up to $200,000,000 of existing mortgages.

PRESIDENT ROOSEVELT: How much does that mean above the government funds for the insurance corporation?

210

MR. FAHEY: How are you going to insure distressed mortgages? I think you are under a clear misunderstanding. The great bulk of these applications are those where people are due to lose their homes. That is what we are faced with through foreclosure.

PRESIDENT ROOSEVELT: How much money have you left?

MR. FAHEY: One billion, four hundred million dollars.

SECRETARY MORGENTHAU: You ought to keep that. How many of those people want to get lower interest rates?

MR. FAHEY: About 35 per cent.

SECRETARY MORGENTHAU: I would like to have the privilege of looking into that.

MR. FAHEY: Sure! By examining the application.

SECRETARY MORGENTHAU: I went all through that for a year. If you have $1,400,000,000 left, I think that should be saved.

PRESIDENT ROOSEVELT: You are talking about existing homes. That is one subject. I understood the chief thing we were talking about was the other subject, which is financing new homes. Is that right? That is a different thing.

MR. WALKER: That contemplates opening up the mortgage market as it now exists. It will be necessary to take care of existing mortgages.

PRESIDENT ROOSEVELT: Why do you have to do that?

MR. WALKER: A lot of the savings banks have loaned up to the limit. All the objections that came from this were directed to new money going out for new construction, and not for existing mortgages.

PRESIDENT ROOSEVELT: I am still perfectly foggy about the whole thing. Can you differentiate between old mortgages and new mortgages?

SECRETARY MORGENTHAU: We did this morning. There are three different plans. One is the plan to lend a man between two hundred and two thousand dollars. Another plan, which we agreed upon in our office this morning, was some corporation would insure private institutions who want to lend to people who want to build new homes.

PRESIDENT ROOSEVELT: Is everybody agreed on that?

MR. WALKER: Yes, everybody is agreed on that.

PRESIDENT ROOSEVELT: The only thing is the third thing, the refinancing of old mortgages. Why do you have to do that at all, outside the funds of the Home Owners' Loan Corporation? Why is that?

MR. HOPKINS: I think there are two distinct things. The part that interests one is the part that will give people work and move capital goods. The third part of this thing is, as I get it, a reform measure, and it comes about by the fact that the Home Owners' Loan has got four billion dollars worth of applications and only two billion dollars. We argued quite a while

211

this morning as to whether or not we would get just as much repair work and new building if we eliminated this entirely.

PRESIDENT ROOSEVELT: Why can't we eliminate No. 3 altogether for the time being?

MR. FAHEY: The insurance of old mortgages?

PRESIDENT ROOSEVELT: Yes.

MR. FAHEY: I think it is absolutely necessary. It is an impossible thing to do. If anybody will show me an organization by which it can be done, I will approve it in a minute. We certainly are not capable of doing it.

PRESIDENT ROOSEVELT: Who is pushing the insurance of old mortgages? Has it got a father? or a mother?

MR. WALKER: It has eight or ten parents.

MR. ECCLES: I met with Mr. Fahey and the Home Owners' Loan group last week and we went over this plan and we agreed to the elimination of old mortgages. Mr. Walker and Mr. Riefler and others have thought that there should be some reform of the mortgage market in order to provide for a long-term instrument and low interest rate. They felt that the other should be included, and this morning, as a result of a compromise of the situation, the Secretary agreed to go as far as one billion dollars on insuring loans on existing properties. I don't think that is going to relieve the Home Owners' Loan to any great extent because 50 per cent was the limit of value upon appraisals. That in itself would practically eliminate the distressed mortgages. However, it would tend, I think, to reduce the interest rates substantially on existing mortgages as a result of the competition that might be created as a result of it. So to that extent it would be a reform. Now the problem is the organization to provide the appraisal mechanism necessary to get insurance on existing properties. Mr. Fahey is correct when he states that he has objected to insurance of existing properties. The building and loan people object strenuously to that. They feel it will take from them the mortgages which they have, and which are 30, 40, and 50 per cent appraisals and are in good standing, because they are unable to reduce interest rates on those existing mortgages down to a point that would enable them to compete with the insured mortgage.

PRESIDENT ROOSEVELT: You say they are unable to?

MR. ECCLES: They say they are.

MR. FAHEY: Mr. President, there is one point on that; that proposal is absolutely impracticable. We cannot see any savings banks or other holders of sound mortgages which are not in distress on a basis of 50 per cent value, and on which they are getting six per cent interest today, where they are going to take five per cent and one per cent more for insurance. In the second place, we don't exactly see how a savings bank or any other bank will be in a position of having part of its mortgages guaranteed and another part not guaranteed, and expect that they are going to get deposits or savings out of the public on such a basis as that. What I point out is that savings banks and insurance organizations, which are the two largest factors in this, say that they see no practical way they could do anything of this sort. Maybe they don't know what they are talking about, but that is what they tell us.

MR. WALKER: This is going to cut your interest rates.

MR. FAHEY: I don't believe it would cut the interest rates for a long time.

MR. WALKER: We do have to get a low interest rate or we cannot achieve the purpose we are setting out to achieve.

PRESIDENT ROOSEVELT: Will the lending of money on new homes through insurance plan number two at lower rates have a tendency to bring down the existing mortgages of building and loan associations?

MR. FAHEY: I don't see how it can. They are coming down somewhat already as a result of new conditions. They are taking the good mortgages at lower rates where they have money in some of the states, but of course that is very spotted, and it is only true in some sections of the country. Insurance companies, in some cases on prime loans, absolutely first-class loans, are renewing them at five per cent or making new loans at that rate. That is a very limited thing.

PRESIDENT ROOSEVELT: You think we ought not to have any new set-up for the old mortgages?

MR. FAHEY: I would strongly advise against attempting to tackle the old mortgages at the present time. I think you have to experiment with this new device, and make some adjustments on it. I think because of the resistance of selfish interests to it that it will take some time before you can get them in line.

PRESIDENT ROOSEVELT: On new legislation, there would be debate.

MR. FAHEY: There is no doubt about that. Take the application of this to the savings departments of national banks: my impression is that you would find a vigorous attack on that in the United States Congress.

MR. WALKER: We are going to get very serious attention from the insurance people if you confine it to new construction.

MR. FAHEY: I don't believe there is any one of the insurance groups that will use it at all. If there is, I don't know who it is. Maybe the Prudential is making some long-term loans. Very few of

	the others have. Certainly if they mean what they say—the large interests in the insurance field—it has no appeal to them at all. They cannot use it.
MR. WALKER:	They make the argument they want the current mortgage market straightened out. If you confine this to new building, that will not be done without getting their own house in order first. If it is confined entirely to new construction, it will have an opposite effect upon them, and we are going to have bitter opposition from them unless we do give them an opportunity to make this apply to current mortgages.
MR. RIEFLER:	I think if this goes down as a new construction program, the insurance companies would "see red," whereas now they seem fairly friendly.
PRESIDENT ROOSEVELT:	What do you think, Homer? How far do you think we ought to go?
ATTORNEY GENERAL CUMMINGS:	I think there are some very great difficulties quite aside from the policy. If you are going into this third group on any extensive scale, I don't know how you are going to do the appraisal work—how you are going to handle the mechanical proposition, even if Congress agrees to it.
PRESIDENT ROOSEVELT:	You think on repairs and new houses we could go ahead?
ATTORNEY GENERAL CUMMINGS:	I should think so.
PRESIDENT ROOSEVELT:	You have had a certain amount of experience on that; what do you think?
MR. JONES:	I am in favor of the new work, both kinds. I am in favor of the principle of the other, but I have not seen the detail of it. I would like an opportunity to read it and understand how it can be applied. I see a good many difficulties, but at the same time I think a good purpose would be served if we can find the solution to that whole subject.
PRESIDENT ROOSEVELT:	John, what is the present situation of the old building and loan companies?
MR. FAHEY:	The present situation is that there are about 2,400 of the best of them that have come into the Home Loan Bank System since last May. There are about 11,000 such associations in the country. Probably three to four thousand of those are on the way out now.
PRESIDENT ROOSEVELT:	What happens when they go out? Do people get their money back?
MR. FAHEY:	They get what there is. In some cases, they have been taken over by state bank commissioners and are being liquidated. In other cases, they are in suspense and are gradually being liquidated, but sales are not being forced. In other cases they are being forced. Some are being reorganized and merged.

Some are in process of being converted into federals. We have a big one out in Toledo, amounting to about ten million dollars.

PRESIDENT ROOSEVELT: Can the RFC provide any funds for those?

MR. FAHEY: No, we recommended that steps be taken along that line. We are pretty sure of this, that if we undertake to carry forward this insurance plan through the Home Loan Bank Board, we would be up against very serious difficulties in the banking system and that a great many good associations, as it goes on here in the next year, would make no progress at all, and would not lend money because they would not have it. Our theory is quite in line with the suggestion of the Treasury and the Director of the Budget. As soon as we can get existing agencies into action and relieve the government from carrying this load, that is what we ought to do, but you cannot do that without strengthening some of these agencies and you cannot do that while the government is providing competition. They tell us all over the country, as they pay out checks on these maturing shares, the checks show clearly that the money is put into the savings banks or commercial banks. They are not getting it.

PRESIDENT ROOSEVELT: What are these savings and loan associations, primarily?

MR. FAHEY: They are mutual thrift associations.

PRESIDENT ROOSEVELT: Why do we apply a different rule than to these other banks?

MR. FAHEY: Our feeling is that we should not.

PRESIDENT ROOSEVELT: The RFC is taking care of the distressed savings banks?

MR. JONES: Yes, we have done that. We have taken care of building and loan associations by lending money, not by capital.

PRESIDENT ROOSEVELT: You are lending money on assets.

MR. JONES: Yes.

PRESIDENT ROOSEVELT: What is the essential difference between the relationship of RFC to savings banks and to building and loan association banks that are in trouble?

MR. ECCLES: The bank deposits are subject to demand. Savings bank deposits can be withdrawn in 30, 60, or 90 days. Building and loan associations sell stock or shares which mature over a period of years. Many have been attempting to perform the functions of a bank by retiring their stock upon demand or approximately so, and have gotten into difficulties as a result of performing a function which they were not set up to perform. I do believe there is a possibility of providing a form of insurance, and we have been working with Mr. Fahey on that matter, and are hopeful of being able to submit a program that would give to the building and loan companies which

215

qualify for membership in the Home Loan Banks a type of insurance that would protect them as building and loan institutions, not as deposit institutions.

MR. JONES: A great many have advertised six, seven, and eight per cent on demand. Whatever is done, if anything, they should be reduced down to conservative principles.

MR. FAHEY: That is absolutely necessary. The only way of doing that, Mr. President, is getting them into the Federal Home Loan Bank system where you can maintain control over them. That is what is proposed by this plan.

PRESIDENT ROOSEVELT: What do you need in order to do that?

MR. FAHEY: We would use this insurance plan and offer it only to those who are in the Home Loan Bank system. We would check them when they come in and make them conform to the requirements.

We left two or three things up in the air Friday—rate of premium, and the question of withdrawal. Those questions were still open to debate when we finished up last Friday. My own belief about it is that we ought to be able to work out these two plans, and our feeling is that the second one is essential if the first one is going to be put into effect. We are morally certain about the results so far as the Home Loan Bank and the lending interests as a whole are concerned.

MR. WALKER: That would be in the nature of a federal insurance plan for building and loan associations, and you would find yourselves the first thing with the same obligations to guarantee principal in the Home Owners' Loan. The plan submitted to us is on the basis of one-fifth, two-fifths, or three-fifths of one per cent. That was not good business. I believe the government would start with $100,000,000 or $200,000,000 and have a federal agency sponsored by the government. I don't see how you are going to avoid later on, if this is not worked out on an insurance basis, some more obligations when we start into the Home Owners' Loan. If you can work out some insurance plan that is sound, I would be inclined to agree. From all the conversation I have heard at the conference I have attended, I don't think the building and loan association crowds are in the frame of mind that they want to go along with that. They want too big a spread, and they do not want a sufficient rate of insurance.

MR. FAHEY: I don't believe that any proposed statute would pass Congress that did not have sufficient safeguards in that respect. We certainly would not want to favor any where the proposed rate is not sufficient. We hold no brief for any particular rate. That does not bother us at all. It is only a question of a workable plan.

PRESIDENT ROOSEVELT: I cannot get it out of my head that these building and loan associations are not banks. Why don't banking rules apply?

MR. JONES: They have not quite as good a grade of management as savings banks. If you do it at all, it ought to be pretty well worked out.

PRESIDENT ROOSEVELT: I suppose they are generally managed by the local plumber, and the national banks are run by the local grocer.

MR. FAHEY: What is the difference between the plumber and the grocer?

ATTORNEY GENERAL CUMMINGS: The plumbers are supposed to stop more leaks! (*Laughter*)

PRESIDENT ROOSEVELT: Have you considered the possibility of placing them on the basis of banks and reorganizing the ones on the edge?

MR. FAHEY: That is what we would like to see take place in order to establish a sound system for the future. We think those that cannot be insured will drop out of the picture, and that it is well that they should.

MR. ECCLES: The present bank insurance plan would not meet the situation.

PRESIDENT ROOSEVELT: Why?

MR. ECCLES: They pay a higher rate of interest, and their funds are not subject to immediate withdrawal.

PRESIDENT ROOSEVELT: I am inclined to think we better go ahead with Nos. 1 and 2, and let you people talk more about No. 3.

MR. FAHEY: You mean the insurance of individual mortgages?

PRESIDENT ROOSEVELT: New mortgages.

MR. FAHEY: What do you say about the old mortgages?

PRESIDENT ROOSEVELT: That is No. 3.

ATTORNEY GENERAL CUMMINGS: First is repairs.

PRESIDENT ROOSEVELT: Here is the point. This whole subject was started with the idea of putting people to work on new work. We gradually discovered that it had some relationship, not very well defined, to existing financing of existing buildings. We are not interested in financing existing buildings from the point of view of putting people to work. That was the original objective, starting what was called the heavy industries. Suppose we confine ourselves to that for the moment and get the legislation for that. As I understand, it is very simple.

ATTORNEY GENERAL CUMMINGS: That would be fairly easy.

PRESIDENT ROOSEVELT: If we could cut out all the frills in the legislation, leaving the details to administration rather than legislation, I think we could come pretty close to writing a bill in two pages which

217

	would allow us to set up insurance. What do you think?
SECRETARY PERKINS:	Mr. Wallace and I thought we would have the insurance lobby on us. They have mortgages left on their hands.
PRESIDENT ROOSEVELT:	But they are being paid right along.
SECRETARY PERKINS:	Sometimes they are not. They want some insurance. They have unsold or unrented houses on their hands. It is the same situation you get in New York slum clearance.
PRESIDENT ROOSEVELT:	All the owners are opposed to putting up any new buildings.
SECRETARY PERKINS:	They would like to go ahead with new financing if they could have some relief on their existing mortgages. I suppose it is insurance companies to whom you look for the capital for the construction work who are going to object if they are not taken care of. It is a political choice as to which group you can best cope with.
SECRETARY MORGENTHAU:	May I say there is much merit in the suggestion just made by the Secretary of Labor. If we assume, as Mr. Fahey says, that we cannot appraise these to any great extent in the next year, then we are not going to loan out a lot of this money; and if, as he says, not many of these agencies will take this money on old mortgages, our obligations are not going to be serious. On the other hand, it will take off our shoulders the insurance crowd, and the savings banks crowd. If they start lobbying, we are going to find ourselves in serious difficulty.
PRESIDENT ROOSEVELT:	You have very little time left if you are going to get any legislation. It seems to me you should get together, if you can, in the next 24 or 36 hours.
MR. FAHEY:	I am willing to agree on anything that will work, but I cannot tell the President of the United States that I think the proposed plan will work when our experience demonstrates that it won't.
MR. WALKER:	Mr. President, I wish you would tell Mr. Fahey to agree on this!
MR. FAHEY:	I will do anything that the President of the United States tells me to do, but I cannot see any way that this can be worked out.
PRESIDENT ROOSEVELT:	Make Frank the chairman; he is very good at making people agree to things. Now John, Henry, and Brother Eccles— is there anybody else in on this particular phase? Frank, get them in a room and tell them no lunch unless they agree! (*Laughter*)
MR. WALKER:	Ten days ago, we were supposed to agree in 48 hours.
SECRETARY MORGENTHAU:	Life isn't long enough, Mr. President.

PRESIDENT ROOSEVELT: You are a young man, compared with Mr. Fahey.

SECRETARY MORGENTHAU: I will put it this way. Life is long enough, but the day isn't long enough. I am glad for Mr. Eccles' services.

MR. JONES: He is a younger man than Mr. Fahey!

PRESIDENT ROOSEVELT: I think we need a steam roller here! Go ahead, and see me tomorrow.

Meeting adjourned at 4:20 p.m.

Proceedings of the National Emergency Council

Joint Meeting of the Executive Council and the National Emergency Council

Held in the Cabinet Room of the Executive Offices, The White House, Tuesday, June 26, 1934, at 2:55 p.m.

[meeting no. 10]
June 26, 1934

Present: the President of the United States; the Secretary of State; the Secretary of the Treasury; the Secretary of War; the Attorney General; the Secretary of the Interior; the Secretary of Agriculture; the Secretary of Labor; the Director of the Budget; the Assistant Secretary of the Treasury; the Assistant Secretary of the Navy; the Assistant Secretary of Commerce; the Administrator of Agricultural Adjustment; the Administrator of Federal Emergency Relief; the Administrator for Industrial Recovery; the Chairman of the Board of the Home Owners' Loan Corporation; the Chairman of the Board of the Reconstruction Finance Corporation; the Chairman of the Board of the Tennessee Valley Authority; the Director of the Emergency Conservation Work; the Federal Coordinator of Transportation; the Governor of the Farm Credit Administration; the Chairman of the Federal Trade Commission; the Adviser on Consumer Problems; the Economic Adviser; the Executive Secretary.

[There is a trend, visible in this meeting, of the NEC "shaking down" into a more modest role. It is characterized, perhaps, by F.D.R.'s remark: "at least it is a clearing house of information" (p. 230). At this meeting, the discussion of major policy issues was rather conspicuously absent, and the burden of discussion related to matters of secondary importance growing out of reports that had been submitted for the agenda. These were efficiently disposed of by the President. Hence the Council functioned quite well at this rather modest decision-making and coordinating level. Also, its role as a source of information for the President on current developments and problems was demonstrated—a role that will be seen to grow in importance.—Editors' note.]

SECRETARY MORGENTHAU: The meeting will please come to order. We will have the minutes of the last meeting of the Executive Council.... Next on the agenda is the question of reallocation of funds of the Executive Council.

MR. WALKER: That is to be signed by the President. We will take that up after he comes in.

SECRETARY MORGENTHAU: We will now have the report of the Secretary of Agriculture in connection with the drought situation and crop conditions....

Next is the report of the Economic Adviser. (*Just as Mr. Riefler had begun reading his report, the President came in.*)

PRESIDENT ROOSEVELT: I am sorry to be late but I have been trying to settle the affairs of the Republic of Colombia during the past hour. Does anyone wonder that the United States is not frightfully popular in the countries of Central and South America! The President of Colombia tells me that their national debt which is owing to the United States, including the citizens of the United States, is on the average of a six and one-half per cent basis, and in addition to that, there is a premium of three and one half per cent, making a total of ten per cent interest, and the other republics which also borrowed up here are paying about fifteen per cent to American bankers and other citizens. That is worse than Jesse Jones! (*Laughter*)

MEMBER: Why couldn't they borrow on better terms than that in Europe? Why is it possible for bankers to exact such terms?

PRESIDENT ROOSEVELT: They did borrow part of it in Europe.

MEMBER: On the same terms?

PRESIDENT ROOSEVELT: About two-thirds here and one-third in Europe.

MR. WALKER: I spoke with some of the Cabinet officers and I tried to get some of the matters out of the way. We are now on the Economic Adviser's report.

PRESIDENT ROOSEVELT: Just before we get to that, what is the situation in agriculture, Henry?

SECRETARY WALLACE: The drought, you mean?[1]

PRESIDENT ROOSEVELT: Yes.

SECRETARY WALLACE: There have been scattered rains during the last ten days.

PRESIDENT ROOSEVELT: Things looking a little better?

SECRETARY WALLACE: I would say, rather, that they have not been getting worse. These rains have not restored the pastures so as to make a great difference; the hay crop is gone and small grain crop is gone. It means that we have to take up these three million to five million head of cattle; but it also means that we are not going to be overwhelmed.

PRESIDENT ROOSEVELT: How is the corn situation?

---

[1] A sampling of the *New York Times* for the spring months of 1934 depicts vividly the drought situation. An article which appeared May 13 (sec. IV, p. 1) says this was the worst drought in 25 years. On July 15, Arkansas was reported to have had but .01 inches of rainfall in 33 consecutive days.

SECRETARY WALLACE:	These rains have been enough to carry the corn in pretty good shape, but we cannot tell much about it until the month of July. These rains are not quite enough. There is necessity for about one inch each week to get a good crop of corn. We cannot tell you about corn until in August, although we can tell you if it is ruined before that.
PRESIDENT ROOSEVELT:	Mr. Riefler, you were in the middle of your report.
MR. RIEFLER:	Yes, sir, shall I start over again? ....
PRESIDENT ROOSEVELT	[after Mr. Riefler had referred to foreign shipments of motor vehicles]: Where are those going?
MR. RIEFLER:	I have not looked at the distribution of them; but I think they are going to the noncontinental markets, where the restrictions do not hold them out.
PRESIDENT ROOSEVELT:	Yes, outside of Europe. The next question is whether information should be made public in regard to emergency expenditures in the various states.
MR. WALKER:	(...) These requests come largely from Senators and Congressmen who would like to go back and give a report to their constituents on these activities.
PRESIDENT ROOSEVELT:	It would make a very bad showing in some states, and much too good a showing in other states.
SECRETARY ICKES:	We have given them information on PWA when they have asked for it, and I don't think we have had any repercussions.
MR. FECHNER:	We have given out information on the CCC.
MR. HOPKINS:	We have been publishing it right along and never had any serious trouble over it.
SECRETARY PERKINS:	But when you put it all together—the CCC and Agriculture and Public Works—it may look bad. I think they should get it independently from each of the agencies.
PRESIDENT ROOSEVELT:	If you put it together, it would require too many explanations. We are not hiding anything from the public at the present time, but let them get the figures from each department.
MR. MYERS:	It is more revealing to have the details than to have the totals.
MR. WALKER:	We have our central information service and it is embarrassing to say we don't have the information.
PRESIDENT ROOSEVELT:	You can ask them what they want and then get it for them.
MR. WALKER:	Get it separately?
PRESIDENT ROOSEVELT:	Yes, if you lump the figures, it is apt to be confusing. Next is the report by the Executive Secretary on the disposition suits already begun by the Justice Department, but for which the appropriations have been diverted, including a report by the Director of Procurement.

MR. WALKER: This is a report, and I don't think there is any need of going into the whole thing. They recommend going ahead with the condemnation suits at Urbana, Illinois; Detroit, Michigan; Fremont, Michigan; Endicott, New York; Fayetteville, North Carolina; Aliquippa, Pennsylvania, and Butler, Pennsylvania; and, for various reasons, held up on those at Moline, Illinois; Kalamazoo, Michigan; Orange, New Jersey; New Rochelle, New York; and Buffalo, New York.

PRESIDENT ROOSEVELT: What are those condemnation suits for?

MR. WALKER: They are for sites for post offices—all post office buildings. Some of these moneys were put aside for other purposes and the condemnation suit stopped.

ORNEY GENERAL CUMMINGS: We thought the defendants were entitled to know whether we were going on, so I asked that this question be settled, whether we are going on and how far.

PRESIDENT ROOSEVELT: Next is the report of the chairman of the board of the Home Owners' Loan Corporation of the purchase of a building. I hear you have bought one.

MR. FAHEY: Yes, Mr. President.

PRESIDENT ROOSEVELT: The price is right?

MR. FAHEY: Yes, we managed to chisel them down about forty thousand less than their original price.

PRESIDENT ROOSEVELT: Have you got it?

MR. FAHEY: Yes, sir.

PRESIDENT ROOSEVELT: Are you going to move in soon?

MR. FAHEY: Yes, sir.

PRESIDENT ROOSEVELT: I thought you looked happier.

MR. FAHEY: It is a fireproof building and it will save us about forty thousand dollars a year in rentals.

PRESIDENT ROOSEVELT: Talking about space, we have discussed on numerous occasions the question of building a Public Records building and taking what might be called the dead or the moribund files out of a great many departments and agencies. The last report I have had is that the Archives Building, which is, of course, eventually to serve an entirely different purpose, will have, in the beginning, a great deal of extra space.[2]

SECRETARY ICKES: Yes, sir; we can put stacks in there for at least fifty years of dead files.

PRESIDENT ROOSEVELT: Yes, so we can put, for instance, the Veterans' War Department files in there and that will give you a lot of space;

---

[2] The cornerstone of the National Archives building was laid in the last days of the Hoover Administration in 1933; the structure was completed in 1935.

	and all you need to do is put two or three people down there with a telephone.
SECRETARY ICKES:	Do you wish us to go ahead?
PRESIDENT ROOSEVELT:	Yes, see that the Archives Building stacks will be sufficient to take care of the dead and semi-dead records. That will save us a lot of space. Next we will have the report of the state directors of the National Emergency Council (. . .).
PRESIDENT ROOSEVELT:	Is there any comment on that by anybody? Do you want any discussion on that? The only question there is whether the state directors should be given additional authority on code enforcement.
GENERAL JOHNSON:	I think if they are given additional authority, they should be confined to that work. We have a director of enforcement. I do not believe one man can do that job and attend to all the other emergency jobs too. Take the state of California, for example; there has been a constant effort to get us to agree to a "transmountain empire" out there. We have several times had most unfortunate experiences. As soon as you let it get out of your hands, they begin to interpret the codes in entire defiance of the policy and for racketeering purposes. I think that so far as the making of policies is concerned, it would be a mistake to disseminate it.
SECRETARY PERKINS:	How many of them asked for more authority in enforcement?
MR. WALKER:	Only two, I think.
SECRETARY PERKINS:	Is Maryland one of them?
MR. WALKER:	Yes.
SECRETARY PERKINS:	Maryland always does, and that would be the worst possible place to give it to them, too.
PRESIDENT ROOSEVELT:	The next thing down here is—I don't know quite what it means—No. 9: "For discussion and decision. Hopkins."
MR. WALKER:	That is mine. The Director of Federal Emergency Relief brought in his report at the last minute, and that is my handwriting there. He was late with his report.
PRESIDENT ROOSEVELT:	Do we give him a chance first? I think it is better to hear what he has to say.
MR. HOPKINS:	There have been wide complaints around here about my not having a haircut. I have a report there which Mr. Walker has, but I don't know whether he wants to read it or not. It is about the drought and relief situation in the country as I see it today.
PRESIDENT ROOSEVELT:	I think it is worth reading (...). I thought you told me only about 125,000 families.

MR. HOPKINS: Mr. President, since last week the drought area has almost doubled, and the number of families has about doubled.

PRESIDENT ROOSEVELT: How does that compare with your report, Henry?

SECRETARY WALLACE: The relief people are just that slow in recognizing the situation. They were slow in recognizing it up to June 10. That is when the situation seemed most desperate. The rains which have come since then have prevented it from becoming more serious, and since that time we are rather maintaining *status quo*.

PRESIDENT ROOSEVELT: Do you think you have most of them on the list now?

MR. HOPKINS: No, I think we will get a big increase in the relief loans this winter, in the Dakotas especially. In most of the drought states I think we have them on now.

PRESIDENT ROOSEVELT: They will run to a total of what, throughout the winter?

MR. HOPKINS: A total of 500,000 families.

PRESIDENT ROOSEVELT: You are going ahead with the allotment due in the other agencies?

MR. HOPKINS: Yes, that has all been done, Mr. President.

PRESIDENT ROOSEVELT: You want a further allotment before I go?

MR. FECHNER: Mr. President, I have a memorandum I would like to present to you.

PRESIDENT ROOSEVELT: You are afraid Mr. Hopkins will try to take away your $50,000,000?

MR. FECHNER: No, I don't think so.

PRESIDENT ROOSEVELT: You are taking the business out of the urban areas.

MR. FECHNER: It was my understanding that Mr. Hopkins would take care of the country boys, and the CCC boys would come from the city.

PRESIDENT ROOSEVELT: I think that is going to be the right way to handle it. The failure of crops is not only going to put a lot of farm boys out of work, but also a lot of city boys.

[The President then read a summary of the reports submitted by members of the Executive Council.]

[Reading of a court decision relating to the power of the ICC to set minimum freight rates] What is the net result now?

ATTORNEY GENERAL CUMMINGS: The ruling is overturned because apparently there was no findings that the ratings were less than reasonable, or noncompensatory.

MR. EASTMAN: That is the lower court. That has not gone up yet.

ATTORNEY GENERAL CUMMINGS: Oh no, that is what they call the three-judge court.

PRESIDENT ROOSEVELT: Where does it go then?

ATTORNEY GENERAL CUMMINGS: To the regular Circuit Court. It could go to the Supreme Court direct, but I don't know what the wishes of the ICC

225

	would be. Do you know?
MR. EASTMAN:	No, I do not. I have not attended those meetings. I should think, myself, it ought to be cleared up.
ATTORNEY GENERAL CUMMINGS:	It is a very important ruling.
PRESIDENT ROOSEVELT	[reading that 786 codes were set for hearings]: Hugh, how are you getting on with the so-called blanket code?
GENERAL JOHNSON:	Everybody is not agreed on it, but I think we will have it out in a day or two now.
PRESIDENT ROOSEVELT	[after reading from the report of the TVA board chairman]: How are you getting on with the Knoxville case?[3]
DR. MORGAN:	That is just waiting for the Tennessee Valley Power Company to approach us again. We did not get together at the time of the negotiation. They are considering how they can approach us again.
PRESIDENT ROOSEVELT:	They did not think we offered them quite enough?
DR. MORGAN:	No; they would like to get enough so that the bond holders will get only a part of what they put in, and the others will get a part.
PRESIDENT ROOSEVELT	[reading the proposals of the Federal Coordinator of Transportation for extensive changes in methods of handling railroad traffiic]: Eighty per cent; how do you account for that?
MR. EASTMAN:	That includes intermediate terminals.
PRESIDENT ROOSEVELT	[after reading a plan for pooling freight cars]: Are you getting anywhere with that?
MR. EASTMAN:	They are reaching an agreement on operations of the plan that never have been agreed to heretofore.
PRESIDENT ROOSEVELT:	Are they going along with the idea of pooling of ownership and maintenance?
MR. EASTMAN:	I doubt whether they do it voluntarily, but as I say, some of the sticking points in the past have been worked out, apparently satisfactorily.
PRESIDENT ROOSEVELT	[after reading of the need for permanent legislation for centralized regulation of transportation]: The Emergency Act expires June 16, 1935. I think after you have a little holiday, and we both get back to Washington, we might talk over the plans for the next session of Congress beginning on the third of next January.
MR. EASTMAN:	Yes, sir.
PRESIDENT ROOSEVELT	[reading the RFC financial statement]: You are pretty nearly through with that, aren't you now?

---

[3] Apparently this refers to the offer by TVA of $6,550,000 for the Knoxville properties of Tennessee Public Service Company. Long court fights followed during the rest of the year over these properties.

MR. JONES: No, there will be a good many more.

PRESIDENT ROOSEVELT: You have authorized a billion?

MR. JONES: I think it will be a billion and three if we complete the job. All these that we have authorized will not be taken. There is some yet to come.

PRESIDENT ROOSEVELT [having read that 11,000 veterans were included in the new CCC enrollees]: Bob, how are those war veterans working out now?

MR. FECHNER: They are doing very well, Mr. President, the reports indicate. Of course, we have had some trouble with a few of the camps. A few of them seem to have been impossible to get straightened out, but there have been very few. I have just gotten another letter from General Hines since I came over this afternoon, urging me to ask you again to permit veterans at camp more than a year. There is a great deal of merit in it.

PRESIDENT ROOSEVELT: They have had a year, which is more than most of the boys have had.

MR. FECHNER: Yes, but the veterans are nearly all married men with families and just simply won't be thrown out.

PRESIDENT ROOSEVELT: You can't get rid of them?

MR. FECHNER: General Hines urges that the rules be suspended in the case of veterans.

PRESIDENT ROOSEVELT: Are they making any effort to find jobs for the veterans?

MR. FECHNER: Yes, the Federal Employment offices under Mr. Persons are doing all they can, but it is hard to get a man forty-five years old a job.

PRESIDENT ROOSEVELT: Do you think we ought to keep them on?

SECRETARY PERKINS: Are there any other veterans who want to take their places?

MR. FECHNER: In some corps areas there are, and in others there are not.

SECRETARY PERKINS: There are nearly 11,000 of them, and they are acclimated so that the hard period of management is over, and with veterans the period of management is very hard. The first two or three months are the hardest ones.

PRESIDENT ROOSEVELT: Go ahead, then, and let them re-enroll, but see if you can make a special effort to find them jobs.

MR. FECHNER: I will take that up with Mr. Persons.

PRESIDENT ROOSEVELT [reading of selection of winter camp sites]: The bill did not go through, did it, authorizing us to give away the camps to municipalities, to counties, and to towns?[4]

MR. FECHNER: No, sir.

PRESIDENT ROOSEVELT: What are you going to do with them?

---

[4] These seem to have been camps closed because work in the area was completed. Judging from figures in the CCC report for 1933-1935, there was considerable fluctuation in the number of camps in each state.

MR. FECHNER: We turned them over to the Director of Procurement, and he is offering them to any other federal agency. Mr. Hopkins seems to be about the only one who can find any use for them at all. I don't know how many Mr. Hopkins has taken over.

MR. HOPKINS: Three hundred.

MR. FECHNER: I was very sorry that the legislation did not go through. I did everything I could and so did Marvin.[5] We tried to get it through but could not do it.

PRESIDENT ROOSEVELT: What is the procedure in case a municipality wants to buy one of those camps?

MR. FECHNER: It has to be put up at public sale and if the municipality offers the highest price they will get it.

PRESIDENT ROOSEVELT: Wouldn't the price really be the scrap value of the entire plant? Isn't that about all?

MR. FECHNER: Yes, we would be lucky if we got that much.

PRESIDENT ROOSEVELT: Shouldn't the municipality be able to be the highest bidder in a case of that kind?

MR. FECHNER: Yes, sir, I think so.

PRESIDENT ROOSEVELT: Is there any way under the law in which the Director of Procurement can ask for bids for a camp and then after bids are received, say to a municipality, you can have it if you will equal the high bid or exceed the high bid?

MR. FECHNER: In my opinion, that would not be legal.

MEMBER: It has been the practice in the past on old federal buildings if the city comes along and makes a bid that is in line with the reasonable value, the government can sell it to them without any trouble. Sometimes they want an old post office building for a library or something of that kind.

DIRECTOR DOUGLAS: I wonder what law that is under?

MR. FECHNER: Admiral Peoples says he cannot do that.

PRESIDENT ROOSEVELT: Will you talk with Peoples about that?

MR. FECHNER: Yes, sir.

DIRECTOR DOUGLAS: It requires an act of Congress to do that, Mr. President.

PRESIDENT ROOSEVELT: You might look into it too, Lew—some way in which a city could say, "We will offer two per cent or five per cent above the highest bidder"—put that in as a bid, knowing pretty well that the highest bid will be on the scrap value of the plant. I would like to give municipalities chances to get these camps without having to pull them down.

MR. FECHNER: There are others in the southern states besides municipalities.

---

[5] This is probably not a reference to Marvin McIntyre, one of the Presidential secretaries. It has not been possible to discover to whom it does refer.

The 4-H Clubs have been very active in trying to make arrangements to buy some of them.

PRESIDENT ROOSEVELT: And the Boy Scouts organizations?

MR. FECHNER: Yes, quite a number of them. They are not municipalities and most of them haven't any money. And yet I think it would be a very desirable thing.

PRESIDENT ROOSEVELT: Probably if those camps are sold at scrap value most of those organizations could raise the money.

SECRETARY PERKINS: Isn't it possible to lease them and postpone the sale date?

PRESIDENT ROOSEVELT: I think that is worthy of looking into. Can you do that?

MR. FECHNER: Only by putting it up at public offer.

SECRETARY PERKINS: Why don't you try that?

GENERAL JOHNSON: Can you, without sale or lease, give them the privilege of using the camps?

MR. FECHNER: No, sir, not under the decision of Admiral Peoples and Mr. Douglas. They both agree that I cannot lend the camps.

GENERAL JOHNSON: Lots of government property is handled that way, very informally.

MR. FECHNER: Mr. Hopkins just tells us he will handle it.

MR. HOPKINS: I think I can handle that under the Relief law.

PRESIDENT ROOSEVELT: I want to avoid tearing them down if they can be of use to somebody.

MR. FECHNER: They are not worth tearing down if they can be sold for any reasonable amount.

DIRECTOR DOUGLAS: There may be provisions in the Relief Acts sufficiently broad to cover that.

PRESIDENT ROOSEVELT: If it is a worthy purpose.

DIRECTOR DOUGLAS: Yes, sir.

PRESIDENT ROOSEVELT [reading report of loan applications to the Home Owners Loan Corporation]: I would say they are getting worse.

MR. FAHEY: The applications are beginning to decline sharply. They were down to twenty per cent for the week ending June 15, which is the lowest figure since last fall, and less than half the peak back in March. We cannot say that that is a permanent trend, but it is dropping very perceptibly from week to week now.

PRESIDENT ROOSEVELT: That is all I have. Have you anything else, Frank?

MR. WALKER: We would like to get that $28,000 which Mr. Douglas sent back to the Public Works (...).

DIRECTOR DOUGLAS: I don't understand, Frank?

MR. WALKER: We had $40,000. Twenty-eight thousand was being held by you for the Executive Council expenses. You agreed to transfer that to us, but instead your transferred it to Public

229

Works. Now I have to get an Executive Order from the President to get it back. Your department recommends that. I thought you knew about it.

DIRECTOR DOUGLAS: You asked for $12,000.

MR. WALKER: You left me only two or three thousand dollars.

DIRECTOR DOUGLAS: I think that will be enough, Frank.

MR. WALKER: Not for a very long time.

PRESIDENT ROOSEVELT: You want to keep the Council going. That brings up the subject of the next six weeks. It looks possible that I may be beyond the three-mile limit on Saturday.[6] I think it is a pretty good idea during the six weeks I am away that you should have a consolidated meeting of the Emergency Council and the Executive Council. Do you see any reason why you should not? It will give the people just one more afternoon to play golf, if you do that. Frank is going off to take a holiday, but somebody will take his place during the interim, and the senior member of the Cabinet in Washington will preside over it.

I think it is just as well to have these meetings once every two weeks for the next six weeks, for at least it is a clearing house of information. I hope very much we are going to have a peaceful time, depending on the labor situation.

I hope everybody will take a perfectly adequate holiday during the course of this summer, as I mentioned before, because of the fact that people don't think straight unless they take a proper holiday; and we have got to keep ourselves in proper condition for a very strenuous fall and winter. In other words, there will not be very much let-up next year. I hope you all will be able to take a holiday, and I think things will be fairly quiet during the next two or three months.

I just want to say one thing that comes into my head, and that is that there is going to be a great deal of shooting at the government of the United States during the next few months, and it is my expectation that a large part of the shooting—not all of it—will come either from merely political sources or will come from people whose toes have been stepped on. I think the situation we are to bear in mind,

---

[6] F.D.R. sailed from Annapolis on July 1, aboard the cruiser *U.S.S. Houston*, for a cruise to various points in the Caribbean area, the Panama Canal, and Hawaii. He arrived back in Washington on August 10, after a cross-country train journey with frequent stops.
The next two meetings occurred during this period; they illustrate the NEC functioning during a prolonged Presidential absence.

probably more than ever before, is that the government is being run less for political purposes and more for the general good than it has been in some time. I think the people who are in this room are a pretty good illustration of the correctness of that statement. In other words, we are thinking about government, and not merely about party; and the more we emphasize that fact, the more it will really be brought home to the public that we are trying to do service regardless of mere party or political reasons. And, incidentally, from the political point of view, we catch more votes doing it that way than the other.

I hope you will all be able to take a holiday, and that it will be a delightful holiday. I expect to get back the fourth or fifth day of August, and remain here during the latter part of the month of August, and remember also one thing— that I am entirely accessible, although I will be a good many miles away physically. Any important matter that you want to let me know about, or consult about, you can send to me by sending a message over to the office of Naval Communications, and they will be able to reach the ship I am on within ten or fifteen minutes, whether it is in the harbor or in the middle of the Pacific somewhere. So, actually, I will not be nearly so much out of touch with things as one might think. As you can imagine, I will have plenty of time. Of course, you may get some "horseback" opinions from me, based on lack of complete information, but I hope you will keep in touch with me in case anything does come up.

I think if the two Councils meet jointly every two weeks during the next six weeks, it will be a very good thing for everybody. I am sorry to be going away, but I think it will do us all good.

Meeting closed 4:20 p.m.

Joint Meeting of the Executive Council and
the National Emergency Council

Held in the Cabinet Room of the Executive Offices,
The White House, Tuesday, July 10, 1934, at 2:10 p.m.

**[meeting no. 11]
July 10, 1934**

Present: the Secretary of State; the Secretary of the Navy; the Secretary
of the Interior; the Secretary of Agriculture; the Undersecretary of
the Treasury; the Assistant Secretary of War; the Assistant to the
Attorney General; the First Assistant Postmaster General; the Assistant
Secretary of Commerce; the Chairman of the Board of the Home
Owners' Loan Corporation; the Federal Coordinator of Transportation;
the Assistant Director of Civilian Conservation Work; the Deputy
Governor of the Farm Credit Administration; the Third Director of
the Board of the Tennessee Valley Authority; the Chairman of the
Federal Trade Commission; the Adviser on Consumer Problems; the
Economic Adviser; the Executive Secretary.

[The key to understanding this meeting is the date. This was
the summer doldrums. In spite of the crisis represented by
the depression, the government still went into partial
suspension during the summer months. (The coming of the
Cold War would decisively change this state of affairs.) The
President was away from July first until August tenth, sailing
to the Caribbean, through the Panama Canal, to Hawaii, the
West Coast, and thence back across the continent. Both the
date, and the absence of the Chief Executive from the
meeting and from the capital as well, are reflected in the high
proportion of assistant secretaries and similar functionaries
sitting in at this session for their absent chiefs.
The lengthy discussion of the recent Executive Order dealing
with personnel classification and compensation is of interest—
in an otherwise colorless meeting—from several points
of view. It suggests the perennial problems of administering
governmental personnel systems, and the cumbersome
rigidity which is the price of an elaborate merit system.
It also suggests the special difficulties of the rapidly expanding
emergency agencies and functions, and the staffing thereof.
This was often done outside the regular merit system, at
least in part because of the near impossibility of moving
rapidly within the confines of civil service procedures. The
Order in question was part of an effort to get things back on
a more orthodox basis in these agencies. Those familiar with

the Ickes *Diary* will be more than prepared for the tart comments of the redoubtable Secretary of the Interior.— Editors' Note.]

SECRETARY HULL: I suppose we might run over the minutes while waiting for other questions to come in. Will you read the minutes?

MR. RICHBERG:[1] The minutes of the last meeting?

SECRETARY HULL: Yes. [Mr. Richberg then read the minutes.] The report of the Executive Director concerning the matter of acceptance of relief funds in payment of Home Owners' Loan obligations is next in order . . . . This is a very interesting question. Is there some comment or discussion by anyone?

MR. FAHEY: Mr. Chairman, there is one phase of it that is not dealt with in that memorandum. It is just this—it was brought up by Mr. Hopkins at a meeting of the Council some time ago—the point being that the relief agencies are making allowances to those on the rolls for rent payments. That is not uncommon, Mr. Hopkins tells me, and if those allowances are made to persons who have had their mortgages refinanced by the corporation, and they do not utilize the money for that purpose, in lieu of rent, it simply means that they are using the money otherwise. It was not our opportunity to go into it further with Mr. Hopkins before he went away on his vacation, but that was contemplated. I think it is rather difficult to rule on it in a general way. I would say that if it was a case of taking relief money, then it is doubtful; but in cases where a relief agency is making the allowance for rent or for housing purposes, that allowance ought not to be made if the home owner is being relieved by the corporation; but if money is being obtained on that excuse, I see no reason why it should not be applied to the payment of interest if we are giving out money to take care of housing. However, the corporation would be very glad to have the view of others on the subject, because it does represent a problem.

SECRETARY HULL: There would not be any way to allow the debtor to elect as to which one of two or more federal sources he would utilize to apply on this sort of item, would there?

MR. FAHEY: That might be done; but it seems perfectly plain to me that a relief agency ought not to make an allowance for rent if it is not being used for that purpose. And, of course, the interest

---

[1] Donald Richberg was appointed Executive Secretary of the NEC on July 1, 1934, to serve during the summer leave-of-absence of Frank Walker, which had been announced in May. Actually, Walker did not return until April 1935, and Richberg served until that time. See also the biographical note in the appendix.

they are paying is in lieu of rent, and very low rent compared with what they would ordinarily pay. I think there are very few occasions of this sort that arise. I don't remember any other coming to us.

MR. COOLIDGE: I think there is also the consideration that the relief agency is not permitted to give funds for this payment in place of rent. This interest piles up and up against the man and in two or three years there will be a large amount against him.

MR. FAHEY: That is quite true; and in some cases it rather invites foreclosure, which is the thing we want to avoid.

MR. COOLIDGE: Yes, it accumulates to a considerable sum.

MR. WILLIAMS: Speaking for Mr. Hopkins' agency, we make it a practice to base allowances upon necessary interest payments as a general policy. Of course, it was in line with that that this offer was made. I don't think this amounts to any large number, generally speaking. It would seem to me a bit unfortunate to make any hard and fast rule here because the situation differs so greatly; and after all, the main thing we are after is to try to help the person who is about to lose his home, and frequently we have to take a different approach in every case.

MR. COOLIDGE: I think it would be rather unfortunate for the Home Owners' Loan Corporation not to have the public feel that their debt was just as good as anybody else's debt.

MR. WILLIAMS: There would not seem to be much occasion for it, because they have a way to save their home.

SECRETARY HULL: I imagine, as you suggest, Mr. Fahey, there is not a very large amount of this improper duplication of benefits received from the government. I don't see how you can check them everywhere. You might in this instance. In those cases where it is improper to receive duplicate benefits, the question of administration would be down to the minimum, I judge.

MR. FAHEY: I think it would be much more practicable, because there are so few cases, to leave them for adjustment between the Emergency Relief Organization and our own, because it is true that the character of the cases would vary so widely it would be very difficult to deal with it under any general rule. I think that would be the best disposition of it.

SECRETARY HULL: If there is no further discussion, I assume it is tacitly understood that the different governmental agencies will go on without any uniform, or general, or fixed policy on the matter, dealing with each situation as you come to it.

The next order of business is a report by Dr. Ballinger concerning the proposed administration of the Executive Order relating to the report of adjustments in salaries paid by emergency agencies.[2]

MR. RICHBERG: This is a report by Dr. Ballinger which I will read in as much detail as you desire . . . .

SECRETARY SWANSON . . . : How many employees have they?

MR. RICHBERG: The Emergency Conservation Work has 9 increases and no decreases; the Home Owners' Loan Corporation has 2,117 increases and 14 decreases; the Federal Home Loan Bank Board and Federal Savings and Loan Division, 100 increases and 104 decreases; Public Works Administration, 1,356 increases and 548 decreases; Subsistence Homesteads, 57 increases and 8 decreases; Soil Erosion Service, 11 increases and 17 decreases; Oil Enforcement, 223 increases and 8 decreases. That makes a total for these employees of $923,732. Roughly speaking, Mr. Secretary, there are something over 3,500—pretty nearly 4,000—increases and something under 600 decreases . . . .

This circular reads as follows, presented because if it does not meet with disapproval we will attempt to send it out . . . .

This is presented in view of obtaining the approval of the Council, first, for sending out rules and regulations to the heads of emergency agencies, and second, for the participation of the Civil Service Commission in sending out instructions.

I think, in addition to that, I might suggest that with respect to the interpretation of the Executive Order, various questions seem likely to arise and we might desire to frame questions for presentation to the Attorney General for interpretation so that there will be no confusion as to the interpretations made.

SECRETARY HULL: What do you say to these suggestions, gentlemen?

SECRETARY ICKES: So far as Public Works is concerned, Mr. Secretary, we sent in just before the end of June a long list of adjustments—increases and decreases. Am I to understand those are going to have to be done over and passed upon one by one, and in the meantime, the person affected to get neither increase nor decrease? Obviously, in the case where no decrease is put into effect, the government can't very well subsequently go in and claim that from the employee. This thing has caused Public Works more headaches than any question that has been before us.

For some six or seven months we have been completely in the air as to our rights, duties, and obligations. Finally this Executive Order was issued. I think that I am well within the mark when I say that the total increase of salaries shown here—something

---

[2] This undoubtedly refers to the draft executive order discussed at the meeting of May 1, 1934. See transcript of that meeting, note 3.

short of a million dollars—has been lost to the government in Public Works alone through loss of efficiency on the part of employees. Our morale is just shot; they never knew whether they were coming or going. Certain practices have been put into effect and then something different is done; and, with all due respect to the Civil Service Commission and the Budget Bureau, it takes us five or six weeks to clear even a necessary emergency employee through the Budget. It takes a similar length of time to clear him through the Civil Service Commission. It is literally now six weeks or two months before you can get somebody on your staff that you need. We are burdened with rules and regulations and demands for information and questionnaires.

If I am any judge, based upon experience, of what will be the effect of this order, we won't know for two or three months more whether we are coming or going. There seems to be a disposition on the part of the various Bureaus to put their recommendation ahead of any department, even on comparatively unimportant matters.

You cannot hire a clerk for a thousand or twelve hundred dollars a year without spending time and effort of various government officials amounting to at least that much before putting that employee on. I don't know any aspect of the government that needs simplification more than this particular matter.

MR. RICHBERG: May I make clear that this Order does not in any way hold up the changes but merely provides a method of reporting them for subsequent review.

SECRETARY ICKES: I made a great effort to find out just what it did do. I don't know. I don't know what this report means. I wish I did. It has to be referred back again to the Attorney General. The Attorney General and the Director of the Budget and the Comptroller General all agree to disagree on the subject.

MR. STANLEY: Don't put us in that class, please!

SECRETARY ICKES: We don't know, if the thing goes into effect, whether the Comptroller General, in his wisdom, will obey the Executive Order of the President or not. We may have to go to the Supreme Court on it. That is literally the situation, isn't it?

MR. STANLEY: I just objected to being put in that class.

SECRETARY ICKES: The Comptroller General didn't agree with your ruling. It had to go back again. My personnel is just shot to pieces. The morale is something to cause angels to weep!

SECRETARY HULL: Is there any further discussion? This suggests the idea of sending out to the heads of emergency organizations the rules and regulations.

SECRETARY ICKES: We have to give out questionnaires to about fifteen hundred employees; and then this Council will have to go over all those in addition to all the suggested changes from other emergency agencies. I don't know where we are going to head in.

MR. RICHBERG: May I read from the Executive Order?

All classifications made pursuant to this order, except those made in accordance with the provisions of the Classification Act of 1923, as amended, shall be subject to review and revision by the Civil Service Commission upon the request of the executive council. In the event any classification made by the head of a department or an agency pursuant to this order is revised by the Civil Service Commission, the revised classification shall be final and effective beginning the first day of the first month after such revision is reported by the executive council to the head of the department or agency concerned.

I understand the object of this is to enable the Executive Council to ask for a review if it deems that advisable.

SECRETARY ICKES: You will have to scrutinize all these and decide whether to ask the Civil Service Commission for a review, and then the Civil Service Commission will render a decision after several weeks or months.

MR. RICHBERG: Your classification goes into effect in the meantime.

MR. FAHEY: I want to support the remarks of the Secretary of the Interior on this subject. I think we have probably had about as much grief as he has had, certainly during the weeks this thing has been pending. It has brought about no end of lost motion in our organization and plenty of jealousy and friction and trouble. It seems to me quite impracticable that any questions of changes in individual cases should come to this Council to take up the time of a group of men around this board to discuss questions whether somebody is going to get fifty or sixty dollars a year more, or be classified as a junior secretary or a common, ordinary stenographer.

Not only that, but certainly so far as we are concerned, the objection to this—which as I understood it was to prevent the emergency activities from paying more than was reasonable for corresponding service elsewhere—just isn't working out with us. On the basis of our estimates after weeks of study, this reclassification is going to cost us about three hundred thousand dollars a year, so far as we have gone; and when we extend it to the country as a whole we don't know how far it is going.

We have about 1,900 employees in Washington at the time, and we need about three or four hundred more, if we had any place to put them, to operate properly; and over the country we have thousands of them, as you know. There is a great discrepancy between the rates in one section and those in another, and this attempt to classify, even with the latitude allowed, is certainly bringing us no end of trouble.

So far as dealing with the matter through the Council is concerned, it seems to me that if these recommendations approved by the responsible heads of departments have to be reviewed by somebody outside quite unfamiliar with the character of the work being done, there is only one cold, practical way to do it, and that is to set up some committee or staff that will approve them unless there is a question involving a general policy, and then let it be passed upon by somebody in the Civil Service Commission or somewhere else.

It seems to me an obvious waste of time if we have got to have hundreds of these things come in here to be passed upon by this Council. Not only that, but I, for one, would say that I think it would be extremely useful if some small committee familiar with this thing could restudy it and consider whether we are on the right tack about it. I very much doubt if we are.

SECRETARY HULL: It does seem that the entire membership of the Council could not well undertake to go through all those details. Evidently, if this course is to be pursued, it should be through a small committee selected for that purpose. What is the pleasure of the members as to the step that shall be next taken? We can either go forward without it, as suggested, by a special committee, or we can let it lie on the table until the members think further.

SECRETARY SWANSON: As I understand it, the adjustment has to obtain until changed. If it is continued until the next meeting of the Council, they could go ahead and adjust the salaries.

MR. RICHBERG *(reading from Executive Order No. 6746)*: "All adjustments in rates of compensation made pursuant to this order shall be reported to the executive council and shall become effective beginning the first day of the first month subsequent to that in which such report is made."

I assume, therefore, that when these adjustments have been made and they are reported to the Council, they become automatically effective, beginning the first day of the succeeding month after some action is taken.

SECRETARY SWANSON: Greater uniformity is needed. Starting all kinds of bureaus that pay more than the regular bureaus produces dissatisfaction. Every man gets what he thinks is just. If you have one man who gets less than somebody else who has less responsibility and less work, he is dissatisfied.

SECRETARY ICKES: Why wouldn't it be a proper policy to consider all these adjustments affirmed unless the Civil Service Commission, upon any investigation it chooses to initiate, raises some question with regard to any particular salaries?

MR. RICHBERG: That would present some questions to the Council, too. We don't want to leave it to the Civil Service Commission.

SECRETARY ICKES: Give them the power to raise any question they desire. I think the emergencies will have ceased before we get to it.

MR. RICHBERG: The purpose of this Order was to submit to the Council the differences in salaries between the employees as a whole and the people regularly employed. If I am properly informed regarding it, the idea was to have the readjustments made in conformity with the general standard and then such report made to the Council as could be analyzed in the office of the Executive Director and then a report made to this Council if there were anything that seemed worthy of the attention of the Council, not to throw the entire matter to the Civil Service Commission. The whole purpose of this request presented here was to have some uniformity about reporting what has been done, so that the report could be analyzed for the later consideration of the Council.

I don't understand that this action would interfere with the readjustments made unless at some subsequent date the Council should find some agency out of line on some policy being pursued.

SECRETARY SWANSON: As to uniformity of salaries, the Civil Service Commission would have everybody employed at uniform salaries, not emergency salaries.

MR. RICHBERG: That is the reason Dr. Ballinger has been assigned to that work.

SECRETARY HULL: Would that include the sending out of this circular?

MR. RICHBERG: If this is approved, we would send out this circular so as to obtain uniform reports; then, after analyzing that, we would report to the Council if there appeared to be anything unusual. I understand Dr. Ballinger has been assigned for the purpose of doing that work, hasn't he, Mr. Ironside?

MR. IRONSIDE: Yes, sir.

SECRETARY ICKES: We called upon the Civil Service Commission and it assigned to us one of its experts in classification, who went over this whole matter with us, and our classification was based upon his recommendations. Why would it be necessary to furnish the Civil Service Commission with information it already has, in order for it to be passed on again?

MR. STANLEY: The water is over the dam, it seems to me.

SECRETARY HULL: Do you desire this to go to the Attorney General?

MR. RICHBERG: I don't think that is necessary. If the question of interpretation arises, it should be referred to the Attorney General so that it would not be referred some to one place and some to another.

SECRETARY SWANSON: Why don't you refer it all to the Civil Service Commission?

SECRETARY HULL: What would be the objection to the Director and his associates giving this matter further investigation and having it ready for the next meeting?

MR. RICHBERG: We would be very glad to follow the directions of the Council. The thought was that we would not want to send out the circular if it did not meet with the approval of the Council.

SECRETARY ICKES: I question it, so far as we are concerned; we have furnished all that information. I don't want the burden thrown on my organization in midsummer. I think we have been classified over there now three times.

MR. HOWES: I don't see how you can reconcile the actions of the different departments unless you handle them in the manner you propose—have them all in a central agency—for the purpose of coordinating the wages in one department with another.

SECRETARY ICKES: They can take the reports we have already sent in.

SECRETARY SWANSON: Why don't this agency take the reports already made and get their approval of those? When you get the moral support of the Civil Service Commission behind salaries, it is worth a great deal to the country.

MR. FAHEY: But, Mr. Chairman, certain classifications for certain types of employment have been fixed. We may pay them a minimum or a maximum for a certain classification. Those have already been determined. We have submitted our list, just as the Secretary of the Interior has, in great detail. It has been passed upon and has become effective, as I understand it. When it comes to engaging additional employees, so long as they are employed within those classifications, and their employment conforms to the regulations laid down, why should it be necessary to take it up for review anywhere? If cases arise outside of those classifications, or in a "twilight zone," and there is any doubt about that, then it would seem to me that that might well be subject to review somewhere; but so long as you have fixed your classifications for stenographers, junior stenographers and clerks of all types, and lawyers, and they are kept within that fixed scheme of things, I don't see why there is any good reason for reviewing every additional case that comes up.

MR. RICHBERG: Mr. Secretary, suppose I make the suggestion that we work with those agencies which have already reported this matter—those that have material available—and I presume that the others will come in in the meantime, before the next meeting of the Council. I see the objection clearly and the great amount of clerical work that has already been done. As a matter of fact, many of the agencies followed the course that the Secretary of the Interior followed and obtained the advice of the Civil Service Commission. Presumably there will be adjustments for all of them.

SECRETARY HULL: Then if it is agreeable, that action can be taken for the present. The report by the Secretary of Agriculture, concerning conditions of crops and their bearing on the production control in 1935 comes next.

MR. RICHBERG: Secretary Wallace, do you want me to read this report which I have from you on that subject?

SECRETARY WALLACE: I think everyone has it.

MR. RICHBERG: Then it is not necessary to read it.

SECRETARY HULL: I don't know whether the members have read it. Have you any questions? Have you read this report?

SECRETARY SWANSON: I read it.

SECRETARY HULL: Mr. Wallace, would you mind stating any particular points in it that might be of interest to the Council?

SECRETARY WALLACE: This chart which I just distributed this afternoon, I think is of very real interest, indicating the way in which farm income a year ago ran away from factory payroll income, going far in advance as a result of that speculative situation; then a very sharp reaction began.

The paying of cotton benefits in September almost brought farm income up to the payrolls. On the whole, the total farm income has been less than the factory payroll income, but the prospect now is, that farm income over the late summer and early fall will be greater than the factory payrolls again. We will be sending out very substantial benefit payments this fall.

As a result of the drought this year, and the advance in farm product prices per unit—which does not necessarily mean any great advance in farm income, although it makes a better showing in price per bushel of wheat and corn, and so on—there is likely to be a feeling in many quarters that the farm program should be abandoned. It would probably be unfortunate, for with ordinary weather next year, with respect to wheat, cotton, and corn, we would again be on the export market with very substantial quantities.

We believe it is exceedingly important that we go ahead in 1935. At the end of that time, however, our carry-overs of wheat and cotton will be down, in all probabilities, to normal unless

241

the weather is exceptionally favorable next year, and it will be worthwhile to reassess the whole picture. It will depend, in considerable measure, to what extent the new policy has been able to build up farm purchasing power.

SECRETARY HULL: What is farm land doing now in the way of increasing values? Is there any increase?

SECRETARY WALLACE: It is perhaps an average of five per cent above a year ago. Our figures for March 1 indicated three per cent above the preceding year. Nobody has any absolutely accurate figures.

MR. MORGAN: It is about that, Mr. Wallace.

SECRETARY WALLACE: About five per cent?

MR. MORGAN: Yes.

DR. DICKINSON: Is there anything in the statement in the paper the other day to the effect that the speculation in farm land is being stimulated by the agricultural programs?

SECRETARY WALLACE: I think it is quite possible it will start next year. There is probably some buying by the city people now.

MR. MORGAN: Some, yes.

SECRETARY HULL: The different farm cooperative measures are all "dove-tailing" in very well, aren't they? So far as I see, they are.

SECRETARY WALLACE: Yes, I think it is beginning to work out much better. The corn-hog checks are beginning to go out now. The cattle buying is proceeding well. The livestock question has been a sore spot, but it is going to be in a very good position next year. It is improving enough now so it will take us off the "hot-spot" to a very material degree.

The situation in the Middle West, because of the lower price of livestock has really been a bad situation.

SECRETARY HULL: You think there are signs of improvement out there?

SECRETARY WALLACE: Yes, the price of hogs is up more than a dollar, and these benefit payments are going out. The Middle West did not share in the agricultural program as the South did last year. That is just beginning to flow in now. I am anticipating there will be somewhat more money flowing into the Middle West than went into the South last fall. That had a very pronounced effect on the South last fall, and I see no reason why it should not have a similar effect on the Middle West during the next three or four months.

In the Dakotas, where they have nothing, it doesn't make much difference what the price is per bushel.

SECRETARY HULL: Next is the report by the Economic Adviser . . . . Any discussion of the report? You feel fairly well satisfied, do you, Doctor, with the present?

MR. RIEFLER: Yes, sir. This small decline is due to several very specific factors. Personally, I think the adjustment will be over about the middle of August, and then I think we can see what the fall situation looks like. There is nothing now to indicate we will not have the usual fall pick-up.

SECRETARY HULL: Next is the report of the state directors of the National Emergency Council.

MR. RICHBERG: I will read the summary of the report . . . . There follows the digest of reports of various agencies.

SECRETARY HULL: Is there any discussion of this report? Are there any late developments in the strike situation?

SECRETARY SWANSON: You mean the longshoremen's strike?[3]

SECRETARY HULL: Yes.

MR. WILLIAMS: From the relief angle, we are having a great number of increases. We have had a three thousand increase in San Francisco in the last three weeks—a thousand a week. That is true in Seattle and in Portland. There is no difficulty, though, from the standpoint of granting relief; that is, the community seems to accept that proposition and it seems to be outside of the controversy.

SECRETARY HULL: That grows out of the strike situation?

MR. WILLIAMS: That grows out of the need of those who are out on strike.

SECRETARY HULL: I had not heard just what was going on in connection with these strikes, whether the differences were being composed by the persons who were giving them attention.

Have you anything to bring up about any phase of the Treasury work?

MR. COOLIDGE: No. From the financial point of view, everything is very quiet.

SECRETARY HULL: Anything from the War Department?

MR. WOODRING: No, Mr. Secretary.

SECRETARY HULL: Anything from the Post Office Department?

MR. HOWES: No, sir.

SECRETARY HULL: Mr. Ickes?

SECRETARY ICKES: No.

SECRETARY HULL: Mr. Wallace, anything further from your department?

SECRETARY WALLACE: I don't think so.

SECRETARY HULL: Or yours, Mr. Dickinson?

DR. DICKINSON: No, sir.

SECRETARY HULL: Haven't you a committee working on some phase of the shipping situation?

DR. DICKINSON: Yes, sir, there is a committee that is gathering data on various types of Merchant Marine policy, trade rates, and payments to

---

[3] The Pacific Coast longshoremen went out on strike in mid-May of that year, and a settlement was not reached until the end of July.

the companies; but that committee is interdepartmental and it is working along very quietly to make available more material by the time the Secretary and the President get back.

SECRETARY HULL: Some gentlemen came in to see me this morning. They say that the ships operating between New York and the east coast of South America might be taken off, sooner or later, and they were very desirous of seeing the government cooperate in any way it might deem at all advisable to secure from two to four new vessels, properly equipped, to take the place of the Munson lines. Is that problem included?

DR. DICKINSON: That whole program is included. Of course, the Munson people are at present in bankruptcy, and their ships are being operated by their trustees. There is another freight line going down the east coast of South America, and the question has been considered for some time as to whether some sort of consolidation ought not to be effected between the freight service and the passenger service down there; but that is a part of the general problem that the committee has in hand.

SECRETARY HULL: I would like to join with those other gentlemen who were in to see me in emphasizing the importance of anything being done that can be done to bring about a suitable line of ships on that route. I notice in traveling down there that there are quite a number of people in those cities who are wealthy, and they are accustomed to taking their periodical trip abroad; but when they step down to the harbor and see well fitted out ships owned by four or five other nationalities, and then look at ours, such as we have there, instead of stepping on our vessels (as they really prefer in most instances) and coming to New York and seeing our country and visiting here and establishing close relations, they step on these more attractive vessels, as you know better than I do, and go to other countries. That is really a much larger problem than at first blush it would seem to be.

DR. DICKINSON: Yes, sir.

SECRETARY HULL: Mr. Fahey, what do you think about the prospects for building activities—renewals, replacements, and repairs?

MR. FAHEY: As you know, on the amendment of our Act a couple of months ago, we were allowed to set aside a certain amount of money which could be used for amortization on the homes we take over. So far, we have had applications for amortization work of that type amounting to about $59,000,000. Of course, that is limited to the homes where we refinance mortgages.

As you know, Mr. Moffett is just taking hold, so far as the Housing Administration is concerned, and we got together this morning to discuss and work out certain plans for collaboration with their work. The indications are that they are going to receive a large number of applications, and also ours are just beginning. We do not anticipate, however, that they will be anything as heavy as they will be with the Housing Administration, because in so large a proportion of the cases, our borrowers are not in a financial condition to incur very great additional obligations, and, of course, we have to exercise care in granting additional loans for purposes of amortization. We have to be satisfied that the home owner is going to be able to carry out the burden. It appears to us now as though we might expend in that direction ninety to one hundred million dollars, but I do not think any more than that. There is provision for as much as three hundred million, but we are very well satisfied that there will not be a demand that would require any such sum as that—certainly not within the next year.

Much is going to depend upon the prompt setup of the Housing Administration and in making clear to the private lending institutions throughout the country what they can do and what they can't do, and stimulating their enthusiasm to go ahead with construction programs. We have every reason to believe it will really go ahead in an effective way between now and fall.

SECRETARY HULL: Are the banking institutions holding up interest rates?

MR. FAHEY: No, there appears to be quite a general softening of interest rates so far as home loans are concerned. In many parts of the country now, the private lending institutions are meeting the rates of the Home Owners' Loan Corporation on the basis of five per cent, and we have a feeling that the trend is toward lower interest rates on home mortgages all along the line. That has begun already. There is no question about that. Some of the cooperative banks and building and loan associations have already begun to advertise loans on a 20-year basis instead of the average of about 12, which has prevailed in the past. They are now very ready to lend on a 15-year basis, and in some cases, as high as 20 years.

SECRETARY HULL *(speaking to Secretary Ickes)*: Are there any new developments in your administration?[4]

SECRETARY ICKES: No, we are getting along a little better than we did for a while. We are hoping that the United States Circuit Court of

---

[4] Secretary Hull is addressing Ickes in the latter's capacity as administrator of the Petroleum Administration. The litigation referred to probably related to the subsequent U. S. Supreme Court decision, Panama Refining v. Ryan, 293 U.S. 388, (1936). The Court invalidated the portion of the National Industrial Recovery Act which provided for regulation of "hot oil."

Appeals in New Orleans will rule in our favor. If they do that, it is going to put us in a better position.

I called in the Standard of New Jersey and the Standard of Indiana to adjust some very bad local price wars and found them very willing to cooperate. I think we are ironing that out.

SECRETARY HULL (*speaking to Mr. Howes*): You had a surplus—or was that just newspaper reports?

MR. HOWES: It was just newspaper reports. We won't know until about the twentieth of the month.

SECRETARY HULL: You won't miss it much, will you?

MR. HOWES: We are making a pretty good showing, I think, but will not know until the twentieth of this month.

SECRETARY HULL: I have heard some comments on the surprising reports to that effect.

I don't think it is necessary to read over these things (*referring to the digest of reports by members of the Executive Council*). You know the contents of the reports.

Have any of you any other question about any phase of your respective bureaus, or departments, or divisions? If you have anything special, we all want to hear about it. Is the relief situation well stabilized?

MR. WILLIAMS: It is about the same. We are not getting new relief families. It has held up, as Mr. Riefler says, and the relief load is staying about the same.

In the drought areas, we are getting increased territory. It is spreading now so that it has practically half of the territory, geographically, of the country in it. There are about 25,000,000 people in that territory, and we have approximately 20 per cent of those people on the relief rolls—five or six hundred thousand families, all told.

In the cities, we are beginning to see this go down. We had, at the end of June, 950,000 people at work on Emergency Relief Work. We dropped about 100,000 compared with the week previous.

SECRETARY HULL: If none of you have anything else on your mind, I suppose we might adjourn.

Meeting adjourned at 3:20 p.m.

Proceedings of the National Emergency Council

[meeting no. 12]
July 24, 1934

Joint Meeting of the Executive Council and the National Emergency Council

Held in the Cabinet Room of the Executive Offices, The White House, Tuesday, July 24, 1934, at 2:10 p.m.

Present: the Secretary of State; the Secretary of the Navy; the Secretary of Labor; the Undersecretary of the Treasury; the First Assistant Postmaster General; the Assistant Secretary of War; the Assistant to the Attorney General; the Assistant Secretary of Agriculture; the Assistant Secretary of Commerce; the Acting Director of the Budget; the Chairman of the Board of the Reconstruction Finance Corporation; the Governor of the Farm Credit Administration; the Administrative Assistant and Budget Officer of the Department of the Interior; the Assistant Administrator of Agricultural Adjustment; the Assistant Administrator of Federal Emergency Relief; the Vice Chairman of the Home Owners' Loan Corporation; the Assistant Director of Emergency Conservation Work; the Executive Assistant to the Chairman of the Federal Home Loan Bank Board; the Commissioner of the Federal Trade Commission; the Economic Adviser; the Adviser on Consumer Problems; the Chief of Consumers' Division; the Executive Assistant; Dr. E. R. Ballinger, Office of the Executive Secretary.

[Here we see F.D.R.'s "clearing house of information" functioning as the NEC carried on in the absence of the Chief Executive and of its executive secretary. (Frank Walker took a leave of absence from NEC work the Spring of 1934 and did not return until April of 1935.) From the vantage point of today, the concern expressed over the issue of Communism and Communist activity in the United States and particularly in the labor movement is interesting. The issue was clearly not being ignored at the time. Secretary Hull seems especially interested in exacting compliance by the U.S.S.R. with the "no propaganda" pledge in the recognition agreement.—Editors' Note.]

SECRETARY HULL: I suppose we might proceed now; the minutes of the last meeting might be read (*Mr. Leggett then read the minutes of the preceding meeting . . . .*)
The minutes are agreed to unless there is some question about them.
Next is a report of the progress of the organization of the Federal Housing Administration . . . . Any question or discussion of this report?
"Report by the Secretary of Agriculture on Drought, Crop

conditions, and Live-stock Purchases." . . . That is a very interesting report. Is there any discussion of it?

This is a further report by Dr. Ballinger concerning the proposed administration of the Executive Order relating to the report of adjustments of salaries paid by emergency agencies.[1]

MR. LEGGETT: This is a report just referring to the actual events since the last meeting of the Council . . . .

SECRETARY HULL: Is it desired that this report be read, or is it the disposition to let the matter lie in abeyance until the President returns?

MR. BURLEW: Mr. Chairman, would it be proper at this time to get the Executive Council to discuss the Comptroller General's opinion[2] in reference to certain points of that Executive Order? If so, I would like to have read a letter from the Secretary of the Interior on that subject.

SECRETARY HULL: If it is desired, any gentleman can be heard. I might offer this suggestion as one that might be considered when we take final action today: I would hesitate a little, myself, to modify or revoke the President's Order without his being present in person.

MR. BURLEW: Naturally we would not expect that; but I thought it might be well to discuss the matter.

SECRETARY HULL: Yes, I think that is very timely and entirely in order.

MR. BURLEW: I have here a copy of a letter from the Secretary of the Interior to the President which might be read, though I don't think it is necessary. (*Mr. Burlew then passed the letter to Mr. Leggett.*) It calls attention to the action of the Comptroller General in connection with increasing of salaries.
(*Mr. Leggett then read the letter . . . .*):

June 20, 1934.

THE PRESIDENT
THE WHITE HOUSE
MY DEAR MR. PRESIDENT:

I have received from Colonel McIntyre the proposed Executive Order covering the classification of emergency positions, and a letter of the Attorney General of June 14 explaining a paragraph which he has inserted in the order prepared by the Director of the Budget.

I am in accord with the Attorney General's viewpoint and I believe the additional language, which provides that adjustments in salaries shall include increases as well as decreases, should be added to

---

[1] See earlier discussion of this same matter during the meetings of May 1 and July 10, 1934. See also note 3, May 1 meeting.
[2] Probably No. A-55907, found in Vol. 14, *Decisions of the Comptroller General*, pp. 14-17, July 5, 1934.

the order. This meets the objective toward which we have been working for many months. It is, however, a controversial point from which the Comptroller General has refused to recede and the Director of the Budget, apparently in an effort to effect a compromise, omitted it from the order. The language conforms to the Attorney General's previous opinion, which so far the Comptroller General has refused to recognize. It involves a principle which I believe is sound legally and which will enable the emergency establishments to deal equitably with the officers and employees. Since the Comptroller General has refused to allow increases under the Executive Order of November 18, 1933, the purpose of that order has been defeated and the one proposed was originally designed to correct that situation.

I recognize, however, that the promulgation of the order in this form will bring to an issue the question whether the Attorney General's opinion on a legal matter supersedes that of the Comptroller General, and any emergency establishment which would undertake to act under the new language would require the support of the Attorney General and yourself to settle the issue.

I hope that you may feel free to sign the order as soon as possible before July 1, since without it several thousand employees in the Public Works Administration and the emergency organizations under the Department of the Interior will be deprived of the five per cent increase due July 1 to employees on a gross basis. The reason for this situation is that, with the exception of a few hundreds recently reappointed on a gross basis because of change of duties, all the other emergency employees here are on a net basis and their status must be changed to a gross basis before July 1 if they are to benefit by the amendment to the Economy Act.

Sincerely yours,
(SGD.) HAROLD L. ICKES
Administrator.

MR. BURLEW: The Comptroller General ruled on July 5, that we cannot make these increases. Of course, we have gone ahead and made them, as have many other establishments; but the result will be suspension. It is quite important that it be settled quickly as to what is done to overcome the action of the Comptroller General.

SECRETARY HULL: What suggestion have you as to the best way to settle it?

MR. BURLEW: Frankly, I have none. It seems to be an impasse that we have not been able to overcome. I don't know whether the Department of Justice has anything in mind or not.

MR. STANLEY: We are willing to give an opinion that the Attorney General's opinion should control, but that does not seem to help. Several of the departments have raised the question. The general order was, in effect, instructing the Comptroller General to follow the opinion of the Attorney General. Naturally, we don't want to suggest that, because our department is affected; but a good many departments have

	approached us and some have suggested that this Council should recommend to the President that an order of that kind be passed. I do not think the Department of Justice ought to suggest a matter of that kind. It ought to come from other departments.
MR. BURLEW:	Mr. Chairman, it seems to me that the Executive Council itself should raise the question because all departments and agencies in the Council are affected. It would be appropriate for the Council to reach a decision on it. Any one department that brings it to the front would be at a disadvantage, it seems to me.
MR. JONES:	May I enquire what is referred to?
MR. BURLEW:	It has to do with increases of salaries under the recent Executive Order. The Comptroller General has held that no increases are legal under the Economy Act.
MR. JONES:	That pertains to the July 1 restoration of five per cent?
MR. BURLEW:	No, not the restoration of five per cent, but the increase of compensation.
DR. DICKINSON:	Then your problem in Public Works is, since these people are on a net basis, the increase is not allowed because they are not on a gross basis less five per cent.
MR. BURLEW:	There are other cases where we increased compensation because the employees were not properly classified; but that is true in all emergency agencies, I suppose. We had to put it into effect.
MR. WEBB:	If you had an expert accountant working for $3,600 and he was so efficient that he was worth $5,000 to you, you could not change him from $3,600; no matter how much he was worth to you, he would still have to continue to get $3,600. We have such a man in the Home Owners' Loan Corporation; and with some 17,000 employees, we are almost daily making changes, promoting men. When they become trained along certain lines, we advance them, but under this Order, it would be impossible to do it. We felt that the matter ought to be discussed here and then perhaps present a petition or request to the President to take this question up when he returns. I think it would be very well to do that. We are in a very embarrassing situation.
MR. JONES:	You have to create a new title?
MR. WEBB:	Yes; if he is an expert accountant you have to make him a chief engineer—something he does not know anything about— before he can get higher pay.
MR. MC ENTEE:	When the payroll of the Civilian Conservation Corps was set up, the maximum salary for foremen in the field was $150

a month. Both the Forest Service and Park Service started many of these men at $110, figuring as they developed, to increase them to $150; but they find out that they can't increase these men. The new men they are paying $150; the men who know the job, and have to teach the others, get $110, while the new men get $150. You know how much "hob" that is raising out in the field. We just can't raise these men.

MR. JONES: The Comptroller rules it cannot be done.

MR. MC ENTEE: It can't be done without changing the title.

MR. STANLEY: It appears to affect a great many people, and I think it is a very important matter. Men in different departments do not know what to do with it.

SECRETARY HULL: The Attorney General has overruled the other official?

MR. STANLEY: We have overruled him, but it does no good.

MR. MC ENTEE: The disbursing officers have tried to change it in the face of the Comptroller's ruling.

MR. STANLEY: The Navy Department suggests that the President pass an Order which would, in effect, instruct the various departments that if there was any dispute between the Comptroller General and the Attorney General, the Attorney General's opinion should prevail; or if there was any dispute between the Comptroller General and any other department, the department ought to submit the question to the Attorney General and his opinion would be binding and final. That would be an Executive Order which the Comptroller General would have to concede to. That was suggested some time ago, but for some reason it was not followed out. That is the only thing we can suggest as a means of straightening it out.

MR. JONES: That is a perfectly good way.

SECRETARY SWANSON: Will the courts sustain the Attorney General's order?

MR. STANLEY: The Comptroller General would be bound by the Attorney General's opinion. The money would already be paid out.

SECRETARY SWANSON: I said I would issue an order paying them and then they would have to go to the courts.

MR. STANLEY: The disbursing officer now is in the Treasury; and he insists on the approval of the Comptroller General. I think the question of bonding companies also comes into it. They have bonded the men.

SECRETARY SWANSON: The only way is to issue an Executive Order and issue a warrant for the money.

MR. STANLEY: There is no doubt about the Executive Order if the President will issue it.

SECRETARY HULL: We will have to wait for action by the President in person.

MR. STANLEY: I think the point Mr. Burlew makes is a wise one, that no separate department should make the request, because it would put them in the position of having the Comptroller General feel unkindly toward them. We don't want to be in the position of suggesting it.

MR. JONES: Doesn't this follow in line with the President's program?

SECRETARY HULL: When that matter was discussed, I was not present, but that is my understanding.

MR. WEBB: The President's Order is not effective because of the Comptroller's position that nothing will happen but suspension of accounts.

MR. JONES: Does this employee get the old salary?

MR. WEBB: We paid the new salary on the fifteenth of July. The question is, shall we put them back to the old salary, which would be very difficult, and demand refund from the employee for the overpayment, or shall we pay them at the new rate on the thirty-first of July?

MR. JONES: Has everybody complied with the increase—all departments—do you know? How many are in this? For instance, we have given increases at the RFC.

MR. LEGGETT: All the reports have not come in yet, but every one that has come in shows increases, I believe; don't they, Dr. Ballinger?

DR. BALLINGER: Yes.

MR. LEGGETT: We will be in exactly the same position on August 1 that we were on July 15.

MR. JONES: The question is whether you are to repeat what you did on July 15.

MR. BURLEW: The Interior Department expects to try to repeat the same thing.

MR. WOODRING: This Executive Order—would that open up the question of raising the salaries regardless of classification? Could a man be advanced from $3,000 to $5,000, regardless of classification?

MR. STANLEY: I don't know that it would go that far. I don't think it has anything to do with that.

MR. LEGGETT: Dr. Ballinger is here and I am sure he can answer your question.

MR. WOODRING: The Comptroller General thinks it would open up to every administrative officer the right to advance employees at his own discretion.

DR. BALLINGER: No, the Executive Order placed upon the heads of agencies the responsibility for classifying positions. If they are classified, the salaries must be within a range specified in the Order for that particular position. Those classifications under the Order are subject to review by the Executive Council so that there is a control of the situation.

SECRETARY HULL: Is it the attitude of the Council that this matter should be referred back to the President on his return, with the recommendation that he take such further action as will make possible the carrying out of this Order, as was originally intended? Is that the attitude of the Council?

MR. JONES: In the meantime, would you include this August 1 payment and leave that to the judgment of the heads of departments? Why wouldn't you do that? Why not let each man assume his own responsibility?

SECRETARY HULL: It would be well to have the consensus of opinion about that, but we haven't discussed that fully.

SECRETARY SWANSON: The issue is whether the Comptroller General's judgment supersedes that of the Attorney General. He claims that there is no requirement that he should follow the Attorney General. Of course, it will be necessary to determine whether the Attorney General is the law officer of the government.

SECRETARY HULL: What is the pleasure of the Council with respect to these August payments that Mr. Jones has brought up?

MR. JONES: Speaking personally, I think it would be well to make them. It is just one more payment. You have made one on July 15, and you don't want to disturb your whole personnel and admit you were wrong.

MR. WEBB: I think it would be very unfortunate if we don't pay them.

MR. JONES: If we pay them, then there will be only two payments instead of one, when the President comes back. I would not hesistate to go ahead and make the August 1 payment. If it has to be undone, we will do the best we can.

MR. WEBB: The position of all the departments would be weakened if we do not do that.

MR. BURLEW: It would be an admission that we were wrong.

SECRETARY PERKINS: I will do whatever the rest of you say is right.

SECRETARY SWANSON: The question of who is the law officer of the government is an important one. We cannot stand and be coerced all the time by the Comptroller interpreting the law. I think we ought to have one law officer. I consult the Attorney General when I can't trust my Judge Advocate General. I think he will keep me out of trouble.

SECRETARY HULL: Have you any comment on this August payment matter, Mr. Attorney General?

MR. STANLEY: No, sir, I do not. I think that the President has indicated that

253

	he desires to follow the opinion of the Attorney General. I do not see how the heads of departments could very well avoid making the payment.
SECRETARY SWANSON:	When will the Attorney General be back?
MR. STANLEY:	He will be back in about a month, but the matter is up to the President now.
SECRETARY HULL:	Unless there is some motion, of course, the heads of departments will exercise their own judgment; and the main question will be referred back to the President with the recommendation which I stated a while ago, unless there is some objection.
MR. BURLEW:	I understand that the question is to be referred back to the President and that the emergency organizations will act as they desire on this matter and take the chance. That is the way it stands?
SECRETARY HULL:	Yes.
MR. WEBB:	Dr. Ballinger is here and I would like to know more about the question of the review and revision by the Civil Service Commission of these classifications. We feel, as far as the Home Owners' Loan Corporation is concerned, that it is entirely appropriate to take up with the Executive Council any changes we would like to make, but as to referring it to the Civil Service Commission, we would like to hear some discussion. We hardly think that is necessary.
DR. BALLINGER:	May I answer your question on that, sir? The Order provides that these classifications shall be subject to review and revision by the Civil Service Commission, but upon request of the Executive Council. If the Executive Council does not request the Commission to act, it will never appear in the picture. With that understanding, it seems to me that the injection of the Civil Service Commission is rather remote.
MR. WEBB:	The request must come from the Council?
DR. BALLINGER:	Yes, sir, it must come from the Council as a request from the Council for classification. That puts it squarely up to the Council whether they wish to review the case or not.
MR. WEBB:	We have to act sometimes very, very rapidly, and when we bring a matter of one or two dozen changes before the Council we get action and that settles it; but if they have to refer that to the Civil Service Commission, I understand it sometimes takes a long time to get it through. It would be hard for us to get along with the delay.
DR. BALLINGER:	The question of delay need not concern you. The Order which the President has signed gives you, as head of the

agency, authority to classify the position and fix the rate of compensation, and that settles it unless at some subsequent date the Council wishes to take action in the case; so there is no delay except the delay on your own part to determine what you want to do.

SECRETARY HULL: Next is the report of the Economic Adviser....

MR. RIEFLER: I made up a somewhat more detailed report this time because it was at the end of a half year, and there are some charts in which I thought you might be interested. These charts are more or less detailed. The first one is based on the American Federation of Labor estimate of employment; the next chart is one which compares the physical output of commodities from factories, factory employment and factory payrolls, and shows them both in the durable goods group and the nondurable goods groups. Nondurable goods remained high; the durable goods are low.

The third chart illustrates this factory employment by breaking down various classes of goods and materials.

The fourth chart illustrates the physical volume of exports and imports and shows that the physical volume of imports has not decreased very much. Most of the decrease has been in prices.

The fifth chart is our price chart showing where we are now in commodity prices.

SECRETARY HULL: That is a very valuable summing up. I am sure we all feel indebted to you. Any discussion of this report?

"The Report on the Operation of the Post Office Department at a Profit in the Fiscal Year 1934." ...

SECRETARY HULL: That is a very gratifying report. The Post Office people are to be congratulated.

The next is the report of the state directors of the National Emergency Council.

MR. LEGGETT: In that connection, we will present only a digest of the report....

SECRETARY HULL: Is there any discussion of that report? Have you anything to bring up, Miss Perkins?

SECRETARY PERKINS: The anticipation of many of these state directors that there will be more labor disturbances is perhaps based upon their conception that these things move in a continuing upward way, whereas a study of labor disturbances indicates that they usually reach their peak in summer. You do not get many new ones breaking out after the first of September. Some may carry over, but we do not anticipate new strikes beginning in the early autumn. My guess is that there will not be serious disturbances after the first of September.

SECRETARY HULL: There are no new developments in the strike situation?

SECRETARY PERKINS: They are all favorable. I think in the situations at present troublesome, we are finding a basis of settlement and adjustment in every case. We have had no "strike wave." We have had relatively few strikes involving relatively few people. There have been more than during the years of depression, but when you compare any other year you will find that, with a few exceptions, the strikes we have had have been very quickly settled—only a few man-hours lost.

When we go through a year or two-year period and compare the man-hours lost, we usually find the loss much less now than in the other periods. This comparison will show a very interesting picture of the labor disturbances; that is, the time lost—economic interference—has been very much better. That has been very characteristic of this period, that the strikes have been settleable and have been settled. I think that can be credited to the intelligent labor policy on the part of the Administration, which is going forward with a proposal of settlement and with the machinery by which settlement can be effected. However, there have been a number of cases where settlement was not easy.

SECRETARY HULL: Do these strikes involve generally the same questions, or a variety of questions?

SECRETARY PERKINS: They involve a variety of questions, but the overwhelming cause—and we analyze them all with regard to the cause, and I think there is never a strike without two or three demands—when you analyze them, the one cause that occurs most frequently is the demand for the privilege of exercising the right of "collective bargaining" which has been guaranteed by the National Recovery Act. It has been the interference with that, or the difference in interpretation of what is meant by that, which has led to some of the disturbances; and the difference in interpretation will probably go on for some time before we come to a general understanding held by all industries and laborers.

SECRETARY HULL: Do you gather any evidence of Communistic interference from outside of this country?

SECRETARY PERKINS: We do not get any trace of it, sir. Whenever a strike proceeds to the point where they have come to a stalemate, as we hear about in the newspapers, the Communists from all over the country, not having been originally participants in the strike,

256

move in to make trouble at the time when they believe bitterness has been established. We have only one or two strikes where we think there is a very large Communist membership in the organization itself. One or two others may have been of Communist motivation, but I see no trace of management outside of the United States.

There has been an abortive fur workers' strike in New York City going on for three months—an excellent time for it. A terrible time would be in the fur season, but that does not begin until the first of August. They have been carrying on the strike through the months of April, May, and June, and it has been merely a strike of excitement and clashes with the police. That has been confined to a union which is largely Communist in its membership. There are two branches of the fur workers' union and they have had an internal battle for seven or eight years, one section being made up of Communists and the other non-Communists.

I think this strike has been a strike of the Communist group with no legitimate purposes. With that exception, I should say we have had no strikes that seem to have been started with Communist agitation. There has been evidence that Communists move in from outside, after trouble starts.

I think the unfortunate publicity habits of both government officials and employers of labor, and the publicity habits of the press itself, have misled us, because apparently the public demands a diet of mustard and pepper, and things must be in exaggerated terms all the time, so that the result has been that very trifling things have been played up in a tone of excitement. I was very greatly distressed by the broadcasting companies, during the period of the San Francisco strike,[3] interrupting every radio program every ten or fifteen minutes with a special strike bulletin. There was not anything to say every ten or fifteen minutes. The people were in conference and there could not be any news. Even though they said the same thing every time—or had three different stories and told them alternately—nevertheless, it was sufficient to keep the whole American people expecting something terrible. If you were trying to agitate the people, you could not have done a better job than that. They engendered a state of mind, and distrust, out of which very serious things sometimes happen. I think the press have played up this whole

---

[3] A general strike was called in San Francisco in sympathy with a shipping strike, and lasted from July 16 to July 19, 1934.

257

strike situation, because trouble is news and disagreement is news, whereas agreement and orderly progress is apparently not news. I think that has exaggerated this whole picture in our minds, and it does put things into heads of people who are the least thoughtful and dependable.

SECRETARY HULL: I might refer to our recognition of Russia[4] some months ago. In their arrangements with other nations for recognition they had only agreed that the government itself would refrain from conducting Communist propaganda in the country extending recognition, but we were able to secure from them an agreement that not only the government but all individuals and persons within the jurisdiction of the government should not be permitted to conduct propaganda in this country.

We are getting quite a lot of complaints that Communistic activities are being conducted in this country. As a matter of fact, I have been following it very closely, ready and even desirous of making a complaint to the Soviet Government whenever the occasion at all justifies it. But, as a matter of fact, we have been able to trace scarcely anything thus far to the government over there or to anybody outside of this country.

In connection with strike activities in this country, we are watching very closely to see whether a state of facts may develop that will justify us in drawing this to the attention of the other government.

Have any of you anything to bring up here today more than what we have had?

Governor Myers,[5] you have been on a trip, and we haven't heard how your department is coming along. Without reading all of this digest, we might ask some of you to tell us the developments in your respective lines. Can you tell us anything that would be of special interest?

GOVERNOR MYERS: I think quite a little, Mr. Chairman. During the past two weeks I have been through the livestock country in Wyoming, Colorado, Arizona, Utah, and New Mexico. The situation is bad. Of course, in Arizona and New Mexico, the drought is chronic rather than emergency. The situation in the northern range states is very seriously complicated by the shortage of forage to carry the livestock through the winter months. The people in the Department of Agriculture are closely in

[4] The United States recognized the Soviet Government in Nov. 1933.
[5] William I. Myers of the Farm Credit Administration.

touch with that, and we depend upon them for their classification of emergency needs in accordance with which we are making emergency feed loans to cattle men.

Serious as the situation is in the area that we cover, I was pleased that conditions were not worse than they are. That means that they are not satisfactory. The stockmen with whom I talked had courage, and were still hoping for summer rains in that range country which would give them water for their livestock and help the situation materially. The most serious retrogression in the last few weeks has been, of course, in the states bordering the corn belt. I have not been into that section and I cannot say much about it. It is going to complicate the work of the Farm Credit Administration in regard to payments on loans, but through the laws that have been passed we are able to handle all loans on a sympathetic basis, requiring the farmer to pay only what he can; and if, on account of causes beyond his control, he cannot make payments, we have the privilege of carrying him until conditions improve.

We continued to make loans at the rate of five or six million dollars a day for the first six months, and reduced fixed charges considerably, and are just making progress.

SECRETARY HULL: Is the Frazier-Lemke Act[6] being invoked?

GOVERNOR MYERS: Very little. It is rather striking, we thought, that in conferences we held in Wichita and Omaha with bankers and with the representatives of the Farm Credit Administration, the question of that bill was not raised. We were discussing credit problems as they apply to the livestock country.

SECRETARY HULL: You think it will not be invoked to any general extent?

GOVERNOR MYERS: That is my belief, that farmers who have debts they are unable to pay must have their debts extended or scaled down in such a way that they can be met. I believe that the principal effect of the bill will be to encourage or scare creditors into effecting reasonable compromises. We have outstanding about $700,000,000 in approved loans that have not yet been closed, and in a large majority of those cases, the debts of the farmers exceed the amount we can loan. The lending policy under the law is to lend a maximum that a farmer can be expected to repay if conditions improve. We have not merely

---

[6] Passed in June 1934, "to make it possible for farmers to reacquire on reasonable terms farms lost through bankruptcy, or to suspend bankruptcy proceedings for five years if creditors would not agree to reasonable terms." Basil Rauch, *The History of the New Deal* (New York, 1934) p. 119.

	transferred the debts, leaving them as badly off as they were before. There has been some indication that creditors are somewhat more ready to compromise. I think the drought will at least have that one favorable effect—that it will speed compromises to a basis that farmers can be expected to repay as conditions improve.
SECRETARY HULL:	Mr. Williams,[7] is there anything from you? What is the trend of the relief situation now?
MR. WILLIAMS:	Why, there is no change, Mr. Secretary, at this time except that in times of drought we are getting, like all other government agencies here, a demand for increased aid. The areas affected are spreading rapidly over into new states, into Arkansas and all of Oklahoma, and coming east, taking up the whole east side of Texas, and have about covered most of Missouri, besides spreading over into Indiana. We have just sent out our August allotments, and we are getting great complaints that they are not adequate. We are impressed with the fact that the amount of money we have now for drought areas is not going to be adequate, as far as we are concerned, to meet the needs of humans and cattle who are unable to avail themselves of any other form of aid. When Mr. Hopkins left he made a grant around $18,000,000 for July, and I have made a grant around $20,500,000 for August. That is barely for the drought. I think that will have to be increased probably five or six million dollars in the next ten days to simply keep the peace; and it will be difficult to do it at that.

We are running into new difficulties in connection with the strike conditions on account of some prolonging a little bit. Madam Secretary says it is true that they are settleable, but at the same time, where they repeat in an area they tend to assume a more complicated character for us. Then, too, they have become more familiar with the fact that they can get aid from us. Generally speaking, however, we are finding very little difference with the Administration in aiding strikers. We have had this development, that in some sections of the Coast our people have been charged with refusing aid to people who are known to be Communists. I have taken steps to see that no discrimination is permitted along that line—that need is the basis of eligibility. I expect more trouble along that line in the future.

GOVERNOR MYERS:	Just one matter of interest I forgot. I talked with the governors in the six states through which I passed, and found they

---

[7] Aubrey W. Williams of Farm Emergency Relief Administration.

260

were unanimous that the government agencies affecting them were doing a satisfactory job, that there was no complaint of the failure to meet the situation insofar as it could be met by the various agencies dealing with the agricultural situation.

SECRETARY HULL: Mr. Jones, how is the business of your organization, and what is the state of mind of private capital these days?

MR. JONES: There is a good deal of private capital, apparently, looking for investment, but it is supposed to be careful and more interested in security than in yield or return. That is reflected by the increasing bond sales.

As for our work generally, our collections continue to exceed our expectations. That, I think, is due somewhat to better conditions, and also to a disposition of people to get out of debt. They want to pay up and feel the freedom of debt relief for a while. That belief has been growing with me for some time. We urge no one to pay. We try to be a generous creditor, and are, and yet payments are coming in much faster than we had expected.

Our loans on cotton, it might be interesting to know, have turned out not very well. While we appropriated $250,000,000 for cotton loans, we loaned only about $101,000,000, but that is all we were asked for, and about 45 per cent of that has been repaid; and that is coming in with some pretty good regularity. We don't force the sale of cotton. We can only force it after it gets to 15c a pound.

On corn loans we appropriated $150,000,000; and in loaning at 45¢ a bushel, of course, we loaned considerably more than the market value of the corn at the time; but corn has gone up and we suffered no loss from either cotton or corn loans. Corn loans are being paid at the rate of some six or seven hundred thousand dollars a day. It is coming in pretty fast.

Our bank work is slow because the banks have no need for the money. There is absolutely no fear in the United States about bank deposits. They feel that either insurance or the Administration is going to see that they are not going to lose their money, so there is no fear. Our work generally is going along very satisfactorily.

SECRETARY HULL: Is there any let-up in the defaults of counties and municipalities and other minor governmental agencies?

MR. JONES: We don't see much of that. That doesn't come to our attention. You see, we have only a very few loans of that character. The loans that we have are in good standing, with a few exceptions. We have very few defaults.

SECRETARY HULL: Is there any other question any one wants to report in which we will be interested?

MR. MARCH: Are banks making loans to their customers generally, or are they not?

MR. JONES: We find a disposition on the part of the banks to make industrial loans. We would like to make loans in connection with banks, and let the banks handle the loans.

MR. MARCH: Is that increasing, do you think, throughout the country?

MR. JONES: Yes, it is. We think we can develop that to a considerable extent. Wherever we make an industrial loan we try to get the local bank to become interested in it and take a part in it, small or large.

SECRETARY HULL: If there is nothing further, I suppose we might adjourn.

Meeting adjourned at 3:32 p.m.

Joint Meeting of the Executive Council and
the National Emergency Council

Held in the Blue Room of the White House,
August 7, 1934, at 2:10 p.m.

Present: the Secretary of the Treasury; the Secretary of Agriculture;
the Secretary of Commerce; the Acting Attorney General; the Acting
Secretary of the Navy; the First Assistant Postmaster General; the
Assistant Secretary of Labor; the Chairman of the Board of the Home
Owners' Loan Corporation; the Acting Director of the Budget; the
Assistant Administrator of the Federal Emergency Relief Administration;
the Assistant Director of Emergency Conservation Work; the Deputy
Governor of the Farm Credit Administration; the Commissioner of the
Federal Trade Commission; the Assistant Adviser on Consumer Problems;
the Second Divisional Administrator of the National Recovery Adminis-
tration; the Economic Adviser; the Executive Secretary.

[Here we find further evidence of the development of NEC
in the direction of a formal information clearing house. At
this stage in the development of the New Deal policies (what
Basil Rauch calls the "first" New Deal—the period symbolized
by the NRA), the established philosophy is fairly well along
and a check on progress is appropriate, while policy decisions
became somewhat less the order of the day.—Editors' Note.]

SECRETARY MORGENTHAU: Is it necessary to read the minutes of the preceding meeting?

SECRETARY ROPER: I would suggest that the reading of the minutes be waived.

SECRETARY MORGENTHAU: Unless there is objection, we will proceed without the
reading of the minutes. Next is a "Report on the Progress of
the Organization of the Federal Housing Administration."

MR. RICHBERG: I have the report here. It is very brief. Unless the Federal
Housing Administration wants to present it itself, I will
read the report....

SECRETARY MORGENTHAU: Are there any questions? Next is the "Report of the Secretary
of Agriculture Concerning the Effects of the Drought upon
the Agricultural Plans."

MR. RICHBERG: Mr. Secretary, do you want me to read this?

SECRETARY WALLACE: Yes.

MR. RICHBERG: I thought perhaps you would like to read it yourself with your
own emphasis....

SECRETARY MORGENTHAU: Any questions? "Report by the Chairman of the Board of the
Tennessee Valley Authority Concerning Certain Operations
in the Tennessee Valley Area."

MR. RICHBERG: This is a brief report, Mr. Secretary. "... The Tennessee Power Company, a private utility which has cooperated with TVA by reducing rates and selling EHFA low-cost electric appliances has sold 6,700 refrigerators, ranges, and water heaters in ten weeks. This is one-fourth as many as it sold in the last 12 years." I assume that means the total of the last 12 years.

SECRETARY MORGENTHAU: I suppose it means that they sold about 24,000 in the last 12 years.

"Report by the Executive Secretary Relative to the Survey of the Governmental Printing and Duplicating Activities."

MR. RICHBERG: This is a preliminary report rather to advise the members of the Council of the report in preparation which will be circularized shortly thereafter....

SECRETARY MORGENTHAU: "The Report of the Executive Secretary Concerning the Classification of Positions and Standardization of Salaries in the Emergency Agencies."[1]

MR. RICHBERG: This has been the subject of frequent recent discussions and there is an effort here to summarize briefly the development of the present problem and present two alternative suggestions for consideration by this Council....

I may point out at this moment that the adjustment under the Order would take place regardless of any approval, only it is required in the Order that they be reported to the Executive Council before they are made effective....

That is, if each specific case were to be reviewed in the office of the Executive Secretary and reports required, there would be complete uncertainty during that period as to the results....

I might call attention to the fact that at the meeting before the last one, when I was present, this matter had some discussion and I think you know about it.

SECRETARY MORGENTHAU: Yes, I do.

MR. RICHBERG: And there seemed to be a great deal of opposition to anything in the nature of a technical construction of the Order as creating confusion and impairing efficiency; but as long as the Order is in effect, the question of construction remains and this suggestion is made as a practical way of administering the Order.

These reports are made to the Executive Council and are

[1] See earlier discussion of this same matter during the meetings of May 1, July 10, and July 24, 1934. See also note 3, May 1 meeting.

filed, and if it is found, in the office of the Executive Secretary, that any particular agency is generally out of line—not as to individual salaries, but in a general way—that matter should then be taken up with the head of that agency with a view to seeing whether it can be adjusted. Then, and then only it should be reported to the Executive Secretary. That is the suggestion, and I think we ought to have something in the nature of an action concerning it and have a common understanding.

SECRETARY MORGENTHAU: This thing has been going on for months.

SECRETARY ROPER: That is a practical suggestion and I think it is the only way of handling it. I would like to ask whether this applies to the emergency agencies.

MR. RICHBERG: That is what it is intended to apply to.

SECRETARY ROPER: How about regular agencies using emergency funds?

MR. RICHBERG: I want to advise that the Order covers all such expenditures.

SECRETARY ROPER: Whether they be emergency or regular agencies?

MR. RICHBERG: Yes.

SECRETARY ROPER: That is what I think also.

MR. RICHBERG: Therefore, the same type of report and action would be taken.

SECRETARY ROPER: I move that the matter be handled as suggested.

SECRETARY MORGENTHAU: Perhaps you should read that again. (*Mr. Richberg then read the applicable paragraph the second time.*)

MR. RICHBERG: I also suggested that in the case of an agency being out of line, the matter would be taken up with the head of the agency before any report, and I suppose that is included in the purpose of your motion.

MR. BATTLE: I second the motion.

SECRETARY MORGENTHAU: All in favor say aye. The motion is carried. Does that clear it up?

MR. RICHBERG: Yes, sir.

SECRETARY MORGENTHAU: Next is the report of the Economic Adviser . . . .

MR. RICHBERG: May I ask one question? I notice the retail sales remain fairly constant in dollar volume; is there a sufficient increase in price levels so that means a distinct decrease in quantity volume?

MR. RIEFLER: No, retail prices have shown very little change. Constant dollar volume ought to mean constant physical volume. We have made a rather extended study and I think we have indicated pretty closely that it should not be done. The price indices are not built up in the same proportions that commodities are, and you get results that are absolutely fantastic in deflating.

The increase in retail volume has been in items such as automobiles and refrigerators. In the ordinary items, there does seem to be a change in quality; that, is consumers want to pay about so much of their budget, and if the price goes up, they buy a slightly different grade but keep on buying it.

SECRETARY MORGENTHAU: "Report of the State Directors of the National Emergency Council."

MR. RICHBERG: I will present the usual summary of these reports....

SECRETARY MORGENTHAU: Any questions?

Next is the digest of reports by members of the Council....

MR. RICHBERG: We have here the regular reports of our different members and this is circularized. Unless it is desired to be read at the present time, shall we rely on the circularization of it?

SECRETARY MORGENTHAU: If everybody has it so that if they are interested they can read it, and as long as the President is not here, maybe we could dispense with it. If that is agreeable, we will omit that.

MR. RICHBERG: There is one matter I would like to speak of in connection with the salary classification. If it is agreeable, as a method of carrying out the Executive Order, we will send out suggestions to the departments regarding the type of salaries to be sent in and other information so that we can obtain more reasonably classified reports to work on. I think that should be done; and as was pointed out, this is a very unsettled condition at the present time. We do not know what adjustments have been and what have not been made.

There is a matter, Mr. Chairman, I wanted to suggest rather as an item of discussion than otherwise. It has been the purpose, of course, of meetings of the Council, in making reports, to have presented a constant picture of the governmental activities, particularly as to the emergency agencies. But we have not available at the present time a certain type of material which in a way, it seems should be at least available for the President at this time, particularly in regard to the emergency agencies, and that I would describe somewhat in this manner: a sort of summarized statement down to date of the objectives of the various agencies that have been established, with a summarized report or condensed statement of how far those objectives have been realized, which could be supported by more voluminous information to be referred to as desired.

I would like to bring this matter up at this time because I feel that, personally, it is a matter of exceeding importance. Every national political campaigner is, in a measure, going to the country with a statement of the problems and achievements of the Administration. I understand that requests have been made to Mr. [Charles] Michelson by various departments and agencies for such information and it should be supplied to those who desire it. It seems to me that far beyond that, from the standpoint of the President, at least, there should be available to him for such use as he thinks should be made of it, and for his own judgment as to the manner in which the general program is moving, summarized reports with supporting material back of them to give different fronts; what the objectives have been of the different agencies established, how far they have been achieved, and what the indications are for the future. I understand that such information has been sought at various times by the President and very earnestly desired; and when I attempted to make a study to see how far such information could be collected through the office of the Executive Secretary for the benefit of the President, I found we simply did not have the information; and it seems to me that each agency of the government in any way dealing particularly with emergency problems—what may be regarded as the "New Deal" program— would desire to present such a statement from the standpoint of its own operations, so that it would not require an action directing that it be done, but something every agency should wish to do; and it seems to me the time is exceedingly short in which that material should be prepared and available.

I suggest for discussion here the question whether it is not desirable for all members of the Executive Council concerned to look to the preparation of such a report.

Some of the reports which have been presented to the Council from time to time are very informative, while some of them are practically devoid of any information whatsoever; and since I have been connected with it, I may say that is conspicuously true of the NRA reports.

JUDGE STEPHENS: I should like to endorse the suggestion very heartily. I have returned from nearly six weeks in San Francisco where I did a great deal of listening and very little talking, and I was very much impressed with the thought that the cooperation of the public with our program would be greatly increased if it were better understood. I found many people are critical with respect to the minor defects and are overlooking the major results. I saw that happen many, many times. I wish we could get the information concerning our objectives, and how far we have attained them, out to the public.

267

	I am sure it would increase public cooperation and sympathy.
MR. MC ENTEE:	Is it your thought on that, Mr. Secretary, that a short synopsis should be submitted to you, or would the general report which the agencies make be satisfactory? They would be rather too voluminous, I think.
MR. RICHBERG:	My thought is that the present time would be a good time for taking stock and preparing an up-to-date report of our objectives, how far they have been accomplished, and what is the prospect of further accomplishment; and that that summarized synopsis should be accompanied by data of such volume as seems to be appropriate and helpful to carry out and prove the point.
	The thought of having this prepared for the President is that instead of suggesting preparation directly for publicity, it could be presented with the utmost frankness and without any effort to window-dress it, so that the President would have the material available for such use as he saw fit to make of it. There is no use fooling ourselves, we might as well *know*.
MR. MC ENTEE:	Oh, yes, that is true. I had in mind that the regular report of the agencies would cover that, but it is rather too voluminous.
MR. RICHBERG:	Some of the agencies are not making any regular reports, and some are transitory. They carry the story along from month to month, but they do not summarize the present condition. They do not all put up a marker and say, "We have arrived at this."
MR. DAVIS:	It occurs to me that as you obtain all these reports from the different agencies and have them edited and improved, and in some instances reduced in volume, you should have them all printed in booklet form and sent to the leading newspapers and perhaps some of the libraries; in other words, get them generally distributed throughout the country so that the information might become more fully disseminated, than would otherwise be the case.
MR. MC ENTEE:	Let me follow the thought; the report you mention would be the bad spots as well as the good ones?
MR. RICHBERG:	The thought I had in mind was to have the entire picture presented, with its good and bad, for the benefit of the President; and that the nature of the material would determine the type of publicity to be used. I think what Mr. Davis says is exceedingly true, that such information should be available for the benefit of those who really want to study—those interested scientifically or preparing speeches—and it is not available now, so far as I can see.

268

MR. DAVIS: There is more or less confusion about the functions of the different agencies which could be clarified by information of that kind.

SECRETARY ROPER: Mr. Chairman, I think this is highly important. I don't believe I have had a conference this summer in which some phases of this need did not arise. There is considerable confusion. We have been doing a great many things. Of course, many persons knit in with the administration and try to make this whole thing a success. I am very heartily in favor of this. I would like to suggest, though, that Mr. Richberg address a communication to us to guide in the matter of uniformity of replies—in other words, to see that statistical data would be put in proper shape.

I find that this confusion referred to applies not only to the agencies that have been in operation, but those which have not yet got into operation. There is something to be said there for the further guidance of the public as to purposes of those; and not only the purposes, but that we are not trying to disrupt and destroy business, that we are trying really to assist business in safeguarding its own future.

A great many of these business people and bankers that I get communications from are weak right along that line, so that we need a clarification, as it were, which the President would know how to shape in the light of the information given him, as to the purposes and objectives of these new agencies. This is a righteous administration and not a destructive administration, as our enemies will try to show.

I am heartily in accord with that suggestion, and I hope Mr. Richberg will communicate with us and give us some guidance so that we may give the information in the form he wishes.

SECRETARY MORGENTHAU: I wish Mr. Richberg would feel that he could also write to anybody in the Administration who makes a speech that seems to be out of tune or out of line with the general policy of the Administration. There certainly have been speeches made the last month or two which could be classified as being unique.

SECRETARY ROPER: I would suggest you confer with Colonel Michelson, who has made a study along this line.

MR. RICHBERG: I spoke to Mr. Michelson about this matter yesterday, because I thought possibly he would be endeavoring to collect material for speeches, etc. I understand he is preparing to send out—I don't know whether he has sent it out—a questionnaire to get certain information, but it does not conflict with this. As a matter of fact, that which I have suggested here would be very

269

helpful along these lines. I did not want to undertake, without discussing it with the Council, to just make a personal suggestion to each member of the Council; but if it does meet with general approval, I would be very glad to write a letter making the suggestion in concrete form.

It seems to me it is entirely possible that at least a summarized statement of activities might be available before the next meeting, when the President will be here, and it might be somewhat in the nature of a pleasing surprise to present such material to him.

SECRETARY ROPER: Fine!

JUDGE STEPHENS: I think there might be some of the new objectives of the regular departments which would be interesting, too.

MR. RICHBERG: May I ask if that may also be understood as a part of the suggestion? Of course, many of the regular departments are carrying on former activities that play a very large part in the entire program, and also some new activities, so that I think this really could properly be presented as a suggestion to practically every member of the Executive Council.

SECRETARY MORGENTHAU: Is there any other business? If not, we stand adjourned.

Meeting closed at 3:00 p.m.

270

Joint Meeting of the Executive Council and
the National Emergency Council

Held in the Blue Room of the White House,
August 21, 1934, at 2:20 p.m.

Present: the President of the United States; the Secretary of the
Treasury; the Secretary of War; the Secretary of Commerce; the Acting
Secretary of the Navy; the Undersecretary of State; the Undersecretary
of Agriculture; the Assistant Secretary of the Interior; the Assistant
Secretary of Labor; the First Assistant Postmaster General; the Assistant
Director of the Budget; the Solicitor General; the Administrator of the
Agricultural Adjustment Administration; the Chairman of the Board of
the Home Owners' Loan Corporation; the Chairman of the Board of
the Reconstruction Finance Corporation; the Chairman of the Board
of the Tennessee Valley Authority; the Federal Coordinator of Transportation; the Governor of the Farm Credit Administration; the Assistant
Director of Emergency Conservation Work; the Assistant Administrator
of the Federal Emergency Relief Administration; the Chairman of
the Federal Trade Commission; the Commissioner of the Federal Trade
Commission; the Assistant Adviser on Consumer Problems; the
Executive Secretary.

[The most valuable thing about these NEC meeting transcripts
is the opportunity provided from time to time to watch,
as it were, the President in an informal context. Here, as earlier
in the transcripts, much of Mr. Roosevelt's own commentary
is devoted to what might be called the "public relations" side
of the governmental enterprise. His keen publicity sense is well
illustrated at this meeting in several subtle ways. In the first
place, note that the report being discussed had been read by the
President primarily with an eye to its public relations
impact. He had, for example, picked out phrases that would
cause trouble if quoted out of context. His sense of "news"
was serving him well, as usual. He also saw the report in
terms of its over-all impact—when put in releasable form—
as a review of the total government attack on the depression
and as one of many needed counterweights to barbed and
distorted comments by the administration's opponents. (It is
interesting to compare Richberg's summary of this report
with the content of the fireside chats of these years, which
also were often reviews of progress and programs initiated,
rather than exhortations, as has been so often assumed.)

new deal mosaic

As to the role of the NEC itself as seen in this meeting, there was less coordination in the narrower sense of the term, but rather education of the agency heads gathered around the table. This frequently was an NEC function: to serve as a forum at which each member could be informed of what others were doing and thereby derive some impression of the over-all program of the government. In other words, the NEC was doubtless a means of counteracting inevitable administrative myopia and as such was clearly filling a "coordinating role" in a broader sense of the term.

Two or three further points deserve passing mention. Note the President's report of his travels about the country and the importance to him of the first-hand look at conditions which such journeys afforded him. Note also that NEC meetings differed little from cabinet meetings in that members at times preferred to have a private word with the President after adjournment rather than bring up departmental matters before the whole group.—Editors' Note.]

PRESIDENT ROOSEVELT: During the past month, an exceedingly interesting volume was compiled for the guidance of Donald Richberg. It is a report from the Executive Secretary of the Executive Council, and comes as a result of a survey made by each department and each agency of its own work. The whole thing has been digested—those two envelopes (*indicating*) contain the bulk of the material—the whole has been digested into this volume of (*turning to Mr. Richberg*)—

MR. RICHBERG: Eighty pages.

PRESIDENT ROOSEVELT: Eighty pages, and it will have to be further digested for public use. One reason for it is that, unfortunately, we suffer at this time, as always, from the press of the country and public speakers who pick out high spots that are not high spots, a very good example of which is a phrase in the report from the Federal Deposit Insurance Corporation which says that a great many banks are in a weak condition. Now if that were to get out—if we were to hand this summary to the press or even distribute it back around the departments—a certain type of newspaper and a certain type of public speaker would at once headline the blazing statement of the Insurance Corporation that a large number of banks were in a weak condition. That, as a sentence by itself, is, of course, wholly misleading. The actual fact is that the Insurance Corporation, under the law, took into the Corporation banks which were solvent. Now a weak bank is not necessarily an insolvent bank. The weak banks we knew were weak when they were taken in under the law. The report of the Federal Deposit Insurance Corporation goes on to make recommendations as to how to strengthen the weak banks. That is just an illustration of how very, very careful we have got to be.

There is also a statement from Dr. [Arthur E.] Morgan that, provided the funds could be immediately released, he could put 10,000 men to work. Of course some bright lad would come along and say, "Where are you going to put them to work?" and he would be put to it to answer that, when what was really meant was that if all the funds were made available, within a reasonable length of time there would be 10,000 people at work.

There are a lot of illustrations here which prove that I cannot go ahead and release this survey. My thought is that Donald Richberg could give us a five or six-minute summary of this report, and having done that, that the eighty-page report, which is all-inclusive, will be redigested for public use and for the press, showing what we have done and where we are going. As such, it has very definite value.

I think if you could go ahead, Donald, and give us a summary of the results of that, it would be very helpful; and it is interesting to know that after he has made a dissecting operation on every department and agency of the government, he is still cheerful and encouraged!

MR. RICHBERG: Mr. President, I cannot give any adequate summary of this eighty-page summary in just a few minutes.

PRESIDENT ROOSEVELT: Make it fifteen or twenty.

MR. RICHBERG: I won't go that far.[1] I should explain that, for the purpose of getting a coordinated view of all the government activities, these reports were digested under main heads so that all the departments and agencies working under a head would have the work considered as a whole. The first was "Industrial Unemployment" as related to private enterprise and to public works.

PRESIDENT ROOSEVELT: I should state that on one page he has classified, in the relationship

---

[1] Richberg's report in the next few pages provides a succinct statement of the scope of economic recovery efforts, and a clear statement of the effects of these efforts. It is an example of how NEC attempted to serve as a central reporting and control agency over the entire effort. Also, the "briefing" F.D.R. received in these reports is revealing.

to the people of the country and the government, every activity under eleven heads. That in itself is an excellent thing.

MR. RICHBERG: I think it is helpful to the general view of the situation. The second is "Agricultural Distress;" third, "Relief of Destitution;" fourth, the "Financial Picture;" and fifth, "Advance in Public Service."

PRESIDENT ROOSEVELT: What do you mean by that?

MR. RICHBERG: That means the advance in various public services that the government itself performs, which may be in the nature of regulatory services or actual direct services.

PRESIDENT ROOSEVELT: Such as the Army and Navy?

MR. RICHBERG: As a matter of fact, the group handled (I can tell from the index, Mr. President) covers the Tennessee Valley Authority, Federal Coordinator of Transportation, the Securities and Exchange Commission, the Food and Drug Administration, and others. Then there is the group of administrative services, under which classification would come the financing of the recovery agencies, furnishing information, and adjustments of the economic situation; and then there is the third classification of promotion of foreign trade. Summarizing the section on the relief of industrial unemployment, I think one or two significant figures can be picked out. In the first place, a statement of the problem is found in the fact that in the Department of Labor report for June 30, 1934, it is shown that the National Reemployment Service received 15,387,508 applications and total placements were 6,951,523. Of course, that is not the measure of unemployment, but it does give a picture of the size of the problem.

PRESIDENT ROOSEVELT: And of the services rendered.

MR. RICHBERG: The National Industrial Recovery Act is classified in two parts. Of course, the main part has reference to the industrial depression. The report from the NRA shows the adoption of 495 codes and 136 supplementary codes covering about 95 per cent of all industrial employees. The President's Reemployment Agreement[2] also covered more than two million employees. There was an increase in employment of 4,120,000 over the low figure of March 1933, and an increase of 2,320,000 allocated

---

[2] One of the provisions of the Act which created NRA authorized the President to enter into agreement with and to approve voluntary agreements among persons engaged in trade or industry, labor organizations, etc., if in his judgment such agreements would aid in accomplishing the purposes of the law. Under this provision, the President promulgated the President's Reemployment Agreement, under which employers subscribed to maintain wages and certain employment conditions.

to the shortening of the hours under the NRA codes which have produced a larger amount of employment than that indicated by the net increases. The codes established minimum wages and maximum hours, and the effect of that was shown in these figures, giving an estimated increase from 58.3 in June 1933, to 62.5 in June 1934, and an estimated increase in wages from 96 in June 1933, to 132 in June 1934. This increase would be divided between an increase in living cost about 9.6 [*sic*] leaving a net increase of 25 per cent in the total payroll of industrial wage earners. The total purchasing power has increased far beyond the cost of living. As to the individual wage earner, the increase in his per capita earnings, the rise in his hourly compensation and a rise in his weekly earnings have been just about the same as the rise in the cost of living, so that on the average he shares his work without losing compensation. He is not better off in his individual standing, but there are more people employed.

PRESIDENT ROOSEVELT: And the country is better off.

MR. RICHBERG: The work week has been reduced approximately six hours on the average for all industries. That is, the average hourly earnings have increased about 26 per cent and wage differentials have been materially decreased.

Under the codes, trade associations have more than doubled in number and labor organizations have had a corresponding increase, more than 2,000,000 having been added to the AF of L. The importance of that is that it marks the organization of industry and labor for concerted effort.

I think the general figures on economic survey which are included in the NRA report, but which come more or less in the report of the Economic Adviser, can be passed over at this time. Probably the most significant figure is the decline in business failures, which from February to May 1934 were more than 40 per cent lower than in 1929.

PRESIDENT ROOSEVELT: That was before the crash.

MR. RICHBERG: Yes; this shows the effect of the NRA codes on the protection of small enterprises, where most of the failures occur.

In corporation profits, there is a rise from a deficit figure of 6.9 to a profit figure of more than 3 per cent in the second quarter of 1934. In this report, there are specific references to particular codes where remarkable advances have been made, such as bituminous coal, automobiles, and oil industry. I quote this one figure from the Secretary of the Interior as administrator of the petroleum industry that petroleum, which had collapsed until oil was selling crude as low as ten cents a barrel, has been restored to a dollar-a-barrel basis; notwithstanding that, oil prices have not advanced materially.

Turning now from that type to Public Works: the Public Works Administration has allocated a grand total of $3,665,000,000 leaving only $35,000,000 not allocated. As to expenditures, 71 per cent of the first appropriation of $3,300,000,000 was allocated to construction projects amounting, as of August 1, 1934, to $1,821,000,000 or about 72 per cent of the total cost of projects under the original appropriation.

Employment increased from zero to 250,000 by December 1, 1933. Those figures obtained through the winter and will increase to about 700,000 in September, to be followed by a gradual decline to 300,000 through the winter and a rise to 450,000 or 500,000 by June 1935.

PRESIDENT ROOSEVELT: Those figures do not include the indirect employment in turning out material for these construction jobs. How much would that be?

MR. RICHBERG: That has been estimated as being from double to triple the number directly employed.[3]

There is one very significant thing in the report of the Public Works Administrator, and that is that the fastest method of spending money has been in federal projects, the most rapid in the building of roads; and of the nonfederal projects, the most rapid has been by loans to railroads, while loans to municipalities and states have produced the slowest results, largely on account of legal difficulties. Of course, various departments are concerned with this, besides the Public Works Administration, including the Department of Agriculture, the Post Office Department, the State Department, Navy Department, War Department, Department of Commerce, and the Department of Justice. All these have been engaged in this program.

PRESIDENT ROOSEVELT: The State Department's activities have been in putting people to work with the Mexican boundary development.[4] (*Laughter*)

MR. RICHBERG: I now move on to the "Relief of Agricultural Distress," which

---

[3] A foreshadowing of the Keynes multiplier theory.

[4] Identification of this reference is inconclusive. The only possibly related item in the public papers is a reconnaisance survey of the Inter-American Highway which was transmitted to the President by Secretary Hull in March 1934. See *Public Papers and Addresses of Franklin D. Roosevelt: 1934. The Advance of Recovery and Reform.* ed., Rosenman (New York: 1938) pp. 133-136.

I do not like to attempt to summarize, but I want to pick out one or two of the highlights of the report which show that the prices of certain agricultural commodities, including benefit payments, had risen in August to 90 per cent of parity or 116 per cent of prewar. On August 6, the prices paid by farmers were estimated to be 122 per cent of prewar prices. That shows that we have approached parity.

The Agricultural Administration reports total farm income from corn, cotton, fruits, vegetables, meat animals, and poultry, including benefit payments, of $5,033,000,000 as compared with $3,881,000,000 the previous year. I think probably that finishes the highlights on the achievement of objectives.

Of course, in connection with the Agricultural Adjustment Administration are all the other services which are rendered in the way of the Commodity Credit Corporation financing surpluses, and there are many figures in regard to that which I would like to summarize, but I think I would probably not pick the most important. They are worthy of much more careful study than can be given that way.

The third major section is "Relief of Destitution." Of course, the central agency for that has been the Federal Emergency Relief Administration, and the problem and what has been done to satisfy it, I think, can be summarized in these figures: in March 1933, 4,569,000 families were receiving relief and the total relief obligations were $81,000,000, including administration. By June, the figure had declined to 3,789,000, with total obligations of $66,000,000. During that period, the number of single resident persons is not available. Since then, the figures have been compiled, and beginning with July, there were 3,900,000 cases involving 15,215,000 persons with total obligations of $60,000,000.

PRESIDENT ROOSEVELT: A month?

MR. RICHBERG: Yes, a month. This is the beginning, one might say, of the present type of administration. Following that program through, we find a decline to the end of September, and then a rise, which dipped off rapidly at the end of the year; but that was only in appearance, because the CWA program took the place of direct relief.

In 1934, the relief rolls have steadily climbed, with a sharp rise April 1, when the Civil Works largely closed. In April 1934, there were 3,800,000 families and 4,447,000 cases, including 16,825,000 persons on relief, with the obligations incurred of $112,527,000 a month.

According to present estimates, there were 4,200,000 cases receiving relief in July, almost one-fourth being employed in work projects, and about a million located in the 18 drought states.

The estimate is made by the administrator that the relief problem will rise to approximately five million cases. He states that probably the trend of relief will be upward for the next eight months, because of the severity of the drought situation and the usual seasonal decline in employment, to five million families in February, 1935.

PRESIDENT ROOSEVELT: Five million families, or five million, including single people?

MR. RICHBERG: I think the single people are included. Is that right?

MR. WILLIAMS: That includes the single people.

MR. RICHBERG: Right in connection with the Federal Emergency Relief, of course, there is a report on the Civil Works Administration and the development of the work program which followed the termination of that.

"Emergency Conservation Work" follows, and I think should be briefly summarized, possibly because of its extraordinary success and the general approval of the work. The total number enrolled in the forest units is 369,838 and the total number of persons employed in payroll administration, etc., approximately 395,000. It is worthy of note that an average of 10,000 men are now leaving the camps each month to go into private employment, as compared with 5,000 a month in the months of October, November, and December of last year. An additional enrollment of 50,000 has been authorized in the drought states. The reports of this work indicate that the success of this program has been realized.

In that program, the War Department has carried a large amount of work in administration of personnel, and in its report I find these figures, that under War Department control, the nonrecurrent cost—shelter, clothing, cost of travel, etc.— averaged $147 per man; and for maintenance, subsistence, etc., $1.71 per man per day; and of the pay, of course, five-sixths, approximately, went back to the dependents, where it relieved the local relief problem.

"Relief of Financial Pressures." Prior to the present administration the major relief was through the Reconstruction Finance Corporation in loans for state relief. I have that under another subhead and would like to postpone that.

The new activities of the present administration have been largely in the nature of relieving financial pressures. The Home

Owners' Loan Corporation reports that since July 13, 1933, up to August 3, 1934, a force of 19,000 employees has handled 1,587,000 applications from home owners and completed 432,000 loans involving $229,000,000 at a gross cost of $1,134 per application. The cost of acquisition is $23.50, which is reported to be far below any similar institution acquiring such loans. The report is made that 432,000 families have been saved from foreclosure and 400,000 will receive relief. The Corporation reports it has noted practical benefit in the real estate market.

Applications dropped from 168,000 in March to 69,000 in July.

The operations of the subsidiaries, I think, may be passed by for the present, although they are important.

The Reconstruction Finance Corporation at first confined most of its activities to loans to financial institutions but many other activities have been added. In its 30 months of operation, the grand total of operations runs to approximately $7,560,000,000. Approximately 900 banks availed themselves of this assistance.

The loans to industry are reported not to be moving to any great extent. The total amount loaned under this plan will probably not be large. Of the applications received, 70,000 have been disqualified by law or policy. The loans to railroads are reported to have saved many important carriers from receivership.

The report of the Federal Deposit Insurance Corporation: On the positive side, it should be pointed out that 14,084 of the nation's banks are insured, the insurance liability being estimated as in excess of twelve billion dollars. More than 97 per cent of the depositors are insured to the full amount of their deposits; and of the total of the 15,700 licensed banks, with total deposits of $45,000,000,000, 90 per cent are members of the Insurance Fund and five per cent are members of the State Insurance Fund.

I think, Mr. President, without trying to endeavor to refer to the other activities, those having to do with public services and administrative services, the most are statements rather than figures. I think it would be very difficult to summarize. Perhaps I have covered the most important figures—except I might refer to the final report of the Adviser on Foreign Trade with its most interesting figure stating that the outgoing accounts of international trade with the United States for the past 38 years have exceeded the incoming accounts by more than twenty billion dollars.

PRESIDENT ROOSEVELT: Approximately the figure of the so-called balance of trade.

This is a perfectly grand job that has been done. I think it will be helpful to everybody if we can get a summary into our hands of this 80-page document which will bring out all the facts in regard to the departments and agencies, what they are trying to do, and the relationship of each to the activities of the broader subdivisions. Any one department may fall into a half-dozen categories, but each one is listed in the proper place so it shows the relationship between the departments or agencies. It is well worthwhile having this to clarify our own minds as to where we are going and what we are accomplishing. The most encouraging thing is that a thoroughly hard-boiled egg like Donald, after reading this thing over with great care, is distinctly encouraged and believes we are getting somewhere.

MR. RICHBERG: I think this is a most enheartening survey of the whole activities of the government. There is one very large gap in it—there is no consideration given to fiscal or monetary policies and their relation to these activities. That would require a special study and survey by those capable of making it.

PRESIDENT ROOSEVELT: In other words, how are we going to finance this? Have we anything else to take up today?

MR. RICHBERG: Instead of the general reports, the only thing is the usual report of the Economic Adviser on economic conditions.

PRESIDENT ROOSEVELT: Where is brother Riefler?

MR. RICHBERG: I think he is on vacation, and while the Council may be getting tired of hearing my voice, this is not long . . . .

PRESIDENT ROOSEVELT: Here are the employment charts if anyone wants to see them.

The Secretary of the Treasury suggests that on the fifteenth of September we are going to add finances to the tune of $1,725,000,000, which is nearly all of it—in fact, all of it, I think—to take care either of bonds or the refunding of notes which are falling due, and the Treasury will not have to ask for any additional money for new expenditures until December. That is very encouraging. This large financing in September will carry us through until practically the end of the year.

I don't think we have any other item. I have nothing else in particular on my mind. I have talked with a good many of you in regard to the things I saw while crossing the country. Of course, I didn't get personally into the most serious part of the drought area. I came through Montana, North Dakota, and Minnesota. I was frankly encouraged by the fact that conditions were not as bad as I had expected them to be from photographs I have seen and figures on that particular section. In other words, the fields are not entirely bare; they are growing wheat and a certain amount of other crops and grass. Up through that section, the principal problem is the livestock problem. In other words, there will be enough for human beings to eat and drink, but not enough for livestock to eat and drink; and our problem is to see that livestock through the winter and prevent the diminution of the livestock to such an extent that we will not have any breeders for next spring.

Farther south, of course, the conditions are distinctly worse, especially in certain sections of Oklahoma, Kansas, Nebraska, and North Texas. Do you want to tell anything more about that, Rex?

DR. TUGWELL: No, sir, I don't think so.

PRESIDENT ROOSEVELT: Or you, Chester; what is your general feeling at the present time, Chester?

MR. DAVIS: I would rather withhold word concerning the livestock situation until the survey, which is now under way, has been completed.

I went out through a portion of the territory—spent some time out there. As to the livestock purchases, we have already bought in excess of three million head of cattle which are being processed for relief distribution. I am hopeful that feed will be available so that we will not have to carry that up to the extreme mentioned by many people—ten million head of cattle. I hope it can be arrested short of that for the very point you mention, that is, maintaining the foundation of livestock in that country.

We will have to do something for sheep, and the machinery is already set up so that in a week or eight days we ought to be actually buying sheep. It is lack of water fully as much as anything else.

I was more encouraged than discouraged with my trip through there. The people have a good deal of reserve courage and resourcefulness, and the effect of all these operations has been to soften the blow of the drought somewhat in these territories in which the loss would have been total, and diffuse the shock of it over the country.

PRESIDENT ROOSEVELT: The important thing, in the last analysis, is the psychology of the people themselves. This is the first time I have been west of the Mississippi since 1932. The difference was perfectly apparent in the faces of the people. You could tell what that difference was by standing on the end of the car and looking at the crowd. They were a hopeful people. They had courage written all over their faces. They looked cheerful. They knew they were "up against it" but they were going to see the thing through; whereas, in 1932 there was a look of despair, not only through that section, but practically throughout the South. That was best illustrated when one day I went through a town in the agricultural section of Tennessee, and Senator Barkley said it was perfectly obvious that the women had only one garment on because they could not afford more than one, and that was a very cheap one; and the men had a sweater and pair of trousers which would possibly hold together for another 24 hours. Of course, as far as the South is concerned, they are richer now than they have been at any time since before the war. Of course, they claim they were rich in 1860, but they were not quite as rich as some of the elderly people claim at this time. In other words, they are richer now than they have been at any time in the history of the country. Do you think I am right about that, brother Davis?

MR. DAVIS: I think you are.

PRESIDENT ROOSEVELT: Taking it by and large, we have to remember to keep our tempers in the next couple of months. There is a very definite effort in the political press to scare the housewife or to scare the head of the family with large headlines in the papers. I read this to the Cabinet the other day, and I think it will interest some of you, as an indication of some of the things we are up against. It was in the New York *Sun* a week ago Saturday, came out that way (*holding up the page*). I had just come back across the country. I know Mr. Dewart, who runs it, very well, and I wrote him this letter, which, of course, was not for publication; it was just to him and nobody else, because I don't think any of us ought to break into print. But I wanted to lay the foundation, so that later on if it is advisable to say something, I will say, "This is nothing new; this goes back to a definite series of small occurrences which might almost be classified by the Attorney General under the term 'conspiracy.' I am sorry you are unable to come to Washington in person, as it would have been far more satisfactory for me to talk with you." I understand he was playing golf that day, but he found his health was such that he could not come to Washington. (*Laughter*)

"On Saturday last, the New York *Sun* published a map of the United States with this caption above it: 'Here Are the Focal Points of Depression-bred Ferment Throughout the Nation.' This map contained these headlines: 'Spirit of Unrest Grips the Nation,' 'Country Disturbed by Conditions not Experienced for More than a Century.' "

Of course, we know the actual number of people on strike during 1934 has been far less than it was in 1921, which very few of us think of as a strike year.

"Another headline was 'Ruined Crops to Force High Price for Food.' In my inaugural address on March 4, 1933, at the time when the United States was rocked by a wave of fear, I said that the one thing we had to fear is fear. The fear that existed at that time was not political nor was it confined to any section or class of the country. That kind of fear has been increasingly eliminated.

"The map carried by the *Sun* and reprinted on Monday morning by the *Washington Post* and which probably will be republished by other papers, contained certain insets,"—not insects—(*laughter*) "as follows: Out on the Pacific Coast the inset relates to strikes which were terminated or are in process of arbitration. The ferment relating to Idaho mentions an individual who is making speeches—Senator Borah. The ferment relating to North Dakota mentions former Governor Langer. The ferment relating to West Virginia mentions that the candidate to the United States Senate [Rush Holt] is one year under the constitutional age limit. The ferment relating to Harriman, Tennessee, speaks of a code compliance matter which had been previously settled.[5] The ferment relating to Springfield, Illinois, relates to the speech of the Republican National Chairman at a political meeting.

"If you were coming to see me, I would have told you what I am now writing you, that any nation in the world must fear fear itself, but that any nation must fear even more those who seek to inject fear into its population. I am very confident, my dear Mr. Dewart, that if you had personally seen a large section of this country or had the personal information which we draw in Washington,"—such as this report today—"you

---

[5] The President refers to a series of difficulties involving the town and the Harriman Hosiery Mills, which had lost the "Blue Eagle" symbol of NRA participation for disobeying a National Labor Board ruling. The resultant protracted controversy with NRA is extensively reported in the *New York Times*, March-Sept. 1934.

would believe with me that in the face of great difficulties such as the world situation, such as the decline of world trade, such as the great human suffering that existed before federal relief became adequate, you would marvel with me at the disappearance of fear as such on the part of the overwhelming majority of American citizens. I have constantly refrained from any criticism of any newspaper that disagreed with me, and that is why I am writing you this letter, which is not for publication, to tell you quite frankly that I consider a front page make-up and map such as appeared in the *Sun* will do more to breed ferment in our country than have all the depression years put together."

It is just as well to take time by the forelock with some of these gentlemen; but taking it by and large, I think we want to keep our tempers the next couple of months, and get across the idea, and I believe it comes pretty close to being true, that the lack of understanding of what the government is trying to do, the principal opposition which comes from lack of understanding, and the principal opposition which comes from politics or from pure cussedness, comes mostly from about ten to fifteen per cent of people whose mental slant is what might be described as being at the extreme right of modern philosophy, and the rest of it is from ten to fifteen per cent of the mental slant that belongs to the extreme left of modern philosophy of civilization; and those two ends— the extreme right and the extreme left—are the people who are causing the criticism and objection that is growing up, that is, where it is captious. Of course, there is a great deal of perfectly legitimate criticism from which we can derive satisfaction and help; but it is rather easy for us to discriminate between the two types.

The general situation is running along fairly well, and I am more confident even than brother Riefler's report outlines, of a better winter, beginning perhaps in October or November. That is just what you might call a hunch on my part.

I don't know of anything else, except that it is good to know that Mr. [Jesse] Jones is taking in more money that he is paying out, as usual. Soon Mr. Jones will have so much money that the Treasury can borrow it all back again. (*Laughter*)

MR. JONES: We can finance the Treasury!

PRESIDENT ROOSEVELT: That's it!

Donald suggests that if anything is said about this report, we should merely say that we had a very brief oral summary of it, that it is encouraging, that it is very informative and very helpful; and that we will give out some kind of summary of it later on. Tell the press that the report has been made and is being summarized for them.

Anything Dan?

SECRETARY ROPER: Yes, I want to get your assistance for two or three minutes after the meeting.

PRESIDENT ROOSEVELT: Has anybody else got anything they want to take up at this time? I have been trying to find another $100,000,000 for FERA in order to tide them through, and if any of you people who are in possession of three [*sic*—free?] funds can avoid spending them all, we can use them for FERA. I consider that of very vital importance so that we can definitely take care of relief work until February sometime. (*Brief conversation so low I could not hear it.*) Mr. Richberg says he knows there are a few millions lying loose. (*Laughter*)

Meeting closed at 3:15 p.m.

Proceedings of the National Emergency Council

[meeting no. 15]
October 2, 1934

Joint Meeting of the Executive Council and the National Emergency Council

Held in the Blue Room of the White House, October 2, 1934, at 2:10 p.m.

Present: the President of the United States; the Secretary of State; the Secretary of the Treasury; the Secretary of War; the Attorney General; the Secretary of the Interior; the Secretary of Commerce; the Acting Secretary of the Navy; the Assistant Secretary of the Treasury; the First Assistant Postmaster General; the Assistant Secretary of Agriculture; the Assistant Secretary of Labor; the Acting Director of the Budget; the Administrator of Agricultural Adjustment Administration; the Administrator of the Federal Emergency Relief Administration; the Administrator of the Federal Housing Administration; the Chairman of the Federal Trade Commission; the Chairman of the National Industrial Recovery Board; the Chairman of the Board of the Home Owners' Loan Corporation; the Chairman of the Board of the Tennessee Valley Authority; the Director of Emergency Conservation Work; the Federal Coordinator of Transportation; the Governor of the Farm Credit Administration; the Adviser on Consumer Problems; the Executive Secretary.

[This meeting was taken up with an examination of the reports submitted by the individual members. The meeting seems to have enabled the President to inform himself of the activities of the various agencies. One could speculate that this was related to a decreasing interest on the part of the President in these activities, because of other calls on his time. In other words, when the programs were in their early formative stages he was absorbed with them and would have had no need for this kind of "briefing." Now that they were going concerns, NEC became a device to enable him to keep track of them with a minimum expenditure of time and attention. The converse of this situation—the impact on the general membership of NEC—is probably a clue to the future of the agency and its decline. This kind of meeting reduced the proceedings to a series of dialogues between F.D.R. and individual members. The subjects of these dialogues contrasted sharply in terms of general interest with, for example, the discussion of general agricultural policy that took place at the meeting of February 20, 1934, above. The low level of general interest this kind of meeting was likely to generate

286

in the group as a whole no doubt contributed to the tendency for substitutes to appear, and for the NEC to decline in interest and significance.—Editors' Note.]

PRESIDENT ROOSEVELT: We are welcoming two new faces to the Council at this time— Jimmie Moffett and Clay Williams.

MR. RICHBERG: And also Mr. Bell.[1]

PRESIDENT ROOSEVELT: Oh, yes, and Mr. Bell.

The first thing on the agenda is "The request by the Federal Emergency Administration of Public Works for the approval of the President to continue special classes of employees at rates of compensation which do not correspond to the salary schedule for emergency agencies." That should be taken up with the Director of the Budget.

SECRETARY ICKES: I don't know how that got in here.

MR. RICHBERG: It came to us through the Executive Council . . . .

PRESIDENT ROOSEVELT: For the general information of all the agencies, when you come to discuss allowances for salaries and per diems for the coming year, if you will take them all up with Mr. Bell he will try to see to it that there are no glaring discrepancies between departments for the same character of work.

The next item is "Request by the Executive Director of the National Emergency Council for funds for the continuation of the activities of the field force now engaged in the Housing program."[2] How much do you want, Donald?

MR. RICHBERG: A million dollars is requested.

PRESIDENT ROOSEVELT: From the Public Works administrator?

MR. RICHBERG: Yes, on allocation. The situation developed out of the refusal of the Budget to allow a retransfer of the money from the Better Housing Administration back to the National Emergency Council. It is my understanding that the Better Housing Administration needs the money itself anyhow, and if this allocation is made to the National Emergency Council

[1] Daniel W. Bell succeeded Lewis Douglas as Budget Director on Sept. 1, 1934. James A. Moffett had been appointed Federal Housing Administrator. S. Clay Williams was Chairman of the National Industrial Recovery Board which had been set up to take over Gen. Johnson's functions as Administrator of Industrial Recovery upon the General's resignation on Sept. 25, 1934.

[2] On Aug. 31, the appointment of regional, state, and district directors for the Better Housing Division of the NEC was announced. State NEC directors were often given additional responsibilities such as this task of acquainting their states with the proposed program under the National Housing Act of 1934.

	we can use it for the Better Housing Division. That is correct, isn't it?
MR. MOFFETT:	The last time I presented it to the President, he thought it ought to come out of the RFC.
PRESIDENT ROOSEVELT:	That is to avoid trouble with the Comptroller General.
SECRETARY ICKES:	It means a lot of money.
PRESIDENT ROOSEVELT:	Get the money from the Public Works Administrator for RFC!
SECRETARY ICKES:	I won't stand on the precedents there. (*Laughter*)
PRESIDENT ROOSEVELT:	The next is "Report concerning characteristics of the urban relief population."
MR. RICHBERG:	This is a report—a very short one—from the Administrator of Federal Emergency Relief concerning the characteristics of the urban relief population as revealed by recent research study....
PRESIDENT ROOSEVELT:	The next is a very interesting report, pretty long to read, but I think probably it is worth reading. It is a report by the Secretary of Agriculture and includes certain recommendations with reference to increase of industrial production and employment. I thought I might read it so that we will at least have it to think over. [The President then read the report aloud, pausing occasionally to ask a question or to comment...] How are they getting along, Chester, with that feed stuff business, that sugar cane from Puerto Rico?
MR. DAVIS:	We are taking out about 1,200,000 tons of mature cane. We are getting figures as to what it will cost for the delivery of that. The cane will be paid for and there will be an added cost for transportation. What it will cost delivered in this country we do not know. And then we are working through the feed section on methods of handling it. The sections of the country that need feed are not accustomed to using molasses feed.
PRESIDENT ROOSEVELT:	What effect does it have on the health of the cattle?
MR. DAVIS:	All right, if you feed it with roughage. I think there are some possibilities in it, but we are not ready to say yet just what it will cost, or how far we can go with it.
PRESIDENT ROOSEVELT:	Of course, that will solve the sugar cane problem in Puerto Rico.
MR. DAVIS:	It will help immensely.
PRESIDENT ROOSEVELT	[Having read a table showing increase in industrial production for the U.S. and five other countries]: These figures relate to industrial production and are quite interesting because of some of the arguments that Great Britain has increased far more than we have, or even that Japan has.

[After reading a proposal to increase industrial production through use of the Surplus Relief Corporation, the Commodity Credit Corporation, and the reorganization of NRA activities and units] I think it is well worth study. You will remember that it was some time in December, I think, of last year that a similar report—I have forgotten who it came from—on housing was referred to a special committee, and they studied over it practically all winter, and out of the study made on that suggestion came the new Housing Administration. Donald, don't you think this should be referred to perhaps a special committee, or the Policy Committee, or the Industrial Emergency Committee for further study?

MR. RICHBERG: The Industrial Emergency Committee, Mr. President, I think, has quite a number of the elements on it that would be interested in it. That includes NRA and the AAA.

PRESIDENT ROOSEVELT: But it does not include Housing.

MR. RICHBERG: I think it would be very desirable to add the Housing Administration to this study.

PRESIDENT ROOSEVELT: Will you go ahead and get that started?

Are there any comments anybody would like to make on that? It is just a trial balloon.

MR. MOFFETT: We have been working on the basis of 1926. If you have forty-one billion dollars in mortgages and if you inject a different price level in there downward, what is going to happen to the mortgage situation as to value? There has been a flight of capital from mortgages now.

PRESIDENT ROOSEVELT: You have been working on the 1926 basis?

MR. MOFFETT: That is what we had in mind. The existing level is about 90. We expect to operate on November first, and we have to take some position at that time as to the appraisal. To my mind, it seems important to restore some value for the existing mortgages, loosening them up through the medium of insurance. If we try to get a brand new price level in there, I don't know just what will happen. New construction is a ten or twenty-year proposition, as I see it. In England they have a long-range program.

PRESIDENT ROOSEVELT: Of course, this is not really from the 1926 level. It is based on the 1923-1925 level.

MR. RICHBERG: Mr. Wallace is not here. I thought possibly some one here could speak on that particular matter.

PRESIDENT ROOSEVELT: How would it affect your work, John?

MR. FAHEY: I was going to say, Mr. President, any program of reviving housing on a broad scale must take into consideration the restoration of the mortgage market. There is just no doubt about that. The mortgage market is improving—there is no question about that. As the result of our distribution of $1,600,000,000 and a continuing distribution of about $200,000,000 a month these institutions are being loosened up; not only that, but confidence in them is being restored. That is particularly significant in connection with the Federals.[3] Almost invariably as these Federals are chartered and opened up, it stimulates a return of public money to them immediately. We have had some very surprising results in that direction. The fact that they have the Federal name, that they are under Federal supervision, that their form of organization is mutual in character, has a tendency to restore confidence even in communities where you would not expect the reaction because of conditions. Where state associations have been reorganized and have taken the Federal name and Federal charters, within a few weeks a flow of money into them has begun.

I agree with Mr. Moffett, that in any approach to the solution of the housing problem—and, of course, I agree it is one of the biggest things that can possibly be done to revive employment—great care must be exercised that you do not undermine the mortgage market which is now reviving very rapidly. I think in that field we must look forward to next spring when the great urge will come, if it is properly planned; and I think it has to be planned very carefully right now. And I do agree with Mr. Moffett that it just cannot be done without considering the mortgage problem, because you cannot go on using enormous sums of public money and expect you are going to get them on bonds and in other directions; we have to get the small saver and the public into this thing.

PRESIDENT ROOSEVELT: This broad report refers only to housing as one of a number of things in which the general suggestion of the vertical tying-in should be carried out. I think the best thing to do would be to have a meeting of the Industrial Emergency Committee and have Mr. Fahey and Mr. Moffett attend, and also such other persons as are affected, and thresh the thing out in a preliminary meeting.

MR. RICHBERG: As to those who might be concerned, I think the broad question involved here as to whether you are pushing your economics toward a lower price level and larger volume by a mechanism of this sort, which will then have very strong effect on all your

---

[3] An apparent reference to the Federal Savings and Loan Associations being set up under the Federal Home Loan Bank Board pursuant to the Home Owners Loan Act of 1933 as amended. The purpose was, in part, to enable the establishment of these Associations in localities without banking facilities.

investments of every type, or whether you are trying to move your prices up, is a very fundamental question. There is no relation of this to any particular price level. It was merely suggested in the report that prices should be brought down and volume of production thereby stimulated.

PRESIDENT ROOSEVELT: Next is the report of the Economic Adviser . . . . There are two charts accompanying that; one is pertaining to cotton textile, and the other is automobiles and steel.

Next is the report of the state directors of the National Emergency Council.

MR. RICHBERG: Mr. President, I have the usual two-page summary of these reports. Do you wish me to read it?

PRESIDENT ROOSEVELT: Yes . . . .

The reports of departments and agencies I can summarize very briefly. They are not very long. [The President then read the reports aloud, with occasional comments or questions.]

[After reading of approved plans for reopening of national banks] That will be pretty well cleaned up by the first of January, I think.

[After reading reference to an injunction against the Secretary of Agriculture] I might add that the Secretary of Agriculture is at this moment on the stand.

SECRETARY DERN [After the President had read a reference to the Philippine Constitution]: The Philippines may not take that up until next fall.

PRESIDENT ROOSEVELT: A year from now?

SECRETARY DERN: Yes.

PRESIDENT ROOSEVELT: They want something more out of Congress?

SECRETARY DERN: No, not necessarily; but I think they are getting more frightened over the situation.

PRESIDENT ROOSEVELT: [After reading of a slum clearance project in Atlanta, Georgia, from the report of the Secretary of the Interior]: Where is that, Harold?

SECRETARY ICKES: One is adjoining Atlanta University, and one adjoining Georgia Tech.

PRESIDENT ROOSEVELT: That is the white one?

SECRETARY ICKES: Yes, that is the white one.

PRESIDENT ROOSEVELT: What is there to that slum-clearance project for Negroes? Is it single houses?

MR. MOFFETT: It is a combination plan. There is a series of small apartments and individual houses and four houses in one.

PRESIDENT ROOSEVELT: What will those rooms cost per month?

SECRETARY ICKES: About five dollars, I think.

new deal mosaic

PRESIDENT ROOSEVELT:	Fireproof construction?
SECRETARY ICKES:	Yes.
PRESIDENT ROOSEVELT:	Are they pleased about it?
SECRETARY ICKES:	Yes, I think it is going to be a great development. There are certain classes of Negroes around those universities that are really above the grade of other Negroes. On that side over next to Georgia Tech, it is more a problem of getting those little houses pushed out.
PRESIDENT ROOSEVELT	[Having read of a slum-clearance project in Chicago]: Tell us something about that.
SECRETARY ICKES:	That is a beauty; it worries the *Chicago Tribune* a lot.
PRESIDENT ROOSEVELT:	Good!
SECRETARY ICKES:	It is on the northwest side. One hundred sixty acres, playgrounds, parks, and nurseries for children so the mothers can go to work; walk-up apartments.
PRESIDENT ROOSEVELT:	Where is it located?
SECRETARY ICKES:	The west boundary is Ashland Avenue.
PRESIDENT ROOSEVELT:	That means nothing to me.
SECRETARY ICKES:	It is southwest of the center of the city, across the river. It is a wornout neighborhood, and we managed to keep the thing quiet. Practically no one knew about it until we clamped our suit down. Part of it is the twentieth ward and part of it is in Congressman Sabath's district.
PRESIDENT ROOSEVELT:	Not much opposition outside the *Chicago Tribune*?
SECRETARY ICKES:	No. The *Tribune* was piqued because I gave out the announcement that we could spend our money somewhere else if they didn't want it. The other papers have been very enthusiastic. The *Tribune* is playing a lone hand.
PRESIDENT ROOSEVELT	[Having read a reference to "hot oil" in East Texas]: What is the exact status of that, Homer, from the prosecution point of view?
ATTORNEY GENERAL CUMMINGS:	It is a difficult and complex situation. I have had several conferences with Mr. Ickes about it, and the Department of Justice and the Department of the Interior are sending down some of our best men to study the situation. They are going in there this week and they will look it over and make specific recommendations as to the course to be pursued.
PRESIDENT ROOSEVELT:	Is the Railway Commission[4] helping at the present time?
ATTORNEY GENERAL CUMMINGS:	That is one of the things we want to find out—whether they are going to help or not. There is also an indication that the attitude of some of the judges has changed. We had a good deal of

---

[4] The Texas Railroad Commission had jurisdiction over oil well production and similar enterprises in the state.

> trouble, you will remember, with the District Court judges, especially Judge Bryant. In order not to make any false start, we are just going to have this little survey made, and then we will decide on a course of action in which the Department of Justice, the Oil Administration, and all others interested will cooperate.

PRESIDENT ROOSEVELT [Having read of the investigation of the *Morro Castle* disaster[5]]: Where does the District Attorney in New York City come in on that, Dan?

SECRETARY ROPER: We are cooperating with him very closely and have supplied him with the testimony and are giving him the benefit of the analysis of that testimony; in other words, we are in touch with him.

PRESIDENT ROOSEVELT: He attended the hearings?

SECRETARY ROPER: Yes, and he has all the testimony. Of course, you know our duties here are rather meagerly defined [in the] statutes, and we are looking to him to pursue the criminal phases of it.

PRESIDENT ROOSEVELT: There was a good deal of public comment on the fact that apparently nothing was done in those hearings to find out exactly what the proctors for the *Morro Castle* had done in handling their witnesses—the members of the crew, etc.

SECRETARY ROPER: For that reason we had many of those witnesses recalled, and the question was put up to me—and there was considerable opposition to it—as to whether the officers and others should be called. We took the position that everybody should be called that might be related in anywise to the sources of information; namely, that if these officers on the ship and their crew had been derelict in any way, we would like to know just what instructions they had from the officers of the company.

PRESIDENT ROOSEVELT: And also from the counsel.

SECRETARY ROPER: That has been done.

PRESIDENT ROOSEVELT: I think it is very important, Homer.

ATTORNEY GENERAL CUMMINGS: I understand he is taking very much interest in it.

PRESIDENT ROOSEVELT: The firm had not tampered with the witnesses, but had given exceedingly careful coaching to all the witnesses and members of the crew of the ship.

SECRETARY ROPER: That is the reason we recalled several witnesses.

PRESIDENT ROOSEVELT: That question is distinctly in the purview of the District Attorney rather than the Department of Commerce.

SECRETARY ROPER: We are pursuing it at this time, Mr. President. We have, of course, our agencies who are charged with inspection and also

---

[5] The steamship *Morro Castle* caught fire and burned off the Jersey coast on Sept. 8, 1934, with considerable loss of life.

293

following up our regulations; but in order that we might check even against our own people in regard to this, we have sought the assistance and have obtained the cooperation of the Acting Secretary of the Navy, and we are putting on each one of these ships as they leave the harbor a man from the Navy for certain of these trips in order that we might make sure that our regulations are correct, that they are not defective and are being carried out; also for the purpose of studying the possibilities of need of further legislation; and we are starting that at once, with the assistance of the Secretary of the Navy. That is having a wholesome effect.

PRESIDENT ROOSEVELT: I think it would be a very good thing if you could send over to the Commerce Department instructions as to how a ship can be made fireproof, because the Navy has had to make ships fireproof for a great many years.

ACTING SECRETARY ROOSEVELT: Everything has to be steel. There is not a bit of wood. Even chairs and other furniture are made of steel.

PRESIDENT ROOSEVELT: I think the coming Congress is pretty apt to pass rather drastic instructions as to materials used in any new passenger vessels.

SECRETARY ROPER: I may state, too, that we have an interdepartmental committee that is studying, as you know, and doing very effective work, and we have charged them also with suggestions of that character. We will be able to present to you at least a preliminary outline of that report some time next week, so you can have ample time.

PRESIDENT ROOSEVELT [Referring to cotton production]: Have you got anything further, Chester, on the use of the ten per cent leeway that you have in taking care of the one, two, and three-bale people?

MR. DAVIS: It seems to me almost impossible to take care of them directly out of the ten per cent. The Act is a taxing statute and it did not mention the small farmer as distinguished from any other kind of farmer.

PRESIDENT ROOSEVELT: Have we any discretion in the matter?

MR. DAVIS: It appears to be very little; the records are incomplete as to what constitutes a small farmer. One man may show he has two bales or three bales and another man may have a number of tenants, each one a one or two-bale man.

PRESIDENT ROOSEVELT: Can not you leave it to the discretion of the county committee?

MR. DAVIS: We are following out that line, but that is a pretty loose way of handling a tax matter.

PRESIDENT ROOSEVELT: Who is going to go behind it?

MR. DAVIS: I think as these allotments are going out, a lot of the complaint dies out. In Georgia, I think there was a misapprehension, but they feel better about it now. That is the report we get.

PRESIDENT ROOSEVELT [Having read of the proposed corn-hog referendum]: They will all say yes, won't they?

MR. DAVIS: Probably not all. They are feeling a little better now than they did last spring.

PRESIDENT ROOSEVELT [Reading figures on distribution of allotments to wheat growers]: What about the winter wheat condition, Chester?

MR. DAVIS: We are planting heavily and depending on that for fall and winter pasture. I think very much of the winter wheat is going in with satisfactory surface moisture conditions.

PRESIDENT ROOSEVELT: What is the total acreage compared with last year?

MR. DAVIS: I do not know what it will be. I have no report as yet. I think there will be a considerable increase. We are not putting any limitation if they want to pasture it. It will be quick feed.

PRESIDENT ROOSEVELT: That is subject to later control?

MR. DAVIS: Yes, and they accept that very willingly.

PRESIDENT ROOSEVELT [Reading of an increase in the processing tax on Burley tobacco]: Why do that?

MR. DAVIS: The average price on Burley last year was not as near the so-called parity figure as it was the year before. There is an exemption from that applying to low value tobacco used for chewing tobacco and twist that is reduced to four cents a pound.

PRESIDENT ROOSEVELT [Reading that NRA had approved 522 basic codes and 167 supplementary codes]: Clay, have you got to the point where you can give us a supplementary report on that?

MR. WILLIAMS: We have only undertaken a survey of our task today and cannot make any report at this time.

PRESIDENT ROOSEVELT [Reading the Farm Credit Administration report that 20,000 farmers with debts in excess of $125,000,000 had obtained settlements]: A pretty good report, that is.
[Reading a report on car pooling] Weren't all the railroad freight cars pooled during the war?

MR. EASTMAN: Yes, they were.

PRESIDENT ROOSEVELT: And did they go back to the old system?

MR. EASTMAN: Yes; of course, that pool was automatic. The great difficulty in the pool is in the handling of the maintenance problem and that was not taken care of properly. That is one of the great objections to pools, at the present time, that the railroads have raised.

PRESIDENT ROOSEVELT: In other words, they might get a car lost and never get it back to repair it?

MR. EASTMAN: They had no adequate means for providing where the repairs

295

would be made, the light repairs as distinguished from the heavy repairs, and so on.

PRESIDENT ROOSEVELT: What is the news of this new organization that Pelley is going to have?[6]

MR. EASTMAN: I think he is going to find his vice-presidents now. That is the most important thing about the whole organization—to get the right personnel. He has been sick, himself.

PRESIDENT ROOSEVELT: Does that new railroad organization concern itself with financial problems as well as management problems?

MR. EASTMAN: They propose to have a section that will deal with financing and accounting, consider general policies with respect to those matters, give advice to individual companies, and so on. They will cover general policies with respect to rates.

PRESIDENT ROOSEVELT: One other question. What is this petition to the ICC for increased rates? Does it cover all rates?

MR. EASTMAN: No, they have endeavored to make a rather careful selection—at least that is the theory—and raise those rates which would be capable of being raised without unduly encouraging competition. Just how successful they have been in that, I do not know. There were about four or five hundred people down there yesterday, I understand, ready to oppose it. Apparently those interests do not regard it as successful.

PRESIDENT ROOSEVELT: When will we have to get a decision from the ICC on that?

MR. EASTMAN: I should think possibly before the end of the year. I know they will endeavor to press it as rapidly as possible. Yesterday, the presiding commissioner refused to allow a railroad witness to testify who had his testimony in the exhibit all ready to read. He said, "It is already written down, so put it in."

PRESIDENT ROOSEVELT: That is practical. It is no particular secret that a number of very large carriers are still in a very bad financial condition; but it looks as if the general railroad problem will come to a head sometime within the course of the next year. That is almost inevitable.

[Reading that charters were granted to 21 federal savings and loan associations, bringing the total to 536] John, are you getting to the end of that now?

MR. FAHEY: Oh, no, no! You mean the granting of new charters?

PRESIDENT ROOSEVELT: Yes.

MR. FAHEY: Oh, no, just beginning. It is going steadily on.

---

[6] The Association of American Railroads, created Sept. 21, 1934, represented a consolidation of the American Railway Association and the Association of Railway Executives; the new organization elected as its president John J. Pelley, president of the New York, New Haven and Hartford.

PRESIDENT ROOSEVELT: How many can the country stand?

MR. FAHEY: You see, we had eleven hundred counties in the United States that did not have any local association at all, and that ought to run up to fifteen hundred or two thousand before we get through; and then there were a great many conversions pending of state institutions to federal charters, and the number of them is increasing all the time. For example, more than two-thirds of all the associations in the state of Oklahoma are applying for federal charters now. It looks as though most of the state would go federal as far as Oklahoma is concerned.

PRESIDENT ROOSEVELT: That would not be a very bad idea for Oklahoma.

MR. FAHEY: No, some of them are trying to beat the efforts of the state, and appoint as many receivers as possible.

PRESIDENT ROOSEVELT [Reading a report of the dollar volume of home loan applications]: Why do you exclude Michigan?

MR. FAHEY: Michigan had some erroneous reports in as to applications on file up there which had to be subtracted. We are trying to make an adjustment up there.

PRESIDENT ROOSEVELT [Having read there were 125,749 foreclosures in 1934]: Gosh! Why is that keeping up so high?

MR. FAHEY: It is beginning to decline now from the peak. The peak was in June of 1933. The month in which this bill was passed was the highest month ever recorded in the United States. For 1932, the total number of foreclosures was about three and one-half times the average for over twenty years. Now it has begun to go down.

PRESIDENT ROOSEVELT: Of these foreclosures, say a hundred twenty-five thousand up to date in 1934, how many of them came to you for help—what percentage, do you suppose?

MR. FAHEY: It is very difficult to say as to those numbers. I would say a comparatively small number, because our experience here is that very few of the applications which we have actually accepted have to be abandoned and allow foreclosure to take place. There were a lot of foreclosures, I think, for other reasons, and then foreclosures beyond our reach, foreclosures on apartment houses, and that includes foreclosures on farms and everything else.

PRESIDENT ROOSEVELT: I see.

MR. MYERS: We have had about 40,000 applications from farmers in the year. In a very large proportion of these cases, we were able to get postponements.

PRESIDENT ROOSEVELT: Yes, all those figures were included.

MR. MYERS: That is right.

new deal mosaic

PRESIDENT ROOSEVELT [Reading the TVA progress reports on Wheeler Dam, and on Norris Dam]: Have they all the foundations in there now?

DR. MORGAN: We are something over a third done with the dam as a whole.

PRESIDENT ROOSEVELT: That is going some! By the time I get down there in November, I will see something.

[Reading that use of electricity at Tupelo, Mississippi had doubled at the end of just six months under TVA rates]: They cut the rate in half and doubled consumption.

DR. MORGAN: The private companies cut their rates about 30 per cent also.

PRESIDENT ROOSEVELT: And they have had an increase?

DR. MORGAN: And their income is greater than it was before the cut.

PRESIDENT ROOSEVELT: That is all there is on that report. Has anybody got anything to take up?

I am going to ask the members of the Industrial Emergency Committee to stay behind about five minutes to take up some new work.

The meeting closed at 3:40 p.m.

Proceedings of the National Emergency Council

[meeting no. 16]
October 16, 1934

Joint Meeting of the Executive Council and the National Emergency Council

Held in the Blue Room of the White House, October 16, 1934, at 2:23 p.m.

Present: the President of the United States; the Secretary of the Treasury; the Attorney General; the Secretary of Agriculture; the Secretary of Commerce; the Undersecretary of State; the Acting Secretary of War; the Acting Secretary of the Navy; the Assistant Secretary of the Treasury; the First Assistant Postmaster General; the Assistant Secretary of Labor; the Administrator of the Federal Emergency Relief Administration; the Administrator of the Federal Housing Administration; the Chairman of the Federal Trade Commission; the Chairman of the National Industrial Recovery Board; the Chairman of the Board of the Home Owners' Loan Corporation; the Chairman of the Board of the Reconstruction Finance Corporation; the Director of the Division of Program Planning of the Agricultural Adjustment Administration; the Third Director of the Tennessee Valley Authority; the Assistant Director of Emergency Conservation Work; the Deputy Governor of the Farm Credit Administration; the Adviser on Consumer Problems; the Director of the Consumers' Division; the Economic Adviser; the Executive Secretary.

[The content of this meeting is similar to the last—self education, interspersed with bits of policy advice and guidance, generously given by the President. One may question how valuable to the members of the group these proceedings were. For the reader interested in the New Deal, this particular meeting illustrates both the breadth and variety of the Administration's program and the way the fertile and imaginative mind of the President played over the whole field of government policy.—Editors' Note.]

PRESIDENT ROOSEVELT: Unless somebody would like to hear the minutes of the last meeting, we will dispense with them.

First is the combined report of the Department of Agriculture and the Agricultural Adjustment Administration concerning the effects of the drought on feed, forage, and livestock. I hope you will bring out the question of how many cows are going to die this winter. A friend of Mr. [Jesse—apparently] Jones wrote him that he expected twenty million head of cattle to die from lack of forage this coming winter. Go ahead and read it . . . [To meet the emergency indicated by the survey of the

nation's feed and forage resources, organization of the Federal Agricultural Corporation is being completed . . . An Executive Order, authorizing the transfer of collateral to serve as a basis for capital stock has been prepared for submission to the President . . . .]
Why do you have to have a new corporation? Is that merely to borrow money from brother Jones?

SECRETARY WALLACE: Yes.

PRESIDENT ROOSEVELT: Does he know about it?

SECRETARY WALLACE: Yes.

MR. JONES: I would like to amend that report in this respect: It mentions getting "a loan of $50,000,000" from us. We have a little term that we use—"up to" instead of "of." That enables them to get any part that is needed. I guess they won't need over $20,000,000 or $25,000,000. How about it?

SECRETARY WALLACE: It may require the whole of it—we may ask for more than that.

MR. JONES: We got him down to $50,000,000.

PRESIDENT ROOSEVELT: I knew you would do it. I am not surprised at all. Probably Henry wanted $50,000,000 in the beginning, and knew if he started you at $200,000,000 he would get what he wanted?

SECRETARY MORGENTHAU: Isn't there any other way?

PRESIDENT ROOSEVELT: Jones comes to you for the money.

SECRETARY MORGENTHAU: Well, theoretically. We have a number of these corporations and they always incorporate to do a great deal more than their particular job. I want to ask two questions. Is this the only way the livestock people can be taken care of? If it is the only way, why don't they confine themselves to that particular job?

PRESIDENT ROOSEVELT: Have they any intention of doing anything else?

SECRETARY MORGENTHAU: That reads that they would be given power to process.

SECRETARY WALLACE: It would be necessary to process some things in order to handle them.

SECRETARY MORGENTHAU: The Surplus Relief Corporation—couldn't they handle this without another corporation?

PRESIDENT ROOSEVELT: That is under Harry Hopkins.

SECRETARY MORGENTHAU: Yes, but we already have a corporation that sounds very much like this one.

MR. JONES: I think this probably almost fits in with Commodity Credit.

SECRETARY MORGENTHAU: Mr. Jones says you have the Commodity Credit.

MR. JONES: There were three other corporations.

SECRETARY WALLACE: Commodity Credit doesn't have enough credit to swing it.

MR. JONES: Enough funds are available there.

SECRETARY WALLACE: Surplus Relief Corporation has funds only insofar as Harry Hopkins puts money into it.

MR. JONES: If we ever lend anything to Harry we never get it back!

PRESIDENT ROOSEVELT: Hear that?

MR. HOPKINS: I heard it, but it doesn't mean anything.

SECRETARY MORGENTHAU: If Commodity Credit Corporation could do it, and it is just a question of increasing the capital, why not increase the capital?

MR. JONES: Do you remember the reasons about that?

SECRETARY WALLACE: We stopped at the capital question.

PRESIDENT ROOSEVELT: The fewer new corporations that have to be brought in, the better. If we can work it through the Surplus Relief and the Commodity Credit, even if we have to amend the charter, it will be much easier because they have very broad powers. I am quite sure that the Comptroller General would also be very keen to use an existing corporation rather than start a new one.

SECRETARY WALLACE: The Surplus Relief has the broadest powers—much broader than the Commodity Credit—and from the standpoint of powers it would be much better adapted, I think.

SECRETARY MORGENTHAU: I think the tendency, Mr. President, should be to less spending agencies rather than more.

MR. JONES: Can you add that capital to the Commodity Credit?

SECRETARY WALLACE: I don't know; I think it would be a legal matter.

MR. JONES: Suppose we pursue that and see—

PRESIDENT ROOSEVELT: Yes, suppose you pursue that and see if you cannot work it through one or both of those existing corporations.

I might just as well mention the fact at this point, because it is on the same general subject, that I have the Executive Order all drawn and approved by the Attorney General, and have been talking it over with a good many people and they all agree that it is rather silly for us to continue two separate bodies, one called the Executive Council and the other the Emergency Council. We thought we would merge the two into one. That seems a practical thing to do at this time. It seems, because the Emergency Council is the operating agency of the directors in each state, we will probably have to retain the name of the National Emergency Council—something along that line. My thought was that if we get that order signed we would consider this as the merged part of the two of them and consider— because we meet once every two weeks—the advisability at times, if we get pressed with work, of having a meeting the other Tuesday. It will simplify things and get rid of one complete organization. I think that is in line with what we have been talking about—trying to simplify things. It becomes sort of a super-cabinet, like the British Cabinet,[1] which contains 22

---

[1] In practical effect, the NEC was enlarged by this consolidation to include

members at the present time, and they have a small executive committee of six which is politically minded.

The next thing on the agenda is the presentation of a confidential chart prepared by the Secretary of the Treasury relating to federal expenditures and receipts, including a memorandum from the Economic Adviser.

SECRETARY MORGENTHAU: I thought this was the better way to do it.

PRESIDENT ROOSEVELT: I think if Mr. Riefler would go ahead and explain this now, it would be fine.

MR. RIEFLER: You all have the charts. There are four of them, and I think you can follow them fairly carefully. If you cannot, stop me.

PRESIDENT ROOSEVELT: These were shown to me the other day, after I requested the charts, and a mere layman could understand . . . .

Before you go on, I want to ask one question on which I am not very clear. In your two top lines of expenditures, does the word expenditures mean the date when it actually goes out of the Treasury, or does it mean the date when, let us say, the material contractor actually puts people to work?

MR. RIEFLER: No, I think this is the time when the expenditure comes out of the Treasury.

PRESIDENT ROOSEVELT: How much lag is there, let us say, on some municipal projects? The municipality is given the money by PWA. They give their bonds in and they have that much credit. They immediately go to a contractor and they say, "We want such and such a number of tons of concrete." The contractor puts his people to work immediately processing that concrete. How long does it take before the money is drawn out of the Treasury?

MR. RIEFLER: Secretary Ickes would know the details much better than I would. I would think that when the actual draft is made it would probably be about a month, but I really don't know for certain.

PRESIDENT ROOSEVELT: I think that is something that ought to be looked into. For instance, take the second red line down here.

---

the agency heads who had been attending the Executive Council meetings. The reference to the British Cabinet could serve as point of departure for the drawing of many parallels and contrasts. NEC could never become a genuine policy-making body because its members were not jointly responsible for government policy as in the British Cabinet, but were rather subordinates of the President, who was solely responsible. The paucity of basic policy decisions made by NEC brings this out. There was no obligation on the part of the President to make policy in and with this group as such. Hence, policy decisions were (and probably must be, given the nature of the American Presidential system) made by the President in any setting he saw fit or that seemed appropriate at the moment.

MR. RIEFLER: That is the actual expenditure.

PRESIDENT ROOSEVELT: Which is the actual expenditure? That is actually out of the Treasury?

MR. RIEFLER: Yes.

PRESIDENT ROOSEVELT: The question is whether that should not be materially higher because the money has already been spent for labor and material.

MR. RIEFLER: It will depend on the agency spending it. Some get their money first and then spend it, and some get it later.

PRESIDENT ROOSEVELT: It would be very difficult to get an estimate. What I am afraid of is that the actual expenditure is a couple of months behind time. That would be worth checking.

SECRETARY MORGENTHAU: That simply indicates that the money is paid by check out of the Treasury.

PRESIDENT ROOSEVELT: Yes, but it doesn't necessarily mean that those people were actually at work on that particular thing within the previous week or two. It might have meant two or three weeks beforehand.

SECRETARY MORGENTHAU: Mr. Bell gets in touch with each spending agency and they give him an estimate thirty days in advance; and then they notify us twice a week.

PRESIDENT ROOSEVELT: What I am trying to avoid is having people say that these two red lines represent the actual number of people at work as a result of that expenditure.

MR. RIEFLER: There would be quite a lag. . . .

PRESIDENT ROOSEVELT: Does that income tax include corporate income as well as personal?

MR. RIEFLER: Yes.

PRESIDENT ROOSEVELT: Where is that decrease shown mostly, in corporate or personal?

MR. RIEFLER: Mostly in corporate, I think.

RNEY GENERAL CUMMINGS: That doesn't touch settlements of old income tax cases?

MR. RIEFLER: I think those estimates are in there.

PRESIDENT ROOSEVELT: It includes all sorts of moneys that they expect you to get back . . . .

Next is the report by the Economic Adviser . . . .

There is one question on that. The fact that the retail trade has held up far better than factory operations—does not mean that we had on hand during the late summer more actual retail goods than we thought we had? In other words, were the shelves more filled up than we thought?

MR. RIEFLER: In the case of textiles, yes. You have two things happening. In the summer of 1933, we had two months of textiles operating higher than they ever operated in the history of the country, and the question ever since then is, where are those inventories?

303

	They went somewhere down the line. When we came out of that, in August or September, the first inventory figures we were able to get showed the mill inventories extremely low.
PRESIDENT ROOSEVELT:	The jobber was holding it.
MR. RIEFLER:	Exactly; the price situation in relation of finished textile prices to raw material prices was such as to rather encourage jobbers to hold until around February. In February, they began to move them, and from February until the present you have had the situation in which the jobber would likely take a speculative position on textiles. I think it is coming very close to a turn in that now.
PRESIDENT ROOSEVELT:	What would you say the condition of the retail store shelves would be now?
MR. RIEFLER:	Department stores represent a very small proportion of the total, and those inventories are just exactly the same as they were last year at this time.
PRESIDENT ROOSEVELT:	You remember what happened. The department stores were taken completely by surprise because of the volume of buying they hadn't expected. The result was that by a week before Christmas they didn't have anything to sell in a great many places.
MR. RIEFLER:	When the drought came along they didn't expect much business; as a matter of fact, the farm income is very good in relation to what it has been. They are getting a huge volume of retail trade.
PRESIDENT ROOSEVELT:	Do you get reports from the manufacturing of retail store goods in regard to orders on hand?
MR. RIEFLER:	In textiles we have them.
PRESIDENT ROOSEVELT:	That is all?
MR. RIEFLER:	That is about all. In general, inventory information is awfully poor. It is difficult to get. I think we have to build it up.
PRESIDENT ROOSEVELT:	Would it be possible to get better statistics on orders received from all manufacturers week by week?
MR. RIEFLER:	You have to build it up line by line, because of the tremendous difference in the kind of goods they are dealing in. Employment payrolls, dollar sales, you can get from everybody. When you get down to inventories and orders, you have to go after it with a rifle and say just exactly what you are asking for. I think that through the NRA we can begin to really get it.
PRESIDENT ROOSEVELT:	I think it is a very important thing to do, because I have the feeling that those statistics will be very helpful. The question mark in my mind is as to how much lag there is, whether our information is not two months late, so far as it can be translated

into existing terms of employment. There is a lag in these figures.

MR. RIEFLER: There is always a lag. What you have to do is to jump from a spring board. You can get completely accurate figures two months ago, and you can get some indications as to the future if we can build it up . . . .

PRESIDENT ROOSEVELT: Next is the report of the state directors for the National Emergency Council.

MR. RICHBERG: I have only the two-page summary of that to read, Mr. President, if you wish.

PRESIDENT ROOSEVELT: Yes. . . .

Next is the summary of departments and agencies. [As the President read this summary aloud, he paused to make comments and to ask questions as follows.]

[Reading of certain treaties signed by the Secretary of State] How many people in San Marino?

UNDERSECRETARY PHILLIPS: I could not tell you that. This is our effort to build up the figures all over the world.

PRESIDENT ROOSEVELT: Bill [Wm. Phillips], one thing I wish you and Dan Roper would have a talk about is this. It is partly national and partly international. The old law of salvage grew up through the centuries, like Topsy, and it is still international law, that when a vessel is in distress, flying a signal of distress and asking for assistance, a rescuing vessel can come, and if the rescuing vessel saves the vessel in distress, it can file a libel for the entire ship saved. It is an unconscionable rule. It ought never to be in international or national law; and it is time we did something about it. The rescuing vessel should be paid for the rescuing service, and nothing more. I am inclined to think it is time for us to take the lead on it.[2] If you and Dan could start the machinery going for a survey of that, I think it would be very helpful. Almost every time we have a maritime wreck, there is a report of some rescuing vessel that stood by but delayed in giving help in order to be quite sure she would become a case for salvage. That came out in a portion of the *Morro Castle* testimony. I don't know what the

---

[2] We found no evidence that this suggestion was followed up to the extent of producing a formal published report, news item, or detectable change in admiralty law. It appears from Martin J. Norris' volume, *The Law of Salvage* (New York, 1958), that the President was correct in suggesting that rescuers are entitled to more than the mere value of their services but, Norris writes: "Generally an award of more than 50% [of the value of the vessel], or a moiety, is rarely allowed. In fact, an award of more than 50% in these days of large values is exceptional."

305

	necessary steps are, it is so long since I was in an admiralty court.
ATTORNEY GENERAL CUMMINGS:	Of course the old salvage law is an unconscionable rule and is generally recognized so, I believe. It grew out of entirely different conditions. I think it would be a very happy thought to have that survey.
UNDERSECRETARY PHILLIPS:	I would be very glad to take it up.
PRESIDENT ROOSEVELT:	You, and the Attorney General. I don't know what it requires. I am not sure that treaties have ever said anything about the rule of salvage. I am inclined to think it is one of those unwritten rules of international admiralty law. It is worth considering, anyway. [Reading a report by the Secretary of Treasury on bond refunding] You are saving on that about fifty million dollars a year?
SECRETARY MORGENTHAU:	About that. [The President, continuing with the Treasury report, read of proposed research into the drugging of race horses.]
SECRETARY MORGENTHAU:	That refers to the so-called saliva test.
PRESIDENT ROOSEVELT:	Are you doing it for greyhounds, too?
SECRETARY MORGENTHAU:	We haven't got to that yet.
PRESIDENT ROOSEVELT:	And racing turtles? (*Laughter*) [Reading the Postmaster General's report on revenues] Oh, by the way, on that, Bill, has there been any discussion about reducing the three-cent postage to two cents?
MR. HOWES:	The department is against that. We all agree it would result in a terrible deficit.
PRESIDENT ROOSEVELT	[Reading of a compromise settlement of indebtedness to the government]: This is one of the largest business houses in the United States. They have been delivering by their own cars instead of sending them through the mail. [Having read from the report of the Secretary of Commerce pertaining to appointment of 25,000 persons to work on the mid-decennial Census of Agriculture] I think this is pretty tough.
SECRETARY ROPER:	May I be permitted to comment?
PRESIDENT ROOSEVELT:	I think comment is very much in order.
SECRETARY ROPER:	This is not our plan; it is theirs. Strange to say, this plan goes back a long time. It is not new. It has been in operation now for about 40 years. We are flowing along the regular course.
PRESIDENT ROOSEVELT:	It goes back, to my certain knowledge, to the first term of Andrew Jackson.
SECRETARY ROPER:	We didn't begin with that.
PRESIDENT ROOSEVELT:	Your apologies are accepted.

SECRETARY ROPER: I thought it was necessary to state the facts, and we did, to Mr. Snell [Rep. Bertrand H., R., N.Y.], that we were following the plan he had approved.

PRESIDENT ROOSEVELT: What did he say?

SECRETARY ROPER: He stopped; he didn't say anything more about it.

PRESIDENT ROOSEVELT: That is very important: "No appointment will be made prior to November 15."

SECRETARY ROPER: I told Snell that.

PRESIDENT ROOSEVELT [reading from the Attorney General's report that active participation in the Lindbergh case had been concluded]: One thing, on that, Homer. How about the retention of those certificates?

ATTORNEY GENERAL CUMMINGS: That is why we said "No federal indictment is being sought." We were careful not to say there was no federal offense committed. But that is such a minor offense compared with the other two, that we didn't think best to push it.

PRESIDENT ROOSEVELT [reading of large and sudden increases in jail commitments in Oklahoma and New Orleans because of violation of revenue laws pertaining to alcoholic beverages]: Aren't these new indictments and convictions under the new Alcoholic Beverage Law[3] going to be a lot more?

ATTORNEY GENERAL CUMMINGS: Yes, that has been a subject of very considerable debate in connection with the budget. From all the information I can get, both as to what is happening now and what happened prior to Prohibition compared to what happened during Prohibition, it appears that when the amendment went out we had a sudden drop in the number of prisoners. Now they are beginning to fill up again, and it is a fair guess that by the time we reach normal conditions we will have just about as many income tax violators in jail as we had before Prohibition—I don't mean income tax, I mean revenue!

SECRETARY MORGENTHAU: Just in alcohol taxes alone, we have over 12,000 people arrested and awaiting trial. Last week the average jail sentence of these people was a little over a year. We had one case in the South where they abducted and tortured a man who gave evidence against them, and these men got 23 years.

ATTORNEY GENERAL CUMMINGS: While we are on this subject, let me say this, that in Southern California they are having great difficulty with the court conditions. They are nearly two years behind their docket. We have not court facilities; we haven't judges enough.

---

[3] A Liquor Tax Bill was enacted into law Jan. 11, 1934; the Twenty-first Amendment to the Constitution ended Prohibition when it was ratified on Dec. 5, 1933.

And even if we sent judges in there, there is no court room available. We discussed with the Post Office Department, and I believe the Treasury Department, whether there might be some way of pushing forward a plan so we could get some courts and then perhaps we could send in the additional judges to help clean up that situation.

PRESIDENT ROOSEVELT: The Chief Justice told me the other day that he had practically no available district judges he could send to Southern California or to southern New York.

ATTORNEY GENERAL CUMMINGS: That condition in Southern California is terrible. It is worse than southern New York, and it is bad enough there. The delay has been due to the fact, I believe (I will be corrected if I am wrong), that it was contemplated there might be a new Post Office building in Los Angeles. Therefore, there was a reluctance to remodel some other building for the Post Office building and we are just stuck there.

PRESIDENT ROOSEVELT: Couldn't you hire space?

ATTORNEY GENERAL CUMMINGS: We could if we had the means; then it would require considerable remodeling. I am more distressed about the court situation there than anywhere else. Outside of New York City and Southern California, our federal courts are pretty well up on their job.

PRESIDENT ROOSEVELT: I am just thinking out loud, but if I could send them up on the third of January a very short emergency message asking for another judge or two in Southern California and another one or two in New York, we might get it through as an emergency message.[4]

ATTORNEY GENERAL CUMMINGS: I think we could make an awfully good case of it.

PRESIDENT ROOSEVELT: Will you take that up for me?

ATTORNEY GENERAL CUMMINGS: That is a very good idea.

PRESIDENT ROOSEVELT [reading]: "The Supreme Court recently determined the William Waldorf Astor estate case favorable to the United States Government. The estate was suing to recover approximately $10,000,000 in income taxes." Had they been actually paid?

ATTORNEY GENERAL CUMMINGS: Yes, they had been paid $10,000,000 away back in 1922. The case has been dragging along.

PRESIDENT ROOSEVELT: We didn't get any additional revenue?

ATTORNEY GENERAL CUMMINGS: No, but we saved about $9,000,000.

PRESIDENT ROOSEVELT [reading]: "A supplemental memorandum on behalf of the Government has been filed in the Supreme Court in connection

---

[4] There is no evidence that the President sent such a message to the Congress.

with the Amazon Petroleum Case calling attention to the reinstatement in the Petroleum Code by Executive Order of the second paragraph of Section 4, Article III."

ATTORNEY GENERAL CUMMINGS: That was to cure the defects that appeared in that record.

PRESIDENT ROOSEVELT [reading from the report of the Agricultural Adjustment Administration]: "Completion of the alloting of permanent tax exemption cotton certificates is anticipated within a week. A referendum on the Bankhead Act is contemplated for late November. More than 90 per cent of the cotton farmers have signed contracts which continue adjustment into 1935." Has anything further been done about the one, two, and three-bale farmer—the little fellow?

SECRETARY WALLACE: Mr. Tolley, do you want to report on that?

MR. TOLLEY: We are working on that. We are doing everything that can be done to give the little fellow a break. That is one of the causes of the apparent delay in getting out the final certificates. Our people report that those one, two, and three-bale people will be quite well taken care of when the final certificates are out.

PRESIDENT ROOSEVELT [reading]: " . . . The program will mean that [sugar beet] growers will get some $15,000,000 more than they would have received if they had sold their present crop in open competition with offshore sugar." Why do they tell me—people in Utah—that the crop is only about 20 per cent of normal? It must be more than that.

SECRETARY WALLACE: Utah is in very bad shape.

PRESIDENT ROOSEVELT: Not as low as 20 per cent, though.

SECRETARY WALLACE: I don't know. There are regions undoubtedly as low as that. When I was there, they expected that because of the shortage of water.

PRESIDENT ROOSEVELT [continuing to read from the AAA report]: "Government Counsel expect a favorable decision in the action brought by the Hawaiian sugar producers." What do you hear about that case?

MR. TOLLEY: Our lawyers participated with the Attorney General's lawyers, and that is the way they feel.

ATTORNEY GENERAL CUMMINGS: They are on pretty good ground, Mr. President.

PRESIDENT ROOSEVELT: I am in the unfortunate position that if the government wins its suit, it makes an awful liar out of me. I told them out in Hawaii that Hawaii was an integral part of the United States.

ATTORNEY GENERAL CUMMINGS: We worked out a distinction that saves your declaration and saves the government point. I told them the same thing when I was out there.

309

new deal mosaic

PRESIDENT ROOSEVELT [reading]: "The State Department has been asked to begin negotiation of a trade agreement with Argentina as a basis for the development of a flax program in the United States. This program would permit the domestic flax industry to supply about one-half of the domestic requirements and insure a fair return to growers..." What percentage do we grow now?

SECRETARY WALLACE: Up to the past couple of years we were growing about half. This is in line with the average a few years ago.

PRESIDENT ROOSEVELT: Does this include flax seed?

SECRETARY WALLACE: This is flax seed. I don't think we can, under the Act, do anything on fiber.

MR. TOLLEY: The Act pertains to flax seed.

PRESIDENT ROOSEVELT [reading from the Reconstruction Finance Corporation report]: "The Corporation has authorized 3,205 loans in the amount of $993,412,582.11 (including outstanding commitments) to 2,423 institutions for distribution to depositors of closed banks..." How about direct loans to industry, Jesse?

MR. JONES: We have authorized about sixteen or seventeen million direct, and we had about $200,000 authorized before. Some of that is coming in direct. We are making a little better progress now. They are learning how to do it. We will never get a great deal of money out of it. I don't believe we will ever get more than $100,000,000.

PRESIDENT ROOSEVELT: Are the Federal Reserve Banks stepping up their loans?

MR. JONES: I think so, but they are considerably behind us, because we had the experience and they didn't.

PRESIDENT ROOSEVELT [reading from the TVA report]: "Service over 68 miles of rural transmission constructed by the Authority was started October 7. This line makes electricity available to some 400 rural homes not heretofore served with power." I wonder where that is?

MR. LILIENTHAL: I think that is in Lauderdale County, northern Alabama.

PRESIDENT ROOSEVELT: It comes from the Wilson Dam?

MR. LILIENTHAL: Yes, sir.

PRESIDENT ROOSEVELT [reading the financial statement of the Home Owners Loan Corporation]: Now, John, where do you and Jim Moffett come in on that question? Aren't you crossing wires on the loans?

MR. FAHEY: No, our loans are confined to the houses we finance. The cost is absorbed into the mortgage. That is under the limitation of the Act. The Federal Housing Administration deals with all others through the banks and lending institutions on that guarantee plan. We have nothing to do with houses outside of those on which we take mortgages.

PRESIDENT ROOSEVELT: Is Jim's campaign for modernization increasing your loans—helping you out?

MR. FAHEY: No, I would not say that, because you will observe that a little less than one-half of all the houses we refinance loans on require some repairs or modernization as a result of the neglect of the last five or six years. And, of course, such repairs are absolutely necessary, because otherwise we are taking a piece of property with a liability against us. I mean we would have to put up for the repairs sooner or later. Our repairs average pretty small. On the other hand, of course, they can loan substantial sums through the Federal Housing Administration.

PRESIDENT ROOSEVELT [reading from the Emergency Conservation report]: "The Labor Department has completed the selection of men and the War Department anticipates that the entire quota of replacements needed to bring the CCC to full strength will be in camps by October 25. Between 300 and 400 camps will be moved from summer locations to winter locations during this and the succeeding month." Is Bob [Fechner] here?

MR. MC ENTEE: No, I am representing him.

PRESIDENT ROOSEVELT: How many new camps are we putting up in the South?

MR. MC ENTEE: I could not tell you offhand, Mr. President. I think I would be hazarding a guess. I can send you a memorandum on that.

PRESIDENT ROOSEVELT: The majority will go back to the same place?

MR. MC ENTEE: Yes; for instance, in Georgia we moved two camps.

PRESIDENT ROOSEVELT: You are getting a good deal of salvage out of the old camps?

MR. MC ENTEE: In some places it pays and in others it does not. A very low grade of lumber was used in the beginning. It splits in tearing them down.

PRESIDENT ROOSEVELT: How are you disposing of the barracks?

MR. MC ENTEE: Mr. Hopkins has taken a number of them. In fact, he would take all that we have. We are experimenting with cutting these barracks into four sections and moving them to the new sites and bolting them together. Experience will tell whether that is profitable or not. We are trying it out.

PRESIDENT ROOSEVELT [reading]: "... through July 31, the CCC had completed reforestation, conservation, erosion prevention and flood control work valued at $236,000,000." That is quite a significant statement.

MR. MC ENTEE: Those figures do not show, Mr. President, the potential savings in years to come.

new deal mosaic

PRESIDENT ROOSEVELT [reading]: "While no attempt has been made to figure the dollar value which has accrued from the fire prevention activities, officials state that the constant presence of more than 300,000 forest workers had made it possible to hold fire losses well below normal expectations." I think it is fair to say that out through the Northwest in forest areas, the presence of these boys literally saved tens of millions of dollars this year.

PRESIDENT ROOSEVELT [reading figures on families receiving relief from the report of the Federal Emergency Relief]: Harry, why so much more increase in single resident persons?

MR. HOPKINS: I think that is due to the fact that a year and a half ago single people could not get relief. They were neglected and kicked around pretty badly. Lately we have been trying to take care of a lot of single people, especially single women. I think that accounts for it, chiefly.

PRESIDENT ROOSEVELT [continuing to read from the Relief report]: "...conditions in drought areas have become worse during the last two weeks. The extent of destitution in these areas becomes emphasized with the approach of winter and extraordinary measures will be necessary not only to relieve suffering but to prevent a wholesale desertion of farms for cities. In order to meet this, it is believed that the rural rehabilitation program must be emphasized in drought areas during the winter."
I wish, Harry, that you would just give us a three-minute report on what you showed me just before the conference about the two rural rehabilitation plants,[5] one in West Virginia and one in Arkansas; they are of particular interest.

MR. HOPKINS: Mr. President, in West Virginia, in the town called Red House, which is on a river with an eight-foot channel (the New York Central goes through it) we purchased 2,300 acres of land. We have taken 150 stranded miners' families and moved those families into that community, where they are building houses themselves. These houses are built out of cinder blocks.

PRESIDENT ROOSEVELT: And they have cellars.

MR. HOPKINS: Yes, and bathrooms. The total cost of the land and the house when completed, including barns and several community houses, will amount to about $1,500 total cost per person.

PRESIDENT ROOSEVELT: Per family?

---

[5] The Subsistence Homestead Program, according to Secretary Ickes, was not one program but several, with Ickes himself involved as PWA Administrator, the Department of Agriculture doing some work, and Harry Hopkins also involved, as indicated here. See *The Secret Diary of Harold L. Ickes* (New York, 1954), Vol. I, p. 288.

MR. HOPKINS: Per family. This is a community type of group where the houses are in the community and the farming land is out beyond. We have already been approached by two or three industries that have inquired whether we would be interested in having them come there.

We will be able to get every cent of our money back over a period of years at interest of three and one-half or four per cent—get it all back.

We believe there is every reason to believe that these miners who have been on relief for two years will be taken entirely off relief rolls and made entirely independent.

In Arkansas, we had a similar situation of a large number of stranded families around old stranded mining communities. There we took a much larger piece of land—about 29,000 acres of cut-over land, but which was very good—the finest land in Arkansas, Mississippi County, the county which raises the most cotton of any county in the United States. We bought that for $2.50 an acre, cleared the land, brought the families down and put up temporary shacks for them. That is nearing completion now—will be completed by the middle of December. About 150 houses have been completed now. The cost of houses of four, five, and six rooms ran from $600 to $950.

PRESIDENT ROOSEVELT: How much land?

MR. HOPKINS: Each house will get from 20 to 40 acres of land. We built a railroad in connection with Harvey Couch down there, and we are going to have electric power and railroad facilities. That is for 700 families.

The total cost—including community houses, school houses, churches and all—the total average cost per family will be about $1,200 when we are all through.

PRESIDENT ROOSEVELT: What are the houses built of?

MR. HOPKINS: Wood. We set up our own saw mills and put these people to running the saw mills.

PRESIDENT ROOSEVELT: The timber comes from the land?

MR. HOPKINS: We got the timber off the land. I believe we are going to make those 700 families entirely self-supporting.

We have another project in Georgia in connection with our submarginal land. We have to move about 400 families. We are making a deal with a big wine outfit—the biggest and oldest in America. They are willing to make a contract with us to take grapes, and the Department of Agriculture have had their men down there and tell us that grapes can be raised,

313

and we are going to do the same thing with four or five hundred families there.

PRESIDENT ROOSEVELT: I hope the W.C.T.U. doesn't get onto that!

MR. HOPKINS: We have literally hundreds of applications to have this thing done. One of the leading industrialists in America told me yesterday that any time we were ready, he would set up six small plants of his, employing from 1,000 to 1,500 men in any community that was agreeable to us, and he would let us pick the men. He claims that, providing we will not go over age 48, he will let us pick the men, and he claims he can train those men and he will make money out of those plants. He is ready to build six plants in any rural communities that we ask him to build in. I am convinced that this has simply enormous possibilities.

The great trick is to keep the cost of buildings down so that the man, when he becomes obligated, does not owe so much money he is never going to get out. We believe we can do this so that he can get out to the tune of eight, nine, or ten dollars a month and pay every cent of it back. There is still an enormous demand for this sort of thing all over the country.

PRESIDENT ROOSEVELT: You saw this Britisher?

MR. HOPKINS: Unwin?

PRESIDENT ROOSEVELT: Yes; he was telling me about their similar plans over there. They are a little more suburban than ours. They give them only about a quarter acre piece of land; but the difference between theirs and ours is that the people they take out of the congested areas and put in the suburban communities remain tenants all their lives. They never get the opportunity to get the title to their homes. They figure the amortization and interest on a 60-year basis. They spread it over very thin and, of course, the annual rent is very low. I think they are probably making a mistake extending it as long as that. That is at least two and possibly three generations, and, of course, we could never, in this country, put through any project which would be based on a continuation of tenancy rather than on home ownership. That is one reason that the British have been so successful. They have kept it on a tenant basis and have spread it over 60 years, and at the end of 60 years you still don't own your home.

MR. HOPKINS: That is what Mussolini does. When they cleared those great marshes they talked about selling the marshes. They really never owned them. There is some merit in that, because it keeps people from going back to town.

314

MR. FAHEY: In some of the British systems, they permit them to acquire shares and those shares are transferred under their laws.

That is particularly true in their garden homesteads. You will remember—going back to the Irish Land Act over 25 years ago—they provided for them to acquire the land and charged only two and a quarter per cent interest, and they actually supplied them with cattle and gave them 28 acres apiece, and gave them 30 years to pay for it.

PRESIDENT ROOSEVELT: Anybody got anything else?

MR. JONES: That is a very interesting report, Harry.

Meeting adjourned at 3:55 p.m.

315

Proceedings of the National Emergency Council

[meeting no. 17]
October 30, 1934

Held in the Blue Room of the White House, October 30, 1934, at 2:25 p.m.

[Joint Meeting of the Executive Council and the National Emergency Council]

Present: the President of the United States; the Secretary of the Treasury; the Acting Secretary of the Navy; the Hon. Wilbur J. Carr, Assistant Secretary of State; the Hon. L. W. Robert, Jr., Assistant Secretary of the Treasury; the Hon. William Stanley, Assistant to the Attorney General; the Hon. Harllee Branch, Second Assistant Postmaster General; the Hon. Oscar L. Chapman, Assistant Secretary of the Interior; the Hon. M. L. Wilson, Assistant Secretary of Agriculture; the Hon. A. J. Altmeyer, Assistant Secretary of Labor; the Acting Director of the Budget; the Administrator of Agricultural Adjustment; the Administrator of Federal Emergency Relief; the Vice Chairman of the Federal Home Loan Bank Board; the Chairman of the Federal Trade Commission; the Chairman of the Reconstruction Finance Corporation; the Director of Emergency Conservation Work; the Federal Coordinator of Transportation; the Governor of the Farm Credit Administration; the Adviser on Consumer Problems; the Chairman of the National Industrial Recovery Board; the Federal Housing Administrator; the Economic Adviser; the Executive Director.

[Here we find a series of examples of F.D.R.'s excellent publicity sense. The opening discussion cautioned against advance budget publicity, and the general precept the President enunciated (p. 318) about how to introduce a program to the public, illustrates this. So also do the various references by the President, to his press conferences, showing that the publicity possibilities of a situation or bit of data were always at the back of his mind. Note also the evidence of the adroit use he made of his press conferences (especially p. 321). His sense of the proper timing of news evidences itself in the use F.D.R. made of the story about consolidating the Executive Council with NEC.

Turning to the development of NEC, we see that this meeting, as the President himself underscored when he noted that only Secretary Morgenthau of the members of the regular cabinet was present (all others had sent second and third string deputies to represent them), illustrates the drop in interest in its work, and hence usefulness. As to substantive policy matters, the President did throw out for discussion the matter of pay scales on relief projects. This issue, which lay at the heart of the Administration's program and brought into focus a series of group demands and theoretical problems, was one that NEC should have been able to thrash out and decide. In practice, clearly, the best that was likely to come out of the meeting were some opinions to add to those which F.D.R. was collecting from many other sources on this issue. Whether NEC ever might have *made* policy decision of this magnitude—with all their political overtones—is doubtful. That the direction of movement was away from such a level of Council activity is clearly shown by the deputizing of assistants for its meetings.—Editors' Note.]

PRESIDENT ROOSEVELT: This is a very small meeting today. I notice there is only one member of the regular Cabinet present; I take it the rest realize it is the last week before election. (*Laughter*)

I asked Donald whether he had a good bill of fare today, with plenty of pie. He said, "No, it is the same old scrambled eggs and bacon." (*Laughter*)

There is one thing that does relate to scrambled eggs and bacon that I would like to suggest before we go on to the regular business, and that relates to the budget. I am a very old hand at budgets, with four years' experience in Albany; and one of the things I discovered was that during the budget examination period—in other words, in the fall of the year—the press is very apt to get all kinds of headline stories about this, that, and the other thing; that some department has come in with an enormous estimate for new work, or that the total of the budget will be such and such an amount, all of which they arrive at by going around and getting that much from one person and that much from another person and putting two and two together. Publicity during the budget-making period is very, very invaluable because it is almost always inaccurate and at least gives the wrong impression! The *New York Times*, I think it was, came out with a large headline—

SECRETARY MORGENTHAU: And a story.

PRESIDENT ROOSEVELT: Yes, and a story,[1] that Public Works is preparing a budget of five million dollars for immediate expenditures and a five-year program for the expenditure of twelve [billion] dollars. Now, of course there is not any five-year program. There is not

---

[1] An article with the headline, "PWA Asks $12,000,000,000 for Five-Year Outlay," appeared in the *New York Times* the morning of this meeting, Oct. 30, 1934.

317

any one-year program in mind at this time. A thing like that
would have to be decided by me and nobody else, and
probably on the thirty-first of December, or maybe the second
day of January; in other words, the last possible moment
before the budget message goes to Congress. I think it is
tremendously important for every department and every
agency to just refrain from talking about budgets until
they come in.

There is another reason, too; the budget is a confidential document which is sent to the Congress and is released by the
Congress and not by the Executive. Even what we call the
preliminary budget for the regular departments and agencies
which will come up to the committees informally the first
week in December—those tentative preliminary budgets for
departments and agencies—will also be entirely confidential,
and if they come out, they will only come out from the
Congressional committees. It is their prerogative, not ours.
Take one simple illustration. I went over one department
yesterday and a number of agencies with the Director of the
Budget, and I pulled out my little old blue pencil and I blue-
penciled right and left and sent them back to those particular
departments and the agencies involved with the request that
they cut the total down by such an amount—so many million
dollars. Now, that is not final. I hope that the department
and the agencies involved will be able to cut approximately
to what I am asking them to cut to. They may have some
comeback that something I eliminated is absolutely essential
to the continuance of the federal government, and, therefore,
these conversations—and they are only conversations that
are going on and will continue to go on until January—are
strictly within the family. Nothing is final, and nothing will
be final until the fourth day of January, so far as any knowledge on the part of the public is concerned. I think we have
to be very, very careful not to talk about the budget.
(*At this point there was a very quiet conversation for a few
moments between the President and Secretary Morgenthau.*)
The Secretary of the Treasury very properly suggests this.
Suppose we have some rather important policy that we are
formulating; it is exceedingly important that the announcement of that policy should be timed right and should go
out in the proper way. As Henry said, if it leaks out a
little here and a little there it takes all the bloom off of it.
I hope you will bear in mind that we are very anxious

to keep all discussion on the budget out of the papers.

SECRETARY MORGENTHAU: I shed tears this morning when I read the *New York Times*— twelve billion dollars!

PRESIDENT ROOSEVELT: When the press comes in tomorrow I am going to tell them they were wrong—it was a hundred and twenty billion! (*Laughter*)

We will dispense with the minutes of the last meeting unless somebody wants them read.

Next is an excerpt from the report of the Federal Coordinator of Transportation.

MR. RICHBERG: The reason for this, Mr. President, is because of the significance in the first litigation, I believe which has been started, and we thought that part of the Coordinator's report might be particularly interesting to the Council. I will read this short excerpt.

[During the week the Coordinator issued an order prohibiting the Louisville & Nashville from discontinuing the interchange of through passenger car with the Chicago & Eastern Illinois and substituting an interchange with the New York Central. The Chicago & Eastern Illinois has for about 50 years participated with the Louisville & Nashville in operating through limited passenger trains between Chicago and Florida, and has developed its line from Chicago to Evansville for this service. It has a large percentage of double track, automatic block signals throughout, and a large mileage of automatic train control. The New York Central has an inferior line between the same points which is primarily a freight line, has little double track, and is not equipped with automatic block signals. The Chicago & Eastern Illinois is in bankruptcy, owing largely to the decline of its coal traffic. The proposed change would cripple it still further. Only a month's warning of the change was given by the Louisville & Nashville. The excuse was the desire to gain the benefit of the large soliciting force of the New York Central. The matter was referred by the Coordinator to the Regional Coordinating Committees, but they found that the lines concerned were within their rights and declined to interfere or intervene. The Coordinator thereupon issued his order, finding that the change would cause duplication in services, and wastes and other preventable expense. The Louisville & Nashville and the New York Central have an opportunity to seek a review of the order by the Interstate Commerce Commission, but may go directly into court. In the meantime the United States District Court has granted a preliminary injunction prohibiting the change in service.]

I assume that was on the request of the Coordinator; is that correct?

MR. EASTMAN: No, that was on the request of the railroads. My order, under the law, is not effective until twenty days after it was issued, so that no injunction could be sought under that order.

319

PRESIDENT ROOSEVELT:	That is your first order, isn't it?
MR. EASTMAN:	Yes, of that kind.
PRESIDENT ROOSEVELT:	As a matter of fact, it really has a great significance, and possibly a greater one than appeared in the statement you have made. Both of the lines are Morgan-controlled and one is in receivership. It was decided, apparently, to let the Chicago & Eastern Illinois road fall by the wayside and kiss it goodbye; having done so, they are now trying to divert the traffic to the Big Four. Am I right about that?
MR. EASTMAN:	That is all assumption. I do not know whether that is true or not. Of course they deny that. The majority of the stock was controlled by the Van Sweringens. They practically lost their control. The Louisville & Nashville is very insistent for doing this. They say that after the service began to decline in connection with the through service of the Illinois Central they used to carry more passengers to Florida and now they carry less. That was due to the inefficiency of the Chicago & Eastern Illinois, which was cutting its expenses to such an extent that they did not advertise and solicit properly.
PRESIDENT ROOSEVELT:	Jesse, does the Chicago & Eastern Illinois owe you any money?
MR. JONES:	Our information is that without this particular traffic the roads are not meeting operation expenses.
MR. EASTMAN:	It not only takes passenger business from them but it would lose as a freight carrier also.
PRESIDENT ROOSEVELT:	It is a much better kept road than the Big Four road.
MR. EASTMAN:	Yes, far better.
MR. JONES:	You say there is a great significance to that, really?
MR. EASTMAN:	Yes.
MR. JONES:	Even beyond this thing you are talking about.
PRESIDENT ROOSEVELT:	Is there any way in which Jesse can intervene to uphold the order as a creditor?
MR. EASTMAN:	I suppose he could. I know the bond-holders could intervene.
PRESIDENT ROOSEVELT:	You might check on that as to whether it would be advisable to consider intervening in support of the order.
MR. JONES:	We sent an order and put our position up to them. In addition to that, Mr. President, I have in mind discussing this whole thing with the New York Central. It looks very much as though they were doing this to make a good buy—buy it for nothing, something like that. Williamson said he would come and see me the next time he was in town, but he was here and did not come in.
MR. EASTMAN:	He will be here tomorrow.
MR. JONES:	I will probably see him tomorrow, then.

PRESIDENT ROOSEVELT: Anything else on that?

MR. RICHBERG: No.

PRESIDENT ROOSEVELT: Next is the report of the Acting Secretary of Agriculture with respect to the possibilities of self-liquidating public works projects in agriculture.

MR. RICHBERG: Shall I read this, Mr. President?

PRESIDENT ROOSEVELT: Yes . . . .

MR. JONES [after Mr. Richberg had read some rather astronomical financial figures]: Mr. President, have you some smelling salts? (*Laughter*)

SECRETARY MORGENTHAU: The gentleman on my left (*Mr. Stanley*) says it sounds like Amos an' Andy. (*Laughter*)

PRESIDENT ROOSEVELT: That wouldn't worry Jesse! (*Laughter*) . . . The Department of Agriculture was evidently reading the *New York Times* this morning.
Next is the report of the Federal Emergency Relief Administrator.

MR. RICHBERG: Do you want me to read this?

PRESIDENT ROOSEVELT: Let Harry read it; it will save your voice.

MR. RICHBERG: I don't mind reading, but it gets monotonous . . . .

MR. HOPKINS: The rest of this concerns the works program and finally a statement on airports. The FERA and the CWA have built, in the past year, more airports than existed altogether prior to the beginning. We have built a thousand airports and landing fields and will have finished two thousand by the end of another six months; so we have doubled the airports and landing fields in America in the last twelve months.

PRESIDENT ROOSEVELT: This is such a clear statement that I am wondering if it would not be a good idea to have it made public.

MR. HOPKINS: If you do, Mr. President, what would you think of doing this in an interchange of letters with somebody, or something of that sort?

MR. STANLEY: It seems to me it is an awfully good answer to Lindbergh.[2]

MR. HOPKINS: A great many people and newspapers are still carrying stories that these cattle are being killed just for the sake of killing them; that food is being destroyed; that the food is not being used. I see it in a few of the opposition papers all the time.

PRESIDENT ROOSEVELT: I would like to give it out in a press conference tomorrow.[3]

[2] Testimony critical of aviation policies of the Administration, given before the Federal Aviation Commission, was reported in the *New York Times*, Oct. 17, 1934, p. 11.

[3] It is interesting to note, as an example of the publicity sense of the President and the conscious use he made of his press conferences to highlight the work of the Administration, that he did just what he here

new deal mosaic

MR. HOPKINS: All right.

PRESIDENT ROOSEVELT: You and Steve [Early] might go over this with me afterwards and perhaps dress it up a little. You have some long words in there.

MR. HOPKINS: Some two-dollar words in there!

PRESIDENT ROOSEVELT: Next is the report by the Economic Adviser . . . .
[After Mr. Riefler had read a summary of the economic situation in the steel industry] On that figure of 25 per cent—the current rate of production—25 per cent of what?

MR. RIEFLER: Twenty-five per cent of capacity. It increases slightly from year to year so that 25 per cent of capacity this year would be slightly larger than last year.

PRESIDENT ROOSEVELT: Is it a fair criterion? In other words, I want to go back to the old steel rail thing—four million tons of steel rail capacity and yet the railroads all say—I think I am right, Joe, that they do not want more than a million tons a year.

MR. EASTMAN: They did purchase around an average of two million tons during the boom period.

PRESIDENT ROOSEVELT: Yes, but wasn't that—a lot of that—specially stimulated?

MR. EASTMAN: They were making over a lot of their tracks with heavy rails. They do not need it right along.

PRESIDENT ROOSEVELT: I am wondering if that 25 per cent is a fair figure to take.

MR. RIEFLER: The best record is that in 1929 we did go along several months with the steel industry running very close to a hundred per cent of the capacity figure. A lot of that capacity is not absolute. I think today that percentage of absolute capacity is very much larger than usual. I doubt very much whether they could run very much above 60 per cent of capacity without having to replace equipment. In 1930 they did increase their capacity quite a bit.

PRESIDENT ROOSEVELT: Is there anything we could do to get them to establish a new parity?

MR. RIEFLER: The NRA steel code authority might take it up. I am not a technician in that field at all.

PRESIDENT ROOSEVELT: Would you speak to them about that? I have been thinking for a long time that that is a very unfair statement to make before the public from week to week. It is not true. Taylor told me

suggested, at his press conference on Oct. 31. In reply to a question about general relief needs for the coming winter, he referred to this report on food surpluses used for relief purposes, explained briefly what was involved, and noted that it had been mimeographed for distribution at the end of the conference. He was careful to point out that the report had been submitted to the NEC, possibly with the incidental purpose of publicizing the work of the Council in general.

himself that if United States Steel could operate at 50 per cent right through they would be very well satisfied.

MR. RIEFLER: They are running around 40 to 45.

PRESIDENT ROOSEVELT: Take it up with them and see what can be done about it. [After Mr. Riefler had read a summary of economic conditions in construction] On that point of construction, I have been making the assertion—throwing out the suggestion to some of these bankers and business men coming in and talking to me about the construction industry, etc. I said this to Brown, president of one of the Chicago banks, talking about no construction going on: "Do you need any new hotels in Chicago?" He said, "Hell, no!" I said, "Do you need any more office buildings?" He made the same reply. I said, "Would your bank lend any money to build a new hotel or office building?" He said, "No." "Would you invest any money in them?" He said, "No." I believe that is true right down through the list of cities in the United States that are over-supplied, but I have no figures to back it up. Would it be possible for you to get the figures on one or two of the larger cities of a million or more?

MR. RIEFLER: We can get totals on that.

PRESIDENT ROOSEVELT: Also one or two second-size cities around three to five hundred thousand, one or two cities of a hundred thousand, and one or two of the smaller type around twenty-five thousand people, and see what, in that 1926-1929 period, was being built. You could make a list of the type of buildings that were being put up and then try to get from somebody in each city an answer to the question, "Do you need any of these buildings—new ones of these types?"

MR. RIEFLER: The whole point on construction is in residential construction. That is what we are pushing.

PRESIDENT ROOSEVELT: I think if it could be brought out, a lot of these people who are talking about the depths to which the construction industry has fallen and that we have to start in building—if we could show what I believe to be true in that period of 1926-1929 probably three-quarters of all the building trade people that were employed, plus three-quarters of all the materials—steel, concrete, marble, etc.—that went into these buildings, went into a type of building which we do not need today and could not possibly use if we did build—I think it would be an awfully good lesson if that fact could be brought out. Will you see if you can bring out something on that?

MR. RIEFLER: Yes, sir.

PRESIDENT ROOSEVELT: That points the way to residential construction as the only thing we can do—that and slum clearance.

[After Mr. Riefler had read from his economic summary on employment: "A critical revision of these estimates is now being made by government agencies on the basis of new Census data which are now becoming available for several important industries for which adequate information has hitherto been lacking. As soon as this revision is completed we will have fairly good monthly figures on about 60 per cent of all of the persons gainfully employed outside of agriculture, as compared with about 35 per cent used in the present estimates."] Why only 60 per cent?

MR. RIEFLER: The rest are in very small trades, proprietor shops, filling stations along the roads, and things like that, and the only way to catch those is the general census. What we are getting now is the census of American business last year, and that covered a lot of firms and industries we never had before. As these figures come out on the machine, we are working them into the estimates, which changes the picture quite a bit. That other 35 per cent is the people pushing buttons and the rest of them that we just can't get without a census.

PRESIDENT ROOSEVELT: Does this new census take care of that?

MR. RIEFLER: That is the thing we are trying to get. With the census this winter we can pass that bill. We have been working our heads off to see if we can't do it with the sampling method, covering every fifth one, and get it more quickly; but in testing those results we find they do not show any accuracy at all. It has not worked out.

PRESIDENT ROOSEVELT: You are trying to do a *"Literary Digest!"*[4]

MR. RIEFLER: We are trying to save time and money. We may be able to find a method that is fairly accurate, but it looks as though it would require a real census for that type of person. Those are the people who have been thrown out during the depression.

PRESIDENT ROOSEVELT: I think there is another thing to consider in talking about the figures of unemployment. The Federation of Labor statement which came out day before yesterday said that there were more people unemployed than the previous month, whatever it was, whereupon a lot of friendly newspapers ran the headline, "Fewer people are employed." Now, of course the two things do not necessarily go together, because there is a growth of population.

---

[4] The *Literary Digest* polls, popular at this time, later fatally misfired on the Roosevelt-Landon presidential campaign predictions in 1936, and the magazine ceased publication shortly thereafter. Mr. Riefler's comments here foreshadow the now extensive use by the federal government of scientific polling techniques.

MR. RIEFLER: The estimate there is about four hundred fifty thousand for the year.

PRESIDENT ROOSEVELT: Is it possible for us to work out these figures to put it on the percentage basis in relation to population so that the two figures would appear together? That would be a more fair way.

MR. RIEFLER: I will see what we can do.

PRESIDENT ROOSEVELT: Yes, see what you can do about it; I think it would give a much fairer picture because, after all, if the country increases about ten million in ten years and a total of unemployed remains the same, at least we are not slipping backwards.

MR. RIEFLER: It is so hard, on the basis of the 35 per cent figures, to make anything out of it. I hate to see them used.

Two weeks ago you asked whether there was a lag in the Treasury's expenditures as they were charged to the Treasury and as they go out to the public. We have been looking into that. This is what we have found. The months in which the Treasury disburses funds does not necessarily indicate the month in which actual expenditures are made; in some types of operations, expenditures to the public take place some time before the account is finally collected from the Treasury, while in other operations the Treasury advances funds some time before they are actually spent. A brief checkup of FERA and PWA accounts indicates that the bulk of expenditures for the Civil Works program and for public roads were not charged to the Treasury until some time after they were made; advances for relief and loans to railroads, on the other hand, have usually been charged at the Treasury before actual disbursement to the public. The question of whether there is a lead or a lag between the timing of these expenditures on the Treasury's books and their actual disbursements to the public, therefore, depends largely on the type of expenditure which predominates in any given month. On balance at the present time, emergency expenditures as charged at the Treasury are probably running slightly higher than actual disbursements to the public. Just now relief is the larger item.

PRESIDENT ROOSEVELT: Next is the report of the state directors for the National Emergency Council.

MR. RICHBERG: In that connection, Mr. President, do you wish me to refer to the functions of the state directors?

PRESIDENT ROOSEVELT: Suppose we do this first.

MR. RICHBERG: All right . . . .

PRESIDENT ROOSEVELT: Next is the digest of the reports by members of the Executive

Council. (*President Roosevelt then read . . . with comments and questions . . .*) ["Work has begun in the preparation of material for the use of the Department at the fourth Pan American Commercial Conference."] When is that going to be held, Mr. Carr?

MR. CARR: In March.

PRESIDENT ROOSEVELT: Where, here?

MR. CARR: No, in Buenos Aires.

PRESIDENT ROOSEVELT: ["A plan has been approved for the organization of an advisory committee to assist the American members of the International Technical Committee of Aerial Legal Experts in the study of international private air law."] I hope it doesn't get into the same mess with international law.

["The U.S. Fleet began its transit of the Panama Canal in its return from the Atlantic to the Pacific, October 24, the 86 ships transiting the Canal in 41 hours."] The two aircraft carriers carried away all the lights and left the canal in total darkness. They were too wide.

["Postal receipts continue to increase as indicated by reports from twelve Federal Reserve cities covering business the first three weeks of October. Increase average is approximately five per cent."] Isn't that a rather better percentage of increase than before?

MR. BRANCH: I think it is, Mr. President.

PRESIDENT ROOSEVELT: ["Gold shipments from San Francisco to Denver amount to $1,727,000,000."] Do you have anything left in San Francisco?

SECRETARY MORGENTHAU: A little.

PRESIDENT ROOSEVELT: ["The effectiveness of the enforcement of Raw Materials Regulations, particularly in Chicago and Cleveland, is shown by the fact that the most prominent raw material suppliers of moonshiners in Cleveland shipped 91 cars of sugar in August, as compared with 41 cars in September, which includes approximately 98 per cent of all sugar reaching illicit stills."] Where are these 41 cars going?

SECRETARY MORGENTHAU: To wholesalers, mostly.

PRESIDENT ROOSEVELT: ["As a result of the investigation of the *Morro Castle* disaster, three of the deck officers and two engineers will be required to show cause why their licenses should not be revoked at hearings to be held at New York next week. The PWA has allotted $180,000 to the Navy Department for the removal of the hull, but the Comptroller General has held that neither that money nor any appropriation may be properly used for the removal work. Conferences are being had with the Comptroller General

326

in an endeavor to obtain his approval of this expenditure."]
That is a mean situation. There is a hull which we cannot
remove, and there are a lot of green hides which are proceeding
to decompose.

["The report of the Section of Car Pooling has been sent to the
Regional Coordinating Committees of the carriers. The ultimate
objective is to have an organization which would acquire
ownership and necessary repair facilities to the cars assigned to
the pool. The immediate objective is the acquisition of the cars
by lease or contract during a trial period. It is proposed that the
pool organization be controlled and handled by the new
Association of American Railroads. Savings in operating
expenses are estimated at $50,000,000 per year and savings in
carrying charges to about $15,000,000 per year."] Joe, are they
cooperative about that or not? They do not like it, do they?

MR. EASTMAN: I don't know as yet because I have not taken it up. I understand
it is coming up before the Association. They have undoubtedly
spent a good deal of time analyzing it and probably will call
some of my men before them to answer questions.

PRESIDENT ROOSEVELT: ["The current rate of incoming applications for farm debt
refinancing is about one-third as large as it was a year ago. The
greatest decrease in the number of applications occurs in the
Southern States; New Orleans district current rate of applications shows a decline of 79 per cent."] Huey Long will
probably take credit for it!

["The volume of business of production credit associations
showed an increase of 18 per cent during the first fifteen days
of October compared to the preceding two weeks; i.e., loans
amounting to $3,488,000 and $2,929,000, respectively."]
Bill, [Wm. I. Myers] on this thing, I wonder if you can give
us some figures to show the number, amount, and extent of
Federal Land Bank loans and Land Bank Commissioner loans
that were in default. Is that worthwhile doing?

MR. MYERS: Yes, we are following that. Only interest commitments are
required for three years, up to October first. There have been
very few delinquents. That includes the United States, with
some areas in severe drought and some areas in rather unsatisfactory condition. Collections are very encouraging. We are
following a very vigorous policy and expect them to pay when
they can. We are getting good cooperation.

PRESIDENT ROOSEVELT: ["After several months of negotiations and mutual inquiry as
to the cost of Portland cement, bids for cement have been
accepted at a price which justifies the (TVA) Authority in

327

purchasing the cement and not building its own plant."] I read in the paper that TVA only awards contracts after applying the screws to industry. There is much complaint about coercion in order to obtain lower prices. However, they got a very, very good price on this cement they are buying, and the prices are based, of course, primarily on the size of the order. I think the cement companies cut about 40 or 45 cents on cement.

MR. EASTMAN: How do they get around the code prices?

PRESIDENT ROOSEVELT: They just *do*, Joe.

MR. RICHBERG: They have no price fixed.

MR. EASTMAN: I have been having joint meetings of the railroad purchasing departments in various regions. One great difficulty they find is that the bids are uniform.

PRESIDENT ROOSEVELT: Yes. ["Negotiations for extensions of the Automobile Code are under way, the proposed changes in the National Electrical Manufacturing Association Code are under joint study, and important pending questions in the Lumber and Retail Solid Fuel Codes are in the process of being ironed out."] Clay, on the lumber retailers code, is that a separate code from the lumber code?

MR. WILLIAMS: The lumber retailers tie in, as I understand it, with the other codes. Mr. Richberg is more familiar in the territory than I am. Am I right, Mr. Richberg, in that understanding?

MR. RICHBERG: I think that is correct, although it is a separate operation.

MR. WILLIAMS: But they have one big code authority and that is divided into so many divisions, and they all have their own code authorities that work out specific prices in that territory. We have a great deal of trouble in that code.

PRESIDENT ROOSEVELT: It is one of the worst things we have, and the chief complaint is not in the price which the actual hewers of trees are getting, but rather from the price-fixing of the lumber retailers.

MR. RICHBERG: I may say that that code is one of the few price-fixing codes. It received the severest criticism when it went through. It never received the approval of the legal division.

MR. WILLIAMS: When they voted on it, the vote was 34 to 1 to retain it in the code authority. But the West Coast is all out of kilt with respect to it. We have a meeting today in Washington state with respect to it. It is about as completely mixed up—that is the "scrambled eggs" you were talking about a while ago, without the bacon.

PRESIDENT ROOSEVELT: The trouble is, they have been getting the bacon.

MR. RICHBERG: They have been losing money on their high prices. They overplayed the market.

MR. WILLIAMS: The thing is inconsistent. They fixed the price and tried to control it. The result was, they brought 4,000 units into operation under the temptation of the fixed price. You have two things, one pulling against the other.

PRESIDENT ROOSEVELT: I think we ought to take some pretty quick action on that.

MR. WILLIAMS: It is on the table, but it has many ramifications, with 35 divisions.

MR. RICHBERG: There is where we get the complaint.

PRESIDENT ROOSEVELT: Yes. ["Two weeks activities, October 15 to October 27 (RFC): total authorizations, $30,428,170; total disbursements, $23,549,366; total repayments, $40,844,374."] Still making money!
["The Corporation has authorized 3,255 loans in the amount of $1,000,307,537 (including outstanding commitments) to 2,451 institutions for distribution to depositors of closed banks of which $117,205,776 has been canceled and $639,537,575 disbursed."] That total of 36 banks that have not been cleaned up—is that coming down?

MR. JONES: That is in the Comptroller's office.

SECRETARY MORGENTHAU: It is right around that number.

MR. JONES: That job is pretty near finished, Mr. President.

SECRETARY MORGENTHAU: I think it is 30 now.

MR. JONES: By and large, the job is pretty well done. I think if we have losses, it will be more particularly along this line than anything else.

PRESIDENT ROOSEVELT: How is the actual liquidation of those loans proceeding?

MR. JONES: Of the closed banks?

PRESIDENT ROOSEVELT: Yes.

MR. JONES: The collections are very good. They are too good; people are still denying themselves anything else, trying to get out of debt. We are trying to devise some means of slowing it down to get them to do something else with part of their money. We are trying to get that spirit all through the organization where we will not suffer because of it. I think there are less than 500 banks that have not applied.

PRESIDENT ROOSEVELT: How many banks are buying back their stock?

MR. JONES: Not many; $66,000,000 all told, and that includes the New York banks up to date.

PRESIDENT ROOSEVELT: ["The Civilian Conservation Corps is at peak strength with an estimated enrollment of 355,000."] Robert, on this, before I forget it; I cut out from the Department of Agriculture estimate an item to clear the land and start actual planting work on this new national arboretum here in Washington which is up in the

329

	Northeast section. I think it is on the Anacostia Creek. Do you know where it is?
MR. FECHNER:	Yes, sir.
PRESIDENT ROOSEVELT:	I cut it out from their estimate. We have no CCC camps right here, have we?
MR. FECHNER:	Yes, we have one right up there on that project.
PRESIDENT ROOSEVELT:	Do you think they can go ahead and do it?
MR. FECHNER:	Yes, we have a camp that was assigned for that particular development. I don't know why it could not do all the work necessary.
PRESIDENT ROOSEVELT:	You might talk with Mr. Bell and the Department of Agriculture about it—anything that might be called cleaning up jobs around the District. You will be able to list them as you go through the department estimates. Instead of doing that, we may be able to do it through CCC.
MR. FECHNER:	We have four camps working right near here now, and just across the river. There is some good news about the CCC. We have made studies about the discharge of men as to what happened to them. We have completed the second group that went out. Of the second group, more than three times as many were employed as we found in the first group that went out, which would indicate that the men, as they are now leaving the CCC camps, are finding employment much better than they were several months ago.
PRESIDENT ROOSEVELT:	Was that contained in the letter you sent to me the other day?
MR. FECHNER:	Yes, sir.
PRESIDENT ROOSEVELT:	Make a memorandum to stick that into it too. ["There are 1,988 Community Campaigns (FHA) under way and 3,110 Community Campaign Chairmen have been appointed. Estimates indicate that for every dollar loaned for alteration and repair work there has been approximately $5.00 of work done for cash."] How do you get that way, Jimmie?
MR. MOFFETT:	That is other bank loans, short term. We are running about one to five.
PRESIDENT ROOSEVELT:	["Mortgage Insurance (FHA): Substantial progress has been made on the development of Rules and Regulations. The matter of proper interest rate to be allowed upon insured mortgages is proposed at five per cent except in the case of states where rates are currently higher. This interest rate would also include the service charge."] About that five per cent, except where rates are higher: I would try to keep it down to that if you can. In some of these states where they are currently higher, they ought not to be. If we can

keep it down to five per cent as generally as possible, it will be a great thing on these mortgages. The trouble is this: take Georgia, for instance; [for] a good many years, the custom has been nine, ten, and twelve per cent. It is just dead wrong. I think if we could lay down the general policy of trying to make the interest rates as uniform as possible throughout the country it would be a good thing. Just because you happen to live in Georgia is no reason for paying ten per cent.

I suggested to the Bankers Association that they pass a resolution as to abnormally high interest rates on mortgage loans; they would not pass it.

["Home Owners' Loan Corporation: . . . (b) applications for 32,252 loans with a value of $106,115,912 were received, bringing the total applications received to date to 1,731,002, with a value of $5,576,700,967 . . ."]

SECRETARY MORGENTHAU: How can the Home Owners' Loan Corporation commit themselves to $5,000,000,000 which is much more than Congress authorized?

MR. WEBB: They don't. Those are only applications.

SECRETARY MORGENTHAU: They continue to receive applications in excess of their authorizations.

MR. WEBB: They have not reached the limit of their authorizations yet—only a billion, seven hundred million out of three billion of the bonds for that purpose. We have rejected, as you will notice, a large number of applications, and while our total applications are now something like five billion, we are certainly not going beyond what is authorized, and could not do so.

SECRETARY MORGENTHAU: The Farm Credit, when they get an application now, and they cannot take it, they notify the man, but the Home Owners' Loan Corporation is taking applications and the man has the reason to believe that they are going to be kept on. It backs up in the territory and makes it very embarrassing.

PRESIDENT ROOSEVELT: You are rejecting them, aren't you?

MR. WEBB: We have rejected about 40 per cent of all the applications.

PRESIDENT ROOSEVELT: Do you notify the applicant?

MR. WEBB: Yes, immediately; not only the mortgagor but the mortgagee.

SECRETARY MORGENTHAU: But you are building up a fabulous debt so that when Congress meets we have to increase the three billion dollars.

MR. WEBB: We have slowed down considerably on both applications and disbursements. You will notice we have cut down considerably.

SECRETARY MORGENTHAU: How many have you approved, waiting to go through the works?

MR. WEBB: I cannot tell you.

SECRETARY MORGENTHAU: I think it is in excess of three billion.

MR. WEBB: Oh, no!

MR. RICHBERG: It really isn't a figure of applications.

MR. WEBB: Forty per cent of those can be eliminated right off. We just give the total figures. That doesn't mean that we expect to deliver that many bonds, by any means.

SECRETARY MORGENTHAU: I still maintain you are building up a situation there that you are going to force us. As I understand your own estimate, you cannot go beyond February. Is that right?

MR. WEBB: We cannot go beyond February.

SECRETARY MORGENTHAU: At the rate you are going you will be out of money by February?

MR. WEBB: Yes.

PRESIDENT ROOSEVELT: Now, T.D. [Webb], could you work up for the next meeting, the additional figures on this? There are two important figures here; one is that the loans to date total $1,780,000,000, and the other figure is the applications totaling $5,576,000,000. Can you break down that $5,576,000,000 into four classifications: (1) the loans already made, which is $1,780,000,000; (2) the loans approved but not yet made, whatever that figure is; (3) the loans still under consideration; and (4) the loans rejected.

MR. WEBB: I think I could give you that quite accurately.

PRESIDENT ROOSEVELT: That would give us a better picture. Then the other suggestion is that you give us the number and amount and extent of the loans in default, so we know how we stand—how it is actually working out.

MR. WEBB: I don't know, but we can give you a good estimate. On that particular point, we are in the same position as the farm people in their collections. Our collections are excellent and are running over four hundred thousand dollars a day. So far the total cash receipts are something over thirty million. In the beginning they had a three-year moratorium on principal, and all that has to be taken into consideration, to see just what the delinquency amounts to. I am satisfied that it is not over 15 to 20 per cent, from what the auditor tells me. We are opening regional offices for the purpose of servicing these loans and keeping up with the delinquencies.

PRESIDENT ROOSEVELT: This also comes back to the Home Loan Bank Board. The outstanding loans seem to be 87 million, whereas last March they were 95 million. That is apparently a credit operation of about eight million dollars.

MR. WEBB: I think, Mr. President, the figure was probably over that. Banks and building and loan associations have been greatly benefited by the operation of the Home Owners' Loan Corporation and the bonds they have gotten. The distressed mortgages we have taken up have given them the money to pay down on their loans. While they are loaning new money, they have paid more than they are loaning out through the operations of the Home Owners' Loan Corporation. The indications are that that will begin to come out from now on because we are about through, with the exception of some special cases we are working on with Mr. Jones. They were up, I think, to about a hundred million. Now it is down to 87 million. That has gone up, if you will notice that report, a little in the past two weeks.

PRESIDENT ROOSEVELT: ["The question of taking an appeal is being considered in the case of the Railroad Retirement Act which was held unconstitutional by the Supreme Court of the District of Columbia."] How are you getting along on that?

MR. STANLEY: The Attorney General has made a statement he is going to take an appeal.

PRESIDENT ROOSEVELT: No similar cases coming up?

MR. STANLEY: No, I think they have pretty well decided to make this the test case.

PRESIDENT ROOSEVELT: [" . . . an appeal has been authorized by the Secretary of the Interior in the matter of the suit by the United States to enjoin a violation of the well-spacing regulations issued by the Secretary."] What is that? What are "well-spacing regulations?"

MR. RICHBERG: The distances they are apart.

MR. STANLEY: The distances of the oil wells.

PRESIDENT ROOSEVELT: ["In connection with the AAA. . . the Supreme Court of the District of Columbia on October 22 handed down an opinion holding the Act constitutional in all respects and particularly with regard to the Hawaiian sugar producers."] Have they appealed from that?

MR. STANLEY: No, not yet; but I assume they will.

PRESIDENT ROOSEVELT: Now the state director question; will you take that up?

MR. RICHBERG: In connection with the functions of the state directors of the National Emergency Council, there has been considerable confusion. I prepared a statement of the functions of the state directors which would go beyond the present activities and define their duties in relation to the emergency agencies. It seems important to have a general presentation of that in order that there may be an understanding.

First, each state director should operate a clearing house for information concerning the federal emergency agencies, answering and referring inquiries from within the state to federal agencies within the state if possible—otherwise to Washington—and spreading information concerning federal activities through publicity channels within the state.

Second, to serve as chairman of a committee composed of the chief state representatives of various federal agencies. Some of the state directors have proceeded along that line. It seems to have a desirable effect, and it ought to be understood so that there will be no misunderstanding as to such activity on the part of the state directors.

Third, to serve as a liaison officer between the federal agencies as a group and the state administration in carrying out the emergency programs. That involves, in many instances, modification of state legislation, and it is rather desirable to have a definite method of cooperation established.

Fourth (and this is one which ought to be very carefully understood and criticized if objected to), to prepare (a) a confidential report to the Executive Director of the National Emergency Council every two weeks (that is what is being done now); and (b) a mirror of public opinion within the state concerning the activities of separate federal agencies and the federal emergency program as a whole.

Then as a second group of functions, B, "The State Director may serve as a direct representative of another federal agency upon its request where either a small volume of work permits it or a new program is being inaugurated." They have been serving for the Federal Housing Administration and the NRA.

PRESIDENT ROOSEVELT: What are they operating under now—Executive Order or order from the Emergency Committee?

MR. RICHBERG: They are only operating under the appointments which were made by the executive director with the approval of the President, long ago.

PRESIDENT ROOSEVELT: But no specific instructions?

MR. RICHBERG: General instructions were given to them, but they were not definite, as they are here, and there has been a great deal of confusion over the fact that they have served as representatives of different agencies; and if they are going to serve in the capacity of furnishing these reports, it seems that their particular functions should be defined so that there will be no misunderstanding. The idea, primarily was to furnish a coordinating, centralizing individual within the state for the benefit of its reflection on the program back here.

PRESIDENT ROOSEVELT: This would have the effect of clarifying the duties.

MR. RICHBERG: That is the purpose. We want it perfectly clear that they are not there as sort of special reporters to watch and report on the other agencies, but rather as a centralizing individual.

PRESIDENT ROOSEVELT: Do any of you have any thought on that suggestion of Donald's that this be prepared along this line to go out to the state directors to give them a practical outline of their duties?

MR. JONES: I see no objection to it.

PRESIDENT ROOSEVELT: I think it would clear the way a bit.

MR. RICHBERG: There is a good deal of misunderstanding.

PRESIDENT ROOSEVELT: What is your general feeling about the personnel of these state directors? Is it pretty good?

MR. RICHBERG: I think it is somewhat spotty; some are very good and helpful, while some are rather mediocre, and some have a vague view of what they are supposed to do. If we can give them a definite job and hold them to it we can test them. Here is one illustration. A man operating particularly as compliance officer thinks that is all he is supposed to do. Then the NRA said "We want a compliance officer." Then the state director wants to know what he was supposed to do now. We have to preserve the integrity of this organization or else dispense with it.

MR. MOFFETT: We are taking thirty of them permanently on November first—full time jobs.

MR. RICHBERG: We have the situation there—some of these men do not want to go to Federal Housing while some of them prefer to go there. We have said, "If Federal Housing wants you, and you want to do that, that is all right with us; we will appoint another state director. If you want to remain state director you are at liberty to say so to Federal Housing."

PRESIDENT ROOSEVELT: Under your plan, the state director could serve as direct representative of Federal Housing provided he also carries on his work as state director. But if he could not devote any time to his work as state director, he would have to resign as such and become Federal Housing Director.

MR. MOFFETT: Thirty of them have resigned.

MR. RICHBERG: We have a very serious problem there, because out of that thirty I think, Mr. Moffett, quite a number have felt that they were being advised to take up this work and were not anxious to do it. They would prefer to remain state directors. I want to clear that up and not have them feeling that we are trying to get them to do it.

PRESIDENT ROOSEVELT: I like this, in general, except for B: "The state directors may also serve as direct representatives of a federal agency upon its request where either a small volume of work permits it or a new program is being inaugurated."

MR. RICHBERG: That applies to Federal Housing.

PRESIDENT ROOSEVELT: I am inclined to think that might be reworded so as to make it clear that he can do it where a small volume of work permits it and does not interfere with his state director work, or that he may do it temporarily for a new agency, but not in such a way as to hurt his work as state director. That would make it perfectly clear. Don't you think so? And of course it is perfectly possible to work out this idea. For instance, in the case of Housing, let the state director be the head for you and accept the responsibility, but give him an assistant mutually agreeable to you and him who would do all the heavy work.

MR. MOFFETT: I believe it will take a hundred per cent of his time on Housing. He has to pass on these mortgages.

PRESIDENT ROOSEVELT: He cannot hold both jobs?

MR. MOFFETT: He will be paid out of the premium of the Home Owners. They will finance the operation.

PRESIDENT ROOSEVELT: Is there any further discussion of this? I suppose the most practical way would be to have an action by the Council—the Emergency Council as a whole—requesting the director to send a letter to all the state directors defining their duties in accordance with this memorandum.

MR. STANLEY: I so move, in order to bring it up.

PRESIDENT ROOSEVELT: You have heard the motion; all in favor, say Aye. (*There was a good volume of ayes.*) It does not need an Executive Order.

MR. RICHBERG: I think this ought to be done or there will be a great deal of confusion.

PRESIDENT ROOSEVELT: I have signed the consolidation Executive Order. The old Executive Council is now out of existence and the new Emergency Council is now meeting. The reason I did not give it out before was I thought it would be good press news for the newspapers tomorrow morning.

There is one other question I wish you would be thinking about—something we can take up when we meet two weeks from today. I wish you would be thinking about it so we can have some real discussion on it, perhaps devoting half an hour to it at our next meeting. It is something that will come up probably during the course of the late fall and winter, and, in a sense, it goes to the root of a great deal of unemployment work that we are doing.

Should there be a distinction in prices paid for labor and materials out of government appropriations for direct relief, for work relief, or for nonproductive public works and those for self-liquidating public projects?

336

If all of these expenditures are on the most economical basis, there will be the largest volume of relief at the lowest cost and the least interference with private employment. On self-liquidating public projects, however, there might be a reasonable claim of unfair competition by the government in obtaining cheaper labor or cheaper material unless the prevailing standards were maintained.

If relief expenditures are on normal competitive basis, the effect is to put relief itself in competition with private employment, increasing the burden of relief and decreasing private employment.

Now, that general subject has a lot of ramifications. The subject came up in the first instance over a year ago—a year and a half ago—when we started the CCC camps. A practical illustration of this is the idea that the pay to these boys should be on the basis of the going pay of the locality, which, in the North would have been for common labor in a good many sections as high as three or four dollars a day, while in the South it might have been as low as eighty cents a day with no board and no lodging. There was a protest when we fixed thirty dollars a month as the standard wage. That included, of course, board and lodging.

As it has turned out, the CCC camp activity has probably been the most successful of anything we have done. There is not a word of complaint—rap on wood. They are performing two kinds of work; they are doing the kind of clean-up, soil-erosion job that you cannot call self-liquidating in the sense that the money will actually come back to the government. That money never will come back to the government except in a very indirect way, except through increase of values of land. They have, however, been doing some other forms of work which will bring in a return to the government eventually—the cleaning of certain forest areas for example, where the government is permitted to cut actual timber and will get that timber as a result of the CCC operation. It is very difficult to draw a clear-cut distinction between what is self-liquidating and what is not.

We are going to have, of course, more public works this coming year, and we are going to have more relief this coming year in one form or another; and the quetsion is, whether we should treat the subject on the basis of making a distinction in what we pay for labor and what the going rate is on the outside in private employment, or whether we should pay the standard wage on the outside. If we pay the standard on the outside, it is going to cost the government a great many millions more.

And furthermore, there is the other side of the picture, that the man who is working for the government, and getting just as much money as he would in private employment, has very little incentive to go back into private employment; but take it by and large, I am inclined to think we ought to make private employment a good deal more desirable and attractive than government employment. On the other hand, we do not want to go and tear down the wage standard which has been arrived at after a long period of constant struggle for organized labor.

There are the two horns of the dilemma. I think it is something we ought to be thinking about and I thought we would take it up two weeks from now.[5] If you will be thinking it over yourselves, we will talk it over at that time.

MR. HOPKINS: Will we take up the possibility of exempting all relief from the codes? If we had complete exemption from all the codes on relief expenditures, we would save millions and millions of dollars.

PRESIDENT ROOSEVELT: As long as you don't break down the minimum wage, child-labor, and short-hour provisions of the code. It is essential to maintain that portion of the codes.

MR. HOPKINS: We are constantly getting bids for goods and then being told that the fellow that bids is not living up to the codes.

MR. RICHBERG: It might very well work out as a means of disposing of a certain amount of surplus stock and improvement in the market situation if it were carefully handled.

MR. HOPKINS: We would buy a great deal more goods. We are in the market to buy ten million tons of coal. They are talking about giving us a price break of a very few per cent which doesn't mean anything. But coal operators tell us if they could get into action they would give us a break of 25 or 30 per cent.

PRESIDENT ROOSEVELT: And at the same time maintain their wage scales.

MR. HOPKINS: And we would buy a lot more coal.

---

[5] The President specifically says here that he wants this subject discussed at the next meeting, but there is no mention of it in the Proceedings for November 13, with the exception of an ambiguous item on the agenda— "For discussion and decision: the 'Critical Problem'—presented by the President at the meeting of October 30, 1934." This absence of continuity in the Council's deliberations may indicate the marginal importance it had come to occupy in the President's day-to-day concerns, suggesting that he looked upon NEC more as a sounding board for his thoughts and ideas of the moment than as a serious policymaking body.

MR. FECHNER: If they gave that reduction, they would maintain their wage scale.

MR. EASTMAN: They would do the same thing for the railroads if they had a chance.

PRESIDENT ROOSEVELT: Would they—and still maintain the labor provisions of the codes?

MR. EASTMAN: It simply means that the production would be by those best organized to produce.

MR. RICHBERG: And by low-cost producers who are located in good geographical positions to supply the needs.

MR. [HENRY] ROOSEVELT: That would apply to the other departments, such as the Navy. We could get all kinds of material cheaper on that basis.

PRESIDENT ROOSEVELT: You would at once run into the obvious criticism, "Why should the government pay less than private companies?"

MR. MYERS: It is a hot potato.

PRESIDENT ROOSEVELT: It is a hot potato both ways. The same thing is involved in two other very important items; one is the building of subsistence farm homes, where Harry Hopkins is doing it at a very low cost because he is using people on relief to do it a good deal lower than can be done by the Interior Department that is not using people on relief to the same extent; and the other thing is slum clearance, and there again we run into the question of the building trades.

MR. RICHBERG: They are not getting any work in that at all. They say they are getting nothing out of it.

PRESIDENT ROOSEVELT: We cannot afford slum clearance operations at the present cost. Instead of three, four, or five dollars, it is costing us nine and ten. This new housing project in the Bronx that everybody talked about as such a grand thing is going to cost $11.50 a room. Who is going into that? They are going to be people of $2,500 and $3,000 a year. It is not going to take care of the family with seven or eight hundred dollars a year, yet those are the people we want to help.

Well, we might think it all over and have a talk two weeks from now.

Meeting closed at 4:10 p.m.

Proceedings of the National Emergency Council

[meeting no. 18]
November 13, 1934

Held in the Blue Room of the White House, November 13, 1934, at 3:00 p.m.

[This brief transcript illustrates both the potential and actual weaknesses of the National Emergency Council as a coordinating mechanism. The President's lengthy commentary on the problem of proliferating interdepartmental committees and his decision to place these committees under the aegis and supervision of NEC suggests the former. One may legitimately reserve judgment on the extent to which any one agency can integrate a coordinating job, and still applaud recognition of the problem and the attempt to meet it.

On the debit side, recall that at the last meeting the President opened the subject of differential rates of payment for materials and labor on government relief projects against comparable costs in the private sphere. Twice Mr. Roosevelt said then that he wanted to discuss it further at the next meeting. Only in the agenda for November 13 is the subject mentioned, however. It never came up during the session, thus illustrating the too casual work habits of the President. Beyond this, collegial efforts at either policy making or coordination or both clearly depend, here and in general, on

the willingness of the Chief Executive himself to follow
through. One must assume that it was Mr. Roosevelt's own
oversight or his deliberate decision not to raise this item on the
agenda before him that caused it to be passed over.—Editors'
Note].

PRESIDENT ROOSEVELT: We have a number of new members today—Mr. Kennedy, Mr.
Peek, Mr. Thomas, Mr. Choate, Mr. Crowley, Mr. McNinch,
and Mr. Sykes. We welcome you to our Council.
I will not be able to attend the next meeting two weeks from
today, but I think the Secretary of State will be here.

MR. RICHBERG: Shall we have a meeting then?

PRESIDENT ROOSEVELT: I think you might have a meeting; there will be a number of
things coming up.
The first thing on the agenda is the minutes of the previous
meeting. Unless there is objection we will waive the reading of
the minutes.
I want to mention one matter, another step in the general policy
of the Council, which I think will probably be fairly useful. As
you know, there have been a good many interdepartmental
committees formed. The Secretary of Labor says she thinks
she belongs to 32 of them! This morning I discovered a
committee which I had appointed six months ago and forgotten
all about—the interdepartmental committee on shipping policy.
It was brought to my attention; and there have been several
similar instances. It occurred to me, and to a good many of us,
that in order to tie in these committees, many of which are
temporary and some of which are more or less permanent, it
would be a good thing gradually, as occasion arises, to make them
subcommittees of this Council, so that we would not forget
their existence. For instance, day before yesterday, we agreed
that there should be some form of clearing-house or coordinating
committee of the credit agencies of the government—RFC,
Home Owners' Loan, Farm Credit, the Housing Corporation,
etc.,—and I went ahead and appointed a committee, I think of
seven or eight, with the Secretary of the Treasury as chairman.
Now probably the Secretary of the Treasury won't let me
forget the existence of that committee, because funds are
involved, but if it were not for his insistence I probably would
forget it; and it is my thought that we should gradually make
these special committees, or the more permanent committees, a
part of the Council so that they could report to the Council

341

meetings. And even if they have nothing to report, they should at least report progress so we would be reminded of their existence, and they would be reminded of the fact that we know of their existence, which is equally important. So, if there is no objection, I think the Council might well consider making this Interdepartmental Committee of Credit Agencies a committee of the Council; and the other committee which I think we could make a part of the Council at once is the Interdepartmental Committee on Shipping Policy. It has nearly completed its work, but it will not make its report until early in December, and when it has given its report there may be other duties or questions which we may assign to that same committee. So, if there is no objection, we will consider both of those committees as committees of the Council, with the request that they report to the regular Council meetings through Mr. Richberg.

(*After a few moments of quiet conversation between President Roosevelt and Mr. Richberg.*) Donald says it would be a good idea for all the other 32 committees to do the same thing. I told him that is his job.

MR. RICHBERG: Then, as a preliminary request, I am going to ask the different committee chairmen if they will send me a memorandum of their existence so that I can proceed with this work.

SECRETARY ROPER: Mr. President, do I understand, for instance, that the chairman of this committee on shipping policy, when he presents his reports, at least for that meeting, is to have admission to this Council and make his report to the Council? In other words, will that chairman be a member for that day of this Council and report in person?

MR. RICHBERG: I would suggest that it might be well to have the chairman of the committee always a member of the Council.

SECRETARY ROPER: You mean—

MR. RICHBERG: I mean when these committees are appointed, each chairman should be, himself, a member of the Council.

PRESIDENT ROOSEVELT: I don't think you can do that. The Secretary of Commerce is the only member of the department who is here, and yet he cannot function as chairman of a half-dozen different committees. I think each chairman better report through the head of his department, the secretary. Then we can ask him in if we need him.

Next is a report on the agricultural position by the Secretary of Agriculture.

MR. RICHBERG: Shall I read this report, Mr. President?

PRESIDENT ROOSEVELT: Yes, you better read it . . . .
"Report by the Administrator of Federal Emergency Relief" . . . .
Harry, these figures showing 20 per cent consisting of people too old to work, mothers with children, and so forth and so on—do you think that total numbers in that 20 per cent are much higher than in 1929?

MR. HOPKINS: Yes.

PRESIDENT ROOSEVELT: Why?

MR. HOPKINS: Because the old people in 1929 were those retired from business and had an income to support themselves, but they lost their capital, and so the number of old people who are dependent now is greater than in 1929.

PRESIDENT ROOSEVELT: A lot of them died in the meantime.

MR. HOPKINS: Yes, but a lot of them are still living. The same thing is true of other persons who were not wage earners.

PRESIDENT ROOSEVELT: How about the percentage of widows?

MR. HOPKINS: The percentage of widows who are dependent now is greater than in 1929. Many of our people think the figure is going to be ultimately higher than 20 per cent.

PRESIDENT ROOSEVELT: But up to the organization of state and national relief, they were taken care of by local relief.

MR. HOPKINS: Yes, by state pension and old age pension; they have never been cared for by federal funds.

PRESIDENT ROOSEVELT: Next is the summary report in connection with the capital reconstruction of insured banks.

MR. RICHBERG: This is a short extract from a longer report. ". . . The balance of the report being of a confidential nature, has been transmitted to the President in accordance with the practice established in the inauguration of the Executive Council." In explanation of that last sentence, I want to call attention to the fact that in order to have these reports freely sent in, there are many things in them which should not be mimeographed on account of the liability of miscirculation.

PRESIDENT ROOSEVELT: "Report by the Economic Adviser." . . . "Report of the state directors of the National Emergency Council."

MR. RICHBERG: I have a short report and a two-page summary, Mr. President . . . .
I should emphasize that this is a summary of the state directors' reports and not the opinions of the executive director.

MR. JONES: Mr. President, may I ask what the criticism was of the Housing Administration not getting the support of the agencies?

MR. RICHBERG: That seems to be a criticism of the bankers, that they did not think the Federal Housing Administration was getting the cooperation of some of the other federal agencies. I say this is the report of the state directors; it may be a very good alibi, Mr. Jones.

MR. JONES: I was just wondering.

PRESIDENT ROOSEVELT: "Report of the members of the Council." (*The President then sketched rapidly through* [*the report*], *asking questions or making comments . . . .*)

["... The beer regulations were signed, the most important of which made mandatory the installation of beer meters by all breweries. The Alcohol Tax Unit seized 575 stills valued at approximately $400,000."] Is that in two weeks?

SECRETARY MORGENTHAU: Yes, two weeks.

PRESIDENT ROOSEVELT: ["... In connection with the amendment to the Appropriation Act, 678 investigators must either qualify in a noncompetitive examination or be separated from the service December 1. Indications are that less than 25 per cent of them passed the examination, so it will be necessary to recruit approximately 500 new men who qualified in the recent examination."] That is in accordance with the Comptroller's ruling?

SECRETARY MORGENTHAU: In accordance with the Attorney General's ruling; and late last night the Comptroller handed down a ruling[1] which has upset things so that we have to recruit about a thousand. Our organization is completely shot. That lets everybody out except about 20 per cent. In fact, we have almost no investigators. Between the two, it leaves us in bad shape.

PRESIDENT ROOSEVELT: I wish you would see the Comptroller General and tell him what a mess it leaves us in.

SECRETARY MORGENTHAU: I think he is right, from a legal standpoint. The Department of Justice didn't—

PRESIDENT ROOSEVELT: The Department of Justice, at our request, didn't go as far as they might have gone.

SECRETARY MORGENTHAU: The Comptroller went the rest of the way. It is just hopeless now. I will see him.

PRESIDENT ROOSEVELT: Will you have a last try at the Comptroller?

SECRETARY MORGENTHAU: I will.

PRESIDENT ROOSEVELT: ["Due to the rapid increase in Japanese importations of cotton textiles into the Philippines during the past two years, it is desirable to take steps to protect the United States interest in the cotton textile trade with the islands. Those interested in the United States shipments became very insistent that this

---

[1] No. A-58496, dated Nov. 12, 1934, and found in Vol. 14, *Decisions of the Comptroller General*, pp. 383-389.

government take some definite action and accordingly a formula was worked out in the State Department designed to stabilize temporarily the situation at its present level. The Philippine Government was advised that legislation along this line be deemed advisable and would be acceptable to this Government. Mr. Quezon is cooperating with the wishes of this Government."]

I might add to that that the Philippine Legislature, I think, adjourned without taking action. A year ago, 80 per cent of all cotton textiles used in the Philippines came from the United States; today, 80 per cent comes from Japan—all in one year. ["The number of depositors in the postal savings system was increased from 2,493,204 in December 1933, to 2,619,546 in September 1934, a total increase of 126,342 depositors."] What do you give them—eight per cent?

MR. HOWES: Yes.

PRESIDENT ROOSEVELT: ["Airplanes manufactured in the United States during the first nine months of 1934 totaled 1,285, of which 673 were for domestic civil use; 306 for military delivery, and 306 for delivery to purchasers in foreign countries. The total manufactured in 1934 represents an increase of 220 aircraft over the corresponding period in 1933."]

You don't know how much of that increase is due to Army and Navy orders, do you, Dan?

SECRETARY ROPER: I don't, sir.

PRESIDENT ROOSEVELT: ["Information is being placed at the disposal of cotton producers needed in voting intelligently on the Bankhead Cotton Act referendum; and plans are being perfected for conducting the referendum."] I thought we had one.

SECRETARY WALLACE: No, not yet.

PRESIDENT ROOSEVELT: When are you having it?

SECRETARY WALLACE: About in December, isn't it, Chester?

MR. DAVIS: About the middle of December.

PRESIDENT ROOSEVELT: [". . . applications for 13,672 loans with a value of $42,000,000 were received, bringing the total applications received to 1,745,496 with a dollar volume of $5,643,000,000 . . ."]

Five billion, six hundred million dollars; John, you have stopped them and told them not to put in any more applications?

MR. FAHEY: I made public announcement of it.

PRESIDENT ROOSEVELT: Fine.

["The Reconditioning Department of the Corporation reports a considerable decline in the number of applications for reconditioning and modernization loans. During the two weeks,

7,673 applications were received, bringing the total to 296,903, amounting to approximately $68,000,000."] Those are gradually going over to the Housing, aren't they?

MR. FAHEY: Not the ones of the mortgages that we refinance.

PRESIDENT ROOSEVELT: They don't?

MR. FAHEY: No, those are repairs, and we have to make them ourselves.

PRESIDENT ROOSEVELT: ["Export-Import Bank of Washington: The only financial transaction entered into by the bank consists of a loan to the Second Export-Import Bank of $1,100,000 which has been repaid. The bank has not functioned actively to date because of its policy that no actual credit transaction will be undertaken with the Soviet Government until it submits an acceptable agreement relating to the Russian indebtedness."] I hope the directors' fees are not eating into the capital of the First Bank.

MR. PEEK: Not yet; they may.

PRESIDENT ROOSEVELT: ["... to date (Export-Import Bank) has authorized ... a loan not to exceed $100,000 to a manufacturer of cotton ginning machinery in connection with the export of its products to Brazil ... "] Thereby encouraging Brazil to manufacture its own cotton cloth!

MR. PEEK: That is part of the idea, I think. There is a question of England shipping the ginning machinery, or the United States.

PRESIDENT ROOSEVELT: They are going to do it anyway.
["... Reconstruction Finance Corporation: ... October 29 to November 9: total authorizations, $21,601,536.10; total disbursements, $36,578,582.81, total repayments, $30,275,150.22."] Bad! Got a six million dollar loss this week!

MR. JONES: I apologize! (*Laughter*)

PRESIDENT ROOSEVELT: ["In the elections on Tuesday, the city of Memphis voted 32,737 to 1,868 in favor of a municipal power system using TVA power."] Aren't you getting out of your watershed, Arthur?

DR. MORGAN: They are coming in. That's their business—it is their initiative.

PRESIDENT ROOSEVELT: You are not going to distribute power in the Mississippi Valley, are you? Do you think that is all right?

DR. MORGAN: Yes; that was their initiative.

PRESIDENT ROOSEVELT: How many miles is it from Wilson Dam to Memphis?

DR. MORGAN: It is a hundred miles from Hickory Dam. The Act says we shall dispose of it within reasonable transmission distance.

PRESIDENT ROOSEVELT: It doesn't limit you to the watershed?

SECRETARY HULL: It is not so far from Tupelo across to Memphis.

MR. JONES: This doesn't represent a completed transaction, does it?

DR. MORGAN: No, we have taken no action.

PRESIDENT ROOSEVELT: ["Intensive studies of major problems are being made (by the National Industrial Recovery Board) for the purpose of formulating policies with respect to the Service Trades, Distributing Trades, the Lumber Industry, Coal Industry, Construction Industry and Retail Solid Fuel Industry, the provisions for price control and production control, and the Labor Provisions of Codes."]

The Secretary of the Interior went down to the East Texas field where, of course you know, we are trying to regulate the outpouring of "hot oil"[2] which, in the place of a natural resource, has been bankrupting everybody, throwing labor out of work and flooding the country with gasoline and oil at the kind of competitive prices that nobody makes any money, and in the end, most people lose their jobs and their business.

We have undertaken down there to handle it by court action; but the difficulty is that while that will undoubtedly apply to interstate oil, there is a question how far we can go on the regulation of "hot oil" which is turned into gasoline right at the well. I told the Secretary of the Interior there was no reason I could see why he should not announce what we have been coming to for a long time, and that is that unless the industry itself can conform to the policy of preventing this unlimited production of hot oil, that about one remedy is left, and only one, and that is the declaration that oil, for two good reasons, is a public utility, and put it in the class with other public utilities, subject to complete government regulation. That seems to be about the only government recourse left.

About the same thing, if we are forced to it in oil, will have to be applied to coal and perhaps lumber. Lumber is another question, depending on whether you call it a natural resource which may be entirely depleted or whether you call it an agricultural problem.

["The (Federal Trade) Commission has approved for transmission to the Senate Part I of its report on Publicity and Propaganda Activities and Expenditures of the Electric and Gas Industries. Volume I of Part II of this report has been finally approved and will also be transmitted to the Senate

---

[2] "Hot oil" was oil produced in excess of state-imposed production quotas, a practice difficult for the states alone to control. Much about the early efforts to deal with "hot oil" may be gleaned from the Ickes diaries, especially Vol. I, *The First Thousand Days* (New York, 1954).

within a few days. Other volumes of the same report are before the Commission for study and approval and all will be ready to be submitted to the Senate before the end of the present month."] Ewin, when was that started—about how long ago?

MR. DAVIS: About a year ago, when the Senate authorized the investigation. They directed a report on propaganda activities of the electric and gas utility interests against public ownership and related subjects.[3]

PRESIDENT ROOSEVELT: But the complete report will be finished this winter?

MR. DAVIS: Oh, yes; in fact, we have finally approved and ready for transmission to the Senate practically all that propaganda report—over a thousand pages in the report we are making to the Senate, which is a resumé of the evidence that is in about twenty volumes of reports of testimony which have already been entered in the hearings and sent to the Senate. We have sent about seventy volumes to them.

PRESIDENT ROOSEVELT: The calendars are finished, aren't they?

MR. DAVIS: Yes, with respect to that phase. We were directed by joint congressional resolution to continue this investigation until the first of January 1936. Most of our investigation from now on will relate to the gas phase of it, and particularly the natural gas, as to which there had been much less investigation than of the electric companies.

PRESIDENT ROOSEVELT: Yes.

["While field work in the milk investigation has been somewhat curtailed by reason of the assignment of personnel to the Textile investigation, yet work in the Philadelphia and New England area is in progress, reports of which will be submitted to Congress in January."] How closely are you working with the Department of Agriculture on that?

MR. DAVIS: Very closely.

PRESIDENT ROOSEVELT: They know what you are doing?

MR. DAVIS: Yes; in fact, they recommended that investigation, and we have been in close touch with them about every phase of it and have obtained all the assistance from them we can. They are very cooperative.

PRESIDENT ROOSEVELT: ["About 9,000 men per month are leaving the CCC per

---

[3] An investigation of public utilities was conducted by the FTC. On Nov. 25, 1934, a lengthy report, described as the third installment in a six-year inquiry, was transmitted to the Senate, covering utility expenditures to influence public opinion through educational institutions. See the *New York Times*, Nov. 26, 1934, p. 3.

month to accept private employment."] That is a rather interesting fact.

["The Federal Coordinator of Transportation has submitted a report showing progress in the development of the legislative program for the coming session of Congress. This report, involving in part tentative conclusions and being of a confidential nature, has been transmitted to the President—in accordance with the practice established in the inauguration of the Executive Council."] Have I got that report?

MR. RICHBERG: It is in your file.

PRESIDENT ROOSEVELT: ["Joint regulations have been approved by the Attorney General and the Secretary of the Treasury covering the sales of liquor forfeited under the customs laws. Negotiations to effect the sale of large quantities of such liquor are now going forward."] Members of the Emergency Council will place their bids with Mr. Choate!

SECRETARY MORGENTHAU: He doesn't handle it.

PRESIDENT ROOSEVELT: ["Suits brought by A. W. Mellon and the Executors of R. B. Mellon for refund of 1920 income taxes aggregating about $390,000,000—"]—three hundred ninety million dollars?—

JUDGE BIGGS: Yes.

PRESIDENT ROOSEVELT: ["—were heard in the Eastern Pennsylvania District Court, October 3."]

["In connection with the National Industrial Recovery Act: (a) the Northern District Court of Alabama held that the Act is unconstitutional and it is proposed to take this case to the Supreme Court by Direct Appeal."] That is a good case.

JUDGE BIGGS: Very good for a test case.

PRESIDENT ROOSEVELT: ["Five persons were arrested on warrants charging the execution and sale of false affidavits which are required to be filed with the Department of the Interior by shippers of petroleum products in violation of the Criminal Code."] That is the East Texas field?

JUDGE BIGGS: Yes.

PRESIDENT ROOSEVELT: Get after them!

Is there any other business anybody wants to bring up?

Meeting adjourned at 4:20 p.m.

349

Proceedings of the National Emergency Council

[meeting no. 19]
December 11, 1934

Held in the Cabinet Room of the White House, December 11, 1934, at 2:10 p.m.

Present: the President of the United States; the Secretary of the Treasury; the Secretary of War; the Postmaster General; the Secretary of the Interior; the Secretary of Commerce; the Secretary of Labor; the Honorable William Phillips, Undersecretary of State; the Honorable Rexford G. Tugwell, Undersecretary of Agriculture; the Honorable James Crawford Biggs, Solicitor General; the Honorable Henry L. Roosevelt, Assistant Secretary of the Navy; the Honorable Daniel W. Bell, Acting Director of the Budget; the Honorable L. W. Robert, Jr., Assistant Secretary of the Treasury; the Administrator of Federal Emergency Relief; the Chairman of the Board of the Reconstruction Finance Corporation; the Chairman of the Board of the Tennessee Valley Authority; the Chairman of the Federal Home Loan Bank Board; the Chairman of the Federal Trade Commission; the Director of Emergency Conservation Work; the Federal Coordinator of Transportation; the Chairman of the National Industrial Recovery Board; the Chairman of the Alcohol Control Administration; the Chairman of the Federal Housing Administration; the President of the Export-Import Banks of Washington, D.C.; the Chairman of the Federal Deposit Insurance Corporation; the Chairman of the Federal Power Commission; the Chairman of the Federal Communications Commission; the Chairman of the Securities and Exchange Commission; the Chairman of the Federal Reserve Board; the Honorable Alfred D. Stedman, Assistant Administrator of AAA; the Honorable W. Forbes Morgan, Deputy Governor of the FCA; the Honorable Willard L. Thorp, Chief, Consumers' Division; the Economic Adviser; the Executive Director.

[This meeting reveals "pure" F.D.R. Voiced here by the President are some of his best informal expositions of New Deal policies that lay closest to his heart—convincing in their force and sincerity. The 1935 session of Congress, the high water mark of reform legislation under the New Deal, was in the offing, and the President apparently decided to take this opportunity to school the members of the Council in simple, direct and even eloquent terms, in the policy proposals that were in gestation, and the reasons for them. The achievement of TVA is recounted anew in moving words that impressed even its chairman so that he requested a copy to take back with him. The shift toward greater dependence upon work relief and more vigorous housing programs is foreshadowed,

and specifically, the public utility holding company legislation is discussed. Miss Perkins also alluded to the preparatory
work being done on the Social Security Act. The discussion
of press conferences is invaluable as an account by the master
himself of some of his own eminently successful techniques.
As to the work of the NEC itself, the discussion of legislative
clearance is of vital importance for the future of policy
coordination. Otherwise, for all its interesting features, this
meeting does rather little to dispel the feeling that NEC
was declining in value. One suspects the President was less
interested in getting the opinions of the members than in
using them as channels of information to a wider public. The
Council's members were being educated but were not doing
better at working together.—Editors' Note.]

PRESIDENT ROOSEVELT: There are quite a lot of things to talk about. The first relates
to a memorandum from the Director of the Budget. On
November 21, the Director of the Budget received a message
from Warm Springs saying that the President was taking
no action with reference to giving a half-holiday except the
half-day before Christmas or the half-day before New Year's.
It has always been done by Executive Order. The Director
of the Budget telephoned that message to all Departments;
but the Director of the Budget was informed that generally
all the departments and agencies did excuse their employees on
Wednesday, November 28, in spite of the message which
was telephoned to the chief clerks of those departments. You
can inform your chief clerks they acted contrary to the
instructions from the Director of the Budget.
I have taken time to talk to quite a number of members of the
Council, and it is generally agreed that these reports[1] we
have been reading take a long time in the reading and do
bring up a certain number of things for discussion, but not
many. I would like to have your point of view. I thought we
could eliminate the reading of these reports on condition
that all members of the Council read them themselves. The
chief point in my reading them was to get them into the
ears of the members of the Council. For you to get them
through the eye is perfectly satisfactory to me; but I think
it is tremendously important that every agency and department

[1] Referring to the reports of all the agencies prepared for each meeting.

351

should know very well the general line of things going on in the rest of the government. That is the object of it. If I hear no insistent demand that I should go ahead with the reading of these reports, which generally occupy an hour and a half, we will see how it works letting the members of the Council read them. What do you think, Miss Perkins?

SECRETARY PERKINS: I am free to say I shall never read them. I *know* I shall never read them. I mean, the amount of reading material of my own department which is laid away for train-travel and bedtime reading is already enormous, and the hour and a half that we spend here is the only time I personally give to the consideration of the memoranda of the other departments. It has been interesting and important to me, but I don't know that it is to anybody else.

PRESIDENT ROOSEVELT: I will be glad to read aloud to you while you eat!

SECRETARY PERKINS: I have always wanted you to appoint a reading master! The only suggestion is that they could be digested.

PRESIDENT ROOSEVELT: They are pretty well digested now.

SECRETARY PERKINS: It is important for us to know.

PRESIDENT ROOSEVELT: I think it is important for everybody to know what is going on in other departments. (*After a whispered conversation with Mr. Richberg.*) Donald says he got it down this time to 22 pages. Let's try it for a week or two and see how you get along. Glance through the 22 pages.

SECRETARY PERKINS: Give us an examination on it.

PRESIDENT ROOSEVELT: Yes, a examination might be a good thing.

SECRETARY PERKINS: An oral test once in a while.

PRESIDENT ROOSEVELT: So, with that new program—the elimination of the time taken on that in the past—it seems to me that we might adopt equally a new program. First of all, a summary of the regular reports made to the executive director which would be sent to each member in advance of the meeting. Then, if any member of the Council wants particularly to bring up something in that report, it would be in that first order of business.

The second thing would be a tentative agenda for me, to be prepared by the executive director, to include for consideration first a report of the subcommittee of the Council; second, specified policy questions which it may be desirable to have explained and discussed—general information; third, arrangements for further coordination; and fourth, matters that should be referred to a subcommittee of the Council for consideration or action. In other words, carried out more in detail, the topic on the agenda would be presented by the President or the executive director to bring the topic before the meeting; then the designated members of the Council would furnish information or comments on the topic; and general discussion would be open in special instances where it seems advisable—as long as we do not get into a debating society. The President then would close the discussion with some expression of opinion, as in the past, by reference or final determination. The general purpose and intent of the meetings would be to keep the members of the Council informed as to the general trend of administration policy and, incidentally, if there is any haziness, the place to bring it up is at the Council meeting and not at the press conference, so that all may have a consistent understanding in respect to the policies. This is the place to have policies discussed by those charged with the administration so that the members will gain a better understanding of the purposes and programs of the administration and at the same time have an opportunity to contribute suggestions, either in the meetings or subsequently.

Touching the general program of subcommittees to iron out interagency relations, there will be a definite responsibility to work out a great many problems now without imposing the burden directly on me. The chairmen of the subcommittees will report progress, as a regular procedure, through the executive director, who will place these reports on the tentative agenda. The report will also be made directly to the President when he so orders. The executive director, as in the past, will handle special matters referred to him by the President, and the general business of the Council. Reports from the members to the Council should be of sufficiently informative character so that they may present a continuing picture of activities; these reports will be digested and distributed, or summaries of them; and if confidential matters are contained in the reports, the President and executive director will use their discretion in not including such matters in these summaries; but they will be called to the President's attention. We have one report today which is of a confidential nature, and that report came straight to me instead of to the Council.

The reports of subcommittees will be available for the agenda of Council meetings; and if subcommittees are inactive, they should be abolished or put on the inactive list to be revived if needed. Later on, Donald is going to present some very interesting figures to you in regard to the number of committees now at work. Upon the request of one or more members of the Council, the executive director will call a meeting of a group of members for discussion. If the discussion of that group indicates the desirability of establishing another coordinating committee or referring the matter to an existing committee, the executive director will put that on the agenda of the Council for the next meeting.

Now we come to the tentative agenda for the National Emergency Council meeting today. First is the report of the Interdepartmental Loan Committee . . . .

Next is the report of the Interdepartmental Shipping Policy Committee . . . .

SECRETARY ROPER: We have already begun the preparation of the report.

PRESIDENT ROOSEVELT: Can't you let me have it before three weeks?

SECRETARY ROPER: Yes, sir.

PRESIDENT ROOSEVELT: Could you let me have it by Christmas?

SECRETARY ROPER: Yes.

PRESIDENT ROOSEVELT: One thing I might interject here is that there are two very important things to remember. If any agency or any department has a happy thought[2] after the fifteenth of January, or has failed before that date to bring to me the proposal for legislation, the chances are that they won't get anything through this session. At the last session of the Congress, we all of us had happy thoughts through until the day Congress adjourned. It delays the action of Congress; it confuses the legislation; it angers the members of the Senate and House; and this year, if you do not get anything in by the fifteenth of January, it probably won't be approved. I will have to say that as a *fiat*. You might just as well all do it. That is due warning. There may be some emergency things that come up afterwards.

SECRETARY PERKINS: Does that include such major things as NRA and National Labor Relations Board reorganization—

PRESIDENT ROOSEVELT: Yes, it does.

SECRETARY PERKINS: —about which there have to be a great many happy thoughts from many sources?

PRESIDENT ROOSEVELT: Of course, after the legislation gets into the hands of Congress, there could be modifications of the general plan; but only something that is not of a new nature. We have got to make

---

[2] Roosevelt's expression for departmental programs either for legislation or appropriation or both.

that rule. I have very insistent demand from the leaders of Congress that that rule be put into effect. That means very hard work.

And incidentally, if you expect to get anything in by way of recommendation for the message of January third, or any messages that will follow in pretty short order between the third and the fifteenth of January, you better get them in by Christmas Day, because I cannot undertake to handle brand new things for the third of January if they are presented to me after Christmas Day. There are limits to my ability to write a complete message for Congress in three hours.

Next is the report of the Industrial Emergency Committee . . . . Next is a special report from the executive director on a survey of interdepartmental committees. Get out your charts.

MR. RICHBERG: Mr. President, at the last meeting,[3] the question came up of finding out the number of interdepartmental committees, how many were alive, how many were inactive, and how they were related. The effort to get the information has been a rather staggering one. Up to date, we have found that there are 124 interdepartmental committees, boards and commissions, which have 224 interdepartmental subcommittees, making a total of 348 interdepartmental arrangements. We have prepared some charts simply as an indication of the size and complexity of this problem and for the further handling of it. I will just give an example of one group. Here, in the overlapping of functions, there are 22 functions carried on by 44 interdepartmental committees directly concerned with foreign trade matters. I give just an example of the charting of that particular group.

PRESIDENT ROOSEVELT: Say that again, just as to foreign trade.

MR. RICHBERG: There are 22 functions carried on by 44 interdepartmental committees. Obviously, there is a great deal of overlapping. The foreign trade work is carried on by 27 bureaus of 20 departments and independent establishments. I point this out particularly because it is a good illustration of activities very closely related that should be coordinated and tied together.

In addition to those committees, there are not listed here 12 other committees which have related functions, such as the Central Statistical Board, the Natural Resources Board, and others. That is one group and there are other groups which I will simply point out in passing, such as that concerned with

_____

[3] See proceedings for Nov. 13, p. 341.

the various problems of economic security and another concerned with public works; here is a chart of the agencies concerned with planning in general; here is a group concerned with public health, general administration, and financial problems; here is another group concerned with the subject of procurement. You may even observe by a mere glance the size of that particular group which includes 78 interdepartmental subcommittees, as to which there are possible duplications. When it comes to statistics, there is far from coordination in that work. We have a very large group concerned with transportation problems, and there is another on science advisory problems. It has been actually impossible to chart these in any way that would be fundamentally effective. These groupings are not those which would probably be permanent. The purpose of trying to chart them is to bring forward the absolute necessity of trying to coordinate these committees into certain fundamental groups which could then be created as subcommittees of this Council and then be connected, through the Council, with the general functions of the Administration. A great many of these exist off by themselves at the present time. They are not connected with any particular group. They have no function in connection with any single agency. They do not report anywhere. They have been created to take care of problems, and a great many of them have been forgotten. A great many of them were at work, but the product of the work does not land anywhere. We could go into greater detail with this but I think that may be sufficient.

PRESIDENT ROOSEVELT: The majority of these are inherited. These organizations have been growing up for years and years.

MR. RICHBERG: The great mass of them are very old. Some have been created to meet vital necessities. In order to get at the problem it is suggested that a committee of the Council make a thorough study of this information which we have obtained for the purpose of recommending to the Council necessary reorganization, consolidation, and abolition of committees with a view to preventing overlapping and duplication. In that connection, Mr. President, I make the suggestion that there are primarily concerned here these departments, going through the list: State, Treasury, Agriculture, Interior, Commerce, and Labor. The other four departments are not so frequently involved in these interdepartmental committees; but if you are going to attempt to coordinate these groups I should think very clearly those six departments should be represented upon any committee charged with that object, as they will be constantly working with those six departments. The committee could be organized by including a direct representative such as an assistant secretary.

PRESIDENT ROOSEVELT: In other words, we have three hundred forty-two now and you want the three hundred forty-third?

MR. RICHBERG: Yes, to eliminate the 342! (*Laughter*) One large boa constrictor to swallow all the others!

MR. JONES: How many have been added in this administration?

MR. RICHBERG: I don't know as we have that. There is an enormous amount of confusion because we had committees reporting which other departments denied existed although they were supposed to be on them. My thought, Mr. President, is that if a committee could be created on which I would suggest possibly that somebody from the National Emergency Council— my office—should act as executive head, as we have gathered the material and we can furnish it and save a great deal of labor. This committee could then eliminate a great many simply by saying that their functions had ceased to exist, and could coordinate a great many, and leave some that would be brought back to the Council with the question as to the desirability of continuing them.

PRESIDENT ROOSEVELT: State, Treasury, Agriculture, Interior, Commerce, and Labor then should need an assistant secretary. Why don't you do it this way. Tell them to go ahead and appoint that temporary committee. How long would it take them?

MR. RICHBERG: I would say that considerable progress could be made within a week or ten days if they got down to the task.

SECRETARY ROPER: Why not suggest the individuals right now and make the committee up?

PRESIDENT ROOSEVELT: Bill (*referring to Mr. Phillips*), will you take it yourself? And how about the Treasury?

SECRETARY MORGENTHAU: Mr. McReynolds.

PRESIDENT ROOSEVELT: Agriculture?

DR. TUGWELL: How about Mr. Wilson?

PRESIDENT ROOSEVELT: Interior?

SECRETARY ICKES: Mr. Chapman.

PRESIDENT ROOSEVELT: Commerce?

SECRETARY ROPER: John Dickinson.

PRESIDENT ROOSEVELT: Labor?

SECRETARY PERKINS: McGrady.

PRESIDENT ROOSEVELT: Go ahead with that; and I would suggest that if they can, we have a meeting a week from Monday. A week from Monday is the day before Christmas, isn't it? That's bad. Could you get it in by the twentieth?

MR. RICHBERG: I would like to designate Mr. [Fred] Ironside to act with that committee.

PRESIDENT ROOSEVELT: Do you think you can report on the twentieth, a week from Thursday?

MR. RICHBERG: Yes.

PRESIDENT ROOSEVELT: That would give me a chance to go over it. I would want to talk with a number of the heads of departments about it before final action.

MR. RICHBERG: As to the future, I would like to make a suggestion in this connection, that if any subcommittees of the Council are established, or if they desire to establish an interdepartmental committee, it would be highly desirable to clear the matter first through the Emergency Council to find out if there is a committee in existence that has substantially the same purpose.

MR. PHILLIPS: May we have copies of the charts now?

MR. RICHBERG: We can run off any number of those for the committee. They are all prepared.

PRESIDENT ROOSEVELT: The next recommendation is as to state legislation.

MR. RICHBERG: This is a very brief one, Mr. President; the current reports from the members of the Council indicate, first, that the Federal Housing Administration is planning to obtain necessary revisions to state laws, and that forty-four legislatures meet in January 1935. In order to avoid confusion and see that efforts will not be made at cross purposes, it is suggested that the heads of these agencies, and such other agencies as may desire state legislation, prepare, through the National Emergency Council, a coordinated program of state legislation which, when approved by the President, could be carried forward in the field by the state directors for the Council. In other words, we are facing difficulty in having a great many agencies of the government desire particular bits of state legislation, which is going to be very confusing.

PRESIDENT ROOSEVELT: There again, we have to set a time limit on it. Most of the state legislatures meet in January—from the first of January to the fifteenth. One of them meets in April. If we are going to get any state legislation, it seems that I have to write a letter to the governor of the state; and if any of you need state legislation, please send in your recommendation to Mr. Richberg in order that a proper letter can be written. I have, for example, this morning received from the Federal

Housing Administrator a request for a letter relating to Title II and Title III of the National Housing Act, which is a very excellent suggestion because the earlier we get it to the governor, the quicker he can get it before his legislature. In some cases, it is advisable to get it to the governor before the first of January for his annual message.

There are some things we cannot include, such, for example, as any request for unemployment insurance legislation, because that cannot be sent out until after my message to Congress on that particular subject.

In Jim Moffett's memorandum he gives a list of the forty-four states, and then he says "there is a possibility that there will be a special session of the legislature in Louisiana which Mr. Long may call at any moment."[4] (*Laughter*)

The Executive Director calls our attention to the report of the Secretary of Agriculture with respect to the cotton program for 1935 . . . .

Having been in the South for more than three weeks, it is perfectly clear to me that the present policy of crop control is working, and it will be continued. The opposition comes from people who cannot be blamed for opposing it. The people who are engaged in ginning—the more cotton they gin, the more money they make; the people engaged in transportation of cotton—the bigger the crop, the more they transport, and the more money they make; and the large firms who handle the export of cotton—all of that element—the middle men—the more cotton they handle, the more money they make, and it is perfectly obvious they would like to handle fifteen million bales instead of ten.

Anybody who has been in the South, however, knows that if you can get proper crop limitation of 25 per cent and get a 12¢ crop instead of having an unlimited crop at 5½¢, the result is that the South is more prosperous than it has been any time except in 1917 to 1919, when everything went crazy with 40¢ cotton down there.

I should say that the South has come back faster, economically, than any other part of the country. There is a real reason why the South should come back faster than any other section, and that is because the South is a great deal farther behind in its social development. Education is, from the Northern point of view, antediluvian. They cannot tax themselves to

---

[4] Huey Long, then Senator from Louisiana, controlled the state legislature with unusual "ease."

provide better education. They have had no taxable values. They have had no wealth from which they could provide better education and a real standard of living. The statistics show pretty clearly that 50 years from now the majority of people will be of Southern origin, because they are the only ones now that have large families. The present generation should be able to increase their standard of living so that the second generation from now will be fairly well along in education. It is one of the most important things we have to figure on, nationally, and crop limitation is one of the things which is working.

We should analyze with great care the reasons for the opposition to the present program. It has been suggested that we go ahead on the McNary-Haugen theory,[5] which means unlimited production, the setting of prices, and the dumping of surpluses for whatever they will bring. I am not willing to go along with that program. It is out of the window. There is no use discussing it any further. If we start dumping wheat, cotton, and other agricultural products on the markets of the world, we are doing a disservice to the rest of the world, and the world can always get back at us by declining to receive our dumping. That is perfectly obvious. It would be a bad thing for the world as a whole, too, for the United States to start a national policy of dumping. So that part of the national policy is hereby made extremely simple.

SECRETARY ROPER: I have another point I would like to discuss with you. I think it is quite a serious matter, too. And the idea that you discussed I acknowledge to be mine, which I have reached after very careful consideration and also from the reports which I am getting from various countries of the world. One thing that is certainly disturbing is the way in which cotton is being brought back to this country—from Brazil, especially, because of that plan.

PRESIDENT ROOSEVELT: All these people want to increase our foreign exports. I would like to increase our foreign exports. But the fact is that for a great many years the world has been increasing its production of cotton. Brazil has gone into it very heavily. They are buying cotton machinery from the United States in very

---

[5]The McNary-Haugen bill, passed in 1927, provided for a series of equalization fees to be paid by the growers of certain staple crops to a Federal Farm Board, which was empowered to use this money to dump crop surpluses abroad, to buy and sell agricultural products, and to make crop loans to farm cooperatives. The bill was twice vetoed by President Coolidge.

large amounts every year in order to build cotton mills and produce their own cotton cloth. India, before the war—in 1913 and 1914—was actually producing only five to ten per cent of its cotton cloth; but today India is producing 80 per cent of its cotton cloth. England cannot help that; and if they cannot, we cannot. You may call it a tendency toward nationalism if you like. The nations of Europe which imported most of their wheat and foodstuffs are growing more and more of the foodstuffs, and no policy on our part is going to change that. We might as well look the facts in the face.

SECRETARY ROPER: My thought has been that we could control the acreage; but whatever is produced over and above our needs we might never get out of this country.

PRESIDENT ROOSEVELT: One fellow reduces his acreage and the fellow next door doesn't; he takes his chance for a higher world price. Each farmer is guessing against every other farmer. They have had plenty of warning of this in days past. When prices were down one would say that next year he would not plant so much, and the fellow next door says, I will outsmart my neighbor, and he plants twice as large a crop.

Next is a report from the chairman of the Federal Deposit Insurance Corporation.

MR. RICHBERG: I merely want to call attention to this report without reading it in full. The report points out that the Federal Deposit Insurance Corporation has been able to fulfill its objective of rehabilitating the capital structure of banks in the Federal Reserve System (with the cooperation of the Federal Reserve Board and the Comptroller of the Currency); it has been obliged to rely entirely on cooperation of state agencies in dealing with nonmember banks. As the banking crisis recedes into the past, its moral suasion will be less and less effective. It is therefore urged that the Corporation be given more positive regulatory and supervisory powers....

PRESIDENT ROOSEVELT: Next is the new manual which is to be brought out.

MR. RICHBERG: I thought everybody here would be particularly interested in this information. Based on its practical experience in providing factual information about government activities through 1,794 Information Offices over the country, and to government officials and employees, the National Emergency Council is revamping its loose-leaf manual, effective January first. This "Daily Revised Manual," with which you are probably familiar, covers primarily the emergency agencies. This new manual, which is now in process of preparation, covers the entire field of government activities. It includes, in addition, charts of the agencies of the government and the personnel heading each agency, followed by the purpose, activities, and so on.[6] It has not followed the practice of the previous manual in giving the information in question-and-answer form. The utility of the manual has been well demonstrated the past year. I just want to read from a letter from Judge Payne of the Red Cross: "Over 1,300 Red Cross Chapters have had copies of the 'Daily Revised Manual,' and it has been of very great value." As a matter of fact, we find, through our Information services, a constant reduction in the amount of inquiries which are going to the departments, which embarrass the mail of every department, because of the use of this manual. I think it is more than paying for itself in the saving of labor resulting from this mass of inquiries wrongly directed. These are put into the hands of all without payment by the departments. Of course, we have to pay for it. They are sold outside the government at a cost price, which has been a dollar and a half and maybe two or two and a half dollars for the new manual....

PRESIDENT ROOSEVELT: A great many have availed themselves of it?

MR. RICHBERG: Yes, a great many. It makes it possible to find information.

JUDGE BIGGS: The Chief Justice seemed quite surprised this morning that Executive Orders were not printed.[7]

MR. RICHBERG: The NRA orders are printed by the thousands.

JUDGE BIGGS: But they are not in a volume where you can go and find them.

PRESIDENT ROOSEVELT: The only Executive Orders that are not printed are the Executive Orders that have no reference to private citizens in any way. The others are printed.

JUDGE BIGGS: You have to go to some department and find them there.

SECRETARY PERKINS: They are not in a gazette.

JUDGE BIGGS: The Chief Justice seemed quite surprised that they are not printed; also, the orders of the Interior Department.

PRESIDENT ROOSEVELT: What happens to the Interior Department and Public Works Administrator's orders?[8]

---

[6] The process which we saw begin earlier in this record advances another step toward the *United States Government Organization Manual* as we know it today.

[7] During argument before the Supreme Court on the "Hot Oil Case" (Panama Refining Company v. Ryan, 293 U.S. 389), which took place Dec. 10 and 11, 1934, the issue of the inaccessibility and careless draftsmanship of Executive Orders was raised. See Robert H. Jackson, *The Struggle for Judicial Supremacy* (New York, 1941), pp. 90-91.

[8] Here follows an examination of a problem raised by the growth of administrative rule-making and orders attendant upon the wide discretion given the new administrative agencies.

SECRETARY ICKES: It depends on the nature of the order. We have no such publications as that referred to. We do not publish them in pamphlet or gazette form; but we do mail them and make them public.

PRESIDENT ROOSEVELT: Executive Orders, from time immemorial, probably, have related largely to things like half-holidays, or extending the time of some seventy-year-old employee for another year— trivial things, purely intragovernment, within the government itself. Those have always been kept at the White House and another file at the State Department. The State Department has the originals, and also a file for inspection. The trouble is that in the Interior Department, for example, and in AAA, by Executive Order I delegated the power to issue what are in effect Executive Orders to the Public Works Administrator, to the Oil Administration, and to the Agricultural Adjustment Administration through the Secretary of Agriculture. Now, those are, in effect, delegated Executive Orders. I think some steps should be taken immediately so that those will be available to the public through the regular sources of information.

JUDGE BIGGS: Those are made by your authority. They are really, in effect, Executive Orders.

PRESIDENT ROOSEVELT: What do you think? Would it be possible to have a file of the Public Works orders and AAA orders kept both in the State Department and the White House also?

SECRETARY ICKES: I wonder if we ought not to publish them in pamphlet form, in view of the position of the Supreme Court?

JUDGE BIGGS: The Supreme Court called attention to the fact that they were not attested by the Secretary of State. We had printed them in our brief, and they wanted the attestation of the Secretary of State—these Executive Orders which have the full force of law. Your regulations are issued under Executive Orders.

SECRETARY ICKES: We have never regarded them really as Executive Orders.

PRESIDENT ROOSEVELT: They are Executive Orders, because I definitely, in the Executive Order setting up the Public Works Administration, the Oil Administration, and the AAA, gave authority to issue such orders. Those were the only ones. I didn't do it with NRA.

SECRETARY ICKES: Should they be attested by the Secretary of State?

PRESIDENT ROOSEVELT: That is a legal question.

JUDGE BIGGS: That is what the Court was complaining of—that we are using Executive Orders that have not been attested.

PRESIDENT ROOSEVELT: An Executive Order is not attested by the Secretary of State.

UNDERSECRETARY PHILLIPS: Yes, most of those on file in the State Department

363

are attested by the Secretary of State.

JUDGE BIGGS: There was one which seemed not to have been.

PRESIDENT ROOSEVELT: Aren't you thinking of proclamations?

UNDERSECRETARY PHILLIPS: No, Executive Orders.

JUDGE BIGGS: It doesn't have the Great Seal on it.

MR. RICHBERG: Isn't it a fact that when they are transmitted to the State Department they come to you without any form for attestation?

UNDERSECRETARY PHILLIPS: But they are afterwards attested by the Secretary of State.

SECRETARY MORGENTHAU: The Treasury gets out all kinds of orders which I think would be most helpful for an attorney. There is not a day that the Treasury does not get out a decision on income tax or customs matters.

JUDGE BIGGS: What is the difference between a proclamation and an Executive Order?

PRESIDENT ROOSEVELT: A proclamation gets the Great Seal on it, and I have to authorize a special paper to get the Secretary of State to put the Great Seal on it.

MR. RICHBERG: Wouldn't it be possible, Mr. President, to have the daily grist of these orders accumulated as much as once a week and printed, the whole document being attested by the Secretary of State?

PRESIDENT ROOSEVELT: No.

JUDGE BIGGS: The Executive Order comes to the Department of Justice; we approve of the form, and then we send it to the Secretary of State. If we want a copy of it, we get it from the Secretary's.

PRESIDENT ROOSEVELT: The NRA orders are different. They are in the form of Executive Orders, but they come straight to the White House and go straight back to the NRA from the White House, and never go to the State Department at all.

JUDGE BIGGS: What the Court was complaining about was this; here is a regulation made by the Secretary of the Interior which makes certain acts offenses. It is the law, and yet you cannot find it. You have to search in that office for them. They are not available to the public.

PRESIDENT ROOSEVELT: The answer is perfectly simple, I think. Congress gave certain executive authority to me in a dozen bills. In some of the bills, such as the Triple A, the National Recovery Act, the Oil Act, and the Public Works bill, I was authorized either by Executive Order or through an administrator duly designated to have the authority to issue Executive Orders on my behalf, to carry out these general administrative functions; in other words, different from any previous legislation. I took advantage of that in certain cases. The public was put on notice when I set up the Oil Administration that the Oil Administrator had the authority to issue Executive Orders on my behalf as Administrator. There was public notice given.

JUDGE BIGGS: That was all explained to the Court; but the Court wanted to know where anybody could get those regulations issued by your authority. That is what they seemed to think ought to be done. Those nine men have their own ideas about things, sometimes.

MR. RICHBERG: A very strong case is made, for example, as to all orders the public is expected to obey. We had it up in the NRA at a very early stage. I think we arranged for the publication and printing, widespread, of every order that anyone was expected to obey; and then we put in a clause requiring them to show cause.

JUDGE BIGGS: Could they all be published in volumes, and be available to the public?

PRESIDENT ROOSEVELT: Of course we ought not to put into that the decisions, for instance, of the Treasury Department. That is a different thing. That ought not to be done.

SECRETARY MORGENTHAU: They are all published.

PRESIDENT ROOSEVELT: Instead of appointing another committee, we have a committee— (*President Roosevelt and Mr. Richberg then held a private conversation for a few moments.*)

MR. RICHBERG: We had a committee from the Council prepare a report.

POSTMASTER GENERAL FARLEY: In some way the Secretary of State could send the orders to the nine men of the Supreme Court.

PRESIDENT ROOSEVELT: In other words, you would like to have the Supreme Court put on the mailing list. That will increase your carrying charges.

I will appoint a committee to make a special study of this, consulting with the State Department, the Treasury, the Attorney General, Interior, and Agriculture. Those are the only ones—not the NRA.[9]

Next is Coordination of the Public Works Program, Relief Program, and Housing Program.

I have three things down here. Donald suggested I might outline to you certain policies. We have a great many people working, and no one person knows what the other person is doing, except myself—right here, nowhere else in the government—as to the coordination of the public works program, the relief program, and the housing program, insofar as new legislation

---

[9] The problem discussed in the last few pages was eventually solved by the passage of the Federal Register Act (July 26, 1935). The Division of the Federal Register, therein provided for, was given the duty of publishing all executive orders, proclamations, and similar documents in periodic volumes.

goes; and nobody knows exactly what is going to be done until the third of January. We are seeking to cut down relief in this sense; there are only two schools of thought, one school represented by a number of very worthy persons who believe we should adopt the dole system in this country because it would cost less. We have somewhere around five million people on relief in the United States today, on a subsistence basis; we can save a great deal of money by just giving them cash or market baskets on Saturday night, thereby destroying morale at the saving of a large sum of money. That is out of the window; we are not going to adopt that policy. The policy is going to be to eliminate that form of relief all we possibly can. That means the adoption of the alternative, which is furnishing work instead of the dole. We are working on that at the present time.[10]

As a part of that work program we come to the question of the housing program. The easiest way is to explain it, once more, in words of one syllable. There are in this country about 120,000,000 people. The government is doing something for three groups of that 120,000,000 people in the way of housing. The richest group for whom we are doing something are people who have borrowing capacity. That is to say, they have either jobs with incomes that go with jobs, or at least form a class of sufficient wealth in the community for banks and other lending agencies to lend money to them. For various reasons, banks and other lending agencies have shown a disinclination to come forward as fast as we hoped they would. We, therefore, have tried to stimulate lending by private agencies through the establishment of the Housing Administration. The Housing Administration has made very great progress—excellent progress. It has operated through the system of the guaranteeing of a percentage of the loan; in other words, the insurance method. They have been lending money so far under Title I of the Housing Act to people—I think I am right, Jim and Dan— with average income of about $2,750 a year. In almost every case, those people already have their own homes and they are borrowing money to improve their existing homes. People in

---

[10] This reference to work relief and the subsequent discussion by the President of other policy innovations contemplated is an interesting example of part of the process of internal policy discussion in the Administration. This work relief decision was embodied in the Emergency Relief Act of 1935 adopted by the session of Congress about to convene. The famous Works Progress Administration was set up to administer this Act. Several other pieces of legislation passed in the 1935 session are foreshadowed in this meeting, for example, the Public Utility Holding Company Act.

this country with an average of $2,750 a year income are rich people. They are far above the average in respect to income; and we are doing a fine job for them.

Next come the people a little lower down the scale, but people who still have borrowing capacity—some form of security to offer to private capital. Those are the people who already had their homes or their farms. Bill Myers and John Fahey are looking after their wants. In other words, the Farm Credit Administration is extending government credit or the credit of the federal farm banks or federal home loan banks is being extended to people who already have property. They are extending it in the form of loans or in the form of reduced interest rates on existing mortgages. Those people come into a lower income group in almost all cases than the people who go to Jim Moffett. There may be 10,000,000 men, women, and children who have taken advantage of the Housing Administration; there might be another 10,000,000 people, or possibly 15,000,000—perhaps 20,000,000 people—who would take advantage of the Farm Credit Administration or the Home Owners' Loan organization. That is about 30,000,000 people in this country.

Below them is the largest mass of the American population— people who have not got enough, either in earning capacity or in security in the form of tangibles, to go either to Moffett or Fahey or Myers. Those are the people who are living—most of them—in un-American surroundings and conditions. They cannot be helped by the Housing, the Farm Credit, or the Home Loan; they are too poor. They cannot go to a bank or a building and loan association or to a private money lender and get money to improve their living conditions. The question comes up, are we licked in trying to help them in their living conditions? A good many real estate people consider we are; and they say the government should not help them. We say, "Will private capital help them?" They say, "No, it can't, but we don't want the government to help them." Are we licked in trying to help these people—forty million of them, men, women, and children? Their answer is, "Yes, we are licked; we must not do anything to help them, because we might interfere with private capital." The answer is, "No, we are not licked! We are going to help them!" I am telling you quite a lot about policies; we are going to help those forty million people by giving them better houses—a great many of them, all we possibly can. Hence, there is no conflict whatsoever in the government's

housing program—never was. They fall into entirely different
social groups. The program of building houses has nothing to do
with the Housing Administration, nothing to do with the Farm
Credit, nothing to do with the Home Owners' Loan. It is an
entirely separate proposition and will have entirely separate
handling. And, incidentally, we will kill two birds with one
stone; we are going to provide better housing, and put a lot of
people to work.

I think it is clear to everybody and there will be no further
question about any conflict, because there is no conflict.

Then we come down to another thing—TVA and electric
power. There have been two confusions of thought, perhaps
among some members of the administration and certainly in the
public mind. I will also set it out in words of one syllable. TVA
is not an agency of the government. It was not initiated or
organized for the purpose of selling electricity. That is a side
function. Am I right on that, Arthur [Morgan]?

There is a much bigger situation behind the Tennessee Valley
Authority. If you will read the message on which the legislation
was based you will realize that we are conducting a social
experiment that is the first of its kind in the world, as far as I
know, covering a convenient geographical area—in other words,
the watershed of a great river. The work proceeds along two
lines, both of which are intimately connected—the physical land
and water and soil end of it, and the human side of it. It proceeds
on the assumption that we are going to the highest mountain
peak of the Tennessee Watershed and we are going to take an
acre of land up there and say, "What should this land be used for,
and is it being badly used at the present time?" And a few feet
farther down we are going to come to a shack on the side of
the mountain where there is a white man of about as fine stock
as we have in this country who, with his family of children, is
completely uneducated—never had a chance, never sees twenty-
five or fifty dollars in cash in a year, but just keeps body and
soul together—manages to do that—and is the progenitor of a
large line of children for many generations to come. He certainly
has been forgotten, not by the Administration, but by the
American people. They are going to see that he and his children
have a chance, and they are going to see that the farm he is
using is classified, and if it is not proper for him to farm it, we
are going to give him a chance on better land. If he should use it,
we are going to try to bring him some of the things he needs,
like schools, electric lights, and so on. We are going to try to

prevent soil erosion, and grow trees, and try to bring in industries. It is a tremendous effort with a very great objective. As an incident to that it is necessary to build some dams. And when you build a dam as an incident to this entire program, you get probably a certain amount of water power development out of it. We are going to try to use that water power to its best advantage.

Insofar as competition goes with other companies—private companies—it comes down to a very simple proposition. There has been, again, a confusion of thought. The power people—not the people who are running the operating companies but the people who have cornered the control of those operating companies in large financial groups called holding companies— have been talking about the attack on utility securities. There is a perfectly clear distinction well expressed by an effort made the other day in New York to get the insurance company to join with the holding companies in opposing the government program. I think it was Mr. Ecker of the Metropolitan who, on being asked to join in the attack, was told that the security bonds—the utility bonds—of the Metropolitan would be jeopardized, made the perfectly simple answer that the larger insurance companies, like the savings banks, if you go through their portfolios of securities that make up their resources against policies, those portfolios will show a very large number of utility bonds; but in every case of the larger companies and the savings banks those bonds are bonds of operating companies. In other words, they represent money that was put into the actual development. It is a pretty fair guess that ninety-nine and a half per cent of the bonds of all the operating company utilities in the United States are worth at least a hundred cents on the dollar today. They are absolutely all right. The only utility securities which are all wrong are the securities of holding companies, which securities represent no cash invested in electrical development itself. They represent merely financial transactions, and therefore, it is a perfectly safe position for anybody to take that the government program does not jeopardize in any way the securities of honest operating companies. If every operating utility company was concerned only with making the interest on its bonds and a reasonable profit on its stock, they could reduce their rates per kilowatt hour to the household users of power throughout the United States and survive, making a good living and an honest profit. Those reduced rates would almost immediately stop the rush of

369

municipalities to put in their own plants. It is a perfectly simple proposition. There is hardly a municipality in the United States, where 3¢ power is possible for the existing private companies, that would seek to put in its own municipal plant if they could get 3¢ power. And in most parts of the United States, the private company can give 3¢ power and make a substantial profit on their investment.

DR. MORGAN: May I have a copy of those remarks for my associates?

PRESIDENT ROOSEVELT: The next thing is the question of foreign trade development and consolidation of subcommittees.

MR. RICHBERG: I only wish to make a suggestion that when this committee takes it up, the problem of the Tariff Commission, NRA, and Foreign Trade Advisory matters should be brought into the consolidation of those committees. I was going to suggest that this was the sort of method that this committee will operate on. These problems would be brought in. I use this as an illustration. They are concerned with all these trade committees.

PRESIDENT ROOSEVELT: We are going to try to limit the number of committees.

MR. RICHBERG: Exactly. These three groups are concerned—Tariff Commission, NRA, and Foreign Trade Advisory. They are all concerned in getting proper coordination of foreign trade.

PRESIDENT ROOSEVELT: Do you want this to come in—NRA Reorganization? We have only one thing, I think.

MR. RICHBERG: And that is that it is operating with administrative efficiency quite impressively at the present time; and also that any suggestions as to NRA reorganization should be cleared through the Industrial Emergency Committee which has that problem particularly in charge. A great many have been brought forward by different departments of the government in regard to that problem. They can be cleared promptly through that one agency.

PRESIDENT ROOSEVELT: The next thing is economic security and the labor policy that goes with it, running also with Public Works—that thing you wanted to talk to me about. We shall probably want to get in Mr. Green and one or two others in talking about the Public Works for the following year's program.

SECRETARY PERKINS: I would like to talk to you very seriously about that. The economic security program will be ready to recommend to you in about a week.[11] It was our thought that we would bring it to you for your study and discussion and not give it out until after you had discussed all our suggestions and perhaps made

---

[11] The Social Security legislation that was passed in the ensuing session of Congress (1935) was the outgrowth of this study.

some other revisions; and it has been our effort to bring in with this a works program in connection with the total program. A special subcommittee is working on the problem of works as a form of providing economic security. The two will be integrated in the general report which will not in any way attempt to say what type of works. There are, in the report of natural resources, as well as in the various studies of housing and building programs, a wealth of suggested material as to what type of works could be utilized.

PRESIDENT ROOSEVELT: The next is a very old subject that was referred to subcommittee number 113. I refer to federal incorporations. This is hoary. It must be a year and a half old. It was also referred to the Federal Trade Commission.

MR. RICHBERG: The chairman of that subcommittee is Harold Stephens, I think.

PRESIDENT ROOSEVELT: The matter was also referred to the Federal Trade Commission.

MR. DAVIS: I have one report with me that I wish to deliver on that subject, and we are preparing some more.

PRESIDENT ROOSEVELT: Has Harold Stephens been working with you on this, or are there two separate reports?

MR. DAVIS: This is separate. You see, the Senate Resolution[12] directed the investigation of gas and electric utilities and also directed the study of recommendations with reference to holding companies and other incorporations. These studies have been in connection with that, and a recent compilation has been made of legal expressions upon the subject of federal incorporation for the past twenty years, embracing practically all declaration made in Congress, in National Platforms, by several Presidents, and economists, as well as resolutions adopted by the American Bar Association, National Manufacturers' Association, and others discussing this subject. We have been conducting several studies through our legal staff of different phases of the question.

PRESIDENT ROOSEVELT: You studied the old theory of John Sharp Williams about twenty years ago that the Secretary of State was talking about the other day? It is not a licensing program nor is it federal incorporations, but establishment of certain rules and regulations by law applying to all state corporations doing interstate business, and yet requiring the state corporations by charter to be incor-

---

[12] Senate Resolution 80 (May 29, 1933) directed a survey by the Federal Power Commission of the cost of distributing electric power. At the time of this meeting, both the Senate and the House were conducting studies on utilities. These discussions recorded here are part of the work that led to the introduction of utility regulating legislation at the next session of Congress and the passage of the Utility Holding Company Act of 1935.

porated. Has that been studied too? That is John Sharp Williams' theory.

MR. DAVIS: Of course, federal jurisdiction necessarily relates to interstate business, and various proposals have been advanced, such as compulsory incorporation and a licensing system or permit system.

PRESIDENT ROOSEVELT: What was it the Senate Resolution asked the Federal Trade Commission to do.

MR. DAVIS: Just to study the subject and make recommendations.

PRESIDENT ROOSEVELT: Only on utilities?

MR. DAVIS: Of course, that relates to the subject; but it is a six-year study of the utilities systems and has given a splendid picture of that question. Now, for instance, on the subject of holding companies which you were discussing a while ago, it has been testified in our investigation that there are institutions where as many as twelve holding and subholding companies were superimposed upon one operating company, none of the holding companies having any tangible assets and none of them having any source of income except all of them milking this operating company; and, of course, there are various suggestions made on the subject of holding companies. One is that they not be permitted, for instance, beyond the first degree. Then, that they not be permitted to charge for service, and things of that kind. Of course, at common law, no corporation could hold stock in another corporation, but most of the states have passed acts which permit corporations to hold stocks in other corporations. This system has grown up.

PRESIDENT ROOSEVELT: On that subject, we might as well lay down more Administration policy, without going into the details or methods of attaining that end. As to the origin of the holding companies—the holding company in most cases started in as a management company with the idea of combining a number of operating companies and putting in unified management. The difficulty with that was that the holding company, if it was the management company, owned stock in the operating company and in order to justify the watered stock of the holding company, charged undue management fees. Now there is no reason why management companies as such should not continue to exist, providing they are paid for the service of management only; and provided they do not hold any stock in any of the companies which they manage. That is rule No. 1.

Rule No. 2 relates to so-called investment companies. An investment trust or investment company is an absolutely legitimate device for you or for me who have not got time to study the field of investment to turn over our money to the investment company for that investment company to use our money for the buying or the selling of investments, to buy bonds and stocks, whichever it may be, or both, which in their judgment have value; and if there is appreciation in those bonds and stocks, to sell and make a profit. That is a perfectly legitimate device. By having a large amount to invest, they can more quickly diversify the investment than the individual can with limited capital. In other words, the investment company is a proven, sound thing; but as soon as the investment trust becomes owner of too large a proportion of the incorporation there is immediately a very natural and human tendency to make an effort to manage that corporation and to tell that corporation what to do and what not to do. Number 2 point is that investment companies must have nothing to say about the management of any of the companies in which they are investors. Those two rules could be carried out in national policy, and it would solve half of the financial troubles we have been in the last 25 years.

MR. DAVIS: Right in that connection, I wish to call attention to another phase which has been developed, and that is that almost without exception, the stock of these holding companies which has been placed on the general market and sold to the general public has been nonvoting stock. In other words, the voting stock is controlled stock and has been held by the management. It does not go to the general public, which, of course, is an answer to the argument that we have public ownership and management through the management of stocks.

DR. TUGWELL: That is an example of the lack of coordination. About a year and a half ago there was appointed a committee to study coordination. We have a report, and this seems about the time for it.

PRESIDENT ROOSEVELT: That was a special committee. The resolution had not passed Congress for the Federal Trade Commission, nor had the Department of Justice been asked to make a report on it.

JUDGE BIGGS: When was that request made to us?

MR. RICHBERG: December 13, 1933. That is the one Mr. Tugwell is referring to. The chairman is Harold Stephens, and the other members are Mr. Tugwell and Mr. Means.

PRESIDENT ROOSEVELT: Didn't that committee report a recommendation of no action at that time?

DR. TUGWELL: No, sir; I think that was a private report I made to you. (*Laughter*)

PRESIDENT ROOSEVELT: We didn't seem to have anything practical at that time. Has that committee reported?

DR. TUGWELL: The report has been ready for some time. The report is all done.

MR. MC NINCH: With reference to holding company and power company legislation that the Federal Trade Commission has been working on, I would say that the Power Commission and the National Power Policy Committee[13] have also been working on that.

PRESIDENT ROOSEVELT: I don't think we need a special committee on that. We have got far enough on it so that the Federal Trade and the Power Commission, the Treasury Department, and the Attorney General's Office will be able to clear up the whole thing. "Needs for further coordination." We are doing a lot of coordinating today. Fine! Go ahead!

MR. RICHBERG: There are three suggestions I would like to bring forward; the first is that there should be a definite understanding as to the manner in which departments and agencies seeking legislation will clear their proposal prior to submission to any member of Congress.

PRESIDENT ROOSEVELT: This is tremendously important. Before any department goes up to Congress, we have got to know what they are going to ask of the subcommittees. Last year I was quite horrified—not once, but half a dozen different times—by reading in the paper that some department or agency was after this, that, or the other without my knowledge.

SECRETARY ROPER: We channeled through the Director of the Budget.

PRESIDENT ROOSEVELT: That was for appropriations. That is a different thing. What I am talking about is legislation. In matters relating to appropriations, you cannot go under the wall through a committee of Congress and ask for something different from what has been referred by the Director of the Budget. But coming down to legislation, there has never been any clearing house. That is about the size of it, and I think, in the last analysis, that has got to be tied in and go through the Emergency Council. In other words, before you go up there, if you are going to ask for any legislative action, it has got to come through Donald Richberg and up to me if necessary. In all probability, it will come to me. A very good example of that is the Navy. They had a personnel bill, which very properly the Secretary of the Navy sent to me before

---

[13] Established by President Roosevelt. This commission was headed by Sec. Ickes, and charged with developing a plan for closer cooperation among public and private interests, whereby national policy in power matters might be unified and electricity be made more broadly available at cheaper rates to industry, agriculture, and domestic users.

he went up and asked for this personnel bill on the Hill. Luckily, he did, because the personnel bill as submitted to him by the Department called for two or three hundred Admirals of Fleet and four or five hundred full Admirals, and Rear Admirals, so that everybody would have been an Admiral. We made very short shrift of that, because that comes up every year from the officer of personnel in the Navy. We always step on it. That is just an illustration of the necessity of clearing through the Emergency Council first.[14]

ASSISTANT SECRETARY ROOSEVELT: We didn't get the Admirals! (*Laughter*)

SECRETARY PERKINS: The difficult problem is that bills are introduced into Congress by any congressman, and he then requests the appearance of the head of the Department to give his views on a particular bill. When the thirty-hour bill is introduced by Mr. Connery, he will certainly desire to know the opinion of the Department of Labor, and I shall postpone appearance just as long as I can. I shall be very busy.

PRESIDENT ROOSEVELT: And before you appear, come and talk to Papa.

SECRETARY PERKINS: But there comes a terrible moment. Do you see?

PRESIDENT ROOSEVELT: Yes.

SECRETARY PERKINS: One is likely to be called on any time. It is very difficult.

PRESIDENT ROOSEVELT: You have to use discretion. When you are asked a snap question, you answer with snap judgment at your own peril. The answer may be wrong. I may have to come out and reverse the position. So it is a great deal safer to find out first. It is a great deal easier to say, "I cannot answer that at the present time."

SECRETARY MORGENTHAU: One Department should not lobby against another, as it happened last year.

PRESIDENT ROOSEVELT: Were there any such cases?

VOICE: Yes, sir!

ANOTHER VOICE: *Yes, sir!*

ANOTHER VOICE: YES, SIR! (*Laughter*)

A MEMBER: It seems to be unanimous.

PRESIDENT ROOSEVELT: I wonder if we can lay down a rule. Put that on the agenda for next time.

MR. RICHBERG: There is one matter which is very complicated which I would like to bring out here. We have had a very elaborate study which means weeks of work through a committee representing different departments and agencies in an endeavor to get some coordination in legal activities of the government. There is

---

[14] For an excellent history of the clearance of legislation, see Richard Neustadt, "Presidency and Legislation: The Growth of Central Clearance," *American Political Science Review* Vol. XLVIII, No. 3 (Sept. 1954), 641. Neustadt quotes the transcript of this NEC meeting.

375

widespread overlapping and duplication to an extreme extent in the legal divisions and staffs. It has reached the stage where it seems to me it is vitally necessary to get definite organization of a committee headed by a representative of the Attorney General for the purpose of bringing about an elimination of these duplications and use of material.[15] As a matter of fact, one Department studies all over again the same thing another department has got out on that same line. There is no basis of exchange of information, no coordination of the work; and unless that problem is ironed out, we have a great deal of unnecessary duplication. We have a great many suggestions in this preliminary report, which was the work largely of a sort of voluntary committee. I think it ought to be organized directly under the Council. My suggestion is that such a committee be appointed, consisting of a representative of the legal staff of each department and agency and headed by a representative of the Attorney General's office to try to bring about a utilization of this study that has already been made.

PRESIDENT ROOSEVELT: Do you need any more committees studying it?

MR. RICHBERG: It needs this: a basis for developing policy. I think that group could get together. It involves the question of publication, also. Different departments pay different prices. They do not exchange information. They arrive at opposite opinions.

JUDGE BIGGS: Our department has been working on that subject for some time.

PRESIDENT ROOSEVELT: That makes committee number 344!

MR. RICHBERG: This is another committee to eliminate committees!

MR. DAVIS: Wasn't there a committee appointed on that?

MR. RICHBERG: A committee has been working on it, but it has not been officially settled.

PRESIDENT ROOSEVELT: If there is no objection, go ahead and get that going and try to get a report on it early in January, so that I can make a report. I would like to make a report to the Congress on that simplification. You know the tendency to have an independent legal staff in every department. The history is that about every twenty years, our federal and state governments get busy and eliminate a large number of these independent legal staffs with the rather definite objective of concentrating them in the Department of Justice, or whatever it happens to be. About every twenty years you clean house and get rid of a lot of supernumerary lawyers and problems of legal work. I think the twentieth year has come.

---

[15] See Ickes' reaction, quoted in the Introduction, p. xxii; see also *The Secret Diary of Harold L. Ickes* (New York, 1954), Vol. I, p. 243.

MR. RICHBERG: One suggestion that does not require a committee, if it is approved of, is with reference to the Central Statistical Board which exists sort of off by itself.[16] My suggestion is that that should be related directly to the National Emergency Council by having the Economic Adviser of the Council act as chairman of that Board.

PRESIDENT ROOSEVELT: I thought he was.

MR. RICHBERG: It is a peculiar relationship. Mr. Riefler, as a matter of fact, is supplied by the Federal Reserve Board, and if he is going to continue as Economic Adviser, he should be paid through the Council.

PRESIDENT ROOSEVELT: Is he paid by the Federal Reserve Board?

MR. RICHBERG: Mr. Eccles presented a memorandum asking why they should pay for a man whose services they do not have.

MEMBER: He is worth paying!

PRESIDENT ROOSEVELT: Is it a question of Civil Service status or anything like that?

MR. RIEFLER: I have none.

PRESIDENT ROOSEVELT: That is unfortunate.

MR. RICHBERG: The Central Statistical Board, of course, is not set up under Executive Order, and if it is made permanent I think the salary ought to come on that budget. That would be the simplest way.

PRESIDENT ROOSEVELT: In other words, you come along with the plan of making it a permanent part of the Emergency Council?

MR. RICHBERG: My point is that instead of creating another independent agency, this should be tied in and then it can be called the Statistical Board of the National Emergency Council.

MR. BELL: We can budget it that way.

PRESIDENT ROOSEVELT: That will relieve the Federal Reserve Board.

MR. ECCLES: We wanted Mr. Riefler back; but inasmuch as they are not going to let us have him back, we expect somebody else to pay for him.

PRESIDENT ROOSEVELT: We cannot let you have him back. We like him too much.

SECRETARY PERKINS: Everybody on the board is a working member of the staff of another department and it is highly desirable that that sort of relation should exist. It is one of the few successful pieces of coordination. At the outset it was regarded as very desirable, not only because of his personal qualifications but because of his direct connection with the Federal Reserve, that he head this Board.

MR. RICHBERG: There is no thought of changing that relationship of the board,

---

[16] Organized Aug. 9, 1933, under the authority of the NIRA, to plan and promote improvement, development, and coordination of federal and other statistical services.

but this work requires a staffing, and that has to be budgeted somewhere. With the Central Statistical Board under the Economic Adviser of the Council and under the Council budget, we could have direct exercise and responsibility, which we have not at the present time. It is off by itself at present. That is my suggestion.

PRESIDENT ROOSEVELT: The chorus of approval which met the broad suggestion of the Secretary of the Treasury that no department or agency should go up to the Hill and advocate the things which step on the toes of other departments shows there is a need of saying something about that general situation. Of course that is perfectly true and goes back to something that has been growing for the past six months or a year. And that is the failure of members of the government to mind their own business, to put it roughly; but it is true. You are, all of you, when you receive the press, at a distinct disadvantage; and only a very small percentage of the heads of departments and the heads of agencies know how to handle the press. It is a special art all by itself. They have been doing it all their lives. They have got you at a disadvantage when they start a press conference. Unless you have years of experience in handling it, you will fall into the traps that they set for you. There are certain rules in handling the press which I will just give you out of a very wide experience.

If some reporter says to you, "Mr. so-and-so makes such and such a remark (referring to somebody in another department); what do you think of it?", the practice has been to comment upon it in the past, in altogether too many instances. There is a definite reason why you should not, and a definite rule not to comment on it at all. In the first place, it catches you cold; you haven't studied it. In the second place, the quotation that is made to you by this member of the press is so phrased, in many cases, as not to represent what the other department actually said. There are many phases of those questions, many trick ways of putting things. Just for example, last Friday one of the members of the press said, "Mr. President, what have you got today about the speech made by the American Ambassador in England, in which he advocated and suggested a much closer working relationship between Great Britain and the United States?" Obviously, he was trying to get me to say, "Why, I am, of course, in favor of close relationship between Great Britain and the United States." If I had said that at that time, it would have been expressed the next morning that the President advocates a working alliance between the United States and Great Britain. In the middle of the Naval Conference, both Great Britain and the United States having some trouble with Japan, it would have become a sensational story—an Anglo-American Alliance against Japan. On the other hand, if I had said, "I have no comment to make on the speech of the American Ambassador," there would have been a headline intimating that the President had dissented with the remarks of the American Ambassador. Either way I answered that question, I would have been in wrong. I said to the young man, "I have not read the speech of the American Ambassador; I cannot answer any quotation from it which you give from memory, and there is therefore no comment upon it." I did not know what he was trying to do. As a matter of fact, I had read the speech, but I could not remember, snap judgment like that, as to whether this young man was quoting the American Ambassador correctly or not.

Remember always that you are at a disadvantage when the press is talking to you, and remember that when they ask you if what you are doing has some relationship to another department, that it is none of your business without coming to headquarters first to find out. They will say to you, "Such and such a commission or such and such an agency has made such and such a recommendation which seems to affect your department." The answer is, you have nothing to say because you do not know what the recommendation has been; you would like to study it first. The general rule is much the simplest, and that is not to comment about what any of your colleagues are doing. Stick to your own last. If you find that something your colleague is doing is actually affecting your department, the Emergency Council and the President are obviously the people to come to to straighten the matter out.

There has been always a great deal of loose talk in Washington. I have met it for years. Remember that when you go out to dinner, the lady that you are sitting next to is probably a sieve to one to three or more members of the press. Remember everything that you say as head of a department at a dinner or a dance or a night club will, ten to one, get to the press inside of twelve hours. How does Drew Pearson live, at one extreme; how does Arthur Krock live, at the other extreme? By the gossip that he picks up in Washington. Some of it is gossip that originates from this group right here. And it was spread either by amiable people who are friends of the Drew Pearsons and

Arthur Krocks, or it is paid for by them. There are a large number of people, many of them your close friends, many of them my close friends, who actually get paid for giving information to the public press. I am sorry to have to say that. But I know the names of a dozen people who are getting paid for nice, juicy information. You would be surprised if I told you their names.

There is probably no place in the world where the press has closer access to the government than in the city of Washington. We attempt in no way to interfere with the freedom of the press, and at the same time everybody knows that talk outside of the official family is going to be published; and everything you tell a member of Congress is going to be published. There has never been such a thing in the last 50 years as an executive session of the Senate of the United States which is supposed to take up absolutely confidential matters of great public purport so important and so secret that they clear the galleries and put everybody out—I say there has never been an executive session that was not fully public property of the press within half an hour. It is an unfortunate commentary on the Legislative branch. I do not want the Executive branch to have that reputation, but today it has that same reputation. I think the time has come to turn the corner. If anything comes up that affects any other department outside of your own, do not answer it. If your toes are being stepped on, come and tell me. I think that covers it.

Now, before we adjourn, two weeks from today is Christmas Day. We won't meet that day, When do you want another meeting? How about the end of next week—how would it do to have a meeting on Friday the twenty-first, and then we can adjourn over to the day after New Year's, Wednesday?

SECRETARY MORGENTHAU: Let's not meet on Friday when so many will be wanting to get away for Christmas.

SECRETARY PERKINS: The four o'clock train is good enough.

SECRETARY MORGENTHAU: But not on the Friday before Christmas.

PRESIDENT ROOSEVELT: At the request of the Secretary of the Treasury, we will make it Thursday the twentieth.

Meeting adjourned at 4:10 p.m.

Held in the Cabinet Room of the White House,
Thursday, December 20, 1934, at 2:15 p.m.

___

Present: the President of the United States; the Secretary of State;
the Secretary of the Treasury; the Secretary of War; the Attorney General;
the Secretary of the Navy; the Secretary of Agriculture; the Secretary
of Commerce; the Honorable L. W. Robert, Jr., Assistant Secretary of
the Treasury; the Honorable A. J. Altmeyer, Assistant Secretary of
Labor; the Honorable Harllee Branch, Second Assistant Postmaster
General; the Administrator of Agricultural Adjustment; the Administrator
of Federal Emergency Relief; the Chairman of the Board of the Tennessee
Valley Authority; the Chairman of the Federal Home Loan Bank Board;
the Director of Emergency Conservation Work; the Governor of the
Farm Credit Administration; the Chairman of the Federal Alcohol Control
Administration; the Chairman of the Federal Housing Administration;
the President of the Export-Import Banks of Washington, D.C.; the
Chairman of the Federal Deposit Insurance Corporation; the Chairman
of the Federal Power Commission; the Chairman of the Federal Communi-
cations Commission; the Chairman of the Securities and Exchange
Commission; the Governor of the Federal Reserve Board; the Honorable
Willard L. Thorp, Chief, Consumers' Division, National Emergency
Council; the Honorable Leon C. Marshall, Executive Secretary of the
National Industrial Recovery Board; the Economic Adviser; the
Executive Director.

___

[The NEC is here seen effectively at work on a variety of
matters, but at a rather low level of policy importance. The
housekeeping problems of hiring personnel are dealt with
efficiently. In general, at least part of the spirit of the early
meetings seems to have been recaptured. Donald Richberg,
the executive secretary, seems in the last meeting and this
to have pushed reports to completion and adoption.
Also, in the last meeting, and this, we note the presence of
considerably more department and agency heads and fewer
deputies. The change may be traceable to embarrassment
at the low point (underscored by the President) to which
attendance of top administrators had fallen since the November 13 meeting. Inevitably, there is some correlation between
the significance and fruitfulness of the discussions and
the presence of persons with sufficient stature in their respective organizations to speak with authority on matters of
concern to their programs.—Editors' Note.]

PRESIDENT ROOSEVELT: We have lost a member of the Council—Mrs. Rumsey. You
have read about her death. Donald has sent a little letter on
behalf of the Council.

381

The first report is that of a subcommittee, the Interdepartmental Loan Committee . . . .

"Report of the Industrial Emergency Committee." . . . Is there any comment on those recommendations?

MR. RICHBERG: They all aim simply to coordinate the committees through the proper channels.

PRESIDENT ROOSEVELT: There is only one section that you have not put in, and that is this: While the responsibility lies with the heads of departments and agencies for the establishment, proper functioning, and timely abolishment of these committees, unless we have some periodic checkup, we won't know whether they have been abolished or not.

MR. RICHBERG: I think as they are reporting through the Emergency Council meetings, it ought to be our function to check up on them.

PRESIDENT ROOSEVELT: Yes, every two or three months check over the list. This shows the abolition of 32 committees and that they have all been asked to justify their existence; and if they cannot do that, they will be abolished. So if you carry that out, I think you can probably abolish about 32. At least, it will be a step in the right direction. It retains 50 committees. It is a good step.

MR. RICHBERG: A great many of them have very definite functions.

PRESIDENT ROOSEVELT: Anybody want to say anything more about that? If not, I take it we can adopt it as the procedure and policy. "Special Reports, Executive Director." The digest of reports has been delivered to members prior to the meeting. Did I get mine? I hope everybody will be able to report that they have read the regular digest of reports that went out ten days ago. I shall begin quizzing you next time, so you better read the report that has been delivered to you.

SECRETARY SWANSON: It is a good report.

MR. MC NINCH: This report didn't come out ten days ago.

PRESIDENT ROOSEVELT: No.

MR. MC NINCH: This one I got at 11 o'clock.

PRESIDENT ROOSEVELT: "Procedure for reorganization of Council Reports." . . .

MR. RICHBERG: This is merely in the form of a suggestion so that there will be no misunderstanding when our representative calls for the purpose of seeing how far we can make the reports consistent. We have prepared here, for instance, some charts which indicate some of the possibilities of presenting biweekly a set of charts which will really give a draft of the various activities, so that the President may have before him something in the way of a vivid picture of change every two weeks. In order to do that, we need some consultation and consistency in the type of reports that are made, and for that purpose, I want to suggest that we undertake the job at the present time. If everybody understands it, there will be no misunderstanding when a representative of the Executive Director wants to discuss with whoever prepares the report the matter of getting it in shape.

PRESIDENT ROOSEVELT: That is a very clear picture of some of the things that we had in the regular biweekly reports. For instance, the last two graphs down here: The first graph shows progress of allotments by the Public Works Administration on federal projects—how fast that money is going out; and then on the other side is the Public Works Administration allotments on nonfederal projects. Obviously, that is not any good unless you have a second line. The first line shows the allotments, but that does not mean that the job is actually started. Your second line shows contracts awarded and day labor started—the actual progress of some of these government jobs. The third line shows the expenditures, the money that has actually been withdrawn from the Treasury for this work—something you (*Secretary Morgenthau, I think the President was looking at*) have been talking about so much. The second chart in the same way breaks down the allotments on nonfederal projects, the second line the municipalities, cities, and so forth; then contracts awarded, day labor started; and third, the expenditures of the Treasury. This proves what I said a month or six weeks ago, that we cannot use as the criterion the mere allotment of money to jobs, for it does not mean it has been spent, nor can we go to the other extreme and merely use the amount that has been taken out of the Treasury. Somewhere in between those is the amount of actual day labor that is at work on the projects, and this middle line shows it.

The same thing applies on the next graph up here—the reconditioning loans of the Home Owners' Loan Corporation. That shows a constantly rising line of contracts actually executed. The next one is the modernization loans of the Federal Housing Administration showing insured loans reported and the federal liability for insurance. The next one is the loans and discounts of Home Loan Banks insurable by the Federal Housing Administration under Title II. We put that in because there is no line under it yet. It will be in operation very shortly, won't it, Jim?

MR. MOFFETT: We have made commitments on a lot of insurance, but the institutions are slow.

PRESIDENT ROOSEVELT: Then above that is the Home Owners' Loan Corporation

383

applications received, applications approved, and loans actually closed. Some are with the Federal Land Banks and the Land Bank Commissioner; and above it is shown the trend of foreclosures in industrial states and the trend of foreclosures in agricultural states—showing that the trend of foreclosures in industrial states is not decreasing, but in agricultural states it is declining. There are a good many other graphs that could be given.

MR. RICHBERG: This is to show what we are working for.

SECRETARY DERN: That will be sent to each department, will it?

MR. RICHBERG: Yes, when we get the proper graphs worked out.

PRESIDENT ROOSEVELT: The executive director wanted to say something about the problem of one job per family.

MR. RICHBERG: Mr. President, there has been some correspondence on this subject with the various departments, and the matter has finally come down to this: It has been suggested that the Council adopt a policy with respect to limiting future appointments in the government service on the basis of one job per family . . . . I believe it was your suggestion, Mr. Attorney General, that rather than attempt to govern it in any formal way we should attempt to limit, so far as possible, the employment of more than one member of a family in government service.

PRESIDENT ROOSEVELT: In other words, we are not trying to legislate on it. We are not trying to disrupt Civil Service legislation; but I think we better just have a gentleman's agreement, everybody here, that when any agency of the government employs any new person in a non-Civil Service job, as a general rule—not always, of course— you should not employ a person who already has a member of his family or her family in a government job.

SECRETARY MORGENTHAU: That is new jobs.

PRESIDENT ROOSEVELT: Yes, new jobs. Do not make it retroactive—do not throw anybody out.

SECRETARY ROPER: How shall we find that out?

PRESIDENT ROOSEVELT: Ask the individuals.

SECRETARY SWANSON: How close do you want the relationship?

PRESIDENT ROOSEVELT: The simplest thing I know is this: occupying a house under the same roof. That practically is the answer to it.

DR. MORGAN: We have gone further than that and provided that no person shall be working under a relative to the third degree.

PRESIDENT ROOSEVELT: That is a good thing, too. This cuts out man and wife; it cuts out any member of the family living under the same roof. It does not cut out father and son if they have separate establishments. Living under the same roof is really the criterion.

384

SECRETARY SWANSON: That is the only way.

MEMBER: Does that apply to those under Civil Service?

PRESIDENT ROOSEVELT: No, if it is planned to fill a Civil Service job, under certificate from the Civil Service Commission, I don't think you can apply the rule. There is nothing in the law that allows it.

SECRETARY ROPER: Suppose the application is made for a non-Civil Service position; shall we inquire as to whether there is a member of the family in the service?

PRESIDENT ROOSEVELT: Yes.

SECRETARY SWANSON: Suppose they tell us that one member of the family has lost his job and they are in danger of losing their home. Any exception in that kind of cases?

PRESIDENT ROOSEVELT: Carry out the rule just as far as you possibly can. In other words, I'll tell you what it comes down to. If you have a family that has no income at all and another family that has got a home with two people in government employ, keeping the payments up, I would rather, as between the two, take care of the fellow who hasn't any home at all.

SECRETARY SWANSON: We have a vacancy in the Civil Service and three names to select from. Do you want the same rule to apply?

PRESIDENT ROOSEVELT: Yes, other things being equal.

ATTORNEY GENERAL CUMMINGS: This applies only to the future. We are not dealing with the past.

PRESIDENT ROOSEVELT: And if you come down to investigating the actual case you may find, as I have in many of them, two people at work for the government, and they come in and say, "We both have to work or we will lose our home;" but if you get down to an intimate examination of the case you will find that they won't lose their home. It is much more convenient, of course, but they can get by, in nine cases out of ten.

SECRETARY ROPER: Isn't there an application to be made here to the relief program along that line, Mr. President?

PRESIDENT ROOSEVELT: Yes.

SECRETARY ROPER: That might be the same proposition.

PRESIDENT ROOSEVELT: I think probably in 85 per cent of the cases in regard to the people on relief we do live up to this rule.

SECRETARY ROPER: It is very important to be sure that that is the case.

PRESIDENT ROOSEVELT: We sometimes find two people from the same family, but it is against the rules and it is a case of chiseling.
"Hiring personnel away from agencies."

MR. RICHBERG: This is merely calling attention to the fact, Mr. President, that on February 19, 1934, the Director of the Budget addressed a memorandum to the heads of all executive departments, independent establishments, and emergency agencies, reading as follows:

385

new deal mosaic

The President has requested me to inform you that it is his desire that no contacts or negotiations be made by officers or representatives of one department or agency with employees of another department or agency with a view to securing the services of such employees before approval is given to such contacts and negotiations by the heads of the organizations concerned . . . .

As there have been various complaints from time to time, Mr. President, it seemed to be desirable to recall attention to this and mention the fact that it is not being carried out.

PRESIDENT ROOSEVELT: We have talked about this on previous occasions. I appreciate the fact that none of us in this room actually does the hiring; nevertheless, everyone of us in this room is responsible for the actions of our personnel officer or chief clerk, the people who do the hiring, and it requires a very, very firm hand on your part over your personnel officers and over your chief clerks to see that this rule is lived up to. Things are a little better, but it is still being observed in the breach. So, please hereafter get hold of your personnel officer and your chief clerk and read them the riot act and tell them if any new case comes up you are going to get a new personnel officer!

ATTORNEY GENERAL CUMMINGS: May I have a word at that point? I think we suffer as much from that as any department.

PRESIDENT ROOSEVELT: Are they robbing you?

ATTORNEY GENERAL CUMMINGS: Yes, and especially the Division of Investigation; and this is what happens. A man comes along in our Division and resigns. He is going to quit. Of course he quits, and nothing happens for 30 days, and then we find another department has him. So it is not a case of hiring them away from us, but by using this device of resignation and then having the thing all fixed so that he knows he is going to be reemployed, they get the desired results.

PRESIDENT ROOSEVELT: I would suggest the next time that happens that you put your J. Edgar Hoover on the case and find out if there was any collusion in it; and if there was, we will fire the personnel clerk or the chief clerk; and Hoover is a good man to do that investigating.

ATTORNEY GENERAL CUMMINGS: He is the one that is groaning about it now. He could give a list of them any time.

PRESIDENT ROOSEVELT: That is just a subterfuge.

ATTORNEY GENERAL CUMMINGS: Yes, just a subterfuge.

PRESIDENT ROOSEVELT: "Directing attention to the report of the Secretary of Agriculture concerning supply and demand relationships in an industrial program." . . .

MR. RICHBERG: I wish to summarize briefly the report of the Secretary of Agriculture, which seems to be one of considerable interest . . .

PRESIDENT ROOSEVELT: I wish you would read this report from the Secretary of Agriculture. It is an extremely interesting thing. A man who came back from France the other day says that over there they make what they call a cheap car—a couple of cheap cars. They sell for $1,600 apiece, the cheapest ones they sell over there. The output, of course, is almost negligible. Gasoline is 60 cents a gallon in France. Instead of there being a car for every five or six people, they have one car for every 200 people. There is no question about it that increased production of automobiles is resulting. I do not know that I have ever heard anybody compare hogs to automobiles before, but it is very interesting and we thought it was worth pursuing.

SECRETARY WALLACE: The automobile manufacturers will say at once that their margin is only perhaps a hundred dollars and that this would suck up their entire margin; but taking into account the reduction in overhead the loss might only be $50.

PRESIDENT ROOSEVELT: I think you better see if you cannot knock off $50 and see what happens.

SECRETARY WALLACE: Some of them would say they could and others wouldn't. We could use this specific illustration.

PRESIDENT ROOSEVELT: Of course, certain industries have gone on the exactly opposite theory. Take the steel industry. They have held up the price even during the depression, in spite of many urgings. And the very first opportunity that came, six or eight months ago, they started to raise the prices, already up to a high level.

SECRETARY WALLACE: Suppose the automobile people should say to the steel people, "We are going to be able to buy so much more stuff; how much of a cut will you make?"

PRESIDENT ROOSEVELT: The automobile people did say that to the steel people, and the steel people said, "No."

MR. RICHBERG: They forced a certain reduction because of coordinated purchasing power; but there were very few that had that power.

That fits in, Mr. President, with the next item here concerning proposed hearings which the National Industrial Recovery Board[1] was planning to hold. I think it is quite important to have it generally understood. The Chairman of the National Industrial Recovery Board reports the following information with respect to policies: . . .

[On a question of general policies of NRA, our study of what should be modified and what should be confirmed has progressed to the point where

---

[1] This Board took over the functions of the Administrator of Industrial Recovery upon Johnson's resignation.

387

we have adopted a definite plan for carrying this work through to finality. The plan involves a series of public hearings at which there shall be (a) consideration of proposed modifications or confirmations of policy on major problems now confronting the Administration, such proposals to be announced in each case prior to the hearing scheduled for consideration of the particular policy; (b) presentation of an analysis of the experience of the Recovery Administration with respect to the particular subject thus scheduled for hearing; and (c) an opportunity for presentation of relevant facts, analyses and suggestions by industry and other interested parties.

The first of these hearings is called for January 9, 1935, on the subject of price-fixing.]

PRESIDENT ROOSEVELT:	Price-fixing—What about Clay [Williams]?
MR. RICHBERG:	He is out of town. Mr. Marshall is here.
PRESIDENT ROOSEVELT:	How are you going to run these hearings?
MR. MARSHALL:	We are going to send notice to all the code authorities involved, and that means to all of them, so that they can come down and present facts and data bearing on the situation.
PRESIDENT ROOSEVELT:	This will not be a general discussion?
MR. MARSHALL:	No; but all interested parties may present their data.
PRESIDENT ROOSEVELT:	Limiting the time?
MR. MARSHALL:	Yes, driving the thing through as much as may be, and yet there will be no discussion at that time of the amendment of any particular code. The procedure that will be followed with respect to the change of any particular code will be determined after we see the outcome of these hearings and the general feeling. It is contemplated that due notice will be given to everybody to bring the policy determination that is arrived at as a result of these hearings into actual operation.
PRESIDENT ROOSEVELT:	How long will this run? I am thinking of the recommendations to Congress. I cannot put the recommendation off much beyond the twentieth of January. Can you have the policy recommendation ready for me by the twentieth?
MR. MARSHALL:	We can have the policy recommendation before the twentieth on all of these. We shall be able to give you our judgment before that time. I think we might be able to get the hearings moved off at the rate of about one a week. There are four or five hearings. Much depends on the result of our first hearing.
PRESIDENT ROOSEVELT:	It won't mitigate against the recommendations of Congress?
MR. MARSHALL:	Not the slightest. These hearings are in the orderly process of the administration of the codes.
MR. RICHBERG:	That is substantially the report.
PRESIDENT ROOSEVELT:	Next is the Secretary of War reporting on the CCC.
MR. RICHBERG:	This raises a specific question that it seems proper to bring forward . . . .

[Under the law, the Civilian Conservation Corps terminates on March 31, 1935. Due to the fact that this organization has demonstrated its worth as a great moral, social, and economic agency, it is reasonable to suppose that Congress will authorize its continuance. Meantime, the Quartermaster Corps is embarrassed by its inability to proceed with the procurement of supplies for the new enrollment. To secure such supplies, amounting to $19,000,000 under orderly procedure of public advertising, followed by an allowance of time for the manufacture of goods not on the market, properly requires about four months. It could hardly be expected that Congressional action will be sufficiently expeditious to enable the Army to procure the necessary supplies without delaying the re-enrollment.]

PRESIDENT ROOSEVELT: Can you do it? How can I give you money I haven't got but expect to get?

MR. FECHNER: How did that come to you? This is a report from the Secretary of War. There is a memorandum on your desk, Mr. President, which I sent over last week on that.

PRESIDENT ROOSEVELT: What did it say?

MR. FECHNER: That if you will authorize it, we have $15,000,000 we can use from funds in hand to buy these materials that will be needed after April first if the work goes on; and a great deal of it will be of such a character that the regular Army could use it if by any chance the CCC work stops March thirty-first, so that there would not be any loss involved. I did not feel I had any authority to authorize the use of this money that is appropriated for current needs in anticipation of what might be needed for next April first.

PRESIDENT ROOSEVELT: I do not want to take away $15,000,000 out of your current fund and not have it replaced by Congress in the next appropriation.

MR. FECHNER: This $15,000,000 is the amount we have set aside for winding up the CCC whenever it stops, so that it won't embarrass us at all.

PRESIDENT ROOSEVELT: Where is the Director of the Budget?

MR. FECHNER: I talked to Mr. Bell about it, and he is willing to have the money used that way.

PRESIDENT ROOSEVELT: Why don't you get the Quartermaster General and Mr. Bell together up to the Hill and speak to the two chairmen about it and tell them that the recommendation is going to Congress for a continuation of the CCC camps, and ask them if they are entirely willing to have this $15,000,000 used that way? Get them to say "Fine! And we will reappropriate it out of the next appropriation!" In other words, I don't want to have it taken out of, let us say, the $300,000,000 we asked for next year.

SECRETARY DERN: That $15,000,000 was not set aside by Congress.

PRESIDENT ROOSEVELT: I know it, but all the same I think you better tell them about it.

MR. FECHNER: I will be glad to do that.

new deal mosaic

PRESIDENT ROOSEVELT: Then you will be ready to go ahead; but if the CCC does not go on that is very fair to the Army because they turned over to you all their old equipment! (*Laughter*)

SECRETARY DERN: They did not get any second-hand equipment from us.

MR. RICHBERG: The problem is this. This affects not only these two agencies but other emergency agencies being carried on by PWA allotments. In other words, if the present act is not extended in some form, you will have a different type of dealing in this whole program.

SECRETARY HULL: That is very interesting.

MR. RICHBERG: It is very vital to a great many agencies. This was brought up in the discussion of the Industrial Emergency Committee,[2] whether it was desirable to extend Title I or attempt a separate piece of legislation. We immediately ran into the PWA problem and the other problems also.

PRESIDENT ROOSEVELT: This also involves, of course, the form in which the Budget will go out, and that has got to be decided upon by the twenty-sixth of this month, because that is about the last date on which we can print the budget. We are going to have a meeting with the Director of the Budget and the Treasury on the twenty-sixth, and I think this is a matter that is really dependent on the form in which the Budget goes up. We may ask for one or two major items or we may segregate them into half a dozen different items; so if you can be there on the twenty-sixth also, Don. Probably the legislation will closely follow the budget recommendations.

  "Policy as to Wage Rates for Public Projects and Relief Work." Have you anything on that? Just for your information—and it should not go outside of this room—the question has been raised, if we go in for direct employment of a very large number of persons on public works, what kind of pay should we give them? We have had three forms of relief running in the past year or year and a half. The first form has been the dole; in other words, cash payment or the grocery store order. There have been two forms of work relief, one roughly known as work relief under the Relief Administration. In the majority of cases we have paid the full labor price in the vicinity—in many cases a good deal more than labor was getting—and we have employed the people two days or three days a week. The projects have not been permanent or valuable projects in a great many cases. It has been a case of the locality scratching its head

---

[2] This Committee was set up in June of 1934, and was merged with NEC at the end of October of the same year.

to find something to give these men to do. I call it cutting grass on the highway. Those men get $3.00 a day and they are employed two or three days a week. The work is not particularly useful, and the amount they get at the end of the week runs from $6.00 to $9.00 a family. If we give up that form of civil works and put these men on five days a week on useful projects, we are confronted with the question of how much to pay them in case they belong above the common labor classification. We have the utmost sympathy for the building trades. A lot of building trades people today are on relief. Although they may be carpenters or bricklayers or plumbers they may be getting work cutting grass on the highway. If we put them on useful permanent public work such as rural rehabilitation or building waterways—work of that kind—shall we pay them the union scale of ten dollars a day or not? There has been a good deal of discussion of it. Whatever we pay them, for five days' work, we will give them a much larger amount in their pay envelope at the end of the week than they are getting at the present time. How far should we carry the theory out? If we should pay them the regular scale, which is, say, $10.00 a day, does that mean that if we happen to have a lawyer on the relief roll, or an architect, who has had a longer technical education than the apprenticeship of a bricklayer, should we pay the lawyer the going wage for a competent lawyer, or should we pay the architect the going wage for a competent architect, even though he is actually laying a water main? In other words, if we go through with the idea of paying the regular scale of the building trades, isn't it logical that we should apply the same thing to the lawyer or architect or skilled craftsman or clergyman or anybody else? They do not happen to be organized, but they have gone through an apprenticeship similar to that in the building trades.

There is a second consideration. If we were to pay the going scale on the outside, there would be no particular incentive to try to find private employment. Most of them would stay put, perfectly satisfied; if they can build houses for the government in the country at $10.00 or $12.00 a day, it is a cinch. It is a permanent job, and at the end of the year they get a great deal more out of it than if they were to be in the regular building trades where if they work 200 days a year they are lucky. Then there is the third consideration. If we pay the going scale on the outside for public works of a kind that would not be built if it were not for giving jobs to the unemployed who are on relief rolls, we cannot afford to do it. We just plain cannot afford it. The general thought at the present time is that we will have to adopt, whether we like it or not, a policy of paying them for work to replace the dole and replace civil works, giving them five days' work a week and making it useful work, and paying them a good deal more than they are getting at the present time. We hope that by that method we would put a lot of other people to work on materials and that as far as possible the men on this new form of work will go off into regular private employment. That seems to be about the best hope we have.[3]

DR. MORGAN: In Eastern Europe, I know, it is in a good many cases the custom to pay the people on almost a subsistence level so that they can always live on it, and then as soon as a real job shows up they leave the government work. They get only 30 to 50 cents a day on government work, and the government gets its work done cheap and it is not interfering with private industry.

MR. BRANCH: Would that apply to contract work also?

DR. MORGAN: No, roadmaking, chiefly.

PRESIDENT ROOSEVELT: As an illustration, two friends of mine—a carpenter and a painter—just hadn't been able to get any work at all and were both working on the roads at $3.00 a day, and they were employed one week two days and the next week three days at $6.00 a week and sometimes $9.00 a week; in other words, from $25 to $26 a month up to $35 or $40 a month. Under this plan, these two poor fellows have been able to get by. Under this new plan, they would get five days' work a week and they would get about $50 a month for their work.

MR. MC NINCH: Would those on public relief work be on the lookout for a job with private industry?

PRESIDENT ROOSEVELT: Yes, there would be a difference in the scale. Some poor devil came to me last spring from the automobile trade. I said, "How much are you making?" He said, "I am making a dollar an hour. I am a machinist getting $10.00 a day." I said, "Is that all right?" "Yes, that's fine." "How much did you make last year?" "I worked 68 days and $680 in the year." But he lost his home. What is the use of making $10.00 a day if you work only 68 days a year? Am I right, Bob?

MR. FECHNER: Yes, labor knows better than anybody else that high wages don't mean anything if you do not get work.

PRESIDENT ROOSEVELT: That brings up one of the other things. I got out of bed on the

---

[3] A previous discussion of this same subject, apparently as yet unresolved by NEC, appears in the transcript of the meeting of Oct. 30, p. 336f.

392

wrong foot this morning. The first thing I read was that fool report from White Sulphur Springs![4] (*Laughter*) They spoke in that report about the maintenance of the "splendid American standard of living." I came over to the shop and Arthur Morgan was the first man I saw. He said, "Mr. President, I want to talk to you about 4,000,000 people who live along the Appalachian Chain who probably as families don't see much more than $25 a year cash per family—the "splendid standard of American living," I ask you! 'Nough said.

"Comparison of Relief Loan this Winter and Last." The executive director says we are about 2,000,000 families less this year than last, and that it is less than the anticipated increase. I would like to hear Harry on that. That is a new one. How do you figure it?

MR. HOPKINS: You have to be careful with those figures. On the first day of November this year, there were a million more families receiving relief than on the first day of November last year.

PRESIDENT ROOSEVELT: How many?

MR. HOPKINS: A million more cases. On the other hand, when CWA got to going on this particular date in December, we had 2,000,000 more families getting work from the CWA and relief than are receiving relief today.

PRESIDENT ROOSEVELT: Why didn't somebody bring that out before?

MR. HOPKINS: We put 4,000,000 families on CWA.

PRESIDENT ROOSEVELT: A lot of people don't understand it. What you mean is this. We have 5,000,000 people on relief rolls today, and last year you had 4,000,000 doing CWA work and 3,000,000 on relief. You had 7,000,000 people last year getting government money. And now you have only 5,000,000. That is an exceedingly important fact, and nobody has ever brought it out before.

MR. HOPKINS: Many of those on Civil Works last year were not on relief. They were drawn from the unemployed.

PRESIDENT ROOSEVELT: Yes, but the government was taking care of 2,000,000 more people last year than this.

SECRETARY MORGENTHAU: Do I understand there are a million more families on relief rolls than 12 months ago?

MR. HOPKINS: If you eliminate the CWA, there are more than that. There were 3,000,000 families on relief rolls a year ago this date.

SECRETARY MORGENTHAU: And now?

MR. HOPKINS: Now 5,000,000.

---

[4] An article on page one of the *New York Times* for Dec. 20, 1934, datelined White Sulphur Springs, bears this headline: "Business Suggests That It Take Lead in Recovery Drive." The report of this business conference is printed on page 18 of the same edition.

new deal mosaic

PRESIDENT ROOSEVELT: The states and municipalities were employing 4,000,000 in addition to that.

SECRETARY MORGENTHAU: But there are more relief cases now than 12 months ago.

MR. HOPKINS: No, that is not true, because we took over half of our CWA from relief rolls. Mr. President, there were more families on relief rolls in America in March 1933, than have been on relief rolls, per se, any month since. The highest relief rolls in America were in March 1933, and from that time on, they went down. We had over 5,000,000 families—not cases—on relief; now we have only 4,200,000 families. Another important thing is that this is the first time since the depression when there was no increase in the relief rolls in November over October and September. Relief rolls have remained flat for the last two months, and I think there is going to be no substantial increase in the month of December over November.

PRESIDENT ROOSEVELT: Can you let me have a memorandum by tonight on that?

MR. HOPKINS: Yes.

MR. RICHBERG: May I make this suggestion for a common understanding of this, for I do think it is very important. If you speak of the load on the federal government, you avoid all confusion as to the figures. The fact is—

PRESIDENT ROOSEVELT: That's right.

MR. RICHBERG: The fact is—you can check me if I am wrong—you had approximately 7,000,000 as a load on the federal government last year. It doesn't make any difference whether they were CWA or relief, they were there.

PRESIDENT ROOSEVELT: Or whether they were listed on relief rolls or unemployed who were not on relief rolls.

MR. RICHBERG: That has to be compared with the total of 5,000,000 this year. I have had to meet that repeatedly. I have been making this statement over and over again. As a matter of fact, there is no proof that times are worse with the theory that the federal government is carrying a higher load, because very clearly the federal government is carrying 2,000,000 less load than last year.

SECRETARY MORGENTHAU: Do you have the figures in dollars?

PRESIDENT ROOSEVELT: I think this particular comparison is one matter that the Council can talk about on the outside, ad lib! (*Laughter*)

MR. MC NINCH: I wonder if we all might have a copy of the memorandum?

PRESIDENT ROOSEVELT: Could you do that?

MR. HOPKINS: Yes.

DR. MORGAN: What I intended to say was that there are probably more than a million people who see not over fifty or a hundred dollars a year in cash.

PRESIDENT ROOSEVELT: And there are a good many others living near by who do not see much more than that. Take the counties that Harry checked up on when he found a majority that had never seen an atlas.

DR. MORGAN: We found 11 counties where the cash income would not be over $25 a year.

MR. MC NINCH: Is their real economic condition as bad as that would indicate?

DR. MORGAN: It is not quite as bad; but in those counties, there is very little gardening. They live on cornmeal and salt pork. There is not the additional income from the home that you ordinarily think of in a well-conducted farm.

MR. MC NINCH: Do you think that quite prevalent in the Tennessee Valley?

DR. MORGAN: It is prevalent over such a large area that I think it would be perfectly safe to say that there are a million people who have an income of from $25 to $100 in cash.

MR. MC NINCH: The only question is whether that is a true index of the economic condition.

DR. MORGAN: In some sections it is a very good index of the economic condition.

SECRETARY ROPER: Is it true of agricultural communities more than industrial?

DR. MORGAN: It is true of the mountain communities where agriculture is very small.

SECRETARY HULL: How much do they go to school there?

DR. MORGAN: In some cases, the school system is largely broken down. We made a study of Lincoln County, West Virginia, where there have been three fortunes taken off that land. The first was timber, the second oil, and the next was gas; and in that county a year ago, 87 ½ per cent were on the relief rolls. They had tuberculosis and pellagra and trachoma. The schools are largely broken down. As to living conditions, a man told me he had never seen worse slums in Europe than in that county. And the gas and oil is still flowing up to Pittsburgh. There are considerable areas where that is a fair picture. They never have been well off.

MR. MC NINCH: I think we should be careful that we do not exaggerate the economic conditions of the people and give the impression that that is a true, rounded-out picture of conditions in North and South Carolina.

DR. MORGAN: I think you are quite correct that it is not a fair picture of the economic condition in those places where there is a decent standard of living; but there are areas where that picture does apply. The day before Christmas last year I was in Kentucky and I watched the average, usual purchase of the people, and it was a ten-pound sack of cornmeal. My son has been working in that country on relief work, and I got pretty direct reports.

There are whole counties where that is not a very exaggerated statement. There are other counties where they are not on a moneyed economy but on a bartering economy where they are quite comfortable with no money.

MR. MC NINCH: I am not familiar with conditions which are quite comparable.

PRESIDENT ROOSEVELT: There are quite a good many places in Georgia where conditions are very bad.

MR. MC NINCH: And in many states of the Union; but I think the government's efforts might possibly be misinterpreted if we should inadvertently exaggerate too greatly or incorrectly their extreme economic plight in a journalistic effort.

PRESIDENT ROOSEVELT: Next on the list is the power policy. Does anybody want to talk about the power policy?

MR. MC NINCH: There are some individuals in the industry who are not in harmony with the spirit of Mr. Carter's (?) [sic] memorial.[5]

PRESIDENT ROOSEVELT: It seems that after the White Sulphur Springs meeting the past week, a large number of people doubted the wisdom of the report that was actually put through. It was by no means the unanimous expression of the opinion of the people who were present, even though they were rather carefully hand-picked.

SECRETARY ROPER: Raskob (?) [sic][6] was the leader of that.

MR. RICHBERG: There was a very strong dissenting voice.

MR. MC NINCH: I am not willing to prophesy what may happen, but I know this. Very soon after the statement was issued, a man in one of the largest set-ups in the country got me on the phone and said he was not going along with any such thing as that proposed.

PRESIDENT ROOSEVELT: With reference to the New York City matters you read about this morning—the City of New York buys a great deal of electricity; so does the federal government. Our electricity in the navy yard was a fairly large bill—$900,000 a year; but after a survey, we found we could produce our own electricity for $300,000 a year instead of $900,000. If I had been a private manufacturer in New York, starting to put up a new factory, I would have asked the same question; which would be cheaper, to buy from New York Edison Company or put up my own power plant? There are a great many folks in New York City that do manufacture their own power. The government is in

---

[5] The editors cannot identify "Mr. Carter." Since electric power is under discussion, it might be Thomas N. McCarter, New Jersey utilities executive, though the *New York Times* indexes no reference to a "memorial" sponsored by McCarter.

[6] Roper was probably referring to John J. Raskob, a former General Motors and Dupont executive, chairman of the Democratic National Committee, and unfriendly to F.D.R.

exactly the same position as a private manufacturer would be. The City of New York ran up against a rate for the street lighting system and found that they were paying for the street lights in New York a higher rate than the individual householder was paying, although they were using several hundred thousand dollars' worth of electricity every year. They could not get any reduction, but they found that for a comparatively small investment they could produce the electricity necessary for the city's needs. And the federal government needs electricity there for the post office and substations. We can save about $240,000 a year. It is a straight business proposition.

SECRETARY ROPER: We effected a large saving in the airways—some $500,000. Investigations had never been made beyond the local companies. There was no competition. However, now that we have investigated it, they immediately come across and we have saved between $400,000 and $500,000.

MR. ECCLES: The question of taxation is not taken into account, which is an important element in the cost of private production. I happen to be familiar with the situation out West, where $15,000,000 worth of preferred stock of a company are owned entirely by the people in the state of Utah and southern Idaho. The company is in default at the present time on its preferred stock. The loss of that income is a tremendous thing to those people. The agitation to put in city plants in order to save to the city is like a two-edged sword, and I think there are two sides to these questions.

PRESIDENT ROOSEVELT: This was an operating company?

MR. ECCLES: Yes, sir.

PRESIDENT ROOSEVELT: Was the preferred stock put into the plant?

MR. ECCLES: Yes, sir.

PRESIDENT ROOSEVELT: It is one of the exceptional cases where an operating company is not making money on its investment.

MR. ECCLES: It is making about two-thirds of the preferred stock dividends. One of the reasons is that the condition of the mining industry reduced the load tremendously.

PRESIDENT ROOSEVELT: In other words, they built it for a different kind of sales from what they are getting at the present time.

MR. ECCLES: Sales have gone down. In other words, they have more productive capacity than they can possibly need at the present time. If there were some way of forcing rates down rather than duplicating facilities that would be—

PRESIDENT ROOSEVELT: The reduction of rates almost inevitably forces consumption up.

397

We would much rather have increased consumption with lower rates than we would to try to duplicate plants.

MR. ECCLES: It would keep the local institutions paying taxes.

SECRETARY SWANSON: I hope you will see that Great Falls is utilized. We have had that through the Senate practically unanimously several times. We could have the cheapest electricity in the United States if that were developed.

PRESIDENT ROOSEVELT: Great Falls just about goes dry sometimes. It would be necessary to handle the Potomac the way they do in Tennessee so that we could have a more continuous flow of water; but that means going to the upper Potomac.

SECRETARY SWANSON: The cheapest power could be made here, where the government is, of any place in the United States.

PRESIDENT ROOSEVELT: We might put McNinch and Morgan on it.

MR. MC NINCH: Coal is really more economical than hydro. Great Falls has been combed over pretty carefully. It is not an extremely economical proposition because of lack of capacity, unless you go way up. I would like to say a word about taxes. I think it is a very real factor. The total tax burden on the industry in America amounts to a fraction less than 13 per cent of the gross operating expense, so that applied to the average rate in America if all taxes were lifted, it would relieve the rate a little more than one-half of one cent, the average rate today being $5\frac{1}{2}\cent$. If all taxes were lifted, that rate would be below $5\cent$, and you would still have a very high rate and one that is unjustifiable. The other thing about income is the consumption, which is steadily increasing, and industry is picking up to such an extent that we have a net eight per cent increase during the first nine or ten months of this year against the corresponding months of last year, an increase in gross revenue with the net almost up to the level of that existing prior to these rate decreases. In another few months I confidently expect to see the net of the operating companies what it was before these decreases occurred.

PRESIDENT ROOSEVELT: Right in line with that, all of us have an exceedingly merry Christmas in view of what some of us feared last September and the first part of October, when everybody was saying that the picture was very black; but we judge not only from the power consumption of the country but also from the postal receipts which are up on the average somewhere around six or seven per cent not only in the smaller communities but in the big cities. In December 1933, there was a general chorus of approval that it was going to be the most prosperous Christmas the country had had in a great many years—certainly since 1930. This year it is going to be an even more prosperous Christmas than last year. You remember also that last year there was a vast flood of money going out in the CWA projects; this year there is no CWA and in spite of it we have a tremendous increase of business. Department stores are showing an increase of from 10 to 25 per cent in their sales over last year. On the whole, I think we can all leave this particular meeting of the Council with a feeling that the country is a lot better off than it was last year, and last year it was a lot better off than it was the year before.

SECRETARY ROPER: The psychology is much better.

PRESIDENT ROOSEVELT: Yes; in New York City the traffic problem—what to do with the cars on the streets—has risen for the first time since 1928.

SECRETARY ROPER: Some stores have had to close their doors in order to wait on the customers.

PRESIDENT ROOSEVELT: Macy's closed at three o'clock the other day and would not let anybody else into the store.
"Civil Service."

MR. RICHBERG: Just a word on that. A question has been raised as to putting agencies that come within permanent legislation under Civil Service. It would be impossible to operate properly with any effort to comply with the Civil Service requirements. I simply want to call attention to that fact.

PRESIDENT ROOSEVELT: Many of the agencies will either become permanent or continue for some time, and as a general policy I would like to see how many people we can gradually bring in under the Civil Service. Is that a correct attitude to take?

MR. RICHBERG: Of course that is highly desirable, but very difficult to handle.

PRESIDENT ROOSEVELT: I don't think we need any drastic order, but we should all study the idea of bring as many as possible in under Civil Service. Does anybody have anything else? If not, we better talk about the next meeting. When is the next Cabinet Meeting?

SECRETARY ROPER: The twenty-seventh.

PRESIDENT ROOSEVELT: We cannot have the next meeting of the Council on January first, which is Tuesday, and we cannot make the second or the third, when Congress meets. We could make the fourth, or put it over to the following week.

MR. RICHBERG: I think we might put it over to the following week.

PRESIDENT ROOSEVELT: I think January 8 would be the best—two weeks from next Tuesday.
I hope you have a very Merry Christmas, and I will see you in two weeks.

Meeting adjourned at 3:45 p.m.

Held in the Cabinet Room of the White House,
Tuesday, January 8, 1935, at 2:10 p.m.

Present: the Vice-President of the United States; the Secretary of State;
the Secretary of the Treasury; the Secretary of War; the Postmaster
General; the Secretary of the Navy; the Secretary of Agriculture; the
Secretary of Commerce; the Honorable Frank J. Wideman, Assistant
Attorney General; the Honorable Oscar L. Chapman, Assistant Secretary
of the Interior; the Honorable Charles H. Fullaway, Administrative
Assistant to the Director of the Budget; the Administrator of Federal
Emergency Relief; the Chairman of the Board of the Reconstruction
Finance Corporation; the Chairman of the Board of the Tennessee Valley
Authority; the Chairman of the Federal Home Loan Bank Board; the
Chairman of the Federal Trade Commission; the Honorable James J.
McEntee, Assistant Director of Emergency Conservation Work; the
Governor of the Farm Credit Administration; the Chairman of the
National Industrial Recovery Board; the Chairman of the Federal
Alcohol Control Administration; the Chairman of the Federal Housing
Administration; the President of the Export-Import Banks of Washington,
D.C.; the Chairman of the Federal Deposit Insurance Corporation;
the Chairman of the Federal Power Commission; the Chairman of the
Federal Communications Commission; the Chairman of the Securities and
Exchange Commission; the Governor of the Federal Reserve Board;
the Economic Adviser; the Executive Director.

[This meeting presents a rather mixed bag of agenda items,
few of them of overriding importance. The absence of the
President accounts in large measure, here as elsewhere, both
for the relative triviality of the business discussed and for the
often inconclusive results. Examples of this kind of item
might be the report of the Committee on Interdepartmental
Committees. The intent here was to prune out useless committees, introduce some order where there was little before, and
the like—all worthy objectives for a coordinating body like
NEC, but not of major importance. The discussion of coordinating the granting of holidays in the various governmental
establishments suggests the same level of integration effort.
At one point, it will be noted, Donald Richberg, the executive secretary, raises a major problem of coordination
arising out of the overlap of departments and agencies in the
housing field. Significantly, there was a clear disinclination on
the part of the assembled officials to pick up this tentative
initiative of the executive secretary, and the matter was dropped

400

with virtually no consideration. Aat another point, Richberg refers to the policy of legislative clearance through the NEC. References are to be found to this same topic in other transcripts, which was clearly one of the most important functions of the Council. Legislative clearance was later to be centralized in the Bureau of the Budget together with the clearance of legislative proposals involving appropriations.—Editors' Note.]

SECRETARY HULL: We are sorry the President cannot be with us. In the meantime, I suppose we might go forward with our program. Among the reports of subcommittees is that of the Interdepartmental Loan Committee . . . .

MR. RICHBERG: I think I might ask in that connection whether the subcommittee on housing legislation covers all those agencies that are concerned with financing or planning the housing work.

SECRETARY MORGENTHAU: I did not attend the meeting. We had RFC, Moffett, and Fahey; I think everybody was there from the lending agencies. I don't know whether Mr. Ickes' organization was represented or not.

MR. FAHEY: Yes, Mr. Secretary, Secretary Ickes was there.

SECRETARY MORGENTHAU: Was everybody there?

MR. FAHEY: As far as I know, yes, sir.

MR. RICHBERG: I didn't know whether they were all represented or not.

SECRETARY MORGENTHAU: They got together and had a good meeting.

SECRETARY HULL: Is there any discussion or comment or disposition with respect to any of these things, or isn't there anything to be done?

MR. RICHBERG: No, sir.

SECRETARY HULL: "Report of the Industrial Emergency Committee."

MR. RICHBERG: That committee has had no meeting, because of the holidays, and so has no report to make.

SECRETARY HULL: "Report of the Interdepartmental Legal Committee."

MR. RICHBERG: This is a brief report which I think will be of general interest. The first part refers to the drafting of legislation, and I think special attention should be called to that so that anyone interested can bring to the attention of the committee any legislation they may desire . . . .

That concerns the question of bringing about a better exchange of information and the elimination of duplication in the various legal staffs in the different departments and agencies, which is a matter of very general interest.

SECRETARY HULL: Is there any discussion of this report?—any comment or suggestion on the part of anyone? I suppose there is nothing further to be done about it at this time.

Next is the report of the Committee on Interdepartmental Committees.

MR. RICHBERG: The following six organizations upon examination have been found to be formal administrative interdepartmental committees, and hence the departments have adjusted their responsibility and records accordingly:

American Marine Standards Committee.
American Standards Association Committee.
Sectional Committee on Safety Code for Lightning
    Protection, Group 1.
Interdepartmental club concerned with special problems
    of Negroes (TVA).
Association of Personnel Officers Committee.
Committee on Fair Consideration for Negroes.

[GROUP I. Abolition by instructions to Departments.

The Committee on Interdepartmental Committees having studied the existing committees, recommends abolition of the following twenty-one committees because (1) their functions overlap those of committees retained, (2) their immediate purpose is accomplished. As the persons interested have raised no objection, the procedure necessary to effect abolition of this type of committee is to issue instructions to the departments.

The Advisory Council
The Federal Contract Board
The Federal Stock Catalog Board
Federal Specifications Board
Executive Committee, American Section, International Scientific
    Radio Union
Interdepartmental Liquor-Importation Committee
Committee to cooperate with the upper Monongahela Valley
    Planning Council
Interdepartmental Committee on Conservation of Hides and Skins
Committee on Increase in Production and Employment
Joint Treasury-Navy Committee
Departmental Committee on Air Transport System
Board of Simplified Office Procedure
Committee to Cooperate with the Subsistence Homesteads Division
Liaison Committee on Aeronautic Research
Committee on Air Transport
Special Committee on Governmental Borrowing
Committee to Coordinate Activities Affecting Banks
Preferred Stock Committee
Deposit Liquidation Board
Committee on Railroad Fixed Charges
Committee to Study Report of Secretary of Agriculture Relating to
    Increasing Employment.

GROUP II. Abolition by Executive Order.

As the Division of Federal Relations, National Research Council, has raised no objection, the procedure necessary to effect abolition is by issuance of an Executive Order.

GROUP III. Abolition by Act of Congress or by Executive Order under Reorganization Act.

Since the United States Council of National Defense has raised no objection, the procedure necessary to effect abolition is by an Act of Congress or by Executive Order under Sec. 16 of the Act of March 3, 1933 (Public No. 428, 47 Stat. 1517).]

SECRETARY ROPER: What kind of personnel has the National Defense Council?

MR. RICHBERG: As I recollect, it is entirely members of the Cabinet. Isn't that correct, Mr. Ironside?

MR. IRONSIDE: Yes, sir. Mr. Dern is chairman.

MR. RICHBERG: Yes, of course.

SECRETARY ROPER: May I ask you to read again concerning the first group named there? I did not exactly get the point in the report with regard to that group.

MR. RICHBERG: That was to be abolished through instructions from the departments concerned. In other words, we will simply send around a memorandum.

SECRETARY ROPER: Then we will get notice?

MR. RICHBERG: Yes; these committees have been abolished and they will be taken care of in the departments.

SECRETARY HULL: That is the only action necessary at this time?

MR. RICHBERG: Yes; if there is no disapproval of the suggestion here made, we will carry it forward.

The following committees are under the jurisdiction of the National Emergency Council:

[Industrial Emergency Committee
Loan Committee
Shipping Policy Committee
Central Statistical Board
Council of Personnel Administration
Federal Board of Hospitalization]

The following committees are retained but are recommended to report to the Council through the departments:

[Cabinet Committee to Study Prices (Through the Secretary of Labor)
Drought Committee (Through the Secretary of Agriculture)
Committee to Consider Tonnage Tax (Through the Secretary of War)
Transportation Legislation Committee (Through the Secretary of Commerce)]

SECRETARY HULL: Number IV reports through whom?

MR. RICHBERG: Through the Emergency Council. The first two do at the present time,—the Industrial Emergency Committee and the Loan Committee.

SECRETARY HULL: How about No. V?

MR. RICHBERG: Those are retained. The Committee has recommended that the following committees be abolished. Objections were raised by the affected agencies because of the character of their functions and, therefore, it is necessary that the abolition and transfer of the functions of these agencies be given further consideration:

National Forest Reservation Commission
Chicago World's Fair Centennial Commission
Interdepartmental Committee on Great Lakes and St. Lawrence River
Mississippi River Commission
Federal Board of Vocational Education

As to those five, the Interdepartmental Committee wishes to continue its consideration because the Committee thought they could be abolished or their functions transferred, but objection has been raised to that and we want to iron the matter out.

SECRETARY ROPER: I am sure the Secretary will understand that the Chicago Fair Commission—we have no objection to that being abolished as soon as we can dispose of it properly. There is no objection to discontinuing it.

SECRETARY DERN: I think both the Mississippi River Commission and the National Forest Reservation Commission should be retained. I think it would be a great mistake to abolish either of them.

MR. RICHBERG: I am merely presenting the recommendations of this committee. Where there was objection, it was thought best to hold the matter over for further consideration. The Committee did wish to report it had considered the entire field. (*Mr. Richberg then read the remainder of the report*).

SECRETARY HULL: May I inquire about the Mississippi River Commission? What agency would assume its functions if it should be abandoned?

MR. RICHBERG: I did not work on this particular matter, Mr. Secretary. I am not familiar with that commission.

SECRETARY HULL: There is a reference to the Board of Vocational Education. Do you know about that?

MR. RICHBERG: I haven't the details.

SECRETARY HULL: Is there any discussion of this report? I assume that unless there is objection the committees under Group I will be abolished in due course—

MR. RICHBERG: There are 21 of them.

SECRETARY HULL: —by instructions to the departments involved. There is no further action called for that I see with respect to those.

MR. RICHBERG: Unless there is a question as to Groups II and III, they will be abolished according to the recommendation.

SECRETARY HULL: Is there any objection to the proposed action on these two groups? (*Pause*) I assume there is no objection.

MR. RICHBERG: There might be some question as to Groups IV and V reporting as indicated, Group IV through the National Emergency Council and Group V through the department head.

SECRETARY HULL: Is there any discussion of this recommendation?

SECRETARY DERN: Which are those?

MR. RICHBERG: Group IV includes the Industrial Emergency Committee, the Loan Committee, Shipping Policy Committee, Central Statistical Board, Council of Personnel Administration, and Federal Board of Hospitalization, and Group V includes the Cabinet Committee to Study Prices (through the Secretary of Labor), the Drought Committee (through the Secretary of Agriculture), Committee to Consider Tonnage Tax (through the Secretary of War), and Transportation Legislation Committee (through the Secretary of Commerce). That is merely a matter of reporting.

SECRETARY HULL: If there is no further discussion or comment or suggestion, the course indicated here will be carried out.

We come now to special reports from the executive director. First is the views of the Department of Agriculture regarding the governmental land policy.

MR. RICHBERG: We bring this report particularly to your attention because it involves a very important subject.

[In connection with the recommendation of the Committee on Interdepartmental Committees relating to planning government structure, there is herewith presented the matter of unification of governmental policy regarding land as viewed by the Department of Agriculture.

Adjustment of agricultural production is one of the outstanding features of this administration, and of course, this adjustment resolves itself chiefly into the problem of land use and means of influencing land use. Besides important agencies in the Department of Agriculture having to do with land, there are other important agencies, such as the Subsistence Homestead Unit, the Soil Erosion Service, the General Land Office, the Bureau of Indian Affairs, the Bureau of Reclamation, and, more remotely, the Office of National Parks, all in the Interior Department; there is in FERA the Rural Rehabilitation organization which, of course, bears importantly on agricultural policy and land use. Other departments have some bureaus that bear on land, also, but in no instance so directly as those mentioned. There are, therefore, such problems of coordination as are provided in the administration of the Taylor Grazing Bill in the Interior Department and regulation of grazing in the National Forests by the Forest Service of the Department of Agriculture; the regulation of forests in a way not inconsistent with the regulation of National Parks; game research and regulation of the Biological Survey in a manner consistent with policies of the Forest Service and the other bureaus mentioned; soil erosion work in the Bureaus of Plant Industry and Chemistry and Soils, as well as in the Soil Erosion Service of the Department of the Interior; regulation of agricultural production throughout the country, generally, and the granting of new homesteads by the General Land Office and development of new irrigation projects by the Bureau of Reclamation provide other problems.

405

[The whole situation thus rather loosely outlined is illustrated in detail by the duplication of effort in soil erosion work. The specific suggestion is that this may serve to bring up for administrative consideration the general problem of a unified policy with regard to land use.

The example of the administrative expedients caused by lack of structural unity is the location in FERA of the land-purchasing unit. Action by this unit is a continual matter of conference and compromise on the part of the three agencies concerned.

It is pointed out that the Farm Bureau Federation at its national convention this month is reported to have adopted resolutions urging wholesale shifts of certain agencies. These resolutions illustrate the fact that there seems to be growing appreciation of the need for some consolidation and unification of agencies in this particular field. While the Department of Agriculture feels that land use is overwhelmingly an agricultural problem, it does not have any desire simply to acquire additional administrative units. Its concern is with the consolidation and unification of those things that are importantly agricultural, and it should like to see the possibilities explored.]

Mr. Secretary, this brings up the question of a very definite need of doing something to avoid duplication and inconsistency. I have another communication from the Secretary of Agriculture on the subject. This particularly involves also the Department of the Interior. The Federal Emergency Relief Administration and other organizations may be also involved. It seems to me it is a matter that should be presented directly to the President for consideration, because at the present time it is causing a great deal of difficulty in the handling of government business. I thought it would be appropriate, since the President is not here today, to bring the matter up as one which is going to be brought to the attention of the President so that those interested, if they desired, could either furnish their memoranda to the President on the subject, or, if they care to furnish them to the executive director, I will bring the whole thing in compiled form to the President. I have a great deal on it already. I want to give everybody who is interested a chance to present their views on the subject.

SECRETARY MORGENTHAU: I think the President has already asked the Director of the Budget to do something with this.

MR. RICHBERG: On the budgetary side?

SECRETARY MORGENTHAU: No, on the question of reorganization and study of land use and soil erosion too, I think.

MR. FULLAWAY: That is a matter Mr. Bell has in charge.

MR. RICHBERG: If that is already under way I am very glad to understand that somebody else is interested in it. I felt it all should be presented to the President.

SECRETARY MORGENTHAU: I think that sort of work has been done by the Director of the Budget and comes through him to the President. I know that the President did ask Mr. Bell to work on that.

MR. RICHBERG: I can conceive that the various budget matters would require coordination. I was looking at it from another standpoint than that of appropriations.

SECRETARY HULL: I suppose you and Mr. Bell can work this out together. Is there any further discussion of any phase of this recommendation?

DR. MORGAN: That would cover all agencies having to do with land use, and it would therefore also involve the Tennessee Valley Authority, which is working on some matters that are involved in the ordinary work of the Department of Agriculture and the Department of the Interior.

MR. CHAPMAN: Did you make any recommendation?

MR. RICHBERG: No; all I desired to do was to get an adequate amount of material showing the views of all those concerned so that it might be compiled and summarized for the President.

SECRETARY HULL: This is intended to be a sort of initial rough basis for proposed unification.

MR. RICHBERG: Yes, in some form.

SECRETARY DERN: (*Said something about flood control, I think; could not understand him, as he spoke very low.*)

MR. RICHBERG: I don't know how that might affect other problems. It is mainly a problem of land use—soil erosion, reforestation and matters of that sort, including flood control.

SECRETARY HULL: If there is nothing further on this, we will pass to the next subject,—a summary of the report of the present position of the Federal Deposit Insurance Corporation.

MR. RICHBERG: Mr. Secretary, this report covers a matter of quite wide interest and I thought it might be desirable to read a brief summary of it . . . .

SECRETARY HULL: Any discussion?

MR. RICHBERG: In connection with this report, Mr. Secretary, at the last meeting we pointed out that we are endeavoring to work up a series of charts to be presented from meeting to meeting. We have one example on the Federal Deposit Insurance Corporation to present and others on the Farm Credit Administration which I would like also to show, including some on the subject of the operation of the Farm Credit Administration. I bring this up because it is our hope to get adequate reports each two weeks so that we can prepare wherever possible a series of continuing charts and have them available constantly to the President and also available for the consideration of the Council as they are prepared. I think it will aid very considerably in giving an understanding of the manner in which some of these agencies are functioning and the progress being made on them.

SECRETARY HULL: Next is Farm Mortgage financing.

MR. RICHBERG: I merely call attention to the report here which is a part of the regular printed report. The particularly interesting matter to which I wish to call attention is the shift which has taken place in the gradual improvement in private financing which went through a definite period of decline. It is pointed out here that 37 life insurance companies show that these companies loaned more money on farm mortgages during the first three weeks in December than in any corresponding period or any month during the past two years for which data is available . . . .

It is interesting to note the slight shifting away from federal financing back toward private financing, although federal financing at the present time is far in excess of the private financing.

SECRETARY HULL: Any comment on this by any one?

"Special problems for explanation or discussion presented either by the President or the executive director;" the first one is concerning holidays during 1935.

MR. RICHBERG: This suggestion is presented by the Acting Secretary of Agriculture.

[The advance decision with respects to the half holiday before Christmas and New Year's day was a great relief to the administrative officers of this Department. On other occasions when decision was delayed or when the excusing of employees whose services could be spared was left to the discretion of each Department, much confusion has resulted. Many telephone calls were exchanged between Departments, each endeavoring to ascertain what action the other would take, and also hundreds of calls were made by employees who desired to learn whether there would be a holiday. The result has been two or three days during which a normal course of business has been seriously interrupted.
I wish to suggest that . . . the Emergency Council consider the preparation of a program covering the year 1935 which will schedule the occasions on which extra holiday time is to be granted. Such a program if adopted and published to all employees affected, should have the effect of introducing a more orderly procedure, reduce the interference with Government business and make it possible for employees to plan their holidays in advance.]

If that suggestion is agreeable to the Council as a whole, Mr. Secretary, the thought was that we would try to prepare a schedule and get it approved in advance and then distribute it so that throughout the government service the matter would be settled long in advance. Perhaps someone will raise questions as to the practicability of that.

SECRETARY HULL: It would be practicable at least to minimize these conditions that are objectionable. That suggestion seems to be timely as well as useful. What discussion is there on this report?

SECRETARY SWANSON: The navy yards always give a half holiday on Saturday. I think the navy yards ought to be excluded and have it left so that we can issue an order. I think it is a good idea in the departments, but not for the large number of people in the navy yards. They have a half holiday every Saturday.

SECRETARY HULL: There seem to have been one or two occasions when the practice has been both ways in the past, and that, I think is what brought this up.

SECRETARY SWANSON: We simply want the right to run the navy yards like a business. We do not want a man to come and work for a little while and then close down.

SECRETARY DERN: We have the same situation.

SECRETARY MORGENTHAU: We have the same situation in the Bureau of Engraving and the mints.

SECRETARY SWANSON: We gave them a half holiday, but at a different time, and they were satisfied.

MR. RICHBERG: I might make this suggestion, that we send around a schedule of the holidays and then get the opinion of the individual departments and whether there should be exceptions in regard to them. In that way we could get the matter worked out to meet the needs of all the departments.

SECRETARY ROPER: I think the suggestion of the executive director is a proper one; namely, to work out a tentative schedule and pass it around to the different departments.

SECRETARY HULL: Are there any other suggestions or comments on this matter? (*Pause*) Then the course suggested by Mr. Richberg will be pursued.

Next is a suggestion from the Secretary of Agriculture on rural housing.

MR. RICHBERG: I have shortened this to present in very brief form the suggestion. [The summary was a four-page closely-typed review of the prevalent substandard conditions in rural housing plus a plan for coping with various needs, and a request for legislation and the financing of research.]

That brings up the problem, Mr. Secretary. I understand that long ago, before I had any connection whatever with the Council—I am speaking from hearsay—there was a very extensive consideration of the overlapping activities in regard to housing. We have something like 34 or 36 different agencies such as the Departments of Agriculture, Commerce

409

and Interior, Federal Emergency Administration of Public Works, Federal Emergency Relief, Federal Home Loan Bank, Federal Housing, National Recovery Administration, Reconstruction Finance, Tennessee Valley Authority, Treasury Department, etc., working on that. I simply call attention to the very great need for some effort to bring together in some method of coordination these numerous divergent activities in connection with housing. At the present time, there is no doubt a great deal of crossfire and duplication in it. I haven't a suggestion to make beyond calling attention to that once more, unless the Council itself desires to take some action to create another subcommittee on this subject. I understood that was in the spirit behind the Federal Housing Administration last spring, but there has not been any such coordination through the Federal Housing Administration; we simply have another agency which is now laboring on the problem.

SECRETARY ROPER: Mr. Chairman, we started it off by transferring our interests in that to the Secretary of the Interior as a Christmas present; so you can eliminate the Department of Commerce.

SECRETARY HULL: Any suggestion about this matter? Any discussion of it in any way? (*Pause*) I suppose no one cares to take it up just now.

DR. MORGAN: Would it be helpful to have such information as you ask for in reference to land purchases to see what the various organizations are actually doing?

MR. RICHBERG: I think we have the information.

DR. MORGAN: Not complete.

MR. RICHBERG: But we can endeavor to complete our information. This program is so involved in some larger issues that I do not wish to suggest any action at the present time, unless somebody else wants to undertake the responsibility of making the suggestion.

SECRETARY HULL: Now we have the question of needs for further coordination.

MR. RICHBERG: That is a general heading, Mr. Secretary. Under that I wanted to call attention today only to two matters not strictly coordinated matters. In the first place, on account of the absence of the President, and at his suggestion, I wanted to say a word about this clearance of legislation, because I think there may be considerable misunderstanding on the subject. The purpose of the suggestions made to the Council at the last meeting were in order to help prepare what might be regarded as purely an act of business for the

President. In other words, all departments and agencies that had no direct channel or clearance were requested to clear legislation through the Emergency Council. I do not think the members of the Council misunderstood, but possibly outside persons did. The purpose was not to have those matters subjected to any review, as far as the Council is concerned, or the executive director, but merely to have them cleared through one place so that they could be transmitted to [the] President with various summaries and aids to show where there might be duplication of effort, or inconsistency of effort, so that the President might have before him the various suggestions in regard to legislation; and it is my understanding that it is his intention to take up with each individual the question of any legislation recommended by the department or agency before any action is taken on the matter. I want to explain that. In other words, these matters are not being held up in the Emergency Council. We are simply compiling matters, making compilations showing where the same subject is covered or more or less duplicated, if that is so, for the benefit of the President. Our compilations will be handed to him, and the matters will then be taken up by conference between the President and the individual agencies or departments concerned.

I do not wish the functions of the executive director in this matter misunderstood, and I also do want it understood that these matters are simply being routed through the Emergency Council to the President. They are not being stopped there.

SECRETARY SWANSON: We have a general order to follow, that when a bill makes a charge on the Treasury it be sent to the Budget.

MR. RICHBERG: This is part of the regulation.

SECRETARY SWANSON: Consequently, I have confined myself to the Budget.

MR. RICHBERG: Those matters all clear through the Budget. There is no necessity for all those matters coming to the Emergency Council at all.

SECRETARY SWANSON: Any bill that increases the appropriations or will increase them, goes to the Budget?

MR. RICHBERG: That is correct. It is only miscellaneous legislation which has no relationship to appropriations, and amendments to existing laws—that type. In other words, if it doesn't come directly from the head of the department to the President himself in normal course, it will clear through the Emergency

Council for the purpose of clarifying. I am exercising the functions of messenger boy under the circumstances, trying to put things all in the proper envelope to see that they go to the proper place.

SECRETARY HULL: You have listed here "Supreme Court Opinion in Oil Case."

MR. RICHBERG: I thought possibly there might be some interest in the subject of the opinion handed down yesterday by the Supreme Court in the oil case.[1] Perhaps it may be desirable to make clear, at least to the members of the Council, the very distinct limitations upon that case. I would be very glad to have anybody else present the interpretation. It is quite clear what the Supreme Court does *not* decide, and I think it will save confusion if there is a general understanding, because so many of the activities of the government are the result of delegations of power to the President. They simply held very plainly that when power was delegated in that sense there must be standards of action laid down and requirements for findings in order to see that the standards had been complied with, whereas in the particular section—Section 9(c) of the Recovery Act—the provision was simply made that the President was authorized to prohibit the transportation of oil in excess of state quotas. There was no standard given on which he should act. There was no direction that he should act. The entire legislative power was left in the hands of the President. The Court at the same time pointed out that that was not true of the codes of fair competition, so that the implication of the opinion is all in favor of the National Recovery Administration acts because the Court pointed out that the conditions upon which the President should act were laid down in the law, and that the law did require findings by the President. And while the Court did not say that that was necessary, they pointed out that it did not create the same objections that were raised to the Section 9(c). I thought the Council should know that there is no sweeping overthrow of the various legislative delegations of emergency legislation which are vitally important.

SECRETARY SWANSON: The Court decided that the Interstate Commerce Commission is legal.

MR. RICHBERG: They said, "You must lay the standard and provide for an orderly carrying out of the standards."

---

[1] The "Hot Oil Case" (Panama Refining Co. v. Ryan, 293 U.S. 388) was decided against the government, and in effect deprived federal authorities of the power to regulate oil production.

SECRETARY HULL: Nothing to do with the subject itself.

SECRETARY ROPER: I would like to ask a question in regard to the reports that are to be made through the Council. Who is to take care of the publicity of it? Shall we look to the executive director for that? For instance, we have great pressure brought to bear upon us the moment any of these reports are complete to interpret them to the public. What shall be the policy in regard to that? It seems to me that those reports are not to be interpreted in the department until they have been considered by the Executive Council and through the Executive Council by the President. I mean those reports that are not required by the Council but required for presidential orders. I would like to pass down to the committee in the Department of Commerce the proper policy with regard to that, just who shall make the interpretation of these reports for the public press.

SECRETARY HULL: Has your organization considered that?

MR. RICHBERG: Mr. Secretary, I think, in the first place, that when an interpretation is made it clearly should come from the body responsible for the report and not from a secondary authority. I do think the suggestion by the Secretary is thoroughly sound, and that is that if the report is going to be made to the Council, it should not be made public until it has been presented to the Council, and then question may be raised whether it is desirable to make it public or not.

SECRETARY ROPER: The Council meets every two weeks. Suppose a report is ready just a day or so after the meeting; it is almost impossible to stand them off until the next meeting. What shall be the procedure? Suppose we get out a report for this Council tomorrow; shall we transmit the report, as soon as it is finished, to the executive director and then cooperate with him in the proposed analysis?

MR. RICHBERG: I suppose you have in mind the Shipping Committee report or some such report where it is an anticipated report of public interest.

SECRETARY ROPER: Right.

MR. RICHBERG: I do not see that there is any distinction between presenting that kind of report and regular reports. It seems to me it is entirely in the hands of the committee, when it is not a subcommittee report to the Council on something the Council is considering as an interdepartmental matter. Would a report of that kind, Mr. Secretary, be addressed to the President?

SECRETARY ROPER: Yes.

MR. RICHBERG: Then I should think the question of publicity would depend entirely upon the action taken in the White House in the matter.

SECRETARY ROPER: Mr. Chairman, in regard to this report, the President has asked us to check up with certain individuals whose opinions we would like to have before presenting it officially to the Council, so that the report is ready, but not quite through the checking process; but it might be ready tomorrow.

SECRETARY HULL: Is there anything further?

SECRETARY ROPER: You might be interested to know that we have the figures which are, we might say, largely reliable, though some are estimataes, of course. The Christmas business is estimated at $3,000,000,000 as compared with $2,627,000,000 last year; so you see there is over $370,000,000 this year over last year.

SECRETARY HULL: Is that fairly complete?

SECRETARY ROPER: I have a rather complete report. I will be glad to turn it over, or furnish a copy to anybody that might be interested.

SECRETARY HULL: I think each of you have a copy of the Summary of Reports. If there is nothing further, we will adjourn.

Meeting adjourned at 3 p.m.

Held in the Cabinet Room of the White House,
January 22, 1935, at 2:20 p.m.

Present: the President of the United States; the Secretary of State;
the Secretary of the Treasury; the Secretary of War; the Secretary of the
Navy; the Secretary of Agriculture; the Secretary of Commerce; the
Honorable L. W. Robert, Jr., Assistant Secretary of the Treasury;
the Honorable William Stanley, Assistant to the Attorney General; the
Honorable William W. Howes, First Assistant Postmaster General; the
Honorable Theodore A. Walters, Assistant Secretary of the Interior;
the Honorable Edward F. McGrady, Assistant Secretary of Labor;
the Honorable Daniel W. Bell, Acting Director of the Budget; the
Administrator of Agricultural Adjustment; the Administrator of Federal
Emergency Relief; the Chairman of the Board of the Reconstruction
Finance Corporation; the Honorable John B. Blandford, Jr., Coordinator,
Tennessee Valley Authority; the Chairman of the Federal Home Loan
Bank Board; the Chairman of the Federal Trade Commission; the
Director of Emergency Conservation Work; the Governor of the Farm
Credit Administration; the Chairman of the National Industrial Recovery
Board; the Chairman of the Federal Alcohol Control Administration;
the President of the Export-Import Banks of Washington, D.C.; the
Chairman of the Federal Deposit Insurance Corporation; the Chairman
of the Federal Power Commission; the Chairman of the Federal
Communications Commission; the Chairman of the Securities and
Exchange Commission; the Governor of the Federal Reserve Board;
the Economic Adviser; the Executive Director.

[The most interesting and important matter discussed in this
meeting is legislative clearance. Again we find that one of the
permanent achievements of NEC was, like the *U.S. Government
Organization Manual*, a more or less accidental by-product of
its activities. Instead of NEC developing into a permanent
coordinating agency, it declined in importance throughout its
brief life and eventually disappeared. What did happen was that
NEC encountered subproblems ancillary to policy coordination about which it *could* take useful action, as in the case of
legislative clearance. Thus permanent, if rather minor,
contributions were made in the integration of policy.—Editors'
Note.]

PRESIDENT ROOSEVELT: The first order of business is a report of the Interdepartmental
Loan Committee . . . .
I think this method of clearing agencies' bills is working
pretty well. It will prevent our crossing wires when they get

up on the Hill; and I have tried to make it perfectly clear to some of the department heads that the reference of these bills through the White House is going to save time and trouble. They fall into three categories; first, the kind of legislation that, administratively, I could not give approval to—it will eliminate that; secondly, the type of legislation which we are perfectly willing to have the department or agency press for, but at the same time we do not want to put it into the category of major administrative bills. Obviously, I have to confine myself to what the newspapers called last year the comparatively small list of *must* legislation. If I make every bill that the government is interested in *must* legislation, it is going to complicate things very much; and where I clear legislation with a notation that says "No objection," that means you are at perfect liberty to try to get the thing through, but I am not going to send a special message through for it. It is all your trouble, not mine.

At the same time I want to add one word of caution in the family, and that is, if you are asked questions about measures or policies advocated by other departments or agencies, your opinion is not necessary to express. We should stick to our own loom. It is much the easiest way. There have been instances in the past two years, and especially in the previous administration, of some very raw cases of one department going up and lobbying against another department of the government on the Hill, and it has made bad feeling and utter confusion. Luckily in the past two Congresses we have had very little of crossing of wires between different departments and agencies of the government. I just wanted to mention that. Now, going back to the question of these bills for a moment; by having them cleared through a central agency it gives somebody else outside the department itself the opportunity to have happy thoughts. For example, take the illustration that came through yesterday—a bill, a perfectly proper measure from the Secretary of War—authorizing the Secretary of War to sell 45 parcels of land totaling not much in the way of acreage—only about 350 acres. I sent word back to Donald to see if he could find out whether any other department or agency of the government would like to use any portion of these 45 parcels of land, and, instead of selling them out of the government to private parties, it might just so happen that some other department or agency could use one of the Secretary of War's parcels of land and keep it in the government rather than selling it out. It would just give everybody an opportunity of knowing what those parcels are and using them if we need them.

MR. HOWES: If someone introduced a bill in Congress and the chairman of the committee writes down to the department head and wants to know if that department has any objection to that particular bill, should we clear through Mr. Richberg on that?

PRESIDENT ROOSEVELT: I don't think you can have any definite rule on that. I think you have to be a little careful. The chief trouble relates to those bills after they have passed and come to me. Last year I vetoed more bills than have ever been vetoed before since the days of Grover Cleveland. That is literally true—about 150 bills, I think it was. After Congress adjourned they dumped them all in my lap. That last week of Congress I had a veto-fest for about a week. In taking up those bills I found in a great many instances that the bills I wanted to veto were accompanied by a letter saying, "We have no objection to this bill," which made it more difficult for me to veto it. They were mostly private claims.

MR. HOWES: And then they follow that up by asking someone from the Department to appear, and I was wondering if we should just do that without consulting you.

PRESIDENT ROOSEVELT: In most cases, yes; but remember that on a close decision I would prefer you to oppose the bill rather than O.K. it. On a close decision I want to veto it. If the con's are just as strong as the pro's, rule in favor of the con's.

MR. MC NINCH: The Power Commission now has three requests for an expression of opinion on bills to establish authorities.

PRESIDENT ROOSEVELT: That is a very particular thing.

MR. MC NINCH: It is a question of policy; would you suggest that we should undertake to clear that?

PRESIDENT ROOSEVELT: Talk with me, because on the establishment of these authorities I am proceeding rather slowly. At least five different territories are wanting to set up authorities. I am not ready— and we won't be ready this year—to set up any new authorities. Take, for example, the Columbia River Basin, where they want an authority covering the whole Columbia River Basin. We are not ready for it yet. The Public Works will not be finished for another two or three years, and until another year has gone by I do not think we want to set up anything like that. My thought is that for the Columbia River Basin we would appoint an unofficial, unpaid advisory committee which might eventually become an authority if it is advisable when

417

	the time comes. Broadly speaking, I do not want any authorities set up this year.
MR. MC NINCH:	I am asking the Engineering Division to make studies, and that will necessarily take considerable time, and we probably will not be ready to express any kind of opinion to the committee any time soon.
PRESIDENT ROOSEVELT:	You have always this thought on the authority: power is only a very minor element, and when it comes to working toward the broader objectives, it should go to the National Resources Board when you get beyond the power.
SECRETARY HULL:	On the question of bills calling for appropriations, the other day some congressman conceived the idea of putting through a bill appropriating $300,000 for a legation building in Finland as a compliment to Finland, and they inquired what the attitude of the Department was. I said that we could say nothing about the matter in any way until it passed the President and the Budget on the appropriations.
PRESIDENT ROOSEVELT:	There again is the question of additional appropriations. If those things are put up to me or the Director of the Budget, our answer is a very simple one. Our Budget has gone through, and it did not include this item. If we once start to approve items in addition to the existing Budget, the Budget is over-burdened, and over-burdened with our approval. In other words, we are ruling against our own Budget. Take the Finland case; I am most sympathetic; I would love to have a legation in Finland, and I can say off the record—and it would have to be off the record—if they stick that in they do it on their own responsibility and they will have to take the chance of having the whole bill vetoed because of that item. It is their baby once the Budget has gone up.
SECRETARY MORGENTHAU:	I am awfully glad Mr. Hull brought that up, for there is the question of $40,000,000 for seed loans.
PRESIDENT ROOSEVELT:	I had four telephone calls in about five minutes, and they keep on telephoning and asking if we will approve additional seed loans. The answer is, "No, it is not in the Budget." There is only one answer. "It is not in the Budget."
SECRETARY SWANSON:	You do not want us to refer to the Budget anything that will increase the Budget that is not already in the Budget. Everything that is an expense is to be referred to the Budget, but they have made up the Budget. You want us to take that responsibility and not dump it on you.
MR. RICHBERG:	I don't think there is anything that will clear through the Emergency Council unless it is a question whether some other

department is interested in the same question. We will be very glad to help iron that out.

PRESIDENT ROOSEVELT: "Report of the Industrial Emergency Committee."

MR. RICHBERG: I have no report.

PRESIDENT ROOSEVELT: "Report of the Interdepartmental Legal Committee." (*Mr. Richberg read . . .*

[. . . As directed by the Council, the Committee has been considering the various proposals for the adequate publication of Administrative Orders which may determine rights and liabilities. At the present time there are before the Congress two measures aimed at effecting such publication.

HR-1403, introduced by Congressman Lewis of Maryland, provides that whenever by statute any Executive Officer or Administrative Board is authorized to determine and make or enforce *any* rule or regulation whether general or specific, violation of which may result in any penalty or liability, criminal or civil, a copy of such rule or regulation *must* be filed with the Secretary of State and thereafter in five days it may become effective.

HR-2884, introduced by Congressman Celler of New York, provides for mandatory publication of Executive Orders, including *all instances of the exercise by the President of any power* conferred on him by statute as well as *all* rules and regulations promulgated by any agency in the Executive Branch of the Government.

Both of these measures were examined in detail, but in the judgment of the Committee they were objectionable because of their sweeping character and the fact that they would seriously hamper administration. . . .])

PRESIDENT ROOSEVELT: Which of those is the Harvard Law School bill?

MR. RICHBERG: The last one, introduced by Congressman Celler.

PRESIDENT ROOSEVELT: I think it is important to have something like that when you get your bill drafted.

MR. STANLEY: We have it drafted now.

SECRETARY HULL: On the question of Executive Orders, Mr. President, there have been a few instances where some of the departments have not forwarded the Orders to the State Department to be published and distributed until many months afterward. People come in and demand information about such Orders and whether they are there or not. If heads of departments would have that attended to, it would avoid some criticism, because sooner or later there will be criticism.

PRESIDENT ROOSEVELT: I think that is good—in one way. You sometimes see penciled chits which have the effect of Executive Orders, and they are not even copied!

MR. RICHBERG: I thought they were all to clear through the Budget and the State Department.

PRESIDENT ROOSEVELT: I don't think anybody clears my penciled chits. You get some of those.

SECRETARY HULL: They do come through to be published and distributed—all Executive Orders.

419

new deal mosaic

PRESIDENT ROOSEVELT: You might publish the one I sent you the other day, suggesting that the distinguished career people in foreign service should work five days a week, eight hours a day! (*Laughter*)

SECRETARY HULL: That is not a bad suggestion.

PRESIDENT ROOSEVELT: "Special Reports from the Executive Director. The Federal Reserve Board;" do you want me to read that?

MR. RICHBERG: I think you would be interested in it. . . .

PRESIDENT ROOSEVELT: "Suggestion of the Secretary of War with respect to scientific work of the Government."
(*Mr. Richberg read* . . . [. . . memorandum on the need for scientific research as a national program to create employment. . . .])

PRESIDENT ROOSEVELT: That is fine! George [Dern], I suggest that you put that in speech form and deliver it to the public! It is all right.
"Report of the Executive Director regarding the cotton situation." . . .
That paragraph about informal approach to the British Government has not been given to the public, has it?

SECRETARY HULL: No.

PRESIDENT ROOSEVELT: That, I think, should be kept confidential. The British Government essentially controls the Indian problem and the Egyptian problem. It means only relations with the British Government and with Brazil—two important factors.
"Report of the Executive Director concerning Government holidays."

MR. RICHBERG: Without reading this report in detail, I may suggest that it be submitted for your consideration along the line of the last meeting—that is, providing uniform determination of holidays in advance. The problem has been explored, and this is the report.

PRESIDENT ROOSEVELT: All right. Next we have "Directing attention to the reports of the Chairman of the Federal Deposit Insurance Corporation."

MR. RICHBERG: These are short reports, Mr. President. . . .

PRESIDENT ROOSEVELT: Leo, tell me, what are you requiring in the way of surety bonds from these banks where there are defalcations? You had a case in Virginia recently, didn't you?

MR. CROWLEY: We have nothing in the law that permits us to do it at all. We are trying to get a new law to cover that.

PRESIDENT ROOSEVELT: Do they carry surety bonds?

MR. CROWLEY: Not sufficient. One had $75,000 defalcation and $5,000 insurance. We are asking for a new law to give us authority to require that.

PRESIDENT ROOSEVELT: "Deputy Governor of the Farm Credit Administration."

MR. RICHBERG: This is a short report which is rather significant. . . .

PRESIDENT ROOSEVELT: "Federal Housing Administrator." . . .

"The Postmaster General."

(*Mr. Richberg read* . . . [The following suggestion with respect to the use of air mail is made by the Postmaster General:

"May I again direct the attention of the other agencies of the Government to the advantages of the use of the air mail service in lieu of telegrams. While franked matter for other Departments is not carried by air mail, yet the new air mail rates afford an opportunity to the Governmental agencies to transmit more complete instructions than is practicable in telegrams and at a lower cost. To obtain the maximum advantage of this service, letters should be sent special delivery, thus obtaining immediate delivery at the office of address. In order to facilitate the use of this combined service, a new 16¢ stamp covering both air mail and special delivery has been provided."])

PRESIDENT ROOSEVELT: Everybody please note that. Tell your chief clerks.

I have here this book of charts on the progress of the various agencies. I hope that you will cooperate with the department in that. Who handles this?

MR. RICHBERG: It is handled by Mr. Ironside, particularly.

PRESIDENT ROOSEVELT: I hope you will cooperate in keeping this data up to date in the director's office, because it is not only very practical, but it gives a view of how fast we are going and where we slip behind.

MR. RICHBERG: We propose to keep this up to date as a book for your desk, and in order to have it up to date and keep the material, we need to have the cooperation of the statistical services in the departments. As far as we have gone we have had it and have been able to get very good results.

PRESIDENT ROOSEVELT: "Special problems for explanation or discussion. Lobbying by Departments"—that has already been covered. "Debts owed by Government employees." . . .

As I understand it, the law prevents the garnisheeing of government salaries. I have not thought about this for a good many years. In the Navy Department, the rule was that the government is not a collecting agency. Our answer was that it was a matter entirely between the creditor and the individual debtor.

MR. DAVIS: I made the suggestion, and I am familiar with that. That, of course, is the general position of our Commission. We refer the complaint to the employee for any comment, and if he admits he owes it, that it is a just debt, we might suggest that he take care of it at different times. We have received a letter from a United States Senator which resulted in making this

421

suggestion. They make these arguments, that employees are exempted from garnishment, and yet they think it is wrong for the government to retain men in its employ who are getting good salaries and who will not pay their just debts. They become pretty insistent about it. For instance, in a particular case—the one I have in mind now—the Senator sent us a certified copy of the judgment. It was an old one, but it has been pressed not only by the creditor in this instance, but by the Senator. It seems that we should do something about it. Of course, we have explained that we cannot force them to pay the debt, and of course they are not subject to garnishment, but they occasionally insist that it is a matter that ought to be dealt with by the government in some way, and our secretary has made some inquiry of other agencies. It seems that there is no uniformity about it. They handle it about like we have, or perhaps pay no attention to it. I am of the opinion that the Post Office Department has more definite rules and procedures along that line than other departments I know of. As I understand it, if it appears to the satisfaction of your department (*speaking to Mr. Howes*) that an employee fails to pay a just debt which he is able to pay, that after warning him you sometimes discharge him on the theory that he is bringing the public service into reproach.

MR. HOWES: If he is doing the best he can, we do not do that.

MR. DAVIS: You do that only when you feel that he could pay it and doesn't.

MR. MYERS: Would it be worth while to consider Federal Credit Unions in the various government agencies? We have one in the Farm Credit Administration, and there has been quite a demand for loans, especially from the lower-salaried employees. Those loans are made to pay up debts, sometimes to pay up loans from these loan sharks, and sometimes to pay hospital bills. Since the workers themselves provide the funds, it stimulates thrift and I think tends to prevent the accumulation of debts of that kind.

PRESIDENT ROOSEVELT: They had a similar organization in the Navy Department a great many years ago—an informal association.

MR. MYERS: I think the general procedure is that it should be a coherent group in a department or agency.

PRESIDENT ROOSEVELT: Do you know of any objection to setting up these credit unions among the units?

MR. MYERS: We will be glad to help them do it.

PRESIDENT ROOSEVELT: It is a voluntary thing. If any question comes up, we will refer them to the Farm Credit Administration for information as to how it goes.

MR. MYERS: About a third of the employees in Farm Credit are now members. We started it about seven or eight months ago.

MR. BLANDFORD: The Tennessee Valley Authority has two such arrangements.

PRESIDENT ROOSEVELT: Of course, as I understand the law with reference to Civil Service employees, if they do not pay their bills, the creditor has a right to file a writ with the Civil Service Commission which militates against these employees when it comes to promotion.

MR. DAVIS: If they are not under Civil Service, the Commission has no jurisdiction. If we can take cognizance of it, of course we do; but just how far to go—that is what we wanted to know.

PRESIDENT ROOSEVELT: "Information regarding policy with respect to answering the Sirovich questionnaire."

He has sent around questionnaires all over the place. The answer is that we are not a collecting agency for any member of Congress. That is very clear. Members of the Senate and House will sometimes come around and ask for lists of employees, the salaries paid them, and so on. The easiest way, I think, is to refer them to the Civil Service Commission. Answering questionnaires is not our function, and you can tell them I said so.

MR. RICHBERG: There is another question allied with that. I think Mr. Fahey has had some experience with it in having questions sent from the members of Congress as to number of employees, and the salaries of employees in particular localities, and the amount of loans disbursed, and things of that kind.

PRESIDENT ROOSEVELT: It is necessary to use a certain amount of discretion in that. If it takes people off their work, you could tell the congressman, "We haven't any money for that; if you will pass a special appropriation bill, we will furnish the information."

MR. FAHEY: We have no difficulty in the matter of furnishing information relative to the amount of loans and that sort of thing because we have that, and it is open to the public; but the difficulty we encounter is in the requests for names and addresses of employees in different places and various sections of the country, the amount of their wages, etc. Back before and during the campaign we had a lot of that—requests by congressional districts, cities, and all that sort of thing; and also many requests for the names of people who got loans, and we took the responsibility of declining to give that information. When Congress or a committee has passed a resolution asking for detailed information concerning employees, we have provided it, although it has oftentimes cost us a considerable sum of money. If we respond to individual requests for the number of employees and the wages they receive, and their names and addresses, we are in trouble. If we do it in one case, we will have to do it in others. We have something like seventeen or eighteen thousand employees now, and of course that list is constantly shifting and changing, and yet we are now beginning to get a new wave of inquiries as to how many employees we have, what their addresses are, the salaries they receive. We do not know what the rest of the departments do if they have corresponding inquiries. We do not want to be discourteous and we do not want to discriminate.

PRESIDENT ROOSEVELT: It is a very simple thing. If it is a congressman, write back and say, "Dear Congressman: Sorry, no funds. Sincerely yours."

MR. FAHEY: But they say we still have some! (*Laughter*)

PRESIDENT ROOSEVELT: And if it is a committee, tell the committee they will have to pass a special appropriation, that you cannot dig into the regular appropriations; we haven't that authority under the law.

MR. FAHEY: Of course, in some cases, it would not involve a great deal of expense, but the difficulty is in establishing a precedent. If we do it for one, we must do it for all. We are up against it if we deny it in one case and agree to it in another.

PRESIDENT ROOSEVELT: You ought to be very hard-boiled.

SECRETARY HULL: You have to be.

SECRETARY SWANSON: I reply, I have no funds.

MR. FAHEY: Is it perfectly proper to say that if we do this in one case we would have to do it in all, and that if we adopted that policy we would have to have the money for it?

PRESIDENT ROOSEVELT: Yes; the appropriation was not made for that purpose.

MR. RICHBERG: It might be suggested by Mr. Fahey that the volume of such requests is so great that he is unable to comply with them.

PRESIDENT ROOSEVELT: "Needs for further coordination." I call your attention to other papers and the summary of report of the National Emergency Council. May I ask you again to read that summary? I won't ask any questions on it.

Is there anything else anybody wants to bring up?

Meeting adjourned at 3:10 p.m.

Held in the Cabinet Room of the White House,
February 5, 1935, at 2:15 p.m.

Present: the President of the United States; the Vice-President of the
United States; the Secretary of State; the Secretary of the Treasury;
the Secretary of War; the Attorney General; the Secretary of the
Navy; the Secretary of the Interior; the Secretary of Agriculture;
the Secretary of Labor; the Undersecretary of the Treasury; the
Honorable L. W. Robert, Jr., Assistant Secretary of the Treasury; the
Honorable William W. Howes, First Assistant Postmaster General;
the Honorable John Dickinson, Assistant Secretary of Commerce; the
Administrator of Agricultural Adjustment; the Administrator of Federal
Emergency Relief; the chairman of the Reconstruction Finance Corpora-
tion; the Honorable John B. Blandford, Jr., Coordinator, Tennessee
Valley Authority; the Chairman of the Federal Home Loan Bank
Board; the Honorable Charles H. March, Commissioner, Federal Trade
Commission; the Director of Emergency Conservation Work; the
Governor of the Farm Credit Administration; the Chairman of the
National Industrial Recovery Board; the Chairman of the Federal
Alcohol Control Administration; the Honorable Stewart McDonald,
Executive Assistant, Federal Housing Administration; the President of
the Export-Import Banks of Washington, D.C.; the Chairman of the
Federal Deposit Insurance Corporation; the Chairman of the Federal
Power Commission; the Chairman of the Federal Communications
Commission; the Chairman of the Securities and Exchange Commission;
the Economic Adviser; the Executive Director.

[The most interesting things in this meeting are perhaps the
lecture the President read to those assembled on the care
and feeding of Congressmen, and the references to Huey Long.
On the first, insight is gained into the problems of executive-
legislative relations as they relate to individual departments.
As to Huey Long, he had supported Roosevelt's program
during the early days of the Administration, and very soon
thereafter became a bitter opponent of the President's measures.
He was removed from the political scene by assassination on
September 8, 1935.—Editors' Note.]

PRESIDENT ROOSEVELT: The first matter is the report of the subcommittee, the
Interdepartmental Loan Committee . . . .
The next is the report of the Interdepartmental Legal
Committee . . . .
Has that been cleared?

425

MR. RICHBERG: That is being handled by Mr. Celler in the House. They are to have a meeting Wednesday, at which time the Committee will appear before the Congressional committee. I think originally Mr. Celler introduced the bill in the House.

VICE-PRESIDENT GARNER: That has been referred to the House and it should also be sent over to the Senate.

MR. RICHBERG: I would suggest that Mr. Stanley is the chairman of the committee, Mr. Attorney General.

ATTORNEY GENERAL CUMMINGS: What committee?

MR. RICHBERG: The Interdepartmental Legal Committee. The bill has gone to the House and the Vice-President suggests that it go also to the Senate . . . .

PRESIDENT ROOSEVELT: Next is the report of the Industrial Emergency Committee . . . .

I might say that that question of the extension of the NIRA[1] has got to the point where in the course of the next week we will be ready to ask the chairman of the committee to come down and talk to us on the whole subject.

VICE-PRESIDENT GARNER: What committee does that go to?

PRESIDENT ROOSEVELT: It goes to the Ways and Means Committee in the House because NIRA went to them before; and to the Senate too, I suppose.

MR. RICHBERG: There was no prediction made as to that yesterday.

PRESIDENT ROOSEVELT: "Special reports from the Executive Director: Consumers' Division of the Council."

MR. RICHBERG: I think this is of interest to a good many of the agencies, Mr. President . . . .

We expect to get some coordination and simplification in that before very long.

PRESIDENT ROOSEVELT: Next is the question of coordination by the state directors for the Council . . . .

MR. RICHBERG: I don't think you want to have this entire report read, but I would like to summarize it.

PRESIDENT ROOSEVELT: It is a very important report, I think.

MR. RICHBERG: This report, I think, has not been mimeographed. We are, for the first time, bringing about some coordination in the field between the various phases of the federal program. This is being done through the state directors acting as coordinator in their field, bringing together the representatives of the

---

[1] This question became academic some three months later with the handing down, on May 27, 1935, of the Supreme Court decision in the "Sick Chicken Case" (Schecter Poultry Corp. v. United States, 295 U.S. 495), in which the NIRA was declared unconstitutional.

federal agencies in their state for discussion and then clearing anything in the way of state legislation. It also provides a basis of information. The result has been quite heartening in finding the extent to which these agencies could be put in touch with each other and learn a great deal that they did not know about each other's work. There are summarized in this report quite a number of activities that have been carried on by this coordinating group. The activities of this group cover state recovery laws to assist NRA, state mortgage laws to conform with FHA, loan insurance, state laws to join and cooperate in the PWA program, and the assumption by the states of their fair share of relief. Also, state agencies to cooperate with National Reemployment Service, authorization of permanent state planning board, state banking laws to strengthen deposit insurance, state laws to integrate savings and loan association activity, and cooperation with the Farm Credit Administration. That just gives an idea of some of the activities going on within the state. There is very great need of coordination. They are also coordinating publicity which needs to be carried forward without constant duplication.

We have a list here of the various problems that have been disposed of by some of the states. I think I might read these, as follows:

ALABAMA	Code compliance by contractors using federal funds strengthened.
ARKANSAS	Close cooperation between CCC and AAA on soil erosion assured.
ARIZONA	Overlapping in housing programs clarified.
COLORADO	Federal Business Association assisted by committee.

PRESIDENT ROOSEVELT: What do you mean by "Federal Business Association?"

MR. RICHBERG: I understand that has to do with purchases. Is that right, Mr. Ironside?

MR. IRONSIDE: They are local groups involved in the rental and exchange of federal property in the field.

MR. RICHBERG (*reading*):

IDAHO	Cooperative agreement between agencies affected corrects conditions under which many counties were falling below their quota of CCC enrollees. Assistance to NRA in obtaining code compliance pledged by purchasing agents of federal agencies.
MONTANA	State director aids in ending misunderstanding between

427

	local chairman of Home Loan Bank and HOLC manager.
NEBRASKA	Misunderstandings with regard to soil erosion between FERA, AAA, Soil Erosion Service and CCC cleared up completely. Code compliance by contractors using federal funds greatly assisted by agencies affected appointing liaison officers to act with NRA.
NEW JERSEY	PWA, FERA, and State Planning Board all started works surveys each duplicating work of the others. Subcommittee with NEC director to make one survey and make results available to all. Code compliance by contractors on work involving federal funds improved by FERA agreeing to submit proposed contracts and bids to NRA for checking.
OKLAHOMA	Committee to assist agency heads in promoting compliance with Code labor provisions, suggesting contracts be checked with NRA.

That indicates the line of work that these state directors are engaged on. I think it is really producing very helpful results.

PRESIDENT ROOSEVELT: "Development of Council Report." . . .

MR. RICHBERG: I want to report on that. I think those who read them will probably agree that the reports are getting very much better. They are more complete and contain more useful information. A special effort has been made to develop these reports agency by agency. I want to say that up to date, special work has been done with these agencies and they have cooperated: Farm Credit Administration, Federal Emergency Relief, Federal Deposit Insurance, Department of the Interior, and the Petroleum Administration, Federal Home Loan Bank System, and the Home Owners' Loan Corporation. As a result of that, I want to call attention to the fact that we are now able to get up this book in increasing size and detail of information from week to week for your desk. It is not intended for reading matter but as a summary of activities up to date.

PRESIDENT ROOSEVELT: "Summary report from the Chairman of the Federal Home Loan Bank Board." This is fairly long and it is very important. It is a very excellent report. Has that been mimeographed?

MR. RICHBERG: I want to present that question, because this is a precedent in getting from the agencies one by one these special reports. This, for example, is the Home Loan Bank Board and the various agencies under it . . . . This is a very comprehensive report of work up to date covering the progress made. It is highly informative. For example, it is the sort of thing that we tried to get out last August when we had this report to the President and we had great difficulty; we are starting anew in this field. One by one we would like to get this uniform type of report. If you desire, we would mimeograph these and send them to all members of the Council. I don't think you would want to take the time to have them read here, but they would be very valuable in detail.

PRESIDENT ROOSEVELT: This gives very good information as to what each agency is doing. I think that is a very good idea.

MR. RICHBERG: The other idea is whether the charts should be duplicated.

PRESIDENT ROOSEVELT: I don't think it is necessary to do that.

MR. RICHBERG: I don't believe it is necessary.

PRESIDENT ROOSEVELT: "Summary report of current conditions." . . . That is only two and one-half pages. Perhaps we might read that.

MR. RICHBERG: I think you will find it very interesting if you care to read it yourself. (*President Roosevelt then read . . .*)
I do not question the accuracy of that but it is an extraordinary increase. I thought that possibly there was some explanation.

SECRETARY PERKINS: I think that is correct.

MR. RICHBERG: I had no question as to its correctness. But it is an extraordinary increase of employment in the nondurable field.

SECRETARY PERKINS: The base line is 1923 to 1925 so that you had your increase when you had your expansion years.

PRESIDENT ROOSEVELT: It means twice as many men working in the nondurable goods field.

SECRETARY PERKINS: The big expansion in that industry took place in 1925 to 1929.

MR. RICHBERG: An enormous percentage has been held.

PRESIDENT ROOSEVELT: Maybe it is one of those true fairy stories. (*The President then read to the end of the report.*)
Where the Federal Reserve mentioned the index of 86, is that on the same basis as the Bureau of Labor statistics?

SECRETARY WALLACE: It is 1923 to 1925.

SECRETARY PERKINS: They are all on the same basis now. We were not originally, but we are now.

PRESIDENT ROOSEVELT: Next is the "National Power Survey." . . . I might say that the electric industry is awake to the desirability of greater uniformity of rates throughout the country. Some of the more farseeing utility heads are working in two separate groups toward the simplification of rate schedules and toward the elimination of various high rates in certain localities, to bring them all over the country down to more normal rates. The question of what is the lowest level does not enter into it. They are trying to eliminate those localities where there is an obvious abuse. They are beginning to show some substantial cooperation with the policy of the Administration.

On the matter of "Special Problems for Explanation or Discussion," there is a question as to the advisability of suspending new activities or legislative proposals concerning the work program. Donald wanted to bring that up, for instance, in regard to housing.

MR. RICHBERG: We have this sort of question coming up frequently, Mr. President, as to the desirability of starting some new activity. I think possibly you would like to present the matter in some way so as to get a uniform attitude toward it upon various requests for legislation in that field or appropriation of funds or allocation of funds to undertake new work.

PRESIDENT ROOSEVELT: I think we should go a little slow the next two weeks with PWA and FERA in the way of planning until we know what Congress is going to give us; in other words, we do not want to start a large staff on some particular survey unless the thing clears through me so that we can keep in touch with what Congress is doing and not go out too far on a limb ahead of them. I don't want to stop the work at all, but I don't want to get too far out on the limb.

The other question is reciprocal aid from states in promoting recovery when they are calling on the federal government for relief of unemployment.

MR. RICHBERG: The problem there, Mr. President, is this. In many instances, there has not been very great encouragement from particular state governments in helping forward some of this legislation and other activities by which the federal government is endeavoring to reduce the load of unemployment, and yet the same state is calling very strongly for its share of any federal aid. It seems to me it is a question of very diplomatic handling. It is not a question of withholding money, but it is very desirable to at least establish a cooperative policy which we have been trying to do in a measure through the state directors. It seems to me it concerns almost every department or agency of the government in some way.

PRESIDENT ROOSEVELT: I would like to discuss that a little more. How would it do to find out first from each of the agencies what states are not cooperating from their point of view? Is that the first step? I think the thing to do is to have each agency let Don know the difficulties which the particular agency has in particular states. If you have no particular difficulty with a state, do not put the name of that state down, but let us know just what the difficulty is so that we can take it up with the appropriate authorities. Of course that applies principally to FERA more than anybody else, I imagine.

MR. RICHBERG: It applies to Public Works also.

PRESIDENT ROOSEVELT: Yes, to a certain extent; but we ought to get the information before we go after the governors.

MR. RICHBERG: That raises the question you brought up some time ago. There have been a great many requests to write letters to the governors. It it getting to be a rather large order with all these various legislative activities.

PRESIDENT ROOSEVELT: I think I sent out four round-robin letters to governors. I want to call a halt.

MR. RICHBERG: Of course, it destroys the effect of a letter from you if you send one each week.

PRESIDENT ROOSEVELT: Yes. I sent out one relating to highway safety, which didn't do any harm, but I don't think it did any particular good. We said we would be glad to cooperate in establishing greater highway safety.

The other question is with reference to the Central Statistical Board.

MR. RICHBERG: The question there is the problem of requesting legislation which might establish it as a permanent body. The suggestion which came to me, Mr. President, was that that work, as I understand, was originally established as a result of four Secretaries meeting—Agriculture, Commerce, Labor, and War. I don't know whether they would desire to take the matter up again at this time for consideration of future developments of the statistical work.[2]

PRESIDENT ROOSEVELT: What do you think about that? Were you chairman of that, Henry?

SECRETARY WALLACE: I think General Johnson was the fourth member, as I remember it.

PRESIDENT ROOSEVELT: Of course, we did excellent work and we have a centralized agency that is operating; but the question is whether it should be made permanent by legislation. I don't think it is necessary, if this new bill is broad enough to give an allocation of money; but it is not as at present drafted. That is the trouble.

SECRETARY PERKINS: It gives an allocation of money to other emergency agencies.

---

[2] The Central Statistical Board was established under the National Industrial Recovery Act of 1933 by Executive Order 6225 of July 27, 1933. It remained in existence until its functions were merged with those of the Bureau of the Budget by Reorganization Plan I of July 1, 1939.

PRESIDENT ROOSEVELT: No.

SECRETARY PERKINS: Statistics are being collected, I think properly, at the present time by volunteer action and by experiment; but it is essential that there be funds.

VICE-PRESIDENT GARNER: There are a lot of useful agencies.

PRESIDENT ROOSEVELT: NRA itself.

MR. RICHBERG: And the National Emergency Council, which is now sitting.

SECRETARY PERKINS: Also the Steel Board and the Textile Board.[3]

MR. RICHBERG: It was understood that it was covered by that.

PRESIDENT ROOSEVELT: But it isn't.

MR. RICHBERG: I am now informed that it was not covered; but there may be a difference of opinion on that.

VICE-PRESIDENT GARNER: You would have to make up your list of these necessary activities, send it to Congress, and let the Rules Committee bring it in.

MR. RICHBERG: Would it be sufficient to allow funds from this?

VICE-PRESIDENT GARNER: If these funds are necessary, then you better send this up to the Appropriations Committee.

PRESIDENT ROOSEVELT: I think if you have a bill to handle that it is all that is necessary.

MR. RICHBERG: I thought we had a bill which had that interpretation in it, and I still think it has. But there is a difference of legal opinion. I should like very much to have the opinion of the Attorney General on the subject.

PRESIDENT ROOSEVELT: The Comptroller General will rule against him anyway!

MR. RICHBERG: That is the difficulty.

ATTORNEY GENERAL CUMMINGS: He does, but my impression is that every time he does, the court has decided that the Attorney General was right.

PRESIDENT ROOSEVELT: That's right!

SECRETARY PERKINS: On that matter of the legislation for the Central Statistical Board, I think it might be very helpful to let Mr. Riefler state now for the benefit of the other members of this group what he has talked over with the various Cabinet officers who have been backing this Board. They have some very real plans for the future.

MR. RIEFLER: The statistical activities of the government have needed coordination for years. Under the emergency powers under which we are operating now we are hampered in some places. We can only operate on statistics that contribute to recovery. That cuts out certain types of statistics though

---

[3] The Textile Labor Relations Board, which replaced the earlier Textile National Industrial Relations Board, and the Steel Labor Relations Board were set up under the Department of Labor by Executive Orders 6858 (Sept. 26, 1934) and 6751 (June 28, 1934). See Leverett S. Lyon *et al*, *The National Recovery Administration* (Washington, D.C., 1935), p. 469.

it includes most of the economic statistics. But it does shut us off from some fields that need coordination. For the purpose of real coordination in that field I think legislation is ultimately very desirable. It is broader than the emergency and is longer in its term.

PRESIDENT ROOSEVELT: Of course you should get a special appropriation for it. You can word it: for the statistical work.

VICE-PRESIDENT GARNER: Put your legislation in the appropriation bill.

SECRETARY PERKINS: Define the duties and objectives in the bill.

PRESIDENT ROOSEVELT: In working up the general question of all the agencies, you will talk with Mr. Riefler about that and see that you get the right language, so we will not be limited in the matter of recovery statistics.

SECRETARY PERKINS: Or the recovery period.

PRESIDENT ROOSEVELT: I want to commend to you the summary of reports of the National Emergency Council. The Secretary of State reports the trade agreement with Brazil has been completed.[4] It was signed with due solemnity on Saturday and created a very favorable impression not only in Brazil but all through South America. One fact that should be noticed is that it involves results not only between Brazil and the United States, but a great many other countries besides. For example, in releasing the duties on Brazilian maté, which is a growingly popular drink in this country, Argentine and Paraguay maté can come into this country on the same basis as Brazilian maté. In the same way, Brazil is reducing her tariff schedules on some 23 or 24 necessary products and so says to the other nations, you can bring them into Brazil on the same basis. So that it is not merely a straight trade agreement between two countries but also opens up business with others and results in increasing the fields of international trade. That is one thing that everybody should remember, that the trade agreements are not limited to the two countries making the agreement but apply also to a great many other countries at the same time, to the general interest of world trade.

The Treasury bill for the use of these so-called "baby bonds" was signed day-before-yesterday.[5] The professional bankers and financiers are of the general opinion that they will not

---

[4] One of the first treaties concluded in the newly adopted reciprocal trade program.

[5] An amendment to the Second Liberty Bond Act authorized the Treasury to issue "United States Savings Bonds" in small denominations (Public Law No. 3, 74th Congress, 1st Session, approved by the President, Feb. 4, 1935).

be very popular. They are to be sold through the Post Office Department. Instead of having to take your bond home and hide it under the mattress, in the absence of a safe in the home, you can leave it in the care of the postmaster, where it will be very safe. We believe that they will be popular. I think I am much more enthusiastic about it than the bankers are and I think the Treasury is, too.

MEMBER: What rate of interest do they carry?

PRESIDENT ROOSEVELT: It is not fixed but will be between two and a half and three per cent.

MR. COOLIDGE: It has a gradual increase in value.

PRESIDENT ROOSEVELT: In other words, you buy a $100 bond for $75. At the end of ten years you get a $100 back, and each year you can cash it for an increasing amount up to the $100; and you can get your cash for it any time you want it.

VICE-PRESIDENT GARNER: Hadn't you better ask the Post Office Department whether their bonds cover this?

MR. HOWES: We had that up, whether we should have increased bonds.

VICE-PRESIDENT GARNER: There might be claims brought against the government.

MR. COOLIDGE: There is not much danger of that. They are all registered and they are not transferable. A person has to prove that he is the one who bought the bond. It is only a receipt for the money.

VICE-PRESIDENT GARNER: He can get it any time he wants to?

MR. COOLIDGE: Yes; the only way we pay them is by check in the man's name.

PRESIDENT ROOSEVELT: It is a very nice looking bond with a picture of Grover Cleveland on it.

MR. COOLIDGE: It is different Presidents.

PRESIDENT ROOSEVELT: There is only one other thing that I want to talk about, somewhat informally, but rather firmly. You have probably read in the press that I had a visit—I should say visitation—from some gentlemen of the lower House,[6] who came down to say that they were being badly treated, and tomorrow they are having a meeting that should not be described as an indignation meeting though it will probably result that way. They came down and made two speeches which were to the general effect that nobody loves them, nobody pays any attention to them. I said, "Don't make speeches; get specific."

Well, some of them have been specific, and they brought out

---

[6] Probably the deputation of six House members, headed by Speaker Byrns, mentioned in *Time*, Feb. 11, 1935, p. 11.

certain things that I think everybody around this table and in this room should keep very closely in the front of their brain all the time. The first general point is that all of your money, my money, your existence and mine, as well as the government's, is dependent on the Congress of the United States. There is absolutely no question about that. We have to conform with the appropriation and we have to conform with the law, and if we give the impression to the Congressmen of the United States that we think they are running things with a high hand, it is going to mean an increasing difficulty in getting appropriations and legislation through the Congress.

They have been specific. A member of the Congress went to a certain agency of the government and did not see the head of that agency but saw a man down the line in a responsible position. He stated his case and the man said, "Why, Mr. So-and-so in the next room handles that matter." He opened the door and said, "Mr. So-and-so, will you come in here. I want you to meet Congressman X." Immediately a voice from the other room said unmistakably, "To hell with it! I am too busy to see any Congressman!"

Of course, that went right straight through the House of Representatives. The matter was taken up. I was so gosh darn mad that I almost fired him out-of-hand! He apologized. His whole agency apologized. He gave as his excuse that he was not feeling well. But that is no excuse. I sent word that if anything like that happened in any other agency of the government or any department of the government, the person will be fired out-of-hand. I am not firing this particular man because I am using him as a horrible example to point to. I am keeping the man that has taught us all a lesson.

The other case related to another agency where a certain division of the office on one day, without explanation to anybody, fired 11 employees and took on 11 other employees. Two or three of the Congressmen from that surrounding territory dug into things. I don't know that the facts are a thousand per cent true, but they say they discovered 11 Democrats had been fired and 11 Republicans appointed in their place. I don't believe that is a thousand per cent true, but even if it was only 8 Democrats out of 11 fired, it was a bad situation.

Most of the members of Congress are fairly reasonable. They have two problems; the first problem is the insistent demand

435

of a lot of political hangers-on who want jobs. In almost every case, as soon as you investigate the political hangers-on you find that 50 per cent of them are not fit for the job and the Congressmen will agree with you. What they complain about more than that is the fact that especially in the new agencies there have been appointed a great many people who went out and worked against the Congressman. That is not just Republicans—not by a jug full. Perhaps it is a Congressman from the South and the election is the primary. It is not the general election. Suppose the Farm Credit Administration or the CCC or something else takes on a man in a Congressman's district and the primary campaign comes on and that federal worker goes out and tries to beat the Congressman. It hurts him just as much as if he went out and worked for the Republican in the North in the general election.

I always go back to an experience in the State of New York. I found one of the departments there—the Highway Department, the State Highway Department—had road gangs, and I found that in the eastern part of my own county there were 30 men on the road gang and there were 20 of them Republicans. I didn't complain. It was all right because it was a Republican district. Twenty out of the 30 were enrolled, registered Republicans. But I was tipped off to the fact that 18 out of those 20 Republicans were actively working for the Republican Party. I drew the line there. That is different.

The complaint from the Congressmen is that in a great many of these appointments by these new agencies, especially, they are not Civil Service people and they are working against the Congressmen. They are not asking that these people work *for* the Congressmen, but they are asking that they be prevented from working *against* them, either for other Democrats or for Republicans, and they are entitled to that.

I think it is extremely important that everyone of you, when you get complaints from Congressmen in any specific case— you can tell them to be specific, that is all right; but when they are specific, don't turn it off by saying in a perfunctory manner that some field agent solemnly says he knows this man has never done anything like that. But you should get a thorough investigation of it and if the evidence is 50-50, don't assume that your field agent is right and the Congressman is wrong. There is too much tendency along that line. Nobody wants to put all these agencies into Administration politics, but we must prevent them from being anti-Administration. If they are not in sympathy with what we are doing, we do not need to use them. And there are a lot of people employed by these emergency agencies who are not in sympathy.

MR. KENNEDY: That has been called to our attention, Mr. President, but what are we going to do about it?

PRESIDENT ROOSEVELT: Fire the fellow! A few good examples of firing people for not living up to these principles would be an awfully good thing.

I am telling these Congressmen that if they do not get satisfaction along these lines to let me know. When you get word from me on the thing, you can know I mean it. These things I mention will—inevitably—eventually get up to me.

SECRETARY WALLACE: In a delicate situation like Louisiana we may have to ask your advice.

PRESIDENT ROOSEVELT: You won't have to do that. Don't put anybody in and don't keep anybody that is working for Huey Long or his crowd! That is a hundred per cent!

VICE-PRESIDENT GARNER: That goes for everybody!

PRESIDENT ROOSEVELT: Everybody and every agency. Anybody working for Huey Long is not working for us.

SECRETARY HULL: It can't be corrected too soon.

PRESIDENT ROOSEVELT: You will get a definite ruling any time you want it.

ATTORNEY GENERAL CUMMINGS: A matter has been called to my attention which is to the effect that the telegraph companies give reduced rates to the government but that the telephone companies do not. I am just wondering whether our telephone bills, which amount to a large amount of money, should not be investigated. I really haven't any idea how much the expenditure is but it must be enormous in all the departments. I was just wondering whether some survey of that should not be made by an appropriate agency.

PRESIDENT ROOSEVELT: I wonder if the Communications Commission should not take up that question.

MR. SYKES: We would be very glad to look into it.

PRESIDENT ROOSEVELT: That came up a few weeks ago. I was told—I don't know whether it was true or not—that the telegraph rate the government gets is actually below the cost of handling those telegrams to the Western Union. I don't think that the government has any right to get a rate that is so low from any private company that the private company loses money in handling the government business. On the other hand, I don't think that the private company should make any large profit off the government rate, because they get a very large amount of business. A very simple example is the press rate. The press rate is extraordinarily low, but I am told that a large part of it goes during the quiet hours of the evening and very early in the morning and that the Western Union and the Postal come out on their press rate service a little better than they used to.

MR. SYKES: Those contracts with the government on telegraph rates were made by the Postmaster General quite a number of years ago. There has been very little change in that contract for a number of years. We have no contracts with the telephone companies at all. We would be very glad to look into that.

PRESIDENT ROOSEVELT: I wish you would look into that, because the same thing applies to the radio companies. The State Department has a special rate, I think, with the radio and cable companies.

SECRETARY HULL: Yes.

PRESIDENT ROOSEVELT: How do we arrive at that?

SECRETARY HULL: It is a little technical and I do not think I can state it accurately.

PRESIDENT ROOSEVELT: If the Communications Commission will take that up, we will appreciate it.

MR. SYKES: Yes, sir, we will.

MR. RICHBERG: There is a committee on the question of cost of communications which ought to take that matter up also.

MR. SYKES: Is there such a committee?

MR. RICHBERG: Yes, there is.

MR. SYKES: I didn't know that. We will be glad to have a member of our Commission on that committee too, if you please, sir.

PRESIDENT ROOSEVELT: The Vice-President makes a suggestion, and it is an excellent suggestion, too, in regard to the federal employees in Louisiana.[7] Of course, the ones who are regular Civil Service employees we cannot touch; but I would like to have a list of all those employees working for the federal government in

---

[7] The discussion of patronage in Louisiana and the importance attached to the matter reflects the general concern at the following gained by Senator Huey Long and the possibility he would become a serious challenge to President Roosevelt for the Democratic Presidential nomination in 1936. See James A. Farley, *Jim Farley's Story* (New York, 1948), especially pp. 50-52; and Arthur M. Schlesinger, Jr., *The Age of Roosevelt: The Politics of Upheaval* (Boston, 1960), pp. 42-68, *et passim* (especially p. 250 f).

Louisiana who are non-Civil Service people. It is a fairly important thing at this time for us to have that information. That brings up another question. If any question arises, I see no reason why you should not take it up personally. If you want advice on individuals and their affiliations in the state of Louisiana, call up Congressman Sandlin and ask him for his recommendation.

That brings up another question. Congressman Sabath sent to one or two agencies a request for a list of all their employees in the state of Illinois. If every Congressman does that for every state, it will cost the federal government about $500,000. They are doing it by individuals, not by committees of Congress; and if they make that request, I think the proper answer is that if the request comes officially from a committee of Congress, of course we will be very glad to answer it, but to do it for individual Congressmen—furnish them with lists of employees—would cost the government so much money that there would have to be a special appropriation for it.

SECRETARY DERN: Congressman Sirovich wants very elaborate information concerning the personnel in my department.

PRESIDENT ROOSEVELT: We are not going to do that.

DR. DICKINSON: I was going to bring up that same thing. We had the impression as a result of what took place that we would need to go ahead with that, but we are informed that the other departments have not done it. We would like directions as to what to do under these circumstances.

PRESIDENT ROOSEVELT: If the questionnaire is sent through the mails to individual names, the department cannot interefere with the mail service of the United States; but if they are delivered in large bundles there is no need of making delivery.

SECRETARY PERKINS: I ought to apologize. The Department of Labor did that. It was referred to the personnel officer in our Department, who is a very competent officer, and it was not until a week later that he learned he did not have to do it.

SECRETARY WALLACE: This last one comes from Sirovich in behalf of a committee.

VICE-PRESIDENT GARNER: He wants the list of names so that he can get this questionnaire to each of the employees.

PRESIDENT ROOSEVELT: They ask all kinds of questions that the average Civil Service employee is unable to answer. They are catch questions.

VICE-PRESIDENT GARNER: You could say, "Now if you will pass a resolution by the Congress we will make an official report." The Secretary of the Treasury could say to the Congressman, "We don't think that this ought to be done, but if the House will pass a resolution, we will make an official reply."

SECRETARY WALLACE: Could we have Mr. Richberg prepare a standard reply?

MR. RICHBERG: Yes.

VICE-PRESIDENT GARNER: It would take considerable labor, and you will have to say that you have no money to do it; but if the House or Senate passes a resolution, then you will officially regard it.

PRESIDENT ROOSEVELT: Yesterday morning one of the employees here came in and said, "Mr. President, have I got to answer this?" I said, "What is it?" It was one of those Sirovich questionnaires. I could not have answered it to save my soul. I said, "I don't understand it, and I don't think anybody else understands it." He said, "Do I have to answer it?" I said, "You tear it up and put it in the waste basket."

MR. HOWES: Where he sends out a franked envelope, that clogs up the mails pretty well, too.

PRESIDENT ROOSEVELT: The Secretary of War is in the real estate business. He has a bill allowing him to sell some very valuable property, and before we give him authority to sell it I thought I would let you all know about it. Some of it could be transferred to some other department. Maybe it has been cleared, but I don't think it has. (*President Roosevelt then read a number of items from the suggested bill.*)

You are all put on notice; if you do not ask for it, the bill is going through. Harold, will you go over that and keep it in the government if you can?

Meeting adjourned at 3:30 p.m.

Held in the Cabinet Room of the White House,
February 19, 1935, at 2:10 p.m.

Present: the President of the United States; the Secretary of State; the
Secretary of War; the Attorney General; the Postmaster General; the
Secretary of the Navy; the Secretary of the Interior; the Secretary of
Agriculture; the Secretary of Commerce; the Secretary of Labor; the
Acting Director of the Budget; the Honorable T. Jefferson Coolidge,
Undersecretary of the Treasury; the Honorable L. W. Robert, Jr.,
Assistant Secretary of the Treasury; the Administrator of the Agricultural
Adjustment Administration; the Administrator of Federal Emergency
Relief Administration; the Chairman of the Reconstruction Finance
Corporation; the Honorable John B. Blandford, Jr., Coordinator,
Tennessee Valley Authority; the Chairman of the Federal Home Loan
Bank Board; the Chairman of the Federal Trade Commission; the
Director of Emergency Conservation Work; the Governor of the Farm
Credit Administration; the Chairman of the National Industrial Recovery
Board; the Chairman of the Federal Alcohol Control Administration;
the Administrator of the Federal Housing Administration; the President
of the Export-Import Banks of Washington, D.C.; the Chairman of
the Federal Deposit Insurance Corporation; the Chairman of the Federal
Power Commission; the Chairman of the Federal Communications
Commission; the Chairman of the Securities and Exchange Commission;
the Honorable J. J. Thomas, Vice-Governor of the Federal Reserve
Board; the Executive Director.

[We find here examples of NEC functions encountered
earlier—NEC as a means of communication to and education
of agency heads by the President, and as a means of coordinating strategy. From this meeting, it appears that legislative
clearance has been shaken down into a routine. Finally, we
catch a glimpse of Presidential legislative strategy in relation
to the holding company problem. Here we see that the
stereotype of F.D.R. as a ruthless politician who bullies
Congress, was exaggerated. At times, he resorted to much
gentler and more subtle methods.—Editor's Note.]

PRESIDENT ROOSEVELT: "Report of Subcommittees; Interdepartmental Loan
Committee." . . .
With the approval of Senator Glass?
MR. RICHBERG: The report doesn't mention that.
PRESIDENT ROOSEVELT: Next is the report of the Interdepartmental Legal Committee.
MR. RICHBERG: That committee is still working. The Federal Register Act
was considered at the first hearing on the bill before the

441

Subcommittee of the House Committee on Judiciary and Messrs. Stanley, MacLean, Wyzanski, Smith, and Townsend testified. The Subcommittee reported it favorably, with certain changes, on February 13 to the whole Committee on Judiciary, which committee is now considering it. Messrs. Stanley, MacLean, and Townsend are keeping in close touch with the matter and are in hopes that the bill will be reported out on the floor of the House with only slight changes.

PRESIDENT ROOSEVELT: Was anything done in the Senate on that—the Senate Judiciary?

ATTORNEY GENERAL CUMMINGS: I don't know. We will take that up.

PRESIDENT ROOSEVELT: "Report of the Industrial Emergency Committee."

MR. RICHBERG: There is only one item to report on that, and that is the fact that Mrs. Emily Newell Blair is now Chairman of the Consumers' Advisory Board of NRA.

MR. WILLIAMS: There is one other change, and that is: Mr. Pelley is taking the place of Owen D. Young on the Board.

PRESIDENT ROOSEVELT: "Special reports from the Executive Director; calling attention to the report of the National Industrial Recovery Board and the Federal Power Commission."

MR. RICHBERG: As stated at the last meeting, we are getting rather full reports from the various agencies bringing their work up to date in report form. We have now a report from the National Recovery Administration which is a rather large document, and another from the Federal Power Commission. These will be sent around to all members as previously promised.

PRESIDENT ROOSEVELT: "Report of the AAA regional adjustment."

MR. RICHBERG: From the AAA there is this brief report. . . .

PRESIDENT ROOSEVELT: Have those regional maps been adopted?

MR. DAVIS: No, Mr. President, these questions are going to be considered, and recommendations will be made after the meeting has been held so that we can have the advantage of regional advice.

PRESIDENT ROOSEVELT: That is a very, very sound thing, but I was not certain about the lines of the map. The thought behind it is excellent. "Report of the Governor of the Federal Reserve Board."

MR. RICHBERG: I will make a little summary of this, Mr. President. First is the decline in the interest rates. It is pointed out that these conditions exist concurrently with a continued rise in the government deficit and the necessity of large-scale government borrowing to finance relief and recovery activities. It has often been said that an unbalanced budget must lead to a failure of "confidence in the government credit," to an increase in the interest rates which the government must pay on new borrowing, and to a sympathetic rise in other rates as the supply of savings normally invested in private enterprise is diverted into government securities. Actually, the course of events in the money market has not borne out this line of argument.

PRESIDENT ROOSEVELT: Don't let Congress know that! (*Laughter*)

MR. RICHBERG: The tables show the decline in interest from 3.62 in 1929 to 2.77 in 1935; municipals, from 4.25 in 1929 to 3.42 in 1935; corporate bonds (AAA), 4.66 to 3.75.

The second point covered by this report is the question of the Federal Reserve Bank loans to industry in which it is pointed out that the amounts are very small comparatively. Also, there has been a recent decline. A partial explanation of the decrease may be found in seasonal influences, in better understanding on the part of borrowers of the kind of loan the banks are legally permitted to make, and possibly in the increased accessibility of the usual sources of loans.

This table shows December 12 to January 9, 1935, total applications 280 as compared with 506 in the previous period. The amount of applications in this period is $18,823,000 as compared with $23,329,000 in the previous period. The total accumulated advances is only $15,318,000.

PRESIDENT ROOSEVELT: The total advances made are much larger, although the number of applications made is much smaller.

MR. RICHBERG: In this last period, that is correct.

PRESIDENT ROOSEVELT: What is the explanation of that? Is Marriner [Eccles] here?

MR. THOMAS: There are fewer loans, but of better quality.

PRESIDENT ROOSEVELT: The actual amount of bank loans is getting bigger each month.

MR. THOMAS: Yes, it is picking up since that report. The actual amount approved by the committee is about $75,000,000 up to now. The actual cash advancements are a little over $18,000,000.

MR. KENNEDY: In previous depressions, the low money rates have been the forerunner of conditions getting very much better. It is because the corporations themselves have been able to avail themselves of those increased earnings. They are not able to do that as it stands today. That is very definitely a severe problem and we cannot possibly decide on cheap money because it is not of any particular advantage to the corporations themselves.

PRESIDENT ROOSEVELT: "Reports and charts from the Secretary of the Treasury concerning federal receipts and expenditures."

MR. RICHBERG: Mr. President, you may wish to read that. These charts were prepared by the Secretary of the Treasury. We have copies here.

443

new deal mosaic

PRESIDENT ROOSEVELT: The Secretary of the Treasury has prepared three charts. We might look at them. (*Mr. Ironside passed out the charts to the members of the Council.*)

The first chart shows the total federal receipts and expenditures showing a net deficit of $4,296,000,000 for the year. During January, the expenditures have fallen below the anticipated level. The receipts are just about in line with the Budget estimate. Receipts, expenditures, and the deficit for the current fiscal year are all larger than for any of the preceding four fiscal years, but for the fiscal year 1936 an increase in receipts, a decrease in expenditures, and therefore a decline in the deficit may be anticipated.

"Federal receipts." That is on the next page. Actual receipts are approximately in line with the anticipated trend, customs and miscellaneous internal revenue being very slightly greater and miscellaneous receipts slightly lower. The actual and estimated receipts for the first six months of the present fiscal year by major components are very closely in line.

"Chart 3." Actual expenditures have been slightly less than the anticipated trend in the case of general and AAA expenditures, while emergency expenditures have been substantially less than anticipated. The top line is emergency and that is pretty far below what we ought to be spending. The actual expenditures total a little below and AAA very slightly below.

"Report regarding the effect on consumption of economic changes during the past two years by National Emergency Council Consumers' Division."

MR. RICHBERG: Mr. President, the Consumers' Division is now working under the direction of Thomas Blaisdell, who has been appointed and is going ahead with that work. This is one of the first reports from that Division. First, total consumers' income has increased substantially since March 1933. According to preliminary estimates, there has been an increase of about 23 per cent in national income paid out since March 1933. Income payments are running between eight and nine hundred million dollars per month higher than at the low point. These estimates place the total for the year 1934 around six billion above the year 1933, which is an increase of 13 or 14 per cent for the year as a whole. The bulk of this increase is available for consumption expenditures.

Second, prices paid by consumers have advanced. Third, the volume of goods consumed has increased.

444

PRESIDENT ROOSEVELT:
MR. RICHBERG:

There has been a great deal of controversy over this matter. Are they all agreed on this answer?

I am not sure that they will all agree. That is why I mention it.

There has been about a ten per cent increase in the income since the low point of 1933. These estimates must be modified by the use of some consumer incomes to pay off debts and by the fact that many consumers with restored jobs have made installment purchases.

There are a few very reliable measures of the volume of goods flowing into consumption. Direct measures of automobile sales are available and these show large increases in 1934, and further sharp increases are in prospect for the first half of 1935.

Fourth, groups of consumers have not fared equally. Three groups in particular have been aided by the various government programs and these three groups undoubtedly have had the largest relative improvement in their status. They are the unemployed, the lowest-paid wage earners, and the agricultural population. The unemployed are best helped by supplying them with jobs. Those still unemployed cannot be said to be helped at all except in a negative sense of provision for subsistence. With Public Works and work-spreading under the NRA there has been an increase of employment since March 1933, estimated at around 4,000,000 men. Estimates place the number still unemployed or on work relief at around 11,000,000.

(b) The group of labor income receivers has been increased in number by approximately 4,000,000 since the low point in March 1933, an increase of approximately 11 per cent. Total dollar income in wages and salaries for this group in December 1934, has been estimated as 20 to 25 per cent larger than in March 1933.

The earnings per employed worker are required to measure the well-being of individual members of the group and the best indications are that these earnings increased on the average of ten per cent for individual income receivers from March 1933, to December 1934.

(c) The farmer in 1932 received what was estimated as only 7.5 per cent of the national income. In 1934, it has been estimated by the Agricultural Adjustment Administration that agriculture received 10.2 per cent of the national income. This increase brings the farmers' share practically back to the position it occupied in 1928 and 1929 before the effect of the industrial depression hit the farmer harder than most other groups.

There is a chart attached to this which shows in graphic form the increase in income in the different groups of the national income.

PRESIDENT ROOSEVELT: "Concerning Interpreting Economic Statistics in the Executive Director's Office."

MR. RICHBERG: I wish to report this for the information of those who may be particularly interested. . . .

SECRETARY PERKINS: May we know who is going to make this survey?

MR. RICHBERG: I am trying to make the survey.

SECRETARY PERKINS: I thought you were using someone from Mr. Hopkins' organization.

MR. RICHBERG: Only to help me get the information. I wanted to get a report on the matter as to how these statistics could be procured. We have not been getting them.

SECRETARY PERKINS: What statistics do you want?

MR. RICHBERG: Current compiled statistics of various kinds—the sort of thing we have had to work out ourselves to prepare these charts.

SECRETARY PERKINS: I wondered if we might know of the nature of them, because if any departments that are supposed to be furnishing statistics have been unequal to the strain we should know it.

MR. RICHBERG: Oh, the departments have done their part! It is the coordination of statistics that we want. The Central Statistical Board was not permitted to produce any statistics of its own; therefore, it was necessary to have another agency to bring together the statistical reports of the departments. That is the work we have had difficulty in getting done. What I am trying to find out now is why we can't get them, or if we can.

PRESIDENT ROOSEVELT: "State Legislation."

MR. RICHBERG: I think there are a great many of the agencies that may desire to know something about the progress toward state legislation. There are 44 states where the legislatures are meeting this year and the state directors for the National Emergency Council and their committees have been assisting in the presentation of these proposals. And by the time of the next Council meeting, we will be able to present a detailed picture of just what has been accomplished in state-federal cooperation.

I am submitting today preliminary reports on the status of this legislation to the heads of the various agencies. This information will be supplemented from time to time so that agency heads will have an unbiased current estimate as to the possibility of enactment in acceptable form in the various states.

PRESIDENT ROOSEVELT: "Administrative Charts—RFC. Twelve major loan categories complete."

MR. RICHBERG: Mr. President, in providing this book of charts for you, we are trying to supplement that with the preparation of a master sheet, every two weeks, on which the major charts will be reproduced. This is not typical because it has some of the major charts and has all of the RFC charts we just received, but it does indicate the type of information, and if there are any members of the Council who desire to have these, we will furnish them in photostatic form.

PRESIDENT ROOSEVELT: Will you have a new one every two weeks?

MR. RICHBERG: Yes.

PRESIDENT ROOSEVELT: I think at the next meeting we better have charts for the members.

MR. RICHBERG: They are broken down here into subcharts. The major charts we can distribute to everybody.

PRESIDENT ROOSEVELT: "Special Problems for Explanation or Discussion. Lists of employees not yet received from certain agencies."

MR. RICHBERG: That refers to the Louisiana situation, Mr. President. We have received some of them. There was a little misunderstanding, I think, and others were sent to you. We have been clearing them through Congressman Sandlin. We have received lists from the Departments of Justice, Agriculture, and Interior, and from RFC, Federal Housing, PWA, National Resources Board, Subsistence Homesteads Division, Soil Erosion Service, NRA, and AAA. That does not include all of them. Congressman Sandlin has expressed particular anxiety to have reports from FERA and Labor, also.

SECRETARY HULL: How about CCC?

MR. RICHBERG: We have none from them as yet.

SECRETARY HULL: They have about 12 camps, I think.

PRESIDENT ROOSEVELT: Will you please get everybody who is not on that list to get in their names to Mr. Richberg for transmission to the Congressman. We have only two regular departments.

MR. RICHBERG: Three.

PRESIDENT ROOSEVELT: Yes, three, and about eight of the agencies. We need all the agencies.

POSTMASTER GENERAL FARLEY: You mean exempted employees?

PRESIDENT ROOSEVELT: Yes.

ATTORNEY GENERAL CUMMINGS: Non-Civil Service.

PRESIDENT ROOSEVELT: Yes.

447

MR. RICHBERG: There is some difference in the type of reports. Some have added to the report of the list of names and the salaries something of the endorsement they had.

SECRETARY PERKINS: You want those who come from Louisiana and those who are working in Louisiana?

ATTORNEY GENERAL CUMMINGS: People working in Louisiana or from Louisiana working elsewhere.

MR. RICHBERG: It is essentially a question of legal residence.

PRESIDENT ROOSEVELT: I think it is very important. I had a session with the Congressional Grievance Committee on Saturday, and our friend Mr. McFarlane played right into our hands. He got off in a very bad start and never quite got back on his feet afterward. He came in with a Congressional Directory and he started proceedings by rising to his feet and saying, "Mr. Speaker!" That brought a general laugh.

And then he said, "I hold in my hand a Congressional Directory. In the Department of State I have checked the names of holdover Republicans. There are 69 holdover Republicans out of 84 non-Civil Service positions." Then he went on with the Department of the Treasury, etc. He finally let me see the book. I turned to the first one he had read off—the Department of State—and I said, "I see you have the Secretary of State listed as a Democrat." He said, "Yes, I believe that is correct." I said, "I see you have the Undersecretary, Mr. Phillips, listed as a Democrat." He said, "Yes." I said, "He was a Republican up to 1932. I don't suppose you hold that against him, do you?" He said, "No." Then I said, "I see the Undersecretary listed as a Republican, Mr. R. Walton Moore." I turned to the Speaker and I said, "I just hate a thing like that; here is a man who served as a Democratic member of the House for 16 years. I thought he would remain true to his Democratic principles. When a man of that long experience in the Democratic party, after such long service in the House, backslides at his age, it is a pretty serious situation." (*Laughter*)

Then I went on and he had all the heads of divisions listed as Republicans. I think most of them are. But I mentioned the fact to him that they have in the State Department the career service, the diplomatic consular service, and all these men who are heads of divisions belong to this service, which is under Civil Service. He didn't know that. About two-thirds of the information he handed in was incorrect.

Then he came to the second part, and that was that the people in the newer agencies who are not under Civil Service should keep their hands out of politics. I think it was a man in Harry Hopkins' organization who was reported the other day as having presided at a political party town meeting and having thereafter gone out and written postcards to all the voters favoring one of the candidates for town treasurer. It was finally brought to me for a ruling and I said, "That man just could not stay." As a federal government employee he was taking part in local politics actively. It is a very difficult thing to know where to draw the line, because obviously they should not take part in state party politics or national party politics while they are doing their federal emergency work, because the work they are doing does necessarily involve passing individual judgment on individuals. That is especially true on relief work or on loan work; and if they are mixed up with party politics even to the extent of a town treasurer, they can always be accused of determining who should go on relief rolls or who should get a loan. They can be accused of partisan judgment and I think it is a much better thing for us to apply the theoretical rule of the Civil Service that they may exercise the duties of citizenship but they must not take part in partisan politics.

The complaint from the Hill is mostly based on the fact that a lot of these employees go out and try to defeat the sitting Congressmen, or that Harry Hopkins has appointed the son of their particular pet enemy within the congressional district— an awful lot of that. They would like to, but they don't dare ask for it—they do not actually say you have got to appoint the people we nominate. They would like to have it made clear to the government, however, that we should not appoint their own particular pet political enemies.

I think if we bear that in mind in the future, we will get much further with the opposition in Congress, which is not a very serious thing; it always happens every year, but it can always be handled by devoting a certain amount of time to it. I don't think it is a very serious thing, but I think we do have to be careful in the way we treat them and the considerations that we give to their complaints. I would be awfully hot if I were a member of Congress and had to put up with some of the things that these Congressmen have had to put up with. I would be inclined to get up on the floor of Congress and say some pretty nasty things about the heads of departments and agencies. I think they have a little complaint on their side. I don't think all the justice is on our side. That is why I repeat, let us try to give them every possible consideration, and at the same time try to keep the merit system at the front in the actual work of the administration.

Have you anything else, Don?

MR. RICHBERG: Nothing else.

PRESIDENT ROOSEVELT: Has anybody anything else? We are through quite early. I would like to report just one other thing and that is this. A great deal of this legislation is clearing very, very well, I think. Proposed legislation is clearing through Mr. Richberg and me, and it is being pretty well received up on the Hill. We have made it pretty clear that it is legislation so far as the actual measure goes, and we want it to originate on the Hill. We do not want to be in the position in this particular year—because we are not in the middle of a crisis as in 1933—we do not want to make it appear that we are sending things up there that they must pass. They understand that now and the feeling in that respect is much better. They are getting cooperation instead of orders and are very happy about it.

MR. MC NINCH: I have been requested to appear before the committee on holding companies and Power Commission bill which is now being considered.[1] They have had their first hearing today. It was the suggestion that they would like me to go as far as I could go in giving it not only Power Commission but Administration approval. I made no response but will appear.

That presents a difficult situation, to my mind. I doubt if you have personally seen or know a great deal about Title II which deals with the extension of the powers of the Power Commission over interstate commerce and some other matters; but you are familiar with the holding-company operation of it which is Title I. As to that, as you very well know, there is a difference of opinion among those with whom you have advised as to how far to go. Do you have any suggestion or do you want to talk with me before I go up there? I certainly cannot give it Administration blessing unless it comes from you.

---

[1] Legislation to regulate public utility holding companies was under consideration in Congress. The holding-company bill (Wheeler-Rayburn Bill) was handled by the Senate Committee on Interstate Commerce (chairman, Sen. Burton K. Wheeler, D., Montana), and the House Committee on Interstate and Foreign Commerce (chairman, Rep. Sam Rayburn, D., Tex.). The Public Utility Holding Company Act (Public Law 479, 74th Congress) was finally passed by the Congress and signed by the President on Aug. 26, 1935.

PRESIDENT ROOSEVELT: It probably is the best policy for each of the government departments concerned to make their recommendations to the two committees. You have the Rayburn Committee, and at the very minute they get through holding hearings there, Senator Wheeler's committee in the Senate is going to start holding hearings.

MR. MC NINCH: I understand not.

PRESIDENT ROOSEVELT: He told me so this morning.

MR. MC NINCH: Did he?

PRESIDENT ROOSEVELT: Whether the two chairmen will bring in a similar bill I do not know. It is one of those very controversial matters which is better, for the time being, to be threshed out more or less in committee and see what kind of bills they are going to bring in. There may be entirely different bills and the situation is so much at cross purposes as to detail. The ultimate objective may be the same but the methods in both bills may be very different. I think we better wait and see how they come out before we settle the question of final administration policy. Everybody is perfectly at liberty to give their own personal views.

MR. MC NINCH: May I ask: Even though that view does not find expression in the bill? Frankly, I am in an embarrassing position.

PRESIDENT ROOSEVELT: That is perfectly all right. I have no idea how it is going to come out.

Meeting adjourned at 2:55 p.m.

Proceedings of the National Emergency Council

[meeting no. 25] March 12, 1935

Held in the Cabinet Room of the White House, March 12, 1935, at 2:15 p.m.

Present: the President of the United States; the Secretary of State; the Secretary of the Treasury; the Secretary of War; the Postmaster General; the Secretary of the Navy; the Secretary of the Interior; the Secretary of Commerce; the Secretary of Labor; the Honorable William Stanley, Assistant to the Attorney General; the Honorable L. W. Robert, Jr., Assistant Secretary of the Treasury; the Administrator of the Agricultural Adjustment Administration; the Administrator of the Federal Emergency Relief Administration; the Chairman of the Reconstruction Finance Corporation; the Chairman of the Tennessee Valley Authority; the Chairman of the Federal Home Loan Bank Board; the Chairman of the Federal Trade Commission; the Honorable James J. McEntee, Assistant Director, Emergency Conservation Work; the Federal Coordinator of Transportation; the Governor of the Farm Credit Administration; the Chairman of the National Industrial Recovery Board; the Chairman of the Federal Alcohol Control Administration; the Administrator of the Federal Housing Administration; the President of the Export-Import Banks of Washington, D.C.; the Chairman of the Federal Deposit Insurance Corporation; the Chairman of the Federal Power Commission; the Honorable Basil Manly, Vice-Chairman of the Federal Power Commission; the Honorable Thomas R. Tate, Director of the National Power Survey; the Chairman of the Federal Communications Commission; the Chairman of the Securities and Exchange Commission; the Governor of the Federal Reserve Board; the Executive Director.

[A somewhat less sympathetic Congress was faced in 1935 with a large number of highly controversial bills. In many ways, this Congress marked the high point in the passage of New Deal reforms, and this 1935 session was one of the most productive of major legislation in history. Out of it came the National Labor Relations Act (the Wagner Act), a gigantic work relief appropriation, the Social Security Act, the "soak-the-rich" tax bill, and the Public Utility Holding Company Act. Roosevelt's comment, "let them talk," indicated his appreciation of Congressional procedure and his knowledge that despite delays, he would get "his" legislation.—Editors' Note.]

PRESIDENT ROOSEVELT: Well, we have one new member with us today—Mr. Prall, the new chairman of the Communications Commission. Glad to see you.

"Report on Subcommittees;" there is only one, the Inter-departmental Legal Committee.

MR. RICHBERG: This is a report of progress of this Federal Register Act, Mr.

President. It has been favorably considered by the House Committee on Judiciary, which voted to report the bill, with some changes.[1] These changes are limitation of the salary of the director in charge of publication operations to $6,000, and requiring each agency within six months to prepare a complete compilation of their effective rules and regulations; and thereafter the administrative committee is to report to the President with respect thereto, and the President is then authorized to determine which of such documents should be published in either special or supplemental editions. That legislation is going forward.

PRESIDENT ROOSEVELT: All right. "Special Reports;" first, "Calling attention to reports of Farm Credit Administration and Federal Housing Administration."

MR. RICHBERG: Those reports were sent out for the meeting of the Council which was not held last week; and the next item—"Agency Operating Charts"—was also sent out, so all members have that.

PRESIDENT ROOSEVELT: "Report of the United States Information Service." . . .

MR. RICHBERG: It seems worthwhile to call attention of the members of the Council to this Service again. There have been some 41,000 inquiries of the Service in the 50 weeks since it was established, located in the National Emergency Council. I will just summarize those; the government departments have made 13,968 of them, Congress 2,000, and the public 25,000. These inquiries vary in great degree, but as they are coming now, they more and more require looking up and some study. They cannot be answered so much by mere reference to a card. There have been so many of these inquiries that there has been prepared a mimeographed pamphlet called "The Digest of the Purposes of Current Federal Agencies" and a master chart of the federal government. Up to date, 12,000 Digests and 20,000 charts have been mailed from the office.

I want to call your attention to the fact that, following definite requests from government departments, and after learning that no other agency was releasing the same material, the United States Information Service has compiled and kept current such lists as the following: telephone lists of government agencies; emergency and other government agencies; personnel officers of emergencies and executive departments; information, press relations, and publications officers; libraries in the United States Government; Cabinet members and their duties; state governors, and state superintendents of banks.

---

[1] The Federal Register Act was passed during the 1935 session of Congress.

Lists of this sort and many others of like nature are being
kept up, and I thought members of the Council might have
their attention called to the fact that a great many inquiries
which they receive can be handled in this manner and save
a great deal of work.

PRESIDENT ROOSEVELT: Do they all know how to reach the United States Information
Service?

MR. RICHBERG: It can be reached either by telephone or by mail. The
telephone is in the Government Manual. I want to make it
perfectly clear that this service is not to discuss policies, but
just simply to direct inquiries to the proper source under
the circumstances.

PRESIDENT ROOSEVELT: "Report Concerning State Legislation." . . .

MR. RICHBERG: I think that, in view of the fact that a great many of the
departments or agencies are interested in this situation,
attention should be called to the fact a large majority of the 44
state legislatures will adjourn during the next two weeks, or
shortly thereafter, with only a comparatively small portion of
the needed cooperative recovery legislation enacted. There
has been quite a little confusion in the way in which the
federal agencies have submitted their legislative suggestions,
which has sometimes prevented state directors for the National
Emergency Council from being completely effective in this
program. In quite a number of instances, the bills were sent
directly to state authorities so that the state directors had no
knowledge of them and could not help in carrying them
forward. I have instances from several states in which that
practically resulted in failure to get the legislation through.
The President, at the meeting of December 11, approved the
procedure by which state legislation should be routed through
the Council, and a number of the departments and agencies
have carried that forward. The state directors are the contact
men with the state governments. Failure to carry out the
instructions has in some instances retarded legislation in getting
all the help that could be obtained. I want to suggest, Mr.
President, that within the next few weeks, when this particular
experience is clearly in mind, and when a great many of the
departments and agencies have seen the result of what has
been done and what has not been done, it might be a good thing
to have a conference.

PRESIDENT ROOSEVELT: I think you might read some of the specific instances of the
difficulties we had.

MR. RICHBERG: In North Dakota, fifteen bills were sent directly by PWA to

454

the governor, but the local representative and the director were not advised. Ten of those bills have no chance of passage. In Ohio, bills were sent direct to the governor. They were found by chance in the office of the Attorney General on the last day on which introduction was permitted. The local representative and the state director had not been advised, and only accidental finding by a state recovery official got them before the legislature.

In West Virginia, fourteen bills were sent directly to the governor. The state director was asked to indicate which of the federal legislation proposed was most urgent to the Administration but was without advice on this subject, and the legislature is likely to adjourn within a week with no action.

In Utah, the governor received three bills—Housing Authorities Law, Eminent Domain for certain corporations, and the Housing Cooperation Law. The governor discussed them with the state director, who had not been advised previously.

This is the kind of slip that does not help us very much.

PRESIDENT ROOSEVELT:
MR. RICHBERG: We are trying a new procedure in a good many ways, and there is not always an understanding of the service to be rendered. I think it has been helpful in a good many instances, particularly in helping the governor understand what was really wanted.

PRESIDENT ROOSEVELT: The next is a report from the Agricultural Adjustment Administration concerning the landlord-tenant relationship, and as that is a comparatively new subject, I thought I would read that myself. Some of you have seen it already. It is a comparatively new thing that we should be keeping in the back of our heads.... Just how many of those are Negroes returning from the North?

MR. DAVIS: I cannot give the racial breakdown. I do not know.

PRESIDENT ROOSEVELT: I think it is pretty heavy—something like a million and a quarter.

MR. DAVIS: We will have a cross-section of it in the survey when it is completed. (*President Roosevelt then read on to the end of the report without important comment.*)

PRESIDENT ROOSEVELT: Next is the report of the Department of Agriculture regarding urban and farmer consumer income. I will read this and then Donald wants to make one or two comments on it which I think probably are justified.... Now, I think there is a catch in these figures relating to the urban income which Donald will explain.

MR. RICHBERG: I think this needs to be pointed out. I understand the urban consumers' income includes relief payments; in other words, they are not a reflection of the earning power of the urban consumer. Now, the farm income, as a matter of fact, does reflect the earning power—

PRESIDENT ROOSEVELT (*interposing*): Much more nearly.

MR. RICHBERG: Yes, more nearly because the benefit payments are payments for the products of labor whereas relief is out-and-out charity. I think this is not entirely fair as a comparison of total purchasing power or income in sections urban and rural and it might be misunderstood by many people. This table might give an unfair impression of the comparative industrial and agricultural conditions.

SECRETARY DERN: Someone told me the other night that the reduction of cotton acreage in the South had thrown a lot of manual laborers out of work and onto the relief rolls.

PRESIDENT ROOSEVELT: That does not check, does it, with what we have?

SECRETARY WALLACE: Yes, I think, to some extent, it is possibly true; but we have endeavored to keep the same number of share-croppers and tenants. Do you have the precise figures for agricultural laborers in the South?

MR. DAVIS: No, unfortunately we haven't and won't have until the farm census is tabulated, unless we could get a pretty good cross-section from FERA. I think the fact of the matter is that the extent to which labor has been released by the agricultural program is far less than the extent to which industrial labor has been released by the curtailment of industrial production, Mr. President. The fact of the matter is, Mr. President, that tenant houses down in the South are all occupied, and in some cases they have as many as two, three, or four families in one house. A part of that is due to the movement from the city to the country, which gives the appearance of a lot of extra people floating around.

PRESIDENT ROOSEVELT: I don't believe that statement holds water.

SECRETARY DERN: I didn't know.

PRESIDENT ROOSEVELT: "Report by the Chairman of the Board of the Reconstruction Finance Corporation Relating to a Certain Railroad Consolidation Proposal."

MR. RICHBERG: I thought this might have particular interest, Mr. President. . . .

[A plan has been agreed to by the eight railroads affected by, or occupying the same general territory, (which, by the way, is more railroads than it can reasonably support), looking to the absorption by seven of these railroads of the Minneapolis and St. Louis Road, which has been in receivership the past twelve years.

Based upon the entire life of the Minneapolis and St. Louis, it seems obvious that it cannot be operated successfully as an independent system. The road has its headquarters in Minneapolis, and extends through sections of four states (South Dakota, Minnesota, Iowa and Illinois) with a total of approximately 1,627 miles. The country served by this railroad is also served by the other and larger systems.

The plan agreed to must be approved by the Interstate Commerce Commission after hearings. It contemplates the abandonment of approximately 400 miles, with the substitution of dependable highway transportation facilities in communities that might be left without railroad service, and, as far as possible, the absorption or protection of displaced labor.]

As this is the forerunner of possible activities that might come out of the Reconstruction Finance Corporation relations with railroads, I thought it might be interesting.

PRESIDENT ROOSEVELT: What will the ICC people do with that?

MR. JONES: Of course, we cannot tell until the various communities make their protests. Every community is going to object. They are not willing to lose a single residence, to say nothing of a railroad. My impression is that the ICC will be sensible about it; but this is the first time I have ever found a case where eight railroads were affected and all agreed to any one thing. However, some of them are beginning to kick over the traces, and it may not go through. They were all in full agreement about two weeks ago, but they are beginning to buck a little about this, that, and the other, and I don't know whether it will ever get to the point. It is obviously the thing if we can work it out. I thought it would be a matter of interest.

PRESIDENT ROOSEVELT: Yes.

"Special Problems for Explanation or Discussion; Lists of Employees not yet Received from Certain Agencies."

MR. RICHBERG: In regard to the Louisiana question, lists of employees showing legal residence have not been received from the following agencies: the Treasury Department, the Post Office Department, the Commerce Department, Tennessee Valley Authority, Federal Home Loan Banks, Home Owners' Loan Corporation, Emergency Conservation Work, Federal Coordinator of Transportation, Federal Deposit Insurance Corporation, and the Securities and Exchange Commission.

MR. KENNEDY: I beg your pardon; we have reported.

SECRETARY ROPER: I think we have reported.

MR. RICHBERG: We will check up on those, sir.

457

MR. FARLEY: We reported we did not have any.

PRESIDENT ROOSEVELT: How did it happen that you did not have any? Don't you have any post offices in Louisiana?

MR. FARLEY: They are not exempt.

MR. RICHBERG: Congressman Sandlin wished to make up some sort of a program of handling the matter.

PRESIDENT ROOSEVELT: This has been going now for about five weeks. Please get them in quickly.

MR. RICHBERG: It is possible that some may have gone directly to the Congressman.

SECRETARY ROPER: I think that is very likely.

SECRETARY SWANSON: You have the Navy Department!

PRESIDENT ROOSEVELT: "Needs for Further Coordination." I thought I would say a word about the problem of financing agencies. The Public Works bill[2] in the Senate has been more or less mangled, as you know, and the objective at the present time is to get it through. I appreciate the fact that a number of agencies think they have not been taken care of. They may have to fold up in June, for instance, the PWA. That is possibly true under the present form of the Senate bill, but necessarily I have to be guided by the advice of the gentlemen in charge of the bill as to the proper procedure to get the bill through, and you will be taken care of. I cannot tell you when or how. The objective in the first instance is to get the bill through the Senate, and then it will come to conference and we will appear and get those matters taken care of in conference, if necessary. If it cannot be taken care of in conference, we will have to get separate legislation.

MR. MC ENTEE: The CCC is in a very tight place.

SECRETARY PERKINS: Also the National Labor Relations Board.

MR. CHOATE: In the FACA,[3] we are still running on our original appropriation.

PRESIDENT ROOSEVELT: The whole question is being handled by the Director of the Budget, and Mr. Richberg of the clearing house! Just shoot everything at them—Bell and Mr. Richberg—and they will take it up in conference and try to get the Secretary of the Navy and the Comptroller General to pass on these questions! (*Laughter*) And if anything is necessary, we will get it by hook or by crook.

---

[2] Through the early days of March, one of the issues involved in holding up passage of this bill was the old problem of whether to pay prevailing wages on work relief projects, or to make wages deliberately lower than those in private employment.

[3] Federal Alcohol Control Administration.

SECRETARY ROPER: In making some contacts, I find that there is some misunderstanding as to the amount of the unexpended balance in the present Public Works unit and the idea, as I get it from rather good sources, is to reduce that present pending bill by the amount of the unexpended balance; that is, the amount of money that has been allocated but not actually appropriated through contractual relationships. They think it is an immense amount. They are talking about a billion dollars. I have not had time to talk with the Secretary of the Interior about it as yet. These sources told me today that they were going to pass the bill, but less the unexpended balance, which they think is about a billion dollars. I think some enlightenment is necessary.

PRESIDENT ROOSEVELT: Much enlightenment is necessary on the Hill.

MR. RICHBERG: A great many bills have been presented involving these agencies. I made a very strong effort to see if we could not get an amendment which would cover the whole question, but I found that the opposition was insuperable, as far as I could discover, and the President has given the ultimate result on it. I want it understood that I have taken up everything that has been presented.

PRESIDENT ROOSEVELT: It is very necessary for us to have a certain perspective on the time schedule. Before the Norris Amendment[4] went through, Congress used to have great difficulty in adjourning before July. In these days, with infinitely more difficulty in the way of legislation and appropriations, this Congress has only been here two months and there are a lot of people who think Congress is going home next week without passing the legislation. If they go home the first of July or in the middle of July we haven't any complaint. But don't think that because legislation has not been passed by this Congress on the twelfth day of March that you are not going to get it. There is a jittery feeling on the part of some that they are not going to get this or that. That, I think, is positively childish. Congress will do a very good job. If they go away on the first of July without enacting essential legislation, they will come back the following Monday in special session! That is perfectly simple. I don't think we need to get jittery

---

[4] The Twentieth Amendment to the Constitution, sometimes referred to as the "Lame Duck" Amendment, was also known as the Norris Amendment because of the role played by Senator George W. Norris of Nebraska in getting it adopted. It was ratified in 1933, and shifted the start of Presidential terms to Jan. 20, from Mar. 4, and the opening of the annual sessions of Congress to Jan. 3.

459

about Congress because of what they have not done in two months. Give them a chance! After all, they love to talk. Let them talk.

SECRETARY DERN: What about the next enrollment for CCC?

PRESIDENT ROOSEVELT: I told the Quartermaster General and Mr. Fechner to go ahead and advertise for it. You cannot let the contracts, but be all ready to go ahead.

SECRETARY WALLACE: The crop loans and deficiency appropriations are very sadly needed at this very moment. That happens to be a case that does not quite fit the bill so exactly.

PRESIDENT ROOSEVELT: If the CCC goes out, 358,000 young men go out of business on the first of April.

We have a report from Mr. McNinch on the federal power survey.[5] (*Copies of charts and so forth were then passed out to the members of the Council and Mr. Manly presented the report . . .*)

Is there anything more?

Meeting adjourned at 3:10 p.m.

---

[5] The National Power Survey was provided for in Executive Order 6251, Aug. 19, 1933, and was to survey power resources, present and future markets, etc. (Senate Resolution 80, May 29, 1933, also directed a survey of the cost of distributing electricity.) See Federal Power Commission, *National Power Survey, Interim Report* (Washington, D.C., 1935).

Held in the Cabinet Room of the White House, April 23, 1935, at 2:10 p.m.

Present: the President of the United States; the Secretary of State; the Secretary of the Treasury; the Secretary of War; the Attorney General; the Secretary of the Navy; the Secretary of the Interior; the Secretary of Agriculture; the Secretary of Commerce; the Acting Director of the Budget; the Honorable William W. Howes, First Assistant Postmaster General; the Honorable L. W. Robert, Jr., Assistant Secretary of the Treasury; the Administrator of the Agricultural Adjustment Administration; the Administrator of the Federal Emergency Relief Administration; the Chairman of the Reconstruction Finance Corporation; the Chairman of the Tennessee Valley Authority; the Chairman of the Federal Home Loan Bank Board; the Honorable Charles H. March, Commissioner of the Federal Trade Commission; the Director of the Emergency Conservation Work; the Governor of the Farm Credit Administration; the Chairman of the Federal Alcohol Control Administration; the Administrator of the Federal Housing Administration; the President of the Export-Import Banks of Washington, D.C.; the Chairman of the Federal Deposit Insurance Corporation; the Chairman of the Federal Power Commission; the Chairman of the Federal Communications Commission; the Honorable James M. Landis, Commissioner of the Securities and Exchange Commission; the Governor of the Federal Reserve Board; the Executive Director.

[This meeting illustrates the two-way flow of information between the President and the agency heads. The meeting opens with discussion of the recurring problem of adequate statistical measures of progress in the fight against the depression—in this case the outflow of money in payments to people engaged in work projects. Several other matters arose on which the President sought information from those assembled. Either he questioned individuals about reports prepared for the meeting, or set up informal committees to pursue a point further. Then, just as the meeting was to adjourn, he launched into a long discussion of the plans for inaugurating the expanded 1935 work project scheme—the famous WPA. Here he was briefing the assemblage for *their* information. Again it is interesting to note that the discussion is set in a framework of the publicity schedule for the release of the same information to the press and public.—Editors' Note.]

PRESIDENT ROOSEVELT: This says there were no meetings of subcommittees held recently.

new deal mosaic

VOICE:	That is good! (*Laughter*)
PRESIDENT ROOSEVELT:	"Agency Operating Charts."
MR. RICHBERG:	I understand these will be sent around tomorrow.
PRESIDENT ROOSEVELT:	You will get those in the morning. Next is a proposal to provide Council members with graphic charts of construction activities of the government.
MR. RICHBERG:	These are little charts that are being worked out, covering the regular activities that are stimulating the heavy industries. The data will include allocations, work in process, and cumulative expenditures, as well as the approximate number of men employed on a full-time basis for the agencies directly engaged in construction, such as Public Works Administration, Tennessee Valley Authority, Treasury Building program, etc. It will also include construction stimulated by operations of the Home Owners' Loan Corporation and the Federal Housing Administration. A sheet of charts will be submitted, reflecting the status of the major departmental activities in the field of construction.
PRESIDENT ROOSEVELT:	Now, before you make those charts in final form, you better delay it about two weeks for the new setup of the work relief bill, because I want an entirely different kind of chart.[1] Here is a very good example. The Treasury Department brought me some figures showing that on $1,200,000,000 worth of allocations for work, most of which were made a great many months ago, the Treasury had only paid out $300,000,000. Of course it relates, in large part, to what I talked about before—the lag between the allocation and the actual work being done. Actually, under the new program, we are going to get weekly reports from every project. Those reports will be based on payrolls. That is the thing that we are looking toward as the objective of this bill, more than anything else—the amount of money paid out to people on relief at the end of every week—and that is going to give us a much better picture than anything we have had before. Allocations don't count; Treasury payments don't necessarily count; there is a big lag there, but the actual number of people employed during the week and the amount they receive in wages is what counts.

1 The President was referring here to the Emergency Relief Appropriation Act of 1935 which had been signed on Apr. 8. The "new setup" he mentions is obviously the machinery provided for by Executive Order on May 6, 1935, which created the Works Progress Administration and procedures for screening project applications, etc.

I think we can get that from this new system. If you will go a little slow on the form of the chart until we work out the new process of getting facts every week, it will help.
"Calling Attention to Certain Reports to be Later Transmitted to Council Members."

MR. RICHBERG: These are summary reports under the Agricultural Adjustment Act, interest on the public debt and ability to pay, external value of the dollar and the balance of payments for 1934; and international trade.

PRESIDENT ROOSEVELT: "Request of Department of State for Development of Regular Report for Use of Foreign Service."

MR. RICHBERG: I thought this matter ought to be called to the attention of all the members, Mr. President . . . . This involves quite a question of policy, Mr. President.

PRESIDENT ROOSEVELT: How long will these statements be?

SECRETARY HULL: Generally about a page.

PRESIDENT ROOSEVELT: The difficulty in doing that is to get a lot of facts into one page without giving the wrong impression. Have you an awfully good man over there that can draft these?

SECRETARY HULL: I let Mr. Phillips and somebody else look after that.

PRESIDENT ROOSEVELT: I am inclined to think it should clear through the director of the National Emergency Council, because most information comes in that way.

MR. RICHBERG: Of course these matters are being prepared in our office.

SECRETARY HULL: That is what I thought.

MR. RICHBERG: The only question is after this has been checked in this manner, if there is any desire on your part to have it cleared in any further way. I think the State Department will exercise judgment as to what is proper to send out if we do not exercise proper judgment.

PRESIDENT ROOSEVELT: I am inclined to think that if you and Phillips have a talk on the mechanics of it, the best way would be to put out a two-page statement, and you can boil it down. Of course, included in that will be other phases of news, such as the passage of the Social Security bill by Congress.[2]

SECRETARY HULL: The outstanding points of interest.

PRESIDENT ROOSEVELT: Yes, I don't think anything further is necessary. Of course, anybody doing these pages knows the risk, because if they do something which is a misstatement of administration policies, the chances are they will lose their heads! But somebody has to do it and take the chance. You get a bright young man in the

---

[2] The Social Security Act was passed by the Congress and signed by the President on Aug. 14, 1935.

Emergency Council and a bright young man in the State
Department who want to take the chance.

SECRETARY HULL: We thought we had instructions from you to do this.

PRESIDENT ROOSEVELT: Oh, we have got to do it! I am certainly not going to edit
everything that goes out.
"Report Concerning United States Government Manual."

MR. RICHBERG: I don't think it will be necessary to take up the time of the
Council with this. We have a report here showing the extent
of use of the Manual.

PRESIDENT ROOSEVELT: "Significant Excerpts from Reports of Council Members."

MR. RICHBERG: These are all in the reports which have been distributed, aren't
they?

MR. IRONSIDE: Yes, but not in full.

PRESIDENT ROOSEVELT: I think these are almost worth reading. . . .

[Both an importer—Halsey Beverage Distributing Company of Newark,
New Jersey—and a rectifier—Hillcrest Distilling Company, Lawrenceburg,
Indiana (wholly-owned subsidiary of Joseph E. Seagram and Sons)—
having violated the provisions of the labeling regulations, received as a
penalty the suspension of their basic permits. These suspensions represent
the first instance in which it has been necessary to take somewhat drastic
action to enforce the labeling regulations.]

Joe, are they going to take those cases to court?

MR. CHOATE: Apparently not.

PRESIDENT ROOSEVELT: Good!

MR. CHOATE: I should say there is one lawyer who is trying to group
together five or six of these companies and get a fee from them;
but he has not yet succeeded.

(President Roosevelt then read the report headed "The
Postmaster General.")

[At the beginning of this fiscal year, July 1, 1934, a Migratory-Bird
Hunting stamp which sells for $1.00 was authorized for the Department
of Agriculture to raise funds for the establishment of conservation areas
for wild game life. The distribution and sale of this stamp has been
handled by the Post Office Department. More than $602,000 has been
collected to date and turned over to the Department of Agriculture.]

PRESIDENT ROOSEVELT: That particular law violated a rule of Congress not to earmark
funds received from taxes, and it is the first instance in a good
many years where a tax has been imposed and then earmarked
for a specific purpose. It is rather interesting. If we can raise
$700,000 a year for conservation of wild game life, I think it is
going to be a very fine thing, and eventually, after we have
spent two or three years more, it will be almost self-sustaining.
Isn't that right?

SECRETARY WALLACE: It would be hard to get [Jay] Darling to admit it, I suppose; but I hope so.

(President Roosevelt then read the report of the Federal Housing Administrator and the report of the Secretary of Labor.)

PRESIDENT ROOSEVELT: Of course this relates to 1934, and the figures for January, February, and March on construction as a whole, including residences, show a very large increase, the best of any since when, Jim?

MR. MOFFETT: Nineteen thirty-two; it shows an increase of 130 per cent.

(President Roosevelt then read the report of the Chairman of the Federal Power Commission.)

PRESIDENT ROOSEVELT: "Report of the Secretary of Agriculture Concerning Soil Erosion Service." This is only a page and a quarter; I am going to read it. It is something that we have very much on our minds. . . .

[On March 25, the Soil Erosion Service was transferred to the Department of Agriculture, together with the unexpended balance of PWA funds allotted to soil erosion work. Legislation making this service a permanent organization is under consideration by Congress.

On April 1, the engineering soil erosion activities of the Bureau of Agricultural Engineering, the soil erosion research of the Bureau of Chemistry and Soils, and the twelve soil erosion nurseries of the Bureau of Plant Industry, all divisions of the Department, were consolidated with the Soil Erosion Service.

As a result, for the first time, the Soil Erosion Service is in a position to administer all the control and research of this important phase of conservation of our natural resources. In addition, the immediate advice and assistance of the Forest Service, the Bureau of Biological Survey and other large research units of the Department will be available. The rcently established Land Policy Committee of the Department will aid greatly in making a fully coordinated program.

Field operations at present comprise 40 erosion control demonstration projects under local supervision on 39,679,000 acres, of which 35,700,000 acres are federally owned, and 3,979,000 privately owned; 12 erosion experiment stations for research work; 12 erosion nurseries for growing trees, legumes and other erosion control plants, and allotment of 570 E.C.W. camps to operate on approximately 3 million acres of additional private lands.

If this activity is further expanded, it is planned to divide the country into districts with separate administrations for the eastern and western regions responsible to the Chief of the Service.]

"Oral Report by Mr. Hopkins."

MR. RICHBERG: That is out.

PRESIDENT ROOSEVELT: "Special Problems for Explanation or Discussion."

The first is comment of the Acting Director of the Budget

regarding reports of agencies to Congress with reference to proposed legislation.

MR. RICHBERG: This is a question of importance, Mr. President. . . .

SECRETARY SWANSON: What about all legislation?

PRESIDENT ROOSEVELT: Certainly it should clear through the Director of the Budget if it involves expenditures. I think that should be made very clear, because some Congressman may have a happy thought which costs money (*laughter*) and bring it down to the head of a department, and the head of the department may say, "Yes, that is a happy thought," and go along with the idea of the brilliant Congressman and gives his approval to it, thereby violating at least the purpose of the general rule we have to clear through the Budget anything that is going to cost money.

MR. BELL: Mr. President, shouldn't we have a circular letter to the departments by the executive director, making that perfectly clear?

PRESIDENT ROOSEVELT: Will you do that?

MR. RICHBERG: Yes, sir.

MR. BELL: I think I would like to have that done.

PRESIDENT ROOSEVELT: "Suggestion Relating to Coordinated Program of Local Tax Legislation."

MR. RICHBERG: It was just pointed out that in the flooding of lands for reservoirs, etc., in the Tennessee Valley, a great deal of land is taken out of taxation. The suggestion was made as to whether there should be a uniform policy.

PRESIDENT ROOSEVELT: That brings up a very nice question that has plagued me for four years. It has not come up here, but it will come up more and more. The federal government goes in and buys a large acreage and we may take away revenue very seriously—land tax revenues—from a local subdivision—county or township. In the state of New York, a great many years ago when they started the Adirondack Preserve, the legislature passed a policy that the government would pay taxes on the land it had taken, in order to save the local government unit. There are two schools of thought, and there is a great deal to be said both ways. My general feeling, after seeing it operate in the state of New York, is that the best thing is to eliminate the payment of tax or compensation and make the local government unit go out of business by consolidating with another government unit. In the long run, it seems to me that is the best policy. If the federal government starts compensating the local government units, we will have an enormous annual compensation bill. I would like to hear from anybody that is interested in it.

DR. MORGAN: I have some opinions on that.

PRESIDENT ROOSEVELT: What do you think?

DR. MORGAN: I think that, so far as future taxes are concerned, that is the right attitude. We are cutting a county in two and the county is altogether too small anyway. It ought to go out of business. On the other hand, we are driving out school districts that have issued bonds. I think for past liabilities there ought to be compensation made, but for continuing future government there should not. As to working out what the past liabilities are, I don't think you can do it by a specific bill. I think if we could get a uniform act to apply over the country that would be the way to do it for past obligations. For future obligations I think you are just right.

PRESIDENT ROOSEVELT: Can we legally take those obligations of the small unit of government?

DR. MORGAN: I don't know whether you can or not by condemnation proceedings. I doubt if you can. But Congress could set up some way of compensation that would be constitutional. At least, that is the problem; it is working out a very decided injustice to subdivisions like school districts.

PRESIDENT ROOSEVELT: Of course the simplest way, likely, would be to get legislation. Suppose you go into a township and buy half the township; the government buys half the land, both in acreage and value; suppose there are $10,000 in bonds outstanding, the government might very easily assume the obligation of 5,000 of those bonds and pay it off in a certain number of years.

SECRETARY MORGENTHAU: The Treasury has a study under way, which we started some time ago.

DR. MORGAN: We have an extensive study and we might work together on it.

PRESIDENT ROOSEVELT: Is there any drive on us to assume taxes?

DR. MORGAN: Yes, there is a bill in Congress now, and they may build restrictions between past obligations and future obligations.

PRESIDENT ROOSEVELT: Does anybody know whether we have done anything of that kind?

MR. BELL: We do it in public parks by returning part of the receipts to the state, and also in the Reclamation Service.

PRESIDENT ROOSEVELT: To the state?

MR. BELL: Yes, and in some cases to the counties.

SECRETARY WALLACE: They do that in connection with forest grazing fees, don't they?

MR. BELL: Yes, and I think also in connection with Indian lands, where they pay the taxes out of trust funds.

PRESIDENT ROOSEVELT: I wish we could get up a memorandum that would cover that

467

subject. I was wondering if you could act as chairman of a very informal committee and call in the different ones and get their expression on it—Agriculture, Interior, and so on.

DR. MORGAN: Also national parks and national forests.

MR. BELL: I would be glad to do that.

PRESIDENT ROOSEVELT: I might have to veto one of these bills and I would like to have something to veto it on.

MR. BELL: All right.

PRESIDENT ROOSEVELT: The next is also a TVA matter. [. . . a suggestion by the Chairman of the Board of the Tennessee Valley Authority regarding a study of the effect of technological unemployment.]

DR. MORGAN: That is not TVA. I don't believe you are going to get a measure of the probability of our recovery from unemployment until you get some rough measure of the degree of technological unemployment. I made a study of three different industries recently, and find that the man-hour cost of production has been cut in two in the past ten years.

PRESIDENT ROOSEVELT: There have been a lot of people dabbing at that, but has there been any real study made on it?

MR. RICHBERG: There have been some very extensive studies.

PRESIDENT ROOSEVELT: I know NRA has done it. Has Thomas done anything at it at all?

SECRETARY ROPER: Yes, we have been working on that. We are including it now in our textile study.

PRESIDENT ROOSEVELT: It is like the fellow that came in that runs the tin mills out in Ohio. He told me the story about how in 1913 and 14, when the factory was built, they turned out a thousand tons a day and had a thousand workmen. But in 1930, along came a man with a machine. They had been using 12 processes, but the machine reduced it to 8 processes and they laid off 400 men. This past year, another man came along with a machine that cut out several more processes so that they can now turn out a thousand tons a day with only 200 men. What he wanted to know was whether he might turn off the rest of the men. I said, "Don't come to me with that; I don't know."

MR. RICHBERG: We have an enormous army of unemployed.

PRESIDENT ROOSEVELT: It seems that the more industries improve, the more unemployment there is.

MR. RICHBERG: The Brookings people suggested a rather extensive study! (*Laughter*)

SECRETARY ROPER: I wonder if some study has been made by the Federal Trade Commission?

MR. MARCH: We made some study on textiles.

PRESIDENT ROOSEVELT: We have individual studies and different industries. What do you think, Harry?

MR. HOPKINS: I think it would be a very good thing to do. I don't think any one has made a deep study of that. Some studies have been biased and some inadequate. I think a study of that might well be made by the government.

PRESIDENT ROOSEVELT: Should a study of that kind be mostly made by sending letters out?

MR. HOPKINS: I think you would have to have field work on that.

MR. MARCH: I think the Federal Trade Commission would be in a position, with the setup we have, to make a very good study.

PRESIDENT ROOSEVELT: Don, suppose you bring in a recommendation on that, because I think that is a matter that would require a couple of million dollars to make a proper study. If we can justify it by employing a large number of white-collar workers, I think it might be worth while. Harry, you have a lot of things on your hands now, since you are Special Assistant Attorney General. (*Laughter*) From the point of view of taking it out of the $4,000,000 and therefore taking people off your relief rolls, would you act on it informally and talk with the Federal Trade Commission and with whomever else you think of?

MR. RICHBERG: NRA has a lot of data on it.

PRESIDENT ROOSEVELT: NRA, and Thomas has more data. Labor probably has some data. Talk it over and bring it in as a potential project.

SECRETARY ROPER: May I review, at the proper time, the suggestion about following costs from the raw material to the consumer so we could have a better knowledge of that?

PRESIDENT ROOSEVELT: That is too big a subject!

SECRETARY ROPER: I know; but would you permit me to make to you a suggestion? I think certain projects could be handled without making it as expensive as you think it would be and at the same time we would have some knowledge as to where these extensive costs are.

PRESIDENT ROOSEVELT: You might bring that also as a potential project. By the way, talking about projects and finding out facts, you mentioned a little while ago that it would cost $15,000,000 to make a census of the unemployed; I noticed Hugh Johnson says it would take $50,000!

SECRETARY ROPER: Let him take it!

PRESIDENT ROOSEVELT: He said that would be the cost if you did it the army way.

MR. RICHBERG: That was an entirely voluntary job.

SECRETARY ROPER: You have a committee studying that now. There are several angles we would like to discuss.

PRESIDENT ROOSEVELT: You might call up Hugh on the telephone. (*Laughter*)

SECRETARY ROPER: Are you ready to receive these projects now? We have a number of them in Commerce.

PRESIDENT ROOSEVELT: Yes, I will be tomorrow.

"The matter of misrepresentation of government departments in soliciting advertising."

MR. RICHBERG: Here is a letter, Mr. President, sent out under the head of the American Federation of Government Employees soliciting advertising from a company for their forthcoming year book. The letterhead carries on it the names of the Departments—Post Office, Treasury, and so on. The Postmaster General called attention to the fact that this puts the government in the position of aiding in the solicitation of this private advertising. It is not a matter that comes under the postal laws, but it is a matter which the government departments might not be interested in having their participation so represented.

PRESIDENT ROOSEVELT: Suppose the First Assistant Postmaster General sends a letter to the heads of the departments and then the heads of the departments should speak to their chief clerks about it.

MR. HOWES: They are asking for quite a sum.

MR. RICHBERG: Two hundred dollars a page.

SECRETARY ROPER: We turned that down immediately.

MR. RICHBERG: The Department of Commerce is listed here. The point is that all the departments are listed on the letterhead, so it gives out a curious official appearance.

SECRETARY ROPER: We have turned them all down.

PRESIDENT ROOSEVELT: "Needs for further coordination."

MR. RICHBERG: I thought, instead of sending around a memorandum, it might be well to present this informally. The president of the American Hotel Association wrote the Postmaster General a letter, the substance of which was that they had received complaints that government employees were asking for special reduced rates. They pointed out that of course hotels never give special reduced rates, but they didn't like to be asked to do so by public officials. It didn't seem to be a matter which could be very well covered in any memorandum, but I thought perhaps I might bring the question up as long as it has been brought to the attention of the Postmaster General.

MR. HOWES: Some of these hotels wrote letters soliciting business.

MR. RICHBERG: That is the absurdity of the situation.

PRESIDENT ROOSEVELT: With several tens of thousands of government employees traveling every day of the year, it is impossible for us to prevent them from asking for reduced rates. It is up to the hotel

470

	manager whether he gives them or not.
ATTORNEY GENERAL CUMMINGS:	Their per diem allowance is so low that they need reduced rates.
MR. HOWES:	When a post office inspector is traveling he wants to put up at a decent hotel, and with the $5-a-day allowance he has to buy his own meals. Lots of these hotels are glad to have them, and offer them 25 per cent off.
MR. BELL:	That was advocated during the regime of General Lord as Director of the Budget. He solicited hotels and got a 25 per cent reduction. The government departments were circularized.
MR. RICHBERG:	They are trying to cut down preferential rates. Compliance under hotel codes has not been very noticeable from the standpoint of labor provisions.
PRESIDENT ROOSEVELT:	Anything else?
MR. RICHBERG:	That is all.
PRESIDENT ROOSEVELT:	Before we adjourn—nothing should be said about it, as it won't come out in the afternoon papers, but it will be the first announcement in regard to the work relief program—setting up an Application and Information Bureau by our old friend Frank Walker.[3] It will be the clearing house for all kinds of projects. That is the reason why I said to the Secretary of Commerce just now that we would be ready to receive his material tomorrow. That Application and Information Bureau under Frank Walker will receive all the applications from the outside—mayors, governors, congressmen, senators, etc., etc.; also all plans from people who have bright ideas. Out of all the bright ideas from the outside, we may get a few good ones that are useful. They will be classified in this bureau and then sent to the appropriate government agencies for report. If it requires engineering, there will be an engineer report on it. Eventually, it will be properly sifted and a report will be made.
	Frank Walker's Bureau will not take final action. In other words, he can recommend plans for further consideration, or he can pass it on with the notation that it is an impracticable, impossible, thing; but nevertheless, he will not be in a position of having to turn it down. That will come to another party who will be along in two days—an allotment party.[4]

---

[3] This division was not officially set up by Executive Order No. 7034 until May 6, 1935. The announcement was indeed made the next day in the press, however. The *New York Times* for the morning of Apr. 24 carried on page one the headline, "F. C. Walker Chosen as Clearing Chief of Works Program."

[4] This refers to the Advisory Committee on Allotments provided for in the same Executive Order mentioned in note 3. The announcement was headlined on page one of the N.Y. *Times* for Apr. 25: "Allotment Board Named."

471

The first step, I think, will probably be the announcement in tomorrow's paper of the setting up of this Bureau. In the carrying out of this relief work, it will save all the government agencies. There will probably be 15 or 20 government agencies administering the actual projects. It will save a tremendous amount of letters, calls, delegations, etc., coming in to take up their time. Frank Walker will receive the delegations. Also, as the work progresses, if anybody wants to know how it is progressing, he will get the information through Frank Walker's Bureau. I think it is going to work out in a fairly satisfactory way. It gives information as to the project, and also whether the project has a chance of being turned down, or finally considered—a very distinct step in advance.

I am going to try, so far as possible, to use existing agencies of the government. After a careful census, it seems fairly clear that we will only have to set up probably two new agencies of government to carry out this work. One of them—the news for the following day—is the Rural Electrification.[5] There is no organization of government today which has ever carried on work of that kind. The other one is a very necessary consolidation of what might be called Rural Resettlement.[6] There have been a number of agencies working on Rural Rehabilitation and Resettlement, and they are going to be consolidated—the whole thing in one new agency.

Then, the following day, we will announce the method of making the allocations; and the day after that, talk about the method of checking on the various elements relating to the progress of the work, such as how we get people off the relief rolls, as to how they get their materials from a central procurement office, as to the machinery for getting people on work relief back into private employment through the employment agency of the Department of Labor, and weekly check of the actual number of people employed, and the actual wages being paid out.

[5] On Apr. 27 the N.Y. *Times* headlined a story thus: "Hopkins is Made Work Relief Guide, Completing Setup." There was, however, no discussion of rural electrification in the press that day. Apparently the President changed his publicity time-table; references to this part of the program did not begin to appear until a few days later.

[6] The President obviously attached great importance to this aspect of the program. On May 1, 1935, he issued Executive Order No. 7027, setting up the Rural Resettlement Administration. The text of this order appears, followed by a lengthy explanatory note by the President, in the 1935 volume of his public papers. *The Public Papers and Addresses of Franklin D. Roosevelt: The Court Disapproves* (New York, 1938), pp. 143-155.

There are one or two things that should be made clear to all interested agencies in regard to these projects. For example, this morning a delegation from New York wanted an allocation of $70,000,000 to complete a link in the New York subway. I said, "How long will it take to build it?" and they said, "Four years." I said—and here is rule No. 1—"We cannot tie up any of the $4,000,000,000 on work which would not be put through until after July 1, 1936. In other words, we can only allocate for work to be done in the course of the coming year."

I talked with the Secretary of War this morning about the Florida Ship Canal. If the Florida Ship Canal is approved as a useful project, it would cost about $125,000,000 to eventual completion. It would take at least six years to build it. Obviously, we cannot tie up $125,000,000 in the Florida Ship Canal right now. I am not saying it is not a useful project. We might ask the War Department engineers how much they could usefully spend in the course of the first year. Suppose they said they could spend $20,000,000 usefully in the course of the first year; then you cannot go ahead and allocate it on that basis. The next thing we do is to go to Harry Hopkins and say, "How many people from that general area have you on relief rolls?" Twenty million dollars would mean approximately 20,000 people. Hopkins comes back and says, "No, I haven't 20,000 people on my relief roll that I can put to work there; I have only 10,000." Immediately, that cuts the $20,000,000 in half, if we employ only local relief people on it. Hopkins may come back and say, "Yes, I have 10,000 people in that general region, and I can bring you in 5,000 people from Georgia, South Carolina, and Alabama, from areas where we cannot find useful work for them." In other words, the amount of the allocation has got to correspond with the people in the area who are on relief rolls.

Then you come down to the fourth criterion, and that is that the work not only has to be done for that allocation before July 1936, but also that at least we are shooting at the mark, and I don't know whether we can reach it in all cases, but on the average we want to spend half the money of the allocation on direct wages for force account.

I will give you another illustration, that of the Casper, Wyoming project. They are building a dam, a canal, and a tunnel—water tunnel. War Department engineers—I think probably very properly—said the cheapest way to do is to do it by contract.

473

SECRETARY DERN: The Reclamation Service says that.

PRESIDENT ROOSEVELT: I sent out word to the Secretary of the Interior, and I said, "Tell me something about the project. If we let it all out by contract, we are not going to put nearly as many people to work off the relief rolls as if we did part of it by force account." They came back—the Reclamation people—and said the first part of the project is the concrete dam and that work has got to be done mostly by experts; the last part of it is a tunnel through a hill, and that takes experts; but in the middle is a 32-mile canal which is mostly ditch-digging, which is a plain, common, base labor job.

I said to Harry, "How many are there in that area?" And he said there were 1,600 people. Then Reclamation comes back and says, "We can put 1,600 people to work in digging this middle project." There you have an illustration of the need of doing the job with the people in need of work in the territory.

Bear in mind, we do not want any project which will run for a long number of years; and we do not want any project which will employ a very small number of people from relief rolls. The money will go farther.

Insofar as possible, the final point is to get as much money back as we can, even if the length of time for the repayment is longer than we have been accustomed to and even if the rate of interest is lower. Therefore, one of our first inquiries as to all projects should be, "Can this be financed through some sort of loan?" Then the government will get the money back; or the project might be like a power project where we may get an income on the interest on the money expended.

Those are the general rules. I think it is well to keep them in mind all the time because I find people coming to me with various kinds of excellent projects which would take a long time to build, and where the government would not get the money back, or would not put many people back to work. In the course of the next few days, we will have a complete picture announced to the public; in the meantime, don't say anything about it.

SECRETARY DERN: All the departments are to initiate their projects through Mr. Walker?

PRESIDENT ROOSEVELT: Yes.

Meeting adjourned at 3:05 p.m.

Held in the Cabinet Room of the White House,
August 6, 1935, at 3:15 p.m.

Present: the President of the United States; the Secretary of the
Treasury; the Honorable Daniel W. Bell, the Acting Director of the
Budget; the Honorable L. W. Robert, Jr., Assistant Secretary of the
Treasury; the Administrator of the Agricultural Adjustment Administra-
tion; the Chairman of the Tennessee Valley Authority; the Honorable
T. D. Webb, Vice-Chairman of the Federal Home Loan Bank Board;
the Chairman of the Federal Trade Commission; the Director of the
Emergency Conservation Work; the Federal Coordinator of Transpor-
tation; the Governor of the Farm Credit Administration; the Chairman
of the Federal Alcohol Control Administration; the Honorable Stewart
McDonald, Acting Administrator of the Federal Housing Administration;
the President of the Export-Import Banks of Washington, D.C.; the
Chairman of the Federal Deposit Insurance Corporation; the Honorable
Eugene O. Sykes, Commissioner of the Federal Communications
Commission; the Governor of the Federal Reserve Board; the Honorable
Harold Merrill, representing Mr. Delano; Brig. Gen. Frank T. Hines, the
Administrator of Veterans' Affairs; the Honorable Harry B. Mitchell,
President of the Civil Service Commission; the Honorable Morris L.
Cooke, the Administrator of the Rural Electrification Administration;
the Honorable L. J. Martin, Executive Officer of the National Recovery
Administration; Dr. Walton H. Hamilton, the Adviser on Consumer
Problems; the Honorable Harris E. Willingham, Vice-Chairman of the
Federal Alcohol Control Administration; the Executive Director.

[This is a significant meeting for a student of bureaucracy.
As has been evident throughout most of these transcripts,
the NEC was envisioned as operating on two levels: the
Washington level, and the state-local level. In the latter
capacity, it represented a unique effort to cope with the
multiplication of field representatives of federal departments
and agencies. Under any orthodox organizational setup, these
field offices, however close their geographic proximity, could
not officially communicate with one another except through
Washington and their home offices. Bureaucratic specialization
and "mission bias" reinforced this tendency. With the appointment of the state directors of the NEC, it was hoped that they
would coordinate the state level. This would give the citizen
a source of information on available governmental services
and personnel in his area, *and* would render unnecessary the
circuitous communication between local offices and Wash-

ington. The lack of enthusiasm with which this scheme was greeted by local field representatives and offices is described by the President. One can well imagine the reaction which this measure evoked. No "upstart" agency of coordination was going to be allowed to alter well-worn paths of communication or burden local officials with an additional level of hierarchy. Joseph Eastman's comment suggests the effort made within agencies to justify their objections.—Editors' Note.]

PRESIDENT ROOSEVELT: We haven't had a meeting of the National Emergency Council for some time because a large number of the members also belong to the Allotment Board.[1] There is only one particular thing that I wanted to call your attention to at this meeting, and that relates to the work of the directors of the National Emergency Council in the several states.

You will remember we combined the Executive Council with the Emergency Council,[2] and our theory was that the directors in each state representing the National Emergency Council would act as a clearing house for all government agencies. That means not only the old departments but also all the other government agencies, including commissions like the Federal Reserve Board, the Federal Trade Commission, and everything else. The idea was very good, but the execution has not measured up to it. The result is, after a pretty careful check, that a good many of these directors find they are not getting cooperation from the other branches of the government. I have a memorandum here, and I suppose the easiest way is to read it. This is the result of a good many complaints:

You asked that I call attention before the Cabinet Meeting. We took this up in Cabinet Meeting last Friday with respect to cooperation between state directors and other federal employees of various executive departments and independent establishments.

These state directors of the NEC have experienced difficulty in many cases in obtaining cooperation from other officials of the federal government, which has resulted in a situation where they are unable to obtain the information they desire; hence, there has been a lack of local cooperation and a lack of local publicity. They are crossing wires in a lot of states on

[1] The Advisory Committee on Allotments organized to carry out the provisions of the Emergency Relief Appropriation Act of 1935.
[2] This consolidation was accomplished by Executive Order No. 6889-A of Oct. 29, 1934.

the publicity end. They are duplicating statements; the figures do not tally, coming from different departments, and there is no clearing house.

In some instances where the state directors have sought information, their letters have been returned to them, the other agencies refusing even to receive the request for information. Beginning next week, the the National Emergency Council proposes to send three employees to make a national survey. The purpose of this survey is to bring about better cooperation between the various representatives of the Executive Departments and the state directors with all agencies—emphasis on the *all*—through these meetings that are to be made continuous affairs and keep on meeting from time to time and all under the leadership or coordination of the director of the NEC. We have got to have somebody, and he is the best man to do it. It is felt the state directors may obtain much authoritative and factual data from local citizens and make possible a better understanding of the work the government is doing throughout the country.

It was suggested then that there be prepared and sent out a letter asking for cooperation, to be signed by my direction and sent out by the members of the Cabinet and the heads of all agencies and departments and independent establishments to the men in the field. The letter requests the men in the field, by the direction of the President, to cooperate with the National Emergency Council state directors, and proposed joint meetings and discussions between the men in the field. I don't know whether these letters are all ready?

MR. WALKER:[3] Yes, they are, Mr. President.

PRESIDENT ROOSEVELT: The letters are all ready and I think it is a thing that is going to count for a great deal, and will relieve a lot of this talk about confusion. There will be one federal agent in each state who will head up everything.

There is one illustration I have in mind of a certain post office in a fairly good-sized city which also houses practically all of the other functions. There is not even a directory tablet in that post office, and you can not find out where Triple A is, or where the Farm Credit or the Home Owners' Loan is, and yet in that particular city there are probably fifteen or twenty government agents and not even a signboard to say where they are in this brand new post office building! You can run all around and inquire where the Home Owners' Loan fellow is,

---

[3] Frank Walker had returned to the position of executive director of the National Emergency Council, taking over from Donald Richberg, who had resigned in June.

	and nine times out of ten they won't know. There is no coordination.
MR. WEBB:	I had that experience in Detroit, myself.
PRESIDENT ROOSEVELT:	Yes, I was talking about that.
MR. WEBB:	I could not find the office and I tried to find out through some of the post office officials and had trouble finding my own office. I didn't know you were talking about Detroit.
PRESIDENT ROOSEVELT:	Do you want to say anything about it, Frank?
MR. WALKER:	I think that is all we need. I would suggest that the President use a photographic copy of the signature and direct department heads to do this, and it might be very effective. I think all we need is cooperation with the department heads so that the men in the field will feel they have authority to do this. In some cases I think they have a doubt in their own minds, and some of them have no enthusiasm.
MR. COOKE:	Would you like them on our mailing lists? We are constantly getting out releases. One or two of your men have already taken quite an active interest, and it might be they would all like to receive our press releases.
PRESIDENT ROOSEVELT:	I think any agency that has releases—and most of them do have—should mail them to the NEC directors. It only means 48 more copies of every release that comes out. It will give them information which they otherwise could not get.
	Then there is one other matter which I think should be stressed in this connection that is not in this letter, but I think the heads of the departments and agencies could well do it, and that is, if one of your field men in any department believes that he is crossing wires with some agency, instead of taking it up with Washington, he should see the NEC director—that is one of his jobs—and tell him his story. He should tell the state director where his toes are being stepped on, tell him about complaints, and let this NEC director try to straighten it out without bothering us here in Washington. Of course, if it is a purely departmental matter he has to take it to Washington. But if it involves another department, instead of having it come here and go to somebody else down the line and back again three times around the triangle, save all that by going straight to the NEC state director and asking him to straighten it out. I think a letter along that line would be a very valuable thing.
MR. WALKER:	We have prepared a letter along that line.
MR. EASTMAN:	Mr. President, I am in some doubt what is meant by independent establishments; take for instance, the Interstate

478

Commerce Commission: would these state directors want to have all of the releases of the Interstate Commerce Commission which consist of decisions of the Commission—about eighteen hundred of them?

PRESIDENT ROOSEVELT: Use your discretion on that.

MR. EASTMAN: How can the ICC cooperate with these men? It is a little difficult for me to see just what the connection is so far as the independent establishments are concerned.

PRESIDENT ROOSEVELT: Take again the case of Detroit; there were three agencies in Detroit that were not even listed in the telephone book. You had to call information to find out where they were. Now maybe the ICC people up there were not listed.

MR. WALKER: I think we are sending out all the information concerning independent agencies that has any application to the state directors. We have an extensive correspondence with them, and then we have a Manual which gives an outline of practically every agency of the government, together with a chart, and I think they get any information that we feel is essential.

PRESIDENT ROOSEVELT: You do not think it would be a good thing?

MR. WALKER: We have sent them the rules and regulations applying to the Works Relief Program and they have a copy of every rule and regulation indexed.

PRESIDENT ROOSEVELT: Perhaps they do not get everything pertaining to Rural Electrification.

MR. WALKER: Our National Emergency Council Directors will be informed as to every project in their state.

MR. COOKE: We have taken up some matters with your Tennessee man and found him very intelligent on the subject, and we thought that somebody had sent him information.

MR. WALKER: Our state directors have had information.

PRESIDENT ROOSEVELT: That takes care of that matter if you will do it from headquarters, Frank.
Have you anything else—any agenda?

MR. WALKER: The President suggested no meetings until October.

PRESIDENT ROOSEVELT: Yes; is there anything else today, Frank?

MR. WALKER: I don't think so.

PRESIDENT ROOSEVELT: Has anybody anything else to bring up?

GENERAL HINES: May I offer a suggestion in connection with the subject just discussed. There is an organization of the various government agencies known as the "Government Business Organization." They have meetings frequently, sometimes once a week in some of the larger cities. It seems to me that if the director of the National Emergency Council could become the head of that

479

organization, it would bring together quickly all these other government agencies that have been functioning for a number of years, and a suggestion to them to get in touch with whoever is head of that organization I believe would solve many of the difficulties.

PRESIDENT ROOSEVELT: Will you make a note of that?

MR. WALKER: Yes, sir, I will.

PRESIDENT ROOSEVELT: Does anybody have anything else? (*Pause*) I don't believe it is necessary for us to meet until probably a month from now—around the middle of September. I hope that as soon as Congress goes away everybody will be able to get a little holiday, even if not a long one. Some people are overworking—a great many are—and should turn things over to an assistant and try to get a holiday.

MR. FECHNER: When are you going to get yours?

PRESIDENT ROOSEVELT: I am going about the end of September. The only way I can get a holiday is to get out of sight of land!

Meeting adjourned about 3:40 p.m.

Held in the Cabinet Room of the White House,
December 17, 1935, at 2:25 p.m.

_____

Present: the President of the United States; the Secretary of State; the
Secretary of the Treasury; the Attorney General; the Postmaster General;
the Secretary of the Navy; the Secretary of Agriculture; the Secretary
of Commerce; the Secretary of Labor; the Acting Director of the Budget;
the Hon. L. W. Robert, Jr., Assistant Secretary of the Treasury; the
Hon. Harry H. Woodring, Assistant Secretary of War; the Hon.
John N. Edy, Assistant Director of the Budget; the Hon. Charles O. West,
Undersecretary of the Interior; the Administrator of Agricultural
Adjustment; the Administrator of the Federal Alcohol Administration;
the Administrator of Federal Emergency Relief; the Federal Housing
Administrator; the Acting Administrator of the National Recovery
Administration; the Administrator of Rural Electrification; the Hon.
Will W. Alexander, Assistant Administrator of the Resettlement Admin-
istration; the Adviser on Consumers' Problems; the Acting Chairman
of the Central Statistical Board; the Chairman of the Federal Communica-
tions Commission; the Chairman of the Board of Directors of the Federal
Deposit Insurance Corporation; the Chairman of the Federal Home
Loan Bank Board; the Chairman of the Federal Power Commission; the
Chairman of the Board of Governors of the Federal Reserve System;
the Chairman of the Federal Trade Commission; the Hon. Joseph B.
Eastman, Commissioner, Interstate Commerce Commission; the Chairman
of the Securities and Exchange Commission; the Hon. David E. Lilienthal,
Member of the Board of Directors of the Tennessee Valley Authority;
the Director of Emergency Conservation Work; the Federal Coordinator
of Transportation; the Hon. Peyton R. Evans, General Counsel of the
Farm Credit Administration; the Hon. Wayne C. Taylor, Vice-President,
Export-Import Banks; the Hon. Lyle T. Alverson, Acting Solicitor of
the National Emergency Council; the Executive Director.

_____

[An interval of over four months had elapsed since the last
meeting of the NEC. The President on August sixth had
forecast a lapse until sometime in September, but this interval
proved longer. Some measure of the vitality of the NEC
experiment is to be gleaned from noting the diminishing
frequency of meetings held, as time went on.

As noted earlier, perhaps the key value of the transcripts is
the insight to be gained into the workings of the mind of the
President in this informal, off-record setting. Nothing comes
out more clearly in these Rooseveltian monologues than his keen
political sense. At this meeting, held some ten or eleven months
prior to the 1936 election, he again stresses the need for educating
the public on the broad activities and achievements of the New

deal. The role of agency heads as Administration spokesmen comes in for particular Presidential consideration. Nothing he says here is more characteristic and yet revealing than his injunction to them to use "simple illustrations that appeal to the average person back home." He answers the query as to the best method of avoiding conflict and *faux pas* in speeches with the suggestion that Steve Early, his press secretary, is the proper man to see. Early was expected to coordinate public relations for the Administration as a whole.

Some recurring items of business come up for attention. Discussion is resumed of clearance through NEC of legislative proposals from the departments and agencies. Testimony before Congressional committees should be cleared so that the official testifying will know the President's position before he appears. Periodic reports of the general status of agency programs are summarized, serving to inform the other members and provide them with ammunition for their public appearances. Finally, in an interchange initiated by Secretary Perkins, the problem of sharpening the statistical tools of the government is again raised. Both the New Deal programs themselves and the methods of measuring economic results were new. The government was to expend much time and effort before the latter were made accurate and dependable.—Editors' Note.]

PRESIDENT ROOSEVELT: This is the first meeting we have had of the Council for a good many months because during the summer and early autumn, as you know, we met as an Allotment Board.[1] There is no reason for continuation of the Allotment Board because there is no further money to allot, which is a practical reason for its abandonment. The National Emergency Council has been going along, functioning in its capacity in the meantime, and a number of new agencies have been added to the Council since we last met—the Social Security Board, Governor Winant; the Interstate Commerce Commission, Chairman Tate; Rural

---

[1] Following passage of the Emergency Relief Appropriation Act of 1935, a Division of Applications and Information was set up in the NEC. The Works Progress Administration itself was also established, as was the Advisory Committee on Allotments. It is this latter that is doubtless referred to. An elaborate project screening procedure was set up involving all of these agencies, with the Advisory Committee as the final arbiter. For a discussion of this machinery, see Louis Brownlow, *A Passion for Anonymity* (Chicago, 1958), pp. 323-325.

482

Electrification Administration, Mr. Cooke; Resettlement Administration, Dr. Tugwell; and the Central Statistical Board, Mr. Rice. Then, in addition to those new agencies, we have three new heads who have not been with us before from the older agencies—Mr. Landis, Chairman of the Securities Exchange Commission; Judge Hoyt, Administrator of Federal Alcohol; and Dr. Hamilton, Adviser on Consumers' Problems. We have an agenda here which Mr. Walker has prepared; I suppose we had better follow it in general. Now that we have begun to meet again, I think it is important that we should proceed as we did proceed up to last spring, with an agenda and meetings perhaps during the winter about every couple of weeks.

In the meantime, during the summer—and this will come out, I think, at the end of the agenda—the directors of the NEC in the several states have been accomplishing what we started last spring, and that is tying in of the various federal agencies in each state, getting them acquainted with each other, preventing the overlapping of functions, and getting the information in such shape that it will be more available to the public.

The first matter is the report on activities of state directors of the Council.

MR. WALKER: The reason for submitting these five or six pages is that the activities of the Council have been broadening out in the field, and I thought it might be well to inform the Council what we have been doing....

I may say in this connection that in the last month the executive director of the National Emergency Council held a meeting in Illinois at which every agency of the government was represented in the state of Illinois, and in addition to that we had all of the adjoining state directors present. A similar meeting was also held in California in which we did the same thing. All the far western and northwestern representatives were present and we had a meeting at that time in which not only the federal agencies were all represented, but many of our senators and congressmen also appeared....

PRESIDENT ROOSEVELT: There has been accomplished in these last few months in the states—through the Washington NEC office—some of the most important work which the government can do in many ways in the next year. Regardless of the question of a national election coming on, and even if this were not an election year, it seems to me that the whole fate of what the govern-

483

ment is trying to do at the present time depends, regardless of the election, on an understanding of the program by the mass of the people in the country. And, again, quite aside from politics, the continuation of the broad program successfully is dependent upon the approval of the people, which, again, is dependent upon their understanding of it.

We face, of course, in this case, largely because it is a political year, not only a lack of understanding but a very large amount of misinformation, part of which is innocent, and a large part of which is not innocent. That being so, we have a very definite task, if we believe in what the government is doing, to get a wider dissemination of information—correct information—a wider dissemination of answers to misinformation which has been handed out by various agencies and individuals, and, therefore, all that we can do to coordinate this whole thing and give a complete picture is going to be a tremendous help in telling the truth and in getting that truth widely recognized.

Just a word of what I might call advice. All of you from now on are going to be called upon more and more to go around the country speaking both to meetings and over the radio and in writing. I think there are three things which should be kept in mind: the first is that each cobbler should stick, insofar as possible, to his last. It prevents confusion if we stick to our own line of business. If you go beyond your own line of activity, I hope you will all try to get the general picture of the dovetailing of all these things into a wider whole as much as you possibly can; and in answering, I think it probably should be the policy of the government not to call people names, but, in a very gentle and happy way, to explain that things which are not proved, though we do not necessarily call them lies, are not exactly the truth and that the truth is as follows, and so on.

The third point, in my judgment, is that you should bring in as much as possible the simple illustrations that appeal to the average person back home. Through the NEC work that has been accomplished through these state agencies, you can get very easily—you know where to go to get it, get it through the NEC—information that appeals to the audience that you are going to address. There is no use telling the audience in Worcester, Massachusetts, John Fahey, about what is being done to develop and put people to work on a reclamation job in Utah. They are not just interested [sic]. Tell them what is being done by the federal government in Worcester County. That kind of information is available everywhere. Now that you know where to get it, use it. Get down to the human element. Don't tell them in Georgia what is being done in Alabama; take the nearest project to where you are speaking in Georgia and tell them about that.

I think we have a great opportunity to give the whole picture, emphasizing our own particular work in that picture and, in emphasizing our own work, bring it down to the locality where we happen to be making that particular point.

I do not know that there is anything further that needs to be said, except to emphasize again the need of a wider dissemination of information. Take, for instance, one thing that occurs to me—we have a good many things coming on. Take Social Security;[2] there is a great deal of misconception in this country about the so-called Townsend plan.[3] Most of the people that are in favor of the Townsend plan are honest people. They believe it will work. The time is coming when we shall have to say it won't work, and at the same time we have to show them what we are doing through the Social Security organization which is starting at the present time. I am just using that as an illustration of the usefulness of not merely denying the other fellow, but of explaining what we are doing so that they will see the whole thing together. There will be many chances during the coming winter and the coming summer to tell the truth in a very simple well-rounded way without flights of oratory. I am very confident that the country understands about the continuation of the general program. For example, we have been trying—Henry Wallace and I—to tie in the work of Agriculture to the cities. The agricultural people are sensible people. They realize that they have a relationship to the urban communities, though sometimes we have to remind them of it. People in the cities, when they find pork chops are going up, are perfectly reasonable, most of them, and if we explain their relationship to the farmers' problems, we are going to get away from the division between city and country. We are

---

[2] The Social Security Act had been passed during the 1935 session of Congress, and the machinery for its implementation was being established.
[3] For a discussion of the Townsend pension plan and the general ferment that surrounded both it and the Social Security plan itself, see James M. Burns, *The Lion and the Fox* (New York, 1956), pp. 212-213, *et passim*; also, Arthur M. Schlesinger, Jr., *The Age of Roosevelt: The Politics of Upheaval* (Boston, 1960), pp. 29-41.

485

going to get away, in the same way, from a division between different regions of the country—North against South, and East against West. I am trying to emphasize the rounded picture, and I think every one of us has a definite responsibility in getting that rounded responsibility across in the next few months.

SECRETARY ROPER: Mr. President, may I make a comment, sir? It is very difficult in many of these communities which we visit to confine ourselves to the subject matter because of the fact that there is going on in this country a broader study and observation of government than ever before.

In order to comply with your suggestions, permit me to suggest that some plan should be worked out by which speeches should be cleared. That, probably, is too much for one man, but I hope attention can be given to the fact that so that we will all speak the same language, and the only way in which I know that can be done is to have these speeches cleared so that they will, as you suggest, tell the truth, and not be inconsistent. When I go into a community to make a talk, on my conception, and then someone else comes along and says exactly the opposite, I am terribly embarrassed.

Now if I may pass on one other thing. The coordination of this work in the field is splendid; I am greatly encouraged about it; but we need more than that, Mr. President. We need better coordination in Washington. There are numbers of questions which come to me as Secretary of Commerce which I am not informed upon as to how I should consider them. For instance, I am frequently approached by somebody who wishes to get a line of information from the head of a bureau or wishes to be put into a bureau to get certain information. I have two cases here that I expect to bring to you personally. Now, the question is, can we not in some way handle that kind of matter through this very Council so that I would know that the man that comes to me really does represent the proper agency and that it is proper for me to give the information. That concerns me very much because it is right before me now.

PRESIDENT ROOSEVELT: The Council has been used for exactly that.

MR. WALKER: We have an Information Service that has been taking care of this. It has been used by a great many of the senators and many of the congressmen, as well as many of the people in the city. People are coming here for various reasons, and the mail is quite a factor. You can get practically any information with reference to the government that is available that we think should be given to the public. The Information Service is being used very effectively and we have a very efficient woman in charge of it. They also make contact with the various departments and notify them what particular branch or department they should go to.

SECRETARY ROPER: I wonder if the bureau heads know of that department.

MR. WALKER: They have been notified of it a number of times, Mr. Secretary.

SECRETARY ROPER: I am not always informed.

PRESIDENT ROOSEVELT: I will give you a practical example without going into the details of this case. If you had asked Frank Walker about this case, you would have known where to get the answer. The answer was the Secretary of the Treasury in this case; and he would have referred you to the Secretary of the Treasury, who would have been able to tell you all about it.

SECRETARY ROPER: I am not sure now that we all understand it.

MR. WALKER: This is a kind of challenge. I would be very much surprised if any member of the Council could call up our Information Service and stump them!

SECRETARY ROPER: We have a rule, in connection with the Census Bureau, that no individual returns of any establishment can be given out. In fact, we publish those statistics, as you know, only in a group of three so that they cannot be analyzed, and the establishment will be protected. Many of these business units desire certain lines of information which it is proper for them to secure in a guarded way, but are not published in the way they wish. For a number of years now, the plan has been in such cases to take the man who is going to dig this information out and swear him in. He thereby becomes an employee of the government. As a matter of fact, that man is there temporarily and it is a sham. He goes out and probably goes into the employ of a concern, and really we are not accomplishing what we think we are accomplishing. I mention that as one of our problems.

PRESIDENT ROOSEVELT: As to a clearing house for what is going to be said, such a clearing house is in process of formation, and for the time being, if anybody is going to make a speech and has any doubt in his own mind about a phrase or a sentence in that speech which might be lifted out and used in an unfortunate way—as has occurred in the past—or there is any question of government policy, if you will ask Steve Early about it, it

487

will be adequately taken care of. But I ask that such requests be made in sufficient time to have it read and not wait until the last moment before the eve of delivery. We have to be very careful about individual phrases and about sentences which can be lifted out and used adversely against us. The machinery is there. Any question of this kind can be referred to Steve Early in the first instance and it will be taken care of adequately. And if you do not do it—if you want to run the risk of going ahead without any check—I can say the responsibility is wholly yours.

SECRETARY ROPER: But the whole speech is what I referred to.

PRESIDENT ROOSEVELT: That will be taken care of. Necessarily, the responsibility must be yours, and we can't have people going around who are members of the Administration getting us into hot water all the time.

The next question on the agenda is the report on the activities of the Social Security Board. They have been trying to operate without any money and they have been doing a very good job. . . .

Has that budget gone up, unofficially, to the Hill?

MR. BELL: No, sir, it has not; I discussed it with you the last time we met, as to whether we would not hold it over for the deficiency in March, at which time they would know more about the requirements.

SECRETARY ROPER: What do you propose to do with the third deficiency bill estimate?

MR. BELL: We are considering it at this time with a view to submitting new estimates.

PRESIDENT ROOSEVELT: In the first deficiency bill to be passed, they will be taken care of—they will be implemented right away, so far as the office work goes?

MR. BELL: Yes, sir.

PRESIDENT ROOSEVELT: Next is the reduction of CCC strength. That is something that I have got to have a conference on with you, Bob, and Agriculture, and Soil Erosion, and Resettlement, to determine how fast we are actually going to cut down.

MR. FECHNER: When do you think we could have that conference?

PRESIDENT ROOSEVELT: Tomorrow.

MR. WALKER: Then we can pass by Nos. 5 and 6 for the present.

PRESIDENT ROOSEVELT: Next is the matter of federal allotment for emergency relief appropriations. Why bring that up? We haven't any money.

MR. WALKER: I suggested that we pass by that.

PRESIDENT ROOSEVELT: The horrid fact might just as well be known, and I am trying to get money back from people who have had it assigned to them.

Next is the report on the matter of payment of taxes by the federal government....

MR. WALKER: It is a very extensive report, Mr. President, and it seems to me that a committee should be appointed to consider it.

PRESIDENT ROOSEVELT: How large a committee do you want on it? You don't want all these agencies, do you? Just the Budget, and the Treasury, and the Department of Justice.

MR. WALKER: That will be ample, I think.

PRESIDENT ROOSEVELT: So you will consider yourselves appointed—the Secretary of the Treasury, the Attorney General, and the Director of the Budget—as a committee of three to study this report that has been made and outline a policy.

No. 8 is the matter of legislation: "(a), Suggested procedure for clearance of legislation; (b), Matters affecting Federal Housing Administration;" and "(c), Matters affecting Home Owners' Loan Corporation."

MR. WALKER: This is rather interesting, I think. (*Mr. Walker then read ... the suggestion ... that testimony before committees of Congress be entirely factual.*)

PRESIDENT ROOSEVELT: We must confine ourselves again to our own business; and we must be factual. There has been altogether too much going before committees of Congress and talking about somebody else's work and venturing all kinds of opinion—evidence which only is the opinion of the person who happens to give it. A very good illustration: I sent out a little while ago, a good many thousands of letters to clergymen and I asked two questions. What does the clergy think, in their own parishes, about the actual progress of relief, how is it working, and did they have any suggestions for methods of handling relief for the unemployed; and the other question related to Social Security, especially the Act that had been passed. Those were the only two questions I asked. Eighty-five per cent of the answers replied to those two quetsions and were therefore of extraordinary value. I had 16,000 answers, and of those 16,000 answers, 85 per cent answered the two questions I had asked. Fifteen per cent of the clergymen undertook to expound their theories on the Gold Standard, and Prohibition, and Agricultural Adjustment, and all kinds of things. They were not answers, just one man's opinion on something that he hadn't been asked about. In all our testimony before Congress and in all our answers to questions, let us stick to our own last and let us be factual about it. That is one of the most important things that has been said in a long time.

MR. WALKER: Someone made the inquiry, Mr. President, anent that, as to what the press might say about it—whether or not we were adopting a system of censorship.

PRESIDENT ROOSEVELT: No.

(*Mr. Walker then continued with the reading...*)

MR. WALKER: December 25, 1935—that is perhaps rather arbitrary, Mr. President.

PRESIDENT ROOSEVELT: Better make it the night of the twenty-fourth. (*Laughter*)

MR. BELL: Mr. President, I think it is important that you consider the procedure with reference to the giving of oral testimony. It is proposed to make that clear through the Bureau of the Budget.

PRESIDENT ROOSEVELT: How do you clear oral testimony through the Bureau of the Budget?

MR. BELL: No, I mean they must first ascertain your attitude. When they appear and give testimony, they should know that what they say is in accord with the program of the President.

PRESIDENT ROOSEVELT: You can do it in this way. Suppose some Congressman has a bill up before a committee; there are so many bills we cannot follow them all. Suddenly the committee calls up, let us say the Secretary of Agriculture; he goes up there and he doesn't know much about the bill, but he knows that he is going to be asked about the bill. It might be a bill that related not only to Agriculture but to Interior and some other department, and he ought to in some way find out what the general attitude is through some kind of clearing house. Suppose it is a fiscal bill, then he would call you up; and he would call up the other departments and find out their attitude. Of course, you can't talk of questions that you do not know about beforehand, but in that case there is always the opportunity to say, "This is something that I don't know enough about at the present time to speak on, and I wish you would let me have until tomorrow to look it up." You don't have to give snap judgment.

MR. FARLEY: I think there should be pretty definite instructions.

PRESIDENT ROOSEVELT: On the question of policy, you are very apt to have some committee chairman call up and say, "What do you think about this policy?" You can answer, "Let me think it over," or "Please reduce your question to writing." Avoid snap judgment over the telephone. There was an illustration just the other day; a resolution was passed through Congress—a House resolution that did not even have to come to me—asking for a certain report on a very important matter from one of the departments. It was a policy matter. The department was asked to send the report up to the committee and nobody outside the department knew about it. We happened to catch it. If the report had gone up in the form in which it was prepared, it would have been absolutely contrary to the policy of the government.

MR. FARLEY: Your policy should be definitely known. Your policy should be *the* policy and it should be known by the different departments so that they will be both for or both against it.

PRESIDENT ROOSEVELT: Take a very practical illustration. The Interior Department has a measure up there to put the Forest Service into the Interior Department, and Agriculture opposes it! (*Laughter*) We haven't got to the point in the last session or the coming session of doing anything about it. What I am saying to the Secretary of Agriculture and the Secretary of the Interior is, don't go up and either favor or oppose the bill.

ATTORNEY GENERAL CUMMINGS: I think that is very important, Mr. President; I have found it necessary to have one special person in my Department reading bills that affect the Department of Justice to be sure something does not happen that we do not know about. We have to watch it like a cat watches a mouse.

SECRETARY ROPER: That is all right if you will veto the bills passed without our knowledge.

MR. EASTMAN: I am sure it is not the intention to apply that policy to the independent agencies, such as the Interstate Commerce Commission. That is the servant of Congress and is directed by law to make reports to Congress. The report of the Interstate Commerce Commission does not go to the President. It goes to Congress, and it is the habit of committees of Congress to ask our opinion on almost every bill that comes up.

PRESIDENT ROOSEVELT: But, again, there you forget that the Constitution provides that the President is the head of the Executive branch of the government. Congress cannot set up the Interstate Commerce Commission as a separate agency and not in any way related to the President. Therefore, the Interstate Commerce Commission I think would be on the wise side if, when asked for an opinion on a matter of policy, they should consult the President.

MR. EASTMAN: Of course, there is a question whether the Interstate Commerce Commission is a member of the Executive branch.

491

Its work is largely legislative, established by law. I have served not only in a Democratic Administration, but in a Republican as well. I know it has certain judicial functions.

PRESIDENT ROOSEVELT: Of course it has judicial functions. It has a great many executive functions, and therefore it cannot be wholly disassociated from the Executive.

MR. EASTMAN: It is a sort of mixture of several things.

PRESIDENT ROOSEVELT: It cannot set itself up as a whole department of the government.

MR. EASTMAN: No, but it does certain things when it is asked by Congress.

PRESIDENT ROOSEVELT: At the same time, who could say that it meets with the approval of the Executive branch of the government?

MR. EASTMAN: I think it would cause a great deal of trouble if all the bills referred to the Commission were referred here.

MR. MC NINCH: Don't you have reference to those bills and proposals that involve policy, not as judicial functions? The Power Commission is an illustration; we consider that we ought to know for certain that it was in harmony with the policy of the Administration; but in judicial matters we do not concern ourselves.

PRESIDENT ROOSEVELT: Take the question whether trucks hitherto completely unregulated, should, as a matter of government policy, be regulated by the government, and having been brought in, be regulated by the Interstate Commerce Commission.

SECRETARY PERKINS: This sounds to me like a very efficient plan, and I think it is; but does it not occur to you that it may bring a great confusion of thinking? For instance, why should one refer to the Bureau of the Budget a question of policy? It seems a peculiar thing to do. Who will determine the policy on a matter of labor legislation?

PRESIDENT ROOSEVELT: During the session, I suppose every day there were two or three three-line or four-line memoranda from Frank Walker, saying, "The Department of Labor wants to know if such-and-such a bill meets with Executive approval." With no delay—not more than 24 hours—I think in about 99 cases out of a 100, he got a memorandum at the bottom in longhand.

SECRETARY PERKINS: I don't remember having asked Mr. Walker, except as a friend, to advise me on those matters. For instance, how does Mr. Walker know—he knows a great many things—but how does he know all the intricacies in labor circles back of a certain bill? I mean, you will have to call outside the staff for a tremendous amount of advice and information before you can possibly come to a conclusion on such a policy.

PRESIDENT ROOSEVELT: But he might recognize the fact that the legislation stepped on the toes of some other department. That has come up several times. The head of the originating department had forgotten to consult the other department. There is no delay; just give one check and that avoids trouble. As a result of it, last year we had infinitely less trouble than the year before.

SECRETARY PERKINS: It is not the delay that bothers me; it is the confusion as to what is policy and how policy is determined. If it is the NEC staff that is to work out these details, why should the Budget Bureau handle it? It has no relationship to policy, ordinarily, except as to whether the income will stand the outgo.

PRESIDENT ROOSEVELT: It is a fiscal matter involving the expenditure of money, one way or the other, it clears through the Director of the Budget.

SECRETARY PERKINS: But you say the Director of the Budget passes upon the question as to whether the project is worth the price.

PRESIDENT ROOSEVELT: No, I beg your pardon; he passes it up to me with a memorandum, saying, "On our present budget, we cannot afford it; but if you want to break the present budget and approve it, it is up to the President." He gives me factual information about finances; that is all.

MR. WALKER: Some departments do, Mr. President; without consulting anybody, the thing is well on its way before anybody knows about it.

PRESIDENT ROOSEVELT: We have had several instances where that has cost the government a good many millions of dollars.

SECRETARY MORGENTHAU: I can say fully half of my time, when Congress is in session, is spent on matters of this kind. I keep not one but a whole staff of people on the Hill working with the committees, trying to keep up with these things. I can give example after example where I had taken up the matter with you and a policy had been settled, and without anybody knowing it the department or agency put it through without our knowing anything about it. It happens every single day that somebody goes up and tries to put something across that we knew you didn't want. This thing will save you all kinds of headaches.

MR. WALKER: I think the next memorandum on the agenda is typical. [Matters of legislation affecting Federal Housing Administration.] They anticipate legislation. We have received a number of inquiries about Title I of the Federal Housing Act.[4] There is a question of policy and also a question of

---

[4] Title I of the National Housing Act (Public Law 479, June 27, 1934) is headed: "Housing Renovation and Modernization."

finance, and this is anticipating it from the field. We have a number of queries from bankers and men who set up machinery to handle loans under Title I. The question is whether it is a good fiscal policy, whether or not you want to do it, whether or not the President feels it a matter of policy that we should carry on. Right now it is not a question of legislation but it will be very shortly.

PRESIDENT ROOSEVELT: There is a little matter involving perhaps a billion dollars of authorized loans. That has got to clear Federal Housing.

MR. WALKER: It is a matter of policy whether the government wants to assume the guaranty that they place behind it.

PRESIDENT ROOSEVELT: That is a matter that will have to be taken up with the Director of the Budget and the Secretary of the Treasury. The next is the Home Owners' Loan Corporation, which is somewhat similar. . . . I will give you my snap judgment. I agree with you, John. Go ahead and inform Congress.

MR. FAHEY: Otherwise, we would go broke.

PRESIDENT ROOSEVELT: That is all right; approval is given.

Next is the effect of statistical inquiries as reported by the Central Statistical Board. . . .

All we need to do on that is to inform the Central Statistical Board that that report is approved and that all the agencies of the government have been told, "No more doorbell-ringing statistical surveys." We have plenty of them going on at the present time. I don't think we need legislation, as a matter of general policy, that there will be no allocations or requests for appropriations for statistical work approved unless they are first cleared through the Central Statistical Board.

MR. WALKER: There is another letter here, I think, from Mr. Rice.

MR. RICE: Yes, sir.

MR. WALKER: After what the President suggested, there is no need of reading it.

MR. RICE: No.

MR. WALKER: For some time we have been gathering reports from the various emergency agencies and the Council has attempted to make a digest to get it all in one book, under one cover, and in something of narrative form. The work is now in process. I have glanced at some of it, and I think the work is being very well done by Mr. Alverson and some of the men of the Council. If it is agreeable, I thought Mr. Alverson might give us some of the highlights of what is being done.

PRESIDENT ROOSEVELT: It is too long to read in toto, but it is an awfully interesting document. It gives a very excellent picture. I recommend that you read this report, if you have a chance, but in the meanwhile, if Mr. Alverson will give us a resumé of it, it will be very valuable.

MR. ALVERSON: Mr. President, it is difficult to give a resumé. As you suggested the other day, I have endeavored to pick the high spots. The report was compiled, as Mr. Walker has suggested, by addressing to all the agencies of the government a request for a general report. Having received that, we then addressed the agencies a great many specific questions about particular matters which it seemed to us should be brought into the report. They have generously responded. We undertook then to divide the report into several heads, such as Agriculture, Industry and Labor, Housing, Power, etc.

The first chapter of the report deals with the program of recovery in respect of agriculture. I may say, too, that the entire report is an endeavor to survey the activities of the federal government in the program for recovery from the time this Administration assumed responsibility in March 1933 down to some recent convenient date.

The high spot in agriculture, I think, is the fact that is well-known—and sometimes not enough well-known—namely, that the figures supplied by the Department of Agriculture show a gross increase of agricultural income of approximately 38 per cent and a net cash increase of approximately 121 per cent. The difference, of course, is accounted for, as Mr. Wallace pointed out in his report to the Council, by the fact that the gross income increased so much more rapidly than did costs of the farmers. The figures also show improvemen in the parity ratio established by law from 61 to 84. That is an increase of approximately 40 per cent. The department figures also show that there was an increase in retail prices of only some 24 per cent.

At the end of the report you will find a statement of costs. We tried to make a survey of the costs to the National Treasury of doing the things that have been done—that the Administration, particularly the AAA has done. To arrive at actual cost, we set down, first, of course, the gross income from processing taxes and like taxes. They have actually collected $900,000,000 in such taxes and there are now held in suspense $126,000,000 of such taxes on account of injunctions. Assuming that the law is constitutional, we have a gross income of something over a billion dollars—a

495

billion, twenty-five million. Payments to farmers amount to
$925,000,000, leaving an excess credit balance of $99,000,000.
Mr. Davis brought to our attention all the various matters
that were fair and proper charges against that program.
We included the cost of the sow-and-pig-buying program,
the drought, relief, diseased cattle purchases.
We also, of course, added the administrative cost of the
Administration, and we found that the net cost in money to
the United States Treasury for the 27 months of operation
has been about $40,000,000, which to Mr. Walker and to me,
seemed to be a highlight because we hear sometimes it was
more than that.
Reflecting this improvement in agriculture, we have the Farm
Credit situation, and the Farm Credit Administration showed
very clearly the great improvement taking place in the farm
mortgage situation. It also shows that the Federal Farm
Mortgage Corporation, which is operating much the same
as HOLC, has actually operated at a profit of $13,000,000
in the time it has been in existence.
Passing on to the section on labor and industry, [we found]
the increase in production has been approximately 34 per cent
and an increase in employment of approximately 26 per cent.
In that connection, Dr. Morgan, of the Tennessee Valley
Authority, wrote Mr. Walker a letter from which, if I may,
I would like to read a couple of sentences.

The Administration will never know the unemployment problem it has
to face and the public will never appreciate the difficulty of the problem
until a survey is made of the unemployment resulting from these
improvements of industrial processes. A brief inquiry by the writer into
about a dozen industries indicates that in these industries improvements
of the past ten years made it possible to approximately cut in two the
labor required. Similar conditions are general. Only detailed knowledge
of this tendency will enable an intelligent program to be evolved.

The other highlight, I presume, in the labor situation is the
disappointing decrease in unemployment; that is to say,
because of the growing population coming into employment fields, we find that the unemployment situation has
improved about 14 per cent. That is to say, assuming the
accuracy of the figures, the first nine months of 1933, the
average unemployment was 13,680,000 and for the first nine
months of 1935 it was 11,700,000, and the small decrease is
thought to be due to the large number of persons coming into
fields of employment.

In the chapter on public fiscal affairs, the outstanding highlight is the reduction in interest cost of public money borrowed. The Treasury reports that at March 1, 1933, it was 3.427 per cent, whereas at September 30, 1935, it was 2.642 per cent; and they have made a hypothetical computation which shows that annual interest on the debt outstanding September 30, 1935, computed by the average interest rate in March 1933, would be some $225,000,000 greater than it presently is.

Under the heading of private fiscal affairs, the Reconstruction Finance Corporation, the Federal Deposit Insurance Corporation, and the Treasury Department report that only a few banks still need capital strength. The RFC reports that its investments in banks have proved to be sound and dividends are being earned in respect thereto; and the Deposit Insurance Corporation reports 14,195 banks insured and that the insured deposits have ranged from the time it has been in existence from 11 billion to 18 billion of insured deposits. Failures involved only $6,250,000 of insured deposits.

In the chapter on housing, it seems that the outstanding fact is that in the years 1925, 1926, and 1927 the families annually newly housed ranged from 400,000 to 450,000 per annum. The families newly housed from 1932 to 1935 ranged from 25,000 to 40,000 per annum.

The Federal Housing Administration reports that January 1 next the outstanding insurance will approximate $450,000,000 which will be divided approximately one half under Title I and one half under Title II. At January 1, 1937, the Housing Administration reports that it expects there will be outstanding insurance of $1,250,000,000 to $1,500,000,000.

The Public Works Administration and the Resettlement Administration, of course, are engaged in the housing field. The Public Works Administration reports that its program, which has received approval, calls for 96,100 rooms at a cost of $126,000,000. That is to say, approximately 24,025 dwelling units. The Resettlement Administration expects to build about the same number of dwelling units to cost about $130,000,000.

The Home Owners' Loan Corporation reports that it is practically through with its loaning operations—expects to be completely through by June 1, 1936, under the present program, and that it expects it will then have outstanding some one million loans aggregating three and one half billion dollars; that is to say, an average of $3,500 per loan. It also reports that, whereas there will be some losses on these loans, it does not expect that the number of mortgages under foreclosure ever will exceed ten per cent of the total number of mortgages.

A report on the federal power program is found in one chapter of the report wherein the Federal Power Commission states that it is operating on a self-sustaining basis, and is now engaged in research to bring together proper facts for guidance. It appears to be a highlight of the inquiry how relatively few reliable statistics were available concerning power. Information which ordinarily one would expect could readily be found does not exist, and the Federal Power Commission is engaged in a survey which it says will furnish such information.

The Tennessee Valley Authority reports progress which is well-known on the Norris and Wheeler Dams, and gives some statistics showing the actual kilowatt-hour consumption in the same territory before and after applications of the TVA rates, showing an increase ranging from 146 per cent to something over 200 per cent.

Under the heading of transportation, the outstanding fact appeared to be, of course, the situation of railroads wherein freight revenues were shown to be down about 45 per cent between 1926 and 1934. Passenger revenues were down 66 per cent at the same time.

The Interstate Commerce Commission said there were no satisfactory truck statistics showing carriage of freight. Now that the Motor Carrier Act[5] has become effective they expect to get proper statistics and exercise proper control.

Another highlight in connection with transportation is in connection with aviation—a relatively small factor now, but with such extraordinary growth that it is a matter of interest. The number of passengers carried increased from 173,000 in 1929 to 850,000 in 1935, the increase in express was from 257,000 pounds to 4,500,000 pounds, and the distance flown increased from 25,000,000 to 60,000,000 miles.

PRESIDENT ROOSEVELT: Between what dates?

MR. ALVERSON: Nineteen twenty-nine and 1935; they used approximately the same number of planes flying 60,000,000 miles as they did

---

[5] This was the legislation consolidating regulation of bus and truck lines under the Interstate Commerce Commission, signed into law by President Roosevelt, Aug. 10, 1935.

in 1929 in flying 25,000,000 miles.

The Federal Coordinator of Transportation and the Interstate Commerce Commission report there is no federal control as to rates and charges for passengers and express, although I believe both those organizations have recommended that some such control be instituted.

Relief statistics, of course, are fairly well-known. In July 1933, there were 3,900,000 cases; in July 1934, 4,397,000 and in July 1935, 4,372,000. We, however, during this year find a rather steady decrease in the relief load from 5,400,000 at the beginning of the year to 4,196,000 in August.

We also find that the burden on the federal government has grown rather out of proportion to the change in the load; that is, more of the load has been put on the shoulders of the federal government than the change in the number of cases would indicate.

The Works Progress Administration reports that its funds will last until March 15, 1936.

The Public Works Administration reports that at the present time it is employing about 275,000 as against a peak of 700,000, that they expect again to attain such a peak of approximately 650,000 to 700,000 in July next year, and that they expect the program will taper off so that at January 1937 the employment will again approximate 250,000.

PRESIDENT ROOSEVELT: I recommend that report as a very good one.

SECRETARY ROPER: When will it be available for us?

MR. WALKER: I think there are some modifications to be made, but it should be ready within the next week or ten days.

SECRETARY PERKINS: I think there are some very great errors in conclusions and interpretations; for instance, they have used the Federal Reserve Index of production which is based on 20, where the base should be 90. The two are not comparable.

PRESIDENT ROOSEVELT: Were those figures from the Central Statistical Board?

MR. ALVERSON: Yes, sir.

SECRETARY PERKINS: They have taken figures that were not given them by the Department of Labor. I think the Department of Labor would not want to be held responsible for them.

PRESIDENT ROOSEVELT: Who is your person on the Central Statistical Board?

SECRETARY PERKINS: Lubin. We have taken the position that we will not give out estimates of that kind. It is a very foolish thing to do. They added to those estimates a large number of persons who were employed, such as agricultural people who went out to work in the harvest season, artists, writers, dentists, and self-employed people, as well as former business men who are never directly looking for employment. The minute times are better, they are going into business for themselves. Probably six or seven million can be accounted for in that way, in addition to which you have your unemployables that ought always to be thought of as being counted in such an estimate. It is very dangerous speculation, and I think others in the government should know.

PRESIDENT ROOSEVELT: Will you look into that?

MR. ALVERSON: Yes, sir.

MR. FAHEY: Can we have copies of that high-spot report, after it has been checked, without waiting for the full report?

MR. WALKER: Wouldn't it be better to wait for the full report? We will have that whole thing in a week.

MR. FAHEY: Accompanied by a summary?

MR. WALKER: This is a summary, Mr. President.

PRESIDENT ROOSEVELT: If you want just the high spots, I am sure Mr. Alverson will be glad to put them in. It does not cover all the report, by any means.

Anybody got anything else?

MR. HOPKINS: Some time ago I agreed—foolishly—to run a placement service for all employees of the government that were displaced. Last month, the government employment services employed 1,000 while only 86 were employed through our placement bureau. Our placement bureau is concerned exclusively with those that have been in government employ and have been dropped. We are not getting anywhere.

PRESIDENT ROOSEVELT: Who are the offending people?

MR. HOPKINS: The Commerce Department is the best. Rural Resettlement hired 329 people and took none of them from us. About 90 per cent of these people have been cleared through the well-known circles. Either we have got to use this or we ought to give it up, because employees are learning that we are not delivering the goods. They are getting very mad about it; they say we are giving them a run-around, and I think it should be made mandatory on all agencies that all employees under $2,000 a year should be employed from the list of people that have been in the government before.

PRESIDENT ROOSEVELT: I think that is absolutely right. I do not know whether any order is necessary, but since every department and agency is represented here we will make a verbal order to that effect. You can keep checking on it, and if there are any violations, let Frank know right away.

MR. FAHEY: Don't you think there should be some freedom in the matter of choice? Some people were weeded out in the process and I don't know who wants them back.

SECRETARY WALLACE: There are some of those folks that we do not want.

PRESIDENT ROOSEVELT: Then we don't have to take them.

MR. HOPKINS: We will send them 10 or 12 for every job.

PRESIDENT ROOSEVELT: If you have some of those 10 or 12 that nobody wants, they just won't get taken on.

Meeting closed at 3:50 p.m.

Held in the Cabinet Room of the White House,
January 28, 1936, at 2:15 p.m.

_____

Present: the President of the United States; the Vice-President of the
United States; the Secretary of State; the Secretary of the Treasury; the
Secretary of War; the Attorney General; the Secretary of Agriculture;
the Secretary of Commerce; the Hon. Charles West, Undersecretary
of the Interior; the Hon. L. W. Robert, Jr., Assistant Secretary of the
Treasury; the Hon. Turner Battle, Assistant to the Secretary of Labor;
the Hon. Charles H. Fullaway, Administrative Assistant to the Director
of the Budget; the Hon. Henry L. Roosevelt, the Assistant Secretary
of the Navy; the Administrator of Agricultural Adjustment; the Administrator of Federal Emergency Relief; the Chairman of the Reconstruction
Finance Corporation; the Coordinator of the Tennessee Valley Authority;
the Chairman of the Federal Home Loan Bank Board; the Hon. Ewin
L. Davis, Commissioner, Federal Trade Commission; the Chairman
of the Interstate Commerce Commission; the Director of Emergency
Conservation Work; the Hon. E. F. Hill, the Deputy Governor of the
Farm Credit Administration; the Adviser on Consumers' Problems;
the Acting Chairman of the Central Statistical Board; the Acting
Administrator of the Federal Alcohol Administration; the Administrator
of Federal Housing; the Administrator of the Resettlement Administration; the Chairman of the Federal Power Commission; the Chairman of
the Federal Communications Commission; the Chairman of the Securities
and Exchange Commission; the Hon. H. P. Seidemann, Social Security
Board; the Acting Executive Director; the Executive Assistant of the
National Emergency Council.

_____

[Though this meeting is one of the longer ones, there are few
matters of importance. The problem of providing adequate
statistics is raised again. In general, the first half or more
of the transcript, in which the President goes over the reports
of the agencies submitted for the meeting, duplicates previous discussions of the same sort. Mr. Roosevelt read or
paraphrased interesting portions, asked occasional questions,
and raised points of interest. One wonders, in spite of the
educational value to the President and to the other members of
the NEC whether the time was efficiently used. Is it not likely
that many of the members were bored listening to recitals
that involved them little or not at all? Comments of this sort
certainly have often been made regarding cabinet meetings
and the same criticism would seem to apply here.
Even so far as the President himself was concerned, one
wonders how fruitful a meeting like this was. Though the
consideration of relations with a particular Congressional

committee may well have been valuable, the exchanges on the use of the intra-governmental personnel placement service, of standardizing holidays, and of granting time off on election day to federal employees, hardly seem of sufficient importance for the President. "Coordination" in a rather trivial sense was exercised, but not on issues that imperatively required the attention of the Chief Executive himself. One must conclude that the NEC was perhaps reaching a point of diminishing return.—Editors' Note.]

PRESIDENT ROOSEVELT: There is not very much emergency business to do. I attended, about two weeks ago, the meeting of the National Emergency Council in New Jersey, and it was a real inspiration to see those people together. Every government agency in the state of New Jersey, including the Army and Navy, was represented; and they had a complete exchange of information. The people, I think, went away from that meeting with the idea that they knew something about the government. How many were there—about 400?

MR. ALVERSON:[1] About 375.

PRESIDENT ROOSEVELT: Nearly 400 people were there, and of course they all go back to their own field to work with a better understanding and appreciation of how to tell the truth about what is going on. That is why the National Emergency Council is beginning to operate all through the country as a factual information service for people of all kinds—something that I think is going to be of extreme value in putting the average citizen in closer touch with his government. How many of those meetings have we had now?

MR. ALVERSON: That was the forty-fifth meeting.

PRESIDENT ROOSEVELT: That is pretty good.

MR. ALVERSON: That is about all of them. We have had one more since then, in Maryland, and that is all of that semi-annual series.

PRESIDENT ROOSEVELT: Those NEC directors in the various states are now getting pretty well organized so that any other agency of government can get information from them about what is going on, as well as any newspaper or organization or private citizen. How many states have that fairly well organized information service?

MR. ALVERSON: I should say all of them, with the exception of Delaware and

---

[1] Frank Walker resigned as Executive Secretary for the second time on Dec. 18, 1935, and was replaced by Lyle Alverson.

New York. We haven't functioned in those two states yet. Of course, we have some places that still need strengthening and reorganization. In the greater number of cases we are quite well organized.

PRESIDENT ROOSEVELT: We have three new members with us today; I don't wish to call them new, for they are old friends—Miss Roche who is the acting administrator of the Federal Alcohol Administration; Charlie March, chairman of the Federal Trade Commission—

MR. DAVIS: Mr. President, he is at home on a very sad mission—because of the death of a relative.

PRESIDENT ROOSEVELT: I didn't know that; but you are a very good substitute, Ewin. Also Mr. Mahaffie, chairman of the Interstate Commerce Commission.

I thought today we would do what we have done on various occasions in the past, summarize very briefly. I think you have given me about 50 pages to read, but I will not read them in full.

The State Department has a paragraph upon frozen commercial accounts in Brazil. The gist of it is that they expect an early agreement on the details of the operation of releasing about $30,000,000 of the serial obligations.

German export subsidies: Germany has given direct assurance that subsidies under a law enacted in June 1935 are not being and will not be granted on exports to the United States.

Japanese competition: There has been a voluntary extension of the agreement with the Japanese Government providing for voluntary limitations by Japanese exporters of importation into the Philippines of cotton piece goods from Japan, and also the Japanese Government has agreed to a voluntary extension of the agreement limiting cotton rug shipments to the United States. Also, there has been a study of general Japanese trade by the Tariff Commission. That study brings all the facts up to the minute.

International balance of accounts: Increasing public emphasis upon the postwar changes in the international debtor-creditor position of the United States, combined with the significance for that position of the gold and capital movement of recent years, has suggested the desirability of more accurate information upon the foreign investments of this country and investments of foreigners in this country and upon current changes in those positions. Preliminary surveys have been instituted with a view to examining the material currently available and those additional materials which would be necessary in order to secure more full and more prompt information upon the international debtor-creditor position of the United States. These studies have been referred to the Executive Committee on commercial policy which has directed the establishment of a subcommittee of experts to survey this subject in more detail and to report to that committee.

Trade with belligerents: The course of American trade in war materials has been kept under constant daily review.

On the question of trade agreements from December 14, 1935, to January 17, 1936, the Division of Trade Agreements has concluded a trade agreement with Honduras which was signed on December 18, 1935, and which is now before the Honduran legislature for approval; has concluded a trade agreement with the Kingdom of the Netherlands which will come into effect on February 1, 1936; has concluded a trade agreement with Switzerland which will come into effect on February 15, 1936, and has continued negotiations looking to trade agreements with Costa Rica, Guatemala, Finland, France, Nicaragua, Salvador, and Spain.

German aviation mission: A German aviation mission will arrive in Washington on February 8, 1936, to discuss questions pertaining to the possible establishment of a transatlantic air transport service between Germany and the United States. Is that zeppelin, or is it heavier-than-air?

SECRETARY ROPER: It is heavier-than-air.

PRESIDENT ROOSEVELT: Which way do they come, Dan? The Northern way?

SECRETARY ROPER: This group is coming to discuss the general situation in line with several other countries. We had one from Latin America some three months ago; and by the way, you may be interested to know that as a result of that mission our people have sold $400,000 worth of equipment. We have had others; the French have sent a group here, and I presume that Germany is just following suit. The British, you will remember, were here about a month ago, and that is all settled. I think that Germany has just opened up the discussion.

PRESIDENT ROOSEVELT: The Treasury Department reports internal revenue collections for the first six months of the fiscal year 1936 in the main groups, such as the income and excess profit tax, showing collections of $560,000,000, which is up $136,000,000; the alcoholic liquor tax collections were $262,000,000, which is up

505

$47,000,000; miscellaneous tax collections were $707,000,000, which is up $77,000,000.

(Vice-President Garner came in at this point and was invited to a chair at the President's right.)

Agricultural adjustment taxes—the less said the better! The figures for this are apparently completely scrambled.

Public debt and interest charge: As of December 31, 1935, the interest-bearing public debt was $29,442,851,490, the computed annual interest charge was $751,306,488, and the computed rate of interest 2.552 per cent. This is the lowest rate during the current fiscal year. The rate of 2.715 per cent, as of June 30, 1935, was the lowest rate for the end of any fiscal year since 1916, when the rate was 2.376 per cent. As of June 30, 1933, the interest-bearing public debt was $22,157,643,120, the computed interest charge being $742,175,955, and the computed interest rate 3.350 per cent. As the result of the refinancing at lowered interest rates since June 30, 1933, the Treasury is now carrying an interest-bearing public debt that has increased $7,285,000,000, with an increase of only $9,000,000 in the computed interest charge. Going back still farther, to the immediate postwar period, the interest-bearing debt on June 30, 1921, was $23,737,352,080, and the computed interest charge was $1,029,917,903. As compared with this period, with its computed interest rate of 4.339 per cent, we are now carrying a debt $5,706,000,000 greater, with an annual interest charge $279,000,000 less.

Expediting examination of income tax returns: Collectors of internal revenue and district heads of the income tax, alcohol tax, intelligence and accounts and collections unit opened a three-day conference January twentieth. The major problem outlined to the conference was acceleration of the examination of income tax returns. Under the former procedure, on returns filed March 15, 1936, for the calendar year 1935, examinations would begin January 1, 1937, to be concluded by December 31, 1937. Under the new schedule, examinations will be concluded, on an average, nine months after filing a return instead of an average of 15 months after filing. In other words, we will save six months.

Post Office Department: The chief information is that the gross postal receipts continue to run between six and seven per cent higher than they did at this time in 1935.

Navy Department: This department has commissioned

several new ships. Twenty-five thousand men were employed on new ship construction and 28,000 men on other projects.

The Interior Department reports that the Comptroller General has recently approved the allotment of $900,000 of PWA funds for work on the Caballo Dam on the Rio Grande River below Elephant Butte Dam, and there has been transferred from the State Department to the Interior Department $1,500,000 for this purpose, bringing the total amount available to $2,500,000. They report that this work is progressing satisfactorily. Charley, do you know if that is part of the boundary flood control project?

MR. WEST: I think not.

PRESIDENT ROOSEVELT: How did you get the money out of the State Department? Why did you (*turning to Secretary Hull*) give them a million and a half?

SECRETARY HULL: It was appropriated to be used in connection with the boundary work.

VICE-PRESIDENT GARNER: This will be for flood control if that project is ever adopted in whole by the two countries.

PRESIDENT ROOSEVELT: The Public Works Administration reports that work is progressing rapidly on projects coming under its jurisdiction and that some difficulty is being encountered in securing engineers for inspection work on the projects involved. At the end of the calendar year 1935, the Public Works Administration had realized approximately $295,000,000 through the sale of municipal and railroad bonds.

The Housing Division has 11 housing projects under general construction and work has been started on the construction of the foundations for 15 other projects, while 9 project sites are being demolished and contracts for 13 projects have been awarded. Work will be begun on the demolition or construction of these projects within the next few days.

(*The President scanned the Agriculture Department report as follows:*)

The Agriculture Department reports that the agricultural situation, while very much improved over that of 1932, is still out of balance with the rest of the country taken as a whole. I have never known it to be in balance, for that matter. In terms of net income per person on farms, the 1935 returns, excluding benefit payments, represented a purchasing power for industrial goods of about 20 per cent below that of the prewar purchasing power and a disparity in relation to the

relative per capita purchasing power of the rest of the population of about 15 per cent. In aggregate figures, this income
disparity comes to about $850,000,000 and benefit payments
scheduled to be paid on the 1935 output of $480,000,000.
It would take an addition of $850,000,000 to bring the per
capita purchasing power of the average person on farms to
the level of the rest of the population. This does not, of course,
provide any offset for the disparity that has existed every
year from 1928 to 1935 inclusive, about $7,000,000,000 in
terms of the present price situation and national income.
Is that a suggestion that we go on paying back?

SECRETARY WALLACE: It is up to Henry.

SECRETARY MORGENTHAU: Don't anybody else say, "It is up to Henry!" (*Laughter*)

PRESIDENT ROOSEVELT: That would be a popular 1936 slogan—put it up to Henry!
(*Laughter*)
With the corn belt needing only a favorable growing season
to create a 200,000,000 bushel addition to carry over and a
similar situation in the South, the problem of maintaining a
balance between the several major areas will undoubtedly be
a most difficult one under any agricultural program that will
be put into effect in 1936. This conclusion emphasizes even
more the necessity for speed in securing the proper legislation and for getting under way. In 1933, delays in getting
the necessary legislation through Congress and having to start
after the South had done most of its planting turned out to
be a costly matter, especially in that it forced us to resort to
a plow-up campaign. Speed is essential if we are to do the
job expected of us in 1936.
(*The President then read and paraphrased from the report of
Federal Emergency Relief Administration as follows:*)
The Federal Emergency Relief Administration reports a
decrease of 21 per cent in the total number of general relief
cases between July 1 and November 30—that is an interesting
thing to remember—and it is estimated that an additional
15 per cent to 20 per cent over the November figures will
appear for December. The decrease in the number of persons
is even larger, 23.4 per cent, which is apparently due to the
fact [that] in the Works Progress Program, work has been
given to family heads in greater proportion than to single
persons. It must be further kept in mind that, in nearly all
instances, persons assigned to Works Program continue to get
relief until receipt of the payment for the first full period of
work performed. The actual decline in number of persons

removed from the general relief rolls would be considerably greater than that reflected in the 21 per cent. It is particularly noteworthy that, for probably half the month of November, persons assigned to projects probably appear on both the Works Program and the relief rolls for this reason. During this same period, the obligations incurred by the relief organizations have fallen off 40.6 per cent while the obligations from federal funds show an even greater decrease—48.5 per cent. At the same time, the obligations from state funds have increased by 10.6 per cent, whereas those made from local funds have decreased by 31 per cent. The decrease in contributions from local funds is probably largely accounted for by the transferring of even larger amounts as local contributions to projects of the Works Program. There are clear indications that in many places the standards of local relief have fallen off with the withdrawal of federal funds.

The Works Progress Administration reports a grand total of 3,612,000 were at work on projects of all agencies operating under the Works Program. That is a little better than promised.

MR. HOPKINS: That includes everybody working in Puerto Rico; it includes 70 or 80 thousand supervisors in CCC. We counted in that every possible person who gets a job out of this Administration. Of course, it will be cut down in the spring.

PRESIDENT ROOSEVELT (*The President continued to read and paraphrase*): There are four main types of public improvements including roads and streets, public buildings, water supply and sewer systems, and parks and playgrounds, which constitute more than 80 per cent of the value of projects which State Works Progress Administrators are operating at the present time. Work on roads, streets, and alleys will comprise about 15 per cent of the total. The construction of schools, federal government buildings, hospitals, community homes, penal institutions, etc., comprises approximately nine per cent. Another nine per cent will go into the improvement of local state and federal park playgrounds. Forestation, flood control, irrigation, water conservation, and similar projects, including air ways, ski jumps, etc., account for about six per cent of the total, and construction activities also extend to a wide variety of miscellaneous projects.

Out of every federal dollar to be spent on Works Progress Administration projects, 77¢ will go to labor and the remaining 23¢ will be expended on materials and miscellaneous costs. All available funds have now been allocated with the exception of $173,068,903, and this amount has been earmarked for specific allocation. Of the total of $4,386,431,097 allocated to date, the Works Progress Administration has received $1,253,128,502; $527,289,000 has been allocated to the Civilian Conservation Corps and a total of $500,000,000 out of this appropriation has been allocated to the Bureau of Public Roads.

Most of the difficulties which beset our complex organization during its initial stages have been by this time ironed out. Recent adjustment in the direction of decentralization by the Treasury, and amendments in our own procedure, have greatly facilitated procurement and the prompt meeting of payrolls. The whole program is proceeding with a remarkable lack of labor difficulties and an enormous amount of genuinely useful work under way. Here are some unemployment estimates. Do we want them? How does Mr. Nathan get these figures?

MR. BATTLE: We have taken the position right along that unemployment estimates are unreliable.

MR. HOPKINS: The Department of Labor has taken the position that they do not know what the figures are. I do not know why any other agency should get out an estimate. I think we are going to get ourselves into difficulty. I noticed that figure was given some publicity the other day.

PRESIDENT ROOSEVELT: I don't think we want to try to get figures of that kind.

MR. BATTLE: We have taken the stand that an estimate would be very detrimental, ranging from 8 to 23 million unemployed.

PRESIDENT ROOSEVELT: What is meant by unemployed?

MR. BATTLE: The estimate of 1933 is purely an estimate and ranged from 8 to 23 million.

PRESIDENT ROOSEVELT: I think you better tell your people not to put down any estimates on total unemployment.

ATTORNEY GENERAL CUMMINGS: Why do these agencies keep giving out figures?

PRESIDENT ROOSEVELT: I don't think any agency has given them out. Will you tell them not to give out any figures?

MR. BATTLE: We have consistently fought giving out any figures. There was an estimate of 11,000,000 of unemployed recently which we have probably scotched.

VOICE: Was Mr. Nathan transferred from the Consumers' Division of the NRA?

MR. HAMILTON: Mr. Nathan is not connected in any way with the Consumers' Division.

SECRETARY MORGENTHAU: Whom does he work for?

MR. BATTLE: I understand he is one of those people who have been transferred around in these recent shake-ups.

MR. HAMILTON: If he was transferred to us he is an invisible import; I have never heard of him.

PRESIDENT ROOSEVELT (*The President then picked up the report of the Federal Housing Administration*): The annual report of the Federal Housing Administration is in process of publication and copies will be forwarded to the Council as soon as printed. This report shows as of December 31, 1935, the total volume of business transacted of $540,000,000 of which $254,000,000 represents 708,405 modernization and repair notes insured, $258,979,239 mortgages selected for the appraisal of 67,029 homes, and $27,030,000 of mortgages accepted on 15 large-scale housing projects. Of the home mortgages selected, 42,147 for $170,594,864 have been accepted for insurance and 6,957 for about $27,000,000 are now under consideration. Residential construction shows for the last seven months of 1935 an average monthly increase over the corresponding seven months of last year of 207 per cent. The volume of residential construction for this period exceeded that for any comparable period since 1931, and December 1935 residential construction was greater than that of any December since 1930.

The Federal Housing Administration contemplates submitting a number of amendments to the National Housing Act.[2] These amendments will be for the purpose of clarifying the present language of the Act, although several changes in policy in connection with the general housing situation are now under consideration. In reference to the extension of Title I beyond its present expiration date on April 1,[3] "we feel (*reading from the report*) that this Title has largely accomplished its purpose. On the other hand, there seems to be an insistent demand for its extension and our judgment is that its extended existence might further assist in the revival of business. However, we feel that it should be extended in somewhat restricted form so that its activities might be gradually reduced." Then they suggest various details. This question arises. Their losses under Title I are being paid at the rate of $85,000 per month; what is being done to pursue to judgment

---

[2] This Act was approved June 27, 1934.

[3] Title I of the Act authorized the Administrator to insure lending institutions against losses suffered because of loans made for repairing, improving, or modernizing property—the so-called "short-term modernization" part of the program.

511

and collection the government's right against the borrowers? Does anybody know?

MR. MC DONALD: Yes, we are going through that by several different methods in order to determine which is the most efficient. We have employed local attorneys; we have organized our own department in the states to try that also; and the third method has been to turn over a certain portion of the delinquent loans to the credit department of one of the large commercial credit companies. The commercial credit people are ahead in collections, whether because they know how better to go about it or whether their system is better, I do not know. We will adopt the method which appears to be best within the next 60 days.

PRESIDENT ROOSEVELT: The Resettlement Administration reports the completion of 33 subsistence homesteads projects begun by the Subsistence Homesteads Division of the Department of the Interior. On January 4, 1936, the Administration had completed construction of 17 such projects. Construction was in progress on ten projects and final plans were being prepared on six projects. They mention four projects and say that they will represent 4,000 dwelling units at an estimated cost of $16,000,000. That is $4,000 per unit. Is that correct?

MR. TUGWELL: Approximately so; it is too early to say yet.

PRESIDENT ROOSEVELT: The administration further reports that $4,000,000 has been set aside for loans to cooperative agricultural and community services in resettlement communities and that $28,000,000 has been set aside for grants to farm families. Also, that $2,000,000 has been set aside for administrative expenses of the farm debt adjustment program. (*Mr. Alverson then handed a memorandum to the President.*) Oh, ho, Dan! (*reading*) "Robert R. Nathan, Chief of Income Section, Division of Economic Research, Commerce Department." (*Laughter*)

SECRETARY ROPER: I just made a note here—I have received a complaint of a general character. I presume I got him through the NRA. (*Laughter*)

MR. BATTLE: I thought he was one Secretary Roper had given us from NRA!

SECRETARY ROPER: No, but I have some you can have!

MR. JONES: On behalf of the other organizations, I want to express thanks to Mr. "Red" Leggett for going out and getting this information. (*Laughter*)

SECRETARY ROPER: What is the sentence that was pronounced on him?

PRESIDENT ROOSEVELT: To quit figuring!

SECRETARY ROPER: All right, but it is pretty difficult to stop a statistician. (*Laughter*)

512

(President Roosevelt next read the Federal Deposit Insurance Corporation Report)

PRESIDENT ROOSEVELT: There is one question which we have raised in the past two or three years. There are four agencies of the government that are still making bank examinations of one kind or another. The Comptroller of the Currency examines national banks and banks in the District of Columbia; the Federal Reserve System examines State banks who are members of the System; FDIC examines State banks not members of the System; and RFC examines banks which are applicants for loans. Can't we standardize that a little more?

MR. JONES: We use the examinations made by the departments, sir, so that we do not bother the banks any more. I think a lot of progress has been made in taking this thing out of so many examinations for the banks. I believe progress is being made, and I believe we can do more, and we will talk more about it. We will see what we can do. The examinations of national banks, at least, I think are being made on a good deal more considerate basis— considerate to the banks. The examiners' reports indicate it.

PRESIDENT ROOSEVELT: When the new Federal Reserve Board is set up,[4] you might have a little conference some day with these four agencies.

MR. JONES: Fine!

(President Roosevelt then read the Federal Home Loan Bank Board report.)

PRESIDENT ROOSEVELT: There is a question raised here. Where is John?

MR. FAHEY: Here.

PRESIDENT ROOSEVELT: John, does the HOLC make proper recourse to government rolls to insure payment to it by government employees?

MR. FAHEY: Yes, so far as I know, Mr. President. You mean employees in our corporation or government employees in general?

PRESIDENT ROOSEVELT: As a whole.

MR. FAHEY: Wherever they are delinquent, we take the question up with the government agencies involved.

PRESIDENT ROOSEVELT: That is being followed, then.

MR. FAHEY: Oh, yes; we are giving it special attention.

PRESIDENT ROOSEVELT: Does the HOLC make recourse to WPA rolls for the same purpose?

MR. FAHEY: I don't know about that.

PRESIDENT ROOSEVELT: I mean the people on relief.

---

[4] A provision in the Banking Act of 1935 changed the name of the Federal Reserve Board to Board of Governors of the Federal Reserve System (Aug. 23, 1935). An Executive Order related to the same matter was issued Feb. 3, 1936, and this may have been what the President had specifically in mind.

MR. FAHEY: Oh, yes, we work with the relief agencies wherever the delinquents are unable to pay in all the states. We have a good many cases where the home owner is unable to pay, but the relief agencies are allowing payments which would approximate rent.

(President Roosevelt then read the report of the Federal Power Commission.)

MR. MC NINCH: Mr. President, since that report was made, we have been advised by the company that it will respond to the order. We didn't know whether they would test it or not.

PRESIDENT ROOSEVELT: They are not taking it to court?

MR. MC NINCH: That is the present status.

(The next report which the President read was that of the Federal Reserve System, and the report of the Securities and Exchange Commission was then read.)

PRESIDENT ROOSEVELT: Homer, when will these cases come up to the Supreme Court? You have the Judge Coleman case and you have your own case.

ATTORNEY GENERAL CUMMINGS: The Coleman case will not get up there for quite a while unless the stockholders kick. I do not know whether they will deem it advisable to press for a constitutionality decision in a case in which the government is not a party. The case in New York—the Electric Bond and Share Company case—is a terrific undertaking.[5] It involves about 20 subsidiaries, and examination of their detailed structure is a task of some magnitude, but we are pressing them as rapidly as possible. Of course, the commission is handling that, primarily.

PRESIDENT ROOSEVELT: Is that the district judge?

MR. LANDIS: Judge Mack.

ATTORNEY GENERAL CUMMINGS: In the southern district of New York.

PRESIDENT ROOSEVELT: How long do you expect that will take?

MR. LANDIS: We expect to go to trial about the middle of March.

ATTORNEY GENERAL CUMMINGS: That is a tremendous undertaking. That is very good time. It is a large order. Of course, these disputes in this district were set on motion in order to give us an opportunity to bring up that test case, and two of the companies are now seeking an appeal on the decision that Judge Bailey rendered there in the district court. We are now resisting their petition for a hearing

---

[5] According to the full text of the report from which the President was reading, both these were cases in which the constitutionality of the Public Utility Holding Company Act of 1935 was at issue. Coleman was the federal judge involved in the case which implicated the American States Public Service Company. The Electric Bond and Share case was finally decided by the U. S. Supreme Court in 1938 (303 U.S. 419) in a manner favorable to the government, and is cited as one of the principal cases which established the validity of the holding company law.

in the Court of Appeals for the District of Columbia which they tried to get from Judge Bailey's court. I think we have blocked them off there. The only concern I have is this very thing you mention. The Electric Bond and Share Company case presents such a wide sweep we tried to get it up so that it can be decided and expedited.

PRESIDENT ROOSEVELT: Can you bring this Electric Bond and Share Company case straight to the Supreme Court?

ATTORNEY GENERAL CUMMINGS: That is what we are planning to do. It will take quite a while for that case.

(President Roosevelt read the Social Security Board report, and also the report of the Tennessee Valley Authority.)

PRESIDENT ROOSEVELT: Where is Guntersville?

MR. BLANDFORD: About 80 miles up the river from Wheeler Dam.

(President Roosevelt next read the report of the Emergency Conservation Work.)

PRESIDENT ROOSEVELT: "Export-Import Banks." Which one? Or, there is only one.[6] I want to have a little talk with you *(turning to Secretary Hull)* and Jesse about closing up the bank altogether. It doesn't seem to be doing anything.

SECRETARY ROPER: The Cuban bank?

PRESIDENT ROOSEVELT: No, the Export-Import Bank.

"United States Government Manual." *(After summarizing this report, President Roosevelt continued.)* Mr. Alverson suggests that the government departments should check a little on getting this valuable book. I find we are getting three copies in the White House and we need only one. Will you make a check and see if you can cut down on the number you have in your departments and save money?

"Allotment of Funds." So that you all save shoe leather in coming to the White House, on January 10 I sent the following letter to Mr. Alverson:

Under date of December 17, 1935, the Executive Director of the National Emergency Council addressed a memorandum to its members concerning the possibility of Federal agencies obtaining future allotments from the Emergency Relief Appropriation Act of 1935.

---

[6] There were, apparently, two Export-Import Banks. The Export-Import Bank of Washington was organized pursuant to an Executive Order dated Feb. 2, 1934; after various extensions of its life, it was made a permanent agency by the Export-Import Bank Act of 1945. The so-called Second Export-Import Bank was authorized by Executive Order on Mar. 9, 1934, and abolished by another Executive Order, May 7, 1936; its records were transferred to the Export-Import Bank of Washington. The text of the report refers only to the "Washington" Bank, though it may have been the "Second" Bank that the President had in mind.

You should advise any Federal agency requesting such allotments that there are no more funds available for projects of the character described in the memorandum.

Very truly yours,

FRANKLIN D. ROOSEVELT.

I have no more money. Tell everybody.

"Representative Cochran," the chairman of a committee that apparently had nothing to do—is that right?[7]

VICE-PRESIDENT GARNER: Expenditures.

PRESIDENT ROOSEVELT: Wrote a letter asking for all kinds of information and reports to be submitted by departments. Cochran's letter asked for, at the earliest date possible, charts of your department, Frank (*McNinch*), three copies. He said they would like to have them cover the general organization, the personnel summary, the financial summary, estimates, etc. He says charts of this character were prepared for the special economy committee in 1932 and they would like to have the information brought up to date. Those reports are being prepared in good faith, but there is, of course, a limit to the amount of time and money that any department can spend on preparing detailed reports for the committees of the House. The reports should be absolutely factual and should not contain any recommendation. They should merely give the minimum of information desired.

ATTORNEY GENERAL CUMMINGS: Congressman Cochran is asking for information about certain cases we handled in certain particular ways. I am wondering what the purpose of it was.

VICE-PRESIDENT GARNER: His committee would not have any jurisdiction. He was making inquiries how you handle law suits?

ATTORNEY GENERAL CUMMINGS: No, not exactly; there are cases that are settled by compromise, and the inquiry was directed to some of the cases on the theory, I suppose, that the Department of Justice is bound to make a report under the statute every year on cases settled. We always do that. They want to delve into it more deeply, I suppose. I was afraid there was some possible political background to it.

SECRETARY ROPER: I got him down to the department in connection with such inquiries, and he told me he had a great deal of trouble in holding down certain members of his committee; that he was being requested to make these inquiries by members of the committee. I think he is easily handled.

---

[7] Rep. John J. Cochran, doubtless in his capacity as Chairman of the Committee on Expenditures in the Executive Departments.

ATTORNEY GENERAL CUMMINGS: There is nothing at all in the least degree embarrassing, so far as that is concerned; but I was wondering how far that was going to be pursued. Once you start on it, there is no end to it.

PRESIDENT ROOSEVELT: I have here the list of what the departments have done to date. The State Department makes a general statement of the department's activities. The Treasury and War are preparing reports. Justice has sent a functional chart to the committee, with a general statement of the activities. The same thing refers to the Post Office Department. The Navy Department says that if at any time the department can present any practical suggestions to the committee, it will make whatever report is deemed necessary. That goes too far; you are not supposed to make suggestions. The Interior Department goes much too far; the Secretary informed the committee that his principal recommendation concerning reorganization is an early consideration of a bill to change the name of the Interior Department. That should not go up. What they want is factual information and not suggestions.

VICE-PRESIDENT GARNER: Those are controversial.

PRESIDENT ROOSEVELT: Stick to the functional chart; don't make any suggestions. "Report on the Personnel Replacement Division." That brings up a question I wish you would all be thinking about. The Administrator of WPA reports the following: (*President Roosevelt then read the report of the Personnel Replacement Division of the Works Progress Administration.*)
This is something you ought to take up, every one of you, with your personnel officers. For instance, in October the emergency personnel was shown by Civil Service report to be 6,972, of which Personnel Replacement Division relocated only 78.

MR. ALVERSON: That is the month when they were just getting started.

PRESIDENT ROOSEVELT: In November there were 1,926 emergency personnel and the Replacement Division relocated only 137.

MR. ALVERSON: The Civil Service Report for December is not yet available as to the number of emergency personnel taken on.

PRESIDENT ROOSEVELT: I do not understand this; how many new people were taken on?

MR. ALVERSON: There were 1,926 in the month of November.

PRESIDENT ROOSEVELT: And only 137 through the Replacement Division; that is bad, and there was a total available of 1,310. In October we took on emergency personnel to the extent of 6,972 people and 1,177 had their jobs terminated, and yet of those only 78 were taken over on the new jobs. In November there were 1,926 new jobs, 1,310 available people, and only 137 were taken on.

517

	The thing has fallen down; what are we going to do about it? Harry, that is partly you and partly Labor, isn't it?
MR. HOPKINS:	We manage that, Mr. President. You could issue an order saying they must get their employees through the Replacement Division; as long as they have discretion to get them elsewhere they will probably do so. The situation has improved. We are getting about three times as many placements, but the ratio of placements by departments is about the same. The Department of Commerce still gives the highest number of jobs. Last month I think all their placements came through this Bureau. But some of these emergency agencies simply won't use this thing and they get their employees from other sources.
PRESIDENT ROOSEVELT:	Which ones, Harry? Name them.
MR. HOPKINS:	I don't have the list in front of me.
MR. ALVERSON:	I don't recall that your report showed them by agencies. If it did, I missed it. Suppose I make a summary.
MR. HOPKINS:	We have it by departments.
PRESIDENT ROOSEVELT:	Any agency wishing to take people other than through the Replacement Division has got to clear through the Director of the Budget and NEC.
MR. ALVERSON:	I have found the list; Public Works took on six, one from Replacement; War Department, 28, 26 through Replacement; Justice took one and none from Replacement; Agriculture, 127 and 11 from Replacement.
PRESIDENT ROOSEVELT:	Agriculture, that's bad!
SECRETARY WALLACE:	We have given a very strong order about that.
PRESIDENT ROOSEVELT:	Oh, Rex, listen to this! You took on 469 and only two from that Bureau.
MR. TUGWELL:	We asked for every one of those from the Bureau and didn't get one. I don't know where the breakdown is, but that is the situation.
PRESIDENT ROOSEVELT:	Will you go after it with a sledge hammer?
MR. ALVERSON:	I will do my best, sir.
MR. MC NINCH:	I would like to testify to the high quality of the employees we get from the Replacement Division. We have, with very rare exceptions, been able to get a very high percentage of good stenographers and comptometer operators, as well as clerical help. We don't go to them for engineers.
MR. TUGWELL:	Maybe all these people are Republicans.
ATTORNEY GENERAL CUMMINGS:	The Civil Service regulations have something to do with it.
PRESIDENT ROOSEVELT:	Do they?
ATTORNEY GENERAL CUMMINGS:	Our stenographers have to have a Civil Service rating.

MR. ALVERSON: No, sir. This matter relates only to people paid for with emergency funds.

PRESIDENT ROOSEVELT: The question of holidays comes up once a year, at least. At a meeting of the National Emergency Council held on January 22, 1935, the following holidays were approved for that year and were effective during the year. There was no departmental closing before Washington's Birthday, Memorial Day, Independence Day, Labor Day, or Thanksgiving Day. A half holiday was given before Christmas and also before New Year's Day. The closing of the departments for the half day before Christmas and New Year's should be accomplished by Executive Order issued early in December. That was done, wasn't it?

MR. ALVERSON: Yes, sir.

PRESIDENT ROOSEVELT: National election day is not a holiday for government workers in the District of Columbia. It is my understanding, however, and that of the acting director of the Budget, that federal employees who reside in nearby Maryland and Virginia are permitted to be absent from duty for the time required to attend the polls. Have you talked with the Budget about that?

MR. ALVERSON: No, sir; Mr. Bell is out of town.

PRESIDENT ROOSEVELT: I think probably we better use the same rule this year as we did last; in other words, the only days that we give any time off with pay are the half day before Christmas and the half day before New Year's. Every department should remember that. Last year one or two departments started rules of their own, and it doesn't work.

In regard to election day—I was talking with Mr. Alverson about this and it seems to me we should extend the rule according to common sense. For instance, if a man votes up in Frederick, Maryland, the rule has been that he could leave on election day and go up there to vote, perhaps taking four or five hours. If he lived in Cumberland, a little beyond there, he could not do it. You have only that one day. My thought is that on election day, any employee of the government would be allowed to take the day off provided he goes home somewhere to vote. If he only votes in Bethesda, he ought to take only the necessary time for that. On the other hand, if he lives in New York, there is no reason why he should not take the night train and be back for work the day after election.

MR. BATTLE: Why couldn't he vote by absentee vote?

SECRETARY ROPER: It could be charged to annual leave.

PRESIDENT ROOSEVELT: No.

MR. DAVIS: I think the custom in the Federal Trade Commission is to permit them, if they want to vote in Great Falls, or Bethesda, or any surrounding Virginia or Maryland town, to let them remain long enough to vote before leaving their homes; or if that is not convenient, to get off in time to get there before the polls close, instead of coming in and then going back and voting and coming back to work again. That is the way the most of them prefer to do, and that is the way we have done.

PRESIDENT ROOSEVELT: Where do you draw the line? What about Cumberland, Maryland?

MR. DAVIS: They don't go back and forth every day there. I was speaking of those who reside in these nearby places. With regard to those living so far away, they cannot do that, and it seems to me the proper thing would be to give them the day off.

PRESIDENT ROOSEVELT: I would be inclined to suggest where they vote in states that haven't absentee ballots, and don't have to miss more than one day—election day itself—that you let them off to vote for the whole day, provided they are back on Wednesday morning; but only in those places where they cannot vote by absentee ballot.

ATTORNEY GENERAL CUMMINGS: What about places more remote?

PRESIDENT ROOSEVELT: You can get to Boston.

ATTORNEY GENERAL CUMMINGS: What about Indiana or Illinois?

PRESIDENT ROOSEVELT: That is too far; just where they can make it in one day.

SECRETARY ROPER: I think it ought to receive a little further attention.

PRESIDENT ROOSEVELT: I wish you would look into that.

MR. ALVERSON: I think Mr. Bell might have some constructive thought on it.

PRESIDENT ROOSEVELT: Yes, take it up with him as soon as he gets back.

MR. ALVERSON: Mr. President, you will recall this report,[8] one copy of which has been submitted to you. Since submitting it we have reorganized the material after submission to practically all the agencies involved, with a view to possibly publishing it in the future. It has not, of course, been made public. We have undertaken, with the assistance of all the agencies, to strike out from the document everything that, as a matter of policy, should not be made public. We have checked it with the agencies for accuracy, and I believe the document is now in sufficient order so that we may distribute it to the members of the Council, stamped as it is, "Personal and Confidential." Mr. Early has given it consideration. Such of the gentlemen

---

[8] The comprehensive document concerning the activities of the emergency agencies which Mr. Alverson summarized at the meeting of Dec. 17, 1935. See pp. 495-499.

as wish to carry these copies with them may do so, and those who prefer may have their copies sent to them by messenger.

PRESIDENT ROOSEVELT: They ought to be held as confidential documents.

VICE-PRESIDENT GARNER: Things here may be more confidential than in committees of Congress. Usually when we take up such matters there, somebody is going to get hold of it some way or other.

PRESIDENT ROOSEVELT: I think this is almost foolproof.

MR. ALVERSON: It is intended to be foolproof.

PRESIDENT ROOSEVELT: I wish you would read these copies, and if you have any suggestions to make regarding things like estimates of the total number of unemployed—

MR. ALVERSON: There is none.

PRESIDENT ROOSEVELT: Or if some statistician is taking 1932 as the low point, which it wasn't, or anything of that kind, I wish you would let the director know for the next edition of the report. It is a very good report. A great deal of it is going to be extremely useful.

MR. ALVERSON: We are constantly besieged with questions which require research on what the government is doing. This book answers about 75 per cent of such questions.

VICE-PRESIDENT GARNER: If you have it where it is foolproof, isn't it a valuable document for the country to have?

PRESIDENT ROOSEVELT: I would suggest that you all read this and bring in any suggestions you have for more detailed information or for changes in the form in which it is presented, and we will get out a second edition around the first of April in such form that it can be made public.

MR. ROBERT: May I say just a word, Mr. President? Inasmuch as I am retiring from the Treasury Department on the sixteenth of February, this will probably be my last meeting with this Council. I have been a member since it was organized, and apropos of what you were just saying, I think if the public could know more about these meetings and about the thoroughness with which the President is in contact with every emergency agency and with the members of the Cabinet, it would be invaluable on the outside. I have had a few occasions with business friends of mine who have been very critical to tell them, not in detail, about such meetings as these. And I believe that this publication, made foolproof, and with a magazine like *Fortune* that could be elaborated, woul be most valuable to this administration.

In conclusion, I want to say that these meetings have been the most instructive and most interesting of anything in the government. It is the most valuable function that is going on.

521

It has been a great privilege and pleasure to me. I assure you I am retiring in full accord with the objectives of the Administration. You will not see me lined up with the Liberty League or the Townsend plan! (*Prolonged laughter and applause*)

PRESIDENT ROOSEVELT: I don't have to tell you that we are all very sorry to see you go.

MR. ROBERT: I am a little like the nigger who ran to the storm cellar when he saw the storm coming. Now that things have cleared up, I am going back.

MR. JONES: Here is an annual report that is full of good material. It is for the calendar year and covers everything we have done. It is very interesting.

PRESIDENT ROOSEVELT: Yes, that goes away back. (*The President turned the report from Mr. Jones over to Mr. Alverson.*)

SECRETARY ROPER: Can we have these reports distributed now?

PRESIDENT ROOSEVELT: They are right here.

(*The members then gathered about Mr. Leggett as he passed out copies of the report.*)

Meeting closed at 3:45 p.m.

Held in the Cabinet Room of the White House,
March 3, 1936, at 2:10 p.m.

_____

Present: the President of the United States; the Secretary of State;
the Secretary of War; the Secretary of Commerce; the Postmaster
General; the Hon. Charles West, Undersecretary of the Interior;
Admiral Adolphus Andrews, representing the Secretary of the Navy;
the Hon. Turner Battle, Assistant to the Secretary of Labor; the Admin-
istrator of Agricultural Adjustment; the Administrator of the Federal
Alcohol Administration; the Administrator of Federal Emergency
Relief; the Administrator of Federal Housing; the Administrator of
Resettlement Administration; the Administrator of Rural Electrification;
the Acting Chairman of the Central Statistical Board; the Chairman of
the Federal Communications Commission; the Chairman, Federal Deposit
Insurance Corporation; the Chairman of the Federal Home Loan Bank
Board; the Chairman of the Federal Power Commission; the Chairman
of the Federal Reserve Board; the Chairman of the Federal Trade Com-
mission; the Chairman of the Interstate Commerce Commission;
the Chairman, Reconstruction Finance Corporation; the Chairman
of the Securities and Exchange Commission; the Hon. Vincent M. Miles,
Member, Social Security Board; the Chairman, Tennessee Valley
Authority; the Director of Emergency Conservation Work; the Governor
of the Farm Credit Administration; the President of the Export-Import
Banks of Washington, D.C.; the Acting Executive Director; the
Executive Assistant, National Emergency Council.

_____

[This meeting adds further evidence of the diminishing
importance of NEC as measured by the importance of the issues
discussed and the amount of "coordination" accomplished.
By 1936, NEC was clearly drifting farther and farther from the
mainstream of policy. Most of this meeting is taken up with
the review by the President of the report prepared by the
executive director. As usual, Mr. Roosevelt read the portions
that he found of interest, interjecting comments and questions.
That this was a reasonably valuable exercise for him, we may
safely assume, since it gave him opportunity to keep abreast
of developments on many fronts and to quiz the responsible
official on the spot.
The kind of detail which caught the President's attention and
about which he sought further information reflects F.D.R.'s
enormous grasp of the minutiae of policy and its implementation—a grasp that was both a reflection of the man and of an
era in which, though the growth of government had been

enormous, the federal establishment was still of such a size and scope that the gifted President could know its operations. Clearly, Presidents in the 1960's face a vastly larger executive establishment and could not begin to find time or energy for such detailed surveillance.—Editors' Note.]

PRESIDENT ROOSEVELT: I have the reports from the departments and agencies, on which Mr. Alverson has done a great job. He has confined almost every report to one page.

We have two new members of the Council with us this afternoon, Mr. Wilford S. Alexander, Administrator of the Federal Alcohol Administration, and Mr. Warren Lee Pierson, President of the Export-Import Bank.

First, the report from departments and agencies. The State Department reports as follows: (*The President then read the report of the State Department down to the end of the paragraph headed "Proposed trans-Atlantic air service between the United States and Germany," ending with the words, "carrying out experimental flights."*)

That relates chiefly to zeppelin flights, doesn't it, Dan?

SECRETARY ROPER: Yes, sir.

(*The President then continued reading the State Department report down to and including, "No reply or payment has been received from Greece."*)

PRESIDENT ROOSEVELT: What did you tell them?

SECRETARY HULL: This is not a regular war debt, you understand; it grows out of an arrangement among the nations back there following the war, and we asked that they keep within the arrangement.

(*The President then finished reading the report of the State Department, the report of the Treasury Department, and the report of the Department of the Interior down to the end of the sentence in the first paragraph which reads, "It terminates the contract on March 1, 1936, when the Government accepted the work."*)

PRESIDENT ROOSEVELT: That has been taken care of?

UNDERSECRETARY WEST: Yes, sir.

(*The President then continued reading down to the end of the paragraph headed "Division of Grazing," the last few words of which are "and a reasonable amount of new construction."*)

PRESIDENT ROOSEVELT: I might say on that that a good many departments are after

Bob Fechner's boys, and of course he has not got enough boys or camps to go around.[1] Very soon I will go over the whole thing and you will have to accept what you are allotted.

MR. FECHNER: You know I wrote you on that, and you OK'd the program, and it has gone out.

PRESIDENT ROOSEVELT: I was talking about possible increases.

MR. FECHNER: Oh, a possible increase!

PRESIDENT ROOSEVELT: That makes you feel better. (*The President then finished reading the report of the Interior Department, that of the Public Works Administration, and the first paragraph of the report of the Department of Agriculture.*) What is going to be the short title of the new soil conservation act?

MR. DAVIS: It is still to be the Soil Conservation Act.

PRESIDENT ROOSEVELT: I noticed in the newspapers they called it the SCAVA![2]

MR. TUGWELL: It will be administered by the AAA, won't it?

MR. DAVIS: I think that is the Secretary's intention.

PRESIDENT ROOSEVELT: You would rather keep the old name?

MR. DAVIS: I don't believe this new name will need to be referred to in the press very much. It would be rather awkward. (*Laughter*)

PRESIDENT ROOSEVELT: We ought to be informed on it. We don't want people calling it the SCAVA!

(*The President then read the first sentence of the second paragraph of the report of the Department of Agriculture as follows: "These basic provisions mean that our Agricultural policy continues to be definitely not a scarcity policy."*) Some of you will want to listen to this, because you may have to make speeches on it during the next few months.

(*The President then continued reading and paraphrasing slightly the remainder of the report of the Department of Agriculture, that of the Agricultural Adjustment Administration, and the paragraph of the Department of Commerce report ending, "possibly indicating a liberal attitude on the part of the committee."*) I hope the Director of the Budget will take note of that. The Secretary of Commerce said they begged him to ask for more funds! (*The President continued the Commerce report down to the end of the sentence, "Included in this testimony has been some criticism of facilities and personnel furnished by the Bureau."*)

---

[1] The President refers to the Civilian Conservation Corps, and the "CCC" camps and their personnel.

[2] The reference is to the Soil Conservation and Domestic Allotment Act which the President had signed two days earlier. Since *D* and *V* sound so much alike, it is very likely the stenographer at the meeting thought Mr. Roosevelt had said SCAVA instead of SCADA.

SECRETARY ROPER: That grows out of the Cutting incident, very largely.[3]
(The President then finished reading the Commerce report and also the Labor Department report down to and including the sentence, "Compared with January 1935, however, there were 470,000 more workers employed and weekly pay rolls were $24,500,000 greater.")

PRESIDENT ROOSEVELT: That is largely seasonal, isn't it?

MR. BATTLE: Yes, sir.
(The President read the next paragraph, ending with this sentence, "Employment in the nondurable goods group in January 1936 was one-tenth of one per cent less than in January 1935.")

PRESIDENT ROOSEVELT: What is the explanation of the discrepancy between this and the newspaper report of the AF of L the other day?[4]

MR. BATTLE: This statement includes a number of groups not affiliated with the unions.

PRESIDENT ROOSEVELT: But the AF of L report was a scare headline report that apparently fewer people were employed in January than a year ago.

MR. BATTLE: That is not what our figures show.

PRESIDENT ROOSEVELT: No?

MR. BATTLE: We are covering 91 industries, the same industries we covered in 1935.

PRESIDENT ROOSEVELT: I wish you would check with those AF of L figures and let me have some kind of memorandum on it.[5]

MR. BATTLE: All right.
(The President then finished reading the Labor Department report and also the report of the Federal Alcohol Administration, which ends with this sentence, "It is reported that this legislation will be passed without opposition at this session of Congress.")

PRESIDENT ROOSEVELT: I hope you are right, Will. *(The President then read the Works Progress Administration report down to the end of*

---

[3] Referring to hearings by a Congressional committee investigating the work of the Bureau of Air Commerce of the Department of Commerce which were an outgrowth of the death of Senator Bronson Cutting of New Mexico in an air crash the year before.

[4] A news item relating to an AF of L report on unemployment, headlined "January Job Loss Biggest in Five Years," appeared in the *New York Times* for Mar. 2 (the day before this meeting), and drew a reply from the President which was the subject of a story appearing on Mar. 4 on page one of the *Times*.

[5] This memorandum was undoubtedly prepared and subsequently formed the basis of the comment by the President, mentioned in note 4 above. He used his press conference of Mar. 3 as a vehicle for his reply to the AF of L.

the sentence which reads, "Seventy-seven cents of every federal dollar spent on WPA projects is spent for labor.") That is worth remembering.

(*The President then read down to the end of the sentence, "Quotas will be cut as such transfers are made."*) The general curve on PWA, public roads, and various other agency expenditures employing relief people shows that we will not reach the peak of the other agencies until about May. Is that right, Harry?

MR. HOPKINS: I think about July.

PRESIDENT ROOSEVELT: As they increase the number of people from relief rolls, it means that Harry's WPA will be decreased by at least the same amount.

(*The President then finished reading the Works Progress Administration report, ending with the sentence, "For single persons, average WPA wage rates were about three times the average relief grant."*) It pays to be single!

(*The President read the Federal Housing Administration report without comment and down to the end of the first paragraph of the report of the Resettlement Administration, the last word of which is "encumbered."*) That is a new word and not a very good one.

MR. TUGWELL: It means "committed to loans."

PRESIDENT ROOSEVELT: That is a terrible word; don't let us use it.

VOICE: Is "obligation" a better word?

MR. TUGWELL: That doesn't mean the same thing.

PRESIDENT ROOSEVELT: The word "encumbered" sounds as though you had something in your hair!

(*The President then finished reading the report of the Resettlement Administration and also the report of the Rural Electrification Administration, which ends with the paragraph, "Bills pending before the Congress, introduced by Senator Norris and Representative Rayburn, provide for a ten-year rural electrification program."*) That, I think, we got straightened out.

(*The President then read the Federal Deposit Insurance Corporation report down to the comparison of banks insured January 1, 1935, with those insured December 31, 1935.*) Leo, what was the reason for that decrease in banks insured?

MR. CROWLEY: We had about 200 mergers and about that many new banks came in. There are only about 1,100 banks outside the fund, and most of those are in the state of Kansas—about 300 in Kansas outside the fund.

(*The President then continued reading and paraphrasing very*

527

slightly down to the end of the paragraph headed "Home Owners' Loan Corporation" in the report of the Federal Home Loan Bank Board.)

PRESIDENT ROOSEVELT: That is very nearly a million loans for homes, which is pretty good. *(The President finished reading the Federal Home Loan Bank Board report and the first part of the Federal Power Commission report down to the second paragraph ending with the sentence, "The Commission is now re-examining all applications and will here-after make such modifying or rescission orders as may be required.")*

MR. MC NINCH: We did that with our own staff, working at night and over-time. We borrowed a part of the Power Survey staff, also. Technically, we might not have had the right to do that.[6]

PRESIDENT ROOSEVELT: Will this be recurring?

MR. MC NINCH: There will be a few from time to time. The job will take many months because it involves connections with more than 3,000 separate corporations. You can see what it means to examine connections and ramifications of so many different corporations. We gave them a bill of health under the statute to protect them in the holding of the office. The commission has already begun combing the rest of them. We have set 26 for public hearing and will set 100 or more.

(The President then read the first sentence under the heading of Export of Electricity to a Foreign Country.)

PRESIDENT ROOSEVELT: That refers mostly to Mexico?

MR. MC NINCH: Yes, and a little in Canada, but the amount there is very small. *(The President then read the remainder of the Federal Power Commission report and all but the last paragraph of the Federal Trade Commission report, ending with the words, "Nineteen Commission orders appealed to circuit court of appeals were decided in the Commission's favor, and in not one case did the court overrule or void a Commission order.")*

PRESIDENT ROOSEVELT: That is good!

(The President completed the report of the Federal Trade Commission and read rapidly through the report of the Interstate Commerce Commission down to the words, "The reported net income of the year after fixed and contingent charges will show a small red figure of $267,538.")

PRESIDENT ROOSEVELT: What does that mean?

MR. MAHAFFIE: They failed by that much to earn their charges.

---

[6] Reference here is to the task of the Commission, under the Holding Company Law, to review applications to hold interlocking directorates in power companies. These required Commission authorization.

MR. ALVERSON:	It refers to contingent charges.
MR. MAHAFFIE:	Yes, they failed by that much to earn their fixed and contingent charges. (*The President then completed reading the Interstate Commerce Commission report.*)
PRESIDENT ROOSEVELT:	Do you know, Rex, how they are getting along with the grade crossing elimination?
MR. TUGWELL:	No, sir; would you like to know?
PRESIDENT ROOSEVELT:	Yes, I have not heard for some time. (*The President then read rapidly through the report of the Securities and Exchange Commission.*) Is that good policy to put it on the local postmaster?
POSTMASTER GENERAL FARLEY:	We are proceeding on the advice of counsel, Mr. President. (*The President next read the Social Security Board report down to the table showing types of plans, number of plans submitted, and number of plans approved.*)
PRESIDENT ROOSEVELT:	How many states does that mean?
MR. MILES:	Twenty-six states, one plan to each state.
PRESIDENT ROOSEVELT:	How about the other states?
MR. MILES:	The other states are waiting for meetings of the legislature. Some are contemplating special sessions. There were about six states contemplating holding special sessions.
PRESIDENT ROOSEVELT:	Next is the Tennessee Valley Authority. I am glad to say that since the last meeting it has become at least in part constitutional.[7] The Norris Dam is close to completion—so close to completion that tomorrow we expect to press the button. Are you going to be here?
DR. MORGAN:	I expect to be down there. (*The President then read down to the end of the paragraph which closes with this sentence,* "Progress has been made in methods of forming, and a new design for a plate machine has been finished.")
PRESIDENT ROOSEVELT:	What are they turning out?
DR. MORGAN:	Types of porcelain never made in America. By the use of electric firing and some mechanical method we believe we can bring that industry to this country. We have some deposits of kaolin that are better than the old Chinese porcelain or any other. We are getting some of the finest porcelain clay in the world, and we think we may bring the porcelain industry here. (*The President read the remainder of the Tennessee Valley report and down to the end of next to the last paragraph of the Emergency Conservation Work report.*)

[7] On Feb. 17—about two weeks earlier—the U. S. Supreme Court decided the case of Ashwander v. TVA (297 U.S. 288), and in so doing upheld the constitutionality of the TVA in part.

529

new deal mosaic

PRESIDENT ROOSEVELT: What happened to that $6,000,000?

MR. FECHNER: I withdrew the request for it today, because we have to go ahead on a definite plan until April first. I could not get any information from the Budget Bureau.

PRESIDENT ROOSEVELT: Where is it? I haven't got it.

MR. FECHNER: It is over at the Budget. Mr. Fullaway kept telling me it was going to be considered. We came to the time where we had to do something about it. We could not wait any longer. (*The President then read the last paragraph of the Emergency Conservation Work report, regarding the number of CCC patients in hospitals.*)

PRESIDENT ROOSEVELT: Isn't your death rate lower than any other place in the country?

MR. FECHNER: It is lower than in the regular Army. The Surgeon General constantly comments on it. It is below the mortality rate for the ages that we have.

(*The President then read the report from the Export-Import Bank of Washington.*)

PRESIDENT ROOSEVELT: The Senate adopted a resolution on February 24 providing for a committee of five to make a study of departments and agencies of the executive branch to determine whether their activities conflict and whether any of them should be coordinated with others, or abolished, or reduced. The resolution [S. Res. 217] provides for an appropriation of $20,000. The committee consists of Senators Byrd, Robinson, O'Mahoney, McNary, and Townsend.

My only thought on that is that if this committee begins to ask for information some time this spring from any department, you better check through Mr. Alverson before anything is done by your own agency or department, in order that you may have a uniform method of giving this information. In other words, we don't want to put any agency to the difficulty of putting a large number of people to work, thereby destroying the ordinary activities of the department, or greatly limiting them, unless we check up first. If the request is unreasonable, it is only natural that we would make a protest; if it is reasonable, we would go through with it. Remember that if this committee asks for information you are to check up with Mr. Alverson first.

Item 3 on the Agenda is the report of the acting executive director on the matter of government telephone calls. Go ahead and read it yourself. (*Mr. Alverson then read Item 3*).

PRESIDENT ROOSEVELT: Will you all please remember that, and speak to your appropriate officers and bureaus all the way down the line. All calls out of town should be on a station-to-station basis.

Item 4, "Report of the Personnel Replacement Division." *(The President then paraphrased closely the first page of the material under Item 4 of the Agenda.)* We have had this up several times before and there seem to be certain agencies that are reluctant to use the Replacement Office. Why, I do not know. Agriculture employed 301 and took only three from Replacement.

MR. ALVERSON: Mr. Wallace's letter in explanation said a lot of those folks were AAA people who were taken over directly.

PRESIDENT ROOSEVELT: Yes, and now we have broken it down.

MR. TUGWELL: The Replacement Service has been reorganized now and maybe we will be able to use it better.

PRESIDENT ROOSEVELT: I have got to begin to crack down on this. The Agricultural Adjustment Administration employed 263 and took none from Replacement.

MR. DAVIS: During what period, Mr. President?

PRESIDENT ROOSEVELT: During the month of December. Commerce took 147, 13 of whom were from Replacement. Labor took 41, and none from Replacement; Electric Home and Farm Authority, 5, and none from Replacement; Farm Credit, 11, and none from Replacement; Federal Communications, 11, and none from Replacement; Federal Coordinator, 56—where is Joe?— none from Replacement; Works Progress Administration, including FERA and NYA, took on 14, all of them from Replacement! Marvelous, Harry, perfectly splendid! *(Laughter)*

MR. FAHEY: He gets the pick!

PRESIDENT ROOSEVELT: FDIC took on four people, all of them from Replacement! Perfectly splendid! Federal Housing—oh, ho—took 58, and one from Replacement!

MR. MC DONALD: They must have been transferred.

PRESIDENT ROOSEVELT: Federal Power, 71, three from Replacement.

MR. MC NINCH: That is a mistake. It should be the reverse figures. I know that!

PRESIDENT ROOSEVELT: Take it up with Civil Service.

MR. MC NINCH: I will.

PRESIDENT ROOSEVELT: General Accounting Office, 118, 38 from Replacement; Home Owners' Loan, 90, and 5 from Replacement; Interior Department, 8 and 1 from Replacement; National Emergency Council, 4 people, and none from Replacement! *(Laughter)*

The Navy took on 50, none from Replacement. Get after that office. Public Works Administration, 166 new people and only one from Replacement; RFC ten, and one from Replacement; Rural Electrification, 39, two from Replacement. This is bad news. Resettlement Administration, 740 new people, 76 came from Replacement, ten per cent. The Treasury, 287, eight from Replacement; War Department, 148 new people, 18 from Replacement; Emergency Conservation, 38, none; National Recovery, 30 and none.

In other words, we took on in the month of December 2,713 new people and only 188 came from Replacement. Now the answer is a perfectly simple one; I suggest that you have another checkup made for some month, January or February, and at the next Council meeting if there is not a very definite improvement in every single agency, I have got to issue an order—I have got to that point—which means you will not be able to take anybody except through the Replacement Service without special permission. I am sorry to say that, but it has come to that.

MR. FECHNER: Who prepared that list?

PRESIDENT ROOSEVELT: Civil Service Commission. Of course if those figures are wrong, you should get the figures corrected.

SECRETARY ROPER: Shouldn't you use the month of March?

PRESIDENT ROOSEVELT: I have gone into this before.

MR. ALVERSON: The Civil Service Commission is rather slow and that is what makes the lag. Mr. Hopkins has the current figures.

MR. MC NINCH: Do these figures refer only to those who have civil service status?

MR. ALVERSON: Oh, no; on the contrary, they refer only to persons employed by emergency funds.

PRESIDENT ROOSEVELT: Where is Dan Bell? I guess he stayed out on purpose. The Director of the Budget, on the 25th of February sent out a Budget circular—a copy of a Budget circular—dated August 11, 1922, which directs the heads of departments and establishments, before initiating a new activity, to transmit in writing to the Bureau of the Budget certain information therein described, for the purpose of seeing if work of the same or similar nature is being done by any other department or establishment, to the end that duplication of effort may be avoided. He says that the provisions of this Circular No. 77 of August 11, 1922 are and always have been in full force and applicable to all government agencies, including corporations. It is brought to the attention of all concerned so that it may be strictly followed.

That is what I call making a discovery!

I thought we would not meet again until about the fifth or tenth of April.

Has anybody anything to bring up?

Meeting closed at 3:20 p.m.

Proceedings of the National Emergency Council

[meeting no. 31]
April 28, 1936

Held in the Cabinet Room of the White House, April 28, 1936, at 2:10 p.m.

Present: the President of the United States; the Secretary of State; the Secretary of the Treasury; the Honorable Stanley Reed, Solicitor General; the Postmaster General; the Acting Secretary of the Navy; the Honorable Charles West, Undersecretary of the Interior; the Secretary of Agriculture; the Secretary of Commerce; the Honorable Turner Battle, Executive Assistant to the Secretary of Labor; the Acting Director of the Bureau of the Budget; the Acting Administrator of Agricultural Adjustment; the Administrator of Federal Alcohol Administration; the Administrator of Federal Emergency Relief; the Administrator of Federal Housing; the Administrator of the Resettlement Administration; the Administrator of the Rural Electrification Administration; the Acting Chairman of the Central Statistical Board; the Chairman of the Federal Communications Commission; the Chairman of the Federal Deposit Insurance Corporation; the Chairman of the Federal Home Loan Bank Board; the Honorable Basil Manly, Vice-Chairman of the Federal Power Commission; the Governor of the Federal Reserve Board; the Chairman of the Federal Trade Commission; the Chairman of the Interstate Commerce Commission; the Chairman of the Reconstruction Finance Corporation; the Chairman of the Securities and Exchange Commission; the Chairman of the Social Security Board; the Chairman of the Tennessee Valley Authority; the Director of Emergency Conservation Work; the Federal Coordinator of Transportation; the Governor of the Farm Credit Administration; the President of the Export-Import Banks of Washington, D.C.; the Commissioner of Labor Statistics; the Acting Executive Director; the Executive Assistant to the Executive Director.

[The proceedings of the NEC settled into a more or less uniform pattern: a review by the President of the agency reports compiled by the executive director, sprinkled with appropriate queries. This pattern of arid discussion, plus the lengthening intervals between meetings bespeak the decline in importance of the Council. At the close of the last meeting, held on March third, the President tentatively scheduled the next for early April. As a matter of fact, as noted, three or four *more* weeks beyond that were allowed to pass before the group was assembled. Three interesting matters in the following transcript might be highlighted. First there is the discussion of federal land acquisition practices initiated by the President, prompted by information gleaned from the White House mail. This illustrates in an interesting and concrete way the general point that has often been made about the care with which F.D.R. had the mail analyzed and the use he made of it as a check on the general state of public opinion. Dr. Lubin's review of the unemployment picture and the intricacies of the statistical problems involved recalls again the problem of government statistics, and foreshadows future developments along the same line, notably, the work of the Council of Economic Advisers established in 1946. The final comment by the President about central clearance of statistical information adds one further (if minor) dimension to the use of NEC and its satellite bodies for central clearance purposes.—Editors' Note.]

PRESIDENT ROOSEVELT: We have a new member with us today, Dr. Lubin, Commissioner of Labor Statistics of the Department of Labor, also Executive Secretary of the Central Statistical Board. I am going to ask Dr. Lubin a little later to give us a rather brief summary in regard to economic and unemployment conditions, bringing us a little up-to-date along the line that we used to get from Dr. Riefler.

The "Summary of Reports" submitted by the members of the National Emergency Council—I think only about 250 pages— and Mr. Alverson expects me to read them. The first is the State Department. (*President Roosevelt then read the first paragraph of the State Department Report, ending with the words "Trade Agreement with Iran."*) We arrested their minister for speeding.

SECRETARY HULL: Yes, and they are a little out of sorts.
(*The President next read down to the end of No. 4 in the second paragraph concerning a trade agreement with Colombia.*)

PRESIDENT ROOSEVELT: That hasn't gone through finally, has it?

SECRETARY HULL: Yes, that is through.
(*The President then finished reading closely the State Department report, and down to the words* [income tax collections for three-quarters of the fiscal year had been estimated at $1,034 millions; actual collections totaled $1,044 millions], *page 2 of the Treasury Department report.*)

PRESIDENT ROOSEVELT: You ought to estimate it closer than that!

SECRETARY MORGENTHAU: We will try to do better!
(*President Roosevelt then continued reading and paraphrasing closely down to the end of the paragraph on "Division of*

Grazing" in the report of the Interior Department.)

PRESIDENT ROOSEVELT: You are not going to kill off all the prairie dogs, are you? (*No answer*) Nobody here from Interior? (*No answer*) (*Undersecretary West, of the Department of the Interior, came in a few minutes later.*)

(*The President continued reading rapidly through the report until he finished the fourth paragraph of the Works Progress Administration report.*) That is something well worth remembering, not only 40 per cent of the workers on PWA projects came from relief rolls, 60 per cent of all other agencies' workers came from relief rolls, but in the CCC 88 per cent came from relief rolls, and in the case of WPA, 90 per cent came from relief rolls. (*The President skipped the Federal Housing report but read it at the close of the other reports.*) (*After reading the first three paragraphs of the report of the Resettlement Administration, with reference to Farm Debt Adjustment Service, the President said:*) Is there any duplication, Bill, in the work of settling these debts between Resettlement and Production Credit?

GOVERNOR MYERS: No, sir; the handling of these local committees, which are voluntary, is under Rural Resettlement. If the debts are such that they cannot be financed through Farm Credit—

PRESIDENT ROOSEVELT (*interrupting*): Haven't you got a Farm Debt Adjustment of your own?

GOVERNOR MYERS: No, sir, it was started by Henry, and was finally taken over by Resettlement. We thought that a lending agency like ours should not be in charge of that.

PRESIDENT ROOSEVELT: So that all the agricultural debt adjustment is in one place?

GOVERNOR MYERS: Yes, sir; there is no overlapping at all. We have no direct relation, but we try to cooperate.

(*The President next read the fourth paragraph of the Resettlement Administration report.*)

PRESIDENT ROOSEVELT: That is something well worth remembering; it is performing a real service.

(*The President then read the remainder of the Resettlement Administration report.*)

PRESIDENT ROOSEVELT: That is something I want to talk about. Is Rex here?

DR. TUGWELL: Yes, sir.

PRESIDENT ROOSEVELT: Rex, there has been a great deal of complaint. I am judging from my own mail—4,000 letters that come, on an average day—and I can tell pretty well what is falling down. At the present the most conspicuous falldown is in our purchase of land. We constantly get letters saying that "some department

536

took an option on my land a year ago—a year and a half ago—two years ago—and I have not been paid for it. They told me I would get a check for it in six months. I made all arrangements to move off. They have not taken my land, and I cannot move off. What am I going to do about it?" The Attorney General's office assures me that the amount of time spent on search and approval over there is very small, and yet the delay continues. Stanley, what is the situation?

SOLICITOR GENERAL REED: The delay is inevitable, in large measure, because of the particular type of title being acquired. It is necessary to search, get affidavit of death of wife, find the children who have moved to Hawaii or Europe, and bring suit for clearance of title. It seems inevitable that there should be a delay.

PRESIDENT ROOSEVELT: The actual delay in the Attorney General's office is not so great.

DR. TUGWELL: No, it is not.

PRESIDENT ROOSEVELT: Is it the Comptroller General?

DR. TUGWELL: That is one bottleneck. I will give you an illustration. We have all been working on this thing, the Comptroller General, the Attorney General's office, and ourselves, especially on lands. You see, the same procedure is used in buying some piece of marginal land at $3.00 an acre as in buying a site for a federal post office in New York City, and in many cases it costs more than the land is worth. I went into the office in South Carolina to look into the matter there and it happened that their courthouse was burned down by General Sherman. Our procedure requires that they go back beyond the period when that courthouse was burned down.

PRESIDENT ROOSEVELT: How about it, Dan? (*Laughter*)

DR. TUGWELL: They have to get affidavits. It is a very difficult situation.

VOICE: Don't let that get out, or there will be a bill in Congress to rebuild that courthouse!

VOICE: Mr. President, WPA is working on it at this very moment! (*Laughter*)

PRESIDENT ROOSEVELT: A lot of these complaints that I get lead me to believe that a lot of the original fault is not with the Resettlement but that men from the Biological Survey, Reforestation, and so on, went to the owners of the property and said, "We would like to have an option on your land; the government wants to buy it." The man assumes something; perhaps he ought not to assume it. He assumes that he has sold the land when he gives an option. He assumes that he will be paid in what he considers a reasonable length of time—two or three months.

537

new deal mosaic

Would it be possible to have a piece of paper in plain English that you would give to the man in which you say, first, this is not a contract to buy; it is an option. You have not sold your land. And second, this does not assure of payment within any specified time; it all depends on the title search, on the funds, on the Comptroller General, so that the fellow won't think he has sold the land and is going to get paid right away.

DR. TUGWELL: We have already done that, and have taken an additional step; we have taken a lease besides the option, so that the fellow is getting something, anyway, and he understands the situation now; but when these options were originally taken, titles were clearer then, so there was not so much delay. With this great increase of buying, all the bottlenecks have shown up. I think the situation will be met within a month or two, but it has been very embarrassing to everybody. We have taken leases on most of these lands, and the situation is not so bad as it was. What really needs to be done, if the government is going to continue to buy forest land and submarginal land, is something which only Congress can do. I explained the situation in a meeting with a number of Congressmen recently, so there is a possibility that we might get some legislation that will be helpful. If we could get a merchantable title instead of one of these fancy titles, that would help the situation, and the government would not stand to lose very much, even if one title for 2,000 acres of $2.00 or $3.00 land should fail.

SECRETARY MORGENTHAU: What do you pay for the lease on top of the option?

DR. TUGWELL: Usually very little; frequently they will lease it to us for nothing. We are just doing it to clear up the situation so that we can do some development work on this land.

PRESIDENT ROOSEVELT: I know something about poor land. I bought 404 acres at Warm Springs from five children in a case where an old gentleman left no will. We got four of the children to sign, but the fifth had committed a murder in Meriwether County about 20 years before, and lit out, supposedly for Arkansas. We searched Arkansas and couldn't find him; so the murderer owns one-fifth and I own the other four-fifths.

SOLICITOR GENERAL REED: If a man in each project devoted himself to clearing up the defects in titles—they are doing that a great deal—it would help considerably. When they don't get the affidavits—don't find the murderer—the title is left open for weeks and months; and the vendor won't work it out. He is shiftless or careless.

DR. TUGWELL: We are putting on a lot of attorneys and they

are going to help this situation.

PRESIDENT ROOSEVELT: I think the essential thing is to be quite certain that the owner of the land is not fooled when we take an option or take a lease, and won't be led to believe that he will get his payment within a specified time.

MR. JONES: I wonder if you took a lot of options that you did not expect to exercise?

DR. TUGWELL: No, we expected to exercise them; but unfortunately, we don't always have control of those things.

PRESIDENT ROOSEVELT: The money does not always stick. An option isn't necessarily a contract to purchase.

SECRETARY MORGENTHAU: We went all through that in New York State and cut a lot of corners.

PRESIDENT ROOSEVELT: I think we will have to get legislation to put in a central system.

SECRETARY MORGENTHAU: You are required now not only to get a merchantable title but a perfect title.

(The President then continued reading and paraphrasing closely down to the end of the Federal Deposit Insurance Corporation report.)

PRESIDENT ROOSEVELT: These fifteen suspensions in the first three months of the year— is Joe here?

VOICE: Leo is here.

PRESIDENT ROOSEVELT: Oh, I had the wrong pig by the ear! *(Laughter)* It isn't clear in the records whether the fifteen banks were insured.

MR. CROWLEY: I might say that out of 53 banks closed since January 1, 1934, 22 were closed because of defalcation within the bank itself.

PRESIDENT ROOSEVELT: How much of that is being taken care of by Fidelity Insurance?

MR. CROWLEY: It is very difficult to do that; for instance, in Bradford, Pennsylvania, we had a defalcation of $1,500,000, and the deposits were about $5,000,000. You cannot carry a surety bond sufficiently large to protect such cases. We are trying to get them to carry a reasonable amount of surety.

PRESIDENT ROOSEVELT: Can you compel that?

MR. CROWLEY: Yes, we have a right to.

PRESIDENT ROOSEVELT: That whole thing stands out as a big accomplishment.

MR. CROWLEY: All those people have been paid within 10 days of the closing of the bank—36,000 of them.

PRESIDENT ROOSEVELT: Really? What happened to that money eventually?

MR. CROWLEY: We move all the accounts in here and hold it, then we take the debt into our fund for a time.

PRESIDENT ROOSEVELT: How long?

MR. CROWLEY: Two years, I believe.

PRESIDENT ROOSEVELT: Is that all?

MR. CROWLEY: Yes.

(The President next read down to the end of the second paragraph of the report of the Federal Home Loan Bank Board.)

PRESIDENT ROOSEVELT: What is the cause of that increase?

MR. FAHEY: Lending more freely. They are borrowing money more freely and lending it more freely.

(President Roosevelt then read the next two sentences.)

PRESIDENT ROOSEVELT: That is the tendency right along—to convert over?

MR. FAHEY: Yes, sir.

PRESIDENT ROOSEVELT: Have most of them converted so far?

MR. FAHEY: Oh, no; there is a good deal of resistance in the states. The commissioners and the state authorities do not like to see them convert. But they are getting more cooperation regularly in state after state.

(The President then read on down to the end of next to the last paragraph of the Federal Home Loan Bank Board report.)

PRESIDENT ROOSEVELT: The tendency in arrears does not show any increase, does it?

MR. FAHEY: It is being reduced some, yes. Adjustments are made; that is, where the home owner is unable to pay in full, we readjust the amount, usually for not more than three months, to see how he works out; and in some cases, of course, where they owe perhaps $25.00 a month of principal and interest and are able to pay not more than $8.00 or $10.00, we accept that temporarily and readjust the debt as best we can.

(The President then read and paraphrased down to the end of the second paragraph of the Federal Trade Commission report.)

PRESIDENT ROOSEVELT: Henry, does this investigation of agricultural income by the Federal Trade Commission duplicate any work of the Department?

SECRETARY WALLACE: Well, perhaps a little; but I have no doubt that can be, and is being, worked out satisfactorily.

PRESIDENT ROOSEVELT: Are you working together on that?

COLONEL MARCH: Yes, we are; the Department of Agriculture has that information.

SECRETARY WALLACE: We have never had any difficulty on that, have we?

COLONEL MARCH: Not a bit! We have worked perfectly together.

(The President then read to the words "without a single reversal" in the paragraph headed "Complaints and other Legal Work.")

PRESIDENT ROOSEVELT: That is very good! *(The President finished reading that paragraph.)* You must be pretty good lawyers!

(The President next read to the end of the paragraph headed

"False and Misleading Advertisements.") What is the news about the Pure Food and Drug Act, Brother March and Brother Tugwell?

DR. TUGWELL: Representative Chapman still has it under control. It should be out in about two weeks.[1]

SECRETARY WALLACE: I understand he would like to have high authority.

PRESIDENT ROOSEVELT: I talked with him on the telephone about six weeks ago; I will do it again. (*The President continued reading down to the end of the second paragraph on page 2 of the Securities and Exchange Commission report.*) Here?

MR. LANDIS: Yes.

PRESIDENT ROOSEVELT: That is going to be one of your major tasks, isn't it?[2]

MR. LANDIS: Yes, sir.

PRESIDENT ROOSEVELT: And the Atlas case and the Equity case are preliminary to that?

MR. LANDIS: They are.

(*The President read the third paragraph on page 2 of the Securities and Exchange Commission report.*)

PRESIDENT ROOSEVELT: How does that compare with last year? It is up, isn't it?

MR. LANDIS: Yes, considerably. I cannot give you the exact figures, but the increase of new money is quite noticeable this year. The proportion is not greater than 14 per cent, but that is triple or quadruple what it was last year.

(*The President referred back to the third paragraph of the Securities and Exchange Commission report.*)

PRESIDENT ROOSEVELT: I like that point, "The Commission is entitled to an injunction even though the defendant may for the moment have repented." That is contrary to the Supreme Court ruling in the other case.

(*The President then read closely the report of the Social Security Board.*)

These 31 states with one or more plans—John, there is not much chance of getting many more states this year, is there?

MR. WINANT: Not more than half a dozen, Mr. President.

PRESIDENT ROOSEVELT: On the other hand, a good many legislatures haven't been in session this year.

MR. WINANT: That is the reason we haven't had many in.

PRESIDENT ROOSEVELT: There has been a pretty healthy response, hasn't there?

MR. WINANT: Yes, especially in behalf of the children. We feel that next year

---

[1] Rep. Virgil Chapman was a member of the House Interstate and Foreign Commerce Committee and joint sponsor with Senator Royal S. Copeland of the Food and Drug bill mentioned. The bill failed of passage at that session of Congress.

[2] This exchange relates to aspects of the task of SEC to implement the holding companies legislation of the year before.

there will be a demand for something like $55,000,000 in the field of old-age grants, $35,000,000 for dependent children, and $8,000,000 or $10,000,000 for the blind.

PRESIDENT ROOSEVELT: When do those payments begin—as soon as they come in?

MR. WINANT: As soon as they come in. We made quarterly payments in advance.

PRESIDENT ROOSEVELT: Is that the thing, Dan, that I sent up a deficiency estimate on?

MR. BELL: Yes, sir, for next year.

(The President read to the end of the third paragraph of the Tennessee Valley Authority report.)

PRESIDENT ROOSEVELT: That means that next year by this time you will have to have the lake pretty well lowered down, doesn't it?

DR. MORGAN: We lower it about the first of January.

(The President read down to the end of the paragraph headed "Pickwick Landing Dam.")

PRESIDENT ROOSEVELT: Arthur, is that an earth dam or concrete core?

DR. MORGAN: The ends are earth, but the center is concrete.

(President Roosevelt read to the end of the Tennessee Valley Authority report.)

PRESIDENT ROOSEVELT: I always think of that perfectly lovely thought that the Government is making fertilizer based, constitutionally, on the national defense! *(Laughter)*

(The President read to the end of the second paragraph of the Emergency Conservation Work report.)

Can you take it all right, Bob—the pressure from the Hill? *(Mr. Fechner merely smiled.)*

(President Roosevelt read the next two paragraphs of the Emergency Conservation Work report and down to the words "from New York" in the quotation.) I wonder why he picked New York. *(Laughter)*

MR. FECHNER: That is where they came from! *(The President finished reading the Emergency Conservation Work report.)*

PRESIDENT ROOSEVELT: Bob, that's all right!

MR. FECHNER: Mr. President, you might be interested to know that last week there was a conference of the Army chaplains in St. Louis. Three hundred and fifty of them have been on duty in the CCC camps and every one spoke in the highest terms of the conduct of the boys.

PRESIDENT ROOSEVELT: We teach them a lot. It is a good job. *(The President read the first page of the Farm Credit Administration report.)* That is interesting.

(The President continued reading down to the end of No. 5 of the Export-Import Bank report.) Well, the Navy will be

glad to know that you are cooperating in putting out Cuban fires! (*Laughter*)

(*The President finished reading the report of the Export-Import Banks of Washington.*)

MR. JONES: I would like the President of the Export-Import Banks to stand!

PRESIDENT ROOSEVELT: I think that report is grand. He has revived what I had come to regard almost as a corpse. It is coming to life again.

MR. JONES: The expense account has been reduced to a minimum.

SECRETARY MORGENTHAU: Fifty thousand dollars a year.

PRESIDENT ROOSEVELT: The only report left is that of the Federal Housing Administration. (*The President read the Federal Housing Administration report down to the end of next to the last paragraph.*) Where is most of that large-scale housing mortgage business?

MR. MC DONALD: It is in the East, principally, Mr. President—Philadelphia, New York, Delaware, Wilmington, and Baltimore.

PRESIDENT ROOSEVELT: Similar to this type across the river here?

MR. MC DONALD: Exactly that type.

PRESIDENT ROOSEVELT: In the suburbs?

MR. MC DONALD: In the suburbs.

PRESIDENT ROOSEVELT: They cannot be considered slum clearance.

MR. MC DONALD: They do not compete at all. I might say with reference to the home mortgages, this week will see a further gain. It is stepping up rather rapidly.

PRESIDENT ROOSEVELT: Mr. Alverson reports that since the last meeting of the Council, he has closely followed the matter of personnel replacement. He says the problems involved are numerous and complex. On the face of all the reports received from the agencies it appears, he says, that the Replacement Organization is filling its functions satisfactorily and that all agencies seem to be complying with my request that they procure their personnel when possible from the Replacement Organization of the Works Progress Administration. I hope you will continue to do so.

The Secretary of Commerce calls our attention to a matter which he has apparently run up against and probably most of you have also. He says: (*The President then read* [Officials of the Department are being continually importuned by members of Congress and others for the appointment of persons from the Civil Service Register and for the administrative promotion of Civil Service Employees.

The Civil Service rules provide that no recommendations shall be received, and no appointments shall be made, on the

ground of religious or political affiliation; also, that all recommendations for promotion shall come only from the persons under whose supervision the employee has served. . . .])
This relates only to Civil Service employees. I think all that needs to be said I can say now and you can quote me if you want to. The Civil Service rules provide that "no recommendation shall be received, and no appointments shall be made, on the ground of political or religious affiliation." That is a perfectly definite rule of the Civil Service Commission, and it is well to live up to it.

SECRETARY HULL: The Congressmen would rather make the recommendation and let it be turned down by the Civil Service Commission than themselves turn it down.

PRESIDENT ROOSEVELT: Just so they can write home and say they have done it.
The Secretary of Commerce also reports as follows: On Friday, March 13 (the date was well chosen), a man representing himself to be [Thomas Lee of the NRA, called the Photostat Room of the Department of Commerce and requested that a photostat operator remain on duty that evening until 9:00 o'clock for the purpose of doing some important work. One of the supervisory employees of the Photostat Room having heard of a similar case occurring in the Works Progress Administration, officials of the latter organization were communicated with and had representatives at the Department of Commerce to observe Lee and see what material he had to be photostated, inasmuch as Lee had recently been removed from the WPA. Lee called and left some valuable documents to be photostated which it afterwards developed he had stolen from offices of the WPA. The representatives of the WPA left the Department with these papers and Lee in their custody. Lee was apparently depending upon the Guard letting him in on an old pass which he had while with the WPA. Report of this incident is made for two purposes; first, to bring it to the attention of the other Departments and Bureaus so that they may guard against a repetition, and second to suggest that steps be taken to reclaim or cancel all building passes when employees are separated from the Service.]
I think that is a very important thing. We have a good many cases where official documents have been either purloined or temporarily taken away and photostated for political purposes or to cause trouble. That has happened in WPA, Interior Department, and probably if we knew it, in some other departments as well.

SECRETARY ROPER: I thought best to bring this up so that others may have notice of it.

PRESIDENT ROOSEVELT: The director reports the second group of state-wide coordination meetings . . .

MR. FECHNER: In connection with that, we are getting a great many requests to prepare exhibits and send to these meetings. That costs a lot of money, and it requires personnel. I have decided, unless I am overruled on it, we are not going to do it. We will send charts. It is just a day or two meeting, and I don't think it is worth it. We will send charts.

PRESIDENT ROOSEVELT: What else do they want?

MR. FECHNER: They want us to set up a typical CCC camp and show the works projects. I just got one from Philadelphia this week. We can't do it. That one down in Richmond yesterday or today—they wanted an exhibit. We can't do it. If we did, it would cost a lot of money.

PRESIDENT ROOSEVELT: It seems to me the only exhibit you could properly furnish to these men would be photographs. You probably have a good many of those.

MR. FECHNER: Oh, yes.

PRESIDENT ROOSEVELT: Photographs of work and camps, and graphs and charts which you have anyway.

MR. ALVERSON: Each one of the state directors undertakes to outdo every other state director, and each of the state directors attends the meeting of some neighboring state, and when they return, they come back resolved to do bigger and better. I have had the feeling that perhaps we are going a little too much in the field of showmanship. On the other hand, that kind of exhibit which the director refers to is the kind that excites the interest. They are much easier to look at than more graphs or photographs. It is a question whether it is worth the expense and work. Mr. President, I want to talk to you at some appropriate time on the setup of these meetings. We had a tremendous amount of publicity and widespread interest. At the same time, I have felt that maybe the direction should be changed a little in order to avoid the possibility of the charge that we are using government money and government time to publicize the Administration in what some people might call an extraordinary manner. We have tried to confine them to purely factual exhibits and to keep away from the emotional.

PRESIDENT ROOSEVELT: Just be factual and not emotional. This next thing proves the case.

MR. ALVERSON: Yes, it does, indeed!

545

new deal mosaic

PRESIDENT ROOSEVELT: The director reports that exhibitions depicting operation and accomplishment of the various departments and agencies of the government have been offered to the cities of Cleveland and Philadelphia for the week of June 8 and 22. There must be something going on in those cities at those dates![3] The director again suggests that it be factual and not emotional.

Now I think if Mr. Lubin could give us a little summary, it would be extremely valuable to us. The work of the Central Statistical Board has been, I think, in the last couple of months directed into perhaps a more useful form than it was last year when we were getting these weekly reports.[4] The particular subject today is principally on employment. You go ahead.

DR. LUBIN: The records of the Department of Labor, together with the records of the Department of Agriculture, and such other data as are available, show that last month about 500,000 people got jobs in private industry. There was only one industry that showed a decline of any importance, and that was anthracite coal. The figures for March were better than for any other March since 1929. The preliminary report shows that April will show an increase almost as good if not better.

Our figures show there are about 40,700,000 people working in private industry, excluding those in PWA, as compared with 46,000,000 working in March 1929.

PRESIDENT ROOSEVELT: Does that include agriculture?

DR. LUBIN: Yes; and it means that private industry, including agriculture, is employing about 5,000,000 fewer people, which is about equal to the number private industry has absorbed.

PRESIDENT ROOSEVELT: In other words, we have come back half way.

DR. LUBIN: This decline of about 5,000,000 as compared with 1929 is found principally in three groups of industry. First, manufacturing, a million and three quarters; second, trade and service, which accounts for a little more than a million; and agriculture with a hundred and ten thousand, a very insignificant figure compared with all the rest.

Now, in addition to these people who were formerly working in industry, but who are not now working in industry, the

---

[3] The national political conventions of 1936, of course; Republicans in Cleveland, June 8, and Democrats in Philadelphia, June 22.
[4] The Central Statistical Board was organized Aug. 9, 1933, under the Authority of the National Industrial Recovery Act and an Executive Order of July 27, 1933, to plan and promote improvement, development, and coordination of federal and other statistical services—according to the *U. S. Government Manual*. It was transferred to the Bureau of the Budget by Reorganization Plan I, July 1, 1939.

population of this country of working age increased by approximately 3,800,000 during the same period. In addition to that, we have to bear in mind that there were approximately two and one-fourth million people unemployed in 1929, so that the problem facing us is the absorption of those formerly unemployed. If there had been no depression—if industry had stayed just where it was—there would still be approximately 5,000,000 to take care of.

PRESIDENT ROOSEVELT: Two and one-fourth million in 1929 and the other 3,000,000 have been added because of the increased population. That is an interesting fact.

DR. LUBIN: Of this group of people to be reabsorbed, about one and one-half million are in rural areas. In other words, the rural population has been increasing proportionately faster than those of working age in the cities. In addition to that, we have in rural areas about 400,000 people who moved to the farms between 1929 and 1933, and still remain, which means that we have close to 2,000,000 in these rural areas who are a problem quite distinct from these people in the cities who must be reabsorbed.

The significant thing about this whole employment problem is that a lot of industries are employing more people than they did seven years ago. This was taken at random; here is beverages, employing 60 per cent more people than in 1929, after prohibition repeal; rayon, 40 per cent more; radio, 30 per cent more.

You will find there are three groups: first, those depending on the farm for their existence, such as agricultural implements; second, industries such as paints, varnishes, and things of that sort; third, new consumable goods industries, such as radio, beverages, and consumable goods industries which have changed their style, such as woolen fabrics, and rayon; the use of paper in making bags and boxes instead of wooden boxes; car shops, where they are making streamlined cars back in 1929 levels. On the other hand, there are the lagging industries, such as building, steam-heating, locomotive, brick, and marble.

PRESIDENT ROOSEVELT: And in between, a vast number of industries practically the same.

DR. LUBIN: Yes. The problem is one of the lagging industries improving, such as building construction materials, transportation, locomotive, and so on. Steam railroads still show 670,000 workers. Whether or not they will be absorbed by railroad transportation is doubtful with the competition of trucks

547

coming into the picture. Construction work still has 800,000 people. Trade and service, which incidentally always lags behind all these other occupations, picking up when they pick up. There is a total of approximately 5,000,000 in the industries.

In spite of that, there is a shortage of skilled laborers in certain areas. In other words, there are geographical shortages of certain skills. In addition to that, employers are refusing to reabsorb certain skilled workers because of the fact that they do not meet the test of efficiency. Good carpenters cannot meet the test of efficiency. The reason for these shortages is the loss of skill, having been out of work for five years, and second, the fact that industry has not trained new workers for these places. Third, people have moved away from industrial centers; fourth, people who have moved away and who are known to be available won't come back. General Motors sends telegrams to people and they won't come back. They say they would rather have a roof over their head and be sure of it than to come back there and work a few months and then be turned out. Men are refusing to go back to their old jobs. If the shortages become acute, industry is going to have to take the responsibility of training people for the work, or increase the hours of the workers.

MR. FECHNER: Aren't they doing that already—aren't they increasing hours instead of taking on new men?

PRESIDENT ROOSEVELT: Yes, they are.

DR. MORGAN: You haven't mentioned technological employment; do you think that is minor?

DR. LUBIN: We are attempting to measure the number of people who are available for employment in this country. Many of those living in rural areas are running tourist houses or a roadside stand and probably making a fairly decent living.

SECRETARY ROPER: May I ask this question with reference to the local District of Columbia Employment Agency; do they make any effort to train people according to their aptitude? It is impossible to get people to work in my garden. When I get a man through that agency, he knows nothing about plant life. I cannot get anybody that understands gardening except an Austrian that I have to appeal to to help me out. If that could be done—just start a model—I think it would spread throughout the country.

DR. LUBIN: Employment agencies are not training workers.

SECRETARY ROPER: Why not?

DR. LUBIN: First, they have no authority under the law.

SECRETARY ROPER: Can't you find somebody who will?

MR. FECHNER: I wonder if it is too soon to draw a conclusion from the swing of the automobile from spring to fall?

PRESIDENT ROOSEVELT: Have you any figures on that?

DR. LUBIN: Although employment did not increase proportionately, the total number of people employed is greater than it was a year ago. How long that level will be maintained, we do not know. At the end of five months of the new system, it is working beautifully; whether it will show well in the summer, we do not know yet.

PRESIDENT ROOSEVELT: Are there any questions any member of the Council have which Dr. Lubin could answer now or look up for us for the next meeting? If so, I wish you would ask them now, because that is what the Central Statistical Board is for.

VOICE: What is the working age?

DR. LUBIN: We have taken 16 as the working age in certain industries and 18 in others. Sixteen is the age for most industries. Most industries have not gone back to child labor. Some have, and it is growing by leaps and bounds. I am assuming that those turned out by NRA are still out. The number involved is not a large number.

VOICE: What is the upper limit?

DR. LUBIN: Sixty-five.

DR. MORGAN: I keep coming across one industry after another that is buying new equipment to avoid taking on new employees. I come across that so much that it seems to me it must be a large problem. We will not get a very clear picture from it until we get into that.

DR. LUBIN: We have looked into that. Mr. Hopkins is working on that, and we are cooperating. Through observation we have found two things to be true; first, there has been no revolutionary discovery in method which has revolutionized industry in the last five years. Even though you have technological displacements, they are going to here and there, and no one industry will be large enough to make much difference in toto. It may affect quite a large number of men.

SECRETARY MORGENTHAU: I want to say that is the most intelligent statement on employment I have heard for a long time.

MR. BATTLE: You asked me to explain the discrepancies between the AF of L figures and ours. I think Dr. Lubin can elucidate on that.

DR. LUBIN: I think the problem with the AF of L figures is that they have made assumptions which are absolutely untenable; for instance, the Department of Agriculture estimated a decline

549

of three per cent in one group of employees and they have assumed that all employment has decreased by three per cent, which, of course, is absurd. We deduct those who are in school, and there are more in school than in 1929, but the AF of L says they are unemployed because if they had jobs they would not be in school.[5]

PRESIDENT ROOSEVELT: When I asked Joe about the lag in transportation employment, one answer that he gave me was the competition of trucks, etc. I think another answer lies in the industries that have not shown a comeback, such as marble, brick, locomotive, cement, structural iron, bolts, etc. If those would come up, they would take up a lot of car space. Is that one of the real answers, Joe?

MR. EASTMAN: That is true, Mr. President.

DR. LUBIN: It is rather significant that the steel industry, in reporting the source of new orders, pointed to the fact that during the past three months the new orders from manufacturers of electrical equipment, such as electric refrigerators, vacuum cleaners, and things of that sort, was greater proportionately than any other group, which means that the purchasing power is being reflected back in the heavy industries.

PRESIDENT ROOSEVELT: In conclusion, I want to suggest that anyone who is going to make a speech or write an article is supposed, before giving out any statistics relating to economics, to clear through the Central Statistical Board. I think we should check both ways through the Central Statistical Board, first, on the figures themselves, and secondly, on the deductions from the figures that we want to give to the public. In other words, we do not want to have a crossing of wires on deductions any more than we want to have a crossing of wires on the figures themselves. The Central Statistical Board is ready to go over any speech you propose to make or any article you propose to write.

Meeting closed at 3:50 p.m.

[The transcript for April 28, 1936 was the last available in the National Archives; the agency trailed off thereafter, but was not legally abolished until 1939.—Editors' Note.]

---

[5] See transcript for meeting of Mar. 3, 1936, notes 4 and 5, and related passages.

APPENDIXES

Appendix A
BIOGRAPHICAL NOTES

ALEXANDER, WILL W. (1884-1956)
Methodist minister, 1901-17; withdrew from ministry, 1917; held various positions with educational and charitable organizations; assistant administrator, U. S. Resettlement Administration, 1935; administrator, Resettlement Administration and Farm Security Administration, 1937.

ALTMEYER, ARTHUR J. (1891-)
Born in Wisconsin; held positions in high school teaching and with the state of Wisconsin, 1914-33; chief, Compliance Division, NRA, 1934-35; member, Social Security Board, 1935-46, chairman from 1937; U. S. Commissioner for Social Security, 1946-53.

ALVERSON, LYLE T. (1893-)
Lawyer, from New York; became solicitor of the National Emergency Council, May 1935; acting director upon Frank Walker's final departure from the Council in Dec. 1935; resigned, Aug. 1936, to return to private business; author of *Chronological Review of Activities of NEC* and of governmental departments and agencies, 1933-1936; lives in New Jersey.

BANKHEAD, JOHN H. (1872-1946)
Lawyer, born in Alabama; admitted to the Alabama bar, 1893; practiced in Alabama; also president, Bankhead Coal Co., 1911-25; U. S. Senator (Dem.), 1931-46; brother of Speaker William B. Bankhead (1874-1940).

BARKLEY, ALBEN W. (1877-1958)
Lawyer, born in Kentucky; admitted to the bar, 1901; prosecuting attorney and judge in Kentucky between 1905 and 1913; House of Representatives, 1913-27; and U. S. Senator (Dem.), 1927-48, 1954-56; Vice-President of the United States, 1948-52.

BELL, DANIEL W. (1891-)
Born in Illinois; entered the Treasury Department, 1911, as stenographer and bookkeeper and moved up to commissioner of accounts and deposits, 1931-35; assistant to the Secretary of the Treasury on financial and accounting matters, 1935-40; Acting Director of the Budget, 1934-39; Undersecretary of the Treasury, 1940-45; in commercial banking since 1945.

BIGGS, J. CRAWFORD (1872-1960)
Lawyer; admitted to the North Carolina bar, 1894; practiced law, held various political and judicial positions there; Solicitor General of the U. S., 1933-35; practiced law, Washington, D.C.

BLACK, EUGENE R. (1873-1934)
Banker; admitted to the Georgia bar and practiced in Atlanta; appointed governor of the Federal Reserve Bank of Atlanta; appointed a Governor of the Federal Reserve Board, Washington, 1933-34. (Father of Eugene R. Black, recently executive director of the International Bank for Reconstruction and Development.)

BLAIR, EMILY NEWELL (1877-1951) Writer, lecturer; active in women's suffrage in Missouri, Women's Com., Council National Defense; Member, Democratic National Committee; assoc. editor, *Good Housekeeping* mag.; chairman, Consumers' Advisory Board of NRA, 1935.

BLAISDELL, THOMAS C., JR. (1895-) Economist; taught at several institutions; professor of economics, Columbia, 1925-33; assistant director, Consumers' Council, AAA, 1933-34; executive director, Consumers' Advisory Board, NRA, 1934-35; economic adviser to the administrator, Resettlement Administration, 1935-36; held positions with Social Security Board, Securities and Exchange Commission, National Resources Planning Board, 1936-43; several wartime agencies, World War II; assistant to the Secretary of Commerce, 1949-51; returned to university teaching, 1951; lives in Berkeley, Calif.

BLANDFORD, JOHN B., JR. (1897-) Held research and engineering positions, and administrative positions in municipal government; assistant to chairman, Tennessee Valley Authority, 1933-34; coordinator and secretary of the Board, 1934-37; appointed general manager, 1937; U. S. representative, Advisory Com. of UN relief and work agency, 1950; lives in McLean, Virginia.

BORAH, WILLIAM E. (1865-1940) Lawyer; admitted to Illinois bar, 1889, and practiced in Kansas and Idaho; U. S. Senator (Rep.) from Idaho, from 1907 to 1940; chairman of the Senate Foreign Relations Committee, 1924.

BRANCH, W. HARLLEE (1879-) Born in North Carolina; newspaperman, *Atlanta Journal,* 1903-33; executive assistant to Postmaster General, 1933-34; second assistant Postmaster General, 1934-38; member of Civil Aeronautics Board, 1938-48; editor, *Panama City News-Herald* (Florida), 1951-59.

BRUÉRE, HENRY (1882-1958) Born in Missouri; extensive career in welfare work and in connection with municipal financial administration until World War I; insurance and bank executive following the war; President, Bowery Savings Bank, New York City, 1931-49; special assistant to the President of the United States in coordination of activities, 1933.

BURLEW, EBERT KEISER (1885-1945) In business until 1910; office of the Adjutant General, War Department, 1910-14; Post Office Department, 1914-23; admitted to the District of Columbia bar, 1921; administrative assistant, Dept. of the Interior, 1923-38; First Assistant to Secretary of the Interior, 1938-43.

biographical notes

CARR, WILBUR J. (1870-1942)
Entered the State Dept. as a clerk, 1892; rose through the ranks in the Department, assistant Secretary of State, 1924-37; Minister to Czechoslovakia, 1937; retired, 1939.

CELLER, EMANUEL (1888-)
Lawyer; practiced law New York City from 1912; U. S. House of Representatives (Dem.), 1923, and reelected continuously to date.

CHAPMAN, OSCAR LITTLETON (1896-)
Practiced law, Colorado, 1929-33; ass't Secretary of the Interior, 1933; Undersecretary, 1946; Secretary, 1949-52.

CHOATE, JOSEPH HODGES, JR. (1876-)
Lawyer; born in New York; practiced law, New York City from 1902; chairman, Federal Alcohol Control Administration, 1933-35.

CONNERY, WILLIAM P., JR. (1888-1937)
Was on the stage and in business; elected from Massachusetts to Congress; served House of Representatives, 1923-37.

COOKE, MORRIS LLEWELLYN (1872-1960)
Engineer; director, Water Resources Section, National Resources Board, 1934; administrator, Rural Electrification Administration, 1935-37; Office of Production Management, 1940-41; chairman, President's Water Resources Policy Commission, 1950-51.

COOLIDGE, THOMAS JEFFERSON (c. 1894-1959)
Banker; other business, Boston, Mass.; special assistant to the Secretary of the Treasury in charge of fiscal affairs, 1934; Undersecretary of the Treasury, 1934-36; returned to private business.

COUCH, HARVEY C. (1877-1941)
Utility executive, born in Arkansas; long career in railroads and electric utility business, organized several electric companies in the Arkansas, Mississippi, Louisiana area; president, southwestern division, National Electric Light Association, 1930-31; member of the board, Reconstruction Finance Corporation, 1932-34.

CROWLEY, LEO THOMAS (1889-)
Corporation official; born in Wisconsin; began work for a paper and supply company of which he became president; chairman, Federal Deposit Insurance Corporation, 1934-45; associated with various wartime agencies, 1942-45.

CUMMINGS, HOMER S. (1870-1956)
Lawyer, born in Chicago; admitted to the Connecticut bar and practiced there until 1933; active in Democratic politics, chairman of the National Committee, 1919-20; appointed U. S. Attorney General by President Roosevelt in 1933 and served until 1939.

DARLING, JAY (J. N. DING) (1876-1962)
Cartoonist for *New York Herald Tribune* and other newspapers since 1917; chief biologist, Dept. of Agriculture, 1934-35; outstanding U. S. conservationist.

DARROW, CLARENCE S. Lawyer, born in Ohio; admitted to the bar in 1878; associated,
(1857-1938) during a long and celebrated law career, with many cases
of national interest including trust prosecutions, legal work
on behalf of the city of Chicago, the famous Scopes trial in
1925, etc.; headed the National Recovery Review Board
by appointment of President Roosevelt to inquire into the
NRA codes, Mar. 1934.

DAVIS, CHESTER CHARLES Born in Iowa; held various journalistic positions, 1911-21;
(1887-) executive positions in the field of agriculture, both private and
governmental, 1921-33; Administrator, Agricultural Adjust-
ment Administration, 1933-36; member of the Board of
Governors, Federal Reserve System, 1936-41; President, Federal
Reserve Bank of St. Louis, 1941-51.

DAVIS, EWIN LAMAR Born in Tennessee; began practice of law, 1899; held Tennessee
(1876-1949) circuit judgeship, 1910-18; served in U. S. House of Representatives (Dem.), 1919-33; appointed to the Federal Trade
Commission, 1933, chairman, 1935, 1940, 1945; served on the
Commission until his death.

DAVIS, WILLIAM HAMMATT Practiced law in New York from 1903; held administrative
(1879-) positions in Washington during World War I; deputy administrator and national compliance director of NRA, 1933-34;
held government board and committee positions thereafter,
including chairmanship, National War Labor Board, 1942-45;
chairman, Atomic Energy Labor Relations Panel, 1949.

DERN, GEORGE H. Engaged in mining enterprises in Utah from 1894; Utah
(1872-1936) legislature, 1915-23; Governor of Utah, 1925-32; Secretary
of War, 1933-36.

DICKINSON, JOHN Lawyer, practiced, Los Angeles, 1922-25; taught at Harvard
(1894-1952) and Princeton, 1924-29; professor of law, University of
Pennsylvania Law School, 1929; Assistant Secretary of Commerce, 1933-35; chairman, Central Statistical Board, 1934-35;
assistant U. S. Attorney General, 1935-37; general solicitor,
Pennsylvania Railroad, 1937; vice-president and general
counsel, 1946.

DOUGLAS, LEWIS WILLIAMS Arizona businessman and politician; U. S. House of Repre-
(1894-) sentatives (Dem.), 1927-33; U. S. Director of the Budget,
Mar., 1933-Aug., 1934; with American Cyanamid Co., 1934-38;
principal and vice-chancellor, McGill University, 1938-40;
American Ambassador to Great Britain, 1947-50.

DOUGLAS, PAUL H. Economist; 1916-33, held various college and university
(1892-) teaching positions and acted as adviser to several governmental

bodies; member, consumers' advisory board of the NRA, 1933-35; U. S. Senator (Dem.) from Illinois, 1948 to the present.

EARLY, STEPHEN T. (1889-1951) 1908-33, held a variety of newspaper and related positions, including a period working on the 1920 Roosevelt vice-presidential campaign; press relations secretary to the President, 1933-45; in private business, 1945-49; Undersecretary and deputy secretary of Defense, 1949-50.

EASTMAN, JOSEPH B. (1882-1944) Lawyer and public official; secretary, Public Franchise League, Boston, 1906-13; member, Massachusetts Public Service Commission, 1915-19; member, Interstate Commerce Commission in 1919; Federal Coordinator of Transportation, 1933-36; director, Office of Defense Transportation, 1941-44.

ECCLES, MARRINER STODDARD (1890-) Banker and businessman; various business and banking positions in Utah; assistant to the Secretary of the Treasury, 1934; member, Board of Governors, Federal Reserve System, 1934-51; chairman, 1936-48.

ECKER, FREDERICK H. (1867-) Metropolitan Life Insurance Co., 1883-1951; President, 1929-36; chairman of the board, 1936-51.

EDISON, CHARLES (1890-) New Jersey director for NRA and National Emergency Council; Assistant Secretary of the Navy, 1937-39; Secretary of the Navy, 1939-40; Governor of New Jersey, 1941-1944; son of Thomas A. Edison.

EDY, JOHN N. (1883-1952) 1905-35, highway engineer and city manager, municipal and county governments in several states; assistant director, U. S. Bureau of the Budget, 1935; city manager, Toledo, Ohio, 1936; with Federal Works Agency, 1939-42; city mgr., Houston, 1943-45; also for Berkeley, Calif., Flint, Michigan, Dallas, Texas.

EVANS, PEYTON RANDOLPH (1892-) Virginia lawyer, civil engineer; counsel, Federal Farm Loan Bureau, 1927-33; Farm Credit Administration, 1933-40; General Counsel, Federal Farm Mortgage Corp., 1935-40; consultant, Washington Publishers Association, 1941-57.

FAHEY, JOHN H. (1873-1950) New Hampshire newspaper publisher; various positions with the Associated Press and as a newspaper publisher; chairman, Federal Home Loan Bank Board and chairman, board of directors of the Home Owners' Loan Corporation, 1933; chairman, board of trustees, Federal Savings and Loan Insurance Corporation, 1934-50.

FARLEY, JAMES A. (1888-) Businessman and politician, including presidency of a building supply company, and chairman, New York State Athletic

Commission from 1924-33; chairman, New York State Democratic Committee, 1930-44; chairman, Democratic National Committee, 1932-40; Postmaster General, 1933-40; resigned to enter private business.

FECHNER, ROBERT (1876-1939) Machinist, foreman, and master mechanic, 1896-1912; executive officer, International Association of Machinists, 1912-33; director, Civilian Conservation Corps, 1933-39.

FERGUSON, GARLAND SEVIER, JR. (1878-1963) Lawyer; practiced, North Carolina, 1900-18, 1921-27; member, Federal Trade Commission, 1927-49; chairman, FTC, 1930, 1934, 1938, 1943, 1947; retired from FTC, 1949; in practice of law after 1949.

FILENE, EDWARD A. (1878-1937) Merchant; president, William Filene's Sons Co., Boston; active in numerous public causes and organizations; ardent supporter of President Roosevelt.

GARNER, JOHN NANCE (1868-) Lawyer; Texas House of Representatives, 1898-1902; U. S. House of Representatives (Dem.), 1903-33; Speaker of the House, 1931; Vice-President of the United States, 1933-41.

GREEN, WILLIAM (1873-1952) Labor leader; rose through ranks of United Mine Workers to be national secretary-treasurer, 1912-24; President, American Federation of Labor, 1924-52.

HAAS, GEORGE C. (1896-) Economist; U. S. Dept. of Agriculture from 1922-27; assistant chief economist, Federal Farm Board, 1930-33; chief economist and Deputy Governor in charge of finance, Farm Credit Administration, 1933-34; director of research and statistics, U. S. Dept. of the Treasury, 1934-.

HAMILTON, WALTON H. (1881-1958) Law professor; taught history and economics at various colleges and universities, 1909-28; Yale Law School faculty, 1928-48; National Recovery Administration, 1934-35; special assistant to Attorney General, 1938-45.

HEALY, FRANK Assistant compliance director, NRA; chief, Govt. Contract and Competition Branch, 1934; with TVA through 1936.

HICKOK, LORENA Writer; newspaper reporter for *Milwaukee Sentinel, Minneapolis Tribune*, Associated Press, " . . . one of the country's best female newshawks, she was assigned to Albany to cover the New York Executive Mansion where she became fast friends with Mrs. Roosevelt;" confidential investigator for Harry Hopkins, 1933-37; active in Democratic politics, both in New York and Washington, D.C.; author of biographies of F.D.R., Eleanor Roosevelt, and Helen Keller; collaborated with Mrs. Roosevelt on *Ladies of Courage*.

558

biographical notes

HINES, FRANK THOMAS Army officer; promoted through the ranks in the Army to
(1879-1960) Brigadier General; staff positions relating to transportation,
World War I; resigned from the Army, 1920; director, U. S.
Veterans' Bureau, 1923-30; administrator, Veterans' Affairs,
1930-45; Ambassador to Panama, 1945-48.

HOLT, RUSH DEW Teacher, 1924-31; West Virginia legislator, 1931-1935; U. S.
(1905-1955) Senator (Dem.), 1934-1941; a controversy raged over the fact
that he was slightly below the constitutional age for a Senator
at the time he was to take his seat. Served several more terms
in West Virginia legislature, starting in 1943.

HOPKINS, HARRY L. Social worker; executive positions with private welfare
(1890-1946) agencies, 1918-31; executive director, New York State Temporary Emergency Relief Administration, 1931, became
chairman in 1932; federal administrator of emergency relief,
1933-35; Works Progress Administrator, 1935-38; Secretary
of Commerce, 1938-40; held various unofficial and official
positions under President Roosevelt during World War II.

HOWE, FREDERIC C. Ohio lawyer, practiced 1894-1909; various governmental,
(1867-1940) elective and teaching positions; consumers' counsel, Agricultural Adjustment Administration, 1933-35; special adviser to
the Secretary of Agriculture, 1935.

HOWE, COLONEL LOUIS MC HENRY Newspaperman; *New York Herald Tribune*, 1888-1915;
(1871-1936) secretary and assistant to Franklin Roosevelt while he was
assistant secretary of the Navy, 1915-1920; Roosevelt's personal secretary, 1920-33; Secretary to the President, 1933-36.

HOWELL, J. CARNEY Investment analyst with a Chicago bank, 1924-28; secretary,
(1899-) Chicago Investors Corp., 1929-32; assistant director of finance,
Agricultural Adjustment Administration, 1933-35; Office of
Emergency Management, 1942-1945; with State Department
and ICA, 1945 to date.

HOWES, WILLIAM WASHINGTON Lawyer; practiced in South Dakota, 1912-1933; active in
(1887-1962) South Dakota politics, legislator; second assistant Postmaster
General, 1933, advanced to first assistant, 1934.

HOYT, FRANKLIN C. Judge; began practice of law in New York City, 1898;
(1876-1937) justice, Court of Special Sessions, 1908-1927; first presiding
justice, children's court, 1915-1933; Federal Alcohol
Administrator, 1935.

HULL, CORDELL Practiced law in Tennessee from 1891; Tennessee legislator
(1871-1955) and a judge, 1893-1907; U. S. House of Representatives,
1907-21, 1923-31; U. S. Senator (Dem.), 1931-33; resigned
to become Secretary of State, 1933-44.

559

ICKES, HAROLD L.
(1874-1952) Lawyer; practiced law in Chicago beginning 1907; active in local politics; Progressive Party, 1912-16; worked for election of Charles E. Hughes in 1916; campaigned for Roosevelt in 1932; Secretary of the Interior, 1933-46; also during this period, administrator of public works, and oil administrator under NRA.

IRONSIDE, FRED A., JR.
(1904-1955) Lawyer; practiced in Montana and Washington, D.C.; general counsel and administrative assistant with the NEC, 1933-35; special assistant to the Attorney General, 1935-37; resigned to return to private practice; died in Arizona.

JOHNSON, GENERAL HUGH S.
(1882-1942) Army officer; attended West Point; resigned from the Army in 1919 as a Brigadier General; associated with Moline Implement Co., 1919-1929; Administrator, NRA, June, 1933-Oct., 1934; columnist and commentator thereafter.

JOHNSTON (sic), KILBOURNE
(1907-) Son of General Hugh S. Johnson; West Point graduate, Army Lieutenant; served in many positions in the NRA organization both during and after his father's tenure as administrator; later served in the WPA for the City of New York and, just prior to World War II, as Asst. Director of Selective Service and as Army Secretary of the Army and Navy Munitions Board; for Johnston's career in NRA see Hugh S. Johnson, *The Blue Eagle from Egg to Earth*, (New York, 1935), p. 215; lives in Ohio.

JONES, JESSE H.
(1874-1956) Builder and financier; in business in Texas; director of the Reconstruction Finance Corporation, 1932; chairman, 1933-39; Export-Import Bank, 1936-43; administrator, Federal Loan Agency, 1939-45; Secretary of Commerce, 1940-45.

KEEZER, DEXTER MERRIAM
(1896-) Economist; college and university teaching and journalistic positions, 1920-33; executive director, Consumers' Advisory Board, NRA, 1933-34; president, Reed College, Portland, Oregon, 1934-42; various wartime agencies, 1942-45; with McGraw-Hill, publishers, 1945-.

KENNEDY, JOSEPH PATRICK
(1888-) Massachusetts businessman and banker; Securities and Exchange Commission, 1934, elected chairman, the same year, resigned, 1935; chairman, U. S. Maritime Commission, 1937; Ambassador to Great Britain, 1937-1941; father of President John F. Kennedy.

KROCK, ARTHUR
(1886-) Newspaperman; reporter, editor, Kentucky newspapers, 1906-23; *New York World*, 1923-27; joined *New York Times*, 1927, Washington correspondent, 1932-53, Washington commentator, 1953 to date.

560

biographical notes

LANDIS, JAMES MC CAULEY (1899-1964) Law school dean; law clerk to Justice Brandeis, 1925; professor, Harvard Law School, 1926-34; member, Federal Trade Commission, 1933-34; member, Securities and Exchange Commission, 1934-37, chairman, 1936-37; Dean, Harvard Law School, 1937-46; subsequently in private practice; consultant to the Kennedy administration.

LANGER, WILLIAM (1886-1959) Lawyer, North Dakota; practiced in North Dakota from 1911; attorney general, North Dakota, 1916-20; Governor, 1933-35, 1937-39; U. S. Senator (Rep.), 1941-59.

LILIENTHAL, DAVID ELI (1899-) Lawyer; practiced law in Chicago from 1923; member of Wisconsin public service commission, 1931; one of the three directors, Tennessee Valley Authority, 1933-46, chairman, 1941-46; chairman, U. S. Atomic Energy Commission, 1946-50.

LONG, HUEY P. (1893-1935) Louisiana lawyer and politician; practiced law in Louisiana from 1915; member, Railroad Commission of Louisiana, 1918-21; member, Louisiana Public Service Commission, 1921-28; Governor, 1928-31; U. S. Senate (Dem.), 1931 until his assassination in 1935.

LUBIN, ISADORE (1896-) Economist; held positions in Washington during World War I; taught economics at various institutions; association with Brookings Institute, 1920-33; Commissioner of Labor Statistics in 1933-1946; chairman, Labor Advisory Board, Federal Emergency Administration for Public Works, 1933-39; vice-chairman, Central Statistical Board, 1933-39; member, Temporary National Economic Committee, 1938-41; Special Statistical Assistant to the President, 1941-45; series of governmental positions since 1945; professor, Rutgers University, 1959-.

MANLY, BASIL (1886-1950) Economist; expert, U. S. Bureau of Labor Statistics, 1908-12; research positions, both public and private; newspaper special correspondent; Federal Power Commission, 1933, vice-chairman, 1933-36, 1942-44, chairman, 1944-45; resigned, 1945; natural gas company executive.

MARCH, CHARLES HOYT (1870-1945) Minnesota lawyer; Federal Trade Commission, 1929; reappointed, 1935-45; chairman, FTC, 1933, 1936, 1941; member, Special Industrial Recovery Board, 1933.

MARSHALL, LEON CARROLL (1879-) Economist; college professor; taught economics and related subjects at various institutions, 1903-33; vice-chairman, National Labor Board, 1934; deputy assistant administrator for policy, NRA, 1934; member and executive secretary, National Industrial Recovery Board, 1934-35; faculty, American University, 1936-.

561

new deal mosaic

MC CARL, JOHN RAYMOND (1879-1940)
Iowa lawyer; practiced law, 1903-14; secretary to Senator George W. Norris, 1914-18, executive secretary, National Republican Congressional Committee, 1918-21; Comptroller General of the U. S., 1921-36.

MC DONALD, STEWART (1880-1957)
Manufacturing enterprises in St. Louis; police commissioner of St. Louis; assistant Federal Housing Administrator, 1935, became administrator later the same year and served until 1940; deputy Federal Loan Administrator, 1940-42; entered private business.

MC ENTEE, JAMES J. (1884-1957)
Began as a machinist in 1902, in labor union activities; executive assistant director, Civilian Conservation Corps, 1933-40, appointed director, 1940.

MC FARLANE, WILLIAM DODDRIDGE (1894-)
Texas lawyer; Texas state legislature, 1923-31; U. S. House of Representatives (Dem.), 1933-38.

MC GRADY, EDWARD F. (1872-1960)
Newspaper pressman; president of Newspaper Printing Pressmen's Union, Boston Central Labor Union, Massachusetts State Federation of Labor; first assistant Secretary of Labor, 1933-37; assistant administrator, NRA, 1933; vice-president in charge of labor relations, RCA, 1946-1951.

MC INTYRE, COLONEL MARVIN H. (1878-1943)
Railroad and banking positions, 1901-08; newspaper work, 1908-18; public relations assistant to the Secretary of the Navy, 1918-22; Washington representative of newsreel companies, 1922-32; member of President Roosevelt's secretariat, 1933-43.

MC NINCH, FRANK R. (1873-1950)
Lawyer; practiced law in North Carolina, 1900; held political positions; Federal Power Commission, 1930, chairman, 1933; Federal Communications Commission, 1937, chairman, 1937-39; Special Assistant Attorney General, 1939-46.

MC REYNOLDS, WILLIAM H. (1880-1951)
Lawyer; law clerk, 1902-1906; Post Office Department, Washington, 1906-13; invesigator and assistant chief, Bureau of Efficiency, 1913-29; assistant to the Director of the Budget, 1932; administrative assistant to the Governor, Farm Credit Administration, 1933; administrative assistant to the Secretary of the Treasury, 1933-39; administrative assistant to the President of the U. S., 1939-45; retired from government service, 1945.

MICHELSON, CHARLES (1869-1947)
Newspaperman; various newspapers from 1896; Washington correspondent of the *New York World*, 1917-29; director of publicity, Democratic National Committee, 1929-40; director of public relations, NRA, 1933-34.

562

biographical notes

MILLER, CHARLES A.
(1867-1944)
New York lawyer; president, Savings Bank of Utica, 1907-32; Reconstruction Finance Corporation, 1932-33; chairman of the board, Savings Banks Trust Co.

MILLS, OGDEN LIVINGSTON
(1884-1937)
New York lawyer and businessman; active in New York politics; U. S. House of Representatives (Rep.), 1921-27; Undersecretary of the Treasury, 1927-32; Secretary of the Treasury, 1932-33; Hyde Park neighbor of Franklin Roosevelt.

MOFFETT, JAMES A.
(1886-1953)
Businessman; started as a clerk, Vacuum Oil Co., 1906, director, 1919-33, and senior vice-president, Standard Oil (New Jersey), 1934-36; Industrial Advisory Board, NRA, 1933; Federal Housing Administrator, 1934-35; chairman of the Board, California-Texas Oil Co., 1936-53.

MOORE, ROBERT WALTON
(1859-1941)
Virginia lawyer, admitted to bar, 1880; Virginia state legislator, 1887-90; U. S. House of Representatives (Dem.), 1919-31; assistant Secretary of State, 1933; counselor of the State Dept., 1937.

MORGAN, DR. ARTHUR ERNEST
(1878-)
Civil engineer, educator; concerned largely with flood control and similar projects, in private practice and government agencies; president, Antioch College, 1920-36; chairman of the board of Tennessee Valley Authority, 1933-37; removed from the TVA board by President Roosevelt, 1938, as result of protracted internal dispute between him and fellow board members, David Lilienthal and Harcourt A. Morgan; president, Community Service, Inc., since 1941.

MORGAN, W. FORBES
(1879-1937)
New York businessman; investment partner in firms; deputy governor, Farm Credit Administration, 1933-.

MORGENTHAU, HENRY, JR.
(1891-)
Various positions with New York State government relating to agriculture and conservation, 1922-33; chairman, Federal Farm Board, governor, Farm Credit Administration, Acting and Undersecretary of the Treasury, 1933; Secretary of the Treasury, 1934-45.

MYERS, WILLIAM IRVING
(1891-)
Professor of farm finance; Cornell University from 1914; leave of absence in 1933 to be deputy governor and later governor of the Farm Credit Administration; president, Federal Farm Mortgage Corporation; director, Federal Surplus Relief Corporation, and the Commodity Credit Corporation; returned to Cornell, 1938; Dean, College of Agriculture, 1943-59.

PEARSON, DREW
(ANDREW RUSSELL)
(1897-)
Columnist, varied career as teacher, lecturer, and newspaperman.

PEOPLES, ADMIRAL CHRISTIAN JOY (1876-1941) — Naval officer; ensign, U. S. Navy, 1900; rear admiral, 1917; various positions and commands in the Navy supply organization, including Paymaster General and Chief of the Bureau of Supplies and Accounts, 1933-35; director of procurement, Dept. of the Treasury, 1933-39.

PERKINS, FRANCES (MRS. PAUL C. WILSON) (1882-) — Social worker; various positions, New York state government including: commissioner, State Industrial Commission, 1919-21, 1929-33; U. S. Secretary of Labor, 1933-45; member, U. S. Civil Service Commission, 1945-53; associated with Cornell University, 1956-.

PERKINS, JAMES H. (1876-1940) — Banker; banking positions in Boston, Albany, New York City; president, City Bank Farmers Trust Co., 1929-; chairman of the board, National City Bank, 1933-40.

PERSONS, WILLIAM F. (1876-1955) — Social worker; LL.B., practiced law in Iowa, 1905-06; various executive positions in business and private welfare agencies, 1906-33; director of enrollment, Emergency Conservation Corps, Dept. of Labor, 1933-42; director, U. S. employment service, 1933-39; executive, private businesses.

PHILLIPS, WILLIAM (1878-) — Diplomat; diplomatic service and State Dept. from 1903; Undersecretary of State, 1933-36; Ambassador to Italy, 1936-41; President's special representative to India, 1943; author of *Ventures in Diplomacy*, 1953.

PRALL, ANNING S. (1870-1937) — President, New York City board of education, 1920; commissioner of taxes and assessments, New York City, 1922; U. S. House of Representatives (Dem.), 1923-35; chairman, Federal Communications Commission, 1935-.

RASKOB, JOHN J. (1879-1950) — Executive, General Motors and Dupont; chairman, Democratic National Committee, 1928-32.

RAYBURN, SAM (1882-1961) — Lawyer; Texas House of Representatives, six years, two years as Speaker; U. S. House of Representatives, 1913, Democratic majority leader, 1937; Speaker, 1941-47, 1949-53, 1955-61.

RICE, STUART ARTHUR (1889-) — Statistician, sociologist; various positions with private charitable organizations, 1913-20; college and university teaching positions, 1923-33; acting chairman, Committee on Government Statistics and Information Services, 1933; assistant director of the Census, 1933-36; Central Statistical Board, 1933-40, chairman, 1936-40; Assistant Director, Bureau of Budget for Statistical Standards, 1940-55; President, Surveys and Research Corp, Washington, 1955-.

RICHBERG, DONALD R. (1881-1960) — Lawyer, practiced in Chicago, 1904-33; co-author of Railway Labor Act of 1926 and National Recovery Act of 1933;

general counsel, NRA, 1933-35; executive director, National Emergency Council, 1934-35; chairman, NRA board, 1935; resigned, to private practice, 1935.

RIEFLER, WINFIELD W.
(1897-)
Economist; division of research and statistics, Federal Reserve Board, 1923-33; economic adviser, Executive Council, 1933-34; economic adviser, National Emergency Council, 1934-35; Institute for Advanced Study, 1935-48; assistant to the chairman, Board of Governors, Federal Reserve System, 1948-60; during the war years, U. S. Minister in London in charge of economic warfare activities; secretary of the Federal Open Market Committee, 1952-60.

ROBERT, LAWRENCE WOOD, JR.
(1887-)
Practicing construction engineer, business positions; assistant secretary of the Treasury, 1933-36; assistant treasurer, Democratic National Committee, 1936-41; has his own architectural and engineering firm.

ROGERS, WILL
(1878-1935)
The famous actor, lecturer and humorist. Born in Indian Territory (now Oklahoma); began his career in vaudeville in 1905; killed in airplane crash in Alaska; memorial statue in Capitol building is placed so as to "keep an eye on Congress."

ROOSEVELT, HENRY LATROBE
(1879-1936)
Marine corps officer, 1899-1920; Lt. Col., 1917; various business positions; Assistant Secretary of the Navy, 1933-.

ROPER, DANIEL C.
(1867-1943)
Lawyer, 1894-1916; various positions in Washington including clerkships to Congressional committees, and first assistant Postmaster General; active in Wilson's campaign for re-election, 1916; vice-chairman, U. S. Tariff Commission, 1916-17; Commissioner of Internal Revenue, 1917-20; practiced law, 1921-32; Secretary of Commerce, 1933-38; Minister to Canada, 1939.

RUMSEY, MARY H.
(MRS. CHARLES C.)
(1881-1934)
Daughter of E. H. Harriman; married Charles C. Rumsey, a sculptor, who died in 1922; philanthropist, patron of the arts; Chairman of the Consumers' Advisory Board of NRA, and Consumers' Division of the National Emergency Council until her death in a riding accident in 1934.

SABATH, ADOLPH JOSEPH
(1866-1952)
Born in Czechoslovakia; LL.B., 1891; magistrate, Chicago, 1897-1907; U. S. House of Representatives (Dem.), 1907-52; served many years as chairman of Rules Committee.

SABIN, PAULINE M.
(MRS. CHARLES H.)
(1887-1955)
Active in New York state Republican politics; resigned, 1929, to organize Women's Organization for National Prohibition Reform, became national chairman; active in Red Cross during World War II; married Dwight F. Davis, 1936.

SANDLIN, JOHN N.
(1872-)
Louisiana lawyer; practiced from 1896; district attorney and judge in Louisiana; U. S. House of Representatives (Dem.), 1921-37.

SIROVICH, WILLIAM IRVING
(1882-1939)
Physician; practiced New York City from 1906; superintendent, Peoples Hospital from 1917; bank executive and labor arbitrator; U. S. House of Representatives (Dem.), 1927-39.

SMITH, ELLISON D.
(1866-1944)
South Carolina House of Representatives (Dem.), 1896-1900; mercantile and agricultural pursuits; instrumental in the organization of cotton producers; U. S. Senator (Dem.), 1909-44.

SNELL, BERTRAND H.
(1870-1958)
New York businessman; N.Y. State Republican Committee, 1914; U. S. House of Representatives (Rep.), 1915-1939.

STANLEY, WILLIAM
(1891-1946)
Maryland lawyer; practiced until 1933; assistant to the U. S. Attorney General, 1933-35; entered practice of law with former Attorney General Homer Cummings, 1939.

STEDMAN, ALFRED DELOS
(1891-)
Newspaperman; various newspaper positions, 1915-33; director of information, Agricultural Adjustment Administration, 1933, and assistant administrator, 1934-39; returned to newspaper work, 1939.

STEPHENS, HAROLD M.
(1886-1955)
Utah lawyer and judge; Assistant U. S. Attorney General, 1933-35; U. S. Court of Appeals for the District of Columbia from 1935; appointed chief judge by President Truman, 1948.

SWANSON, CLAUDE AUGUSTUS
(1862-1939)
Virginia lawyer; U. S. House of Representatives, 1893-1905; Governor of Virginia, 1906-10; U. S. Senator (Dem.), 1910-33; Secretary of the Navy, 1933-39.

SYKES, EUGENE O.
(1876-1945)
Mississippi lawyer and Justice of State Supreme Court, 1916-24; Federal Radio Commissioner, 1927; reappointed, 1930 and 1933; Federal Communications Commission, 1934-39; entered private practice.

TATE, HUGH M.
(1882-1938)
Tennessee lawyer and Chancery judge; Interstate Commerce Commission, 1930-37.

TATE, THOMAS ROUSE
(1888-)
Director, National Power Survey, 1934; "an engineer with extensive practical experience, formerly chief engineer of one of the leading consulting engineering firms;" chief, various govt. commissions, 1936-42; consulting engineer for Chas. T. Main, Inc., 1949-51; assistant project manager, Sariyar hydro-electric project, Nallihan Baraji, Turkey.

TAYLOR, MYRON CHARLES
(1874-1959)
Lawyer; U. S. Steel, chief officer and chairman of the board, 1932-38; member, Industrial Advisory Board, NRA, 1933-35; President Roosevelt's personal representative to the Vatican, 1939-50.

biographical notes

TAYLOR, WAYNE CHATFIELD (1893-) Economic adviser; banking and investment positions, 1916-32; executive assistant to the administrator, Agricultural Adjustment Administration, 1933-34; assistant to the special adviser to the President on foreign trade, 1934-35; appointed vice-president and trustee, Export-Import Bank, 1935; assistant Secretary of the Treasury, 1936-39; Undersecretary of Commerce, 1940-45; president, Export-Import Bank, 1945-46; with ECA and Mutual Security Agency, 1948-52.

THORP, WILLARD LONG (1899-) Economist; college and university teaching positions, 1921-33; director, U. S. Bureau of Foreign and Domestic Commerce, 1933-34; member, Federal Alcohol Control Administration, 1933-35; director, Consumers' Division, National Emergency Council, 1934; chairman, Advisory Council, NRA, 1934-35; with Dun & Bradstreet, 1935-45; Assistant Secretary of State, 1946-52; professor, Amherst College, 1952-.

TOLLEY, HOWARD R. (1889-1958) High school teacher, 1906-12; Coast and Geodetic Survey, 1912-15; U. S. Dept. of Agriculture, 1915-30; assistant chief, Bureau of Agricultural Economics, 1928-30; professor of Agricultural Economics, 1930-36; leave of absence to join Agricultural Adjustment Administration, 1933; administrator, 1936-38; chief, Bureau of Agricultural Economics, 1938-46; economist, United Nations Food and Agricultural Organization, 1946-51.

TRENT, DOVER P. Born in Oklahoma; worked with Chester Davis on contracts for cotton production, 1934; Assistant Director, Commodities Division, AAA, 1936-37.

TUGWELL, REXFORD GUY (1891-) Economist; taught at various institutions beginning in 1915, including Columbia University, 1920-37; Assistant Secretary of Agriculture, 1933-34, Undersecretary, 1934-37; Governor of Puerto Rico, 1941-46; professor, University of Chicago, since 1946.

UNWIN, SIR RAYMOND (1863-1940) Englishman, chief technical officer for building and town planning, Ministry of Health; chief adviser to Greater London Regional Town Planning Committee, 1929-33. Unwin's experience was drawn upon in 1934 in connection with the programs provided for in the National Housing Act of that year. (See *New York Times*, Aug. 19, 1934, Sec. II, p. 14, col. 2.)

VAN SWERINGEN, MANTIS J. (1881-1935) AND ORIS P. (1879-1936) Associated together in real estate and railroad ventures; headquarters in Cleveland, Ohio.

WALKER, FRANK C. (1886-1959) Montana lawyer; treasurer of Democratic National Committee, 1932; executive secretary of the Executive Council and executive director of the National Emergency Council, 1933-35 (with some interruption of tenure); Postmaster General, 1940-45; chairman, Democratic National Committee, 1943-44; returned to private business, 1945.

WALLACE, HENRY AGARD (1888-) Iowa politician and statesman, son of Henry C. Wallace (Secretary of Agriculture under Harding and Coolidge); editor, writer for family publication *Wallace's Farmer*, 1910-33; Secretary of Agriculture, 1933-40; Vice-President of the United States, 1940-44; Secretary of Commerce, 1944-46; Progressive candidate for President, 1948; retired to farm.

WALTERS, THEODORE AUGUSTUS (1876-1937) Iowa teacher, 1900-06, and lawyer, 1906-33; Attorney General of Idaho, 1917-20; first assistant secretary, Department of the Interior, 1933.

WEAVER, ROBERT CLIFTON (1907-) Economist; adviser, Negro affairs, Dept. of Interior, 1933-37; special assistant to administrator of U.S. Housing Authority, 1937-40; admin. assistant, OPM, WPB, 1940-42; Administrator, Housing and Home Finance Agency, 1961 to date.

WEBB, THOMAS DWIGHT (1867-) Businessman and banker; vice-chairman, Federal Home Loan Bank Board, 1933; member of FHLB board through 1947.

WEST, CHARLES FRANKLIN (1895-1955) College and university teaching, political science, 1920-30; U.S. House of Representatives, 1931-35; special assistant to the governor, Farm Credit Administration, 1935; Undersecretary of the Interior; private business, 1940-47; professor of political science, 1947-50.

WHEELER, BURTON K. (1882-) Montana lawyer; Montana House of Representatives, 1911-13; U.S. Attorney, district of Montana, 1913-18; U.S. Senator (Dem.), 1922-47; Progressive candidate for vice-president, 1924; in private law practice since 1947.

WHITESIDE, ARTHUR DARE (1882-1960) Organized National Credit Office, 1912, president until 1931; directing head of R. G. Dun & Co., from 1931; Dun consolidated to form Dun & Bradstreet, Whiteside became president, later director; adviser to and member, Industrial Recovery Board, NRA, until 1935.

WILLIAMS, AUBREY WILLIS (1890-) Social worker; executive director, Wisconsin Council of Social Work, 1922-32; field representative, American Public Welfare Association, 1932-33; field representative, Federal Emergency Relief Administration, 1933-35; assistant administrator, WPA; director, National Youth Administration, 1935-39, administrator, 1938-45; newspaper editor, 1945-.

WILLIAMS, JOHN SHARP (1854-1932) Mississippi lawyer and cotton planter; U.S. House of Representatives (Dem.), 1893-1909; U.S. Senator, 1911-23.

biographical notes

WILLIAM S. CLAY (1884-1949)
North Carolina lawyer; R. J. Reynolds Tobacco Co., assistant general counsel, 1917, president, 1931, and chairman of the board, 1935; chairman, National Labor Board, 1933-34; chairman, National Industrial Recovery Board, 1934-35.

WILLIAMSON, FREDERICK E. (1876-1944)
Railroad executive; joined New York Central as clerk, 1889, became president, 1932.
U. S. Dept. of the Treasury, 1934-.

WILSON, MILBURN LINCOLN (1885-)
Born in Montana; extensive career in farming, agricultural economics and extension work; U. S. Dept. of Agriculture, Assistant Secretary, 1934-37, Undersecretary, 1937-39; recipient of first "Distinguished Service Award" from Dept. of Agriculture, 1947; Ford Foundation international technical assistant, 1953-.

WINANT, JOHN G. (1889-1947)
New Hampshire legislator; governor of New Hampshire, 1925-26, 1931-34; chairman, Social Security Board, 1935-37; assistant director, International Labor Office, Geneva, 1935, and 1937-39, director, 1939; ambassador to Great Britain, 1941-.

WOODRING, HARRY H. (1890-)
Kansas banker; governor of Kansas, 1931-33; Assistant Secretary of War, 1933-36, Secretary of War, 1936-40.

[The biographical entries are as complete as it was possible to make them at time of publication.—Editors' Note.]

Appendix B

RULES AND REGULATIONS OF THE NATIONAL EMERGENCY COUNCIL

The functions and duties of the National Emergency Council and the executive director thereof are hereby prescribed pursuant to the Executive Order No. 6433-A, dated November 17, 1933.

(1) The National Emergency Council shall be composed of: the Attorney General; the Secretary of the Interior; the Secretary of Agriculture; the Secretary of Commerce; the Secretary of Labor; the Director of the Budget; the Administrator of Agricultural Adjustment; the Administrator of Federal Emergency Relief; the Administrator for Industrial Recovery; the Chairman of the Board of the Home Owners' Loan Corporation; the Governor of the Farm Credit Administration; the Chairman of the Federal Trade Commission.

(2) The duties of the National Emergency Council:

(a) The members thereof shall act in a capacity advisory to the President and to the executive director.

(b) It shall consider and deliberate upon all problems presented to it by the President or its members.

(c) The members thereof from time to time shall make and file with the Council such reports as may be required.

(d) It shall refer to the executive director all matters wherein the policies or activities of the various governmental agencies are in conflict.

(3) The Council shall meet on alternate Tuesdays at a time and place to be designated. At the conclusion of its meeting, the Council shall recess and later reconvene with the President, at which time it shall report the result of its deliberations.

(4) Any member absenting himself from a meeting shall delegate a representative with full authority to act in his place and stead.

(5) The duties of the executive director:

(a) He shall act, subject to the approval of the President, on all matters wherein any conflict of policies or activities between the various agencies exists.

(b) He shall act, subject to the approval of the President, for the joint and several benefit of all of the agencies of the government.

(c) He shall act upon all matters referred to him by the President and shall consider and act upon all matters referred to him by the Council.

(d) He shall effectuate the purposes for which the National Emergency Council was created pursuant to the Executive Order herein referred to; fix the compensation, and prescribe the duties and authority of all officials and employees; and make such expenditures as may be necessary.

Appendix C
BRIEF CHRONOLOGY OF THE NATIONAL EMERGENCY COUNCIL

JULY 16, 1933	Executive Council created. Frank Walker appointed executive director.
NOVEMBER, 1933	President sets up central statistical board under Executive Council to achieve clearance of all government statistical reports.
DECEMBER 6, 1933	National Emergency Council created by Executive Order to serve as coordinating agency and enforce AAA, NRA; supply information to public; protect consumer interests. Emergency Council and its director, Frank Walker given more "teeth" than Executive Council. The latter will continue to exist. The Executive Council is *advisory*; Emergency Council is to be *directive*.
JANUARY 7, 1934	3,000 county councils organized under the supervision of the Bureau of Economic Education (headed by Professor Paul Douglas), a staff agency of NEC. These councils are to be representative of local populations, charged primarily with protecting consumer interests.
JANUARY 12, 1934	Frank C. Walker appoints 44 state Emergency Council directors. They will have the responsibility within their territories of directing compliance with NRA codes and AAA marketing agreements and protection of consumer interests.
JANUARY 31, 1934	First state directors meeting held in Washington. Roosevelt and Economic Recovery administrators explain program to them. F.D.R. stresses the "nonpolitical" role they are to play.
MARCH 14, 1934	NEC announces formation of United States Information Service to assist public in finding their way through the maze of government operations.

572

APRIL 7, 1934	Consumer Councils are set up with Mary Rumsey as head of Consumer Division of NEC.
JUNE, 1934	Frank Walker takes leave of absence; Donald Richberg, General Counsel of NRA, appointed as his replacement.
OCTOBER 31, 1934	The Executive Council is abolished and consolidated with NEC. Donald Richberg is appointed director of reorganized NEC. NRA brought under closer control of NEC.
DECEMBER 24, 1934	NEC issues first *United States Government Manual* describing functions of various governmental agencies. (*Organization* was added to title in 1949.)
APRIL 23, 1935	Donald Richberg becomes head of NRA, replacing General Hugh Johnson. Frank Walker returns to head NEC and Division of Applications on Work Relief Projects.
JUNE 5, 1935	Franklin Delano Roosevelt reconstitutes NEC under Emergency Relief Appropriation Act of 1935.
SEPTEMBER 9, 1935	Consumers Division work to be carried on by NRA Consumers Advisory Board.
DECEMBER 19, 1935	Frank C. Walker resigns as Director of NEC. L. C. Alverson appointed as Acting Executive Director.
OCTOBER 23, 1936	NEC attacked as a political propaganda machine by Al Smith.
SEPTEMBER 21, 1937	Franklin Delano Roosevelt orders end and transfer of NEC functions, records, and equipment to the Bureau of the Budget.
JULY 1, 1939	NEC legally abolished as Reorganization Plan No. 1 becomes effective.